AF683638

FROM INSTINCT TO SELF: SELECTED PAPERS OF W. R. D. FAIRBAIRN

FROM INSTINCT TO SELF: SELECTED PAPERS OF W. R. D. FAIRBAIRN

Volume II: Applications and Early Contributions

EDITED BY
ELLINOR FAIRBAIRN BIRTLES
DAVID E. SCHARFF, M.D.

JASON ARONSON INC.
Northvale, New Jersey
London

This book was set in 10 point Baskerville by Lind Graphics of Upper Saddle River, New Jersey, and printed and bound by Haddon Craftsmen of Scranton, Pennsylvania.

Copyright © 1994 by Ellinor Fairbairn Birtles and the Fairbairn Trust
Introduction copyright © 1994 by David E. Scharff

10 9 8 7 6 5 4 3 2 1

All rights reserved. Printed in the United States of America. No part of this book may be used or reproduced in any manner whatsoever without written permission from Jason Aronson Inc. except in the case of brief quotations in reviews for inclusion in a magazine, newspaper, or broadcast.

Library of Congress Cataloging-in-Publication Data

From instinct to self.
Includes bibliographical references and index.
Contents: v. 1. Clinical and theoretical papers—
v. 2. Applications and early contributions.
1. Psychoanalysis. 2. Psychotherapy. 3. Fairbairn,
W. Ronald D. (William Ronald Dodds) I. Birtles,
Ellinor Fairbairn. II. Scharff, David E., 1941– .
III. Fairbairn, W. Ronald D. (William Ronald Dodds)
[DNLM: 1. Psychoanalysis—collected works. 2. Psycho-
therapy—collected works. 3. Psychoanalytic Theory—
collected works. WM 420 F9305 1944]
BF109.F78A25 1994 150.19′5 94-6784
ISBN 1-56821-080-9 (v. 1)
ISBN 1-56821-251-8 (v. 2)
ISBN 1-56821-366-2 (series)

Manufactured in the United States of America. Jason Aronson Inc. offers books and cassettes. For information and catalog write to Jason Aronson Inc., 230 Livingston Street, Northvale, New Jersey 07647.

THE LIBRARY OF OBJECT RELATIONS

A SERIES OF BOOKS EDITED BY
DAVID E. SCHARFF AND JILL SAVEGE SCHARFF

Object relations theories of human interaction and development provide an expanding, increasingly useful body of theory for the understanding of individual development and pathology, for generating theories of human interaction, and for offering new avenues of treatment. They apply across the realms of human experience from the internal world of the individual to the human community, and from the clinical situation to everyday life. They inform clinical technique in every format from individual psychoanalysis and psychotherapy, through group therapy, to couple and family therapy.

The Library of Object Relations aims to introduce works that approach psychodynamic theory and therapy from an object relations point of view. It includes works from established and new writers who employ diverse aspects of British, American, and international object relations theory in helping individuals, families, couples, and groups. It features books that stress integration of psychoanalytic approaches with marital, family, and group therapy, as well as those centered on individual psychotherapy and psychoanalysis.

Refinding the Object and Reclaiming the Self
David E. Scharff

Scharff Notes: A Primer of Object Relations Therapy
Jill Savege Scharff and David E. Scharff

Object Relations Couple Therapy
David E. Scharff and Jill Savege Scharff

Object Relations Family Therapy
David E. Scharff and Jill Savege Scharff

Projective and Introjective Identification and the Use of the Therapist's Self
Jill Savege Scharff

Foundations of Object Relations Family Therapy
Jill Savege Scharff, Editor

From Inner Sources: New Directions in Object Relations Psychotherapy
N. Gregory Hamilton, Editor

Repairing Intimacy: An Object Relations Approach to Couples Therapy
Judith Siegel

Family and Couple Therapy
John Zinner

Close Encounters: A Relational View of the Therapeutic Process
Robert Winer

The Autonomous Self: The Work of John D. Sutherland
Jill Savege Scharff, Editor

Crisis at Adolescence: Object Relations Therapy with the Family
Sally Box, Beta Copley, Jeanne Magagna, and Errica Moustaki Smilansky, Editors

Personal Relations Therapy: The Collected Papers of H. J. S. Guntrip
Jeremy Hazell, Editor

Psychoanalytic Group Therapy
Karl König and Wulf-Volker Lindner

Psychoanalytic Therapy
Karl König

From Instinct to Self: Selected Papers of W. R. D. Fairbairn, vol. I: Clinical and Theoretical Contributions
David E. Scharff and Ellinor Fairbairn Birtles, Editors

From Instinct to Self: Selected Papers of W. R. D. Fairbairn, vol. II: Applications and Early Contributions
Ellinor Fairbairn Birtles and David E. Scharff, Editors

Object Relations Therapy of Trauma
Jill Savege Scharff and David E. Scharff

Object Relations Individual Therapy
David E. Scharff and Jill Savege Scharff

How to Survive as a Psychotherapist
Nina Coltart

Reclaiming the Legacy of Erich Fromm
Mauricio Cortina and Michael Maccoby, Editors

A Primer of Kleinian Therapy
Irving Solomon

Contents

PART III: EARLY CONTRIBUTIONS TO PSYCHOANALYTIC THEORY AND PRACTICE

PART IV. APPLIED PSYCHOANALYSIS

PART V: TOWARDS A PSYCHOLOGY OF ART

PART VI: BOOK REVIEWS, LETTERS, AND AUTOBIOGRAPHICAL MATERIAL

List of Photographs

Preface

When I began work on Ronald Fairbairn's papers and archives in 1988, I found a collection of early lectures and unpublished papers dating from 1927 to 1937. These were the result of his academic work as a lecturer in psychology under the discipline of mental philosophy at Edinburgh University. The first professor of psychology at Edinburgh University, James Drever, was installed as late as 1932. These papers can be divided broadly into five main areas. I will place these in the order of their importance for later developments in his work: (1) discussion papers on current and new theories of psychology, including psychoanalysis (e.g., James, McDougall, Freud, Glover, Hollingworth, Hertzberg, and Head); (2) critiques of Freudian theory; (3) applications of psychoanalysis (e.g., to child psychology, child abuse, adolescence, education, and sexual offenders); (4) medical lectures (e.g., on psychopathology and neurology; (5) philosophical psychology (e.g., Hobbes, Berkeley, Galton, and James).

I have placed philosophical psychology at the end of this hierarchical list not because the subject itself has little relevance to the development of Fairbairn's psychoanalytical thought. It is in fact its main basis, but by this stage of his intellectual development the philosophical basis of his thought was already in place and the lectures on philosophy referred to have minimal connection with his psychoanalytical thought. This omission comes with some reservations on my part in the case of Hobbes, for the object of Hobbesian psychology, the 'defensive individual', was absorbed into psychoanalytic theory by Freud because Freud himself was a member of a culture which subscribed to this view of human nature.

It seemed to me that, on the one hand, the lectures and papers we have published in this volume provide crucial insights into the development of Fairbairn's psychoanalytical thought, and on the other they were of historical significance in the development of psychoanalysis. This project has enabled me to fulfil my personal intention to ensure the publication of Fairbairn's early writings, which I consider are of importance to the history of ideas. It was also important to me that Fairbairn's later papers should be easily accessible to clinicians and scholars. It is, therefore, with great satisfaction that I welcome the publication of the two volumes which we have entitled *From Instinct to Self.*

I hope that the publication of *From Instinct to Self* will revitalise interest in Fairbairn's work and lead to a radical reevaluation of his contribution to psychoanalysis. I also hope that his wider contribution to disciplines such as education, sociology, social psychology, and aesthetics will be recognised. Such recognition would contribute to an appreciation of Fairbairn's position within twentieth-century thought.

So it has been a privilege and a personal pleasure to have the opportunity to collaborate with David Scharff in the publication of the most important of these. David's knowledge of Fairbairn's ideas and his enthusiasm for the undertaking have been of great encouragement to me. I consider myself very fortunate to have worked with David, who has such a keen understanding of the issues addressed by Fairbairn in his writings.

Ellinor Fairbairn Birtles
London 1994

The opportunity to join with Ellinor Birtles in editing Fairbairn's previously uncollected and unpublished papers came as an unexpected opportunity and privilege. Fairbairn's thinking had long been at the center of my own writing and teaching, but it was not until Jock Sutherland's wife, Molly, asked me and my wife, Jill, to review his papers after his death that the idea of publishing Fairbairn's uncollected papers emerged. At the same time that Jill Scharff began to plan to collect Sutherland's papers, I came across Jock's folder outlining his idea for republishing *Psycho-Analytic Studies of the Personality*, with the addition of some of the later papers. It seemed obvious that the project should be carried out. Alan Harrow and Murray Leishman of the Scottish Institute of Human Relations were supportive and put me in touch with Fairbairn's daughter, Ellinor Birtles, who was already working to compile and understand the corpus of Fairbairn's papers and notes, and who was beginning to write about the philosophical background and implications of object relations theory.

I am grateful to the Fairbairn family, particularly to Ellinor for her trust and for the opportunity she afforded me. Collaboration with Ellinor has been a chief pleasure of the work in collecting these papers. We have found our areas of interest to be complementary. Her unfailing energy and good will, and her willingness to share this project which meant so much to her, has meant a great deal to me.

David E. Scharff, M.D.
Washington, D.C. 1994

Acknowledgments

We are both grateful to all who have contributed to and facilitated the work of collecting and editing these two volumes: To Molly Sutherland for access to Jock's papers and ideas; to Alan Harrow, Murray Leishman, and their colleagues of the Scottish Institute of Human Relations, where many of the papers and notes are housed, for their support and encouragement; to James Grotstein who had already begun aspects of this work and who not only graciously gave way but continued to lend enthusiastic and generous support to us. The staff of the library of Edinburgh University, especially Mrs Jo Currie of Special Collections, helped cheerfully with access to Fairbairn's library and with references to works of his contemporaries. We also extend special thanks to Michelle Benjamin, Hermi Dauker, and their colleagues at *The British Journal of Medical Psychology* for their unfailing helpfulness. We would also like to thank the Librarian in Psychology Library of London University; Deidre Morley, Liverpool Council for Voluntary Service; Miss Pearl King, archivist, and Jill Duncan and Paula Lavis at the library at The Institute of Psycho-Analysis; Cosmo Fairbairn for his translations and checking of Janet; Josephine Lomax-Simpson for all her help and encouragement in so many ways; Diane Barnett for guiding my (EFB) footsteps towards computer literacy and Dean Casswell for his invaluable help with a recalcitrant disk; Elizabeth Foulkes for her interest and the volume of Foulkes' papers; and John Clarke for his patience and encouragement to pursue the study of Fairbairn's thought.

The emerging psychoanalyst: Fairbairn just before his marriage in 1926.

Introduction: Working towards the Theory of Object Relations

The writings which we have selected for this volume consist of papers of historic interest, first, in the development of Fairbairn's own contribution to psychoanalysis and, second, in the history of psychoanalysis. The early academic papers in Part I demonstrate the rigorous nature of Fairbairn's critique of Freud. The extent to which Fairbairn was able to work through the inconsistencies and anomalies which he encountered in his study of Freudian theory enabled him to detach himself from unquestioning allegiance to existing psychoanalytic hypotheses and prepared the ground for the object relations theory of the personality which consolidated his thinking.

As we discussed in the Introduction to Volume I, pp. xiii–xiv it was Fairbairn's philosophical background which gave him the intellectual skills required to subject psychoanalytic theory to a comprehensive critique based upon a nonmechanistic epistemology. Because this capacity was allied to wide experience of the actual effects of psychical disturbances in adults, children, and adolescents, his revisions of psychoanalysis were firmly rooted in clinical practice. In addition, Fairbairn's academic post as a lecturer in psychology gave him the opportunity to acquire a thorough and up-to-date knowledge of that discipline. This had the effect of distancing him from the intellectual stance which Freud had adopted from his entrenchment within the positivistic scientific methodology of neurology. Fairbairn had the advantage of access to new research into instinctive reactions in human beings which had not been available to Freud.

Fairbairn's philosophical background, which encompassed the origins of the 'unconscious' or 'subconscious' aspects of human minds in the philosophies of Schopenhauer, Von Hartmann, and Nietzsche, for example, was of particular relevance to the critical appreciation of psychoanalysis. This study of the 'unconscious' was combined with an exposure to Kantian ideas of mental structures as 'givens' inaccessible to consciousness and a thorough and prolonged study of the experience of 'that which is other' in the philosophies of Hegel and Lotze. He understood the dialectic of human experience mainly through the work of Aristotle and Hegel. Finally, through his study of the psychological researches of William James and James Drever into affective reactions, Fairbairn was enabled to propose a theory of affect which incorporates intrinsic meaning within psychic reality.

In his doctoral thesis, entitled here 'Dissociation and Repression' (Chapter 1, this volume), Fairbairn discusses these unconscious phenomena. The actual effects of dissociation and repression had assumed dramatic proportions in the hysterical injuries which were a feature of the First World War. In 1915 Fairbairn had the opportunity to visit the hospital in Edinburgh run by W. H. R. Rivers (Sutherland 1989). It was this visit which motivated him to become a psychotherapist.

Fairbairn began his critical analysis of Freud with a discussion paper on *The Ego and the Id* in 1928 (see Introduction to Part II, this volume, for Fairbairn's reservations and questions for further study). Freud, drawing on the topographical nature of anatomy, physiology, and neurology had imprisoned his metapsychological concepts of the Ego, Id, and Superego within the same topographical methodology. Fairbairn's struggle with these concepts continued in two papers, published here as 'The Superego' (Chapter 2), where he consolidates the groundwork from which his later theory of endopsychic structure was developed.

In Chapter 3, 'Libido Theory Re-evaluated' we have printed an important paper which, in effect, refutes Freud's idea of instinct as a theory of psychic energy, individuation, or human motivation. On the face of it, the paper appears a long and even pedantic analysis of libido theory and the pleasure principle. However, Fairbairn presents an alternative to impulses in the form of 'reactive tendencies'. Such tendencies come into operation as a result of reality experience, and their effects rely not upon arbitrary gratification but upon emotive meaning states. By this substitution Fairbairn effects a reorientation from impulse to object relations. Although this is not spelled out, Fairbairn is assuming a twentieth-century theory of organic functioning in which energy is a characteristic of structure. It is because of the implicit shift of emphasis that this piece of work throws so much light upon Fairbairn's later theorising. It can also be seen to bring into focus modern thinking about adolescent disturbances and eating disorders, demonstrated in Fairbairn's discussion of erotogenic zones and aversions.

The historic interest of all the early papers which we have included in Parts II, III, and IV is considerable. For example, the paper on child assault (1935) (Chapter 4) represents a contribution to the biennial Mental Hygiene Conferences which were prestigious during the 1930s. The particular conference in 1939 at which the paper, here entitled 'Sexual Delinquency' (Chapter 14), was delivered was opened by the Duke of Kent. Fairbairn's paper opened proceedings on the second day. Chapter 5, 'The Nervous Child', represents a contribution to the contemporary debates on the treatment of mental handicap, eugenics, and child rearing. It should be read in the context of the introduction of the Child Guidance movement to Scotland. The Child Guidance movement was initiated in America and became an important factor in the treatment of disturbed children in Britain. Its influence has continued under the aegis of such clinics and child psychologists working in the education system. The papers here entitled 'Imagination and Child Development' (Chapter 6), 'A Critique of Educational Aims' (Chapter 19), and 'Psychoanalysis and the Teacher' (Chapter 20) are set against the development of the debate about education in Britain during the 1930s. This debate was continued after the Second World War and culminated in the Education Acts enacted in the 1940s and 1950s. The debate has been addressed again in Britain, so it is still ongoing.

'Arms and the Child' (Chapter 18) is a contribution to the understanding of the psychology of the political philosophy of fascism. Fairbairn was much affected by a visit which he made to Germany in 1933, the year of Adolf Hitler's rise to power, during which he witnessed physical oppression. Fairbairn's concern was further consolidated by his reading of Hitler's *Mein Kampf* (1934). However, it is the fostering of aggressive characteristics exhibited by Man and enshrined in the conventional upbringing of children which is Fairbairn's real target in this paper. The problem of delinquency is addressed by Fairbairn in chapters 14 and 22. In these Fairbairn is working within the general context of the 'punishment' or 'cure' debate. Fairbairn's position is that while rehabilitation is possible and desirable both for the individual delinquent and for society, cure is impossible on the grounds that the specific delinquency exhibited by an individual is part of character. Since it is developmentally incorporated, the only cure would be dissolution of the personality. But the development of the expertise to achieve rehabilitation requires intellectual, legal, and financial commitment. The debate between the merits of punishment and those of rehabilitation still remains unresolved in Britain and the United States. Fairbairn's main contention is that the exacerbation of infantile dependence, in the form of punishment by deprivation, will merely consolidate sexually delinquent or antisocial characteristics.

The papers in Part II represent Fairbairn's early work on child development and psychopathology. In these he demonstrates his willingness to challenge accepted ideas of child assault and to refocus attention upon the effects experienced by the child. The historic interest of these papers is also considerable because we find an association of conventional ideas regarding, for example, homosexuality or genital orientation, as depicted in 'Child Assault', 'Male Pseudohermaphroditism', and 'Features in the Analysis of a Patient with a Physical Genital Abnormality' (Fairbairn 1931), combined with an 'object relations' focus. In these particular cases, with some reservations in the case of homosexuality, the genome programme offers to contribute to knowledge of genetic structure and ultimately to the psychological effects of such anomalous conditions. Seen as a problem of historiography, these papers highlight the difficulties faced by any individual theorist in confronting his own historicity while he struggles to formulate a new paradigm within the existing parameters of his own culture. In Fairbairn's case conventional ideas of homosexuality can be seen to inhibit the development of his notions of object relationships.

'Adolescence' (Chapter 7) was developed out of Fairbairn's extensive work on adolescence, which is noted as his special contribution to the development of psychology at Edinburgh University in the 1928–1929 academic year. Dr (later Professor) Drever's special topic was 'Emotion and Sentiment', while that of another colleague, Dr Mary Collins, was 'Delinquency and Defect'. Fairbairn continued to lecture on adolescence to a variety of students until 1935.

The papers in Part III represent an insight into the topics which were seen at the time to be of particular importance to the development of psychoanalysis. We discuss the particular relevance of aggression in the Introduction to Part III of this volume. 'The Psychology of Anxiety' (Chapter 10) is of specific importance to Fairbairn's own development, for anxiety in situations of perceived deprivation in infancy is a state which he later saw as contributing to ego splitting. Therefore, it is also a state which activates the techniques of defensive symptom formation he described so graphically (1941 and 1943a), replacing 'unpleasure' within the mental economy by an instinctual opposition of affective states. Fairbairn views affective states as connecting aspects of experience to structure, thus providing a link—comparable to that proposed in twentieth-century physics through the theory of relativity—to the close relationship between energy and psychic structure (see editors' introductory notes, *From Instinct to Self: Volume I,* pp. xv–xvi and *Volume II*, pp. 415–416).

The two papers on art in Part V represent an attempt on Fairbairn's part to make a contribution to the philosophy of aesthetics. Western aesthetic ideas originated in Ancient Greece, where centres such as Epidaurus combined the ideal of physical well-being with mental health. This was to be achieved through communal participation in physical activity and theatre in an aesthetically constructed environment. Painting and sculpture were seen as a mirror of the real world, while beauty was a universal abstraction. In Europe in the late eighteenth and nineteenth centuries, ideas of enlightenment associated with the changing status of the individual in society were applied to aesthetics. The outcome was that the artist was credited with the capacity to reveal the 'truth' in his artifacts. The expressive content of the work was also given greater status as a representation of the reality of emotion. This was apparent in Goethe's fiction and poetry while his *Theory of Colours* (Goethe 1840) influenced both Turner and the German Expressionist painters. Freud had written that man's motivation was secret and questionable; at the same time, Marx's political analysis suggested that the apparent order of society concealed the motives of those in authority. The status of the artist as 'the revealer of the truth' was thus consolidated by the claims of psychoanalysis and Marxism. In addition, both psychoanalysis and Marxism called into question accepted cultural mores in relation to the individual.

For all these reasons the aesthetic debate in the 1920s and 1930s was focused on the relationship between 'form' and 'content' as expressed in a work of art. So we can appreciate why this relationship seemed important to Fairbairn when he attempted to construct a psychology of art. Freud had tried to demonstrate the validity of psychoanalysis as a tool to uncover the secrets of the artist's psyche. In his study of Leonardo da Vinci, Freud (1910b) utilised the theory of infantile sexuality to validate what he saw as Leonardo's 'pathological' homosexuality without due attention to the context within which the actual work of art was created, nor to some details of the work itself (see Dickson 1985, pp. 146–148). Freud's (1914c) work on Moses similarly divorced the statue from its intended context (see Fuller 1988, pp. 32–33). Such attempts may say more about the symbolism of Freud's own Germanic culture than perhaps he realised. Freud (1907/1917b) did attempt in 'Gradiva' to demonstrate the validity of his theories of dreams and repression through direct analysis of Jensen's story *Gradiva* (1903; see Freud 1917b). However, the attempt remains methodologically dubious since Freud treated a fictional account as though it were clinical data. That is, Freud was relying upon the notion of the artist as 'the revealer of truth'.

Fairbairn's two papers on art represent an attempt to provide a new direction: a meaningful account of the relationship between the artist, the art object, and the viewer which articulates the psychological perspectives of each of the three participants with the artifact in a middle role as 'that which communicates' with both the artist and the viewer. In this way it appears to fulfil a role analogous to that performed by internal objects in the psychic life of the individual. Maintaining this focus we can see how Fairbairn expands our understanding of the psychic processes involved in encounters with that which is other. Despite its inadequacies, Fairbairn produced a general hypothesis upon which to develop a new psychology of art.

In Part VI we have published three of the numerous reviews which Fairbairn contributed in his lifetime. Many of the books he reviewed were only very loosely connected with psychoanalysis, but most have contributed to the development of medicine or science in our time.

The three letters written between 1942 and 1954 are included because they demonstrate Fairbairn's consistent willingness to address issues raised by others and the vehicle of exchange of ideas with his colleagues. It is clear from this small sample that he was prepared to give his time and a courteous, thoughtful response to any request on his views, whether it be from a like-minded colleague, such as Brierley, or one whose work was a considerable distance from his own interests. The final letter is particularly interesting because it is on a subject he was later to write about, and because it was written to his disciple and close friend, John Sutherland, who did so much to extend the range and influence of Fairbairn's ideas.

The final entries, 'The Impressions of the 1929 International Congress of Psycho-Analysis' and the 'Autobiographical Note', are subjective accounts. The former is of historical interest in its focus on the questions actually debated at that Congress. Many of the issues which captured Fairbairn's attention have remained questions for debate in psychoanalytic circles to this day.

Fairbairn's contribution to psychoanalysis has been neglected, underrated, and misconstrued. This is partly because the only prior collection of his writings in *Psycho-Analytic Studies of the Personality* (1952b) did not provide a clear definitive statement of his theoretical position (which at that date was incomplete), while many of his ideas have been accepted as the bedrock of psychoanalytic practice (see Volume I, p. xii) but separated from its theoretical origin in Fairbairn's writing. The papers in Volume II provide evidence of the early date at which Fairbairn formulated his ideas. Fairbairn's work has been commonly accepted as a *revision* of Freud rather than the fundamental reorientation of psychoanalysis it actually was. Where Freud assumed human nature to be dualistic, Fairbairn assumed human nature to be holistic (see Introduction to Volume I, p. xvi). Fairbairn substituted 'man in existent relationships' (Heidegger's phrase was 'being in the world') for 'man in a struggle for survival against others'—the Darwinian view. Fairbairn's alternative view of human nature demanded a nonmechanistic scientific methodology. In Fairbairn this takes the form of an account of energy and structure in mutual relationship or, in psychoanalytic terms, his theory of endopsychic structure. This is reinforced clinically by his view of the analyst as active within the psychotherapeutic relationship (Chapter 4, Volume I). What Fairbairn introduced was not a simple shift from instinct theory to object relations; both of these aspects, namely, instinct theory and object relations, are contained in Freud, as Susan Isaacs (1943) emphasized (see p. 228, this volume), but a new paradigm for psychoanalysis, in which the socially oriented human individual is seen as a self-organising unity.

The academic papers in Volume II of *From Instinct to Self* provide a previously unknown source for the study of the history of psychoanalytic ideas, while the unpublished lectures provide contextual material. This volume allows us to study Fairbairn's mature academic critique of Freud alongside his early published psychoanalytical writings. It documents the beginning of Fairbairn's progression towards his new paradigm for psychoanalysis. The inclusion of papers and unpublished lectures covering wider issues, such as those in Parts II, IV, and V, enlarges the perspective of the volume to embrace child development and psychopathology as well as psychoanalysis as applied to the allied fields of dentistry, sociology, education, religion, and aesthetics. When taken together with the clinical, theoretical, and methodological papers in Volume I, the material in Volume II forms an indispensable adjunct to the only previous collection of Fairbairn's work, *Psycho-Analytic Studies of the Personality* (1952b). Taken together these three volumes elucidate Fairbairn's contribution in a way which none of them does in isolation. Volume II of *From Instinct to Self* is therefore essential for a full appreciation of Fairbairn's contribution to the development of psychoanalytic theory and practice. It provides a fascinating insight into the mind and intellectual development of a singular man. We hope that students and scholars will find the rediscovery of Fairbairn to be as exciting a journey as we have.

Ellinor Fairbairn Birtles
David E Scharff
London and Washington, D.C. 1994

I

EARLY CONTRIBUTIONS TO THEORY

INTRODUCTION TO PART I

In the lecture and class discussion notes he saved, Fairbairn documented his meticulous study of Freud during the fifteen years before his own major revision of analytic theory, where we have already noted that he frequently quoted Freud and stated his agreements and disagreements carefully. There were in addition drafts of papers which Fairbairn apparently intended to make into a psychology textbook which would offer an explication and critique of Freud. This project must have had to have been set aside when he left the university post for full-time practice and then was superseded by his new thinking on object relations some years later. The legacy of these years of study and teaching comes through in his later writing, but the early writing is of interest in itself. We have reprinted here three items we considered the most significant, all published here for the first time. The first is Fairbairn's thesis, 'Dissociation and Repression', which was submitted in 1929 in application for the M.D. degree to Edinburgh University. Second, we have combined two of three lectures Fairbairn wrote on the nature and origin of the superego, entitled 'What Is the Superego?' and, 'Is the Superego Repressed?' in Chapter 2. These have been edited to omit repetitive material which was also repeated in the third of these lectures, which is therefore omitted. Finally, we have included 'Libido Theory Re-evaluated', which was originally intended to be a paper entitled 'The Libido Theory and the Pleasure Principle Interpreted in Terms of Appetite'. In these comments, we want to set the stage for these documents by setting them in the context of Fairbairn's teaching and study.

A SEMINAR ON *THE EGO AND THE ID*

In an extensive set of lecture notes made for an Edinburgh University psychology discussion class, dated 2 November 1928, Fairbairn set out to teach students about Freud's *The Ego and the Id* (1923b), published five years earlier. He began by noting that the book was important because

> Hitherto, Freud had concerned himself largely with the problem 'What is Repressed?'. Here Freud attacked the problem of the nature of the repressing forces. The most important of the theories in this book is the Superego. The most important thesis about the Superego is that it is unconscious. (1928b)

Fairbairn then worked methodically through the five chapters of the book, showing careful attention and understanding to a topic now long familiar to anyone knowledgeable about psychoanalysis. For our purposes, it is of interest that on the final page of his lecture notes he appends a list called 'Points for Criticism in "The Ego and the Id" '. We reprint that list below in order that the reader may see what issues Fairbairn was already considering in 1928 concerning Freud's structural theory.

POINTS FOR CRITICISM IN "THE EGO AND THE ID"

1. Thesis that mind is essentially unconscious.
2. Topographical method.
3. Identification of Consciousness & Perception.
4. Id being made = forces released in Instinct-dispositions.
   Conception of nature of mind should be structural as well as dynamic.
   Freud tries to get at structure but fails.
5. Freud speaks of original identification as if it were conscious. Is this consistent, e.g., when he speaks of Ego acquiescing in the object-cathexis or defending itself against them by repression.
6. Conception of mind as consisting of Entities.
   These spoken of anthropomorphically, even when supposed to be unconscious.
7. Whole problem of Identification.
   Is it due to setting up abandoned object inside mind?

X[1] 8. Inadequate account of why Superego is unconscious.
X 9. Problem of whether or not Superego is repressed.

10. Theory of Bisexuality.
11. Theory of Store of displaceable energy.
12. Question arises "What & where is the resistance?"
13. Question of relationship of Superego & Id difficult to understand.

[1]Editors' note: These X's placed by Fairbairn were apparently meant to mark the major points he wished to develop in his own thinking or in class discussion. Perhaps the material of the three papers on the superego was presented to this class at a later date.

> Superego appears opposed to Id.
> Yet conflict between Ego & Id appears to merge into conflict of Ego with Superego.

In these notes, we can hear the major questions which haunted Fairbairn not only about *The Ego and the Id* but about Freud's theory more generally. Some of them he took up in his M.D. thesis, written at about this time, and in lectures and papers given soon after this seminar, but others only came to resolution fifteen years later when he settled on his object relations theory—such questions as the place of the id, the need for positing a dynamic structure, and the problems of identification and of the anthropomorphic entities of mind can be seen to be resolved through the concept of the internal object. He worked more immediately on the nature of the repressed in the lectures reprinted in this section, but he did not resolve the questions he retained about the nature of the superego itself until late in his theory building, when he finally decided that the superego was a composite structure made up of the ideal object, the rejecting object, and the anti-libidinal ego (Fairbairn 1963a).

FAIRBAIRN'S M.D. THESIS

In Great Britain, graduate doctors receive an equivalent of a Bachelor of Medicine, such as the Medicinae Bachloris, Churigica Bacheloris, signified by the letters 'M.B., Ch.B.' printed after one's name. The Doctorate in Medicine, or M.D. degree, is an advanced academic degree associated with an honored status and is obtained by the submission of a thesis on a scholarly topic to a university faculty of medicine. Fairbairn's M.D. thesis took up the topic of 'The Relationship of Dissociation and Repression Considered from the Point of View of Medical Psychology' and was submitted on 30 March 1929 to Edinburgh University in fulfilment of the requirements for his doctoral thesis.

This scholarly treatise is of increasing historical interest as psychology and psychiatry rediscover dissociation as a developmentally normal, stage-specific capacity of children which, under traumatic conditions, often sets the stage for some of the most serious personality disorders, including multiple personality.

The thesis examines the relationship between dissociation and repression. After reviewing the literature on both, he describes dissociation as the more general category of which repression is a special case of particular importance for psychopathology and psychoanalytic theory. He adds to the existing literature the ideas—which he believes to be original—that dissociation phenomena can be divided into three categories: (a) dissociation of mental content which is *irrelevant* to the attention of the subject, (b) dissociation of *incompatible* content, and (c) dissociation of the *unpleasant*. Repression, he holds, is a special form of dissociation to be grouped in this last category, the unpleasant, and is to be differentiated from other forms of dissociation of the unpleasant in that repression of the dissociated elements essentially consists of tendencies belonging to the mental structure itself, while in the less striking forms of dissociation of the unpleasant, the dissociated elements consist in large part of the mental content:

> In simple dissociation of the unpleasant, what is dissociated is part of the mental content which is felt to be unpleasant because of its relations to a prevailing tendency. In repression, what is dissociated is part of the mental structure which is felt to be unpleasant because of its relation to the organised self. [p. 74]

What Fairbairn was trying to do may in retrospect seem to turn on a fine point, but we can watch him, through the body of the thesis, arguing for the active force of repression by the main part of the personality, which he has the foresight here, as in the lectures on the superego he gave shortly after submitting his thesis, to call the *organised self*. He contrasts the force of most dissociation as instigated by a part of the mind to make *contents* unconscious, with repression in which the central organized self acts against a part of its own structure, which has what he calls a *tendency* towards the elements which have to be actively repressed because of the pain of conflict they would bring if they were allowed to become or remain conscious.

In the light of modern views of dissociation as involving a discontinuity of parts of the mind and of mental functioning—rather than a split of contents alone—the argument Fairbairn makes has probably become outdated. Repression might now be seen as the general or perhaps less pathologized mechanism, while dissociation has come to be more closely associated with severe splits in the personality and with such concepts as hypnogogic states and multiple personality. Nevertheless, modern theorists view dissociation of parts of the personality, as did Fairbairn, as a normal process throughout life, but one whose prominence at certain periods in early childhood predisposes to severe pathology and severe splits in the functioning self or ego if traumatic conditions overwhelm ego capacity. Thus, repression can still be viewed as a subcategory of dissociation, but now it can be seen as a more normal one having to do both with ordinary splitting and with covering up of conflictual material and of parts of the personality at war with the central organized self. Dissociation can be thought of as associated with splits of consciousness and of self-states of the personality, with loss of the self's integrative capacity. Both dissociation and repression can now be seen—with the help of the later theories contributed by Fairbairn and others—to exist on a continuum from normal, nonpathological examples to pathological extremes, with repression ranging from the normal sorting of material into unconscious internal object relations to the severe depletion of personality in schizoid states, while dissociation ranges from a mechanism which gives us the capacity to daydream, to one marking the severe non-integration of multiple personality or hypnogogic states.

While Fairbairn's thesis stands as an early document with a contribution in its own right, it stands more importantly as a milestone on the road to his later work on the centrality of splitting and repression in the organization of personality. In his papers of the 1940s concerning the repression of mental structures themselves, Fairbairn abandoned the discussion of the difference between repression and dissociation which had occupied so much of his scholarship in the lectures on the superego and the M.D. thesis. In the M.D. thesis we can see Fairbairn working with the ideas which came to fruition when he formulated this object relations theory of the personality a dozen years later. By then his thinking about dissociation had been transformed beyond easy recognition to the processes contained in the universal 'splitting of the ego.' In his later formulation, splitting was inevitably paired with repression to reject painful content and to build unconscious structure compartmentalized away from consciousness. These internal structures, he said, are themselves in dynamic relationship and themselves simultaneously able to initiate or potentiate repression of other internal self-and-object structures. The formulation posits the interaction of repressed content with the evolving structure of the mind which must contain it. He saw this sort of interaction as equally relevant for the pathological organizations of both neurotic personality and multiple personality disorder.

The significance of this study can perhaps best be understood with reference to Fairbairn's paper twenty-five years later, 'On the Nature of Hysterical States' (*From Instinct to Self: Volume 1, Chapter 1*), where he puts this earlier interest in differentiating repression from dissociation in perspective. There he noted that the earlier interest of psychology in dissociation had been largely overtaken by the concept of repression which had come to form the cornerstone of psychoanalytic theory, but not without the loss of the direct understanding that the concept of dissociation offered for the more severely split ego-states such as those found in multiple personality. As we have noted, his understanding of repression had changed over those intervening years to focus on the idea that repression was always paired with splitting of the personality—a form of dissociation in a more pervasive and comprehensive form. By then, he had also moved away from the problems of trauma in early life and in war which had been part of his earlier experience. These severe situations are ones in which the central ego's capacity to repress is overwhelmed, and in which the splits in the ego therefore become so severe that subpersonalities or states of being evade the integrating capacities of a central organized self. His early work with such traumatized children, briefly documented in his paper on child assault (Chapter 4, this volume) and his papers on the trauma of war ('The War Neuroses' [1943a] and 'The Repression and Return of Bad Objects' [1943b]), published in *Psycho-Analytic Studies of the Personality* [1952b], had brought him clinically close to these phenomena so likely to be expressed in severe splits of the ego and dissociative states, but his later theory did not deal extensively with these phenomena. It seems likely that the early work with abused children and his continuing work with war casualties—perhaps along with his experience as a combat officer in the First World War—deeply influenced him and is the reason his final theoretical formulations remain so useful in studying these forms of severe psychopathology.

THE SUPEREGO

Fairbairn took up the thread of his inquiry into the nature of psychic structure when, on 2 November 1929, he gave a lecture entitled 'What Is the Superego?' to the Scottish Branch of the British Psychological Society. This lecture is reprinted here for the first time as the first section of Chapter 2. This is one of the three papers given about this time on aspects of the superego, described in *The Ego and the Id* by Freud in 1923. This lecture gives a careful explication of the superego itself and is noteworthy for its close attention to the phenomena of the ego's identification with the parents and the incorporation of lost love-objects within the ego in the process of setting up the superego. Fairbairn traces the development of the concepts by Freud from 'On Narcissism' (1914a) to the conceptions of *The Ego and the Id*, focusing on the growth of the concept of the ego-ideal as the nucleus of the superego and the later addition to this nucleus of the abandoned object-choices which are incorporated through secondary identification. He reviews the concept of the Oedipus complex and its role in the installation of the superego, raising one or two questions along the way: Is the superego mainly a composite of direct, primary identifications, or is it a congregate of lost objects? He also points to Freud's citing of the phenomenon of multiple personality as evidence for this type of organization of the mind, describes the relationship between the three components of the mind now identified, and ends with a consideration of the superego as somewhere between what psychology has called the Complex, 'a sentiment loosely connected with consciousness', and that of 'secondary personalities' exhibited graphically in the situation of multiple personality. The superego, he ends by suggesting, may not fit precisely with either of these phenomena, but 'it would yet appear to be a psychical organization of a similar order'.

The lecture 'Is the Superego Repressed?' also printed here for the first time as Part II of 'The Superego', refers to Part I, 'What Is the Superego?' Its review of Freud's postulation of the superego includes a graphic analogy which Fairbairn contributed to illustrate the reason why the id and the superego are both repressed. It is, he says, just like a patient who would not be content to turn his eyes from a surgical wound if he could still see the doctor's knife to remind him of the threat. So we must blind ourselves to the superego as well as to the id if we are to avoid the unpleasant material which both sides of the internal conflict call to our attention.

In this lecture, Fairbairn repeatedly uses the term *organized self* to describe the principle of Freud's use of the term *ego*, especially before he focuses more specifically on the mechanisms exercised by the ego as agent of repression. The term *organized self* is of interest because of Fairbairn's later use of the term *ego* in a way which implied that he was actually talking about an organization of the self. When Guntrip made this point to Fairbairn many years later, Fairbairn is said to have agreed (Sutherland, personal communication).

The nature of the repressing agency and of the content of the repressed continued to interest Fairbairn for many years. In this lecture the fine points of the superego as both agent of repression and object of repression are discussed at length, but at the end, Fairbairn suddenly invokes the work of his M.D. thesis on the relationship between dissociation and repression to suggest that the superego may not, after all, be repressed, but may represent itself a dissociated structure, cut off from the mainstream of mind, not because it is in conflict with the ego, but because it is incompatible. In that case, he said, it would continue to oversee repression from its unconscious and dissociated position. This fine point does not hold up logically any longer, but in its argumentation we can see Fairbairn working towards the understanding of the role of splitting in mental structure which later became paramount among his theoretical concerns.

In his critical evaluation of the superego concept, Fairbairn is led to conclude that Freud's identification of the superego as a physical structure was mistaken, although he fully agreed that the phenomenon of the superego is clinically confirmed by psychoanalysis. On this basis Fairbairn used the Freudian notions of disassociation and repression to clarify the actual nature of the superego. Having identified the anomalies contained within Freud's theory of repression, Fairbairn employed these to recharacterize the superego in functional rather than structural terms.

Fairbairn's eventual formulation of superego theory depended on the assumption of the integral quality of personality. The ego or self is initially inexperienced but genetically integrated and orientated towards participation, that is, towards relationships with objects. Early experience is never perfect from the point of view of the infant, and, in consequence, reactive instinctual responses and the associated affects become an integral feature of these early relationships. The need for the child to perceive his parents as 'good' leads to a moral defence (Fairbairn 1952b, p. 93). Children define themselves as bad in order that their security can be maintained by the good parents they construct. That which is felt to be bad in the self leads to guilt, expressed psychically by the punitive nature of the superego function. In Fairbairn's late view of psychic structure, the superego is not a separate structure but an ego function. Thus, the strength of the superego as perceived by the analyst will be dependent on the extent to which the child was actually frustrated or persecuted by the parents. Aspects of the superego function may be repressed and then dissociated from the conscious ego within the endopsychic structures, but, as we have previously noted, even in repression these are maintained in object relational structures. Several ego structures, conscious and unconscious, participate in the superego functions. This outcome of Fairbairn's analysis of the conscious and unconscious modes of functioning of the superego is discussed in this paper and in the earlier one, 'What Is the Superego?' Although his later work (1944, 1946a, 1949, 1951a) is based on these assumptions, it is not specifically stated there.

In these lectures, Fairbairn assumes that the individual lives in reciprocity with social and cultural forces. Freud's view was that morality, or conscience, is imposed upon us, while Fairbairn thought we absorb and react to social and cultural mores as a necessary and positive function of being human. Problems arise when mores are nonparticipatory, that is, they have ceased to be reciprocal and have become authoritarian. As Fairbairn would see it, they have come to perpetuate dependence on authority (see 'Arms and the Child,' Chapter 18). As a result of Fairbairn's identification of superego phenomena as ego functions, he could provide a more plausible account of the results of deprivation and persecution in relationships (e.g., criminality, the behaviour of abused children) than Freud was able to do.

THE STUDY OF LIBIDO THEORY

Another of the unpublished academic works written at this time which continued the line of thought of the M.D. thesis is one of substantial significance which was originally called 'The Libido Theory and the Theory of the Pleasure Principle Interpreted in Terms of Appetite'—a paper written in 1930 and intended for publication in *The British Journal of Medical Psychology*.

Here Fairbairn developed an early formidable critique of Freud's dualism and its effects upon his theoretical formulations. Fairbairn regretted that Freud and psychoanalysis in general have dissociated themselves from participation in the general development of psychology. He used the writings of psychologists McDougall and Drever, along with those of Jung, to propose a reorientation of instinct theory. Fairbairn was thus enabled to identify Freud's notion of libido as an appetitive tendency. This, he argued, is as true of sex as of any other manifestation. He rejected McDougall's (1908) proposed associations and hierarchical instincts in favor of Drever's notion of 'instinct-interest'. Using the results of the psychological research into 'instinct-experience', which allowed Drever (1922) to identify the appetitive and reactive tendencies, Fairbairn saw the reactive tendencies as factors designed to promote adaptation to reality in the individual. Because adaptation to reality is a necessary assumption in Fairbairn's reorientation from Freud's instinct theory based upon the gratification of drives, towards the new one based upon object relationships, his arguments here have substantial significance for his future theoretical developments. In addition, Drever's reactive tendencies effect emotional responses in proportion to the extent to which they are facilitated or obstructed. This led Fairbairn to see affect not simply as emotional colouring but as a complex subjective experience of a relationship between the ego or self and that which is other—the object within psychic reality. This subjective experience of relationships is, of itself, a hermeneutical experience, inserting the element of subjective evaluation into the process. This was supported by Fairbairn's use of Stout's (1927) mental levels (see Fairbairn's response to Susan Isaacs' [1943] paper in Chapter 15, and our discussion of that paper on pp. 227–228). We can see a clear correspondence between such ideas and those in his later work. These early papers are evidence that while Klein's work acted as a catalyst in the development of Fairbairn's work, it was not the source from which it was derived.

A defining characteristic of the appetitive tendencies is the immediacy of the need for satisfaction. Fairbairn's discussion of Freud's theory of erotogenic zones introduces a reorientation along the lines of Drever's ideas on the functioning of these tendencies. Fairbairn identifies nausea as an affect of aversion, rather than an appetite, whose aim is the removal of an organic state. He notes the parallel between the affect of nausea and the activities of escape and unpleasure-avoidance. He proposes that nausea and repression are modes of unpleasure-avoidance and discusses their roles in symptom formation, speculating on 'the part which [nausea] may be presumed to play in the initiation of repression and the promotion of culture' (p. 155). (This insight on nausea and repression might throw light on the development of such syndromes as anorexia and bulimia.) Fairbairn continues by noting the connection between nausea and smell aversion in Freud's remarks on organic repression and bodily odors. His conclusions are that Freud's 'libidinal aims' 'are determined by specific appetitive tendencies belonging to the innate endowment of man, while the erotogenic zones correspond . . . to the "significant zones" of the specific appetites' (p. 156), thus diminishing the significance of erotogenic zones in psychoanalysis and substituting a structural bodily correspondence between the bodily activity and the organ involved in the activity. For instance, Fairbairn suggests that the activities of physical exercise and libidinal feelings are promoted for those areas in which the erotogenic zone is the musculature.

This early work provides another aspect of the theoretical basis for a theory of personality which is not rooted in a mind–body dualism. It supports a hermeneutical theory of subjective experience based on object relationships, a theory incorporating intrinsic affect as a component of psychic reality in the form which it assumed in the final theory. It provides an explanation of limited early cognitive functioning and of adaptive techniques not dependent on a division between ego and id.

1. DISSOCIATION AND REPRESSION

OBJECT OF THESIS

The object of this thesis is to consider the conceptions of Dissociation and Repression with a view to determining in what way, if any, the processes are related to one another. These two conceptions have played a part of unrivalled importance in modern psychopathology, but no satisfactory attempt seems to have been made to determine the exact nature of their relationship to one another. The conclusions reached in this thesis regarding their relationship constitute, so far as the writer is aware, an original contribution to the subject.

MEDICINE AND PSYCHOLOGY

The task imposed by the aim of this thesis involves an exploration of ground which is common to medical science and psychology. While these two sciences are rightly differentiated from one another both as regards aim and subject matter, an unnatural divorce between them is detrimental to the interests of both. The subject matter of medicine is disease in the human organism, and its aim is twofold: (a) to understand the nature of disease (The Science of Medicine); (b) to devise and apply methods of cure (The Art of Medicine). On the other hand, the subject matter of psychology is the behaviour of the organism; and its aim is to interpret behaviour in terms of inner experience. The "mental processes" of which the psychologist speaks are the laws of behaviour interpreted in such terms, and the study of these processes constitutes the science of Psychology. Corresponding to the Art of Medicine we may also recognise an Applied Psychology, the object of which is to apply knowledge of mental laws to the solution of various problems of life. Although the science of medicine and the science of psychology are thus distinct, there is a considerable area of common ground in their respective provinces. After all, disease is not an entity. When disease is present, it is the organism that is diseased; and the presence of disease affects the organism's behaviour, which is the subject matter of psychology. Further, there are certain types of disease in which the chief symptoms are aberrations of behaviour. Conspicuous among such diseases is that group which is commonly designated "Functional Nervous Disease": a group which includes the psycho-neuroses and certain of the insanities. It is in relation to this group of diseases that a knowledge of the laws of behaviour is of particular value to medical science. As a matter of fact, whatever debt medicine already owes to psychology is due largely to the light which psychology has thrown upon the nature of these diseases. It may be added that the debt is not one-sided, and that the study of this group of abnormal phenomena by clinicians has exercised a profound influence upon the psychology of normal mental processes.

Although during the last thirty years there has been unmistakable evidence of a rapprochement between medicine and psychology to the mutual benefit of each, it is none the less true to say that the two sciences have not yet recovered from the effects of an unnatural divorce. The divorce between medicine and psychology is of comparatively recent origin. If we trace back the history of both sciences, we find that they have a common origin in Religion. Among primitive peoples the doctor is the witch-doctor. Disease is attributed to the influence of "spirits", and treatment proceeds on lines conforming to this belief. The measures which are taken to combat disease are such as are calculated to influence the spirits concerned. Since these spirits are anthropomorphically conceived, it is easy to understand that primitive medicine is ultimately based upon the conceptions of human mental process prevalent in the community. Medicine and psychology are thus seen to derive their lineage from a common source. They are both children of the primitive animistic conception of the universe. Even after the day when physical science began to evolve out of magic and the effects of physical forces in causing disease began to be realised, the animistic theory of disease was only very gradually abandoned. The physical and animistic theories existed side by side, and the former only gradually grew at the expense of the latter. In Greek and Roman times it is true that a medical science based on physical conceptions reached a high degree of development, but the medical man had a formidable rival in the priest of Aesculapius. Even after the dawn of the Christian era medicine remained intimately connected with religion. The development of Arabian Medicine perhaps constitutes an exception to this generalisation, but this was only a more or less localised interlude. In Christian countries medicine remained a prerogative of the Church. It was only after the Renaissance had stimulated interest in physical science that a proper science of medicine based on physical conceptions began to establish itself on a solid foundation. This movement reached a climax towards the close of the nineteenth century, when the rise of physiology and neurology inclined medical men to interpret all forms of disease, including mental disease, in exclusively physical terms. This phase has by no means passed, but in the latter part of the nineteenth century a reaction against extreme materialistic conceptions of disease began to make itself felt in the medical world. This reaction was the outcome of considerations resulting from the study of two groups of phenomena: (a) the phenomena of Hypnotism, (b) the phenomena of Hysteria.

The scientific study of hypnotism may be said to have begun when Mesmer astonished the cultured circles of Vienna in the latter part of the eighteenth century by introducing them to the phenomena of so-called 'Animal Magnetism'. The prejudices of the medical and scientific world and the extravagances of the Mesmerists themselves led to the discrediting of the whole subject, but it is interesting to note that the explanation put forward by Mesmer to account for the phenomena was a physical one. He attributed them to the action of 'magnetic fluid'. No further light was thrown upon the subject until the time of James Braid, the Manchester surgeon, who in 1843 embarked upon an investigation of the phenomena of mesmerism. These he was at first inclined to regard as the effects of fatigue, and the explanation which he offered was couched in physiological terms. Later, however, he substituted a psychological explanation, in accordance with which "suggestion" was regarded as the main agent in producing the hypnotic state. The view that the hypnotic state was due to suggestion created little interest until it was revived by Professor Bernheim of Nancy, who, under the inspiration of Liébeault, published his book *De la Suggestion* in 1884. The Nancy School held that hypnotism was simply normal sleep induced by suggestion and that it could be produced in any individual by suitable methods. There arose, however, a school of investigators in Paris who took up a somewhat different view. This was the school of the Salpêtrière Clinique, among whom the leading figure was J. M. Charcot (1825–1893). Charcot's investigations were conducted among the nervous patients who attended the clinique, and this fact doubtless explains the conclusion which he drew as to the nature of hypnotism. He recognised the intimate connection of hypnotism and suggestion, but he regarded both as pathological. He regarded them as phenomena of hysteria. The acrimonious controversy which arose between the Nancy and Salpêtrière schools as a result of the divergence of their views is happily now an affair of the past. It is now generally agreed that both views embodied a truth, but that neither view was wholly true. It is to the Nancy School that we owe recognition of the facts that suggestion may take effect in a normal individual and that there is an intimate connection between suggestion and hypnotism. It is to the Salpêtrière school, on the other hand, that we owe the knowledge that increased suggestibility is a characteristic of certain pathological states, of which hysteria is the most notable. It is to the Salpêtrière also that we owe those researches which have led to recognition of the part played in functional nervous disease by psychological processes.

The outstanding figure of the Salpêtrière School was undoubtedly Charcot (vide Freud 1893a). While Charcot was essentially a neurologist, his clinical insight led him to recognise that it was impossible to disregard the importance of mental processes, so far, at any rate, as hysteria was concerned. In his introduction to the famous work on hysteria, by his pupil, Janet, he expresses his opinion in these words: "L'hystérie est en grande partie une maladie mentale" ("Hysteria is in great part a mental disease" [1911, p. 447]). It was, however, in the influence which he exerted upon two of his pupils rather than in his own views upon functional nervous disease that his importance for psychopathology chiefly lies. These pupils were Pierre Janet and Sigmund Freud. It is upon the work of these two men that the whole structure of modern psychopathology is founded.

Although Janet and Freud both owe their inspiration to a common master, their researches have led them along different paths. The starting point for the researches of both was the disease to which Charcot's clinical teaching had directed their attention, viz. hysteria; but Janet in Paris and Freud in Vienna each pursued his own path more or less indifferent to the other. Both modified Charcot's pronouncement that "Hysteria is in great part a mental disease" into the proposition that hysteria is *essentially* a mental disease (Janet 1911, Freud 1893c). Each reached the conclusion that all the hydra-headed symptomatology of hysteria was the expression of one fundamental psychological process. They differed, however, in their views as to the nature of this process, as well as in the terms which they adopted to describe it. Janet developed the conception of "Dissociation", while Freud developed that of "Repression".

The independence of the paths, which, as a matter of history, these two investigators have pursued in the formulation of their views, has led to a situation which is not altogether satisfactory so far as medical science is concerned. It has led to a division of medical thought into two camps, so far as functional nervous diseases are concerned. Between these two camps there is very little coming and going. One school interprets functional nervous disease in terms of the process of dissociation, the other in terms of the process of repression. The two conceptions are thus generally regarded as alternatives for purposes of explanation, though, as Rivers points out (1924), some writers seem to use the two terms indifferently, without considering whether the conceptions involved are identical or not. In psychological circles, on the other hand, the situation is different. Both conceptions have been widely adopted into psychology, but, as far as psychologists are concerned, it would be as untrue to say that they are regarded as alternatives as it would be to say that they are regarded as identical. It remains true, however, that little attempt has been made, either in medical or psychological circles, to consider what relationship, if any, exists between the two processes of dissociation and repression. It is the aim of the present thesis to attempt to supply this want.

DISSOCIATION AND REPRESSION

While it is true to say that little attempt has been made either by medical writers or psychologists to consider the relationship of dissociation and repression, it would be incorrect to say that no such attempt has been made at all. Of the attempts made the most notable are those of Dr. W. H. R. Rivers and Professor William McDougall. It is interesting to note that both these psychologists are also medical men.

Rivers' views upon this subject are to be found in Chapter X, of his *Instinct and the Unconscious*. There he expresses his view that dissociation is essentially a state resulting from "suppression": "suppression" being the term Rivers employs to describe the process of "repression" as ordinarily understood. He thus uses the term "dissociation" to describe a state in which suppressed experience may persist. He conceives it not as a passive state, but as a state characterised by independent activity of the repressed elements. He further assumes that this independent activity carries with it independent consciousness (Rivers 1924). From this summary it is plain that Rivers had a very definite idea of the relationship of dissociation and repression, but his view of this relationship cannot be regarded as satisfactory. It is unsatisfactory for several reasons:

1. The first point which invites criticism is the narrowness of his conception of dissociation. The fact that this narrowness is the result of a deliberately imposed limitation in no way minimises the defect. That it was deliberately imposed is evident from the following quotation

> I propose therefore to use the term 'dissociation', not merely for a process and state in which suppressed experience acquires an independent activity, but shall assume that this independent activity carries with it independent consciousness. In some cases in which we have obviously to do with independent activity as shown by behaviour, it may not be possible to demonstrate the existence of independent and dissociated consciousness, but I believe it will be convenient to limit the term 'dissociation' to cases where there is evidence of this independent consciousness. [Rivers 1924, p. 76]

By thus limiting dissociation to cases where there is evidence of independent consciousness, Rivers excludes many phenomena which seem best explained in terms of this process. The undesirability of confining the use of the term

Fairbairn in uniform 1915

'dissociation' to cases where there is evidence of independent consciousness will be shown in due course.

2. If Rivers' conception of dissociation is subject to criticism, the same holds true of his conception of repression, or, as he prefers to call it, 'suppression'. 'Suppression' is conceived by Rivers as the psychological correlate of that physiological function of inhibition, which the higher and later evolved elements of the nervous system exercise over the lower and more fundamental structures. "The suppression which I have been considering in the last two chapters", he writes, "is only one aspect of the universal physiological property of inhibition" (Rivers 1924, p. 31). This identification

is perhaps the natural result of Rivers' researches in collaboration with Henry Head and J. Sherren on the physiology of the nervous system; but that it involves a stultifying of the conception of repression will be shown later, when the nature of repression is discussed. That such a process of inhibition as Rivers describes does actually exist need not be disputed. The researches of Head and his colleagues leave no room for doubt about the existence of a physiological process of this nature; and psychologists universally recognise the existence of an analogous process, for which they too employ the term 'inhibition'. It must be insisted, however, that this process is not the process of repression.

3. The third great weakness of Rivers' position follows from those to which attention has already been drawn. It lies in the fact that he regards dissociation as a narrower concept than repression. That he does so is evident from the following passage: "I assume, therefore, that suppression often exists without anything which we can regard as dissociation, that in many cases the suppressed content exhibits no form of independent activity with no evidence that it is accompanied by any form of consciousness" (1924, p. 77). Since, in his opinion, dissociation is a state resulting from repression, it is obvious from this passage that, of the two concepts dissociation is taken by Rivers to be very much the narrower. It will be one of the main objects of this thesis to show that this interpretation of their relationship is the reverse of the truth.

The most recent attempt to formulate the relationship between dissociation and repression is that found in Professor McDougall's "Outline of Abnormal Psychology". The difference between McDougall's formulation and that of Rivers is well shown by the following quotation from the book (McDougall 1926) in question: "There are good grounds for distinguishing the process of repression from that of dissociation, as also the state of continued repression from a continuing state of dissociation" (p. 234). According to McDougall, therefore, the two processes are radically and fundamentally distinct. Indeed the distinction between them constitutes the keynote of his book. He erects upon it a tentative classification of the functional nervous disorders. In this classification he distinguishes two groups of disorders: one group characterised by dissociation, the other by repression. The chief representatives of the group characterised by dissociation are hysteria among the psychoneuroses and manic-depressive insanity among the psychoses. The group characterised by repression includes neurasthenia and obsessional neuroses on the one hand, and dementia praecox and paranoia on the other. In formulating his views upon this subject, McDougall appears to have been markedly influenced by the theories of Dr. C. G. Jung of Zürich, and in particular by Jung's theory of psychological types. This theory was originally expounded by Jung (1917), and more recently in his work entitled "Psychological Types" (1923). As is well known, Jung (1917) distinguishes two main temperamental types: the Extrovert and the Introvert. A person, he says,

> is extroverted when he gives his fundamental interest to the outer or objective world, and attributes an all-important and essential value to it: he is introverted, on the contrary, when the objective world suffers a sort of depreciation, or want of consideration, for the sake of the exaltation of the individual himself, who then monopolising all the interest, grows to believe no one but himself worthy of consideration. [p. 288]

Jung's distinction between these two types was based upon a study of the mentality of hysteria and dementia praecox. His studies led him to infer a temperamental difference between these two types of patients, and, starting from this observation, he was led to extend this classification to normal persons. The extrovert temperament was regarded as predisposing to hysteria, the introvert temperament to dementia praecox. McDougall appears to have been impressed by the appositeness of this classification; and he proceeded to adopt it with this modification, that, instead of recognising two distinct types, he conceived a temperamental scale with the extreme extrovert at one end and the extreme introvert at the other. This modification, however, did not affect the broad lines of Jung's classification, and McDougall's further views appear to have been developed on this basis. Accepting Janet's observation that dissociation was a characteristic of hysteria, he looked around for a process which might be regarded as characteristic of dementia praecox. This he found in the Freudian process of repression. Once these two processes had been attached to Jung's two psychological types, a place was found in the scheme for other functional affections besides hysteria and dementia praecox.

The theory of functional nervous diseases, which McDougall was thus led to erect under the influence of Jung, was not without support derived from his own findings. He regarded it as supported not only by the clinical observation of patients suffering from the various functional disorders, but also by striking experimental evidence. One train of evidence was derived from his experience that the extrovert type was more susceptible to hypnosis than the introvert type. This conformed with the statements of Charcot and Janet that dissociation and liability to hypnosis were both distinctive characteristics of the hysteric, and with his own finding that in neurasthenia and dementia praecox hypnosis was peculiarly difficult to produce.

Another train of evidence was derived from a consideration of the bearing of experiments which he had conducted in the years 1912–1914 on the influence of stimulant and depressant drugs upon mental process (McDougall 1926). The experimental material used was a model windmill, the arms of which were rotated at a rate of three revolutions per second. When such a model is watched from an angle of about 25° to the plane of rotation, the arms appear to reverse their direction periodically. The first observation, which McDougall made, was that the rate of alternation varied with different subjects in conformity with the general rule that introverts experienced rapid alternations, extroverts slow ones. The second observation was that the rapidity of alternation could be altered for any given subject by the exhibition of either stimulant or depressant drugs: stimulant drugs producing an increase, depressant drugs a decrease of rapidity. Subsequently McDougall interpreted this in the sense that these drugs altered the position of the subject on the introvert–extrovert scale, the depressants, including alcohol, favouring extroversion, the stimulants favouring introversion. The special susceptibility of extroverted persons to extroverting drugs and of introverted persons to introverting drugs was a necessary corollary. These conclusions were then related to the findings of the Committee appointed by the Liquor Control Board during the recent war to investigate the effects of alcohol: findings which McDougall interpreted as showing that alcohol favours dissociation. The susceptibility of the extrovert to alcohol was thus further evidence of the liability of the extrovert to dissociation. The inference that the introvert, on the other hand, was specially subject to repression was supported by the findings of psychoanalysts to the effect that repression and introversion are constant companions.

It is in considerations of this nature that McDougall finds support for his thesis that dissociation and repression are two distinct, or indeed opposed, processes. Both are methods of dealing with mental conflict, but they are different methods. Dissociation terminates conflict by effecting a separation of the conflicting elements, and thus provides a solution of conflict, however poor. Repression, on the other hand, merely obscures conflict by preventing one set of tendencies from gaining direct expression in consciousness (McDougall 1926).

Whatever else may be said about McDougall's interpretation of dissociation and repression as two distinct psychological processes, it is certainly the most interesting attempt which has been made to define their relationship. Examination of the theory, however, reveals many difficulties in the way of accepting it; an indication of their general nature is all that is necessary. Everything depends upon his ability to preserve the distinction which he formulates so definitely; yet this is just what he finds it impossible to do. Following Janet, he regards hysteria as characteristically a product of dissociation. Yet it was from the study of this same disease that Freud was led to formulate his theory of repression. If McDougall finds in hysteria all that is typical of dissociation, Freud finds in it all that is typical of repression. Further, if McDougall is right in saying that dissociation provides a solution of conflict, then it would seem that hysteria is the last disease in which to find evidence of its presence; for in no functional disease are the symptoms more changeable or more easily aggravated. As a matter of fact, McDougall (1926) is quite unable to preserve intact his distinction between the two processes. He is forced openly to admit that "Conflict and repression prepare the way for, and may produce, dissociation" (p. 226). In another place, referring to a case of traumatic hysteria, he says: "In cases such as case 3, where recovery from some simple dissociative disability is slow and gradual, or long postponed, we have to believe, I think, that the continuance of the dissociation is favoured by an active repression" (1926, p. 238). He even goes so far as to say: "It is possible, although in my opinion the evidence does not warrant this view, that no dissociation takes place without some previous repression that prepares the way for it" (1926, p. 238). These admissions seem to render meaningless the distinction which he takes such pains to establish. If the two processes of dissociation and repression are so intimately connected and interact so constantly, McDougall's differentiation seems to be theoretically unjustifiable and is contradicted even by many of his own clinical observations.

The unsatisfactory nature of the theories of Rivers and McDougall regarding the relationship of dissociation and repression has led the writer of this thesis to seek a solution of the problem in another direction. In spite of the failure of the two theories which have been examined, they have served a useful purpose in clearing the ground and in indicating by their very failure the lines along which a solution may be sought. Rivers regarded dissociation as a state which might result from repression. To distort his view slightly, one might almost say that he regarded dissociation as a special form of repression. McDougall, on the other hand, suggests that they are wholly distinct processes. The most obvious remaining alternatives are either: (a) that the two processes are identical, or (b) that repression is a special form of dissociation. The former of these alternatives—viz. that the two processes are identical—is rightly rejected by McDougall (1926). The impossibility of accepting it will be evident when we come to discuss the various phenomena in which the process of dissociation manifests itself. These include sleep, the hypnotic state and states produced by alcohol and fatigue—conditions which can hardly be said to provide evidence of repression, unless indeed, following Rivers, we equate repression and inhibition. That we cannot follow Rivers, however, in identifying repression and inhibition will be shown when we compare Rivers' theory of repression with that of Freud. For the present, it will suffice to say that we cannot follow him because one of the most obvious features of these states is the relaxation of repression. It is in a man's dreams, in his cups and in fatigue that repressed tendencies are most ordinarily released.

If then it is impossible to regard dissociation and repression as identical processes, the alternative remains that repression is a special form of dissociation. That this is the case will be *the main conclusion of this thesis.*

Before we are in a position to draw this conclusion, however, it is necessary to consider the nature of each of these processes separately in some detail. Until this is done, it is impossible to see in what way repression can be regarded as a special form of dissociation. The necessity for this task arises from the fact that the two conceptions were formulated largely in relation to the needs of clinical medicine. They were framed primarily to promote the understanding and explanation of symptoms met with in clinical work. Whether these conceptions were compatible with the general principles of mental process recognised by psychology was a purely secondary consideration. This is particularly true in the case of the idea of repression. After all, Janet, to whom we owe the theory of dissociation, was a psychologist as well as a medical man; and, although he worked with a psychology which is obsolete, his ideas can readily be expressed in more modern form. On the other hand, Freud, to whom we owe the theory of repression, regarded general psychology with indifference, if not with contempt. Consequently his psychoanalytical theory has been developed in complete independence of psychological ideas, and it has been formulated in highly metaphorical and anthropomorphic terms. Of this the idea of "The Censorship" is a good example. The close connection of such a metaphorical concept as "The Censorship" with Freud's theory of repression illustrates the need to determine what the exact psychological nature of the latter process is. This need is intensified by the fact that, when Freud introduced his theory of repression, he made no attempt to relate it to Janet's theory of dissociation, although this was already on the field.

In what follows it is proposed to devote attention first to the process of dissociation, then to the process of repression; finally, when the nature of each has been discussed, it will be possible to consider their relationship to one another, and to show how the present writer comes to regard repression as a special form of dissociation.

DISSOCIATION

The term "Dissociation" is ordinarily applied by both medical and psychological writers to cases in which elements of mental life, which are ordinarily conscious, become split off from the main body of consciousness and maintain a high degree of independence. The dissociated elements have been described by some writers as parts of the mental content (e.g., "ideas", "memories", etc.), by others as aspects of mental functioning (e.g., "tendencies", "habits", "emotions", etc.). Others again, preferring physiological to psychological terms, have described the dissociated elements in terms of systems of neurons. Whatever form the descriptions take, however, the important fact remains that the dissociated elements seem to exist or function independently of the personal consciousness. It is this cutting-off of mental elements from the personal consciousness which constitutes the essential feature of dissociation.

The conception of dissociation was first formulated by Pierre Janet, who was Professor of Psychology in the Collège de France, and Director of the Psychological Laboratory in the Clinique of the Salpêtrière. Janet combined a considerable psychological acumen with eminence as a neurologist, and he holds an important place in the modern movement to bring psychology into relationship with medicine. This movement, which began to be effective towards the close of the 19th century, is proving of incalculable advantage to both sciences; and Janet is one of the leading figures in the history of this important development.

The hypothesis that mental elements may exist outside the limits of ordinary consciousness was not a new one. As Dr. Bernard Hart (1926) points out, this hypothesis may be found in one form or another in the writings of various modern philosophers, before the day when psychology differentiated itself from philosophy as an independent study. One form which this hypothesis took was to the effect that, outside ordinary consciousness, lay elements of a like nature to those which are conscious but differing from them in intensity. These elements were conceived as being of such a low degree of intensity that they escaped awareness. The "petites perceptions" of the philosopher Leibniz were of this nature (Leibniz 1705). Such elements correspond to what psychologists in later times have described as "The fringe" of consciousness (James 1891). In accordance with this conception we may imagine a field of consciousness analogous to the field of vision. Items which occupy the centre of the field are in the focus of attention and are vividly conscious, but, as we pass outwards from the centre of the field, we encounter items which are progressively less and less characterised by awareness. Ultimately we come to items of which awareness is minimal, and, if we pass beyond these, we leave the field of consciousness altogether. In the case of the field of vision many images, which fall on the periphery of the field, ordinarily escape notice; but that we are not altogether unaware of such images is shown by the fact that change or movement or the appearance of some unusual character in the image at once attracts attention, and there is a tendency for the eye to move in such a direction that the image may fall on the fovea. Similarly the sensations derived from the pressure of our habitual garments upon the body are not ordinarily attended to; but, if our collar comes off the stud, we at once notice the absence of the usual pressure sensations; we cannot, therefore, have been wholly unaware of the tactual sensations which the collar previously produced. Such phenomena are perfectly familiar, and the conception of mental elements characterised by a minimum of consciousness has a recognised place in psychology. The conception of extra-conscious mental elements in this sense, however, is quite different from the conception of extra-conscious elements involved in the process of dissociation. The mental elements involved in this latter conception are elements of which there is no personal awareness at all (not even minimal awareness).

To those who, following Janet, recognise a psychological process of dissociation, the dissociated elements do not cease to be mental because they have no place in consciousness. To philosophers and psychologists of the older school who regard "mental" and "conscious" as synonymous terms, the conception of dissociation can, of course, only be accepted on the hypothesis that the dissociated elements maintain an independent consciousness of their own outside the main, personal, consciousness. Whether this be so or not, the conception of dissociation remains, so far as its essential nature is concerned, relatively unaffected. There are certain medical writers and certain schools of physiological psychologists, of whom the American Behaviourists are the most notable, who reject the theory of extra-conscious mental processes in this sense altogether. Such authorities prefer to substitute a purely physiological theory of dissociation, explaining the phenomena concerned purely in terms of synaptic resistances and inhibition. There does not, however, seem any reason to deny the existence of dissociated mental elements because there are dissociated paths in the nervous system. After all, the relationship between body and mind is intimate, and one would expect a certain analogy to exist between mental processes and the physiological processes to which they are related. Further, if extra-conscious mental processes are excluded from the purview of physiology this holds equally true of conscious processes. Indeed the Behaviourist school are logical enough to recognise this fact, and make an attempt to describe human behaviour without any reference to mental states at all. The task of physiology, of course, is to interpret the physical aspects of life in terms of physical conceptions; but, if any attempt is to be made to interpret the mental aspects of life, it is legitimate to introduce those psychological conceptions, which the mental facts to be explained appear to demand. The psychological conception of dissociation is of this nature.

The hypothesis that there exist mental processes, quite outside the personal consciousness, and which are not merely processes exhibiting a weak or minimal degree of consciousness, seems to be implied in the philosophy of the eighteenth century philosopher Immanuel Kant (1781). A definite conception of "Unconscious" mental states finds a prominent place in the philosophy of Schopenhauer (1819), and about the same time it is given a definitely psychological setting by Herbart (1816). These processes are conceived as different in character from those occurring in consciousness, but are regarded as capable of influencing and modifying the conscious processes themselves. It was to explain certain phenomena of conscious life that the existence of these unconscious processes was inferred. It appears to be through the medium of von Hartmann that the conception of unconscious mental processes was kept alive until modern times. The importance of von Hartmann (1842–1906) lies chiefly in the influence which his writings exercised upon Freud in the formulation of his well-known theory of the Unconscious. That the time was ripe for a conception of extra-conscious processes is evident from the fact that, in the latter half of the nineteenth century, Edward Carpenter, Höffding, F. W. H. Myers, William James and Janet, as well as Freud, all began to turn their attention to the consideration of "unconscious" or "sub-conscious" processes. Of the writers mentioned, Myers, James, Janet and Freud were all led to the hypothesis of extra-conscious mental states through the consideration of abnormal phenomena. Myers was led to this hypothesis through the study of the phenomena of spiritualism, James through the study of unusual religious experiences, Janet and Freud through the study of hysteria.

The clinical interest in the phenomena of hysteria, which directed the attention of both Janet and Freud to the existence of mental processes outside personal consciousness, was largely due to the inspiration of their teacher Charcot. The debt which these writers owe to Charcot's clinical teaching at the Salpêtrière has been explicitly acknowledged by both. Janet, however, does not seem to have been subject to the philosophical influences which affected the course of Freud's thought. The dual influence of philosophy and clinical experience upon Freud's views may be gathered from his paper on "The Unconscious" (1915e). Speaking of the justification of the conception of the unconscious, he says:

> In many quarters our justification is disputed for assuming the existence of an unconscious system in the mind and for employing such an assumption for purposes of scientific work. To this we can reply that our assumption of the existence of the unconscious is *necessary* and *legitimate*, and that we possess manifold *proofs* of the existence of the unconscious. It is necessary because the data of consciousness are exceedingly defective; both in healthy and in sick persons mental acts are often in process which can be explained only by presupposing other acts, of which consciousness yields no evidence. These include not only the parapraxes and dreams of healthy persons, and everything designated a mental symptom or an obsession in the sick; our most intimate daily experience introduces us to sudden ideas of the source of which we are ignorant, and to results of mentation arrived at we know not how. All these conscious acts remain disconnected and unintelligible if we are determined to hold fast to the claim that every single mental act performed within us must be consciously experienced; on the other hand, they fall into a demonstrable connection if we interpolate the unconscious acts that we infer. [pp. 110, 111]

It is thus evident that Freud's conception of the unconscious is not a mere generalisation based on observed clinical facts. It is a hypothesis on a grand scale, postulated in order to explain these facts. As Dr. Bernard Hart points out (1927), this hypothesis differs from a generalisation, just as Newton's hypothesis of gravitation differed from Kepler's generalisation that planets move in ellipses round the sun. It is here that we see the influence of the philosophies of Schopenhauer and von Hartmann upon Freud's thought. Although it was clinical interest that directed Freud's attention to the phenomena which led him to frame the hypothesis, he formulated it as a general law of the human mind.

Like Freud, Janet was led to formulate his conception of dissociation from a consideration of the clinical facts of hysteria and allied conditions, but his conception was of the nature of a generalisation rather than a hypothesis strictly speaking. From his observation of what he calls "The accidents of hysteria", such as anaesthesiae, paralyses and amnesiae, he came to the conclusion that in all cases there was a narrowing of consciousness. He did not formulate a general law of the mind, but contented himself with making a generalisation about a limited class of facts, which came under his notice in clinical work. This he frankly admits in the chapter entitled "L'Hystérie au point de vue psychologique" ("Hysteria from the Point of View of Psychology") in his work *L'Etat Mental des Hystériques* (1911). His observations showed him that certain functions, memories or ideas, which are present in the normal person, are absent in the hysteric, and that consciousness is thereby impoverished. From this he concluded that these elements are cut off from consciousness. Further, he noted that, though these functions, memories and ideas have escaped from consciousness, they do not cease to give evidence of their activity. He therefore inferred that they persist in the mind in independence of the main body of consciousness, and called them "subconscious".

The class of fact which led Janet to formulate his conception of dissociation is too well known to require more than a brief description. An example is the freedom from accidental injury which a hysterically anaesthetic limb enjoys. This phenomenon stands in striking contrast to what occurs when the anaesthesia is of organic origin. Janet's inference was that the sensations were not abolished but only cut off from personal consciousness. The "Yes or No" phenomenon, also found in cases of hysterical anaesthesia, received a similar interpretation. To elicit this phenomenon the patient is blind-folded and told to say "Yes" when he is touched on a normal limb, "No" when he is touched on an anaesthetic limb. It is frequently found that such a patient responds as appropriately to a touch on one limb as to a touch on the other. This indicates that sensation from the anaesthetic limb is not altogether absent from the mind, although it is absent from consciousness. Similarly, a hysterically blind patient is usually able to avoid obstacles placed in his path. In cases of hysterical paralyses, the power to move the paralysed limb by voluntary effort is lost, but its position changes in a manner impossible for a limb affected by organic paralysis. If the patient falls, the paralysed limb may be used in such a way as to save the patient from injury. In hysterical paralysis the appearance presented is thus what one would expect if the power to move the limb remained and the patient had forgotten how to move it. Further, it is found that lost powers of sensation and movement may be regained under hypnosis, the inference being that these powers have never been properly lost but only cut off from ordinary consciousness. The amnesiae of hysteria are likewise recoverable under hypnosis; and, although a hysteric may have an amnesia for a certain group of facts, his actions are often influenced by these facts in the absence of conscious knowledge.

In all such phenomena as these Janet concluded that the mental processes concerned were not abolished but only cut off or dissociated. Somnambulisms and fugues were likewise explained as the result of dissociation; here, however, the dissociation is on a vaster scale. When simple amnesia occurs, there is no wholesale impairment of the continuity of personal consciousness; in somnambulisms and fugues, on the other hand, the continuity of consciousness seems to be cut across abruptly and a new consciousness, apparently having nothing in common with the normal consciousness, is substituted for a period. At the end of this period the old consciousness re-emerges as suddenly as it disappeared, and the temporary consciousness vanishes. Similarly, in the hypnotic trance the normal state of consciousness is replaced by an artificial state in which forgotten memories, inaccessible to normal consciousness, may be revived. When the normal state is restored, on the other hand, any events which took place in the hypnotic trance are immediately forgotten, unless the hypnotiser has given an injunction to the effect that they should be remembered. The phenomena of hypnotism were thus classed by Janet with somnambulisms, fugues and the other symptoms of hysteria. All were explained as illustrations of the same process of dissociation, whereby certain mental elements are cut off from the personal consciousness without thereby ceasing to have a place in the mind.

It is not altogether clear from Janet's writings whether or not he regards the mental elements, which have suffered dissociation, as maintaining an independent consciousness of their own apart from the consciousness of the main personality. The word "sub-conscious", which Janet uses to describe such dissociated elements, implies on the face of it that they do not possess the characteristic quality of consciousness. There are passages also in which he speaks of the dissociated elements as if this were his real view. Such a passage may be found in his work entitled "L'Etat Mental des Hystériques" (Janet 1911), where he says:

> Sans insister sur ces questions purement psychologiques, je me contente de faire remarquer que les études sur quelques formes particulières d'anesthésie, et en particulier l'étude du champ visuel, sont venues confirmer notre conclusion générale. Dans tous les cas, même dans le dernier, les sensations n'ont pas disparu absolument, elles sont simplement devenues subconscientes parce qu'elles sont sorties du champ de la conscience. [1911, p. 66]

> Without stressing these purely psychological questions I will just point out that the studies on some particular forms of anaesthesia, and in particular the study of the field of vision have confirmed our general conclusions. In every case, even in the last, the sensations have not disappeared completely, they have simply become subconscious because they have come out of the field of consciousness. [1911, p. 66] [Trans. C. Fairbairn 1993]

From this passage there can, of course, be no doubt that Janet regards the missing sensory elements in hysterical anaesthesia as preserved in the mental sphere; i.e., his theory is one of psychological not of physiological dissociation. This must be his meaning when he says that the sensations have not disappeared absolutely but have simply become subconscious. If the sensations, however, have not disappeared, the question arises whether they have preserved an independent consciousness of their own. From this passage taken at face value, it would appear that they are regarded as being properly unconscious: "They have left the field of consciousness." The passage quoted, however, proceeds in a fashion which modifies this interpretation of Janet's (1911) meaning. It proceeds thus:

> Le rétrécissement du champ visuel peut être considéré comme l'emblème de la sensibilité hystérique, en général. La perception personnelle, la conscience que *nous* avons *nous-mêmes* des faits de conscience est moins large; elle ne parvient plus à réunir la quantité normale des faits ordinairement perçus. [1911, p. 66]

> The contraction of the field of vision may be considered as the emblem of hysterical sensibility in general. The personal perception, the consciousness we have ourselves of the facts of consciousness is narrower; it no longer succeeds in reuniting the normal quantity of facts ordinarily perceived. [1911, p. 66, Trans. C. Fairbairn]

These further sentences indicate that Janet is using the word "consciousness" in two senses: (a) as the quality of consciousness in general, (b) as the personal consciousness. It would appear that he is using it in the latter sense when he says that "the sensations have become sub-conscious simply because they have left the field of consciousness". If this be so, it follows that in speaking of "sub-conscious" sensations Janet merely means sub-conscious in relation to the main personal consciousness. He does not mean to imply that the sub-conscious elements have not some consciousness of their own. Indeed, the general tenor of his views seems to suggest that an independent consciousness is maintained by the dissociated elements. While it is difficult to find a passage in which Janet states this view explicitly, it is certainly the logical inference of his conception of dissociation. This, at any rate, is how Dr. Bernard Hart (1926) interprets him, and contrasting Janet's "sub-conscious" with Freud's "Unconscious", he expresses the opinion that the divisions of the mind included under dissociation are divisions of consciousness. "Janet's 'sub-conscious'," he says

> comprises those instances of dissociation where the lack of integration is such that there is a lack of mutual awareness between two streams, but in every other respect the processes concerned have all the attributes of consciousness. The division of dissociation is, therefore, a division within consciousness. [p.248]

The present writer has been unable to find an explicit statement by Janet to this effect, but at any rate it is the logical outcome of the conception of dissociation as he framed it.

What Janet leaves to be inferred from his views has been explicitly formulated by other writers, who have derived their inspiration from Janet's work. Among these may be mentioned Professor Morton Prince, who is perhaps the most notable of those who have applied the idea of dissociation to the explanation of abnormal mental states. Most of his attention was devoted to the study of cases of multiple personality, which he explained as due to a dissociation of consciousness. These cases, of course, lend themselves more easily than any other phenomena known to psychopathology to an interpretation based on the division of consciousness. This is evident in the case of Miss B. whose mental state is studied in Morton Prince's work *The Dissociation of a Personality* (1919). Miss B.'s life history was characterised by periods in which her normal personality appeared to be replaced by the totally different personality of "Sally". The two personalities had mental characteristics as different as any two individuals, and they had a separate set of memories. Miss B. was not aware of Sally's existence, but Sally was aware of Miss B. as an external personality. Cases of this nature led Morton Prince to formulate the view that the individual personality was capable, under conditions which favoured dissociation, of being split up into two or more separate entities, each of which had a consciousness of its own. The evidence led him to the conclusion that, when one of these personalities occupied the stage, the other personalities or personality persisted in a state which was none the less conscious because dissociated. To this state he gave the name of "Co-conscious". Where the dissociation involved elements too few to constitute a separate personality, he believed that there resulted such phenomena as the anaesthesiae, paralyses, amnesiae, etc., to which Janet had called attention; in all cases, however, the dissociated elements have, in his view, a detached consciousness of their own, and they are described as co-conscious. Accordingly, he divided those phenomena which appear to influence behaviour without appearing in the personal consciousness, into two groups: 1. The unconscious, which consists in neurological dispositions and processes, 2. The co-conscious, which consists in dissociated mental elements, which, while outside personal awareness, are yet characterised by a consciousness of their own (Prince 1910). The Co-conscious he regarded as identical with Janet's "Sub-conscious" (Prince 1910).

Rivers (1924) adopts an essentially similar view regarding dissociated mental elements. Taking the fugue as the most characteristic product of dissociation, he concludes that the existence of an independent consciousness is the most characteristic feature of dissociation. Rivers, however, differs from Morton Prince in that he recognises the existence of mental elements which, while inaccessible to the personal consciousness, are yet unaccompanied by a consciousness of their own. Such elements, as already indicated, he describes as "suppressed experience", and in this category he includes many of the phenomena which would be described by Janet as "sub-conscious", and by Morton Prince "co-conscious". "Suppression", as he conceives it, is a wider concept than "dissociation," which, for him, amounts to a special form of suppression. It is that form of suppression in which the suppressed elements retain a consciousness of their own.

Rivers' view of dissociation raises the question whether the existence of independent consciousness in the dissociated elements is a satisfactory criterion for differentiating dissociation from other mental processes. McDougall (1926), discussing dissociation, disputes the advisability of adopting this criterion. Not that McDougall denies the fact that such an independent consciousness may exist. On the contrary, in discussing automatisms, such as fugues, somnambulisms and hysterical fits in Chap. XII, he brings forward considerations which, to use his words, "point strongly to the view that in all automatic actions we have to do with expressions of a subsidiary stream of conscious mental activity, which we may best describe by the term 'co-conscious activity', following Dr Morton Prince" (McDougall 1926, p. 255). McDougall (1926) believes, however, that the existence of co-conscious activity is not an essential or necessary feature of dissociation. Accordingly, in the following passage, he protests against the use of the phrase "dissociation of consciousness", and suggests "dissociation of the personality" as a substitute:

> Many authorities write of "dissociation of consciousness"; Janet has used more frequently the expression "disaggregation of consciousness". This way of speaking is, it seems to me, unfortunate; for it begs two of the great questions raised by the phenomena: first it implies the questionable assump-

> tion that consciousness is an aggregation, that the stream of normal thinking is, somehow, compounded of elements of consciousness capable of independent or separate existence; in short, it assumes the truth of some form of the atomistic psychology. Secondly, it implies that, in the dissociated state, elements of consciousness that should have become aggregated in the main stream have some sort of existence or subsistence in a collateral stream; and this also is a disputable assumption. It is better, therefore, to speak of dissociation of the personality. [1926, p. 234]

McDougall's contention appears to be well-founded. One cannot help feeling that to seek the differentia of dissociation in the presence of independent consciousness is to pursue wrong lines. What is distinctive about the dissociated elements is not independent consciousness but independent activity. That consciousness may accompany this activity is theoretically possible, and the facts of certain conditions, such as multiple personality, indicate that this may sometimes be the case. This, however, is mainly a matter of theoretic interest, and leaves on one side the essential problems of dissociation in their more important and practical bearing. It is without doubt this fact which explains the absence from Janet's writings of explicit statements regarding the presence or otherwise of an independent consciousness accompanying dissociated states. Janet's attention was focussed upon the essential features of dissociation, and he did not find the presence of an independent consciousness in the dissociated elements to be one of them. Hence the problem involved did not attract his explicit attention. Co-consciousness is implied in his view, but that is all.

It is to another feature of the process of dissociation that Janet looks for its essential nature. This feature is independence of activity as against independence of consciousness. This is perhaps due to the fact that it was the study of the ordinary symptoms of hysteria rather than of the fugue and the multiple personality that led him to the idea of dissociation. In one of his lectures at Harvard University in the autumn of 1906, he summarises his view of hysteria as follows: "Hysteria is a form of mental depression characterized by a retraction of the field of personal consciousness and a tendency to the dissociation and emancipation of the systems and functions that constitute personality" (Janet 1907, p. 332). In this definition Janet singles out two processes as constituting the essential features of hysteria: 1. Retraction of the field of personal consciousness, 2. A tendency to dissociation and emancipation of the systems and functions that constitute personality. These two processes are, however, merely two aspects of one and the same process. This single process is, properly speaking, the process of dissociation itself. It is a process whereby certain mental elements or functions are excluded from personal consciousness, and this inevitably involved a narrowing of the conscious field. Whether the excluded elements or functions themselves maintained consciousness of their own, and, if so, whether they invariably do so are questions about which we need not concern ourselves unduly. These are secondary considerations which do not affect the fundamental nature of dissociation itself.

It seems desirable, therefore, to look for the characteristic feature of dissociation where Janet found it: in the exclusion or cutting off of certain mental elements from the field of personal consciousness, which is thereby narrowed. This may also be expressed by saying that it is a narrowing of the conscious field whereby certain mental elements are cut off; but it is the cutting off that is the characteristic feature.

The value of Janet's conception of dissociation as a process whereby mental elements are cut off from personal consciousness has been widely recognised by psychologists, and indeed may now be said to have found a place in orthodox psychology. There are, however, certain features of Janet's formulation, which, although they may escape the notice of medical clinicians, yet prove unacceptable to most psychologists. Fortunately, they do not affect the conception in its essential nature; but, if inconsistency between medical and psychological ideas is to be avoided, it is essential that they should be recognised.

The chief weaknesses of Janet's formulation, which are two in number, have been admirably pointed out by Bernard Hart (1926). The most important of these weaknesses is dependent on the fact that Janet set out with a psychology which is now recognised on all hands to be misleading. This is the so-called "Associationist Psychology", which traces its ancestry to the philosophers Locke, Berkeley and Hume, and which dominated psychological thought in France and Britain until the opening of the present century. Indeed, although it is now discountenanced, its influence is not even yet dead. According to the Associationist School, the content of the mind is made up of a number of separate items or ideas, which are compounded together to form more complex products, but which are in themselves simple and indivisible. This atomistic conception of mind-stuff is untrue to the facts of the mind, just as an analogous idea would be untrue of the physical organism. The organism functions as a whole, and, while various aspects of its functioning may be distinguished and separately described, the organism does not consist in a collection of separate functions, one of which may be subtracted without vitally affecting all the others. Thus it is inconceivable that the bile-secreting function of the liver should be "dissociated" from the rest of its functions, leaving the liver's activity unaffected except for the loss of this one function. Similarly, the mind does not consist in an aggregation of separate elements or functions, one of which can be split off from the rest without any effect except its loss. Yet this is the atomistic conception of the mind which Janet accepted from the Associationists, and it introduces a weakness into his formulation of the process of dissociation.

The other great weakness of Janet's formulation was due to hisenslavement to the spatial metaphor. He modelled his conception of the field of consciousness upon the field of vision, which has a spatial reference. He observed in hysterics a concentric narrowing of the visual field, which resulted in the exclusion of peripheral images from conscious perception (vide Janet 1907). Yet one of his patients with a visual field of 5° could be reduced to a paroxysm of terror, if the image of a lighted match fell on the peripheral field. Such cases led him to assume a dissociation of the peripheral field of vision. Janet (1911) ascribed to consciousness in general a field based on the analogy of the visual field: "Le Rétrécissement du champ visuel peut être considéré comme l'emblème de la sensibilité hystérique, en général" (p. 67). ("The contraction of the field of vision may be considered as the emblem of hysterical sensibility in general") (1911, p. 78, trans. C. Fairbairn). He thus described dissociation in general as if it involved a cutting off of part of a spatial field. This is a useful metaphor, but, since the mind is not in space, the metaphor, if pressed too far, leads to an over-simplification of facts too complex to be expressed so simply. Janet is not the only medical psychologist who has been misled by applying the spatial metaphor too rigidly to mental processes. Freud has committed the same mistake. His original division of the mind into the Conscious, the Pre-conscious and the Unconscious, and his later division of it into the Ego, the Id and the Superego are both conceived too much in spatial terms, and this constitutes one of the chief weaknesses of his theory, as it does of Janet's.

Under the influence then, of the Associationist psychology and an enslavement to the spatial metaphor, Janet conceived dissociation as the separation of a mental element or a group of elements from the main aggregation of such elements which he conceived to constitute the mind. The unsatisfactory nature of this view is best realised when we consider such a large-scale dissociation as is involved in cases of multiple personality. In such cases it is often found that certain elements find a place in more than one of the dissociated personalities. Sometimes, too, the barrier raised by the dissociation is, so to speak, permeable in one direction only. This is best seen in cases which exhibit "Co-conscious" phenomena. Here we have not merely an alternation of personalities, but evidence suggesting a co-existence of the personality which is in abeyance at the moment. Thus in the case of Miss B., recorded by Morton Prince (1919), the secondary personality Sally was aware of Miss B.'s thoughts and activities as those of another person, but Miss B. was totally unaware of the very existence of Sally. Similarly, in the hypnotic state a patient has access to the memories of the normal state, but no memories of what occurred in a hypnotic state are accessible to the normal consciousness, unless a suggestion is given to that effect. Such phenomena are hard to reconcile with Janet's description of dissociation as a process whereby a number of mental elements are separated 'en masse' from the totality of the mind. This is pointed out by Bernard Hart (1926).

A further objection to Janet's notion of dissociated mental elements existing in a isolated state is raised by Dr. T. W. Mitchell (1921). As Mitchell points out, "Thoughts and feelings cannot be left floating about in the void, unclaimed by any thinker" (p. 33). He adds that "While the patient is awake and aware of some things, dissociated sensations or perceptions may provide evidence of a concurrent discriminative awareness of other things, as effective as that which characterizes the sensory or perceptive activity of the conscious waking self" (p. 34). This fact may be illustrated by the "Yes or No" phenomenon of hysteria, to which reference has already been made. This phenomenon shows that, although sensations from the anaesthetic limb are not consciously appreciated, the function involved is not cut off from the structure of the mind—a fact which is obscured in Janet's formulation of dissociation. In this respect Freud's conception of "Repression" is more satisfactorily formulated; for, although, according to Freud, repressed elements are unconscious, he still regards them as part of the structure of the mind and as capable of influencing behaviour.

Janet's associationist and spatial pre-conceptions thus impose a profound limitation upon his conception of dissociation, and introduce insuperable difficulties in the application of the conception to many of the phenomena which it ought to be able to explain. To quote Bernard Hart:

> Dissociation does not separate the mind into pieces, it only produces more or less independently acting functional units, each such unit comprising material which may be peculiar to itself, but which may just as well form a part of any number of other functional units. The distinguishing character does not lie in the material of which it is composed, but in the set or pattern. Instead of regarding dissociation as the splitting of conscious material into separate masses, it must be regarded as an affair of gearing, the various elements of mental machinery being organized into different functional systems by the throwing in of the appropriate gear. [1926, p. 247]

The conception of dissociation, which Bernard Hart advocates as a substitute for the spatial conception of Janet, is described by him as "The functional conception". Interpreted in this sense, the conception of dissociation has been widely accepted by psychologists, but medical writers too often cling to the original spatial formulation. In the interests of clarity and conformity to the facts of the mind, it is desirable that medical thought should adapt itself to the "functional" conception of dissociation.

Interpreted in the functional sense, dissociation is a phenomenon of the mind which is not necessarily abnormal. Undoubtedly it is in abnormal mental states that the process is seen in its most striking form; but it may also be observed in perfectly normal individuals under certain conditions. The conditions under which dissociation occurs in normal individuals seem, therefore, to deserve some consideration, if the true nature of dissociation is to be properly understood. Attention must consequently be devoted to this aspect of the subject, and, for reasons which will appear shortly, the nature of the material dissociated will be specially noted.

Emotion in itself is a perfectly normal phenomenon of the mind, but dissociation appears to be one of its invariable accompaniments. Since Professor William McDougall first formulated his theory of Instinct (1908), it has come to be recognised that, when any deeply-rooted innate tendency is profoundly stirred, a feeling-state is liable to make its appearance. Certain of these innate tendencies have associated with their activity emotions which are quite characteristic—the instinct of pugnacity, for example, having associated with it the characteristic emotion of anger. When an instinct is powerfully appealed to, Nature appears to have provided that all other tendencies *irrelevant* to the situation in hand should be inhibited. The importance of this arrangement is evident when we consider how much the survival-value of the instinct of escape would be compromised, if, in a danger-situation, the activity of other tendencies were not temporarily suspended. In such a situation, it is of obvious advantage that all the activities of the organism should be directed to the end of escape, and to that end alone. If, therefore, the object of the instinct of escape is to be attained, it is of first-class importance that no competing tendency, e.g., food-seeking or mating, should be allowed any opportunity of expression. The emotion which tends to develop, when the tendency of escape is aroused, is, of course, the emotion of fear; and its function would seem to be to reinforce the tendency with which it is associated by filling consciousness to the exclusion of all else. This involves the exclusion from consciousness of all that is *not relevant* to the situation. There is at once a narrowing and intensifying of consciousness—exactly what Janet showed to occur in the case of hysteria. In a word, the development of emotion involves a process of dissociation. What holds true of the emotion of fear holds true of emotion in general. To quote Dr. James Drever (1921):

> The most interesting of the psychical effects of emotion is probably the narrowing and specializing of consciousness. When under the influence of a strong emotion we may become blind and deaf to everything which is not relevant to the end determined by the emotion; we may forget principles and resolutions; we may even temporarily break away from what might be described as characteristically the whole trend of our life activity. In all these cases the psychological process known as 'dissociation' is involved, and some kind and degree of emotional dissociation is a matter of everyday experience.

> This is more than the mere regulative function of feeling. It is a definite blocking of those connecting paths in the nervous system—and in the mind—which normally ensure the due balance and control of our various interests and activities. In extreme cases an individual may lose control of fundamental muscular and sensory mechanisms. Speech may be lost, and the control of still earlier and more primitive functions and co-ordinations may disappear. Usually this dissociation is merely temporary, and normal conditions are restored as the emotion passes away. Occasionally, however, more or less permanent dissociations may take place, when the case becomes distinctly pathological. Numerous instances of such pathological dissociation occurred during the war, and in their various forms were all popularly included under the designation "shell-shock". [p. 35]

From this statement it is evident that, although the development of emotion may result in an abnormal degree and extent of dissociation, a tendency to dissociation is a perfectly normal accompaniment of emotion. Further, if we consider the nature of the elements or functions which tend to be dissociated under the influence of emotion, they are seen to be those elements or functions which are *irrelevant* to the situation with which the organism is faced at the time.

The influence of emotion in producing dissociation did not escape the notice of Janet. Indeed, he drew particular attention to this phenomenon. Thus Chapter VI in part II of his "L'Etat Mental des Hystériques" (1911) is entitled "L'Amnésie et la Dissociation des Souvenirs par L'Emotion" ("Amnesia and the Dissociation of Memories by Emotion"). In this chapter he studies the case of Irène, a young woman of twenty-three, who for two years had suffered from a hysterical state characterised chiefly by hallucinatory somnambulisms and a profound amnesia. These phenomena were traced by Janet to the influence of intense emotions experienced at the death of her mother. He concludes that in this, as in other cases which he studied, emotion was responsible for the dissociation which had developed. Thus, towards the end of the chapter in question he says: "Enfin la précédente étude mettait en évidence le rôle considérable de l'émotion pour produire cette dissociation de la synthèse mentale." (1911, p. 532). ("Finally, the preceding study showed the considerable role of emotion in producing this dissociation of mental synthesis.") The phrase "Dissociation of mental synthesis" draws attention to a feature of Janet's views to which reference will be made later: the view, namely, that dissociation is the result of a failure of mental synthesis. Janet interprets the rôle played by emotion in producing dissociation in terms of this general conception. This is not the place to criticise his conception of mental synthesis, but his observation that emotion favours dissociation admits of no dispute.

Another group of phenomena, which Janet (1911) attributes to failure of mental synthesis, are the phenomena of suggestion. Influenced by the clinical studies of Charcot and Babinski, he regarded the phenomena of suggestion as specially characteristic of hysteria. He did not go so far as Babinski, whom he quotes as saying "A phenomenon is hysterical when it can be produced through suggestion and cured through persuasion" (Janet 1907, p. 325). But Janet (1907) did regard suggestibility as a pathological phenomenon, and he classed it as one of the great stigmata of hysteria. He says "A tendency to suggestion and subconscious acts is the sign of mental disease, but it is, above all, the sign of hysteria" (p. 289); and again "I have never seen a finely suggestible subject who was not clearly hysterical" (p. 290). This view is undoubtedly an exaggeration, although there can be no question about the suggestibility of hysterical patients. Janet himself admits, albeit somewhat grudgingly, that suggestion may take place with subjects who are not hysterical. In the "Revue Philosophique" of 1888, he himself described a case of remarkable suggestibility in a man convalescent from acute delirium. He admits that the conditions, which make suggestion possible, arise in various infective diseases, in intoxications and alcoholism, in nervous diseases like neurasthenia and Chorea, and also in the case of imbeciles (Janet 1911); but he is careful to add: "Il faut avouer qu'il y a une maladie particulière qui réunit d'une façon merveilleuse les deux conditions essentielles de la suggestion, la conservation de l'automatisme et la diminution de la synthèse personelle: c'est l'état hystérique" (p. 237). ("I must confess that there is one special illness which reunites in a marvellous way the essential conditions of suggestion, the preservation of automatism and the diminution of personal synthesis: that is the state of hysteria") [trans. C. Fairbairn]. It is impossible at the present time to follow Janet in the opinion that suggestion is an abnormal phenomenon. While it must be admitted that, in certain abnormal conditions like hysteria, suggestibility assumes a pathological form, the psychology of rumour proves beyond question that normal individuals are amenable to the influence of suggestion. The fact is that suggestion is a phenomenon of dissociation. The reason that suggestibility was found by Janet to be such an important stigma of hysteria lies in the fact that hysteria exhibits dissociation in such a marked degree. Dissociation is not, however, necessarily an abnormal phenomenon. It is only abnormal when it gets out of hand. We have already seen that it is a necessary accompaniment of emotion, and, although excessive emotionality is pathological, emotion itself is not. Similarly, suggestion in itself is a perfectly normal process due to dissociation; it only becomes pathological if dissociation is excessive.

Suggestion, in the psychological sense, has been defined by McDougall (1921) as "A process of communication resulting in the acceptance with conviction of the communicated proposition in the absence of logically adequate grounds for its acceptance" (p. 83). Rivers regards it as a process corresponding to the cognitive aspect of the gregarious instinct (1924, p. 91); but, be that as it may, it is essentially a social phenomenon involving a personal relationship. It is a "Method of exerting personal influence by which one individual is brought to accept from another a statement, opinion, or belief, and to act upon it, without having, or seeking to have, adequate logical grounds for its acceptance" (Drever 1921, p. 51). Drever goes on to say:

> The general condition upon which suggestion depends may be best described by saying that, when any idea presents itself in our consciousness, which involves believing or acting in a certain way, any factors which prevent opposing ideas rising in consciousness will tend to make us believe or act in accordance with the idea presented, and so far therefore make us suggestible. The extent to which opposing ideas can be prevented from rising in consciousness will be a measure of suggestibility. This prevention of the rise of opposing ideas is of the nature of dissociation, which we have already met with as a characteristic phenomenon of emotion. Suggestion might therefore be described as a means of producing dissociation, and suggestibility as the tendency for dissociation phenomena to manifest themselves under certain special conditions. . . . Conditions which favour suggestion are in the main conditions which, directly or indirectly, inhibit opposing ideas. [pp. 52–53]

This passage shows with admirable clearness the part played by dissociation in the phenomena of suggestion; it also gives us some insight into the nature of the material which is dissociated when suggestion becomes effective. The nature of the dissociated material becomes evident from the statement that "the extent to which opposing ideas can be prevented from rising in consciousness will be a measure of suggestibility". It is "opposing ideas" that are dissociated in suggestion. Every idea that is *incompatible* with the suggested idea is cut off from acceptance and from motor expression. In the case of suggestion, therefore, it is *incompatibility* with the content of the suggestion given that determines what ideas and tendencies shall be dissociated.

Allied to the dissociation which occurs in suggestion is that which occurs in hypnosis. As we have already seen, the Nancy School went so far as to say that the hypnotic state was simply ordinary sleep induced by suggestion. This view is certainly an over-simplified explanation of a complex phenomenon, although, under Bernheim's influence suggestion is now universally employed to produce hypnosis. Whatever be the fundamental character of the hypnotic state, however, exaggerated suggestibility is certainly one of its most characteristic features. This being so, we should expect to find evidence of dissociation in the hypnotic state, and indeed hypnosis furnishes us with perhaps the most remarkable example of a dissociated state. It is familiar knowledge that almost any dissociation of which a human being is capable may be produced in a hypnotised person. Anaesthesiae, paralyses, rigidity, contractures and all the host of phenomena familiar in hysteria may be induced or removed at the word of the hypnotist. The subject may also be made to exhibit characteristics so foreign to his normal character as to remind us of the phenomena of multiple personality. That the hypnotic state is characterised by a process of dissociation may also be gathered from the amnesia, which, unless a suggestion be given to the contrary, prevents the subject, on the restoration of normal consciousness, from recalling the events of the séance—an amnesia which is absolute, unless the hypnotist gives a suggestion to the contrary. Here again the nature of the dissociated material seems to be determined by *incompatibility* with the suggestions of the hypnotist.

The similarity of the hypnotic state to ordinary sleep is witnessed by the name "hypnosis", which, as is well known, is derived from the Greek *υπνοϛ* for 'sleep'. Whether the Nancy School is right or wrong in describing the hypnotic state as one of sleep induced by suggestion, at any rate ordinary sleep furnishes another typical example of dissociation. Whatever be the physiological conditions of sleep (and of these there appears to be no certainty among physiologists), in its psychological aspect sleep displays all the characteristic features of dissociation. As we sink into sleep, there is a progressive development of functional anaesthesiae, paralyses and amnesiae. The functions of sensation, perception, thought and memory quit the field of consciousness. Feelings and emotions vanish, and the powers of voluntary movement desert us. Attention lapses, and the field of consciousness becomes progressively narrowed, until it is completely bereft of content and a state of unconsciousness ensues. All this is typical of dissociation as observed in the phenomena of hysteria and hypnosis. As in these conditions, the dissociated functions are not lost. The sleeper adjusts his position and makes more or less adapted movements such as pushing back the clothes if he is too hot. These activities occur, however, without the intervention of consciousness. Similarly, the sensory functions are not abolished with consciousness; otherwise, it would be impossible to understand how sounds could awake the sleeper. It is a significant fact, in this connection, that not all sounds do awaken the sleeper. He can sleep through sounds to which he is accustomed, however loud these may be; but even the faintest sound may awaken him if it is a sound which would have a marked significance for him in waking life, that is, if it appeals to a powerful innate or acquired interest. Thus a mother may sleep through a thunderstorm and yet awaken at the faintest sound from her baby. Facts such as these show that the various mental functions are not abolished in sleep. They are merely dissociated. In normal sleep the dissociation is more massive than is usual in hysteria or hypnosis—although the hysterical and the hypnotic trance remind us that massive dissociation is not confined to normal sleep. When sleep is deep, dissociation may be said to be total; but in the lighter degrees of sleep dissociation is less extensive—as is evident from the occurrence of dreams. That some degree of dissociation is present even in light sleep may be gathered from the ease with which dreams are forgotten. Here we have another example of amnesia dependent upon dissociation.

If we proceed to consider the nature of the mental elements which are dissociated in sleep, we are faced with a difficulty which did not meet us in the case of the dissociations produced by emotion, suggestion and hypnosis. In the case of emotion we find a dissociation of all those thoughts, interests and tendencies, which are *irrelevant* to the tendency activated by the situation with which the organism is faced. In suggestion and hypnosis we find a dissociation of all that is *incompatible* with ideas present to the subject. In sleep, however, there seems to be a dissociation of all mental content whatsoever. Sleep appears to be primarily determined by the need of the organism for rest, and, at first sight, it seems a pointless task to try to bring the dissociated material under any classification at all. A little consideration, however, shows that the task is not so hopeless. The fact that the need for rest determines the onset of sleep itself provides a clue. If we study the behaviour of a person seeking sleep, we find that he withdraws himself so far as possible from all sources of sensory stimulation. He seeks a quiet and dark room, lies down in a bed where he is protected from extremes of temperature, and, by relaxing his muscles, renders himself as far as possible immune from kinaesthetic sensations. He thus takes measures to prevent the occurrence of stimuli which fill consciousness with content and stir powerful tendencies. He puts himself under conditions which favour a lapsing of the ordinary interests of the day. If, however, the last condition is not fulfilled, and his mind is occupied with thoughts carried over from the day's activities, sleep is likely to be deferred, even though the other conditions are secured. Normally, however, when the need for rest makes itself felt, the interests of the day automatically sink into abeyance. This may be interpreted as a dissociation of all mental content which is *incompatible* with the innate rest-seeking tendency. Another interpretation is, however, possible, when we further consider how naturally the interests of the day lapse when the need for sleep makes itself felt. This automatic lapsing of ordinary interests suggests that, under the influence of fatigue, the objects and thoughts which usually excite attention have temporarily lost their power of doing so. They have become *irrelevant* for the time being. Indeed, we may say that, when the need for rest becomes acute, the whole world becomes irrelevant; hence the massive dissociation of sleep.

The truth of this interpretation becomes evident, when we consider the well-known fact that, if a fundamental tendency or deep-seated interest is appealed to by a situation of great emergency, sleep may be deferred for almost incredible periods. This was a common occurrence in the recent war. Another confirmation of the view suggested is to be found in the observation that a sleeper may be wakened by a minute stimulus bearing on a deep-seated interest, even when a much greater stimulus with no such significance leaves sleep undisturbed. Attention has already been drawn to the liability of a sleeping mother to awake at the slightest sound relevant to her interest in her child. Another example may be found in an every-day observation of war-time. The gunner, who sleeps undisturbed by the sounds of his own guns in action, may be wakened by an enemy shell-burst which is not so loud, or even by a whisper of warning from a comrade. Additional support for the view that sleep is a dissociation of the irrelevant may be found in the study of animal behaviour. McDougall (1926), in a discussion of the states of fatigue and sleep, has drawn attention to the insight into the nature of these processes, which he gained from observing the behaviour of his dog. His observations played an important part in leading him to the formulation of his "Hormic Psychology" in general. He observed that, in the absence of a situation which appealed to an instinctive tendency and thus stirred an interest in his dog, the animal tended to sink into a state of quiescence and sleep. Thus he writes:

> My dog, left alone in a quiet spot, grows quiet; his nose sinks down upon his paws, and presently he dozes. But let any one of a limited number of things occur, and instantly he is all excitement and activity, putting forth a most copious flow of energy. And the things or events that provoke such sudden outbursts of energy are those that appeal to his instincts. [1926, pp. 61–62]

McDougall interprets this observation in the sense that the dissociation leading to sleep tends to occur in the absence of circumstances that activate any powerful tendency. It would seem, therefore, that, when no strong interest is appealed to, the environment becomes *irrelevant*, and it is this *irrelevance* which determines the massive dissociation of sleep in its psychological aspects. This irrelevance may, of course, be determined either internally or externally. It may be determined, on the one hand, by the need for rest or by poverty of interest; on the other hand, it may be determined by monotony of the environment (a well-known cause of sleep among listeners, when a dull sermon is in progress). In either case, however, sleep appears to be a *dissociation of the irrelevant*.

A process of dissociation similar to that which occurs in sleep, is witnessed in all states of fatigue which fall short of sleep. In its physiological aspects fatigue appears to affect the nervous system by raising the synaptic resistances. On the principle expounded by Hughlings Jackson, those functions of the nervous system which are latest evolved are the most unstable. Consequently, fatigue products may be conceived as affecting most easily the synapses involved in the association paths, leaving relatively unaffected those neuron-systems which correspond to fundamental activities. The physiological effects of fatigue would thus seem to result in relative isolation of the more stable neuron-systems, which thus tend to function independently, if activated by an appropriate stimulus. This is, of course, the phenomenon of physiological dissociation. When we consider the psychological aspects of the fatigue-state, we find the analogous phenomenon of psychological dissociation. In fatigue there is a tendency for activity to become automatic and unrelated to consciousness. The fact that activity tends to be withdrawn from awareness and from conscious control seems to account in some measure for the mistakes which a fatigued person is liable to make in the performance of a skilled activity, such as type-writing or driving a motor-car. It has been a frequent defence, when a signalman has been charged with negligence leading to a railway accident, that he was worn out as the result of nursing a sick person in his hours off-duty. In such cases it is common for the accused person to say that he did not notice that a signal lever was pulled back. This does not mean that the relevant visual sensations were absent; it means that these sensations were out of relation to the general consciousness. They had become irrelevant for the time being as a result of the need for rest. In fatigue, therefore, as in sleep, it is a case of *dissociation of the irrelevant*.

A similar dissociation to that produced by fatigue appears to occur as a result of the action of depressant drugs. Of these drugs alcohol may be regarded as typical. The effect of alcohol in producing dissociation has been investigated in considerable detail by McDougall (1926), who makes reference to the result of his investigations in Chapters III and XXVIII. McDougall points out that it is the blunting of the critical side of self-awareness by alcohol, which constitutes its charm for those who seek escape from anxiety, care and mental conflict. As a result of its action considerations based on the higher sentiments are banished from the field of consciousness, and the more primitive instinctive tendencies gain an opportunity for expression. The removal of the critical functions from the conscious field leads to an absence of self-control, and the tendency of the moment fills consciousness. To quote McDougall (1926), "both introspectively and objectively this lack of self-control is clearly discernible in every stage of alcoholic intoxication" (p. 70). In the first stage, this is evident in the fact that conversation loses its normal restraint. In the second stage, sense perception and skilled movements are disturbed. The significance of visual and auditory sensations is imperfectly realised, unless they are definitely relevant to the tendency of the moment. Movements are ill-adjusted, and the subject is often unaware that movements have taken place until he observes their results: e.g., until he finds he has upset a glass or burnt the tablecloth with a cigarette. The drinker himself realises that many movements occur without his conscious initiation or intention. In the third stage, the impoverishment of consciousness is carried still further. The drinker becomes an automaton, almost wholly unaware of where he is or what he is doing; and the tendency is for consciousness to disappear altogether and for sleep to ensue. It is evident, then, that the psychological phenomena produced by alcohol are characteristic of the process of dissociation. The higher sentiments and the ideals temporarily desert the conscious field, and various sensory and motor functions are cut off from consciousness. There is, further, a tendency to subsequent amnesia for the events which take place while the effects of alcohol are present. In a word, there is evidence of that narrowing of consciousness which Janet found to be typical of the process of dissociation; in the production of this phenomenon alcohol may be taken as representative of the depressant drugs as a whole, and, in certain diseases a similar effect appears to be produced by the action of toxic products.

If then we take alcohol as representative of the whole group of dissociating drugs and toxins, it is not difficult to determine the nature of the mental elements and functions which are dissociated. It is evidently a case of *dissociation of the irrelevant*. The drunken man is oblivious of all that is irrelevant to the tendency of the moment. Confirmation of this interpretation is found in the fact that a drunk man may be instantly sobered, if a situation arises which appeals strongly to some deep-rooted interest which had previously been in abeyance. Thus, the receipt of bad news or a serious threat to life has frequently been noted to exercise a sobering effect. In such a case a large body of dissociated thoughts and functions cease to be irrelevant, and the effects of dissociation are overcome.

A particularly interesting example of dissociation is that which seems to occur in most people in the presence of illness in general. Attention has already been drawn to Janet's admission that suggestion may be a feature of other illnesses besides hysteria. The response, which patients admitted to a hospital for incurables make to any suggestion of an ultimate cure, has come under the personal observation of the writer. This holds true even when the suggestion is conveyed in subtle and unimpressive ways. Another aspect of this phenomenon is the dissociation in a patient's mind of knowledge that his condition is incurable or even that the hospital, in which he finds himself, is a hospital for incurables only. Another observation which the writer has made is the extraordinary dissociation of medical knowledge which doctors and nurses show in relation to their own condition when they are ill themselves. This, of course, occurs chiefly when their illness is of a menacing character: e.g., when signs of cancer, which would be obvious to them in a professional capacity, are present in themselves. This extraordinary feature is particularly frequent among nurses. The reason that it is less frequent among doctors appears to be, that, in their case, medical knowledge is more thoroughly organised, and, therefore, less liable to dissociation from the main personality. That it does occur in doctors, however, has come under the writer's observation. This form of dissociation is to be distinguished from the dissociation produced in illness through the action of bacterial and other toxins. It is not a generalised dissociation, but a dissociation of a particular group of facts, which, if brought to bear on the sufferer's condition, would lead to an acute degree of unpleasure. It is thus psychologically and not physiologically conditioned. Here we find ourselves confronted, so far as the dissociated material is concerned, with a type of dissociation different from any which has been hitherto considered. Our consideration of phenomena of dissociation has so far led us to recognise dissociation of the irrelevant and dissociation of the incompatible. Here we are confronted with an example of another and very important form of dissociation, viz. *dissociation of the unpleasant.*

In the course of our enquiry we have now been led to consider in some detail certain of the chief conditions under which the normal mind exhibits phenomena of dissociation. The conditions to which attention has been devoted are:

1. Emotion.
2. Suggestion.
3. Hypnotism.
4. Sleep.
5. Fatigue.
6. States produced by depressant drugs.
7. Physical illness in persons of normal mentality.

The study of these various conditions seems to indicate conclusively that dissociation is an every-day phenomenon of the normal mind, and that it can only be regarded as pathological when its action is ill-placed or excessive. It is perhaps natural that medical writers should have concentrated their attention upon its pathological aspects, because medicine is primarily concerned with disease; but exclusive concentration upon pathological phenomena does not always lead to clarity of thought. Physiology has learned many lessons from pathology, it is true; but pathology owes a debt to physiology also. Similarly in the mental sphere; although psychology is deeply indebted to psychopathology, psychopathology in its turn has something to learn from normal psychology. Indeed, one of the greatest needs of psychopathology at the present time is to bring its conceptions into line with what is known about normal mental processes. It is because it seems to the present writer that the current conception of dissociation has been based too exclusively upon the study of abnormal phenomena of dissociation that so much attention has been devoted in this thesis to a description of its normal manifestations. Only when normal as well as abnormal dissociation is studied can the full significance of the process be properly understood.

The importance of recognising normal as well as abnormal manifestations of dissociation may be gathered, when we consider the theory which Janet advances to explain the dissociative process. While Janet's formulation of the conception of dissociation must put psychopathology (and psychology also) forever in his debt, the theory, which he puts forward to explain it, has serious limitations. These limitations would doubtless have been avoided, if Janet had paid more attention to the normal manifestations of dissociation. Had he done so, it is doubtful if he would have explained dissociation as due to a failure of mental synthesis. Yet this is the explanation which his study of the phenomena of hysteria leads him to offer. His observation of hysterical patients led him to summarise the various "accidents" and "stigmata", which they exhibit, under the formula "retraction of the field of consciousness" (Janet 1907, p. 303). This he (Janet 1907) interpreted as due to "A special moral weakness, consisting in the lack of power, on the part of the feeble subject, to gather, to condense the psychological phenomena, and assimilate them to his personality" (p. 311). Hysteria thus comes to be regarded as "A malady of the *personal synthesis*" (p. 332), due to "a depression, an exhaustion of the higher functions of the encephelon" (p. 333); it is the result of various circumstances in which the nervous tension is lowered. As a consequence of this lowering of nervous tension, Janet holds that "Consciousness, which is no longer able to perform too complex operations, gives up some of them" (p. 334). This process of giving up complex mental functions because the personal consciousness has not strength to retain them is, for Janet, the essence of the process of dissociation.

Janet's theory, that dissociation is due to a failure of mental synthesis dependent on lack of mental energy, has two important implications: both of which impair the usefulness of his conception of the process. These implications are: 1. That dissociation is a negative or passive process, 2. That it is essentially an abnormal process. These features of Janet's conception of dissociation set it in marked contrast to the conception of repression which Freud was led to formulate from the study of hysterical phenomena. According to Freud, repression is an active, dynamic process. It is not due to failure of mental energy as a result of which certain elements fall out of personal consciousness; on the contrary, to use Freud's words, (1915c in Freud 1924) "The essence of repression lies simply in the function of rejecting and keeping something out of consciousness" (p. 86). Further, once the study of hysteria had led him to recognise the process of repression, it was not long before he began to seek for evidence of its presence in various phenomena of everyday occurrence among normal individuals. The first of such phenomena in which he recognised its presence were 1. the minor mistakes to which normal individuals are subject, e.g., slips of the tongue, the mislaying of objects, and the forgetting of familiar names, 2. dreams. The word "repressed" first occurs in Freud's writings in a paper "On the Psychical Mechanism of Hysterical Phenomena" written in collaboration with Breuer (1893b), but it was only in a paper entitled "The Defence Psycho-neuroses" (Freud 1894) that he first formulated the idea of repression in a definite form. Yet, already he had published a paper on "Forgetting" (Freud 1898), in which he applied the conception of repression to the explanation of such ordinary experiences as when a name, the hour of an appointment or some significant fact appears, for no obvious reason, to slip out of the mind. This paper was later embodied in *The Psychopathology of Everyday Life* (1901). Meanwhile the year 1900 had witnessed the appearance of his famous "Traumdeutung" (Freud 1900), in which the conception of repression is applied to the elucidation of the problems of the dream.

Freud's conception of repression as an active, dynamic process stands in marked contrast to Janet's conception of dissociation as a passive process due to failure of mental energy—a contrast all the more remarkable in view of the fact that it was to explain the same phenomena that the two conceptions were originally framed. That the study of hysteria should lead Janet and Freud to such different ideas of the process involved is, however, not difficult to understand. It is largely due to the preconceptions with which they started. Janet's interpretation is influenced by the atomistic psychology which he inherited from the associationists. Freud's interpretation, on the other hand, was influenced by the atmosphere created in Teutonic countries by the philosophies of Schopenhauer and von Hartmann. It remains true, however, to say that, if Janet had, like Freud, sought confirmation of his views among the phenomena of every-day life, he would probably have modified them considerably. If he had recognised the existence of normal as well as of abnormal dissociation, it is difficult to imagine that he would have explained it as due to a mere failure of mental synthesis. The study of normal phenomena of dissociation, which has been undertaken in the preceding pages makes it impossible to accept the view that dissociation is essentially a passive process. The fact that it is an essentially *active* process is best realised when attention is directed to the *nature of the material* which is subject to dissociation. In the preceding study special attention has been directed to the nature of this material, and it was found that, in the phenomena considered, the dissociated elements and functions could be classified as falling under one of three categories:

1. The irrelevant.
2. The incompatible.
3. The unpleasant.

The fact that in each case the dissociated elements fall under one of these categories seems to the writer to provide a key to the understanding of the process of dissociation.

It is mainly as a result of failure to pay adequate attention to the nature of what is dissociated, that Janet fails to do justice to the conception of dissociation, for which we owe him such a debt. His attention was directed mainly to a description of the process itself and, in a lesser degree, to a description of the conditions or "Agents provocateurs" which favour its development, e.g., emotion, physical disease, psychical trauma, etc. (Vide Janet 1911). He devoted little, if any, attention to the dissociated material itself. In the case of Freud, on the other hand, it was reflection upon the mental content involved that led him to his conception of repression as an active and dynamic process. Both writers were struck by the prominence of amnesia in the symptomatology of hysteria. It is true that Janet (1907) asks his readers "To put in the first line, as the most typical, the most characteristic symptom of hysteria, a moral symptom—that is somnambulism" (p. 23); but he adds later, "It is amnesia that is the stigma of somnambulism" (p. 125). While recognising the importance of amnesia as a characteristic of hysteria, however, Janet was content to note that part of the mental content had been cut off from consciousness and to seek an explanation of this fact in the appearance of psychic weakness which the process in itself seemed to imply. Freud, on the other hand, while also recognising that consciousness had suffered a loss of content, found an explanation in the nature of the content itself. As the result of his efforts to revive the forgotten memories of his patients, he found that these patients had in each case "enjoyed good health up to the time at which an intolerable idea presented itself within the content of their ideational life" (Freud 1894, p. 61). It was in the *intolerable* nature of the idea that Freud found the key to the amnesia involved. It was for this reason that he designated hysteria as a "Defence Psychoneurosis" (1894), and that he came to regard repression as a dynamic process whereby consciousness is protected from intolerable mental content. Since, however, no one, even the most normal, is entirely exempt from the influence of intolerable ideas, Freud was able to extend the process of repression to cover many phenomena which cannot reasonably be regarded as pathological and to recognise repression as a process which occurs in the normal mind. From this point of view, repression is only regarded as pathological when, as in the case of hysteria, it gives rise to symptoms which unfit their victim for normal life.

In view of the fact that Freud framed his conception of repression in the light of the mental content upon which he found repression to be exercised, it has seemed desirable to remedy Janet's failure to adopt a similar procedure in the case of the conception of dissociation. It is for this reason that attention has been drawn in the preceding pages to the nature of the mental elements involved in the process of dissociation. The consideration of various dissociation-phenomena in the normal mind has led to the conclusion that, at any given time when dissociation occurs, the mental content which is involved is either irrelevant, incompatible or unpleasant in the light of the situation with which the organism is faced.

Dissociation of the *irrelevant* was found in our analysis to occur conspicuously in states of fatigue and sleep and under the influence of depressant drugs. Dissociation of the *incompatible* was found to occur under the influence of emotion, suggestion and hypnotism. This type of dissociation is also seen in what may be described as "Dr. Jekyll and Mr. Hyde" phenomena. The church-warden who overcharges his customers during the week without being conscious of an inconsistency is the subject of a dissociation of this kind. A similar dissociation is perhaps also involved in the stamping out of unsuccessful methods which is a feature of trial-and-error learning. Dissociation of the *unpleasant* was illustrated in our analysis by the failure of many persons suffering from organic disease to recognise the gravity of their condition, even when they possess the knowledge which would seem to make such an inference inevitable. In such cases it is the unpleasantness of the facts that cuts them off from the operation of the critical faculties. The tendency of the average person to shelve thoughts about his own death is another example of this form of dissociation, as is his tendency to speak of "the good old times", remembering the pleasant features of the past to the exclusion of the unpleasant. Another example of dissociation of the unpleasant is to be found in the frequently noted phenomenon that a person, faced with a grave emergency, may experience no emotion but impassively note trivial and unimportant features of the environment. David Livingstone records that an experience of this sort occurred to him, when a lion was mauling his arm. This instance is quoted by Rivers (1924) as an example of repression but it would seem to partake rather of the nature of a simple dissociation of the unpleasant. A certain group of "shell-shock" cases so frequently seen in the war appears also to be best explained as due to a dissociation of this sort. This is particularly true of cases in which amnesia or functional blindness followed a traumatic experience.

Acts of forgetting furnish an interesting group in relation to the classification of dissociated material into the irrelevant, the incompatible and the unpleasant, because each of these categories may be illustrated in the forgotten content. Most of our forgetting perhaps, is forgetting of the irrelevant. This is due to the fact that, when we are faced with any given situation, our attention is selective. Professor William James (1891) drew attention to this point, when he described selection as one of the cardinal functions of consciousness. Consciousness, he says, "is always interested more in one part of its object than in another, and welcomes and rejects, or chooses, all the while it thinks" (1891, p. 284). Later he adds: "We do far more than emphasize things, and unite some, and keep others apart. We actually *ignore* most of the things before us"; and again, "Millions of items of the outward order are present to my senses which never properly enter into my experience. Why? Because they have no *interest* for me. *My experience is what I agree to attend to"* (p. 402). In accepting these statements, we must recognise, of course, that the "agreeing" and "ignoring" of which James speaks are not voluntary processes, but spontaneous processes determined by distribution of interest. In this sense the ignoring process is simply an example of dissociation. When we forget the name of a person, whose name ought to be familiar, this is commonly due to a tendency in us to ignore his existence because we are not interested in him. This, indeed, is usually the way in which the person concerned is inclined to interpret it. Much of our forgetting, therefore, is due to selectivity of interest. What does not interest us tends to be ignored. In other words, what is irrelevant tends to be dissociated.

Not all forgetting, however, can be explained as due to dissociation of the irrelevant. Forgetting may also be due to dissociation of the incompatible. Many of the acts of forgetting, which Freud (1901) describes, appear to be of this nature. Freud explains them, of course, in terms of "repression". That, in the writer's opinion, he is wrong in doing so follows from the view of repression which will be developed later; as the relationship of repression to dissociation has not yet been examined, it is sufficient to point out here that many such acts of forgetting are examples of dissociation of the incompatible. This seems to be the case when we forget where we have put a borrowed article, which we have been asked to return before we have finished with it. This common phenomenon appears to be due, not to the fact that the lost memory is irrelevant, but to the fact that it is incompatible with a desire.

An act of forgetting may also be due to dissociation of the unpleasant. The tendency to forget an unpleasant fact is so familiar as to need little illustration. The "nouveau riche" tends to forget the circumstances of his early life; the man in financial difficulties tends to forget about a bill; the fastidious patient is more likely to forget to take an unpleasant than a pleasant medicine.

Among acts of forgetting we thus find examples of dissociations belonging to each of the three categories. It must be remembered, of course, that certain phenomena may fall into more than one category. Thus, the forgetting of an inconvenient appointment may be due to the fact that its fulfillment is incompatible with our purposes and unpleasant at the same time. In such cases, however, it is usually found that one aspect is predominant, and it is possible to classify most dissociation-phenomena under one or other of the three categories.

The fact that acts of forgetting provide such a comprehensive field for the study of dissociation in its various forms accords well with the importance which the phenomenon of amnesia played in the development of both Janet's and Freud's views. "Amnesia" says McDougall (1926) "is one of the most common forms in which dissociation reveals itself. Without unduly straining the sense of the words, it may be said that every dissociation is an amnesia" (p. 235). While it would be a mistake to regard amnesia as co-extensive with dissociation, as McDougall seems to do, it remains true that the process of forgetting is perhaps the most representative of all the manifestations of dissociation. The forgotten material may show any of the three characteristics which tend to provoke dissociation. It may be irrelevant or incompatible or unpleasant; but it always seems to possess one at least of these characteristics. The question now arises whether it is possible to find a comprehensive term which shall embrace all three categories of dissociated material. To find such a term does not seem an easy task, but, for want of a better, the term "*Unacceptable*" may be suggested. Dissociation then may be defined in the following terms: *Dissociation is a mental process whereby unacceptable mental content or an unacceptable mental function becomes cut off from personal consciousness: such mental content or function being regarded as unacceptable if it is either irrelevant to an active interest, incompatible with an active interest, or unpleasant in relation to an active interest.*

From this point of view, Dissociation must be regarded as another aspect of that process of Selection, which James regarded as one of the cardinal functions of consciousness and which Drever (1922) describes as a fundamental "characteristic of the psychical" (p. 29). This way of regarding dissociation has several implications, which may now be considered.

1. Dissociation is in itself a *normal* process, although, like other mental processes, it has a pathology of its own. This point need not be stressed, as many pages have already been devoted to a description of various normal dissociation-phenomena. Attention may, however, be drawn for a moment to certain phenomena which occur in cases, which exhibit an unusual *absence* of dissociation. Such a case came under the writer's observation, when he held the post of Assistant Physician in the Royal Edinburgh Hospital for Mental and Nervous Diseases. The patient was a man well up in years, who was of defective intelligence, and had spent a large part of his life in the Hospital. This patient showed a most astounding memory for details which would have been irrelevant to an ordinary person. He could name the birthday of practically every person who had been on the Staff of the Hospital since his admission, and he could name the dates on which each had come and departed. Other cases of a similar nature have frequently been noted in literature. In all such cases, memory is characterised by an absence of selection, and defect of dissociation which must be regarded as pathological. The phenomenon of "total recall", which so frequently characterises the reminiscences of unintelligent persons, is another example of what happens in

the absence of an adequate degree of dissociation. It may also be suggested that the prolific and disconnected nature of the conversational stream so characteristic of mania is due to the same cause. While, however, an inadequate degree of dissociation is abnormal, it nonetheless holds true that an excess of dissociation is abnormal also: whether it be a general excess or an excess relating to certain material only. The researches of Janet render it needless to stress this point, which is generally recognised at the expense of the fact that dissociation is not necessarily abnormal.

2. Another implication of the view of dissociation which has been reached is that it is an essentially *active* process. This fact has been largely obscured as a result of Janet's formulation. Janet's explanation of dissociation as the result of a failure of mental synthesis shows that he conceived it as a passive process: something that tended to occur automatically unless considerable energy was expended in preventing it doing so. According to this view, dissociated mental elements would seem to "get lost" rather than to be "cut off". This point of view, as has already been pointed out, is the result of Janet's failure to study the nature of the dissociated material. If the analysis which has been undertaken in this thesis is correct, the characteristic feature of dissociated material lies in the fact that it is in some way unacceptable to the subject. This being so, it is difficult to regard dissociation as a passive process of lapsing. It seems more reasonable to seek a rationale of the process of dissociation in the nature of the material which is dissociated. It would be difficult to find a rationale of war, apart from the realisation that the combatants are hostile. Similarly, if what is dissociated is unacceptable material, it seems likely that it is because the material is unacceptable that it comes to be dissociated. Dissociation, therefore, in its psychological aspect, would seem to be a process directed towards an end: the end being *exclusion from consciousness of the unacceptable*. It is, therefore, essentially an active process, not a process such as Janet (1911) describes it when he says: "La synthèse étant trop faible, certaines catégories de sensations, d'images ou d'idées sont *laissées de côté* . . . " (italics not in original) (p. 634). "The synthesis being too weak, certain categories of sensations, of images, or ideas are *left on one side* . . . " (p. 634, trans. C. Fairbairn). Janet's way of representing the process in this passage obscures the real nature of the process of dissociation. It is not a question of elements passively dropping out of consciousness or of being left aside, but rather of their being actively cut off from consciousness. Perhaps it is better still to describe the process from the point of view of consciousness, and to say that it is a case of consciousness, so to speak, "turning away from" what is unacceptable. This metaphor of "turning away" is perhaps preferable to that of "cutting off" in that it brings the process of dissociation more in line with what we know of the process of selection. Either metaphor may, however, be usefully employed. We may avoid a horrible

sight either by holding up our hands to cut off the view or by looking in another direction. The effect is the same in either case, and in either case activity is involved. Whether, therefore, we conceive dissociation as a process whereby the unacceptable is cut off from consciousness, or as a process whereby attentive consciousness avoids the unacceptable, in either case it is an active process.

3. Brief reference may be made to a third implication of the view of dissociation at which we have arrived. It is an unconscious or *unwitting* process; that is to say, the subject is not aware that the process is going on, he can only be aware of the results of the process. That it is not a consciously controlled process is evident to anyone who has made an effort to go to sleep when sleep did not come. All that the would-be sleeper can do is to put himself under the best conditions for dissociation to occur. This is what we do when we go to bed. The process of dissociation is, however, not only not consciously controlled, it is not conscious at all. The hysterical patient may know that a limb is paralysed because he cannot move it, but the dissociative process itself is not in consciousness. Further, the patient may not even be aware that the dissociation has taken place. This fact has been pointed out by Janet (1907):

> When you watch a hysterical patient for the first time, or when you study patients coming from the country, who have not yet been examined by specialists, you will find, like ourselves, that, without suffering from it and without suspecting it, they have the deepest and most extensive anaesthesia. [p. 161]

From these considerations it is evident that dissociation is an unwitting process.

4. A fourth implication of the conception of dissociation, which has been reached, is that the process is in line with a fundamental *biological* process. Drever (1922) describes three fundamental characteristics of the life-process of living organisms and points out that these are specially characteristic of that aspect of the life-process which we call "psychical". These three characteristics are 1. Conservation, 2. Selection, and 3. Cohesion. Conservation is represented by all that is involved when we speak of "learning by experience". If conservation is the basis of all mental development, selection is what determines the direction development will take. If all experience were conserved, learning by experience would be impossible. We should never learn to do a thing properly, if all our errors were conserved on equal terms with our successes. Selection is necessary if progress is to be possible. The most obvious psychical manifestation of selection is found in all that is signified when we speak of "attention", but "interest" more nearly expresses the range of its operation. Conservation and selection are, however, inadequate without cohesion. What is conserved under the influence of

selection is not conserved as a mere aggregate, but as an organised whole. All the phenomena of "association" are to be included under the broader concept of cohesion. *Dissociation*, on the other hand, comes under the category of selection, and is thus in line with a fundamental biological tendency. Dissociation is ultimately an expression of selection in its negative aspect, but, since it involves rejection, it is nonetheless active on that account. Rejection is determined by some ruling interest; and, whether it be a case of dissociation of the irrelevant, dissociation of the incompatible or dissociation of the unpleasant, in each case active rejection is involved. Of the three manifestations of dissociation, dissociation of the unpleasant must be regarded as the most primitive. The activity of the unicellular organism seems to consist either in approximation to food and favourable conditions or withdrawal from noxious stimuli. So far as we can imagine the psychical life of such an organism, we must regard it as characterised almost exclusively by states corresponding to pleasure and unpleasure, according as its fundamental tendencies are facilitated or impeded. Selection at this level is selection of the pleasant; dissociation may be conceived as dissociation of the unpleasant. At a higher level of life, when the multicellular stage is reached and organs are developed, we may conceive that dissociation of the irrelevant is added to dissociation of the unpleasant. This may be conceived as occurring when the stage is reached at which the phenomenon of a life-cycle appears. When this stage is reached, what is relevant at one phase of life becomes irrelevant at another phase of life. Here perhaps we find the key to the development of dissociation of the irrelevant, whereby stimuli effective at one phase become ineffective at another. At a still higher level in the scale of life, when the nervous system has become organised in such a way as to render a variety of movements and co-ordinations possible, we may conceive the establishment of the third form of dissociation: dissociation of the incompatible. By this agency functions incompatible with the prevailing activity are rendered inoperative, and stimuli which would produce behaviour incompatible with the prevailing interest are rendered incapable of producing a reaction.

Although the hierarchy of dissociation-functions, which has been sketched in the last paragraph, is admittedly speculative, yet the writer feels that it gives some biological justification for the view of dissociation which has been reached in the present section of this thesis. This view may be summarised in a modification of the definition already given, as follows: Dissociation is an active mental process, whereby unacceptable mental content or an unacceptable mental function becomes cut off from personal consciousness, without thereby ceasing to be mental: such mental content or mental function being "unacceptable" within the meaning of this definition if it is either irrelevant to, incompatible with, or unpleasant in relation to an active interest.

REPRESSION

The conception of repression was originally introduced by Freud to explain the same group of phenomena which had led Janet to formulate his conception of dissociation. The history of the development of Freud's views shows that he pursued a path independent of that of Janet. As Mitchell (1921) points out, some years before the publication of Janet's first work, Freud's interest had been intrigued by the fact that some of the symptoms of a hysterical patient, whom Breuer and he were treating by hypnotism, were permanently relieved after some forgotten episodes in her life were recalled in the hypnotic state (vide Freud 1893b). Breuer had for some time realised the therapeutic value of reviving forgotten memories under hypnotism, but it was left for Freud to develop from this observation the whole body of psychoanalytic theory, centering, as it does, round the concept of repression. It was this observation that led Freud (1893b) to state his conclusion "that hysterical patients suffer principally from reminiscences" (p. 29). The two facts which attracted his notice about these reminiscences seem to have been, 1. that they were related to experiences of a distressing or traumatic kind (Freud 1893b), 2. that they were "not at the disposal of the patient in the way that his more commonplace memories are" (p. 31). In relation to this second point, Freud noticed that it was only under hypnosis that the memories could be restored in any but the most inadequate way. The fact that memories withdrawn from the possibility of ordinary recollection could be revived with intense vividness under hypnosis led Freud (1893b) increasingly to the belief "that splitting of consciousness, which is so striking in the well-known classical cases of 'double conscience', exists in a rudimentary fashion in every hysteria and that the tendency to this dissociation—and therewith to the production of abnormal states of consciousness, which may be included under the term 'hypnoid'—is a fundamental manifestation of this neurosis" (p. 34). Freud's reference to 'splitting of consciousness' and 'dissociation' as fundamental characteristics of hysteria reminds us at once of Janet's theory. Indeed Freud is careful to add, in the following sentence, that "this view is in agreement with those of Binet and the two Janets". This reference, in a paper written in 1893 (Freud 1893a), to Janet's conception of dissociation raises the question whether Freud was not indebted to Janet for the conception which led subsequently to his theory of repression. This is what Janet himself claimed in a paper read before The International Congress of Medicine in London in 1913. While, however, Freud was undoubtedly aware of Janet's investigations as they were published, it would be wrong to say that he was inspired by them. On the contrary, what inspiration he received from the Salpêtrière was due to Janet's teacher, Charcot, with whom Freud studied in 1885–1886. It was on his return to Vienna from Paris in 1886 that, in collaboration with his senior colleague Breuer, he made the observations about hidden memories which led subsequently to his theory of repression. These observations had been made and subjected to reflection (although they had not been published) before the appearance of Janet's first work. There is every justification, therefore, for regarding Freud's and Janet's theories as being independent developments deriving their impetus from the inspiration of a common teacher—Charcot.

The conception of repression has thus been developed by Freud in independence of Janet's conception of dissociation. Freud and his followers have usually regarded it as an alternative and more satisfactory conception elaborated for the explanation of a common body of facts. The actual fact that there exists, in hysteria and other pathological states, a body of mental elements cut off from personal consciousness is not in dispute between the two schools. In so far as the term "dissociation" is used to describe the existence of such a state, Freud is prepared to recognise the existence of dissociation, and occasionally he uses the word itself. Thus in 1910 he writes "Psycho-analysis, too, accepts the hypothesis of dissociation and of the unconscious" (Freud 1910a, p. 107). Where his theory differs from Janet's is in the explanation of this state of dissociation. According to Janet's theory the splitting of consciousness is a *primary* feature of hysteria; for Freud it is a *secondary* feature (1893b, p. 60). What led Freud to regard it as a secondary feature was his consideration of the material which is dissociated. His observation of the *painful* nature of the dissociated material led him to the view that the dissociative process was of the nature of a *defence*. Since defence is an active, not a passive process, he was unable, like Janet, to attribute the process to a mere failure of mental synthesis resulting from lack of mental energy. Freud's first difference with Breuer—the prelude to their final separation—appears to have arisen over this point. In a paper "On the History of the Psycho-analytic Movement", Freud (1914b) expresses himself thus:

> The first difference between Breuer and myself came to light in regard to a question concerning the finer psychical mechanism of hysteria. He gave preference to a theory which was still to some extent physiological, as one might call it; he wished to explain the mental dissociation of hysteria by the absence of communication between various psychical states (states of consciousness, as we called them at that time), and he therefore constructed the theory of "hypnoid" states, the effects of which were supposed to penetrate into waking consciousness like unassimilated foreign bodies. I had taken the matter less academically; everywhere I seemed to discern motives and tendencies analogous to those of everyday life, and I looked upon mental dissociation itself as an effect of a process of rejection which at that time I called *defence*, and later called *repression*. [pp. 291–292].

The idea that the dissociative process was essentially one whereby consciousness is defended against unbearable ideas only came to Freud after he had given up using hypnosis as a method of reviving forgotten memories. In the earlier days of his association with Breuer, he followed his colleague in using hypnosis to effect that revival of memories which had been found to result in the relief of symptoms. As time went on, however, he found that there were some patients who were difficult or impossible to hypnotise. In attempting to revive memories in these unhypnotisable patients, he adopted the procedure which he had seen Bernheim use in trying to revive in the waking consciousness of patients events which had taken place in the hypnotic state. In the attempt to revive forgotten memories in unhypnotised patients after this fashion, Freud found himself compelled to exercise a certain element of pressure. This fact led him to conclude that there must be some force in the patient's mind actively opposing his efforts: a force which he designated "Resistance". It was not long before he drew a further conclusion—the conclusion, namely, that the force which prevented the revival of forgotten memories was the very force that had originally banished the memories from consciousness. It was to this process that he gave the name of "Repression"—a conception which he regards as "The foundation-stone on which the whole structure of Psycho-analysis rests" (Freud 1914b, p. 297), and yet "Nothing but a theoretical formulation of a phenomenon which may be observed to recur as often as one undertakes an analysis of a neurotic without resorting to hypnosis" (p. 298).

For Freud (1915c), therefore, "The essence of repression lies simply in the function of rejecting and keeping something out of consciousness" (p. 86). This being the essential function of repression according to Freud, what are its other characteristics? From Freud's writings we may isolate two as the most important:

1. Repression is conceived as an *active* process. This is evident from a remark which follows shortly after that which was last quoted:

> The process of repression is not to be regarded as something which takes place once for all, the results of which are permanent, as when some living thing has been killed and from that time onward is dead; on the contrary, repression demands a constant expenditure of energy, and if this were discontinued the success of the repression would be jeopardised, so that a fresh act of repression would be necessary. We may imagine that what is repressed exercises a continuous straining in the direction of consciousness, so that the balance has to be kept by means of a steady counter-pressure. [1915c, pp. 89–90].

2. Repression is an *unconscious* process—a fact which is better expressed in Rivers' terminology by saying that it is "unwitting" (1924, p. 16). This feature Freud's "Repression" shares with Janet's "Dissociation". That repression is unwitting is inferred by Freud from the ignorance which the patient

shows of the fact that such a process is at work in his own mind. Not only is he unaware that repression has taken place at all, but he is unaware of the resistance which the therapeutic effort to revive repressed material to consciousness invariably meets (Freud 1923b).

If these, then, are the main characteristics of the process of repression, what, we may next ask, are the main characteristics of the repressed material according to Freud's scheme? These again are two in number:

1. The repressed material in *unconscious*. Freud (1915e) thus rejects the idea which seems to be implied in Janet's "Sub-conscious", that material which is cut off from personal consciousness has a consciousness of its own. "What is proved", he says, "is not a second consciousness in us, but the existence of certain mental operations lacking in the quality of consciousness" (p. 103). The known cases of "double conscience", he holds, prove nothing against his view: "They may most accurately be described as cases of a splitting of the mental activities into two groups, whereby a single consciousness takes up its position alternately with either the one or the other of these groups" (pp. 103–104).

2. The other great characteristic of repressed material, in Freud's scheme, is that it is *unpleasant*, or rather it is of such a character that, if it became conscious, it would cause unpleasure. Already in 1896, speaking of the "Defence Psycho-neuroses" (Freud 1896b) he states that what is repressed is "an intolerable idea which was in painful opposition to the patient's ego" (p. 155). It is essentially the same fact which he is expressing when he says that the aim of the resistance is "to avoid the 'pain' that would be aroused by the release of the repressed material" (Freud 1922, p. 20).

Such being the main features involved in the Freudian conception of repression, "Repression" in his sense, though not in his words, may be defined as *an active mental process essentially consisting in the exclusion from personal consciousness of certain mental elements whose appearance in consciousness would cause unpleasure.*

The next task which falls to our enquiry is to examine the process of repression with a view to determining whether or not Freud has conceived it in a satisfactory fashion. If now we turn to this task, we shall do well to direct our attention, not to the psychosis or psychoneurosis, but to a phenomenon which is not necessarily pathological, viz. the dream. Freud was the first to realise adequately the importance of the dream in mental life, just as he was the first to formulate the concept of repression; and it is significant that in his "Introductory Lectures on Psycho-analysis" (1916–1917), he makes the study of the dream (Book II) the basis upon which he develops his general theory of the neuroses (Book III). Further it was mainly through Freud's "Traumdeutung", published in 1900, that the medical and psychological world were introduced to the theory of repression. If, then, we turn to the examination of Freud's dream-theory, we find the whole crux of the theory to lie in the concept of *distortion*: a concept with which that of the "Censorship" is intimately connected. The importance of the concept of distortion is evident from a note in Chap. VI of the "Traumdeutung", where Freud writes: "I consider this reference of dream-disfigurement to the censor as the essence of my dream-theory" (1900, p. 287).

According to Freud's theory,

> We should then assume in each human being, as the primary cause of dream formation, two psychic forces (streams, systems), of which one constitutes the wish expressed by the dream, while the other acts as a censor upon this dream wish, and by means of this censoring forces a distortion of its expression. [1900, p. 121]

The dream, therefore, owes its distinctive character to two facts,

1. that there is a barrier to the entry of the latent dream-thoughts into the dream-consciousness;

2. that this barrier may be passed, if the dream-thoughts are suitably modified.

The existence of the barrier and the necessity for distortion of the dream-thoughts, if they are to pass the barrier, are explained as an expression of the process of repression. The metaphor of the censorship (Freud 1900) is designed to convey the impression that the barrier, which the dream-thoughts meet, is not merely a static obstacle but something dynamic—something more like a commissionaire turning people back from a door than a rail across the entrance. The dynamic nature of the barrier is to be inferred from the amount of dream-work which appears to be necessary to enable the dream-thoughts to enter consciousness (Freud 1900). For many years previous to the publication of his "Traumdeutung", Freud had spent much of his time in the attempt to elucidate the meaning of both his own dreams and those of patients. The results of his analysis of the factors entering into dream-formation led him to the conclusion that, so far at any rate as the majority of adult dreams are concerned, the mental elements which seek expression in the dream are prevented from reaching consciousness in their original form owing to their incompatibility with the conscious aspirations of the dreamer (Vide 1900, p. 120). It was this incompatibility which led to the resistance which the dream-thoughts encountered; and it was this incompatibility which made the process of distortion necessary, if the dream-thoughts were to enter consciousness at all. Freud had already reached the conclusion that the symptoms of hysteria were the products of just such a process of distortion, and that the rationale of this process was to be found in a similar incompatibility between conscious and unconscious elements in mental life. It would thus seem evident that any theory of repression conceived along the dynamic lines indicated by Freud must be intimately bound up with the process of distortion as illustrated in the dream. It is, therefore, a matter of vital importance to determine whether Freud is right or wrong in attributing the characteristic features of the dream to a process of active distortion.

Of the modern theories of the dream which dispense with the idea of distortion, that of Rivers is the most noteworthy. Rivers (1923) accepts Freud's distinction between the manifest and the latent content of the dream, but he finds himself unable to follow Freud in attributing the change of latent into manifest content to a process of distortion. For the term 'distortion' he substitutes 'transformation' (1923, p. 4). According to this conception, the manifest content is spoken of as coming in to being through a transformation of the latent content. His explanation of the process of transformation is dependent upon the general view that mental life is arranged in strata or levels, comparable to those represented in the nervous system. In sleep, the higher levels are in abeyance, and only the lower levels are functioning. Like Freud, he regards the dream of the human adult as intimately concerned with mental conflict, but he goes further in this direction, and finds the essential function of the dream to be "the solution of a conflict by means of processes belonging to those levels of activity which are still active in sleep" (Rivers 1923, p. 17). In sleep only the lower levels of experience are functioning, and, therefore, the attempted solution is necessarily mediated by those processes of thought which are typical of the lower levels. It is the translation of the conflicting elements into terms of primitive thought that constitutes 'transformation' (e.g., Rivers 1923, p. 81). The apparent disguise of the dream-thoughts is, according to Rivers, due to the fact that the primitive ways of thinking released in sleep are unfamiliar to the higher, rational processes of thought which characterise waking consciousness.

Whether the characteristic features of the manifest dream-content are due to a process like Freud's "distortion" or to a process like Rivers' "transformation" is a matter of no small importance for our concept of repression. Indeed it is hardly an exaggeration to say that this question constitutes a vital issue. According to Freud, the nature of the manifest content is determined by the necessity of overcoming a resistance to the appearance of the latent content in consciousness. According to Rivers, the nature of the manifest content is determined by the primitive or infantile character of the mental processes which assert themselves when the inhibitory influences of more evolved mental processes are withdrawn in sleep. It is evident, then, that no two dream-theories could be more fundamentally opposed than those of Freud and Rivers. According to Freud, the necessity for transformation is a function of the *conscious*; according to Rivers, it is a function of the *unconscious*. This fundamental opposition has its roots in a difference over the interpretation of the phenomenon which Freud describes as "distortion".

Among the advantages of Rivers' theory may be cited: 1. Its greater simplicity; 2. The fact that it accords with the general impression which a dream gives of being of a piece with primitive modes of thinking. The use of symbols and the dramatic representation, which are such prominent features of dreams, are in line with what we know of the thought of children and savage races. It is unquestionable that some dreams are capable of being interpreted along these lines, particularly war dreams; and, after all, war dreams formed the bulk of the material which Rivers studied. On the other hand, any student of the subject, who has made a collection of the dreams of patients in civil life, must have come across innumerable dreams which are incapable of such an easy interpretation. An example may be quoted from a collection of many thousand dreams, which has been made by the present writer in the course of psychotherapeutic practice. This dream, which may be called "The Spaniel Dream", has been selected because it illustrates the presence of distortion in an exceptionally pointed and dramatic manner. It demonstrates the presence of distortion, in that the whole movement of the dream consists in a gradual break-down of the transformation-process. As the dream progresses, the transformation is undone under our very eyes. The gradual break-down of distortion, which is observed, enables us to realise that there really is distortion there at the start, and that the earlier phases of the dream are the products of just that dream-work, of which Freud inferred the existence, and of which he found the object to be the concealment of the real meaning of a dream from the dreamer. In this case the dreamer was a young woman suffering from a complex psycho-pathological state, which did not conform to any of the recognised groups, but which included obsessional and hysterical features of a very advanced kind. She described the dream as "a real nightmare", and it occurred when she was on holiday, staying at a boarding-house, where she met a young man who attracted her interest and with whom she went for several motor-runs.

The "spaniel" dream. The beginning of the dream was not well remembered, but it had to do with being out for a motor-run. Later, the dreamer was in a house with some others. A young, black spaniel was there also. As the party turned to leave the room, the spaniel leaped up in a playful way at her bare arm or bare leg. She could not recall which of these limbs it was, but it was held out in a horizontal way. The dog was trying to take her limb into its mouth, but was prevented from doing so by the dreamer, who said to it pleasantly, "No, you don't." So far the dream was accompanied by no affect, but now the nightmare part began. Immediately after she had checked the puppy, it became seized by some terrible distress. It seemed as if its upper jaw had become inverted, and it writhed on the ground in terrible agony, wildly pleading by a dumb look in its eyes, and holding out its front paws for help. It was desperate to have its jaw turned back into the proper position. The dreamer felt that the desperate plight of the animal had come about because she had not let it do what it wanted; but she was also conscious of a certain feeling of aloofness. She felt very sorry for the animal, but she did not want to touch it in any way. She experienced a callous, "Fate-being-fulfilled" sort of feeling. All the time, the dog was writhing on the ground, making the most terrible sounds. Then a young boy appeared and tried to help by putting a stick down its throat several times. This was a horrible part of the dream, and unpleasant affect became pronounced. It became still more pronounced, when the dog, as such, disappeared, leaving behind only the throat into which the boy was thrusting his stick. The throat then gradually changed its appearance and became just a big, fleshy opening, which, just as the dreamer awakened, she recognised as the vaginal opening. During the last phase of the dream, the unpleasant affect gradually increased in intensity, and, when she awoke, it was to find herself in a state of abject terror.

The interest of this dream lies in the extraordinarily clear way in which the undoing of the process of distortion is depicted. As we follow the progress of the dream, we are able to observe the dream-work being undone step by step. This enables us to reconstruct the process whereby the dream-work was originally effected. In the earliest part of the dream, the centre of interest is an apparently ingenuous symbol—a young, playful black spaniel. It is notable that in this part of the dream there is absence of affect. As the dream progresses, the dog's throat becomes the significant symbol; and this development is accompanied by the appearance of unpleasant affect. The dog's body then fades away and only the gaping throat is left. As the symbolisation progressively breaks down, unpleasant affect increases in intensity. Eventually symbolisation breaks down completely; the meaning of the preceding symbols is robbed of all uncertainty, and the patient awakes in terror. When such a dream is considered, it is impossible to doubt that the manifest dream in its earlier phases is the product of the process which Freud describes as "Dream-work". It is equally impossible to doubt that this process of dream-work partakes essentially of the nature of "distortion" rather than of simple "transformation". Further, it is impossible to avoid the impression that the function of the earlier symbols of the dream is that of effecting a *disguise*, and that the object of this disguise is to hide from the dreamer's consciousness the true meaning of the dream-thoughts.

Dreams like the 'spaniel' dream, in which the symbolism is seen gradually to break down during the course of the dream, are a much less common phenomenon than a dream-series in which each successive dream shows less and less evidence of distortion, as the dream-thoughts become more insistent. Such a dream-series may occur during the course of a single night or may be spread over several nights. A clear example of such a series is afforded by a sequence of two dreams, which another of the writer's patients recorded as having occurred on the same night. The patient in question was a middle-aged woman, whose career as a teacher had been seriously compromised by a succession of break-downs. These tended to occur after she had held any post for a time. The length of time varied, but in all cases she eventually found the strain of teaching too much for her and felt compelled to resign. She was a good teacher, but she would stay up all night in an excess of conscientiousness preparing her lessons for the next day. The result was that, in due course, she would become completely exhausted and show irritability towards the children under her charge. Her memory would desert her in the class, and she would become dissatisfied with herself. She would struggle to continue her work to the end of the term, but usually found herself quite unable to do so, and had, reluctantly so far as her conscious intentions were concerned, to surrender altogether in a state of depression. This patient was attractive to men, but her case was complicated by a congenital defect which made marriage out of the question. She had neither a vagina nor a uterus, although it would appear that the clitoris was present and there was every reason to believe that the ovarian secretion was not absent. The two dreams in the short series to be quoted were simple in character, but this is perhaps no disadvantage for demonstrating the point, to illustrate which they are cited.

The first dream may be called *"The hole in the stocking" dream*. The dreamer was looking over her shoulder at the heel of her stocking. The stocking was thick and made of wool: "Like the old-fashioned hand-knitted stockings", to quote the dreamer's words. As she looked at the stocking, she noticed that it was a mass of holes and of run-down stitches. She experienced surprise at the condition of the stocking. There were some people present, and one of them gave a little laugh, whereupon she said apologetically, "These were new just the other day and they were strong because of being hand-knitted and being of thick wool; I cannot understand it".

The second dream may be called *"The Nudity Dream"*. In this dream, the dreamer found herself standing naked before a young nephew. The two were seriously discussing something of grave import, but no memory of the subject of discussion could be recalled by the dreamer on awaking. All that the dreamer could remember was that she said to her nephew in a tone of reproach "Surely you don't expect me to go like this".

The deeper meaning of this dream-sequence need not be discussed here, but it had a bearing on the dreamer's physical disability. What is relevant to our discussion, however, is the fact that the holes in the stocking in the first dream appear to be the symbol of the nakedness which appears in the second dream, where symbolism has, partly at any rate, broken down. We cannot help regarding the symbolism of the first dream as the product of dream-work. It bears all the evidence of a process of distortion, and this distortion would appear to be meaningless unless its function is to disguise the true meaning of the dream-thoughts from the dreamer's consciousness.

When the significance of dreams such as those which have been instanced is considered, it is evident that the symbolisation partakes of the nature of distortion rather than of simple transformation. Its essence is *disguise*. The interpretation of such dreams puts a strain upon Rivers' theory which it is unable to bear. If dream-symbols are merely the natural expression of primitive thinking, it is difficult to see why, in the "spaniel" dream, the object symbolised successively by the dog, the dog's throat, and the throat as such should necessitate a process of transformation at all. The object symbolised seems to be itself a natural symbol for primitive thought—indeed it seems to be a more natural content of primitive thought than of any other kind of thought. It is primitive 'par excellence'.

It is true that, according to Rivers' theory, dreams are not simply primitive thinking, but attempts to solve conflicts *in terms of primitive thinking* (vide e.g., Rivers 1923). Even so, however, the only solution which seems to be offered is that of disguise. The only function which transformation effects is to translate the conflict into terms in which its real significance is obscured. This may be easier to do on the plane of primitive thinking, and presumably this is why, in normal people, such phenomena occur typically in sleep—when psychical functions are eliminated from above downwards. Nonetheless, the value of transformation in the attempted solution of conflict seems to be inextricably bound up with the distortion thereby produced. Any theory of dreams, therefore, which fails to do justice to the presence of an active process of distortion must be regarded as inadequate.

If this be true, we are driven to a dream-theory modelled more after the lines of Freud than after the lines of Rivers. We may accept from Rivers the view that the dream is a characteristic product of primitive thinking which occurs when the inhibition of superimposed higher thought-processes is withdrawn; but we must recognise the presence, in a very large class of dreams, of a definite process of distortion. This process of distortion may be a special feature which only occurs when primitive thinking is occupied with mental conflict, but, in so far as it is present, we must regard it as evidence of a process of repression conceived after Freudian lines. Distortion, of course, is a process which occurs quite readily in primitive thinking, because primitive thinking is non-rational in character. When the higher thought-processes are active, perhaps "rationalisation" is a more natural process than distortion; but, be that as it may, the essence of both processes is to be found in the resistance, which seems to oppose the entry into consciousness of mental content of a certain kind. When the higher processes are active in waking life, this resistance manifests itself in a most uncompromising way; it does not manifest itself at all readily as distortion, because distortion is not a natural expression of rational thought. When primitive thought-processes are released, as in sleep or in cases of psychical regression, the resistance manifests itself as distortion, because, although distortion is incompatible with rational thought, it is by no means incompatible with *non*-rational thought. Further, the resistance shows itself in less uncompromising form in distortion than in any process possible to rational thought; and it is for this reason that dreams "open up the straightest road to the knowledge of the unconscious" (Freud 1904, p. 268). It is for a similar reason that the dream has been selected as a field for the study of the process of repression.

It is with a view to throwing light upon the process of repression that attention has been specially directed to the phenomenon of distortion in the dream. The dreams quoted seem 1. To prove beyond all question that distortion does occur in dreams; 2. To show that distortion partakes of the nature of repression as conceived along the lines indicated by Freud. This is not to say that *all* dreams exemplify distortion, or for that matter, that repression is a necessary feature of all dreams. On the one hand, distortion may be absent because (despite Rivers) there may be no conflict finding expression in the dream-thoughts. Waking consciousness is not necessarily concerned with material involving repression; and there is no reason to suppose that the dreaming consciousness inevitably is so either (whatever Freud may say to the contrary in reference to adult dreams). On the other hand, distortion may be absent owing to the fact that repression has broken down. This is what seems to have occurred in the final phase of the 'spaniel' dream. It is to be noted that, when this break-down of repression occurred in the dream, the unpleasant affect became extreme and the dreamer awoke.

This raises the question of the relation of affect to the dream. It is a striking feature of dreams that situations, which would inevitably provoke emotion in waking life, frequently appear to provoke no emotion in the dream; but it is a still more striking feature that situations, which would be indifferent in waking life so far as affect is concerned, may be accompanied by intense emotion. Thus one of the writer's patients dreamed about jumping from one rock to another across a roaring torrent of considerable breadth, yet this dream was free of the fear which would undoubtedly have been felt if the necessity for such a feat had arisen in waking life. On the other hand, in another dream the same patient was filled with terror at the sight of an ordinary cushion lying on the floor. Such phenomena are interpreted by Freud as indicating that "the dream is less rich in affects than the psychic material from which it is elaborated" (Freud 1900, p. 371). Whenever emotion appears in the manifest dream, it is derived from the latent dream-thoughts; but absence of emotion in the manifest dream does not necessarily imply its absence in the thoughts from which the dream is elaborated. Suppression of affect thus comes to be regarded as a feature of dream-formation, and this feature, like that of distortion, is attributed to the action of the censorship (Freud 1900, p. 372). Suppression of affect and distortion are thus both products of repression in the dreamer's mind. The appearance of affect in the dream-consciousness must, therefore, be regarded as a failure of repression, just as a breakdown of distortion has a like significance.

Rivers (1923) agrees with Freud "that affect may be absent or at any rate inappreciable in the manifest dream when it is evidently present in the deeper dream-thoughts of which the manifest dream is the transformed expression" (pp. 65–66). His views on the significance of affect in the dream were based on his study of anxiety dreams in soldiers suffering from war-neurosis. In bad cases the nightmare generally occurred as a faithful reproduction of some terrifying scene of warfare without evidence of any transformation. As improvement in the patient's condition occurred, it was noticed that transformation began to make its appearance. Such cases suggested to Rivers (1923) that:

> There is a definite relation between the amount of transformation and the intensity of the affect. They suggest that the intensity of affect is inversely proportional to the amount of transformation, a suggestion in harmony with the view of Freud that one of the results of the transformation of the latent into the manifest content of the dream is to lessen or inhibit its affective character. [p. 67]

He took exception, however, to Freud's theory that every dream is a disguised wish-fulfillment. The study of war-dreams suggested, on the contrary, that terrifying dreams were the expression of painful experience which the patient desired not to experience again. From this he concluded that "so far as desire enters into causation, the dream is the direct negation of a wish, the wish not to be subjected to the repetition of a painful experience (Rivers 1923, p. 68). There was thus a conflict "between a process in which an experience tends to recur to memory and a desire that the experience shall not recur" (1923, p. 68). Attention has already been drawn to Rivers' theory that the dream is an attempted solution of a conflict in terms of the primitive thinking, which is the only thinking available in sleep. In accordance with this theory, the anxiety-dream is necessarily regarded as "a failure of solution" (Rivers 1923, p. 69).

We have already seen that Rivers' failure to recognise the presence of disguise in dream-transformation vitiated his theory that the dream is simply an attempt to solve mental conflict in terms of primitive thinking; but it is a notable fact that both he and Freud agree in regarding the appearance of affect in the dream as due to a failure of repression. The rationale of the sudden waking of the dreamer from an anxiety-dream seems to be that, when the repressive processes at the disposal of the dreaming consciousness are overwhelmed, the more extensive repressive resources of the waking consciousness have to be called in. The awakening of the dreamer under such conditions is of interest for two reasons. First, it is of interest because it suggests that distortion functions as a process protective of consciousness against inroads from the unconscious. It thus has its 'raison d'être' in the conscious (as Freud's theory implies), not in the unconscious (as Rivers' theory implies). Secondly, study of the conditions of waking from anxiety-dreams leads us to see the superiority of a theory of repression conceived on the Freudian model over Rivers' theory of repression. According to Rivers (1924), repression is really equivalent to inhibition conceived after the model of modern neurological theory. The later evolved mental processes repress more primitive modes of mental functioning, just as the later evolved cortical functions inhibit those of the thalamus and sub-cortical structures. When the higher control is removed, the repressed functions manifest themselves. This way of regarding repression has two implications which it is impossible to accept.

First, if Rivers were right, dream-distortion would become a phenomenon, not of repression, but of lack of repression. The unsatisfactory nature of this position need not be elaborated. It follows from the conclusion, which has already been reached, that disguise constitutes the essence of distortion.

Let us turn to the other implication of Rivers' view (1924). It is to the effect that repression depends upon a distinction between higher and lower mental structures. Repression becomes characteristic of the action of higher processes as such upon all primitive processes which fail to be assimilated by fusion. The importance of this distinction need not be denied, but it is not a distinction which helps us to understand repression. We have seen that the symbolisation of the anxiety-dream is characterised by disguise. It was this fact of disguise that gave Freud the clue to a distinction of infinitely greater value for the understanding of repression than that between "higher" and "lower": viz. the distinction between "conscious" and "unconscious". Study of the anxiety-dream shows that the function of repression is not to prevent primitive mental processes from interfering with higher mental processes, but to prevent certain unconscious mental processes from disturbing consciousness: whether it be the primitive consciousness of the dreamer or the higher consciousness of waking life.

The most striking features of the anxiety-dream would seem to be 1. the tendency of distortion to break down, 2. the tendency of the dreamer to awake. The implications of these facts would seem to be:

1. That the function of distortion is to prevent the appearance in consciousness of mental content, the appearance of which would be accompanied by unpleasant affect;
2. That, when distortion breaks down and unpleasant affect does appear in consciousness, this is a sign that the process of

repression has failed at the primitive mental level of the dreaming consciousness;

3. That, when repression fails at a primitive level, the higher mental processes, which have been in abeyance during sleep, are mobilised and the dreamer wakes;
4. That, when the higher mental processes of the waking consciousness become active, the repressive functions of the sentiments and ideals serve to check the further development of the repressed content in consciousness.

In the light of these inferences, Freud's (1900) dictum that "the dream is the guardian of sleep, not the disturber of it" (p. 197) must be interpreted as meaning that distortion serves the purpose of preserving consciousness from the unpleasant affect which would result, if repressed tendencies succeeded in manifesting themselves in recognisable form. We are thus led by the study of the anxiety-dream to the conclusion reached by Freud (1915c), that repression is a process whereby consciousness is preserved from unpleasant affect.

This conclusion does not require us to follow Freud in adopting a general theory of psychological hedonism. It merely involves our recognising that repression is essentially a hedonistic process. It is a process whereby unpleasant mental content is kept out of consciousness, or, to express the same fact in another way, it is a process whereby consciousness is enabled to avoid the unpleasant. That a tendency to avoid the unpleasant may be a determining factor in conduct is too common an observation to make it necessary to stress the point. Behaviour determined in this way is described by psychologists as "appetitive" in character (e.g., Drever 1921). It is a primitive type of behaviour, which in the human being is normally subordinated to the "reactive" type of behaviour, which characterises the activity of the more highly evolved instinctive tendencies, such as aggression, flight and sex. It would seem to be appetitive behaviour to which Freud refers, when he says that the "primary" mental processes obey the "pleasure-principle", (1911, p. 14). No one who has any experience of neurotics will deny the possibility of finding persons whose conduct is largely determined by a tendency to avoid unpleasure. Their inability to face the sterner facts of life, their liability to break down under strain or responsibility, their dilettantism and their inability to tolerate a frustration of their desires are all evidence of an exaggeration of the natural tendency to avoid unpleasure. Yet these are the very people who exhibit the symptoms which have led to the recognition of the process of repression. Such phenomena provide striking confirmation of Freud's view of repression as a *process whereby consciousness is spared unpleasure. Repression is thus seen to be an expression of the general tendency of the organism to avoid the unpleasant.*

With this conclusion our enquiry into the essential nature of the process of repression comes to an end. The result of our enquiry is to show, that, in general, repression is best conceived along the lines indicated by Freud, who originally isolated it as a distinct mental process. Repression will accordingly be defined as follows: *Repression is an active mental process whereby certain mental elements, the appearance of which in consciousness would cause unpleasure, are excluded from personal consciousness without thereby ceasing to be mental.*

THE RELATIONSHIP OF REPRESSION TO DISSOCIATION

The conceptions of dissociation and repression have now been subjected to such analysis as has seemed necessary to determine their essential nature and to enable satisfactory definitions of the two processes to be formulated. It now remains to consider the relationship between the two processes. Now that the ground has been cleared, this task should not prove difficult. If the definition of repression, which has just been given, is compared with the definition of dissociation previously reached, it is evident that repression is just a special form of dissociation. *Dissociation* was defined as: An active mental process, whereby unacceptable mental content or an unacceptable mental function becomes cut off from personal consciousness, without thereby ceasing to be mental—such mental content or mental function being "unacceptable" within the meaning of this definition if it is either irrelevant to, incompatible with, or unpleasant in relation to an active interest. *Repression* has just been defined as: An active mental process whereby certain mental elements, the appearance of which in consciousness would cause unpleasure, are excluded from personal consciousness without thereby ceasing to be mental. It is, therefore, obvious that repression is in its essence just dissociation of the unpleasant.

While, however, repression must be regarded as dissociation of the unpleasant, it does not follow that all dissociation of the unpleasant is necessarily repression. As a matter of fact, the two processes are not co-extensive. Dissociation of the unpleasant is the more extensive process of the two, and repression is just a special form which it takes under certain definite conditions. The problem that remains is to discover what these special conditions are. When we have answered this question, we shall have determined the exact relationship between the two processes. In seeking the answer to our question, we shall do well to look in the direction which has already proved so fruitful in our enquiry, and devote our attention to the nature of the material involved in the process under consideration. Our remaining task is, therefore, to enquire into the nature of the material involved in the process of repression. It is here if anywhere that we ought to find the differentia of repression from simple dissociation of the unpleasant.

In his earlier writings Freud (1896a) described repression as "arising through an unbearable idea having called up the defences of the ego" (p. 207). Writing in 1905 of the views which he propounded in 1894–1896, he says:

> I had put it forward as a condition of the pathogenic effectiveness of a given experience that it must seem to the ego intolerable and must evoke an effort towards defence. To this defence I had referred the mental dissociation—or as it was then called, the dissociation of consciousness—of hysteria. If the defence succeeded, then the unbearable experience and its affective consequences were banished from consciousness and from the memory of the ego. [1905b, p. 278]

It is thus evident that in his earlier writings Freud regarded the repressed material as consisting of unbearable *ideas* and unbearable *experiences with their affective consequences*. This is in line with his original dictum that "hysterical patients suffer principally from reminiscences"—a dictum which appears in the same paper (Freud 1893b) in which he first uses the word "repress". That Freud should have originally regarded the repressed material as consisting of ideas and memories is what we should expect from the circumstances under which he came to formulate the conception of repression; for, as Freud (1914b) points out, it was the resistance of unhypnotised patients to the recall of memories that led him to recognise the presence of such a process.

In Freud's later writings, however, we notice a significant change in terminology. In his later works, he speaks less of "ideas" and "memories" and more of "impulses", "instincts" and "unconscious tendencies". Thus in 1915 he writes: "One of the vicissitudes an instinctual impulse may undergo is to meet with resistances the aim of which is to make the impulse inoperative. Under certain conditions, which we shall presently investigate more closely, the impulse then passes into the state of 'repression' " (1915c, p. 84). In his later description of repression, therefore, what is described as being repressed is not an unbearable idea but an instinctive impulse, which, by the "attainment of its aim", would "produce 'pain'" (p. 84). This change of terminology, which is a feature of Freud's later as contrasted with his earlier writings, is highly significant. It indicates a movement in the direction of regarding repressed material as consisting *not in parts of the mental content, but in elements of mental structure*. This is well illustrated in a passage where Freud (1922) says:

> It over and again happens that particular instincts, or portions of them, prove irreconcilable in their aims or demands with others which can be welded into the comprehensive unity of the ego. They are thereupon split off from this unity by the process of repression, retained on lower stages of psychic development, and for the time being cut off from all possibility

> of gratification. If they then succeed, as so easily happens with the repressed sex-impulses, in fighting their way through—along circuitous routes—to a direct or substitutive gratification, this success, which might otherwise have brought pleasure, is experienced by the ego as 'pain'. ["pain" = German "Unlust"] [p. 6.]

The realisation that repressed material is composed not so much of ideas and memories as of tendencies having their ultimate basis in the instinctive endowment of the individual was, in large part, due to an observation, which the exigencies of psychoanalytic technique made increasingly clear, as experience was gained. It was found that the aim of bringing the content of the patient's unconscious into consciousness was not fully attainable:

> The patient cannot recall all of what lies repressed, perhaps not even the essential part of it, and so gains no conviction that the conclusion presented to him is correct. He is obliged rather to *repeat* as a current experience what is repressed, instead of, as the physician would prefer to see him do, *recollecting* it as a fragment of the past. [Freud 1922, pp. 17–18]

This observation, the truth of which has been confirmed by the present writer in his own experience, naturally led to a concentration of interest upon repressed tendencies, as against repressed mental content. Another fact which contributed to this change of view-point was the fact that not only the repressed elements, but also "the motives of the resistances, and indeed the resistances themselves, are found in the process of treatment to be unconscious" (Freud 1922, p. 19). Realisation of the significance of the fact, that the resistances are as unconscious as the repressed elements, led Freud to amend an inadequacy in his mode of expression. "We escape ambiguity", he says, "if we contrast not the conscious and the unconscious, but the coherent ego and the repressed. . . . We may say that the resistance on the part of the analysed person proceeds from his ego" (1922, p. 19). The "coherent ego" is, of course, part of the mental structure not of the mental content. It corresponds to what is described in more orthodox psychological terms as "The organised self"—a hierarchical organisation of the sentiments and ideals based on the fundamental instinctive tendencies. If, then, the conception of repression is to be satisfactorily formulated, it must be expressed in terms of mental structure rather than of mental content. This being so, repression is to be regarded as *a process whereby certain mental tendencies are denied conscious expression, if their incongruity with the structure of the organised self is such that the conscious expression of these tendencies would cause unpleasure.*

Although Freud in his later works (e.g., *Beyond the Pleasure Principle* and *The Ego and the Id*) has been led to realise that repression primarily involves elements of mental structure rather than elements of mental content, it must be recognised that his realisation of this fact has been somewhat inadequate. This is largely due to the fact that his views have been elaborated in too great an independence of general psychology. Thus, instead of using ordinary psychological terms, he speaks, e.g., of "Repression of an instinct-presentation", understanding by this expression "an idea or group of ideas which is cathected with a definite amount of the mental energy (libido interest) pertaining to an instinct" (Freud 1915c, p. 91). He thus comes to divide the manifestation of an instinctive tendency into a "group of ideas" and a "charge of affect", which may be separated from it and attached to another group of ideas. This way of speaking of affect as if it were a form of floating mental energy which could be attached to this or that part of the mental content is highly misleading, and it obscures the fact that mental content is only significant in relation to an active tendency. The true interpretation of phenomena of repression, so far as mental content is concerned, appears to be that mental content is only liable to be repressed in so far as it is the expression of instinct-interest which is repressed. Thus we can only speak of "repressed memories" in the sense that memories activated by repressed tendencies tend to be kept out of consciousness because the tendencies which activate them are themselves denied conscious expression.

The reference which has been made to Freud's division of "an instinct-presentation" into "a group of ideas" and "a charge of affect" raises another question besides that of the bearing of repression upon mental content. This is the question of the relation of repression to affect. Psychoanalytic literature is full of such expressions as "unconscious hate", "unconscious love", "unconscious sense of guilt". In so far as such expressions imply the existence of an emotional state which is unconscious, their validity must unquestionably be denied. An emotion is a feeling-state, and to speak of an unconscious feeling-state is to give voice of an absurdity. Freud (1915e) has discussed this question. He writes:

> We know, too, that to suppress the development of affect is the true aim of repression and that its work does not terminate if this aim is not achieved. In every instance where repression has succeeded in inhibiting the development of an affect we apply the term 'unconscious' to those affects that are restored when we undo the work of repression. So it cannot be denied that the use of the terms in question is logical; but a comparison of the unconscious affect with the unconscious idea reveals the significant difference that the unconscious idea continues, after repression, as an actual formation in the system Ucs, whilst to the unconscious affect there corresponds in the same system only a potential disposition which is prevented from developing further. So that, strictly speaking, although no fault be found with the mode of expression in question, there are no unconscious affects in the sense in which there are unconscious ideas. But there may very well be in the system Ucs affect-formations which, like others, come into consciousness. [pp. 110–111]

From this quotation it is evident that Freud recognises the psychological absurdity of speaking of an unconscious or repressed affect, though he gives his sanction to the usage for descriptive purposes. The usage is certainly convenient, but it must nonetheless be deprecated, unless it is clearly understood to be nothing more than a "façon de parler". Many medical writers—not only psychoanalysts—have confused the issue by speaking as if pent-up emotion could be held under repression in the unconscious. It must be insisted that, in cases to which such a description applies, what is repressed is not emotion but a tendency, which, if it reached conscious expression, would give rise to an emotional state.

If then we must conceive "the repressed" as consisting essentially of tendencies belonging to the structure of the mind rather than of parts of the mental content, such as "ideas" and "memories", the question arises: how does this help us to differentiate repression from simple dissociation of the unpleasant? It helps us, because it directs our attention to the *source* of the repressed material. We have already noted the fundamental tendency of the organism to withdraw from the unpleasant. All organisms tend to avoid unpleasant stimuli. In an organism with a primitive mentality this process of withdrawal seems simple enough. An unpleasant sensory stimulus is received, and withdrawal takes place. Even at quite a primitive mental level, however, it must be assumed that an unpleasant experience leaves some sort of memory-trace, so that, when a similar stimulus is received again, the organism's experience is different from what it was on the first occasion. One must assume that the second experience of the organism includes at least a dim sense of familiarity, and that behaviour is in some way modified as a result of the first experience. Only so is it possible to explain that adaptation of behaviour, which is one of the differentia of living organisms from inorganic matter. Only so, can learning by experience be conceived as possible. Only so, can the establishment of such a phenomenon as a conditioned reflex be envisaged. The mental level, at which memory-traces influence behaviour solely in virtue of the modification which they introduce into the second or subsequent experience of a given situation, is described by psychologists as the "perceptual level" of mental development. At this level, memory consists at best in recognition. There is no such thing as a memory-image. This is the level of mental development which characterises the vast majority of living species. For such an animal, there are unpleasant perceptions and unpleasant situations, and these activate behaviour of withdrawal; but there is no such thing as an unpleasant memory or an unpleasant idea.

A complication is, however, introduced at the next level of development, which is characterised by the possibility of memory images, and which is described by psychologists as the "ideational" or "imaginative" level. If the human race is excluded from consideration, it would seem from experimental evidence that only some of the higher animals reach this level of development. At this level, behaviour may be modified by the explicit revival of memory-images of former experiences. It is only when this level is reached that dissociation of unpleasant mental content can be conceived in any sense other than is involved in mere withdrawal from an unpleasant stimulus when it is presented. Once this mental level is reached, however, the conditions are present, which render dissociation of unpleasant mental content possible in the sense in which the phrase would commonly be understood. At this level, it is correct to say that an unpleasant memory or idea may be "dissociated". It would be incorrect, however, to speak of mental content as being "repressed".

Repression would only appear to be possible when the highest—the "rational" or "conceptual"—level of mental development is reached. This stage, so far as we know, is only reached in the case of man. The chief characteristic of mental development at this level is that ideas can be related to one another, concepts can be formed, consequences can be envisaged and general principles can be inferred or applied. It is on account of his possession of these capacities that man's ability to learn by experience is so infinitely superior to that of all other living species known. It is in virtue of these capacities that man is able to adapt his behaviour in a manner superior to that of "trial and error" learning. It is only when this level is reached that it is possible for an organism to attain self-consciousness, to appreciate the existence of various tendencies within the self and to recognise incompatibility between its own conflicting tendencies. It is, therefore, only at this level, if our analysis of repressed material has been correct, that repression becomes possible. Repression is only now possible because it is only at this level that the conscious expression of a tendency incompatible with that organised body of sentiments and ideals, which constitutes the self, can be recognised as such. It is only when such a tendency is capable of being recognised as incompatible with the self that its recognition can cause unpleasure.

These considerations lend point to the suggestion already made that it is to the *source* of the repressed material that we must look, if we would understand what it is that differentiates repression from simple dissociation of the unpleasant. *In simple dissociation of the unpleasant, what is dissociated is part of the mental content which is felt to be unpleasant because of its relation to a prevailing tendency. In repression, what is dissociated is part of the mental structure which is felt to be unpleasant because of its relation to the organised self.* It is only in the latter instance that we can properly speak of *"conflict"*—a term which is generally used to describe the state which provides the essential condition of repression. This difference between repression and simple dissociation in relation to the *source* of the material involved may perhaps be expressed more pointedly in another way. Whereas in simple dissociation of the unpleasant the dissociated material is of *external* origin, in the case of repression the dissociated material is of *internal* origin.

At first blush it may seem incorrect to say that in simple dissociation of the unpleasant the dissociated material is of external origin, if we include under this heading dissociation of unpleasant ideas and memories. These are part of the mental content; is it not absurd, it may be asked, to say that these are of external origin? The answer to this question is that it is not absurd, because ideas and memories have their origin in the experience of events which *happen to* an individual. All the examples of dissociation of the unpleasant, which were cited in the section of this thesis devoted to "Dissociation", showed a dissociation of mental content determined by events. When we speak of "The good old times", what are dissociated in our minds are the memories of unpleasant events. The same holds true of many of the dissociations witnessed in "shell-shock" cases. Our shelving of thoughts about our own death is determined by our experience of the deaths of others. The failure of patients suffering from fatal disease to recognise the gravity of their own condition is a failure to recognise the significance of an event which is happening to them. The dissociations of the kind which occurred to Livingstone, when he was being mauled by a lion, are all dissociations determined by the unpleasantness of events.

Repression, on the other hand, is exercised in relation to tendencies springing from the innate instinctive endowment of the individual concerned. These tendencies may, of course, be activated by situations in which the individual is placed, but the menace, against which defence is directed, has its roots in the nature of the individual himself. It is the tendencies which he possesses that are intolerable, rather than the situations which provoke these tendencies. The danger is internal, not external. It is endo-psychic. This is well illustrated in the case of the patient whose 'spaniel dream' has been recorded. What provoked the distortion in this dream was the presence in the dreamer of sexual desires which were in conflict with her ideals and sentiments. The object of repression in such cases is to preserve consciousness from the unpleasant affect which would result, if the presence of strong impulses irreconcilable with the organised self were to make itself felt in consciousness. In the dream in question the impulses did eventually reach conscious expression, with the result that the patient awoke in terror—fear being the natural emotion in the presence of any danger whether external or internal in origin. The object of the distortion in the earlier part of the dream was to prevent conscious realisation of the unacceptable tendency, which was too insistent to be denied expression altogether. So long as the significance of the impulse involved was concealed by distortion, unpleasant affect was avoided, but, as soon as repression began to break down, unpleasant affect began to make its appearance. It is just the appearance of such unpleasant affect that the process of distortion is calculated to prevent; and it is in the possibility of preventing the development of such unpleasant affect that the rationale of repression is to be found.

These considerations lead us to a conclusion which is at first sight paradoxical: the conclusion, namely, that what is unpleasant to consciousness about the repressed tendencies is the fact that they are pleasant. This paradox is realised by Freud, as is evident from the following passage:

> It is not easy in theory to deduce the possibility of such a thing as repression. Why should an instinctual impulse suffer such a fate? For this to happen, obviously a necessary condition must be that attainment of its aim by the instinct should produce 'pain' instead of pleasure. But we cannot well imagine such a contingency. There are no such instincts; satisfaction of an instinct is always pleasurable. We should have to assume certain peculiar circumstances, some sort of process which changes the pleasure of satisfaction into 'pain'. . . . Such a satisfaction is pleasurable in itself, but is irreconcilable with other claims and purposes; it therefore causes pleasure in one part of the mind and 'pain' in another. We see then that it is a condition of repression that the element of avoiding 'pain' shall have acquired more strength than the pleasure of gratification. ['Pain' = 'Unlust' in German] [Freud 1915c, pp. 84–85]

What makes the satisfaction of an instinctive impulse painful is, of course, the fact that it is irreconcilable with the organised sentiments and ideals, which constitute the main body of the personality. The satisfaction of repressed tendencies is pleasurable in itself, but the mere fact that it is pleasurable makes it all the more intolerable from the point of view of the organised self, with which the tendencies are in conflict. The prime condition for the possibility of repression would thus seem to be the existence in the mind of instinctive tendencies which have not been organised into the hierarchy of sentiments and ideals which form the self, although they may exhibit a minor organisation of their own. This seems to be the state of things to which Freud intends to refer, when he speaks of a "fixation" (vide, e.g., Freud 1915c, p. 86). Another term, which is commonly used in this connection in psycho-pathological literature, is the word "complex". This word was originally introduced by Jung of Zürich to designate minor organisations of instinctive tendencies which are out of relation to the main personality and which thus remain unconscious. The word has since been used by McDougall, Bernard Hart and others as equivalent to "sentiment", but it seems to be more usefully employed in its original sense, as indicating a minor organisation of tendencies out of relation to the sentiments and ideals, and so liable to repression. Where such independent organisations as the complex assume a more extensive form, they would seem to constitute those "secondary personalities" to which Morton Prince and others have devoted so much painstaking investigation. It would seem that any instinctive tendency is theoretically capable of leading to complex-formation and so provoking the process of repression, but, since the sex instinct is, of all the instinctive tendencies, that most difficult to assimilate into the personality in the modern civilised world, it is the tendencies related to this instinct that seem to be most frequently involved. Freud goes so far as to say that the sex-tendencies are involved in every case; but, although the psycho-neuroses of civil life seem to afford evidence in favour of his view, the experiences of war seem to show that tendencies of self-preservation are capable of functioning in a manner so much at variance with the organised self as to provide occasion for repression.

Whatever the exact nature of the tendencies involved, however, the essential feature of the process of repression remains unaffected. Its nature is best understood in the light of the term, which Freud originally employed when he first isolated the process—viz., that of "defence". Defence, however, is a feature which repression shares with all forms of dissociation of the unpleasant. The difference between repression and simple dissociation of the unpleasant lies in the fact, that in the first case the menace, from which protection is sought, is of *internal* origin, whereas in the second case it is only of *external* origin. In simple dissociation of the unpleasant, the defence is directed against mental content determined ultimately by *events that happen* to the individual. In repression, the defence is directed against *tendencies which form part of the mental structure* of the individual himself.

The distinction, which has now been established between repression and other forms of protective dissociation, enables us to understand two characteristic features of repression, which have led many writers to regard it as a completely separate process. These are:

1. The relatively permanent character of its effects.
2. The high degree of activity which it seems to involve.

As regards the first of these features: the relatively permanent character of repression as compared with other forms of protective dissociation is readily understood, once we recognise that, in the case of repression, the source of danger is endopsychic. The source of the unpleasant affect which is threatened, and from which defence is sought, is to be traced ultimately to the instinctive tendencies, and these form part of the permanent structure of the mind. Freud picturesquely describes the source from which these tendencies spring as the "Id" (Freud 1923, p. 28), but this term merely exemplifies the confusion which results, when attempts are made by medical writers to explain mental processes in independence of general psychology. The "Id" is an unnecessary and redundant term for what are familiar to psychologists as the innate instinct-dispositions. It is the permanence of the instinct-dispositions, which gives rise to the impression of the relative permanence of the effects of repression.

As regards the high degree of activity which strikes the observer as characterising the action of repression, this is also traceable to the source of the material. It was probably the contrast between the enormous amount of activity, which appears to be involved in repression, and the relatively small amount of activity, which appears to be involved in simple protective dissociation, that led McDougall (1926) to remark "Dissociation terminates conflict; but repression, in itself, does not" (p. 226). We have already indicated that "conflict" is only applicable where repression is concerned; but, be that as it may, the high degree of activity involved in repression is readily intelligible in the light of the enormous amount of energy with which the instinct-dispositions are endowed by nature. It is because these instinctive tendencies are, biologically speaking, the dynamic of all action, that, when any of them is repressed, repression must necessarily involve a degree of activity which is found in no other form of dissociation.

CONCLUSION

Now that the relationship between repression and dissociation has been determined, the task which the writer set before him in his thesis is concluded. All that remains to be done is to summarise the conclusions reached.

SUMMARY

1. The conception of dissociation has been subjected to examination, and the conclusion has been reached that dissociation should be regarded as: An active mental process, whereby unacceptable mental content or an unacceptable mental function becomes cut off from personal consciousness, without thereby ceasing to be mental—such mental content or mental function being regarded as unacceptable if it is either irrelevant to, incompatible with or unpleasant in relation to an active interest.

2. The conception of repression was then considered, with the result that repression was found to be: An active mental process, whereby certain mental elements, the appearance of which in consciousness would cause unpleasure, are excluded from personal consciousness without thereby ceasing to be mental.

3. On the assumption that these conclusions regarding the essential nature of the two processes are correct, it follows that repression is to be classed with dissociation of the unpleasant.

4. The consideration of various phenomena illustrating repression and dissociation of the unpleasant showed that repression is a special form of dissociation of the unpleasant: viz., that form which occurs when the dissociated elements consist of tendencies belonging to the instinctive endowment and thus forming part of the structure of the mind itself.

5. This last conclusion led to a modification of the definition of repression, as a result of which it came to be regarded as: A process whereby certain mental tendencies are denied conscious expression, if their incongruity with the structure of the organised self is such that the conscious expression of these tendencies would cause unpleasure.

6. This final definition of repression suggests that, whereas the term "mental conflict" is applicable to conditions giving rise to repression, it is not applicable to the conditions which give rise to other forms of dissociation.

ORIGINAL CONTRIBUTIONS TO THIS THESIS

Attention may be directed to certain features of this thesis, which the writer believes to constitute original contributions to the subject under discussion. These are:

I. The analysis of dissociation-phenomena into three categories depending on the nature of the mental elements dissociated. These categories are (a) dissociation of the irrelevant, (b) dissociation of the incompatible, (c) dissociation of the unpleasant.

II. The view that repression is: (a) a special form of dissociation of the unpleasant, (b) differentiated from other forms of dissociation of the unpleasant in virtue of the fact that, in the case of repression, the dissociated elements consist essentially in tendencies belonging to the mental structure, whereas in other forms of dissociation of the unpleasant the dissociated elements consist in part of the mental content.

2. THE SUPEREGO

I. WHAT IS THE SUPEREGO?

The title of my paper today takes the form of a question—What is the Superego? It is rather a dangerous proceeding, I know, to give one's title an interrogatory form—because it suggests that the question asked is merely rhetorical; it suggests that the audience does not know the answer and that the speaker has the answer up his sleeve. It reminds one of those impossible riddles, which some people delight to put to the unwary, in the firm expectation that the answer will be "I give up; you tell me the answer." Such questions serve all too frequently merely to foster positive self-feeling in the propounder of the riddle; or, to employ somewhat Freudian terminology, they gratify the desire to play the role of sophisticated father towards the ignorant and enquiring child. I trust, however, that my paper today is not the outcome of a desire "to play the heavy father" towards a gathering which is ill-suited to play the part of the ignorant and enquiring child. I believe my question to be a **bona fide** question addressed to myself as much as to you.

Perhaps, after all, it will turn out that I am really the enquiring child and that you are playing the role of heavy parents. For I have no doubt that some of you have an answer to my question ready. I can almost hear somebody say "The answer is as easy as stealing buns from babies. The superego is all rot." There are doubtless others, who, without being so blunt in their reply, would still be inclined to regard the superego as just another of those mythical creatures which Freud purports to have discovered in the course of his remote journeys in the unexplored and uncharted territories of the unconscious—creatures such as would have delighted the heart of previous travellers like de Mandeville and Baron Munchausen. This is certainly the attitude of many psychologists towards the psychical entities which Freud describes in his various works. From this point of view the superego and the id are merely the last of a series of specimens which Freud has presented to that zoological collection, which already includes among its finest examples the phoenix, the griffin and the unicorn.

This extreme point of view is, however, in the eyes of the present speaker quite unjustified. In my opinion, whatever the superego is, it certainly *is*. Personally, I have seen sufficient evidence of its activity to be convinced of its existence. In considering the existence of the superego, however, it is important to distinguish two questions which are *really* separate. Whether the *entity* of the superego exists is one question; whether the *phenomenon* of the superego exists is quite another. As regards the first question, it may be remarked that modern psychology has good grounds for being shy of entities. The progress of psychology has been too much impeded in the past by the assumption of entities, for the modern psychologist to welcome their introduction at the present day. The old maxim is a sound one—"Entia non sunt multiplicanda praeter necessitatem." It is a different matter, however, when it comes to a question of recognising phenomena. The existence of the superego as an entity may be justly questioned; the existence of the superego *as a phenomenon* admits, in my opinion, of no doubt whatever.

A gifted young man with a moderate sufficiency of this world's goods and without the embarrassment of debt took a good degree at a British University. He would have been described by everyone who knew him as eminently "steady". As far as could be judged, his life was free of the various entanglements in which a young man sometimes finds himself involved. He was offered a government appointment, upon which envious eyes had been cast by numerous candidates. In spite of competition, however, he was the selected candidate. Fortune appeared to smile, except in one particular. He had been engaged to be married, but his engagement had been broken off—under what circumstances we do not know. One day he remained at home for no obvious reason, when all the other members of the household had gone out. When the servant returned and entered the kitchen, she was conscious of an overpowering smell of gas. The door of the gas-oven stood open and a quilt was stuffed into the aperture. From underneath the quilt projected the body and legs of the young man; his head was in the oven. The gas was turned full on and he was dead. On a table in his room lay his papers and his will neatly arranged. His affairs were all in order. What was it that led him to commit suicide?

We cannot ask the young man himself what his motive was. If we could have done so, it is as likely as not that he would have been unable to satisfy our psychological curiosity. He would probably just have told us that he was "fed up with everything". If we ask the man in the street for his explanation, we should probably be told that "the poor fellow was disappointed in love"; but many engagements are broken off without so tragic a result. What is the motivation of so extreme a measure? Let us ask the psychologist. If we do so, we shall perhaps find difficulty in eliciting a convincing explanation—at any rate, if he confines himself to the more customary psychological conceptions. Freud would say that the young man was driven to death by his superego. I knew the young man, and I am inclined to accept Freud's explanation in its essential features.

But now we come back to our original question—What is the Superego? Whatever it is, there are two statements which may be made about it at the very outset. First, the conception of the superego is not a mere speculative abstraction spun by the theorist in his study. It is a hypothesis framed primarily to explain a large group of very puzzling facts encountered by the psychotherapist in the course of his clinical work—facts such as the compulsive rituals and ceremonials of the obsessional patient and the delusional sense of guilt and suicidal tendencies of the melancholic. The conception framed to explain these clinical facts has, however, subsequently been extended to cover a number of phenomena which lie outside the immediate province of psychopathology, but which illustrate some of the darker and more mysterious workings of the mind.

Secondly, the facts which the conception of the superego was introduced to explain are not trivial and unimportant facts. On the contrary, they comprise some of the most vital and significant phenomena of human conduct. They include facts which are bound up with individual destiny upon this earth, facts which may involve the issues of life and death.

It is thus impossible for us as psychologists to brush aside the Freudian conception of the superego as unworthy of serious consideration. The importance and the seriousness of the facts which it is designed to explain alone forbid us to dismiss it as an extravagant notion simply because it is formulated in terms unfamiliar to general psychology. The theory of the superego may be unpsychological and the term itself perhaps mystical, but the actual phenomenon of the superego may be observed by everyone who puts himself in a position to observe it. The fact remains that, apart from the tendencies ordinarily described as "repressed", and indeed over and against and opposed to these tendencies, there exists in the mind and largely in the unconscious a more or less independent organisation of psychical elements, which exercises an uncanny influence over individual, and perhaps national, destiny. Freud calls it "the superego". If we do not like the term, it is up to us as psychologists to find out what it really is. It is the function of this paper to try to determine the direction in which we must look in order to discover the psychological nature of this strange phenomenon.

Freud's theory of the superego was first described in the work which he published in 1923 under the title of *Das Ich und das Es* (*The Ego and the Id*). As Freud points out in this work, the fundamental premise upon which psychoanalysis is based is the division of mental life into two spheres—the conscious and the unconscious. The existence of the unconscious was an assumption, but Freud regarded it as an assumption which was absolutely necessary for the explanation and understanding of certain pathological mental states. For explanatory purposes he found it necessary in his clinical work to postulate the existence of mental processes which could produce all the effects of ordinary conscious processes but which lacked the attribute of consciousness. In the descriptive sense all these processes are unconscious, but Freud was very soon led to distinguish two groups of such processes. One group gave the impression of being merely "latent"; such processes are capable of becoming conscious under appropriate circumstances; and this group was described as constituting "The Preconscious". The other group of processes, however, seemed to be unconscious in a dynamic as well as a descriptive sense, they are unconscious because there is a resistance to their appearance in consciousness. These processes were therefore described not as latent but as "repressed", and they were regarded as constituting "The Unconscious" proper. It is thus evident that Freud's conception of the unconscious is dependent in its origin upon the theory of Repression.

In the further course of psychoanalytic work Freud found it necessary to assume the existence in the mind of a coherent organisation, which included the conscious and the preconscious and which controlled the approaches to action. This organisation at once suggests to our mind what is familiar to psychologists as "the organised self". Freud, however, designated it as "The Ego", and he conceived repression to be one of its special functions. Repression appeared to be a function designed to deny expression in consciousness and in action to certain tendencies, which analysis showed to stand in opposition to the Ego. The original object of psychoanalytic treatment thus underwent a modification. Its task came to be not simply to make consciousness conscious, but to remove the resistance of the Ego to concern itself with the repressed tendencies.

Now one of the most striking observations of psychoanalytic practice is to the effect that the patient is actually unaware of the resistance by which he is dominated. Accordingly, once the conception of the Ego had been framed, it was only a matter of time till the implications of the view that the resistance emanates from the Ego should force themselves upon Freud's attention. Since the resistance emanates from the Ego and since the patient is unconscious of his resistance, it is evident that there is something in the Ego itself which is unconscious and which behaves exactly like the repressed, in so far as it produces profound effects without being conscious. This discovery made it impossible for Freud to retain his original view that psychoneurotic disease was the result of a simple conflict between the conscious and the unconscious. For the original antithesis between conscious and unconscious it became necessary to substitute an antithesis between the organised ego and what is repressed and dissociated from it. This new antithesis, which was formulated in Freud's work entitled *Beyond the Pleasure Principle* in 1922, involved a complete remodelling of the conception of the unconscious. The unconscious could no longer be regarded as consisting simply of the repressed. It became necessary to recognise the presence in the unconscious of elements which were not repressed and which were not simply latent. Since these elements necessarily fell within the compass of the ego, Freud came to regard the ego as composed of unconscious as well as of conscious and preconscious elements. The result of this development of Freud's thought was to direct his attention to problems of mental structure. It is with these problems that he attempts to deal in *The Ego and the Id*.

The theory of mental structure elaborated in *The Ego and the Id* (Freud 1923b) is expounded in topographical fashion. According to the scheme adopted, the matrix of the mind, which is regarded as primarily unconscious, is described as the Id. The id is primitive in character and loosely organised; in it all impulses are generated, and it is thus the source of all the activity of the organism. The psychological nature of the id is, therefore, not difficult to establish. It quite evidently consists of the primitive instinctive dispositions.

The ego according to Freud's scheme, is differentiated out of the id. It is described as that part of the id which is modified by contact with the outer world. It thus arises in the course of experience. It is described as the organ of perception, and it includes consciousness. It also includes the preconscious and must therefore be the storehouse of such memory-residues as escape the action of repression. It controls or attempts to control the motor functions; volition must therefore be regarded as characteristic of its activity. The id, as we have seen, is really the source of all impulse, but the motor pathway passes through the ego. The impulses generated in the id arise as an expression of the inner nature of the organism; they arise in complete independence of the conditions prevalent in the outer world and without regard to their suitability to the situation of the moment. This is what Freud means when he say that the impulses of the id are governed by the "pleasure principle". In contrast to the pleasure principle, which characterises the activity of the id, he postulates a "reality principle", which comes to characterise the activity of the differentiated ego. Since the ego is the organ of perception, it naturally performs the function of modifying the impulses of the id in conformity with the situations presented by the external world. As James Glover (1926) points out, so far as the ego is active at all, its function is 'reactive' rather than 'impulsive', whereas the reverse holds true of the id. The ego is thus seen to be essentially an adaptive structure.

So far, the psychological nature of the id and the ego is fairly clear. The id consists of the raw, primitive, loosely organised, innate instinct-dispositions; and the impulses generated in these dispositions are id-impulses; these impulses are the ultimate source of all the organism's activity. It is the instinctive tendencies and the impulses generated in them which forms the material for repression; and it would therefore seem that the repressed lies, primarily at any rate, within the confines of the id. The ego, on the other hand, is not quite so simple. Its chief feature, perhaps, is that it has a monopoly of consciousness. In virtue of this fact, it is described by Freud as being the organ of perception. Since the preconscious also falls within the confines of the ego, all the phenomena of memory properly belong to it as much as do those of perception. It is evident indeed that the cognitive functions as a whole belong to the ego. The ego embraces all that is involved in "learning by experience". We must also assume that the whole of affective life takes place within the confines of the ego. The fact that the ego has a monopoly of consciousness makes this inference inevitable. It is true that Freud sometimes speaks of repressed affects. But he explicitly admits in one passage that this is not an exact method of expression; he admits that affect properly speaking is necessarily conscious. As regards conation it would seem that all the higher forms of conation are ego-functions. The ego must be responsible for that mysterious but important process, mediated by affect, whereby cognitive processes are enabled to modify impulse. Since we know that modification of impulse is largely achieved through inhibition, we shall expect to find the function of inhibition included in the ego's repertoire. This appears to be the case, both with regard to that form of inhibition which manifests itself as conscious control and with regard to that form which occurs below the level of consciousness. Since repression is a form of inhibition in the wide sense of the term, repression is essentially a function exercised by the ego upon impulses arising in the instinct-dispositions of the id. Finally if the id consists in the primitive instinctive tendencies, we must ascribe to the ego all the higher organisations of these tendencies which are developed in the course of the individual life-history. To the ego therefore belong the sentiments and ideals, and indeed the character itself.

After this brief consideration of the psychological nature of the id and the ego, it is time for us to turn our attention to the superego. According to Freud the superego is differentiated from the ego, just as the ego was differentiated from the id. The ego as we have described it so far is the ego as it would be, if the superego were not differentiated from it. The superego, therefore, lies within the boundaries which have so far been drawn round the province of the ego.

Let us now examine the considerations which led Freud in the first instance to recognise the superego as an independent structure differentiated from the original ego. Although it was only in *The Ego and the Id* (1923b) that he explicitly formulated the conception of the superego, this conception was the culmination of a train of thought initiated about ten years previously. In a paper published in 1914 under the title "On Narcissism: An Introduction" Freud (1914a) first gave technical significance to a term which has since been replaced by the term "superego", but which is used as a synonym for the latter in *The Ego and the Id.* The term in question is that of "the ego-ideal".

The passage in the paper 'On Narcissism' in which Freud (1914a) originated the technical use of the term 'ego-ideal' is, curiously enough, a parenthetical passage. It is a passage in which he tries to offer an explanation of the differing degree in which repression affects different individuals. In his attempt to deal with this problem he writes as follows:

> We have learnt that libidinal impulses are fated to undergo pathogenic repression if they come into conflict with the subject's cultural and ethical ideas. . . . Repression, as we have said, proceeds from the ego; we might say with greater precision; from the self-respect of the ego. The very impressions, experiences, impulses and desires that one man indulges or at least consciously elaborates in his mind will be rejected with the utmost indignation by another, or stifled at once even before they enter consciousness. The difference between the two, however—and here we have the conditioning factor in repression—can easily be expressed in terms of the libido-theory. We may say that the one man has set up an *ideal* in himself by which he measures his actual ego, while the other is without this formation of an ideal. From the point of view of the ego this formation of an ideal would be the condition of repression. [pp. 50–51]

The ego-ideal thus comes to be regarded by Freud as the most powerful factor favouring repression. Its power to aid repression is due to the fact that its formation increases the demands forced by the ego upon the id. Having once introduced the conception of the ego-ideal, Freud (1914a) proceeds to apply this conception to the subject of Narcissism to which his essay is devoted. The term 'narcissism', it may be remarked, is a term used in psychoanalytic literature for a condition in which 'libido' (i.e., interest deriving from the sex-instinct) is directed towards the self. It is believed to exist in a pathological form in megalomania, but it is also held to be a phase through which every infant passes at one stage of development and it is believed to be not wholly absent in the normal adult. Psychoanalytic writers also offer evidence for the belief that libido is capable of being transformed from a love-object to the ego and vice versa. Such evidence is provided, for instance, by the fact that, the deeper a man falls in love, the more he overvalues his love-object and the more he undervalues himself in relation to her. It is also claimed that, if a love-object is lost for any reason, the bitterness of loss tends to be mitigated by a process whereby the love-object is reinstated within the ego—a process which would appear to belong to the imaginative level of mental activity. By this process, whereby the love-object is reinstated within the ego, it is believed that libido attains a narcissistic satisfaction. To return to the ego-ideal—Freud (1914a) envisages the possibility that narcissistic satisfaction may be derived from the ego-ideal, of a similar kind to that derived from a reinstated love-object.

In this connection he writes:

> It would not surprise us if we were to find a special institution in the mind which performs the task of seeing that narcissistic gratification is secured from the ego-ideal and that, with this end in view, it constantly watches the real ego and measures it by that ideal. If such an institution does exist, it cannot possibly be something which we have not yet discovered; we only need to recognise it, and we may say that what we call our *conscience* has the required characteristics. Recognition of this institution enables us to understand the so-called 'delusions of observation' or, more correctly, of *being watched*, which are such striking symptoms in the paranoid diseases. . . . Patients of this sort complain that all their thoughts are known and their actions watched and overlooked; they are informed of the functioning of this mental institution by voices which characteristically speak to them in the third person ('Now she is thinking of that again' . . . 'Now he is going out'). This complaint is justified—it describes the truth; a power of this kind, watching, discovering and criticizing all our intentions, does really exist; indeed, it exists within every one of us in normal life. The delusion of being watched presents it in a regressive form, thereby revealing the genesis of this function and the reason why the patient is in revolt against it. For that which prompted the person to form an ego-ideal, over which his conscience keeps guard, was the influence of parental criticism (conveyed to him by the medium of the voice), reinforced as time went on, by those who trained and taught the child and by all the other persons of his environment. [Freud 1914a, pp. 52–53]

It is this notion of the ego-ideal which forms the basis of the conception of the superego, which Freud (1923b) elaborates in *The Ego and the Id*. In this work he makes use of the ideas, originally expounded in his essay "On Narcissism", that loss of a love-object may be mitigated by a process whereby the object is reinstated within the ego—a process to which he gives the name of 'identification'. He attaches great importance to this process, and envisages two far-reaching possibilities:

1. that this process of identification may be the sole condition under which the tendencies of the id can give up their objects of attachment (and thus the sole condition of sublimation);
2. that perhaps the character of the ego is nothing but a precipitate of abandoned object-choices incorporated by the process of identification.

Freud next proceeds to point out the profound importance of the earliest identifications of childhood, and he claims that the ego-ideal has its origin in the identification of the child with the parent-figures. Freud does not, however, regard the *primary* identifications of the child with the parents as reinstatements of lost objects of interest. The parent-figures are the first objects of interest and, therefore, cannot be lost objects in the first instance. The primary identifications are *direct* identifications which have not been preceded by object-choice. It is only later that object-choice develops, but, when it does develop, the parents too are the first objects selected. Normally, however, the parents are not selected on equal terms. It is usually the parent of the opposite sex who becomes the chief object of love and, as far as this parent is concerned, object-interest largely takes the place of identification. The identification with the parent of the same sex, however, persists in strength. Thus it comes about that the superego, which has its origin in the earliest identifications of the child, comes to partake predominantly of characteristics derived from identification with the parent of similar sex.

Now the importance of this identification with the parent of similar sex lies in the fact that this parent becomes the chief obstacle to the child's enjoyment of the object-relationship which he has formed to the other parent. Thus in the case of the male child, the father becomes his chief rival for the mother's love; this is the natural result of the intimate and privileged relationship of husband and wife. The situation which arises is, of course, that described by Freud as "the Oedipus situation". In this situation the child chiefly loves and seeks the love of the parent of opposite sex, while the parent of the same sex serves as a frustrating figure. The significance of this situation for the formation of the superego lies in the fact that the frustrating parent is the parent with whom the primary identification has remained strongest. It is the persistence of this identification with the frustrating parent that calls the mechanism of repression into being. This mechanism saves the child from the unpleasure of an intolerable situation, in which his love-object of one parent is in conflict with his identification with the other. Repression saves him unpleasure by rendering the intenser elements in his love for the parent of opposite sex unconscious.

While the child's object-relationship to the parent of opposite sex is thus regarded as tending to undergo repression, his identification with the frustrating parent is believed by Freud to persist as the main element in the superego. It is not the only element which goes to the formation of the superego, however; for the object-love directed to the parent of opposite sex does not wholly replace the primary identification with this parent, which precedes it. The superego derives an element from this source also; and this element does not differ materially from that derived from the frustrating parent. On the contrary, the parent of opposite sex becomes frustrating also

Ronald and Mary Fairbairn with their daughter, Ellinor, in 1929

to the degree that she or he proves inaccessible to the child. In so far as this parent, whose love is sought, proves inaccessible to the child, the child suffers a deprivation of the love-object; and this deprivation operates in the same way as the loss of a love-object does in the case of an adult. The child compensates for the partial loss of his love-object by a *secondary* process of identification; in this way the partially inaccessible love-object comes to be reinstated within the ego, and this reinstated love-object becomes incorporated in the ego-ideal or superego. It thus comes about that the superego is built up on a nucleus of two identifications with frustrating figures—figures, be it noted, which are the most significant figures in the child's life. The various, and often numerous, prohibitions to which a child is subjected by parent-figures in his early years readily become organised round this primitive nucleus; and it is in this way that the superego develops those characteristics which have led to its recognition in the course of psychoanalytic investigation.

Although the superego is originally formed within the ego, it is regarded by Freud as becoming gradually differentiated from it and as already attaining a high degree of independence before the age of five [years] is reached. The persistence of the superego as an independent formation is attributed in the main to three facts:

1. The identifications with the parents are the original identifications in life.
2. They occur at the most immature period of life.
3. They involve the most vital personages in a child's existence.

The independence which is attributed to the superego enables us to understand the chief characteristics which it appears to possess. Of these characteristics, five are of special importance:

1. The superego is, to use Freud's words, "less closely connected with consciousness than the ego" (Freud 1923b p. 35). According to Ernest Jones (1926) "it is probable that the superego may be partly conscious, partly preconscious and partly unconscious; further that its relationship to consciousness varies at different times" (p. 305). He ascribes the fact that the superego is less conscious than the ego to the nature of its relation to outer reality. The only outer situation to which it is really relevant is the attitude of the parents to the child in infancy. It has no real relevance to the environment of the normal adult, though it influences the attitude of the adult to his environment. The fact that the superego does not correspond to any actual situation in adult life is suggested by Jones as the main cause of its loose connection with consciousness.

2. Although there is evidence that the superego is subject to a process of independent organisation during life, it remains throughout at a more primitive level of organisation than the ego. This feature must be connected with the fact that the superego is so largely outside the field of consciousness; and it may be illustrated by the power exercised over quite intelligent people by irrational superstitions. Superstitions are held to be due to the operation of the superego; and they seem to correspond to a childish fear of parental wrath and vengeance dating from a stage of development at which the child is unable to appreciate real values.

3. With the primitive nature of the superego is bound up the fact of its irrationality. Its irrationality would appear to depend on the fact that it originated in a purely emotional relationship. The delusions of persecution which characterise paranoia form a good example of irrational beliefs engendered through the activity of the superego. The persecution in such cases is real enough, but the real persecutor is the superego and not the imagined enemies.

4. The superego exercises a function which is best described as one of criticism and condemnation. This feature is the result of the origin of the

superego in an identification with frustrating parents. "The function of the superego" says Jones (1926) "is to criticise the ego and cause pain to the latter whenever it tends to accept impulses proceeding from the repressed part of the id" (p. 304). The intensity and even ferocity of this critical and condemning function is difficult of comprehension for those who have not been in a position to observe its operation in psychoneurotic and psychotic patients. An uncompromising superego is capable of driving its victim to all extremes of self-torture and even to suicide. In cases where the repressed tendencies, with which the superego is in conflict, are projected, it is also capable of instigating conduct of the utmost cruelty. Many of the most bloody persecutions of history would appear to be best accounted for in this way.

5. The superego is imperfectly oriented to reality. This characteristic it shares with the id. In the case of the superego, however, the orientation to reality is less imperfect than in the case of the id; for, although the situation to which the superego is oriented is a childish one, yet it is a situation which has been actually experienced, whereas the impulses of the id arise solely within the inborn instinctive tendencies.

Of the five chief characteristics of the superego, which have now been described, it will be noticed that there is only one which is not shared with the id. Both the superego and the id are primitive and irrational. Loose connection with consciousness and imperfect orientation to reality are common features to both. It is the only one of the five characteristics ascribed to the superego, that is not shared by the id—whereas the function of the id is to engender impulse, it is the function of the superego to frustrate the impulses of the id.

The fact that the superego should possess so many characteristics in common with the id is of no small importance for our present enquiry, as will shortly be pointed out. Meanwhile let us direct our attention to that feature of the superego which, as we have just seen, differentiates it so markedly from the id. Whereas it is the function of the id to engender impulse, it is the function of the superego to frustrate the id's impulses. This frustrating function of the superego is, of course, dependent for its origin on the fact that the superego originates through the identification of the child with frustrating figures. The presence of this identification, however, does not involve the abolition of the thwarted tendencies. The two incongruous elements persist side by side. The result is a conflict in the child's mind between his natural object-love, which is regarded as proceeding from the instinctive endowment of the id and his uncompromising attitude to the same tendencies absorbed, by the process of identification, from the parents as thwarting figures. It is a conflict between the superego and the id, and this conflict causes acute unpleasure to the ego. The bitterness of the conflict is assuaged by the process of repression. Repression operates upon the tendencies of the id, and dulls the edge of conflict by preventing these tendencies from gaining access to consciousness. Now repression is "a protective mechanism, the object of which is to defend the ego from the unpleasure" (Freud 1915c), which the appearance of the repressed in consciousness would produce. Repression is, therefore, necessarily regarded as a function of the ego. It occurs, however, as the result of the uncompromising attitude of the superego to the id's tendencies (Freud 1923b). The superego is thus, so to speak, responsible for the initiation and continuance of repression. It is on this account that Freud comes to speak of repression as being carried out by the ego "in the service and at the behest of its superego" (Freud 1923b p. 75).

While it is not difficult to understand the role played by the superego in initiating repression and in thus effecting the imprisonment of offending id-impulses in the unconscious, it is not quite so easy to see why the superego should sink so largely into the unconscious itself. Yet that it does so is borne out by the experience of every psychoanalytic worker. The easiest explanation of the loose connection of the superego with consciousness would be that repression operates upon the superego just as it operates upon the id. From this point of view repression would be regarded as a process which imprisoned in the unconscious both parties to the conflict between superego and id. The position is, however, difficult to reconcile with the part played by the superego in the initiation of repression. It is true that in the case of hysteria Freud believes that the superego itself becomes subject to repression (vide Freud 1923b), but it does so only in a secondary fashion. The superego is held to be loosely connected with consciousness apart from any secondary process of repression to which it may become subject. The explanation of this feature appears to be twofold. First, as Jones (1926) points out, the situation in relation to which the superego develops, is a situation of childhood without real relevance to the environment of the normal adult. Secondly, even where the superego itself is not subjected to repression, its intimate association with the process of repression is sufficient to bind it to some extent with the repressed in the unconscious. This appears to be Freud's meaning when he speaks of the very free communication, which is possible between the ego-ideal and the unconscious instinctive trends, as explaining why the ideal itself is so largely unconscious and inaccessible to the ego (vide Freud 1923b).

Now that we have considered Freud's account of the origin of the superego and examined its most important characteristics as he describes them, it is possible for us to appreciate the relevance of the practical manifestation attributed to it. The phenomena in which its activity is discerned all seem to indicate the existence in the mind of just such an independent organisation as Freud claims the superego to be.

In the passage about the ego-ideal already quoted from Freud's essay "On Narcissism", we saw that Freud (1914a) regarded the phenomenon of 'conscience' as exhibiting all the characteristics appropriate to the functioning of the ego-ideal. In *The Ego and the Id* (1923b) he ascribes conscience to the working of the superego. When conscience is active in any individual, that individual experiences a characteristic feeling about certain of his own impulses. In so far as these impulses merely threaten to pass into action, their ideational content has an emotional colouring which we express by describing the impulses as "wrong" or "wicked". In so far, however, as they actually pass into action, or even in so far as we allow ourselves to entertain them, they give rise to a very definite emotional state which we designate as "a sense of guilt". Freud regards the sense of guilt as due to tension between the superego and the ego. He believes this state of tension to arise when repressed id-tendencies find expression in activities permitted by the ego. This being so, it is natural to ask why Freud does not content himself with the word 'conscience', instead of inventing the term 'superego' to convey an old meaning. The answer to this question is that the word superego does not simply convey the old meaning. 'Conscience', as the derivation of the word implies, is applicable only to a *conscious* sense of guilt. Freud (1923b), however, brings forward evidence to support the view that there is such a phenomenon as an "unconscious sense of guilt"—a designation which he later abandoned, owing to its psychological unsoundness, in favour of the term "Strafbedürfnis" (anglicised as "need for punishment"). The term "superego" is thus wider than the term "conscience", because it covers the unconscious Strafbedürfnis as well as the conscious sense of guilt.

Evidence of an unconscious need for punishment is chiefly forthcoming in psychoneurotic and psychotic symptoms. Reference has already been made to those delusions of being watched and delusions of persecution which are so characteristic of paranoia. Sometimes in such cases the still small voice of conscience is replaced by a hallucinatory voice shouting insults from the ceiling. In paranoia, however, neither the sense of guilt nor the guilty impulses are conscious. Here we have a complete contrast with the state of things in normal conscience, where both the sense of guilt and the guilty impulses are consciously realised.

Perhaps the most definite clinical evidence of the activity of the superego is to be found in that "clinging to illness" which is so characteristic of the neurotic patient. It is a familiar fact to all who come into contact with neurotic patients that they give the impression of not wanting to be better. As Freud (1923b) says:

> There is something in these people that sets itself against their recovery and dreads its approach as though it were a danger. . . . In the end we come to see that we are dealing with what may be called a 'moral' factor, a sense of guilt, which is finding atonement in the illness and is refusing to give up the penalty of suffering. . . . But as far as the patient is concerned this sense of guilt is dumb; it does not tell him he is guilty; he does not feel guilty, he

> simply feels ill. This sense of guilt expresses itself only as a resistance to recovery which it is extremely difficult to overcome. [pp. 71–72]

It is the factor to which Freud here refers that explains the impossibility of reasoning a neurotic out of his symptoms. The neurotic, like the sinner, cannot be reasoned with; if he is to be changed, he must be converted. That is to say, the relationship between his superego and his ego must undergo a change.

A somewhat similar manifestation of the superego is to be found in the case of the "victim of misfortune". There are some people who are "always dogged by ill-luck". I once knew a man of this sort whose career consisted of one long series of mischances, which never appeared to be due to his own fault. He was just always unlucky. He could not even go for a ride on his motor-bicycle without having an accident. Destiny and fate, however, are frequently found to be determined by internal and not external forces. There is even a proverb to the effect that "fortune helps those who help themselves". Unfortunately there are many who cannot help themselves because their superego won't let them. As Maeterlinck (1898) says in his *Wisdom and Destiny*—"There are some who are wholly unable to support the burden of joy" (p. 13).

Now that some indication has been given of the direction in which we must look for practical manifestations of superego activity, it seems desirable to offer a sample of the psychoanalytic evidence upon which the theory of the superego is based. Any psychoneurotic case which is subjected to thorough psychoanalysis is capable of supplying material apposite to this purpose; but I shall select for illustrative purposes a case of my own in which the phenomenon of the superego was particularly marked.

The patient in question was a woman teacher of middle age, whose career had been blighted by a series of nervous breakdowns. She was an exceedingly efficient and conscientious teacher, held in high favour by her education authority. So conscientious was she that although most of her life was spent in primary schools and although she had a complete mastery of her work, she would often sit up until the early morning hours preparing her lessons for the next day. This excess of conscientiousness is a feature of some significance as indicating the presence of a very exacting ego-ideal. Such demands did her ideal make upon her powers, that, by the middle of each term, her physical and mental resources were taxed to the utmost limit; it was then as much as she could do to continue working. Under this strain, as can be readily understood, she would begin to find her memory playing her tricks and constant mistakes leading her into difficulties with her class. Her work would thus genuinely deteriorate, with the result that she was spurred to still further efforts. The harder she struggled, the worse her work became and the more she fell short of her ideal. She thus became involved in a vicious circle of a very distressing kind. Her difficulties were increased by the fact that, when she became overwrought, her control of her class began to suffer. Now her ideal of efficiency at work was only matched by her ideal of discipline. She could not bear the slightest inattention, far less the slightest insubordination among the members of her class. The behaviour of the class was measured by the same standard of perfection which she demanded of herself. This was a standard too exacting for the ordinary child; but, as, during the passage of the term, her demands upon herself increased, so did her demands upon the children. Her irritability and even harshness was only mitigated by a supreme effort of self-control. The more she exacted from the children, however, the more incapable did she become of exacting it.

The general result of her efforts to attain perfection in her professional duties was only to make her failure more pronounced. Both schoolwork and discipline deteriorated, and on this account self-reproach was heaped on self-reproach. Frequently the breaking-point was reached before the term ended; and there was then nothing left for her to do but to throw in her hand and ask to be relieved of her duties. The moment her professional responsibilities were removed, an extraordinary transformation scene would usually take place. The stress imposed by her ideal was relaxed with the cessation of her duties, and her troubles vanished as if by magic. On such occasions she would return home to be the life and soul of the family circle—a fact which naturally gave rise to some comment, but of which the psychological explanation is not far to seek. With the relaxing of the tension between her ego and her ego-ideal, she passed into a period of slight elation. This phenomenon is a familiar one in cases of manic-depressive insanity; for in this psychosis a patient may go to bed a melancholic and come to breakfast the next morning in a state of mania. In our patient the slight maniacal reaction would be of short duration. After a few weeks, the tension between her ideal and her ego would begin to reestablish itself. She would then begin to reproach herself with being idle and useless. She would begin to feel herself a parasite upon her parents. A longing for independence would arise and would increase in intensity until she was driven to fling herself into the maelstrom once again. After this cycle of events had been repeated a considerable number of times, she came to the conclusion that it was necessary for her to abandon her work for a prolonged period. She hoped that a year or two of rest would set her right. Her hopes were not to be fulfilled, however. She now began to suffer every few weeks from short periods of depression. As such a period of depression approached, she felt herself struggling for some days against some nameless, unrecognisable force in herself, which, she felt, was somehow threatening to overwhelm her. She would feel utterly miserable; and thoughts of self-destruction would never be far away. Eventually she would find herself unable to resist this nameless force any longer. She would then collapse on the nearest chair, often in a flood of tears. When this crisis was reached, she would experience relief from the extreme tension from which she had been suffering, but would feel utterly and completely crushed. She would then retire to bed, and lie there for several days in a somewhat regressive state, spending her time reading, thinking and sleeping. While in this condition she would allow no one to enter her room except her mother, who attended to her every want as if she were a child. During this period, indeed, she actually did, psychologically speaking, become a child again. The superego had won, and her childish identification with her mother had the field all to itself. She was shut off by the walls of her room from the whole world except the frustrating parent, to whose power she surrendered herself unconditionally for a space.

Many of the dreams which this patient produced during the course of treatment provided excellent material for the study of the superego. Take for example the following dream:

> I seemed to be the object of the most vindictive and relentless persecution at the hands of people whom I think of as Bolsheviks or revolutionists and whose conduct towards me was unreasonable and entirely unmerited. I found myself time and again among a big company of people, trying to mingle with them quietly and escape notice, and, just when I was feeling a sense of security, someone recognised me, rushed at me, and ill-treated me. I felt that to explain my innocence was useless when dealing with such bigoted people. I remember one occasion when I was sitting in a back bench and with every seat occupied like a class in a school. Suddenly I was recognised by a woman in the seat in front who turned round. This person denounced me aloud and people on every side rushed at me in a hostile way. I think certain papers were taken from me and examined or something.

In the dream which followed, the dreamer and her sister were rummaging in a small outhouse in the grounds of a large house. [This outhouse seemed to represent both a summer-house and a lavatory.] Suddenly a loud bell rang—a secret bell, the spring of which they had inadvertently touched and the object of which was to warn those in the big house of their property being invaded. They were quite conscious of being where they had no business to be, but were unconscious of any intention to do harm. They were alarmed and worried, but did not attempt to escape.

During the course of analytic treatment, the patient was asked to associate freely to these dreams. Let us look at the "Accusing Woman Dream", in this the more significant of the patient's associations are as follows:

- former dreams in which the patient had felt helpless before people who were prejudiced against her;

- former dreams about being young and innocent and being run after by unreasonable people, who were always grown up;
- a tyrannical schoolmaster, in whose school she was a pupil as a child;
- associations about coming for treatment, during which, in a significant *lapsus linguae*, she used the phrase "coming to school" instead of "coming for treatment";
- then associations about one of the breakdowns during her career as teacher, her feeling that she dare not let herself go because something seemed always to be threatening her;
- memories of her mother making her do housework in childhood, when she did not want to do so;
- the resentment she had felt when her mother showed her how to do things properly;
- always wanting to go and play outside, instead of helping her mother in the house;
- associations about her maternal grandfather (who, it may be remarked, indulged her very markedly as a child, and who largely took the place in her affections which would have been occupied by her father if he had not been a somewhat insignificant and ineffective personality);
- a funny feeling she used to have that her maternal grandfather belonged to her and had no relationship to her mother;
- a feeling that, while she was frolicking with her grandfather, as she often did, her mother was in the background watching her and just waiting for a chance to reprove her;
- never thinking of her mother as a person who played with her;
- recollections of her father amusing her on Sunday mornings;
- lastly, various associations about playing in forbidden places and being chased away by persons in authority.

On being requested to associate specially to the figure of the accusing woman in the dream, she thought (1) of a sister with whom she had nothing in common, (2) of a woman who had a rupture with her mother, (3) of her own mother. Then followed some interesting associations in the course of which she said that, when she was well, she disliked being at home, because the house was dominated by her mother and she desired independence. She added that, when she was depressed, she felt cowed and afraid to do anything on her own initiative; she then relied on her mother for everything. The associations to the single dream of the accusing woman thus seem to furnish striking evidence for the existence in the dreamer's mind of a psychical complex possessing all the features of the Freudian "superego". The drift of the associations leaves no doubt that there was some *primitive organisation in her mind condemning and frustrating her spontaneous activities*. The origin of this organisation evidently *dated from childhood and was derived from the child's interpretation of her mother's attitude* towards her. The child interpreted her mother's attitude as one of uncompromising criticism towards her happy, spontaneous activities—especially when these took the form of play with her father and her maternal grandfather, who played the role of father-figure. There is also *evidence of a sense of guilt*, showing that *the child had identified with the maternal attitude which she resented*. The child's attitude to her father and grandfather, on the other hand, was that of object-love. In particular, she loved and sought the love of her grandfather; and she resented having to share this love with her mother, who was her great rival for his affection. The child's attitude to her mother was, of course, quite *primitive* and *irrational*; but it was appropriate to the mentality of a young child and was quite justified by the situation from a child's point of view. It was quite out of place, however, in so far as it persisted as an important factor determining the patient's adult behaviour in adult situations. It was an attitude *imperfectly oriented to reality* even in childhood; for the mother seemed to be a kindly, unselfish woman with a strong maternal instinct, albeit somewhat dominating in the home. Finally, this attitude on the part of the patient was *largely unconscious* until analysis brought it to light. So far as it was conscious, it appeared in the form of a general excess of conscientiousness and a particularly strong sense of duty towards her mother. The characteristic conscious attitude of the patient towards her mother is best expressed in the patient's own words—"My mother is the very best of mothers". Indeed, although she disliked domestic work, she was conspicuous among her sisters for her efforts to assist her mother in every possible way—so conspicuous, perhaps, as to suggest the presence of a reaction-formation against contrary impulses. This appearance of a reaction-formation against repressed tendencies must be regarded as a manifestation of superego activity.

The case, which has now been considered at some length, has been introduced in order to illustrate the class of clinical data which support the conception of the superego. Such data, which might be multiplied indefinitely, seem to justify the assumption of a more or less definite organisation in the mind, which is at once independent of the organised self or ego and in conflict with the repressed tendencies springing from the primitive instinctive endowment or id. The Freudian superego is just such an organisation.

What then is the psychological nature of the superego? The attempt to answer this question necessitates our returning to a statement made earlier in our enquiry. After considering the five chief characteristics of the superego, we noted that only one of these characteristics was not shared with the id. Deferring consideration of the characteristics of the superego which are shared with the id, we proceeded to devote our attention to the characteristic which differentiates it from the id. This characteristic we saw to lie in the fact that, whereas it is the function of the id to engender impulse, it is the function of the superego to frustrate the id's impulses. It is this characteristic which puts the superego in line with the ego as against the id. For the function involved is an adaptive function, although the adaptation in question is much more primitive than that exercised by the ego. It is time now to return to those characteristics of the superego which ally it to the id. These were its primitive nature, its irrationality, its loose connection with consciousness and its imperfect orientation to reality.

The presence of so many common characteristics in the superego and the id enables us to attach some meaning to a statement of Freud's, which at first sight appears quite anomalous—the statement, namely, that "the superego is always in close touch with the id and can act as its representative in relation to the ego" (Freud 1923b pp. 69–70). The similarity between the superego and the id also enables us to understand how the relationship of the ego to the superego in many respects resembles that of the ego to the id. It enables us also to understand how the adaptive functions of the ego come to be interfered with as much by unconscious factors having their source in the superego as by unconscious factors having their source in the id. The fact that so many characteristics are shared by the superego and the id is of special importance for our enquiry, because it suggests that the ultimate psychological nature of the superego may have something in common with the psychological nature of the id. We have seen that the id is made up of the primitive instinct-dispositions, and we shall, therefore, expect the instinct-dispositions to enter into the constitution of the superego. Since the superego is differentiated as the result of experience, however, it cannot be regarded as composed of simple unorganised instinctive tendencies. It must be regarded as an organisation of these tendencies. Now the higher organisations of the instinct-dispositions with which the psychologist is familiar are the sentiments and ideals. The sentiment is defined by William McDougall, following Shand (1920), as "an organised system of emotional tendencies centred about some object" (McDougall 1908 p. 122). An ideal may perhaps be defined as organisation of sentiments centred about some idea. However that may be, the sentiment must be regarded as the typical organisation into which the innate instinct-dispositions are integrated in human beings. The suggestion may, therefore, be advanced that the superego is an organisation of instinct-dispositions partaking of the nature of sentiment. If this suggestion be accepted, we must regard the formation of the superego as proceeding according to the pattern of sentiment formation. This, of course, is putting the matter rather too simply; for the superego frequently gives the impression of being more complex than the simple sentiment. We must remember that the phenomenon to which Freud eventually came to apply the term "superego" was originally designated "the ego-ideal", and that the two terms are used synonymously in *The Ego and the Id*. Perhaps the term "ego-ideal" is the preferable of the two; for it may well be that the superego is actually an "ideal" in the strictly psychological sense. If the superego is too complex to be a simple sentiment, then we must regard it as an organisation of sentiments; and, if it is an organisation of sentiments, then it may not be out of place to regard it as some sort of "ideal".

It is not necessary, however, to debate the point whether the superego is strictly speaking a sentiment or an ideal. The fact is that the degree of development attained by the superego varies within wide bounds from individual to individual. It may well be that in some individuals it remains more or less of a sentiment, while in others it more or less attains the status of an ideal. In some individuals it may even undergo such a degree of development as to assume the dimensions of a subsidiary personality. This possibility appears to have occurred to Freud. At any rate, he envisages the possibility that the phenomenon of multiple personality may be the product of just such a process of identification as he believes to be responsible for the formation of the superego. He digresses from his main argument in Chapter III of *The Ego and the Id* expressly to hazard this speculation.

> Although it is a digression from our theme, we cannot avoid giving our attention for a moment longer to the ego's object-identifications. If they obtain the upper hand and become too numerous, unduly intense and incompatible with one another, a pathological outcome will not be far off. It may come to a disruption of the ego in consequence of the individual identifications becoming cut off from one another by resistances; perhaps the secret of the cases of so-called multiple personality is that the various identifications seize possession of consciousness in turn. [1923b, p. 38]

Be that as it may, there is no doubt that during psychoanalytic treatment some patients come to regard their own superego, when it becomes revealed through analysis, as possessing all the characteristics of an alien personality. Whatever degree of development the superego attains, however, in individual cases, the superego may be described in general terms as *an organisation of sentiment*. This organisation may be elaborate and extensive, or it may be feeble and restricted; but the term "an organisation of sentiment" seems the best term to describe the psychological character of the superego.

That the psychological nature of the superego is to be sought in that department of psychology which deals with the formation and organisation of sentiment is the main conclusion of our enquiry. It is in this direction that we must look for an answer to the question which formed the title of this paper—"What is the Superego?" If, however, we answer this question by the statement that the superego is a sentiment-organisation, we must recognise that it is not an ordinary one. It differs from an ordinary adult sentiment-organisation chiefly in three respects, (1) in its primitive and childish character, (2) in its independence of the organised self, (3) in its loose connection with consciousness. Of these three characteristics of the superego, it would seem reasonable to suppose that the first two—its primitive character and its independence—are accounted for by the third, viz. its loose connection with consciousness. It is presumably because it is out of relation to the adaptive function of consciousness and thus unable to develop in conformity with the fruits of widening experience that the superego remains primitive and independent. If we seek an answer to the further question which now arises—why the activity of the superego is so largely withdrawn from consciousness—we are faced with a somewhat formidable problem, which demands separate treatment. Briefly, however, it would seem that the answer can only be derived from an examination of the conditions under which the superego arises in the child. It must be to the intimate association of the superego with the process of repression that we must look for an explanation of the loose connection of the superego with the adult consciousness. We must believe that the intimacy of the contact between the superego and the repressed in the primitive conflict between them is the responsible factor. Although there are objections to regarding the superego as being itself subject to repression, except perhaps in a secondary sense, yet we must regard it as tending to be dragged into the unconscious together with the tendencies for the repression of which it is so largely responsible. If we can imagine this process occurring, there need be no difficulty for the psychologist in conceiving of the existence in the mind of an active independent sentiment-organisation largely withdrawn from consciousness. A conception of this nature is already familiar to psychology in the form of "the Complex", a psychical structure, which may be roughly defined as "a sentiment loosely connected with consciousness". At the other end of the scale, psychology has become familiar with the phenomenon of "secondary personalities". If the superego is usually more organised than a complex and less organised than a secondary personality, it would yet appear to be a psychical organisation of a similar order.

II. IS THE SUPEREGO REPRESSED?

Our [prior] consideration of the features described by Freud as characterising the superego enables us to understand the relevance of the practical manifestations attributed to it. We have seen that the superego originates in an essentially empathetic relationship towards frustrating figures, who are at the same time the most vital individuals in the environment of the child. We should, therefore, expect the function of the superego to manifest itself in activities, which may be somewhat anthropomorphically described as criticism of, condemnation of, antagonism to certain impulses originating in the instinctive tendencies. [We have also considered Freud's (1914a) association of 'conscience' with 'ego-ideal' as well as his (1923b) redefinition of the 'ego-ideal' in terms of the 'superego'; followed by the discussion on Strafbedürfnis (the need for punishment) in the neuroses and psychoses. [See pp. 93–94 above.] The clinical evidence upon which Freud's theory is based is derived from the psychoanalytic treatment of neurotic patients. [Here Fairbairn cites the two neurotic cases—the man "dogged by ill-luck" and the woman teacher. (See pp. 94–98 above.]

There seems to be no lack of evidence for the superego as a *phenomenon*; but what is the superego psychologically? When we come to attempt to answer this question, perhaps the best point to start out from is the relationship between the superego and the id. Certain points of similarity between these two structures have already been noted [above] and reference was made to their close association in the production of functional nervous disease. The clinical findings of psychoanalysis suggest that the origin of functional nervous disorder is to be sought in some special form of the frustration of impulse. The term "repression" has been applied to this particular form of frustration. Now the characteristic function of the id is to engender impulse, and the characteristic function of the superego is to prevent certain impulses being accepted by the ego. We should, therefore, expect the common features of the two structures to depend upon the fact that the resultant of their interaction determines what impulses the ego shall accept. Since the superego is a frustrating or inhibiting structure, we should further expect its special province to lie within that sphere of mental life which is concerned with the organisation of instinctive tendencies. These tendencies have, of course, an organisation of their own which is innate and which therefore would appear to belong to the structure of the id. This innate organisation of the instinctive tendencies is capable, as is well known, of modification by experience even at the impulsive or perceptual level of mental life. It is in this way that the behaviour of most animals comes to be modified. In man, however, the emergence of the imaginative and conceptual levels of mental life enables the expression of the innate tendencies to be modified in a much more drastic way. The typical organisations of impulse, with which we are familiar on the imaginative and conceptual planes, are, of course, sentiments and ideals. It would seem, therefore, that it is in this direction that we must look for the true nature of the superego.

That we will not look in this direction in vain is evident, when we review some of the superego's characteristics. The origin of the superego is ascribed, by Freud (1923b) as we have seen, to an emotional relationship between the child and its parents. The ordinary emotional relationship of this sort with which we are familiar in everyday life is the sentiment of love. This would lead us to expect that the relationship, upon which the superego is founded, likewise partakes of the nature of sentiment,—albeit, the fact that the superego arises in infancy would suggest that here we are dealing with something more primitive than any sentiment with which we are familiar. It may be objected here that a sentiment of the nature of filial love involves an object-relationship, whereas the superego is founded on an identification in feeling. This objection, however, does not amount to much, for it is obvious that sentiments commonly involve an identification in feeling as well as an object-relationship. A consideration of the sentiment of patriotism renders this obvious. Not only is our country the object of our affection, but we also *feel with it*. If it is humiliated we are humiliated; if it triumphs, we triumph also.

The suggestion that the superego is an organisation after the manner of sentiment is supported by other considerations. When a sentiment is profoundly stirred, it gives rise to emotion, the character of which depends upon the particular instinctive tendencies aroused. The stirring of the superego likewise gives rise to emotions of a varying character. In the case of the functional nervous disorders, this emotion frequently takes the form of fear or anxiety. It may also take the form of anger (an emotion specially prominent in paranoiacs) or of negative self-feeling as in melancholia. Another example of negative self-feeling, ascribed by Freud to the action of the superego, is the inferiority response, however, it is the complex emotion of guilt, which is a derivative of shame and negative self-feeling. In its relation to emotion, therefore, the superego is akin to sentiment. The special connection traced by Freud between the superego and the phenomenon of 'conscience' is also significant in this respect; for 'conscience' would certainly be classed by psychologists within the sphere of sentiment. The irrational features of the superego are also compatible with all we know of sentiment. For the Great War [1914–1918] is sufficiently recent in our memory to convince us of the extremes of irrationality to which sentiments like patriotism may lead men.

There are two characteristics of the superego, however, which may be cited as differentiating it profoundly from sentiment as this is commonly understood. These are—(1) its independence of the ego; (2) the looseness of its connection with consciousness. Let us take the first of these points, its independence of the ego. Now Freud's description of the way in which the ego is differentiated from the id through contact with the outer world reminds us of the way in which an individual's character is built up through experience on a basis of the instinctive tendencies. So close is the parallel that we seem justified, for the purposes of our psychological enquiry, in translating the term 'ego' into 'character' or 'organised self'. According to Professor William McDougall (1908) character is built up of sentiments arranged in a hierarchy under the dominance of a master-sentiment. Strength of character depends partly on the nature of the master-sentiment and the position of other sentiments, but mainly upon the degree of organisation attained. Where this organisation is loose, character is weak. In the sentimentalist, each sentiment has an unusual degree of independence, with the result that it may be stirred in a more or less isolated fashion without relevance to the character as a whole. It is, therefore, obvious that the term independence is a relative one when applied to the relation of any particular sentiment or group of sentiments to the character as a whole. There are individuals in whom one sentiment or group of sentiments preserves a remarkable degree of independence. Independence of the organised self, therefore, provides not an absolute but only a relative distinction between sentiment and the superego.

Consider now the loose connection of the superego with consciousness. Is this a feature which differentiates it completely from what we know as sentiment? The superego is largely unconscious. But is this true of sentiment? Here we come upon a difficulty as to the use of the word "unconscious". In one sense of the word, every part of the *structure* of the mind is unconscious; only function can be conscious. In this sense sentiment and superego, being both structural, are alike unconscious and indeed must be so. But Freud uses the word "unconscious" indifferently of both structure and function. When he says the id is unconscious, he is speaking (or ought to be speaking) of something structural which *must* be unconscious; when he says an impulse or a desire is unconscious, he is speaking of something functional, thus he is speaking of something that might equally be unconscious or conscious. As a matter of fact, Freud frequently uses his structural terms in a way which shows that he is speaking of their function as well. Thus when he says that the superego is loosely connected with consciousness, he means that *its function* is loosely connected with consciousness. Once we are clear on this point, the question arises whether a sentiment can be loosely connected with consciousness in the same sense. Typically, of course, the expressions of a sentiment are conscious. We know that we love our country, we know that we love our children. That a sentiment need not be wholly conscious, however, is evident from such common remarks as "I didn't know how fond of the place I was until I had to leave it". That a sentiment may also be unconscious, when it is in embryo, is evident from the intelligibility of such a remark as "I suddenly realised that I loved her". Further, that psychology recognises the possibility of something of the nature of unconscious sentiment is evident from the adoption into psychology of the word "complex". A sentiment may be said to merge into a complex in so far as it is unconscious. When we say that a person's action is the result of a complex, we mean that it is the expression of a sentiment-formation, of which the person is unaware. The hatred of the Arab for the Jew may be a sentiment, but Mr Hilaire Belloc's hatred of the Jews is suspiciously like a complex. He knows that he hates the Jews but the source of the hatred is doubtless withdrawn from his awareness. Certainly the reasons which he gives for his hatred have the flavour of rationalisations. It is thus evident that the loose connection of the superego with consciousness does not invalidate the suggestion that there may be a community of nature between the superego and the sentiments.

The conclusion is thus borne in upon us that, in all probability, the superego is a formation of the nature of a sentiment operating mainly in the unconscious. This being so, we have travelled some distance toward the aim of our enquiry—which is to determine the psychological nature of the superego. That we have not yet reached our goal, however, is evident from the fact that the typical manifestations of the superego are not by any means those which we are accustomed to regard as typical of the sentiment. The psychoneurosis, for example, is not a characteristic product of an ordinary sentiment. Yet it was in an attempt to explain psychoneurosis that the theory of the superego was evolved. It is evident, therefore, that, if the superego partakes of the nature of sentiment-formation, it is not a sentiment or a body of sentiments in the ordinary sense. It must possess some special features, which put it in a class by itself. To what characteristics in Freud's description must we look for a clue to this distinction? There are two characteristics of the superego which seem to meet our requirements. These are:

1. the primitive and childish nature of the superego
2. the intimate association of the superego with the process of repression

The primitive nature of the superego stands in sharp contrast to the high degree of development which seems to characterise the familiar sentiment-formations of the adult. The sentiment of patriotism, for example is subject, even in an uneducated person, to considerable elaboration on the conceptual level. It embraces thoughts about national welfare and cooperation which cannot be ascribed to a mere identification with the community at the imaginative level. It is highly elaborated and integrates a wide group of the individual's activities, though, of course, in many people it is narrow and bigoted. Similarly the sentiment of love is elaborate and comprehensive, including in its scope thoughts about the ultimate welfare and happiness of the loved person. The superego on the other hand is narrow and bigoted in the extreme, and conceptual elements appear to be wholly absent. The primitive features would appear to depend upon the period of life at which it is formed. The superego originates in the child's identification with parents who are imagined as arbitrary and irrational beings like the gods of the Greek myths (who indeed perhaps derive their characteristics from this source). To the infant, the parents must indeed appear very much as his gods did to the ancient Greek—mysterious creatures who come and go the child knows not why, creatures whose actions he cannot understand, creatures who sometimes indeed appear benevolent, but who at other times thwart and obstruct his activities for no reason obvious to his undeveloped mind. Moreover, just as it is the inexorability and recalcitrance of external objects that leads us to our conception of a reality outside ourselves, so it is that the child realises the presence of his parents most acutely, when they thwart him or at any rate appear to him as a menace. The superego, therefore, if it partakes of the nature of a sentiment-formation, stands in contrast with the familiar sentiments, because it is a formation retaining a very childish and primitive character. It is like those "nests" of primitive cells, which according to one theory of the origin of cancer, persist unaltered in character in some part of the body, while the cells around undergo the normal process of differentiation and specialisation. According to this theory of cancer, the primitive cells lie dormant for a period of years, only to flare up into furious activity, when the time comes. To the end the cancer cells remain primitive and unorganised, and since they are outside the economy of the body, their activity has all the appearance of being due to a foreign agent. The superego resembles the cancer cell in the fact that it retains its primitive character and functions outside the spheres of the organised self. Every sentiment, of course, passes through a phase in which it is primitive and unorganised just as all the cells in the body do; but the special feature of the superego is that it persists in this primitive and unorganised state. It always remains childish, like a colony of aborigines in a civilised state.

If we ask why the superego remains childish, we are brought to a consideration of the second of the two characteristics of the superego, to which we said we must look for a clue to the distinction between the superego and the sentiment. This characteristic is the intimate association of the superego with the process of repression. In his essay Freud (1914a) said that, from the point of view of the ego, the formation of an ego-ideal becomes the condition of repression (p. 51). In *The Ego and the Id* (Freud 1923b), he says that the ego carries out repressions, "in the service and at the behest of its superego" (p. 75). According to Freud, therefore, although the superego is not the repressing agent itself, it provides the condition of repression. Ernest Jones (1926) defines the function of the superego thus—"It is to criticise the ego and to cause pain to the latter whenever it tends to accept impulses proceeding from the repressed part of the id" (p. 304). It is evident from this somewhat anthropomorphic statement that repression is a mental process whereby the individual is saved the unpleasure which would otherwise result from the irreconcilability of his instinctive tendencies with the superego. Now we know the fate of the repressed impulses; they are imprisoned in the unconscious. We can, therefore, imagine the association between the superego and the impulses which it thwarts being so close that, as the latter pass into the unconscious, the former tends to do so likewise. If a medical student turns squeamish at a surgical operation, he can hardly avoid the unpleasantness of the situation by cutting the patient off from his field of vision, and allowing his eye to rest on the surgeon with his knife. If he wants to save his feelings he must exclude both surgeon and patient from his sight. In the same way we can conceive that the child's identification with the thwarting parent must pass into the unconscious in proportion as the thwarted impulses are repressed.

If this be so, it is easy to understand how the superego differs from other sentiment-formations. It differs from them (a) because it is primitive and childish, (b) because it is loosely connected with consciousness. Its primitive nature and its loose connection with consciousness in turn are both to be traced to the fact that the superego is so intimately associated with the process of repression. It is cut off from the organised self, or perhaps one ought to say "the self in process of organisation", in the earliest years of childhood, and it retains throughout life the primitive character which belonged to it at the time when it was cut off. It must be admitted, however, that just when we seem to be reaching a satisfactory conception of the superego, a considerable difficulty arises. It arises over the fact that Freud does not claim that the superego is wholly unconscious; he merely says that it is "less closely connected with consciousness" (1923b, p. 35) than the ego. Ernest Jones (1926) is more explicit, when he says—"It is probable that the superego may be partly conscious, partly preconscious and partly unconscious; further that its relation to consciousness varies at different times" (p. 305). If we respect this conception of the superego as capable of being partly conscious, we must interpret the superego as including whole sentiment-formation which results from the child's identification with his parents. Our view must then be that this sentiment-formation becomes unconscious and remains primitive up to the point that it is involved in repression. The presumption then is that, in so far as the superego is characterised by consciousness it is incorporated in the other sentiments with which we are familiar, such as filial love or other sentiments derived from it. In support of this view may be brought the fact that, as the submerged superego is brought to consciousness in psychoanalytic treatment, it becomes related to the organised self and loses its pathogenic power. It must be pointed out, however, that, under these circumstances it becomes part of the ego, and loses the primitive characteristics, which are attributed to the superego in Freud's works. It would, therefore, seem preferable to exclude from the denotation of the superego concept all conscious elements, and to reserve it solely for the unconscious formation.

If we restrict the use of the term in this way, however, we bring into the foreground another difficulty which was already implicit in our attempt to explain the loose connection of the superego with consciousness. The explanation of this feature was found to lie in the intimate connection of the superego with repression. We said that the child's identification with the thwarting parent was, so to speak, dragged into the unconscious together with the impulses which were repressed on its account. Our statement prompts this question—"Since repression is a function of the ego must not the superego be regarded as repressed equally with the impulses which conflict with it?"

In general Freud's position as regards this point is quite clear. "We know" he says "that as a rule the ego carries out repression in the service and at the behest of its superego" (1923b, p. 75). This statement taken alone implies, that while the superego does not actually repress, it is not subject to repression either. This general statement, however, must not be taken out of its context. It is introduced into a passage where Freud expressly states that in hysteria repression is found operating against the superego. He is led to this inclusion in the attempt to explain why the sense of guilt is unconscious in hysteria. The whole passage reads thus:

> The hysterical type of ego defends itself from the painful perception which the criticisms of its superego threaten to produce in it by the same means that it uses to defend itself from an unendurable object-cathexis[1]—by an act of repression. It is the ego, therefore, that is responsible for the sense of guilt remaining unconscious. We know that as a rule the ego carries out repressions in the service and at the behest of its superego; but this is a case in which it has turned the same weapon against its harsh taskmaster. [Freud 1923b, p. 75]

One may go further and venture the hypothesis that a great part of the sense of guilt must normally remain unconscious, because the origin of conscience is closely connected with the Oedipus complex which belongs to the unconscious.

This statement of Freud's to the effect that the superego may itself be subject to repression does not affect our general conclusions regarding the psychological *nature* of the superego; but it becomes evident that, if our ideas regarding the psychological *function* of the superego are to be properly clarified, it will be necessary for us to consider more carefully the exact relationship of the superego to the process of repression. It is when problems

[1]W.R.D.F. intended an explanatory note here, but there is no evidence of its content.

of this nature arise that we realise the weakness of the topographical and anthropomorphic method, which Freud employs in formulating his conceptions. If we accept this method as adequate for the elucidation of the subtleties of the human mind, certain problems almost escape attention. It is only when we attempt to determine the exact psychological significance of Freud's theories, that we realise some of the problems involved. If we conceive the id, the ego and the superego as topographical entities, the relationship between them is analogous to the political relationship between the European powers. The relationship of the ego to the id and the superego is then after the model of the relationship of Elizabethan England to the rival powers of France and Spain. Queen Elizabeth would put herself now at the disposal of France, now at the disposal of Spain; at times she would try to effect a compromise; at other times she seems to have tried to shut her eyes to the demands of both.

It is thus that Freud (1923b) comes to speak of the ego as "a poor creature owing service to three masters and consequently menaced by three several dangers; from the external world, from the libido of the id and from the severity of the superego" (p. 82). It is thus that he comes to speak of the ego turning the weapon of repression, which it originally wielded at the behest of the superego against the harsh taskmaster itself. The complex structure of the mind, however, defies division into hard and fast entities, whose activity can be adequately represented in anthropomorphic terms. Indeed Freud himself shows that he realises the limitations of this method of exposition, when he says "One must not take the division between the ego and id in too hard-and-fast a sense" (Freud 1923b p. 52). The difficulty of preserving the integrity of the three entities becomes greatest, when Freud is discussing their deeper relationships. It appears when he discusses the possibility that superego formation in successive generations may lead to a deposit being left behind in the hereditary endowment of the individual. Freud (1923b) accepts this possibility as a fact, and thus reaches a conclusion which reminds us of the theological doctrine that conscience is inborn. This means that phylogenetically the superego becomes incorporated to some extent with the id: "Through the forming of the ideal, all the traces left behind in the id by biological developments and by the vicissitudes gone through by the human race are taken over by the ego and lived through again by it in each individual" (p. 48). The result of this view is to render intelligible the apparently paradoxical statement that Freud makes in a neighbouring passage which reads, "whereas the ego is essentially the representative of the external world, of reality, the superego stands in contrast to it as the representative of the internal world, of the id" (1923b, p. 48). This paradoxical statement, that the superego stands in contrast to the ego as the representative of the id, shows how difficult it is for Freud to preserve the hard and fast distinctions which his topographical method of description necessitates. It also brings us back to the problem whether the superego is repressed. If the superego comes to stand in contrast to the ego as the representative of the id, it is difficult to avoid the conclusion that the superego must itself be subject to repression.

Before accepting this conclusion, let us examine more carefully the relationship of the superego to repression. That there is a very close relationship between them is evident. To the closeness of this relationship we have already seen reason to attribute that loose connection of the superego with consciousness of which Freud speaks. The conclusion, which we reached regarding the loose connection of the superego with consciousness, was that the emotional identification of the child with the thwarting parent tended to sink into the unconscious together with the impulses repressed on its account. This conclusion is supported by the following passage from Freud (1923b),

> The way in which the superego came into being explains how it is that the earlier conflicts of the ego with the object-cathexes of the id can be carried on and continued in conflicts with their successor, the superego. If the ego has not succeeded in mastering the Oedipus complex satisfactorily, the energic cathexis of the latter, springing from the id, will find an outlet in the reaction-formations of the ego-ideal. The very free communication possible between the ideal and the less instinctual trends explains how it is that the ideal itself can be to a great extent unconscious and inaccessible to the ego. [pp. 52–53][2]

The sinking of the superego into the unconscious owing to the freedom of communication existing between it and the repressed tendencies at once suggests the view that repression must extend its activity from the repressed tendencies to the associated superego. If this be so, the superego too must be regarded as repressed. This view would find support in the difficulty experienced during psychoanalytic treatment in dragging the superego into consciousness. When this task is undertaken a resistance is encountered similar to that encountered in the case of the repressed tendencies. On the other hand, we gain the impression, in psychoanalytic treatment, that whereas the resistance to the emergence of the repressed tendencies is supported by the superego, the resistance to the emergence of the superego is not similarly supported by the repressed tendencies. To use Freud's terms, we may say that, whereas the superego supports the ego in resisting the admission of id-impulses to consciousness, the id does not support the ego's resistance to admitting the superego to consciousness. Further it is found that, in any given case, the intensity of repression varies more nearly with the strength of the superego than with the strength of the instinctive impulses. Thus, in the case

[2]Again, W.R.D.F. intended an explanatory note here, but there is no evidence of its content.

of the perversions, the obvious ineffectiveness of repression appears to be due less to the strength of perverse impulses than to weakness of superego formation. The material derived from psychoanalytic treatment of the pervert supports this interpretation; for, in the case of the pervert, probing of the unconscious reveals little that is characteristic of the superego. If then the strength of repression varies with the strength of the superego rather than with the strength of the repressed impulses, it would seem as if the superego functioned as an agent of repression.

Clinical experience with psychoanalysis thus seems to suggest that the superego is more allied to the resistance than to the repressed. This is in keeping with what we know of the history of the superego concept. It will be remembered that Freud was led to this concept not through consideration of repressed material but through consideration of the repressing agent itself. In the early days of psychoanalysis, it was natural that theoretic interest should be mainly confined to the newly discovered field of the repressed. It was only after this field had been to some extent explored, that attention began to be directed to the nature of the repressing agent itself. The source of repression evidently lay in that part of the mind which fell outside the boundaries of the repressed and to which the term 'ego' was applied. Since the patients were unaware of the existence of the repressed, the resistance evidently had its source in unconscious regions of the ego. It was through investigation of these regions that Freud was led to formulate his conception of the superego. It is thus evident that the very conception of the superego is dependent for its origin upon a distinction between the superego and the repressed.

That the superego abets the process of repression rather than be subject to it is not only implicit in the conception of the superego; it is an explicit feature, which Freud's investigation of the repressing agency led him to embody in the conception. Thus, in his essay "On Narcissism", in which the term "ego-ideal" was first given technical significance, he writes as follows—"Repression, as we have said, proceeds from the ego. . . . From the point of view of the ego this formation of an ideal would be the condition of repression" (Freud 1914a, pp. 50–51).

We have seen that the ego-ideal was the precursor of the superego in Freud's theory, and in *The Ego and the Id* (1923b), he makes it plain that he regards the superego in turn as the condition of repression. Although he finds the superego itself subjected to repression in hysteria, he holds that "as a rule the ego carries out repressions in the service and at the behest of its superego" (p. 75). According to Freud, the ego-ideal has "the task of effecting the repression of the Oedipus complex" (p. 45). This statement is best understood in the light of a previous passage, where he discusses the emergence of the superego out of the Oedipus situation in childhood:

> The broad general outcome of the sexual phase governed by the Oedipus complex may, therefore, be taken to be the forming of a precipitate in the ego consisting of these two identifications [i.e., the father-identification and the mother-identification] in some way combined together. This modification of the ego retains its special position; it stands in contrast to the other constituents of the ego in the form of an ego-ideal or superego. . . . The ego-ideal had the task of effecting the repression of the Oedipus complex, indeed it is to that revolutionary event that it owes its existence. Clearly the repression of the Oedipus complex was no easy task. The parents, and especially the father [i.e., in the case of the boy], were perceived as the obstacle to realization of the Oedipus wishes; so that the child's ego brought in a reinforcement to help in carrying out the repression by erecting this same obstacle within itself. . . . The more intense the Oedipus complex was the more rapidly it succumbed to repression (under the influence of discipline, religious teaching, schooling and reading) the more exacting later on is the domination of the superego over the ego—in the form of conscience or perhaps of an unconscious sense of guilt. [pp. 44–45]

It is evident from the passage, which has just been quoted, that the superego originates, not as a product of repression, but as an agency promoting repression. Whether or not the possibility exists of circumstances arising in the mind which may lead to the superego itself later becoming subject to repression, is a question which will be considered later, but this possibility does not affect the main issue regarding the essential relation of the superego to repression. As regards this essential relationship, study of Freud's account of the origin of the superego makes it plain that the superego is an organisation distinct from the repressed.

If then we come to the conclusion that the superego does not originate through being repressed and therefore is not by nature repressed, the question arises how we are to regard the process by which it becomes cut off from the ego or organised self. We have already come to the conclusion that it sinks into the unconscious simultaneously with the impulses which are repressed on its account, and we explained this fact as due to the close association between the superego and the repressed involved in the process of repression. The matter cannot be left there, however; it remains to be determined, what the process is whereby the superego is cut off from consciousness. If this process is not to be conceived as one of repression, how is it to be conceived?

If we cast around in Freud's writings for a clue which shall help us to answer this question, our attention cannot but be attracted by a passage, where Freud (1923b) makes reference to the phenomenon of "multiple personality". For one reason or another, references to this remarkable phenomenon are conspicuous by their absence in Freud's writings; yet cases of multiple personality provide the most striking examples known to psychopathology of the wholesale cutting off of mental elements from the rest of the mind. The relative neglect of the problems of multiple personality by psychoanalytic writers is partly to be explained as due to the coincidence that these cases have seldom been brought to analysis; but it seems likely that there is a deeper reason. Psychoanalytic theory has been built up upon the concept of repression. "The doctrine of repression" says Freud (1914b) is "the foundation-stone on which the whole structure of Psycho-Analysis rests" (p. 297). The possibility therefore presents itself that the reason why the phenomenon of multiple personality has received so little attention at the hands of Freud is that in this phenomenon repression is not involved. If the possibility that multiple personality is not a phenomenon of repression be envisaged, Freud's infrequent references to the phenomenon become all the more important; for in these we ought to find some clue to Freud's views about a form of dissociation other than repression. Let us therefore turn to a passage where Freud (1923b) expressly interrupts his exposition of the part played by "identification" in the formation of the superego, in order to throw out a hint as to the origin of multiple personality:

> Although it is a digression from our theme, we cannot avoid giving our attention for a moment longer to the ego's object identifications. If they obtain the upper hand and become too numerous, unduly intense and incompatible with one another, a pathological outcome will not be far off. It may come to a disruption of the ego in consequence of the individual identifications becoming cut off from one another by resistances; perhaps the secret of the cases of so-called multiple personality is that the various identifications seize possession of consciousness in turn. Even when things do not go so far as this, there remains the question of conflicts between the various identifications into which the ego comes apart, conflicts which cannot after all be described as purely pathological. [pp. 38–39]

This passage, be it remembered, is intercalated in Freud's account of how the first identifications of the child (i.e., those with his parents) go to form the nucleus of the superego. The inference seems, therefore, justified that the process which leads to multiple personality is of a similar nature to that whereby the superego is formed. We have seen reason to conclude that the splitting off of personalities from the main personality is due not to repression, but to a process of simple dissociation. It, therefore, seems reasonable to look to this process for an explanation of the cutting off of the superego from the organised self.

In Fairbairn (1929a) our examination of the phenomena of dissociation and repression led us to the conclusion that Dissociation is a process whereby mental elements become cut off from personal consciousness in virtue of their being either irrelevant to, incompatible with or unpleasant in respect of active interests in the personality. We also found repression to be a special form of dissociation of the unpleasant—that form which occurs when the dissociated elements consist of mental tendencies so incongruous with the organised self that their appearance in consciousness would cause unpleasure. This being so, it would seem as if the cutting off of the superego from the organised self were due to dissociation of the incompatible. In this way we can explain the relegation of the superego to the unconscious without resorting to the difficulties of regarding it as repressed.

3. LIBIDO THEORY RE-EVALUATED

The object of the present paper is to consider the meaning for psychology of two important Freudian theories, viz. the "Libido" Theory and the theory of the "Pleasure Principle". The point of view to be adopted in what follows is that, while these two conceptions (like most of Freud's conceptions) embody truths of fundamental importance, the terms in which they are at present formulated are not necessarily final. Indeed it seems desirable that their present formulation should be superseded by a formulation framed in terms familiar to general psychology. Only so can the truths embodied in these theories come to exercise their just influence upon psychological thought.

The chief interest, from the point of view of general psychology, of the libido theory and the theory of the pleasure principle lies in their significance for problems concerning

1. the nature and classification of the instinctive tendencies
2. the mode of operation of these tendencies

It is in relation to the first group of problems that the libido theory is most significant, whereas the theory of the pleasure principle is primarily concerned with the second. Both groups of problems are, however, involved in either theory. That this should be so is plain when we consider the possibilities that the nature of a tendency may determine its mode of operation and that the mode of operation of a tendency may prove important for its classification. In the discussion which follows, accordingly, no attempt will be made to keep the two groups of problems separate. The libido theory will first be considered in all its relevant bearings, and later the theory of the pleasure principle will be introduced into the discussion on a similar basis.

The most outstanding feature of the libido theory lies in the fact that it represents so impressive an attempt to interpret the whole field of human behaviour and character-formation from a genetic standpoint and to establish fundamental principles for the understanding of both the normal and abnormal phenomena of mental life; and thus to throw light upon the manner in which various deviations from the normal occur and to provide means whereby abnormality may be removed or prevented. An attempt of this nature is so much in keeping with the spirit of modern scientific research that it must of itself command the attention and admiration of every psychologist. Such attempts are somewhat rare in modern psychology; for modern psychology (in reaction against the introspective psychological systems of the past and at the behest of the experimental method) is for the most part content to study restricted mental problems in comparative isolation. The Behaviourist Psychology seems to provide the only other modern example of a systematic attempt to provide a comprehensive explanation of human conduct, normal and abnormal, from a genetic standpoint. The Behaviourist Psychology has, however, succeeded in commanding the attention of the psychological world in a way which the libido theory has failed to do.

Both systems have encountered considerable criticism on the grounds of one-sidedness; but, whereas in the case of the libido theory the tendency is to criticise it and then banish it from the field of serious thought while the Behaviourist Psychology is allowed to remain within that field in spite of any criticisms. From the psychoanalytic point of view, this fact is readily explained as due to the operation of repression activated by the prominence assigned to sex in the libido theory. As, however, this explanation will only seem convincing to those who have already adopted a psychoanalytic

On holiday in Scotland c. 1930

standpoint another reason for the greater neglect of the libido theory may be suggested. Whereas both the Behaviourist Psychology and the libido theory have been criticised as one-sided, the direction of the alleged one-sidedness differs in the two cases. The one-sidedness attributed to the Behaviourists is, so to speak, in the vertical plane, whereas that attributed to psychoanalytic theory is in the horizontal plane. If Behaviourism appears to be "bottom heavy", the libido theory appears to be "lopsided". The Behaviourist system is criticised on the grounds that it describes the mental edifice only in terms of the basement (i.e., the physio-biological level), but it covers the whole ground-plan. The libido theory, on the other hand, is criticised on the grounds that it describes one wing of the building (i.e., the sex instincts) as if it were the whole building, and therefore does not cover the ground-plan even though it surveys the one wing from foundation to roof.

That psychological criticism should, from the beginning, level the charge of "pansexuality" against the libido theory is easily understood; for, in terms of this theory, the sex-tendencies are ascribed a scope and an importance which is novel to psychology for many instinctive tendencies which are ordinarily regarded as quite independent are ascribed to the libido. For example the "parental instinct" comes to be represented as a libido manifestation through the mechanism of the "Oedipus" situation and "the instinct of curiosity" has been credited with a sexual origin. Even the "instinct of aggression" tends to be brought within the fold of the libido under the guise of "sadism". The libido theory thus appears to extend the sphere of the sex tendencies in such a way as to give them an almost exclusive position in the economy of the psyche.

In spite of the fact that an instinctive monism appears to follow so naturally from the libido theory, the empire of the libido in the human mind was never regarded by Freud as absolute. Even in his original formulation of "the theory of the Libido" (1905c), Freud makes it plain that he does not regard the libido as the sole instinctive force at work in the mind. This is evident from the following quotation:

> We have determined the concept of *libido* as that of a force of variable quantity which has the capacity of measuring processes and transformations in the spheres of sexual excitement. This libido we distinguished from the energy which is to be generally adjudged to the psychic processes with reference to its special origin and thus we attribute to it also a qualitative character. In separating libidinous from other psychic energy we give expression to the assumption that the sexual processes of the organism are differentiated from the nutritional processes through a special chemisus. [p. 77; pp. 74–75 in 4th edition]

From this quotation it is evident that even in his original formulation of the libido theory, Freud recognised the existence of a second group of instinctive tendencies based upon nutritional needs. Here we find a real clue to the weak spot in the Freudian theory of instinct. The psychological weakness of the Freudian theory of instinct does not lie in its monism (for it is not monistic); its weakness lies in its dualism. This essential dualism of Freud's theory of instinct becomes progressively clearer in his later works. Thus in 1910, five years after his original formulation of the libido theory, we find him writing as follows:

> Our attention has been drawn to the significance of the instincts in the conceptual life; we have learnt that every instinct seeks to come to expression by activating those ideas which are in accordance with its aims. These instincts do not always agree with one another, and this frequently results in a conflict of interests; the contradictions in the ideas are merely the expression of the battle between the various instincts. Of quite peculiar significance for our efforts towards elucidation is the undeniable opposition between the instincts which serve the purposes of sexuality, of gaining sexual pleasure, and those others which aim at the self-preservation of the individual, the ego-instincts. Schiller said that we can classify under 'hunger' or under 'love' every active organic instinct of our souls. . . . The light thrown by psychology on our cultural development has shown us that culture is acquired essentially at the cost of the sexual-component instincts, . . . we have been able to recognise . . . that those sufferings we call the neuroses derive from the manifold ways in which these processes of transformation fail in regard to the sexual component-instincts. [Freud 1910a, pp. 108–109]

Although, in this passage, Freud does not actually exclude the possibility that there may be other instincts falling outside the two groups specially referred to, he does attach "quite peculiar significance" to the opposition between the sex-instincts and the ego-instincts. In the following paragraph he refers to them as "the two fundamental instincts", and the assumption that they are the fundamental instincts becomes the working basis of this grand theory of instinct. This practical dualism arose as a result of the process of thought whereby Freud's attention became diverted from a consideration of the repressed to a consideration of the forces of repression. In earlier phases of his thought Freud's attention was concentrated on the investigation of the repressed and the libido theory was the outcome of his reflections. It was only later that the nature of the repressing forces began to occupy his serious attention and that he came to detect in the process of repression the operation of "the ego-instincts". It was then that his original dualism of "the Conscious" and the "Unconscious" came to be replaced by a dualism of instincts—the sex-instincts and the ego-instincts.

In Freud's paper "On Narcissism" (1914a), we find this dualistic theory of instinct expressly formulated:

> In the complete absence of any theory of the instincts which would help us to find our bearings, we may be permitted, or rather, it is incumbent upon us to work out any hypothesis to its logical conclusion, until it either fails or becomes confirmed. There are various points in favour of the hypothesis of a primordial differentiation between sexual instincts and other instincts, ego-instincts, besides the usefulness of such an assumption in the analysis of the transference neuroses. I admit that this latter consideration alone would not be decisive, for it might be a question of an indifferent energy operating in the mind which was converted into libido only by the act of object-cathexis. But, in the first place, this differentiation of concepts corresponds to the distinction between hunger and love, so widely current. And, in the second place, there are biological considerations in its favour. The individual does actually carry on a double existence: one designed to serve his own purposes and another as a link in a chain, in which he serves against or at any rate without, any volition of his own. The individual himself regards sexuality as one of his own ends; while from another point of view he is only an appendage to his germ-plasm, to which he lends his energies, taking in return his toll of pleasure. . . . The differentiation of the sexual instincts from the ego-instincts would simply reflect this double function of the individual. Thirdly, we must recollect that all our provisional ideas in psychology will some day be based on an organic sub-structure. This makes it probable that special substances and special chemical processes control the operation of sexuality and provide for the continuation of the individual life in that of the species. We take this probability into account when we substitute special forces in the mind for special chemical substances.
>
> Just because I try in general to keep apart from psychology everything that is not strictly within its scope, even biological thought, I wish at this point expressly to admit that the hypothesis of separate ego-instincts and sexual instincts (that is to say, the libido-theory) rests scarcely at all upon a psychological basis, but is essentially supported upon facts of biology. So I shall also be consistent enough to drop this hypothesis if psycho-analytic work itself should suggest as more valuable another hypothesis about the instincts. So far, this has not happened. . . . Let us be fully aware of the possibility of error; but do not let us be deterred from carrying to its logical conclusion the hypothesis we first adopted of an antithesis between ego-instincts and sexual instincts (an hypothesis to which we were impelled by analysis of the transference neuroses), and so from seeing whether it turns out to be consistent and fruitful, and whether it may be applied to other affections also, e.g., to schizophrenia. [pp. 35–37]

Freud has been quoted at some length, because the passage in question illustrates several points of importance for our enquiry. Not only does it bear witness to the essential dualism of his theory of instinct, but it also contains an admission on the part of Freud that this theory is based primarily on biological and not upon psychological considerations. The guarded manner in which he affirms his hypothesis of a dualism of ego-instincts and sex-instincts also prepares us for future modifications of his theory. In *Beyond the Pleasure Principle* (1922) such a modification is recorded. This modification consisted, however, not in an abandonment of the dualistic standpoint, but in the establishment of a new dualism: "Our standpoint was a dualistic one from the beginning and is so to-day more sharply than before, since we no longer call the contrasting tendencies egoistic and sexual instincts, but life-instincts and death-instincts" (p. 67).

Historically, this change was forced upon Freud as the result of his adopting the conception of "Narcissism" in an attempt to bring the libido theory to bear on the problems of schizophrenia. The inflation of the ego and the depreciation of the outer world, which is so characteristic of the schizophrenic, came to be explained as due to libido being withdrawn from outer objects and directed towards the ego itself. Further, the study of libido-development in children convinced Freud that the narcissism of the schizophrenic was only secondary narcissism arising through regression to a primary state of narcissism which he concluded to be the state of the young infant. The view that narcissism is the primitive state of the young infant appears to be modified in *The Ego and the Id* (1923b) in accordance with the conception of the id developed in that work: "Now that we have distinguished between the ego and the id, we must recognise the id as the great reservoir of libido mentioned in my introductory paper on narcissism" (p. 38ff.). In accordance with this conception, the ego-cathexis of libido in primary narcissism itself becomes a secondary form of cathexis: "Through the study of the libido-development of the child in its earliest phases it became clear that the ego is the true and original reservoir of the libido, which is extended to the object only from this" (Freud 1922, p. 66).

The ego thus took its place as one of the sexual objects and was immediately recognised as the choicest of them. Where the libido thus remained attached to the ego it was termed 'narcissistic'. This narcissistic libido was naturally also the expression of the energy of the sexual instinct in the analytical sense which now had to be identified with "the instinct of self-preservation", the existence of which was admitted from the first. Whereupon the "original antithesis between the ego-instincts and the sexual instincts became inadequate" (Freud 1922, p. 66).

Once the ego-instincts had come to be incorporated by Freud in the libido, it became important for him to find another group of instincts to complete his dualism—the preservation of a dualism of instinct being apparently necessary to support the theory of repression. It is not difficult to understand Freud's selection of "the death instincts" for this purpose. All dualisms tend to be dualisms of opposites, subject and object, mind and matter, Ahura Mazda and Ahriman, God and Devil and love and hate, conscious and unconscious, individual and race—all these typical dualistic antitheses illustrate this tendency in dualistic thought. It is therefore easy to understand how, when Freud resolved the dualism of (self-preservative) ego-instincts and (race-preservative) sex-instincts into the unity of the life-instincts, he should come to postulate a group of "death-instincts" to provide the necessary antithesis.

The argument by which Freud (1922) reaches the concept of the death-instincts is somewhat complex and obscure. The fundamental observation upon which it is based is that, under stress human beings show a tendency to reinstate former situations. Thus children repeat, in their play, everything (pleasant or unpleasant) that has made a great impression upon them; and similarly neurotics tend, under the influence of anxiety, to reproduce in their dreams and in the transference phenomena situations belonging to their past, even when these are necessarily painful. Such phenomena are taken by Freud to indicate the existence in living beings of a "repetition-compulsion" which is more fundamental than the pleasure-principle, which he had hitherto regarded as the primary process of motivation. By the way of the repetition-compulsion his argument leads him to the conclusion that every organism tends to seek death—not directly indeed, but by the path laid down in the evolutionary process for its particular species. This death-tendency then provides the necessary antithesis to the life-instincts, which Freud requires to complete his dualism of instinct. No attempt need be made here to outline his argument more fully. It is sufficient for our purpose to recognise that the concept of the death-instincts was a necessary development of the progress of Freud's thought if the dualism of instinct with which he started, was to be preserved. The reference which Freud (1923b) makes to this development of his thought may, however, be quoted with advantage:

> As a result of theoretical considerations, supported by biology, we assumed the existence of a death-instinct, the task of which is to lead organic matter back into the inorganic state; on the other hand, we supposed that Eros aims at complicating life by bringing about a more far-reaching coalescence of the particles into which living matter has been dispersed, thus, of course, aiming at the maintenance of life. . . . The appearance of life would thus be regarded as the cause of the continuance of life and also the cause of the striving towards death; and life itself would be a conflict and compromise between these two trends. The problem of the origin of life would remain a cosmological one; and the problem of the purpose and goal of life would be answered dualistically. [pp. 55–56]

This quotation draws attention to the important fact that, like Freud's earlier dualism of sex-instincts and ego-instincts, his later dualism of life-instincts and death-instincts is based upon biological, and not psychological, considerations. The whole development of Freud's theory of instinct, indeed, goes to show that it is not a psychological theory at all. It is a biological theory of instinct and this fact alone leads us to expect to find it weak on the psychological side. It is true that psychology and biology are intimately related sciences, but their problems are different, and distinctions which are valid for the purposes of the one may be invalid for the purposes of the other. One cannot help feeling that many of the difficulties which Freudian theory presents for psychologists are dependent on this fact.

Of all the Freudian conceptions his theory of the death-instincts is one of the least satisfactory. Perhaps its most interesting feature is the example it provides of the general tendency of theories of the Unconscious to issue in a philosophical pessimism. This tendency, which finds its classic instance in the philosophy of Schopenhauer, might well give one furiously to think, and the momentous questions which it raises will one day attract the attention they deserve. These questions, however, are foreign to our present purpose, which is concerned rather with the problem of the classification of instincts. It is equally unnecessary to enter here into any detailed discussion of Freud's theory of the death-instincts, as C. P. Blacker (1929) has devoted a special paper to the subject. For our present purpose it will be sufficient to indicate reasons for believing that the very conception of a "death-instinct" contains an inner contradiction. All instincts are essentially expressions of life. *The instincts with which an individual is endowed are simply the characteristic ways in which life manifests itself in members of the species to which it belongs*. Unless the term instinct is interpreted in this sense, it is difficult to attach any meaning to it at all. *All* instincts are therefore "life-instincts" in the last resort. This remains true even of those instincts which operate in such a way as to cause death. It is of the first importance here to distinguish between the issue of an act and its biological end. The aggressive tendencies frequently issue in the death of the object against which they are directed; but it must not be inferred that the death of the object is necessarily the biological end of these tendencies. On the contrary, their biological end is much more restricted; it is simply the elimination of an obstacle or menace; even if this involves the death of a being which constitutes such an obstacle or menace, the death of this being, is simply incidental. The hunting instinct of the carnivores provides perhaps the most extreme example of a death-dealing instinct; yet even here the biological end served is not the death of the victim but the sustenance of the carnivore's own life. Similarly when the little girl tells her mother that she will throw her out of the window, it is as absurd to attribute to her a "death wish" as it would be to attribute to her a "spinal fracture wish". The aim behind her remark is simply the elimination of a source of danger. A death-wish is only (strictly speaking) possible for a mental organisation sufficiently advanced to realise that killing is the safe permanent measure of elimination; and even here it is not death but elimination that is primary. Sadism itself is misinterpreted if it is regarded as having the death of the object as its aid. After all, the mourning of the sadistic widower can be quite as genuine as that of a more normal man; for the sadist depends for his satisfaction upon an object-relationship, which is abolished with the death of the object. Innumerable examples could be cited to illustrate the same point. The oral sadism of the infant actually depends for its satisfaction upon the continued presence of the mother and not upon her death, which would be experienced as frustration. Similarly, the primitive aim of anal sadism is not destruction of the faeces but their preservation; otherwise it would be difficult to understand how anal sadism could lead to that prizing of gold which is as characteristic of the spendthrift as of the miser (for the spendthrift is as miserable as the miser, when he has no gold to spend). The dependence of sadistic satisfaction upon the continuance of the object in the case of national groups has been illustrated by Freud (1930) in his latest work *Civilization and Its Discontents*:

> I once interested myself in the peculiar fact that peoples whose territories are adjacent, and are otherwise closely related, are always at feud and ridiculing one another, as, for instance, . . . the English and Scotch and so on. . . . One can now see that it is a convenient and relatively harmless form of satisfaction for aggressive tendencies, through which cohesion among members of a group is made easier. The Jewish people, scattered in all directions as they are, have in this way rendered services which deserve recognition to the development of culture in the countries where they settled; . . . it is quite intelligible that the attempt to establish a new communistic type of culture in Russia should find psychological support in the persecution of the bourgeois. One only wonders, with some concern, however, how the Soviets will manage when they have exterminated their bourgeois entirely. [pp. 90–91]

Even the amazing phenomenon of self-destruction in human beings is incorrectly interpreted, if it is regarded as having death as its aim. Self-destruction is best understood as resulting either from the incidental result of the insatiability of aggressive impulses which have come to be directed against the self or from the overpowering intensity of impulses to escape from a danger which has become insufferable so that any form of escape becomes preferable to none. In either case self-destruction results from the operation of tendencies (aggression and escape respectively) which fall essentially within the category of life-instincts. Although in this case the tendencies attain only an extreme pathological expression, yet the tendencies of aggression and escape are in themselves life-preservative in aim. After all the organic world provides many examples of the exuberance of life leading to death, where there can be no question of "death instincts". Cancer leads to the death of the victim, and the death of the malignant cells themselves follows on that of their host; but it seems unnecessary to call in a death-principle to explain a result which so obviously lies at the door of Eros. After all even Eros himself cannot both eat his cake and have it.

Recent experiments on tissue culture seem to suggest that, given sufficiently favourable conditions, tissue growth may go on indefinitely through cell multiplication unaccompanied by death. In *Beyond the Pleasure Principle* Freud (1922) refers to similar experiments conducted by Woodruff on infusoria, but lays stress on the fact that, unless the nutrient medium is repeatedly changed, the animalcules die of the products of their own metabolism. From this he infers that a death-principle is present, even where it is obscured by artificial conditions. It would be more reasonable, however, to infer from such experiments that death depends upon conditions which are in the last resort external. Death seems best interpreted as a failure of adaptation—a failure which may occur either because extra-cellular conditions are so unfavourable as to preclude permanent adaptation or because the organism finds adaptation to extra-cellular conditions an insuperable task. This principle may be applied to multicellular organisms. It may well be, as a quaint friend of the writer has suggested, that the excretory organs are really the vital organs of the body, because it is the excretory organs that determine the constitution of the pericellular fluids. However this may be, no useful purpose appears to be served by retaining for psychological theory the troublesome conception of the "death-instincts".

It now becomes a question how Freud's theory of instinct would fare, if the death-instincts were eliminated from his dualism. Assuming such elimination to have taken place, the modifications which would involve least disturbance to his exciting theory would be either (1) the acceptance of an instinct-monism, or (2) the substitution of some other group of instincts for the death-instincts in the existing dualism. In this connection it is interesting to note that in Freud's recent work entitled *Civilization and Its Discontents* (1930) it seems possible to detect the beginning of a change in standpoint. This change of standpoint lies in the direction of the second alternative mentioned above—that is to say, the substitution of another group of instincts for the death-instincts in his scheme. It is true that Freud (1930) does not go so far as to make a deliberate substitution of this nature; but in *Civilization and Its Discontents* (1930), he does introduce the conception of an "instinct of aggression", which may well be destined to replace that of the "Death-instincts" in his theory of instinct: "If it should appear that the recognition of a special independent instinct of aggression would entail a modification of the psycho-analytical theory of instincts, I should be glad enough to seize the idea" (p. 94). He adds, however, in the next sentence: "We shall see that this is not so, that it is merely a matter of coming to closer quarters with a conclusion to which we long ago committed ourselves" (p. 94). In the meantime, therefore, Freud (1930) does not seem disposed to develop the conception of an instinct of aggression further than is implied in the statement that "This instinct of aggression is the derivative and main representative of the death-instinct we have found alongside Eros, sharing his rule over the earth," (pp. 102–103). From this quotation it is evident that Freud still retains the conception of the death-instincts; but it does seem significant that he should have come to regard them as finding their main expression in an "instinct of aggression", secondary though he may hold it to be. Why he should retain the conception of the death-instincts as primary instead of reversing the relationship and making the instinct of aggression primary is difficult to see; for in the same paragraph from which the last quotation is taken we find Freud (1930) writing "In all that follows I take up the standpoint that the tendency to aggression is an innate, independent, instinctual disposition in man" (p. 102). Perhaps the reason is to be found on a previous page, where, after a summary of the considerations which led him to his theory of the death-instincts, he writes: "The conceptions I have summarized here I first put forward only tentatively, but in the course of time they have won such a hold over me that I can no longer think in any other way" (pp. 98–99). Were it not for the hold that the conception of the death-instincts has won over Freud, it is difficult to believe that the train of argument developed in Freud (1930) could have failed to lead him to substitute the instinct of aggression for the death-instincts in his dualism.

The fundamental observation which compelled Freud to recognise the existence of an instinct of aggression is implied in the title of the work *Civilization and Its Discontents* (*Das Unbehagen des Kulture*). It was reflection upon the discontent accompanying the growth of civilization that led him to take this step. The idea of a conflict between the demands of culture and the natural sexuality of man has been familiar to psychoanalytical thought, so long as no profound attempt was made to analyse the psychological nature of the forces productive of culture. The conflict seemed easily enough explained in terms of the prevailing dualism of the moment (conscious and unconscious, the ego and the repressed, ego-instincts and libido, death-instincts and life-instincts). In his most recent works, however, Freud has turned his attention to the task of analysing the factors productive of culture—a task to the accomplishment of which he brought his preconceived theory of the death-instincts as an important part of his equipment. This part of his equipment, however, turns out to be somewhat of an embarrassment in the argument developed in *Civilization and Its Discontents*, for the analysis of culture undertaken in this work goes to show that the process at work in culture itself

> proves to be in the service of Eros, which aims at binding together single human individuals, then families, then tribes, races, nations, into one great unity, that of humanity. Why this has to be done we do not know; it is simply the work of Eros. These masses of men must be bound to one another

> libidinally; necessity alone, the advantages of common work, could not hold them together. [Freud 1930, p. 102]

If then culture itself is a phenomenon of the evolution of the libido, it becomes a problem to explain the extreme antagonism of culture to sexuality. That socialisation of the libido should involve restriction of the individual's sexual life Freud regards as quite an intelligible result of the economics of libido-distribution. But whence arises the bitter antagonism of culture towards sexuality? In attempting to explain this antagonism Freud (1930) feels driven to conclude that it must be due to the presence of some disturbing influence independent of the libido; and that he traces the disturbing influence to the universal presence in men's minds of a powerful instinct of aggression is evident from the following quotation:

> The existence of this tendency to aggression which we can detect in ourselves and rightly presume to be present in others is the factor that disturbs our relations with our neighbours and makes it necessary for culture to institute its high demands. Civilized society is perpetually menaced with disintegration through this primary hostility of men towards one another. . . . Culture has to call up every possible reinforcement in order to erect barriers against the aggressive instincts of men and hold their manifestations in check by reaction-formations in men's minds. Hence its system of methods by which mankind is driven to identifications and aim-inhibited love-relationships; hence the restrictions on sexual life; and hence too its ideal command to love one's neighbour as oneself, which is really justified by the fact that nothing is so completely at variance with original human nature as this. [pp. 86–87]

If then it is the instinct of aggression that stands opposed at every turn to the evolution of the libido, one would have expected Freud to assign to it the place in his dualism hitherto occupied by the death-instincts. As we have already seen, however, Freud is too much in the grip of his theory of the death-instincts to take this step; he therefore compromises by making the instinct of aggression a derivative, albeit the main representative, of the more ultimate death-instinct. The procedure of deriving the instinct of aggression from the death-instincts is made easier for Freud by the fact that (in Freud 1922) he had already seen reason to derive the aggressive component of sadism from the same source. Thus he says: "Sadism is properly a death-instinct which is driven apart from the ego by the influence of the narcissistic libido, so that it becomes manifest only in reference to the object" (p. 69). At the time *Beyond the Pleasure Principle* was written in 1920 it was "manifestations of the destruction instinct fused with erotism" that Freud was concerned to explain; in *Civilization and Its Discontents* what forces itself upon his attention is the "universality of non-erotic aggression and destruction" (Freud 1930, p. 99).

He interprets the origin of non-erotic aggression however in a similar way—as the expression of death-impulses which have become deflected outwards towards external objects. Thus the "innate, independent instinctual disposition" of aggression, which Freud has found to have so stupendous a role in the life of man, is finally brought within the fold of the death-instincts.

It seems a pity, when Freud has come so near to freeing himself from the unsatisfactory theory of the death-instincts that he should have missed the opportunity to do so. Would it not have been more satisfactory, one is compelled to ask, if his recognition of the importance of the aggressive instinct had led him to give it primacy over the death-impulses, and to make the latter the derivative phenomena? No student of psychopathology could reasonably deny the existence of death-impulses, but the conception of "death-instincts" is based upon dubious considerations *derived not from psychology but from biology*. The conception of an aggressive instinct, on the other hand, is founded upon a wealth of *psychological* observations and has received general recognition among psychologists. Would it not be more natural to regard death-impulses (where the existence of such can be substantiated) as instances of the instinct of aggression being deflected *inwards from external objects to the ego* than to regard aggressive impulses as instances of death-instincts being deflected *outwards from the ego to external objects*? It seems doubtful if there is a single psychoanalytic observation at present explained in terms of the instinct of aggression.

While, however, it must be maintained that a dualism of "sex instincts" and "aggressive instincts" would be much more satisfactory from a psychological standpoint than the dualism of "life-instincts" and "death-instincts", the question arises whether any dualistic classification of instinct at all can be regarded as psychologically sound. It is unquestionable that the Freudian dualism of instinct has provided an invaluable working hypothesis for psychopathological theory, at the present this is the only hypothesis that sheds any real light upon the etiology and nature of the psychoses and psychoneuroses. It also provides a hitherto unrivalled working basis for psychotherapeutic practice. Here it may be noted among its advantages for psychotherapeutic practice the fact that a dualism is easily understood by patients. In this fact, however, we may also perhaps scent a danger. Our suspicion of this danger is confirmed when we consider how readily the Freudian dualism in its later forms has lent itself to the explanation of the larger problems of cultural and social evolution. Indeed, the manner in which Freud has come to speak of "life-instincts" and "death-instincts", as "Eros" and "Thanatos", "Love" and "Hate", forces upon us the recognition that he is no longer concerning himself with psychological tendencies, but with *cosmic forces*. We feel that we have left the restricted terrain of psychology behind and have now been carried far into the realm in which philosophy and religion hold their sway. We feel we are in the atmosphere in which the Greek philosophers moved, and are reminded of Empedroles' attempt to explain the universe in terms of the cosmic principles of 'Love' and 'Hate'. We also feel our feet are on religious soil—on the battleground of God and the Devil, Ahura-Mazda and Ahriman, the Spirit of Light and the Spirit of Darkness.

It could hardly be expected that Freud himself should fail to recognise the connection of the dualism which has figured so prominently in religion and his own dualism of Love and Death or Destruction. Thus in *Civilization and Its Discontents* (1930), when discussing his "assumption of the existence of a death-instinct or a destruction instinct" he writes:

> Those who love fairy-tales do not like it when people speak of the innate tendencies in mankind towards aggression, destruction and, in addition, cruelty. For God has made them in his own image, with his own perfections; . . . The devil is, in fact, the best way out in acquittal of God; [pp. 99–100]

And in a footnote Freud adds "In Goethe's Mephistopheles we have quite an exceptionally striking identification of the principle of evil with the *instinct of destruction*." Freud infers here that the religious dualisms are the products of the conflict which rages in men's minds between the libido and the instincts of death and destruction. There is another side to the question, however. Is it not possible that Freud's theory of instinct is itself developing into something of a religious system? A tolerable case might perhaps be made for the thesis that psychoanalysis is at present tending to acquire the character of a religion—with Eros as its God, Thanatos as its devil, and analytic procedure as the means of grace whereby the guilt-oppressed mortal is relieved of his burden of sin reconciled to Eros and freed, so far as is possible for mortals, from the intolerable tyranny of Thanatos.[1] However this may be, dualisms are so characteristically associated with philosophic, religious and ethical systems that their appearance in scientific writings always raises the suspicion that the bounds of strict science have been transcended. The present writer would be the last to dispute the possibility that the mysteries of the Universe may be best understood in terms of a dualism; but such ultimate questions do not lie within the province of psychology as a science, and it seems obvious that Freud's dualistic theory of instinct leads him outside that province.

The question now arises whether an improvement could be effected in the Freudian theory of instinct if it were converted from a dualism into a monism by the dropping of the death-instincts from his scheme. The unsatisfactoriness of the conception of the death-instincts has been noted in

[1]It may be noted in this connection how often the theories of psychoanalysis are described as 'doctrines', e.g., in *Collected Papers, Volume I* (Freud 1924), where we find the sentence "The doctrine of repression is the foundation-stone on which the whole structure of psycho-analysis rests" [WRDF's emphasis] (p. 297).

an earlier paragraph. It has also been pointed out that, if this conception were eliminated from Freud's theory of instinct, the simplest modifications of the theory would be either (1) substitution of some other group of instincts for the death instincts in his dualism, or (2) abandonment of instinct-dualism in favour of an instinct monism in which the libido figures as the universal instinct. We have further noted certain features in Freud's most recent thought which seem to indicate a tendency on his part to lean towards the former alternative; but we have seen reason for believing that along that path lies, not psychological science, but philosophic and perhaps even religious speculation. It is now time to ask whether adoption of the second alternative would prove more fruitful. If the death-instincts are eliminated from the Freudian dualism, is it possible to frame a satisfactory theory of instinct in terms of libido alone? That this alternative has repeatedly presented itself to Freud as a possibility is evident from the frequency with which he makes reference to it in his writings—always, however, to reject it as unsatisfactory. Such a reference is found, for example, in *Civilization and its Discontents* (1930) in a passage in which he outlines the historical development of his theory of instinct, and explains how the introduction of the conception of narcissism necessitated a revision of his earlier classification of the instincts into ego-instincts and sex-instincts. As we have seen, the concept of narcissism involved the resolution of the ego-instincts into manifestations of the libido, with the result that Freud was faced with the alternative of either finding another group of instinct to complete his dualism or embracing an instinct monism. Freud (1930) describes the state of his thought at this stage in the following words:

> Since the ego-instincts were found to be libidinal as well, it seemed for a time inevitable that libido should become synonymous with instinctual energy in general, as C. G. Jung had previously advocated. Yet there still remained in me a kind of conviction, for which as yet there were no grounds, that the instincts could not all be of the same nature. [pp. 96–97]

This conviction led Freud, as we know, to formulate (on biological grounds) his theory of the death-instincts; and, while we may question the validity of this procedure, we must also recognise the essential soundness of Freud's conviction that the instincts cannot all be reduced to forms of the libido.

To reduce all the instincts to libido is equally unsatisfactory in whatever sense the term 'libido' is interpreted. If the Freudian sense of the word is retained, this step involves the thesis that the sexual tendencies are the only innate tendencies in man, and we are left with a theory of instinct which indeed justifies designation of "pansexuality", which has so frequently been applied to the Freudian system by hostile critics. The truth is, however, that Freudian thought depends for its validity upon the assumption that there do exist in the psyche tendencies which are not sexual in character—tendencies which are distinct from the libido from the beginning of life and which come to operate in antagonism to it. Unless the presence of such tendencies is recognised, the fundamental concept of 'repression' is undermined and Freud's distinctive contribution to the understanding of human behaviour, both normal and abnormal, has to be sacrificed. Quite apart, however, from the needs of the Freudian system, it is manifestly not true that the sexual tendencies are the only innate tendencies in man. Locomotion for example is an innate tendency; so are the instincts associated with fear and anger; yet it would be absurd to maintain that these are inherently libidinous tendencies, so long as we interpret the term 'libido' in the Freudian sense. It is, therefore, only when the term is used as Jung uses it that we can attach any reasonable meaning to the idea that all the instincts are manifestations of the libido. In defining the term 'libido' in his "Psychological Types" C. G. Jung (1923) writes "In my view, this concept is synonymous with *psychic energy*" (p. 371).

According to this usage, it is perfectly reasonable to say that all the instincts are channels of the libido, for libido now simply means the energy which manifests itself in all psychical activity, instinctive or otherwise. The view that all distinguishable forms of instinctive activity are simply differentiations of some ultimate psychical energy ("libido", "élan vital", "life-force") need not be disputed. There are many arguments in favour of such a hypothesis, and it has been adopted by many psychologists (among whom Spearman is a conspicuous example). The general theory of mental energy, however, leaves quite untouched the problems with which we are concerned when we seek to classify the human instincts. Whether or no we find the facts of mental life to be simplified for us by the concept of physical energy, there still remains the problem of determining the simplest analysable modes of instinctive activity in which such mental energy manifests itself. The concept of mental energy is thus more or less irrelevant as far as the classification of the instinctive tendencies is concerned. It will only become relevant to our theories of instinct (and that in a secondary way) if it can be shown that mental energy is capable of being diverted, so to speak, from one instinctive channel into another; but, whether such diversion of energy is possible or not, it is important to know what natural channels are open to it as the result of the hereditary endowment of man. To say that there is only one instinct is equivalent, of course, to saying that there are no instincts at all; for if there is no differentiation of instincts, it is plain that the word "instinct" becomes meaningless (as indeed the Behaviourists hold it to be). It is evidently impossible, therefore, to develop a theory of instinct along monistic lines. If we believe in instincts at all, we must endorse Freud's conviction that the instincts cannot all be of the same nature.

Since then there appears to be no satisfactory way of escape from Freud's dualism along the lines of instinct-monism, it becomes necessary to consider other possibilities. We have seen that, if there is such a thing as instinct at all, there must be more than a solitary instinct. But why should we only recognise *two* instincts? If there is a differentiation of instincts at all, it seems inherently improbable that only two should be differentiated in the course of evolution. It is easy, of course, to see how Freud's theory of instinct came to assume the form of a dualism. After his classic discovery of the process of repression, his attention was naturally directed to a consideration of the repressed. His investigation of the repressed showed it to consist of memories, ideas and impulses deriving their significance from the sex-instinct; and the raison d'être of repression was seen to lie in a conflict between the repressed sex-tendencies and the organised self or "ego". Since the process of repression was thus seen to turn upon a conflict involving instinctive tendencies it became necessary for Freud to adopt some working theory of instinct. Feeling that the psychology of instinct was in a drastic state, he fell back in utter perplexity upon Schiller's aphorism "that hunger and love make the world go round" (Freud 1930, pp. 94–95). These two biological principles of hunger and love provided an antithesis between the self-preservative and the race-preservative tendencies, which corresponded in a remarkable way to the antithesis between the repressing forces of the ego and the repressed sexual tendencies. It was thus that Freud came in the first instance to adopt his dualistic classification of instincts into ego-instincts and sex-instincts; and, although the progress of his thought has since led him to substitute the death-instincts for the ego-instincts in his scheme, his theory of instinct has retained its original dualistic character. If then we analyse the circumstances under which Freud came to adopt a dualistic theory of instinct, it is not difficult to see the two main influences by which his thought was determined. These are:

1. the desirability of finding a theory of instinct which should establish the antithesis of the repressing and the repressed upon an instinctive basis;
2. the tendency to fall back upon general biological considerations in the absence of any acceptable psychological theory of instinct.

It is the influence of these two factors and not a detached examination of the whole field of instinctive life that led Freud to adopt his original dualism of the sex-instincts and the ego-instincts; and the influence of the same factors is still apparent in his subsequent dualism of the life-instincts and the death-instincts. The latter dualism like the earlier was adopted to meet a special need of psychoanalytic theory and it was based upon biological rather than psychological considerations. Under these circumstances it is inevitable that the Freudian dualism in all its forms should prove unsatisfactory as a psychological theory of instinct, however useful it may have proved as a working hypothesis in psychoanalytical thought; for it is difficult to see how any theory of instinct dictated by a special purpose and advanced on grounds which are not psychological but biological could satisfy the criteria of psychology. To satisfy these criteria a theory of instinct must above all else satisfy the demands:

1. that it should be based upon a comprehensive survey of the manifestations of instinctive activity as a whole;
2. that it should primarily depend for its support upon strictly psychological considerations.

Psychology is a biological science, but it is not biology. It studies the same facts as does biology but it studies them from a different point of view. Its special province is to interpret the behaviour of living organisms in terms of inner experience. While the facts which it studies are phenomena of behaviour, it interprets behaviour, so to speak, from the inside; and its explanations are mainly couched in terms of thought and feeling. One of the more obvious phenomena of behaviour demanding explanation is the fact that members of the same species tend to behave in certain characteristic ways in relation to certain characteristic situations; some of these situations appear to be in the main externally conditioned (i.e., determined by environmental contingencies); others again appear to be in the main internally conditioned (i.e., determined by well marked organic states). In either case behaviour is more or less specific. In the human species this specificity of behaviour is less marked than in any other species, but even in man a number of very characteristic behaviour patterns may be discerned. It is this fact that has given rise to the theories of instinct *both* in biology and in psychology. All theories of instinct explain the phenomena in question by assuming the existence of innate dispositions which determine the individual to behave according to patterns characteristic of the species; these hereditary dispositions are described as 'instincts'. Biology, however, is interested in instinct rather than in instincts, whereas the reverse is true of psychology. Biology concerns itself with the more general problems raised by instinctive behaviour, e.g., the place and function of instinct in the organic world, the conditions under which instinctive behaviour arose and the steps of its evolution, its utility and weaknesses, its survival value, etc. In so far as the biologist is interested in the classification of instincts, he classifies them (quite naturally and legitimately) according to the role they play in furthering such fundamental biological ends as the preservation of the individual and the maintenance of the species. The psychologist, however, concerns himself with narrower problems. He is less concerned with the general significance of instinct in the organic world than in describing instinctive behaviour as he finds it—particularly in human beings—and formulating the laws which govern it. Above all he is interested in the inner aspect of instinctive behaviour; as a consequence, the terms in which he describes it are predominantly terms of thought and feeling and the laws which he formulates are mainly laws of experience. The psychologist therefore classifies instincts according to the observed patterns which behaviour actually exhibits and according to the nature of the experiences which it affords, quite apart from the biological ends which are served. From these facts it inevitably follows that a strictly psychological classification of instincts must differ widely from a biological classification, and that there is no necessary correspondence between the two. Thus from the biological standpoint, sexual and parental activities may be grouped together on the grounds that both have as their aim the maintenance of the race; from the psychological standpoint they may be distinguished on the grounds that they exhibit different behaviour-patterns and yield qualitatively different experiences. Again, biologically speaking, aggression in the search for a mate falls into a different category from aggression in the interests of self-preservation, whereas, from a psychological standpoint, aggressive behaviour is of the same quality, whatever biological aim it serves. Again while self-preservative aggression and flight serve the same biological ends, they exhibit totally different behaviour and are associated with totally different psychological experiences, as is evident when we consider the difference between the emotions of anger and fear. From what has been said it is thus evident that the Freudian dualisms of ego-instincts and sex-instincts, and of life-instincts and death-instincts, depend upon considerations which are in no sense psychological.

Of all the strictly psychological classifications of instinct which have so far appeared the most satisfactory would seem to be that originally proposed by Dr James Drever in his *Instinct in Man* (1917) and repeated with slight modification, in *An Introduction to the Psychology of Education* (Drever 1922). This classification has the psychological merits of corresponding to recognisable behaviour-patterns and of being based upon an analysis of instinct experience. In these respects Drever's classification is reminiscent of that proposed by Professor William McDougall (1908) in *An Introduction to Social Psychology*. Like McDougall, Drever makes the affective aspect of the instinct-experience central. He differs from McDougall, however, in that he does not regard the affective element of the instinct-experience as necessarily emotional. McDougall writes: "Each of the principal instincts conditions, then, some one kind of emotional excitement whose quality is specific or peculiar to it" (1908, p. 47), and he regards this specific emotional excitement as constituting the affective element of the instinct-experience. Drever (1922), on the other hand, writes: "We have declined to admit that this affective element is emotion, as McDougall contends, while accepting his general teaching, we prefer to designate it 'instinct interest' or 'instinct feeling' " (p. 58).

This does not mean that Drever denies the association of specific emotions with specific instinctive tendencies. He agrees with McDougall in recognising this association; but he regards emotion as only developing out of instinct-interest when a tendency is either obstructed or facilitated; each such tendency is thus regarded as being capable of giving rise to two emotions—a positive "joy" emotion and a negative "sorrow" emotion. Drever thus recognises the existence of instinctive tendencies which have no corresponding emotions;

in the case of such tendencies the instinct-interest never undergoes emotional development, although its obstruction and facilitation do give rise to unpleasure and pleasure respectively. This standpoint enables Drever to bring under the category of instinct many recognisable tendencies which can only be included in McDougall's scheme on the assumption that there exist emotions so colourless as to escape detection. Drever's deeper analysis of instinct-experience thus renders possible a classification of the instincts which is not only better worked out but more comprehensive than that of McDougall.

Although Drever's classification of the instincts is mainly based upon his analysis of instinct-experience, he also takes into account the situations which call for the instinctive behaviour and the manner in which instinctive tendencies operate. The conclusion which he reaches is that several distinct classes of instinctive tendencies may be recognised:

> We can first of all distinguish two great groups of tendencies which appear to differ fundamentally from one another from a psychological standpoint. One group is characterized by the fact that the tendency is evoked by experiences which are disagreeable or agreeable, and, as it were, because of the disagreeableness or agreeableness, while the end sought has reference merely to this disagreeableness or agreeableness. Such tendencies may be designated "appetitive," but of course "aversions" must be included as well as "appetitions". The second group is characterized by the fact that the tendency is evoked as the reaction to a certain object or situation, which is apprehended, while the end sought is with reference to that object or situation, and may be pursued independently of any immediate disagreeableness or agreeableness. This group may be appropriately designated "reactive" as opposed to "appetitive". Theoretically the distinction appears quite clear and valid. When we seek, however, to apply it practically, it is not without its difficulties. . . . But a closer examination of such cases will probably convince us that the distinction still remains. The comparison of hunger with anger will bring it out clearly. Using the word "hunger" to mark the tendency not the complex of sensations we may say that this tendency is directed towards the removal of the "uneasiness" from which it originates. But in the case of anger aroused, say, by a blow, activity is directed not towards the removal of the uneasy sensations caused by the blow, but towards the destruction of the agent from which or whom the blow emanates. . . . In the second place, among both appetitive and reactive tendencies we can distinguish between tendencies which are relatively specific, and tendencies which are relatively non-specific or general. In this case the two types pass into one another as far as the human being is concerned, but at the extremes they are quite clearly distinguishable. The specificity of one type is a specificity both of evoking conditions and of response; the non-specificity of the other type is similarly non-specificity both of evoking conditions and of response. Among the appetitive tendencies hunger and the tendency to prolong or seek agreeable experiences, and among the reactive tendencies fear and play, may be taken as adequately representing the two types. [Drever 1922, pp. 49–51]

Drever thus divides instinctive tendencies into two main groups—'appetitive' and 'reactive', and within each of these groups distinguishes 'specific' from 'general' tendencies. In addition to these two distinctions, however, he points to a third distinction which may be drawn within the sub-group of 'specific reactive tendencies', namely that between 'simple' and 'emotional'. By an 'emotional' tendency he means a tendency which is specific to varying degree as regards situation and response, and which is liable to give rise to specific joy and sorrow emotions, according as its operation is facilitated or obstructed. By a 'simple' tendency he means a tendency which is characterised by a specific response to a specific situation but which never, of itself, gives rise to any specific emotion of either polarity.

In the light of these three distinctions Drever's classification takes the following form:[2]

Table 3-1
Instinctive Tendencies

Appetitive		*Reactive*		
General	*Specific*[3]	*General*	*Specific*	*Simple Emotional*
Unpleasure avoidance	Hunger	Play		
Pleasure seeking	Thirst	Experimentation	Prehension	Flight
	Rest	Imitation	Organ adjustment	Pugnacity
	Exercise	Sympathy	Locomotion	Curiosity
	Sex	Suggestibility (?)	Vocalization	Self Display
	Nausea			Self Abasement
				Parental
				Gregarious
				Hunting
				Acquisition
				Courtship
				Repulsion (?)

The above scheme cannot, of course, be regarded as perfect in detail, but it includes most of the recognisable human reaction-patterns; and it is based upon the view that all forms of human activity have an instinctive basis. The grouping of the instinctive tendencies is interesting and seems to

[2]This table is reproduced from *An Introduction to the Psychology of Education* (Drever 1922, p. 57).
[3]The present writer (Fairbairn) would add the excretory functions of urination and defaecation to this list.

correspond to real distinctions. The relegation of the "emotional" tendencies to a special group enables Drever to bring under the category of instinct all classes of innate human reactions, whether associated with specific emotions or not. Drever thus puts the conception of instinct on a broader basis than does McDougall. Emotion, he holds, is not a necessary accompaniment of instinctive activity. Even in the case of those tendencies which are classed as 'emotional' because they are capable of giving rise to specific emotional states, emotion is seen to be an exceptional rather than a usual accompaniment of their operation. This feature of Drever's conception of instinct must appeal strongly to psychoanalysts, who have arrived independently at a similar conclusion. The distinction of 'general' and 'specific' tendencies is also not without interest from the psychoanalytic standpoint. According to Drever, the general tendencies are tendencies (e.g., play and imitation) which "do not normally determine specific ends or interests, but attach themselves, as it were, to the ends and interests determined by the specific tendencies, more especially those of the 'emotional' group" (Drever 1917, p. 167). Thus, while the general tendency of play may be recognised as having characteristics which 'sui generis', it manifests itself in activities which may be aggressive, sexual, parental, hunting, etc. It is this feature of the general tendencies which "explain the fact that they have no accompanying specific emotion" (Drever 1917, p. 167).

Activity on the part of the general tendencies does, however, modify the expression of the specific tendencies. Thus,

> in a hunting game, for example, there is, in addition to the specific interest, developing it may be into emotion, of the hunting instinct, the play interest itself, which, while it never can itself become emotional, yet modifies throughout both the emotion and the behaviour of the hunting instinct. [Drever 1917, p. 167]

In the operation of the general tendencies, therefore, we find a functional blending of instincts which manifests itself both in objective behaviour and in subjective feeling (interest). Such functional blending of instincts may also be observed to occur where the specific tendencies alone are concerned. Thus, when two or more specific tendencies are evoked simultaneously by the same situation, the specific affects or emotions concerned fuse so as to produce an affective state which, while analysable into its components, is quite distinctive, and the resulting behaviour is a complication of the forms of behaviour of the individual tendencies in question. These fusion-phenomena seem to be regarded by Drever as of considerable importance for mental development. For in formulating seven fundamental laws of mental development in *An Introduction to the Psychology of Education* (1922), Drever makes them the basis of two of his laws—"the law of fusion of feeling or emotion" and "the law of complication of behaviour" (pp. 73–74). Here we are reminded of Freud's conception of the fusion and defusion of instincts, a conception which was foreshadowed in Freud (1922, pp. 68–69) which was expressly formulated in Freud (1923b, p. 79) and which is assuming growing importance in psychoanalytic thought. The most important feature of Drever's classification of the instincts is, however, his distinction between the appetitive and reactive tendencies. This distinction is of considerable interest in the light of psychoanalytic thought and on this account it demands special attention here.

If reference is made to Drever's classification of the instincts with the special purpose of comparing the tendencies assigned to the appetitive and the reactive groups, it will be noted that the two classes of tendency differ in important respects. First and most obviously they differ in the class of situation with which they are concerned. The situations with which the *appetitive* tendencies deal are essentially *internal*, whereas the *reactive* tendencies are concerned with situations which are essentially *external*. The appetitive tendencies are oriented towards the satisfaction of *basic organic needs*, more or less regardless of outer conditions. It is to outer conditions, however, that the reactive tendencies are directed; they are primarily adaptive in character.

In the second place, the appetitive and reactive tendencies differ in the kind of feeling-state which accompanies their activation. The stirring of the appetitive tendencies characteristically manifests itself in consciousness as a state of uneasiness which is perhaps best described as "a craving" (Drever 1917, p. 247). In the case of the specific appetites, the craving appears to have a special quality according to the particular need which demands satisfaction; but the word "craving" appears inappropriate, however, to describe the feeling-states which characterise the reactive tendencies as such. On the contrary, the affective element which is present when the reactive tendencies are stirred is best described as "object-interest". The character of this object-interest differs in the case of the various reactive tendencies—i.e., it differs according as the object is apprehended as preponderantly fearful, thwarting, unusual, etc. In all cases, however, the object-interest differs essentially from the uneasiness of appetite. Here it may be objected that under certain conditions a feeling-state of uneasiness does accompany the stirring of reactive tendencies. This contention may be freely admitted, but it does not compromise the validity of the distinction—as the following three considerations will show.

1. Firstly, it may be pointed out that there is no reason why appetitive and reactive tendencies should not operate simultaneously, each contributing its characteristic quality to the resultant feeling-state. Indeed this phenomenon is far from unusual, where sexual behaviour is concerned it is particularly common to find the appetitive and reactive tendencies of sex

operating in conjunction. Here it must be remembered that in drawing his distinctions Drever is not describing tendencies which operate in isolation; he is merely analysing instinctive experience into its elements. These elements usually occur in combination, but they are none the less distinguishable. A behaviour-scale may be constructed with pure appetitive behaviour at one end and pure reactive behaviour at the other; most behaviour falls at some intermediate point on the scale; but the extremes are easily distinguished. Within the sphere of sex, we find an example of almost purely appetitive behaviour in the act of masturbation. The interest which a man feels in conversing with a beautiful woman, on the other hand, is almost purely reactive in character. Sexual intercourse with a person who is loved, however, involves both the appetitive and the reactive tendencies of sex in intimate combination. It is not every specific reactive tendency, of course, that has, like that of sex, a corresponding appetite; but the general appetitive tendencies of pleasure-seeking and unpleasure-avoidance readily function in conjunction with every other tendency and indeed appear to provide an ever present, though varying, background for the operation of all of them (cf. Freud's "primary process").

2. Secondly, there is no difficulty about admitting that a feeling of uneasiness or craving may complicate the object-interest of the reactive tendencies even where no appetitive tendency is simultaneously stirred. That, under certain conditions, a feeling of uneasiness does occur in connection with the reactive tendencies themselves cannot be disputed. It is certain, for example, that a person in whom the tendency of escape is powerfully stirred experiences just such a sense of uneasiness as is found in the case of unsatisfied appetite. Here, however, it is important to note the conditions under which such a state of uneasiness arises. It occurs in connection with a reactive tendency only when the activity concerned is impeded or frustrated; thus the frightened man only experiences uneasiness in so far as flight is prevented or is ineffective. Now this is precisely the type of situation in which, as Drever points out, emotions of negative polarity (the "sorrow" emotions) develop. The activity of reactive tendencies is thus seen to give rise to uneasiness and to "sorrow" emotions under precisely the same conditions. The conditions are conditions of frustration, i.e., failure of adaptation. The state of uneasiness, therefore, is seen to arise in connection with the reactive tendencies only in as they cease to be adaptive—in other words, only in so far as they acquire an appetitive colouring. From these considerations two important inferences may be drawn:

1. that the reactive tendencies tend to undergo "regression" to a non-adaptive appetitive level when they suffer frustration;

2. that emotion (in its "sorrow" form, at any rate) is essentially a regressive phenomenon.

These two inferences appear particularly significant in the light of psychoanalytic findings for non-adaptive appetitive behaviour and emotionality are characteristic features of the neurotic personality, and we know from psychoanalysis how incapable the neurotic is of tolerating frustration.

3. Thirdly, in considering the possibility of uneasiness arising in connection with the reactive tendencies, we must remember that after all there are such phenomena as "acquired appetites". It is thus possible for experiences provided by the activity of the reactive tendencies to become sought for their own sake apart from object-reference. This phenomenon occurs, of course, only through the cooperation of the general appetitive tendency of pleasure-seeking, which seems (in varying degree) to form a background for all the differentiated forms of instinctive activity. The fact that the general appetitive tendencies underlie the operation of all other instincts need not, however, blind us to the distinction between the "uneasiness" of appetite and the "object-interest" of the reactive tendencies.

A third important distinction between the appetitive and the reactive tendencies is to be found in the manner of their activity. The appetitive tendencies are characterised by a certain *urgency* which the reactive tendencies as such seem to lack; this urgency has doubtless a biological basis, for the appetites are concerned with the most fundamental organic needs. The reactive tendencies, on the other hand, serve subsidiary ends. They give the impression of having been elaborated in the course of evolution to supplement the appetitive tendencies and make them more effective. They appear to have been superimposed as adaptive mechanisms upon the more or less blind appetitive desires. The appetitive tendencies are more primitive and less adaptive. They are protopathic in their sensory and effective aspects and their expression has an explosive character, in accordance with their nature, they demand *immediate satisfaction*; hence their feeling of urgency. It is different with the reactive tendencies. Having been evolved as adaptive mechanisms, they are oriented to outer conditions rather than to inner organic states. In their sensory and effective aspects they are predominantly epicritic; their motor expression is on the whole graded and discriminative. A long sequence of complicated acts (as in sex courtship) have commonly to be performed before their end is attained. Hence, so long as their activity is progressing in the right direction, *delayed satisfaction* is all that they demand. It is true that, in the face of obstructions they may develop an urgency reminiscent of the appetites, but this is the exception that proves the rule. We have already seen that these are just the conditions in which a reactive tendency is liable to undergo appetitive regression through the development of emotion. In the absence of such appetitive regression, the activity of the reactive tendencies is distinguished from that of the appetitive tendencies by a lack of urgency and a tolerance of delay in the satisfaction of instinctive aims.

The appetitive and the reactive tendencies thus differ in respect of:

1. the kind of situation with which they are concerned
2. the kind of feeling-state which characterises them
3. the way in which they seek satisfaction

As regards these points, the appetitive tendencies are seen to possess the following features:

1. the situations which activate them are internal situations constituted by organic needs and the aim of the tendencies is to satisfy those needs
2. the feeling-states experienced in these situations are states of uneasiness or tension best described as cravings
3. the tendencies demand immediate satisfaction

In the case of the reactive tendencies, on the other hand:

1. the stimuli to activity are provided by external situations or external objects, and the aim of the tendencies is successful adaptive behaviour in relation to these
2. the feeling-states experienced in these situations partake characteristically of the nature of "object-interest" rather than of uneasiness
3. the tendencies seek their goal by adaptive behaviour which characteristically involves postponement of satisfaction

When we consider these outstanding differences between the appetitive and the reactive tendencies, we are at once forcibly reminded of Freud's distinction between "the pleasure principle" and "the primary process" on the one hand and the "reality principle" and the "secondary process", on the other. Activity determined by the pleasure principle is seen to correspond to appetitive behaviour, and activity determined by the reality principle is seen to correspond to reactive behaviour. Whichever terminology is adapted, the same facts are being described; Drever's terminology, however, seems preferable to Freud's because it is based upon an analysis of instinctive behaviour in general and issues out of a comprehensive classification of the instinctive tendencies. Drever's terminology also makes it possible to bring psychoanalytic findings into line with general psychology.

While the general correspondence between the above mentioned distinctions is obvious, the question now arises how far correspondence is exact.

The appetitive tendencies obviously follow the pleasure principle, but some expressions of the reactive tendencies would be regarded by Freud as following the pleasure principle also. The difficulty vanishes, however, if we bear in mind what has already been said regarding the liability of the reactive tendencies, when frustrated, to acquire an appetitive colouring with the development of emotion. Such expressions of the reactive tendencies as appear to follow the pleasure-principle really illustrate appetitive regression of this kind, and thus do not upset the correspondence which has been noted between Freud's and Drever's distinctions.

The correspondence between reactive behaviour and activity determined by the reality principle may be better appreciated if we introduce the conception of mental levels. Following Stout (1927), we may distinguish three levels:

1. the perceptual
2. the ideational
3. the rational

The perceptual level is characterised by a 'here and now' consciousness and behaviour at this level is in response to present stimuli, only modified by *implicit* traces of past experience. At the ideational level, behaviour is complicated by the capacity to revive *past* experience *explicitly* in the form of images; in the case of the higher ideational activities the images may take the form of novel combinations of elements derived from former experience. At the conceptual level, behaviour is further complicated by the capacity to apprehend the relationships of situations and objects which are either perceived or ideally represented. The distinction between the appetitive and the reactive tendencies is a distinction belonging essentially to the perceptual level. In the lowest animals behaviour appears to be exclusively appetitive in character. As we ascend the scale of life we note the emergence of reactive tendencies, which become more differentiated and more highly organised the higher we ascend. The appetitive tendencies persist underneath, as the fundamental basis of behaviour even in the highest organisms, but the prominence of the role played by the reactive tendencies is an index of adaptation to reality. So long as the perceptual level is not transcended, however, the reactive tendencies only enable the organism to achieve a moderate degree of adaptation to reality. Innate behaviour-patterns as they are, the reactive tendencies are more or less stereotyped in their manifestations at the perceptual level; for, although learning by experience undoubtedly occurs at this level, it is limited in its scope by absence of the capacity to revive past experience explicitly and to combine and recombine images. In the whole animal world, man appears to be the only species in which ideational processes (as against perceptual processes) play any significant roles; and it is to the development of this capacity that man's immediate ancestors owe that superior power of adaption to reality which gave them primacy in the animal kingdom. One effect, however, of man's attainment of the ideational level is that the outlines of his inborn instinctive reaction-patterns are obscured by acquired habits. It is for this reason that, when we desire to study the native instincts in man, we must concentrate our attention so far as possible upon behaviour at the perceptual level—a fact which has been too often neglected by those attempting to classify the instincts.

The outlines of the instinctive reaction-patterns in man are still further blurred by processes belonging to the conceptual level. The capacity to apprehend relationships between situations or objects and the constituent elements of both is, so far as we know, the highest function of adaptation to reality. It is this capacity which has fashioned for man the mighty instrument of Science, which has made possible for him not only an unparalleled adaptation to his environment but considerable adaptation of the environment to his own needs. In this development linguistic symbols have played the same part as that played by simple sensory images at the imaginative level.

The conception of mental levels has been introduced into this discussion primarily to clarify the statement that reactive behaviour corresponds to activity determined by the reality principle. From what precedes we see:

1. that the distinction between appetitive and reactive behaviour belongs essentially to the perceptual level
2. that, while the appetitive tendencies always remain the fundamental tendencies of human nature, it is by means of the superimposed reactive tendencies that adaptation is effected
3. that the ideational and conceptual levels have been developed in man in the interests of adaptation
4. that while the appetitive tendencies belong essentially to the perceptual level, the reactive tendencies function also at the ideational and conceptual levels
5. that, while the outline of the various reactive tendencies (which can be readily distinguished at the perceptual level) is blurred at the higher levels by the nature of the adaptive process characterising these levels, the instinctive tendencies remain the dynamic of all human activity.

The conception of mental levels thus helps us to understand how "the reality principle" comes to express itself through the reactive tendencies, and how it does so with varying degrees of adequacy. We note how the adaptive function of these tendencies increases as we pass from the perceptual to the ideational and again from the ideational to the conceptual levels. The various levels correspond presumably to phases in the mental evolution of mankind—the higher levels having been superimposed upon the lower as they emerged. A parallel process of mental evolution may be noted in the history of the individual. In the infant the appetitive tendencies largely hold the field, although even in infancy the reactive tendencies are not unrepresented. As development proceeds, the reactive tendencies assume more and more prominence at the same time manifesting themselves progressively at higher levels. It is in this way that the reality-principle gains whatever victory it is fated to achieve.

Unfortunately, with many individuals the victory of the reality principle is all too incomplete, and such fruits of victory as are at one time gained may subsequently be lost. Psychoanalytic investigation has shown this to be what happens in the case of the neurotic. From a psychoanalytic point of view, the neurotic regressive tendency to abandon the reality-principle in favour of the pleasure principle is a tendency which is regarded as being set into operation by the frustration of instinctive impulses. This interpretation gains additional significance, however, if we adopt the distinction between appetitive and reactive tendencies and the conception of mental levels outlined above. We then see that in the psycho-neuroses there appear signs of a general level in mental functioning and of a tendency on the part of behaviour to assume a more appetitive and less reactive character. A marked feature in all cases is proliferation of the ideational at the expense of the conceptual function—hence the prominence of phantasy symbolism and dream. The encroachment of the perceptual upon the ideational function is less obvious, of course, in the psycho-neuroses than in the psychoses. In the final stages of dementia praecox, indeed, mental life appears to have regressed almost completely to the perceptual level; but this is an extreme case. Even in the psycho-neuroses, however, some encroachment of the perceptual upon the ideational functions may be detected—as when, during psychoanalytic treatment, the patient responds not by free association but by re-enacting in his relationship to the analyst situations belonging to the years of childhood. Together with the general lowering in level of the neurotic's mental functions goes the tendency of his behaviour to acquire an appetitive colouring. This characteristic shows itself in a definite strengthening of the appetitive tendencies. Any or all of the specific appetites may become exaggerated, particularly that of sex (as is evident from the role played by masturbation in the neurotic's history); but most prominent of all is the exaggeration of the general tendencies of pleasure-seeking and unpleasure avoidance (described by Freud as the dominance of the "Lust-Unlust" Principle). Reactions become influenced to an abnormal extent by inner organic states, with the result that conduct becomes unstable and inappropriate to outer circumstances; feelings of uneasiness and tension invade consciousness to a disturbing degree; and there is inability to tolerate postponement of the satisfaction of impulses.

Just as psycho-neurosis is characterised by a fall in the level of mental functioning with substitution of appetitive for reactive behaviour, so recovery from psycho-neurosis is characterised by a rise in the level of mental functioning with substitution of reactive for appetitive behaviour. It appears to be because psychoanalytic technique enables such a rise in level to take place that psychoanalysis is so useful in the treatment of the psychoneuroses. Psychoanalytic technique, based as it is upon the Free Association Method, aims at eliciting from the patient trains of thought which are undirected by conscious purpose and influenced by considerations of logic; i.e., it is concerned primarily with processes at the ideational level. In so far as the patient tends to express his deeper trends by re-enacting situations of his early life in relation to the analyst, he is reacting to the treatment at the perceptual level. It is one of the analyst's aims to induce him to revive in memory the original situations upon which his behaviour towards the analyst is modelled. In so far as this aim succeeds, the patient's reactions are being raised from the perceptual to the ideational level. It is not sufficient, however, that certain functions operating at the perceptual level should be raised to the ideational level, for another feature of the neurotic is that his ideational processes (phantasy, etc.) proliferate and run wild at the expense of his conceptual functions. By the use of the free association method the nature, the extent and the intensity of the patient's ideational processes is revealed. Free association as such can do little more than reveal the richness of the ideational processes; and this is probably one of the reasons why auto-analysis is of such limited value. Free association does, however, provide a vast amount of unsuspected material for the conceptual functions to work upon, and thus affords these functions an unusually favourable opportunity of establishing relations between the ideational contents of the mind. For the achievement of this important task the fact that the patient is required to tell the analyst every thought that arises is of quite special importance; for language is a conceptual function and the patient's attempt to express his thoughts in words involves some degree of conceptual mastery of the ideational material. Here it may be remarked that some of the periods of silence which occur in the course of analytic treatment appear to be due not so much to the patient's resistance as to his inability to express his thoughts in words. This difficulty is, of course, more marked when the patient's reaction is at the perceptual than when it is at the ideational level. It is of the utmost importance, however, that the patient should be required to make a maximum effort to express his thoughts and feelings in words; for whatever success he meets in doing this is so far a victory for the conceptual functions. The interpretations offered by the analyst, on appropriate occasions, aid the conceptual function by enabling the patient to grasp more fully the relations existing between his various ideational processes. In this way the material produced in free association is placed at the disposal of the conceptual processes which, as we have seen, constitute the highest manifestation of the reality-function known to us. In "the completely analysed person", who is the ideal man of psychoanalytic thought, all the mental processes of both perceptual and ideational levels would presumably be integrated at the conceptual level.

Now that the distinction between the appetitive and the reactive tendencies has been seen to correspond to Freud's distinction between the pleasure principle and the reality principle, the question arises whether the same distinction may not also find itself represented in the libido theory. When we approach this question, we are at once reminded of the distinction drawn by Freud between the 'aim' of the libido and its 'object'. This distinction was introduced in *Three Contributions to the Theory of Sexuality* (1905c) where the libido theory was originally propounded; and it has played an important part in the subsequent development of psychoanalytic theory. It is now held as an integral part of psychoanalytic theory that in the history of the individual the libido undergoes both a regular process of evolution as regards its object and a regular process of evolution as regards its aim; and the various symptom-complexes found in the psychoses and psycho-neuroses, as well as certain character traits and perversions, are attributed to characteristic disturbances in one or other (or both) of these evolutionary processes.

What Freud (1905c) means by the 'object' of the libido is plain enough; he means an external object (usually a person) to which libido is attached and in relation to which satisfaction is sought. This being so, it is evident that the relationship of the libido to its objects is essentially a phenomenon of reactive behaviour; and in this object-relationship we discern above all the activity of the reactive tendency of sex. It must be recognised, however, that other reactive tendencies besides that of sex are involved. This fact has not escaped Freud's attention, although the part played by other reactive tendencies in the development of the object-relationships of the libido has been obscured by the limitations of his dualistic theory of instinct. Thus he explains the phenomena of sadism and masochism as due to the fusion of the death-instincts with object-libido and ego-libido respectively (Freud 1905c).

If, however, for Freud's instinct-dualism we substitute a classification of the instincts such as Drever's, we must recognise the possibility of countless situations arising in which one or more of the other reactive tendencies will be stirred in conjunction with the reactive tendency of sex. When this happens, we may assume that functional fusion will occur between the simultaneously activated instincts. Some of these other tendencies also will undergo functional fusion with the sex-instinct more commonly than will others. In the case of such of them as are constantly aroused in association with the sex-instinct, it must be inferred from what we know of the laws of mental growth that functional fusion will give rise to more or less permanent connections in the mental structure. The data of psychoanalysis suggest to us permanent connections of this nature are formed in the earliest years of life and certain reactive tendencies in particular become integrated with the sex-instinct in a specially intimate way. Of such tendencies the parental instinct and those of curiosity, self-display, self-abasement and aggression (or "pugnacity" in Drever's terminology) are the most notable. When we consider the manifestations of the parental instinct, we cannot help noting a certain sexual element in the behaviour of parents towards their children; the different treatment accorded by a parent to children of the same and those of opposite sex cannot escape even the most superficial observation. On the other hand, in romantic love we find the sexual attitude influenced by that tender feeling which is characteristic of the parental instinct. The fact that behaviour of a distinctively parental quality appears to be exhibited even by children of tender years (e.g., towards dolls, pets or younger children) makes it possible to surmise an early origin for the association between the sex and parental instincts.

The instinct of curiosity certainly forms intimate connections with the sex-instinct in early years. From this fact it has been inferred that all curiosity is sexual in origin. Observation of the behaviour of animals, however, leaves no doubt that novelty is the element in a situation which stimulates the behaviour characteristic of curiosity. The intimate connection of curiosity with the sex interest in children is best explained as due to the fact that no subject is so closely guarded from childish enquiry as the sexual life of its parents. Here we may discern the operation of an important principle of instinctive life, which is borne out again and again by the facts of psychoanalytic investigation, and which may be formulated as follows—*when an instinctive tendency is activated by an appropriate situation, instinct-interest is intensified in proportion as satisfaction is withheld.* In the light of this principle we can well understand how curiosity comes to be directed with special intensity towards sexual objects; for in no other sphere is satisfaction so consistently withheld. It is interesting to note here how curiosity having once acquired a markedly sexual colouring through frustration may, after undergoing repression, come to be directed again toward non-sexual objects through the process of sublimation.

The closely related but mutually opposed instincts of self-display and self-abasement also form intimate connections with the reactive sex-tendency at an early stage in life. The union between self-display and the sex-instinct finds its most obvious expression in exhibitionism—a phenomenon which for anatomical reasons comes to expression most obviously in the boy. In the girl, on account of the absence of the penis, exhibitionism comes to expression in a less direct form than in the boy. Thus clothes, which in the case of men are exploited in the interests of repression, have an exhibitionistic value in the case of women. The association between self-display and the sex-instinct appears also to have an important bearing upon the formation of the "female castration complex". In the case of the girl sexual self-display is frustrated not only by social convention but by the stepmotherly hand of Nature, who has failed to endow her, as the boy has been endowed, with the magic phallus. If circumstances are unfavourable, the effect of this inferiority is either (1) to stimulate the instinct of self-abasement and produce submissive behaviour towards men, or (2) to stimulate the acquisitive and aggressive tendencies. In the latter case, we find a host of pathological phenomena which have been amply described in the psychoanalytic literature dealing with "the female castration complex". The acquisitive tendency manifesting itself in such symptoms as vaginismus and over-valuation of the only child (who comes to symbolise the penis in the unconscious), while the aggressive tendency manifests itself in frigidity and husband-persecution (the supreme portrayal of which in literature is to be found in Strindberg's tragedy of "The Father"). While the tendency of self-display fuses with the sex-instinct to produce exhibitionistic impulses, the tendency of self-abasement seems to fuse with the sex-instinct to produce behaviour characterised by modesty; and, just as sexual self-display is more marked in men than in women, so sexual self-abasement is more marked in women than in men. In addition to its more obvious influence upon sexual behaviour, the tendency of self-abasement appears to play some part in the production of the phenomenon of "the superego". According to Freud's (1923b) account in *The Ego and The Id*, the superego arises in the child because the parents constitute for him not only object-figures to whom his libido becomes attached but persons with whom he identifies himself in feeling; it is through the child identifying himself with the parents as frustrators of the libido and introjecting this identification into himself that the superego is believed to come into being. It may be surmised, however, that the tendency of self-abasement comes into operation in the formation of the superego. This tendency is one which is readily activated in the child in relation to the parents. The feeling-state which constitutes its instinct-interest is rather difficult to describe in words (perhaps the phrase "sense of submission" describes it as well as any); but, when the tendency undergoes relative obstruction, the negative emotion which develops appears to be that of "shame". When we recall that Freud describes the superego as the source of "guilt", we can appreciate the part played by the tendency of self-abasement in the formation of the superego; for "guilt" as an actual experience is a complex emotional state in which the simple emotion of "shame" appears to be an important constituent.

Of the various reactive tendencies which fuse with the sex-instinct in its object-relationships perhaps none is of such importance as the tendency of aggression. As we have already seen, the importance of this instinct has now been explicitly recognised by Freud, although he still interprets it as but one manifestation of his "death-instincts". It seems probable, however, that, in this interpretation Freud has reversed the real relationship and that such phenomena as seem to support the theory of the "death-instinct" are really expressions of an instinct of aggression. If we make a broad survey of human and animal behaviour in the search for distinctive behaviour-patterns, none stand out with better definition than those appropriate to the instincts of sex, escape and aggression. Unless, therefore, the conception of instinct is abandoned altogether, it seems necessary to recognise the instinct of aggression as one of the best established and one of the most important of instinctive tendencies. Its special importance is none the less recognised by Freud because he calls it by another name. That a peculiar antithesis exists between this tendency and the sex-instinct is evident not only from the facts upon which Freud bases his dualistic theory of instinct but from a study of the phenomena of religious, ethical and philosophic thought. At the root of all religion and philosophy there may be discerned a fundamental dualism which appears clothed in various forms but which consists essentially in the same antithesis. God-Devil, Good-Evil, Love-Hate, Infinite-Finite; all these and other similar antitheses present the same great contrast between a constructive, uniting, integrating force on the one hand and a destructive, dividing, disintegrating force on the other. This fundamental antithesis appears to be represented in the nature of man in the conspicuous contrast between the aims of the sex-instincts and the instinct of aggression. Whether the essential dualisms of religion and philosophy are the product of a conflict between the two instincts in man or whether the contrast between these two instincts is but one expression of an antithesis which pervades the organic world and the universe itself need not be discussed here. It seems reasonable to suppose, however, that the conflict between these two instincts in man arises as the result of a more universal antithesis of cosmic processes. This, however, is not a question for psychology to settle. The fact remains that, while the operation of many distinguishable instinctive tendencies may be discerned in human behaviour, a peculiar significance appears to attach to the relationship existing between the instincts of sex and aggression. This fact is borne out by the results of psychoanalytic investigation; and the importance of Freud's observations remains unaffected by the rejection of his dualistic theory of instinct. It must be insisted, however, that the instinctive tendency to which Freud applies the designation of "the death instincts" is really the tendency of aggression.

Here reference may be made to the fact that a number of psychoanalytic writers, being dissatisfied with Freud's theory of "death instincts", prefer to explain the relevant phenomena in another way.

> The assumption of the existence of a death instinct or a destruction instinct has aroused opposition even in analytical circles; I know that there is a great tendency to ascribe all that is dangerous and hostile in love rather to a fundamental bipolarity in its own nature. [Freud 1930, p. 98]

In accordance with the tendency to which Freud refers, it is assumed that the "hate" element in the well known ambivalent attitude of the neurotic to his love-objects is simply "love" with a negative sign. While, however, love and hate are in a sense opposites in that they involve incompatible attitudes to the same object, it is only a metaphor to say that they are opposite polarities of the same sentiment. The so-called polarity of "love-hate" is not parallel, for example, to the polarity of "joy" and "sorrow" emotions described by Drever. The positive and negative emotions described by Drever arise according as one and the same instinctive tendency is relatively facilitated or obstructed; it is thus strictly accurate to describe them as of opposite polarity. The relation between "hate" and "love" is different. Each has its own bipolarity. Each may develop a positive "joy" polarity if satisfaction of the appropriate impulses is facilitated; each may develop a negative "sorrow" polarity, if satisfaction is obstructed. The joy of satisfied love is not the same thing as the sorrow of unsatisfied hate, nor is the joy of satisfied hate the same thing as the sorrow of unsatisfied love. Yet this would inevitably be the case if "love" and "hate" stood to one another in a simple relationship of bipolarity. We must, therefore, recognise that love and hate are affective phenomena of fundamentally distinct instinctive tendencies; unless this were so, indeed, the concept of ambivalence would contain an inner contradiction. If love is regarded as a phenomenon of the sex-instinct, hate must be regarded as a phenomenon of the instinct of aggression. It is because love and hate derive from separate tendencies that they are able to occur in conjunction in relation to the same object. It is not difficult to see how this occurs. While the appropriate stimulus for the reactive tendency of sex is the presence of a sexual object (or, of course, the idea of such an object), the appropriate stimulus for the aggressive tendency is the presence of an obstacle (or the idea of such an obstacle). The aggressive tendency is thus liable to be activated when any other tendency is baulked or frustrated; for frustration involves the presence of an obstacle. If the frustrated tendency happens to be the sex-instinct, and if the sex-object itself is apprehended as the source of frustration, it is easy to see that the sex-object will also become the object of aggressive impulses. It is in this way that the sentiments of love and hate come to be entertained for the same persons and that a state of ambivalence is constituted. Freud therefore appears to be justified in his conclusion.

While there are thus cogent reasons for drawing a clear distinction between the reactive tendencies of sex and aggression, it must be recognised that in real life important relations are established between them from the earliest period. Such a relationship is found in the phenomenon of ambivalence. Psychoanalytic investigation has traced the origin of ambivalence to the affective relationship of the child to his parents in early years. The parent-figures are the most significant figures in the child's life. They are the first objects of his love, but in so far as they deny satisfaction to his longings (as, to some degree, they inevitably do), they also erect the most formidable barriers which his love encounters. It is also from the parent-figures above all that the child seeks to elicit signs of affection, yet the degree of affection meted out to him is all too liable to leave his exorbitant demands unsatisfied. It thus happens that the child's original love-objects are also the original sources of frustration in his life, and that, by stirring the aggressive tendency in him, they become objects of hate without ceasing to be objects of love. In the normal person this ambivalent attitude is largely outgrown as development proceeds. Under favourable circumstances, however, it may persist and affect the individual's attitude to the love-objects of later life. In the psychoneuroses and psychoses, there appears to be an actual regression to ambivalence on the part of the patient. The relative disappearance of ambivalence in normal development is explained by Freud as due to "fusion" of the love and hate components in the child's attitude to his love-objects. He explains the reappearance of ambivalence in psycho-pathological states as due to a regressive process of "defusion", whereby the fused components separate out again. This interpretation of the phenomena in question appears to provide the best explanation available. Indeed the general conceptions of 'fusion' and 'defusion' may with advantage be given a wider application; for they illumine its relationship of the sex-instinct to other instinctive tendencies besides that of aggression.

Among the resultants of fusion between the two reactive tendencies of sex and aggression the phenomenon of sadism is the most conspicuous. The sexual behaviour of the sadist has a markedly aggressive colouring; and sexual gratification leaves him unsatisfied, unless the aggressive component attains gratification in the sexual act. A certain degree of sadism appears to characterise normal sexual life. Indeed when there is complete absence of all sadistic elements in sexual behaviour, this must be regarded as evidence of repression and it raises the suspicion of an alternative ambivalence. A greater degree of sadism appears to be normal in men than in women. The reverse is true as regards masochism, which appears to have a greater place in the sexual life of the normal woman than in that of the normal man.

We have now seen that, in so far as the libido is directed towards *objects*, it is an expression of the *reactive* tendency of sex complicated by fusion with other reactive tendencies. Let us, therefore, return to Freud's distinction between the 'aim' and the 'object' of the libido and consider whether the 'aim' of the libido may not be derived from the *appetitive* tendencies. Here a certain difficulty is introduced into our discussion by the fact that Freud (1905c) uses the term 'aim' in two different senses. More commonly he employs it to signify "the action towards which the impulse strives" (Freud 1905c, p. 1); but he also uses it in the sense of 'goal', as is evident when he writes "The aim of an instinct (impulse) is in every case satisfaction (1930)." To avoid confusion between the two meanings Dr Healy and his collaborators suggest that the word 'goal' should always be employed instead of 'aim' in its latter sense satisfaction, and that the term 'mode' should be substituted for 'aim' when the former sense is intended, since "the action towards which the impulse strives" (1905c) constitutes the mode in which satisfaction is attained.[4]

Alike where 'goal' and 'mode' are concerned, however, the conception of libidinal aim is bound up with the theory of sexual impulse adopted in *Three Contributions to the Theory of Sexuality* (Freud 1905c). The interpretation of the sexual impulse upon which Freud bases his libido theory is made plain in the opening sentences of this work.

> The fact of sexual need in man and animal is expressed in biology by the assumption of a 'sexual impulse'. This impulse is made analogous to the impulse of taking nourishment, and hunger. The sexual expression corresponding to hunger not being found colloquially, science uses the expression 'libido'. [p. 1]

Here the sexual impulse is described as the expression of a "sexual need" analogous to the appetite of hunger; and we at once recognise in this description a description of the appetitive (as against the reactive) tendency of sex. It is this interpretation of the sexual impulse that Freud adopts in formulating his libido theory. When he speaks of the 'libido' apart from its relationship to an object, we must therefore understand him to refer to the appetitive sex-tendency. That we are justified in this interpretation is further evident from a subsequent passage, where, after reviewing the phenomena of sexual inversion, Freud (1905c) registers the conclusion that "the sexual impulse is probably entirely independent of its object and is not originated by the stimuli proceeding from the object" (p. 31). From this appetitive character of the sexual impulse as described by Freud, follows the appetitive quality of its "aim". "The source of the impulse is an exciting process in an organ, and the immediate aim of the impulse lies in the elimination of this organic stimulus" (Freud 1905c, p. 31).

If we take 'aim' here in the sense of 'goal', the aim of the libido is to achieve satisfaction through such activity as relieves tension or uneasiness of organic origin. The goal of the libido is thus determined by the general

[4]See Healy, Bronner, and Bowers, *The Structure and Meaning of Psycho-analysis*, 1930, p. 91.

appetitive tendencies of unpleasure-avoidance and pleasure-seeking. As regards the 'mode' in which satisfaction is sought, this depends upon the organ concerned in the production of uneasiness. The 'aim' of the libido in the narrower sense of the term is thus determined by the activities appropriate to relieving tension originating in a given organ. This brings us to the consideration of another and very characteristic feature of Freud's libido theory—viz. the conception of partial impulses and erotogenic zones. According to this conception the genitals are not the only organs capable of giving rise to sexually exciting stimuli; on the contrary, any organ of the body is capable of becoming the seat of such stimuli and thus functioning as an erotogenic zone. The study of sexual perversions, however, convinced Freud that this erotogenic function was characteristically associated with certain definite regions of the skin and mucous membranes. Of these the mouth and anus, together with the genito-urinary organs themselves, are by far the most significant. Owing to the pleasures associated with sucking (and later eating) on the one hand and the excretory functions on the other, these regions come to function in the child as "predestined erotogenic zones". Since the 'aim' of the libido (in the sense of 'mode') is ultimately determined by the source of the stimulus, its most significant aims ('modes') are those of genital, anal and oral origin. If then the general aim (goal) of the libido is determined by the general appetitive tendencies of unpleasure-avoidance and pleasure-seeking, we may surmise that the special aims (modes) of the libido are determined by the specific appetitive tendencies.

In the light of these considerations we are tempted to look for a correspondence between the special aims of the libido and the specific-appetitive tendencies. If we now proceed to indulge this temptation, we find ourselves confronted by certain difficulties. The specific appetitive tendencies appearing on Drever's list are those of hunger, thirst, rest, exercise, sex and nausea. The first difficulty which occurs to us, therefore, consists in the fact that, whereas the anal and urinary aims are of great importance for the libido theory, Drever's list of specific appetitive tendencies does not include the excretory activities. These activities, however, are not represented anywhere else in Drever's classification. If they were to be included, there is no doubt about the group into which they would fall. They possess so obviously appetitive a character and the behaviour which they determine is so specific, that there need be no hesitation about including 'urination' and 'defaecation' among specific appetitive tendencies. Drever himself, in a verbal communication, has expressed himself as willing to admit them to this group.

A second difficulty might arise out of the fact that certain of the specific appetitive tendencies included in Drever's list seem unrelated to any of the "predestined erotogenic zones" expressly emphasised by Freud. It might be argued that this could hardly be the case if there really were a correspondence between the specific aims of the libido and the specific appetitive tendencies. This difficulty might perhaps be met by falling back upon Freud's (1914a) claim that "we can make up our minds to regard erotogenicity as a common property of all organs" (p. 41), but it seems desirable that some further effort should be made to dissipate the difficulty. In the case of three out of the six specific appetitive tendencies mentioned by Drever, there is a close correspondence with libidinal aims having their source in well-defined erotogenic zones. The appetite of sex (interpreted in a restricted sense) may be taken to have its corresponding zone in the genital apparatus, while the mouth seems to provide a zone common to both the appetite of hunger and that of thirst. Here it seems appropriate to consider how it comes about that two specific appetites should arise in relation to a single zone. The clue seems to lie in the fact that in the infant at the sucking stage the two appetites of hunger and thirst are undifferentiated. It is only later, when the teeth begin to develop and solid food comes to be sought, that hunger and thirst become distinct and give rise each to its appropriate activity. What actually happens when the teeth appear would seem to be that the appetite of hunger becomes differentiated out of a primitive appetite of hunger-thirst, leaving thirst to represent the original tendency in a modified form. Here it may be noted how much more closely the activity of drinking resembles the primitive activity of sucking than does that of eating. This differentiation of the hunger appetite would seem to give rise to that difference in libidinal aim which, according to the present form of the libido theory, is believed to distinguish the second from the first oral stage of libido-development.

So far, then, as the appetitive tendencies of sex, hunger and thirst are concerned, there is no difficulty in finding a correspondence to certain of Freud's classic erotogenic zones. The same applies in the case of the two excretory tendencies which have been added to Drever's list. In the case of the three remaining tendencies (those of rest, exercise and nausea) our task is not so easy—especially since the main zones have already been allocated to other tendencies. When we consider the tendencies of rest and exercise, however, we cannot help being struck by the fact that these are the only specific tendencies of which we have direct evidence in the case of the infant before birth. All that we know about the behaviour of the unborn child is that periods of exercise alternate with periods of rest. On these grounds alone it seems reasonable to infer the existence of corresponding appetites; but in adult persons also exercise-making and rest-seeking activities seem sufficiently characteristic to justify this inference. Assuming the inference to be valid, we may now ask how far it is possible to find corresponding erotogenic zones. That the satisfaction of the appetites of exercise and rest can give rise to sensuous pleasures need not be doubted. In the welcome "glow" accompanying exercise and the ecstasy of relaxation following effort we seem to experience just such sensuous pleasures—pleasures, moreover, which appear to have a certain specificity. The specific element in these experiences would seem to have its chief sensory source in the musculature. We may therefore regard the musculature as providing an "erotogenic zone" corresponding to the appetites of exercise and rest. From this point of view, epilepsy and catalepsy may both be interpreted as pathological expressions of muscle-eroticism, epilepsy being a phenomenon of the exercise-appetite and catalepsy being a phenomenon of the rest-appetite. The rest-appetite seems also to play an important part in mystical experiences; for in these experiences muscular relaxation is found accompanied by ecstatic pleasure.

The only specific appetitive tendency on Drever's list which has not yet been related to the conception of erotogenic zones is that of nausea. This tendency differs from the other specific appetitive tendencies in that it is not properly an appetite at all but an *aversion*. In spite of its organic origin it gives rise to a sense of uneasiness and, when this uneasiness attains a certain intensity, it demands immediate satisfaction; satisfaction is achieved through the act of vomiting, which relieves the uneasiness and which has as its aim the removal of the organic state which initiates it. In its capacity as an aversion the tendency of nausea is not without parallel among the instinctive tendencies. It shares this feature with the general appetitive tendency of unpleasure-avoidance, and, among the reactive tendencies, with the specific tendency of escape. The parallel between the tendency of nausea and those of escape and unpleasure-avoidance provides some interesting reflections. The process of repression has been shown by Freud to be one expression of the general tendency to avoid unpleasure ("the pleasure principle"). Repression may indeed best be regarded as the characteristic manifestation of unpleasure-avoidance, when the source of unpleasure lies in an inner tendency (as against a stimulus from without). Now Freud has also shown that the tendency to avoid unpleasure in general and the process of repression in particular attain an especial prominence in the lives of those who develop neurosis. Inability to tolerate unpleasure and excess of repression may indeed be regarded as the most characteristic feature of neurotic individuals. There is only one other feature of neurotics which can be said to rival this one in importance; and that is their undue liability to experience distressing anxiety. Anxiety is best regarded as a chronic form of fear; fear in turn is, as we have seen, the negative emotion which recurs when the tendency to escape is at once activated and frustrated. The chief characteristic of neurotics thus seems to lie in hyperactivity on the part of two of the three distinguishable "aversion" tendencies. This raises the question whether the tendency of nausea may not also be unduly excitable in the neurotic. That this is so in the case of hysteria would seem to be borne out by the special liability of hysterics to develop neurotic sickness as a symptom.

The part played by the tendency of nausea in symptom-formation is, however, of secondary interest in comparison with the part which (if the ensuing speculations prove to be well-founded) it may be presumed to play in the initiation of repression and the promotion of culture. The natural stimulus of nausea is disgusting food; and the biological aim of nausea is to prevent the organism from eating unwholesome substance. The chief sensory channel by means of which the disgusting is discriminated is not, however, the sense of taste but the sense of smell. Through this agency of smell the organism is enabled to exclude a number of unwholesome substances from its diet without the necessity of taking them into its mouth. So closely linked is the tendency of nausea with the sense of smell that an unpleasant odour is in itself sufficient to produce the feeling of nausea. This fact may be related to certain speculations recently advanced by Freud (1930) in *Civilization and its Discontents*. These speculations do not form part of Freud's main argument in this work, but they arise out of the conclusion (reached in Chapter IV) that the sexual life of civilized man is seriously disabled:

> It sometimes makes an impression of being a function in process of being atrophied just as organs like our teeth and hair seem to be. One is probably right in supposing that the importance of sexuality as a source of pleasurable sensations . . . has perceptibly decreased. Sometimes one imagines one perceives that it is not only the oppression of culture, but something in the nature of the function itself, that denies us full satisfaction and urges us in other directions. [pp. 76–77]

In a footnote to this passage (p. 77) and in a previous footnote (p. 66) Freud speculates as to what it is in the nature of sexuality that has led to this process of spontaneous atrophy. He concludes that the most important influence at work is the change of attitude towards bodily effluvia which appears to have resulted in the human species from the adoption of the erect posture. On man's adoption of the erect posture the sense of smell, which plays such an important role in the animal world, became completely overshadowed by the sense of sight. This change must have had portentous effects upon the sexual life of men, since in animals it is mainly through the sense of smell that the male is attracted to the female on heat. In man visual impressions have largely come to replace olfactory impressions as stimuli of sexual excitement. To this fact Freud attributes the relative disappearance in man of that periodicity of the sexual impulse which characterises animals; for in the sexual sphere, visual stimuli are more or less constant, whereas olfactory stimuli assume importance at a certain phase in the female cycle. While the sources of sexual excitation have thus largely lost their periodicity for the male, the organic periodicity of the female none the less persists. Its original psychical effect, however, is now reversed. For modern man the menstrual period, with its characteristic odours, deters rather than attracts. The "taboo of menstruation" is thus traced by Freud to the "organic repression" of olfactory stimuli. It is to the same "organic repression" that he attributes the taboo imposed upon "anal erotism". On the assumption that these speculations are well-founded, it becomes a matter of interest to determine the actual mechanism of organic repression. In our search for such a mechanism it is natural for us to recall the connection already noted between repression in general and the aversions of escape and unpleasure-avoidance. The connection of these two aversive tendencies with repression suggests the possibility that the aversive tendency of nausea likewise possesses a repressive function. The suggestion may therefore be hazarded that in the somewhat humble tendency of nausea lies the mechanism of the "organic repression" of which Freud speaks. Of all the innate tendencies probably one is so readily activated by the sense of smell; and, owing to its aversive character, no part of the innate endowment of man seems better fitted to produce that repression of interest in bodily odours which distinguishes man so notably from other mammals. If this be so, it is not difficult to understand the difficulty of relating the nausea-tendency to any of Freud's erotogenic zones. For nausea alone among the appetitive tendencies possesses the character of an aversion.

From the considerations advanced in the preceding paragraphs it would appear that such difficulties as present themselves when we attempt to relate the aims of the libido to the specific appetitive tendencies are by no means insuperable. On the contrary the correspondence seems sufficiently remarkable to justify us in concluding that the various "aims" of the libido described by Freud are determined by specific appetitive tendencies belonging to the innate endowment of man. Similarly, the "erotogenic zones" from which, according to Freud, the aims of the libido derive their characteristic colouring, are seen to correspond to what may be called "the significant zones" of the specific appetites.

II
CHILD DEVELOPMENT AND PSYCHOPATHOLOGY

INTRODUCTION TO PART II

The papers in this section establish a basis for Fairbairn's understanding of child development, an understanding which was advanced and comprehensive for his day. Before an extensive literature on child analysis was begun under the aegis of work by Melanie Klein and Anna Freud in the late 1930s and 1940s, there were few analysts who had much experience with children.

In his obituary of Professor Robertson, the first professor of psychiatry in Britain, Fairbairn wrote 'the best illustration of Robertson's devotion to the ideals of preventive medicine as applied to mental and nervous disease is to be found in his responsibility for the opening of the "Edinburgh University Psychological Clinic for Children and Juveniles" ' and set up with 'the whole-hearted co-operation of Professor Drever'. This clinic was established as a result of Robertson's interest in the work carried out by the original university 'psychological clinic of an informal character' which Professor Drever instituted in 1923 (Fairbairn 1932a, pp. 401, 402).

Fairbairn worked in the Clinic for Children and Juveniles from 1931 to 1935, where he had particularly extensive experience with children subjected to physical and sexual abuse. He had also conducted intelligence testing of 'deaf and dumb' children in Donaldson's Hospital, a large specialist institution in Edinburgh where they were segregated and often thought to be mentally subnormal. A control group for this study consisted of pupils from Edinburgh's most prestigious girls' school. Fairbairn concluded that the IQs of the deaf children were normal.

It is only in the light of these extensive experiences that we can understand the depth of his interest in the early splitting processes—including those of clinical dissociation—which we now believe to be so profoundly accentuated by early trauma. Object relations theory, which sheds so much light on the relationship between the rejecting or persecuting object and the anti-libidinal ego, is rooted in these experiences. The depth of Fairbairn's early clinical work with children makes more persuasive his statement that a child who is in relationship to a bad object feels he is bad because association with a bad object makes the self feel bad (Fairbairn 1944 in 1952b, pp. 63–68). His experience sheds light on the theory of conditional and unconditional badness in which he proposed that a child with a bad object has no hope of improving the situation, that is, feels 'unconditionally bad,' while a child who feels 'conditionally bad' feels the object is only acting badly because the child himself is bad. The 'conditionally bad' child has the hope of improving the situation if he can improve his own 'bad' behavior, while the 'unconditionally bad' child has no source of hope because there is no hope of finding a good object.

CHILD ABUSE

'Child Assault', published in 1935, is a little-known but remarkably forward-looking assessment of the issues of child abuse. We do not know of a comparably thoughtful or well-informed piece in the literature of the time. It aimed not only at making a clinical contribution but also at promoting informed debate on the important but unacknowledged issue of the psychological effects of child sexual abuse. Fairbairn hoped that adequate legislation could be enacted as a consequence of this debate. The most important features of this paper include (1) his emphasis of the nature of the child–adult relationship in relation to child abuse, (2) his classification of each type of activity in terms of degree of its pathogenic effect on the victim, and (3) the classification of effects on the victim in terms of guilt reactions. The violence done to the child is brought about by the inequality between the adult perpetrator and the child victim, not by the mere presence or absence of actual physical force or cooperation (p. 269). Thus, it is in the distorted aspects of the child–adult relationship that the psychological damage resides. Today, we would see it in the violation of physical and mental integrity through coercion by someone the child looks to foster safety and integrity.

Besides being a paper still notable for its common sense, it is prescient in identifying assault on boys as far more common than previously noticed, and in raising the proposition that homosexual assault may be even more damaging than heterosexual. Fairbairn makes the point that society is reluctant to acknowledge these areas of doubly perverse assault. His recommendations for treatment of the victim offer encouragement to rational thinking by caregivers and family, while at the same time he is sensitive towards the perpetrator, who by the definition of having a sexual interest in children must suffer from a perversion and should therefore be accorded psychological evaluation and psychotherapy.

The weakness of the paper stems from the era in which it was written, a time when medical ideas of homosexuality differed radically from those held today. Freud himself supported the view of homosexuality as a nonpathological variant of development, but the predominent psychoanalytic view nevertheless considered homosexuality as deviant, while legal and religious codes defined it as a moral and legal perversion.

Fairbairn was eager that this paper should receive widespread attention. His correspondence documents that he circulated it to various societies and individuals with the aim of promoting social action. One such organization which acknowledged his contribution was the League of Nations.

CHILD DEVELOPMENT AND PATHOLOGY

Fairbairn gave many lectures which document his interest and familiarity with child development and its vicissitudes. We have reprinted three in this section. Taken together with those reprinted as chapters 18, 19, and 20, they indicate the extent of his knowledge and interests.

On 14 December, 1932, Fairbairn presented a talk, 'The Nervous Child,' to the National Council of Women and the Edinburgh Women Citizens' Association. His explanation of the emotional basis of disturbance gives direct illustration of the depth of his understanding of emotional disturbance in children, although this talk was given to a lay audience.

The lecture was a frank polemic with a threefold purpose: (1) to educate women in aspects of nervousness in children and to suggest environmental improvements to avoid its occurrence, (2) to lobby for more resources to be made available for treatment of 'nervous children,' and (3) to reply to a conference he had attended in 1931 on 'eugenic sterilization.' This was a topic of great debate throughout Europe and of particular relevance because of the Nazi regime.

Fairbairn's main thrust is that childish fears and nervousness have a basis in the facts of the child's own experience, although fears also result from children's perception of loss when there has not been a demonstrable outward experience of loss. In either case, these fears are real to the child, even if some fears are the result of misinterpretation by the child due to inexperience. The fear of loss and the accompanying anxiety are identified by Fairbairn as the primary causes of nervousness in children. Situations which exacerbate such fears will cause or increase disturbance on the part of the child.

Fairbairn identifies anxiety as a chronic form of fear and argues that there is no fear without a cause: '[T]he nervous child is simply the anxious child' (p. 192). Fairbairn emphasises that parents and educators who appreciate the world from a child's viewpoint can mitigate anxieties suffered by the child. Situations such as the birth of a sibling should be handled in such a way as to reduce the anxiety of children who understand a new baby as a loss of

Ronald Fairbairn c. 1895–1896

parental attention for themselves. He further suggests that educators should become aware that excessive discipline is also likely to cause anxiety.

'Imagination and Child Development', a lecture to Parents' National Educational Union on 1 February, 1934, is an early piece on the application of analytic thinking to child development and education. It is remarkably advanced for its time and shows Fairbairn's range of understanding and knowledge about child development, as well as demonstrating his capacity to make sense of psychological material for a lay audience.

Fairbairn gave several versions of lectures on adolescence to medical and psychology graduate students between 1929 and 1935. Some are elementary, others extremely thorough. Taken together, they demonstrate his extensive knowledge and interest in physical and psychological developmental processes during adolescence. Much of his information was based on a close reading of the then classical study of adolescence by G. Stanley Hall (1904), but as in all his lectures, Fairbairn added his own thoughts. The lecture on adolescence reprinted here was given to the Missionary College in April 1930. Of all the lectures on this topic, it is the least concerned with a detailed review of the literature and of the details of physical and social development. It also gives the most coherent statement of Fairbairn's own views. It presages his formulation of an object relations view of the personality by considering that it is the adolescent's move from the original family to the family of procreation which is at the center of the reorientation of adolescent interest, brought on and shaped by the new biological capacity for reproduction and its reshaping of the sexual drive.

It is fitting that object relations theory has made sense of the understanding of the way pubertal changes in both boy and girl produce a new and 'strange' body which seems to be another self to the growing adolescent. When the new body has to be integrated into the adolescent's perception of the self, this discontinuity is a central stimulant to the formation of a new identity. Failures in this adjustment lead to a sense of personal estrangement, since the adolescent's own body seems alien, as if a different person has taken possession of the self. While Fairbairn could not flesh out these matters in these early lectures, his contribution of object relations theory lent the tools which have helped others to make sense of these and many other developmental problems.

The final paper in this section is a brief communication from 1953, 'Male Pseudohermaphroditism.' It is a follow-up to the paper in *Psychoanalytic Studies of the Personality* on the analysis of the woman with a genital abnormality, and it demonstrates Fairbairn's continuing interest in the physical aspects of development. Although understanding of the problems of sex role assignment and ambiguous sexual identity in the genetic and hormonal disturbances of physical gender have surpassed what was known in Fairbairn's day, this brief report is reprinted here as a historical footnote to his earlier psychological study.

4. CHILD ASSAULT

The company to which the present remarks are primarily addressed is engaged in considering what further steps should be taken by the community for the moral protection of children. One of the most important subjects for deliberation is the problem of child assault; and I have been invited to discuss this problem in its medical and psychological aspects. I interpret this invitation as indicating some public recognition of the impossibility of treating these two aspects of child assault separately. So intimate is their connection indeed that I shall take as my subject the *medico-psychological* aspect (rather than medical *and* psychological aspects) of the problem of child assault. I shall do so because, if psychological considerations are excluded, such medical problems as remain are of secondary importance only.

In approaching the problem of child assault from the medico-psychological angle we find three groups of problems awaiting our attention. These are (1) the nature and classification of offences, (2) problems relating to the victim, (3) problems relating to the offender.

For the present purpose these problems may be conveniently approached in the light of the 'Report of the Departmental Committee on Sexual Offences against Children and Young Persons in Scotland' (Fleming 1926). With this report as a background, let us review each of the three problems in turn.

I. THE NATURE AND CLASSIFICATION OF SEXUAL OFFENCES

Sexual offences against children may be classified both according to the quality of the act and according to the respective sexes of victim and offender. The following is a list of the chief offences classified according to the quality of the act:

Sexual Offences Classified According to the Quality of the Act

1. Offences involving the natural sex act (other than incest), e.g., rape and defilement of girls.
2. Offences involving manual interference.
3. Exhibitionistic offences involving either
   a. the exposure of the victim, or
   b. the exposure of the offender.
4. Offences involving gross physical perversions of the sex act (i.e., offences in which unnatural parts of the body are concerned).
5. Incest.

All of these groups of offences must be regarded as involving serious psychological consequences in the victim. It is therefore regrettable that, in the 1926 Report, attention is so largely centred upon the group involving the normal sex act, for, while offences of this class are the most obvious, they are neither the most frequent nor, except when they are also incestuous, the most serious in their consequences. The relative frequency of the various offences which we are considering is extremely problematical; but, so far as pathogenicity is concerned, I should arrange them in the following order:

Offences Arranged in Order of Pathogenicity

1. Incest—most pathogenic.
2. Offences involving gross physical perversions.
3. Offences involving the normal sex act (other than incest).
4. Offences involving manual interference.
5. Offences involving exposure—least pathogenic.

Here I venture to submit that, *in so far as the seriousness of these various offences in the eyes of the law does not correspond to their seriousness as judged by psychological standards, changes should be made in the law.*

Offences may also be classified according to the respective sexes of victim and offender. According to this classification two general types of offence may be recognized: (1) heterosexual offences, (2) homosexual offences. Each of these general types includes two sub-groups corresponding to the sex of the victim. Thus we have:

Offences Classified According to the Respective Sexes of Victim and Offender

1. Heterosexual offences.
   a. Committed by a man against a girl.
   b. Committed by a woman against a boy.

2. Homosexual offences.
   a. Committed by a man against a boy.
   b. Committed by a woman against a girl.

The possibility of this second classification makes it desirable to inquire how far the Committee responsible for the 1926 Report were justified in prefacing their consideration of the various classes of offence by the following statement (*vide* §15): "For convenience, we assume generally that the victims are girls. Our statistics include offences against boys—chiefly lewd and libidinous practices—of which no separate statistics are available, but we know the number of detected offences of this kind is very small, and no purpose would be served by considering them separately."

In expressing this opinion the Committee of the 1926 Report appear to differ from the Committee of the English Report 'On Sexual Offences against Young Persons' published in 1925; for in the latter report offences against boys are taken into consideration to some extent. While the Committee of the 1926 (Scotland) Report were obviously not blind to the prevalence of offences against boys, I cannot agree with them that no purpose would be served by considering such offences separately. On the contrary, I interpret the fact that the number of detected offences of this kind is so small as a special argument in favour of further inquiry. If the problem of sexual offences against children is to be satisfactorily dealt with, it is essential to ascertain the prevalence of all classes of offence. My own observations have driven me to the conclusion that *offences against boys are much commoner than offences against girls.* If my conclusion is correct, it seems to me important that it should be publicly recognized.

There is another important fact distinguishing offences against boys, viz. the fact that, *while offences against girls are generally heterosexual in character, offences against boys are usually homosexual.* While, therefore, offences against girls appeal more to the popular imagination, offences against boys are more unnatural. The fact that public opinion is less alive to the prevalence of offences against boys seems to me attributable only in part to the fact that offences against boys are more difficult to detect. It is also due in part to the fact that offences against boys do not involve the risk of what may be described as a "traumatic pregnancy"; but it is chiefly due, in my opinion, to the existence of a "blind spot" in the public conscience for such offences. The existence of such a blind spot may be illustrated by the case of a young man who was charged with indecent exposure before women. Two women happened to be in the vicinity, and it was the complaint of these women that led to the charge being laid. The fact of a boy being present was ignored. Yet the presence of the boy was the keynote of the offence. It required only a superficial psychological examination to show that the offender was a homosexual, and that it was the presence of the boy that conditioned the exposure. When the facts of a homosexual offence are forced upon public attention in an unmistakable fashion, as in the trial of Oscar Wilde, the public feeling aroused is proportionate to the unnaturalness of the offence; but, otherwise, it is less disturbing to the public conscience to ignore what is not thrust upon public notice. It may be formulated as a general principle that, *the more unnatural an offence is and the greater the abhorrence in which it is held, the stronger is the tendency of society to ignore its existence unless it is forcibly obtruded upon public attention.* This is but an example of the wider psychological principle that, the more unpleasant a fact is, the more the human mind tends to ignore it, so long as it is capable of being ignored.

It is impossible to determine the exact proportions of the four groups of offences to which I have just called attention; but it is quite possible to form a rough estimate of their comparative frequency. I should estimate their comparative frequency as follows:

Comparative Frequency of Heterosexual and Homosexual Offences

1. Homosexual offences against boys—extremely common.
2. Heterosexual offences against girls—common.
3. Heterosexual offences against boys—uncommon.
4. Homosexual offences against girls—rare.

Perhaps I should add that this estimate of frequency takes no account of those cases in which infants are sexually stimulated by unscrupulous women. Although this practice appears to be common in the East, it is impossible to estimate its prevalence in this country; but it is probably commoner than is usually recognized. If taken into account, it would swell the number of offences falling into the categories of heterosexual offences against boys and homosexual offences against girls. So far as older children are concerned, homosexual offences against girls are very seldom recorded; but cases in which women take advantage of boys are less uncommon. I recall a case of the kind which came under my notice some years ago. A boy of about twelve presented himself at the out-patient department of one of our hospitals with the story that he had been kicked on the sex organs at football, and had been sent to get the injury attended to. The so-called injury turned out, however, to be an obvious manifestation of primary syphilis. The true facts of the case were difficult to elicit, as the boy stuck to his story with great pertinacity; but eventually he revealed the fact that he had been taken advantage of by a woman who lived in the same house. This woman had made a practice of coercing him into such sexual relationships as he was capable of, and it was from her that the boy had acquired venereal infection. His natural reticence regarding the source of infection turned out to have been reinforced by powerful threats.

This case is significant, not only as indicating the possibility of heterosexual offences against boys, but also as challenging us to inquire what constitutes an assault. An offence of this character, committed by a woman against a boy, obviously demands a certain degree of co-operation on the part of the boy—much more co-operation than is necessary in the case of an offence committed by a man against a girl. This raises the question of how far co-operation on the part of the victim affects the gravity of an offence. In answer to this question, I submit that, where the offender is an adult and the victim a child of, say, under fifteen years of age, the psychological nature of the offence is unaffected by the question of consent or co-operation. It is to be remembered that there are other forms of coercion besides physical violence, and that children are eminently suggestible, especially where a grown-up person is concerned. The authority and prestige of an adult in themselves have a considerable coercive value for the child. It is upon this fact, rather than upon the effects of physical force, that parents and teachers rely in the training of children. *When the authority of an adult is employed to induce a child to co-operate in a sexual offence, it is difficult to see that the psychological character of the offence is in any way affected by the mere absence of physical violence*—particularly if, as is so commonly the case, persuasion is accompanied by threats or the promise of rewards. Here again it seems desirable that the provisions of the law should conform to psychological principles.

From what has emerged from our discussion of the nature of sexual offences, I would select the following statements for special consideration:

1. Public concern over offences which involve a normal sex act tends to distract attention from offences which may be more serious.
2. The more disturbing an offence to the public conscience, the less likely it is to attract attention.
3. Although homosexual offences are both more unnatural and more frequent than heterosexual offences, the public conscience is more sensitive to heterosexual offences.
4. Although offences against boys are commoner than offences against girls, the public conscience is more sensitive to offences against girls.
5. While offences against girls are usually heterosexual, offences against boys are usually homosexual; i.e., irrespective of the sex of the victim, the offender is usually male.
6. The psychological nature of an offence remains unaffected by consent or co-operation on the part of the victim, if the victim is under about fifteen years of age.

II. PROBLEMS RELATING TO THE VICTIM

The chief questions demanding consideration under this heading are (1) the effects of sexual assault upon the victim, (2) the after-treatment of the victim.

1. The Effects of Sexual Assault upon the Victim

What are the effects of a sexual assault upon the victim? According to the 1926 Report (§ 128): "The after effects of sexual assault or malpractice vary greatly with the nature of the offence and the temperament of the victim. Such an experience may induce fear, disgust, hysterical anxiety, or sexual perversion in varying degrees."

This statement may be accepted as giving a sufficiently accurate description of the facts, but it requires expansion. The emotional reactions of fear and disgust represent, of course, *immediate* effects, while hysterical anxiety and sexual perversion represent two characteristic forms of *after*-effect.

As regards the immediate effects, it would be more accurate to say that the emotional reaction of the victim is one of mixed feelings. On the one hand, the experience tends to satisfy an inborn instinctive tendency, viz. the sex instinct; on the other hand, the experience usually arouses feelings of horror, disgust and shame—a group of feelings which may be conveniently classed under the general heading of "anxiety". The relative proportion of these two conflicting groups of emotional reaction varies from case to case, but it is usual for the anxiety reaction to predominate.

The remote effects or sequelæ of a sexual assault completely eclipse the immediate effects in importance. As in the case of the immediate effects, so in the case of the remote effects two conflicting types of emotional reaction may be distinguished. On the one hand we have a group of reactions dependent upon the stirring of the sex instinct; on the other hand we have a group of reactions characterized typically by anxiety. Which of these two groups of reaction shall dominate the picture appears to depend upon the extent to which *guilt* is activated in the child's mind. If little guilt is activated, sexual behaviour is promoted. If much guilt is activated, mental conflict will ensue and some manifestations of anxiety will inevitably develop. I speak of "guilt" rather than a "sense of guilt", because one of the great discoveries of modern psychopathology is that the conscious sense of guilt is no adequate measure of the burden of guilt in the mind. In other words, guilt may be largely unconscious. If, however, unconscious guilt becomes sufficiently intense, it produces reverberations in consciousness; and these reverberations usually take the form of neurotic anxiety and other nervous symptoms.

It may be taken as an invariable rule that, whatever other effects a sexual assault may have, it powerfully reinforces the sexual propensities of the victim. No child is free of sexual propensities in some degree, and a strong sexual stimulus cannot fail to activate these propensities. In the absence of the inhibiting influence of guilt, therefore, some form of sexual behaviour may be expected as the sequel of an assault. Of such sequelæ the commonest are as follows:

Common Sequelæ of Assault in the Absence of a Guilt Reaction

1. Bad sexual habits of a personal kind.
2. Heterosexual behaviour characterized by licence and lack of restraint; e.g., in females, prostitution; in males, rape and defilement of girls, consort with prostitutes, etc.
3. Perverse sexual practices of varying degrees of gravity; e.g., exhibitionism, homosexual practices.

On the other hand, when the activation of sexual impulses in the victim is accompanied by a profound stirring of guilt, the sequelæ characteristically take the form of nervous symptoms such as the following:

Common Sequelæ of Assault in the Presence of a Guilt Reaction

1. General nervousness and anxiety.
2. Special fears, e.g., fear of the dark, fear of being alone, fear of going to school, fear of germs.
3. Sleeplessness and nightmares.
4. Nervous habits, e.g., bed-wetting, nail-biting.
5. Nervous twitching and restlessness.

While the two types of after-effect which I have just described, i.e., the "sexual" and "anxiety" types, must be regarded as distinct and indeed alternative forms of reaction, yet they are not mutually exclusive; for they may occur in all degrees of combination, according to the varying proportions in which sexuality and guilt are stirred by the assault. It should be added that the fact of an assault being experienced at the hands of an adult markedly aggravates both types of after-effect in the child. Adults as a class are naturally regarded by children as the source of all the prohibitions and taboos imposed upon the child's behaviour. An assault by an adult thus introduces an anomaly into the child's world. On the one hand, it produces demoralization; on the other hand, it intensifies mental conflict, and thus enhances the probability of neurotic developments.

2. After-treatment of the Victim

The after-treatment of children who have experienced a sexual assault presents at once a difficult and an important problem. The Committee responsible for the 1926 Report were unanimously of opinion (*vide* § 130) that, except when the offence is actually committed by a parent, "most of the victims will get the best after-care if they are left with their parents in their usual environment". This opinion seems to be psychologically justified; for to remove the child from its usual environment only serves to make it feel that it is being victimized for an offence which was really committed against it, and thus to intensify guilt or create resentment. It is undoubtedly a wise policy that, in accordance with the Committee's recommendation, the usual tenor of the child's life should be interfered with as little as possible. I cannot help feeling, however, that the Committee were less happy in their unqualified pronouncement that "it should be part of the duty of the doctor who examines the girl[1] to advise the parents not to discuss the incident with her in any way, but to help her to forget all about it". This recommendation seems to me to require qualification in the light of modern psychological knowledge.

The opinion that the victim should be encouraged to forget the traumatic experience "as soon and as completely as possible" also appears in § 128 of the Report; but here it is prefaced by the wise advice that the child should "be led to take a sensible view of the occurrence". What the Committee would regard as "a sensible view" is unfortunately not specified; but, if what they have in mind is the promotion in the child of an objective and unemotional attitude towards the experience, their advice is in complete conformity with psychological findings. Apart from the provision of safeguards against the risk of future traumata, *nothing in the way of after-treatment could be more important than to encourage the victim to substitute an objective attitude towards the traumatic experience for the emotional attitude which naturally arises in the first instance.* It is because it is so extremely important for the victim to achieve this objective attitude that I take exception to the unqualified statement that the child should be encouraged to forget the incident as soon and as completely as possible. The Committee's recommendation was, of course, inspired by a very proper desire to prevent parents making sensationalistic capital out of the assault of a child, and so aggravating the intensity of the child's emotional reaction. At the same time it must be pointed out that to encourage the child to forget the incident is really to make the incident a taboo subject; and one of the most marked features of a taboo is that it makes objectivity of attitude impossible. No subject upon which the taboo of silence is imposed can possibly be regarded unemotionally, and a "hush-hush"attitude

[1]An example of the preoccupation of the 1926 Committee with offences against girls.

to an incident which is already overcharged with emotion is simply calculated to endow it with a still further emotional charge.

An unqualified recommendation that the victim of a sexual assault should be encouraged to forget the occurrence appears to be based on the assumption that the banishment of a painful memory from consciousness is equivalent to its banishment from the mind. This, however, is very far from being the case, as is shown by the fact that traumatic memories which have been forgotten are capable of revival. That such memories are capable of revival is perhaps the most surely established finding of modern psychotherapy. All recent advance in the understanding and treatment of neurotic disorders is based on the discovery (made by Breuer and Freud over forty years ago) that nervous symptoms can be relieved by the bringing to consciousness of highly emotional memories which have been completely forgotten. It was found to be a feature of such memories that they were uniformly painful in character; and it came to be recognized that it was the painful nature of these memories that led to their being forgotten. It further became apparent that such memories were not so much "forgotten" in the ordinary sense as "repressed" or banished from consciousness owing to their being the subject of intense emotional conflict. What happens, therefore, when a painful memory is repressed is simply that it is, so to speak, driven underground into the depths of the mind, where it is inaccessible, instead of remaining on the surface, where it can be dealt with. It may now be taken as established (1) that there exists a natural tendency in the mind for memories associated with painful emotional conflict to be actively repressed from consciousness, and (2) that excessive repression of such material provides the conditions necessary for the development of subsequent nervous symptoms.

The chief task of modern psychotherapy consists in an attempt to revive repressed emotional conflicts. The object of this procedure is twofold: (1) to relieve the inner tension underlying "nervous" symptoms by promoting the discharge of the super-charged emotions attached to repressed mental conflict, and (2) to promote the insight necessary for a conscious solution of mental conflicts which, so long as they remain unconscious, must necessarily remain unresolved and so pathogenic. If, then, it has been found that nervous symptoms can be relieved by the revival of material which has already been repressed, it seems undesirable to encourage a child to repress conflictful material which is still fresh in the memory, and which is capable of promoting neurotic developments in the event of repression.

It is important to recognize that the repression of individual memories is only an incident in the repression of mental conflicts associated with such memories. The ultimate object of repression is the banishment from consciousness of the conflicting elements themselves. As we have already seen, the usual effect of an assault upon a child is not only to stimulate sexual impulses, but also to activate guilt. Guilt is activated quite irrespective of any cooperation or consent in the act on the part of the child, because the average child has learned to regard everything to do with sex as a forbidden subject. Here then we have a conflict between the sexual propensities on the one hand, and all that stands for guilt on the other. So far as repression takes place, both the sexual propensities and the guilt are simultaneously repressed in a state of emotional tension, with the result that, though the conflict disappears from consciousness, it continues unabated in the depths of the mind. Not only does it continue unabated, but it is actually increased in intensity, for, since the conflicting elements are denied expression, their pressure inevitably rises. The result is that, down in the depths of its mind, the child grows at once more sexual and more guilty, and thus becomes a candidate for neurotic symptoms in the future. In order that this eventuality may be avoided, it is of the utmost importance that every effort should be made to prevent excessive repression occurring, as it is so liable to do in the victim of an assault. The measures best calculated to achieve this end would appear to be the following:

1. The parents should be advised to adopt an unemotional and matter-of-fact attitude to the incident, in order that guilt may be mitigated and grounds for reticence may be reduced; for it must be remembered that the ultimate source of both guilt and reticence is fear of parental disapproval.

2. An unobtrusive effort should be made to provide the child with an opportunity to ventilate the memory of the traumatic incident, and to work off its emotional reactions in an atmosphere which is free both of sentimentality and of moral indignation; if the parents cannot be relied upon to adopt the requisite attitude, arrangements should be made for some appropriately qualified person, during the course of an interview, to represent the traumatic incident to the child in its proper perspective.

III. PROBLEMS RELATING TO THE OFFENDER

Let us now turn our attention from the victim to the offender. In the case of the victim our attention was occupied with *effects;* in the case of the offender our attention will be occupied with *causes*. If therefore our sympathies naturally ally themselves with the victim, yet the offender is the more deserving of our study; for it is the offender himself after all who constitutes the ultimate problem. It is particularly important that, in approaching the subject of the offender, we should temporarily divest ourselves of all feelings of moral indignation and strive to attain an objective outlook. If, following tradition, we give ourselves over to moral indignation, our energies are more likely to be occupied in devising punishments for the offender than in discovering how offences are caused and how they may be prevented. In what follows I propose to consider (1) causative factors in the offender, (2) the treatment of the offender.

1. Causative Factors in the Offender

The ultimate source of sexual offences is the sex instinct—an instinct which is universally present in mankind, and which forms part of man's instinctive endowment. While this statement may appear a truism, it is perhaps less obvious, although equally true, that civilization is a complicated and precarious mechanism for controlling man's various instinctive tendencies—particularly, perhaps, those of sex and aggression (two tendencies which come to simultaneous expression in the act of sexual assault). These instinctive tendencies, if allowed uncontrolled expression, would of course render social life as we understand it quite impossible; and it is only through the operation of inhibition and repression—mental agencies which function as barriers to the natural expression of instinctive impulses—that social redirection of these impulses can possibly occur. Part of the price we have to pay for the advantages of living in a civilized society is our constant exposure to the risk of a breakdown of repression, accompanied by a break-through of primitive impulses in the case of either social groups or individuals. When such a break-through occurs in the case of an individual, society regards him as a criminal; and he becomes a criminal either (a) because character-formation has been so weak and repression so inadequate as to leave the primitive tendencies insufficiently tempered, or (b) because repression has been so excessive as to deny all expression to primitive impulses until they reach a state of explosive tension. Sexual offences committed by adults against children well exemplify just such a break-through of primitive tendencies, which have failed to undergo normal modification in the course of development and have persisted in a distorted and exaggerated form.

It will be noticed that throughout I have gone upon the assumption that the offender is an adult. This assumption has been made, *not* because the offences under consideration are more commonly committed by adults than by children (for the contrary is the case), but (1) because, as we have already seen, offences committed by adults are more serious in their consequences upon the victim, (2) because such offences indicate a more serious departure from normality when the offender is an adult. Sexual behaviour on the part of children partakes largely of the nature of play, and is due to the stirring of inborn propensities which have not yet been brought under proper control. Sexual offences committed by adults are the expression of the same propensities which dictate sexual behaviour in children, but they fall into a different category for two reasons: (a) because a greater measure of control is to be expected of a grown-up person, (b) because a child does not constitute a natural sex object for a mature individual.

In the light of these considerations we seem entitled to draw certain general conclusions:

1. Offences should be evaluated in relation to the normal developmental history of the sex instinct; i.e., offences which may be regarded as relatively slight aberrations at an early stage of development must be regarded as gross aberrations at a later stage of development.
2. The adult offender is distinguished by an absence of the relationship which normally exists between the strength of the sex impulses and the factors controlling these impulses.
3. Such a disturbed relationship between the strength of the sex impulses on the one hand and controlling factors on the other may be due either to an abnormal strength of the sex impulses or to defects of character formation, or (as is commonly the case) to both of these causes.
4. The adult offender is further characterized by an arrest in the normal development of the sex instinct; and this arrest in development imparts to the sex instinct a primitive character, which, in an adult, is definitely unnatural, and which may even be regarded as perverse.

If these conclusions are justified, it becomes a question whether any grown-up person committing a sexual assault upon a child (other than an assault upon a maturing adolescent of opposite sex) can be regarded as a normal person. In other words, the question arises whether such an offence is not in itself evidence of abnormality in the offender. This question cannot be answered by reference to any available criminal statistics, for we have no guarantee, under prevailing conditions, that the proportion of offenders found to be irresponsible on the grounds of insanity and mental defect (the only grounds which are at present regarded as justifying such a finding) provides any indication of the real situation. Such a question could only be answered if every offender were submitted to an adequate medico-psychological examination—which is very far from being the case at the present time.

Further pursuit of this topic would inevitably lead us to a discussion of the vexed question of criminal responsibility. This question is too far-reaching to be discussed in the present instance; and, in any case, the concept of criminal responsibility is a legal rather than a psychological concept. I submit, however, that the question of criminal responsibility is less important than a knowledge of how crime is motivated, how it may be prevented, and how the criminal should be dealt with both in his own interests and those of the community.

So far as concerns our present subject, I shall refrain from making any pronouncement regarding the proportion of offenders who should be held irresponsible on medico-psychological grounds. Nothing can be more certain, however, than that many offenders who are at present committed to prison should be dealt with as medical cases. I shall content myself with drawing attention to the chief forms of abnormality which appear to dispose offenders to commit sexual offences against children. These are:

Abnormal Conditions Predisposing to Sexual Offences against Children

1. Insanity.
2. Mental defect.
3. Encephalitis lethargica.
4. Epilepsy.
5. Perversion.

I shall say a few words about each of these conditions.

1. *Insanity*. No one, I think, would be inclined to dispute that an offender who is found to be demonstrably insane should be treated as a medical case rather than as an ordinary criminal. On this point legal and medico-psychological opinion are in complete accord. From such statistics as are available, however, it would not appear that many offenders come under this category. According to the figures quoted in the 1926 Report, out of 1343 cases traced by the police during the three years to July 31st, 1924, only 20 offenders (i.e., 2½%) were found to be insane. More reliability may be attached to this figure than to other figures relating to offences against children, because an insane offender is more likely both to be brought to book and to be recognized as abnormal than any other class of offender. At the same time a certain proportion of offenders who are only in the incipient stages of insanity are bound to escape recognition in the absence of routine medico-psychological examination.

2. *Mental defect*. Overt mental defect, like insanity, is generally recognized as a condition justifying the treatment of an offender from a medical rather than a penal point of view. According to the figures quoted in the 1926 Report, however, mental defect would appear to be an even rarer condition than insanity among offenders. Out of the 1343 offenders traced by the police in the triennial period already mentioned, only 3 (i.e., about ¼%) were found to be mentally defective. It is impossible to place much reliance upon this figure for two reasons: (1) It is difficult to believe that the incidence of mental defect among offenders (about 2 per 1000 according to the above figure) is so much lower than its incidence in the community as a whole (about 8 per 1000

according to the Lewis Report of 1929). (2) In the absence of a routine psychological examination, it is unlikely that any but the most glaring cases of mental defect will attract notice.

One great difficulty accompanying any attempt to assess the significance of mental defect among offenders arises out of the fact (so frequently ignored) that mental defect is not an entity but a matter of mental level, and so subject to graduations. In this connection it may be pointed out that mental level is most conveniently and most practicably assessed in terms of native intelligence. There are all degrees of intelligence from genius to idiocy, just as there are all degrees of height from gigantism to dwarfism. There is an average intelligence, just as there is an average height; and, just as a dwarf is a person who is unusually short of stature, so a mental defective is a person who is unusually short of intelligence. To ask how low a person's intelligence must be to qualify him as mentally defective is like asking how small a person must be to qualify him as a dwarf. In both cases the standard is arbitrary and depends upon purely practical considerations. The highest category of mental defect recognized in the Mental Deficiency Act of 1913 is that of "feeble-mindedness"; and feeble-minded persons are defined as "persons who require care, supervision and control for their own protection and for the protection of others". According to psychological convention, any person with an intelligence which is less than 70% of the average is regarded as mentally defective.

If I seem to have digressed, I have done so deliberately on account of the misconceptions which prevail on the subject of mental defect. There is an erroneous tendency, even among many who ought to be better informed, to regard mental defect as a well-defined entity, and to attach too much importance to the part it plays in the causation of all sorts of social ills, including those which we are now considering. This development I feel to be unfortunate, because it distracts attention from much more important factors. Thus a whole section of the 1926 Report is devoted to mental defect in the offender, to the exclusion of conditions which play a much greater part in the causation of offences. After all, the vast proportion of mental defectives are docile and harmless enough, as a visit to any ordinary institution for mental defectives will soon convince the dispassionate observer.

At the same time there can be no doubt that the figures quoted in the 1926 Report give a very inadequate indication of the prevalence of mental defect among sexual offenders. In the absence of routine psychological examination, as I have already indicated, only the most glaring cases of mental defect will attract attention. Yet, so far as sexual offences are concerned, the high-grade defective is undoubtedly a greater menace than the low-grade defective. Low-grade defectives are neither so numerous nor so likely to be at large in the community. Further, they have not sufficient intelligence to make them really dangerous. High-grade defectives, on the other hand, have sufficient intelligence to commit a serious assault, while they lack ordinary self-control. Still more dangerous is that large group of individuals who stand on the borderline of mental defect without actually crossing the borderline, and who accordingly fall outside the provisions of the Mental Deficiency Act. Such individuals, combining as they do a sufficiency of intelligence with an insufficiency of self-control, are, so far as my experience goes, much more likely to commit sexual assaults than are out-and-out defectives.

The mention of borderline cases draws our attention by an easy transition of thought to a class of offenders who constitute a very special difficulty. I refer to the group of so-called "moral imbeciles". In the Mental Deficiency Act of 1913 moral imbeciles are defined as "persons who from an early age display some permanent mental defect coupled with strong vicious or criminal propensities on which punishment has had little or no deterrent effect". This definition has been the subject of endless criticism. Indeed, nowadays, it is rare to find anyone who has a good word to say about it. For one thing, the category created by this definition is redundant, since a person who from an early age displays some permanent mental defect can be certified as defective quite irrespective of any vicious or criminal propensities which he may display. The mere existence of a redundant category is, of course, harmless enough; but in this case the result is disastrous, for the definition excludes from the category of moral imbecile the very class of case for which the category should be reserved. It excludes individuals who, while *not* displaying any marked defect of intelligence, yet *do* display strong vicious and criminal propensities which cannot be influenced either by punishment or by any other measure. The great danger of such individuals consists precisely in the fact that their vicious and criminal propensities are *not* combined with any other mental defect. It is their intelligence that makes them so particularly dangerous.

This class of individual presents a very real problem. So far as my experience goes, a much greater proportion of sexual offenders belong to this category than to any legally recognized category of defective. In the present state of the law, it is quite impossible to deal with such offenders in a satisfactory manner. They cannot legitimately be brought under the categories of insanity or mental defect; yet to treat them as normal persons is out of the question. Ordinary penal treatment is perfectly useless both from the remedial and from the preventive point of view; and it is unfair both to the offender and to the community—to the offender because he is incapable of self-control, and to the community because, after the offender has served the usual sentence, he leaves prison more inclined to commit fresh offences than when he went in (this being his typical reaction to enforced restraint).

3. *Encephalitis lethargica.* One of the most distressing conditions which are found to predispose to sexual offences is the disease of encephalitis lethargica, popularly known as "sleepy sickness". This is an acute endemic disease which

affects the brain, and which as a rule leaves this organ permanently damaged. In the case of those attacked in early life one of the most unfortunate sequels of the disease is found to be an impairment of self-control accompanied by an intensification of primitive urges. In such cases uncontrolled behaviour is particularly liable to manifest itself in the sexual sphere, with the result that many post-encephalitics become sexual offenders. I recall one case in particular—the case of a youth who for nearly two years kept the mothers of a whole district in a constant state of apprehension lest their young daughters should be assaulted. Owing to defects of the Mental Deficiency Act as it applies to Scotland, and to a lack of co-ordination between the various authorities then concerned (the education authority, the parish authority and the police), this youth was able to roam about committing countless offences in spite of the efforts of his parents to keep him under control and to induce the authorities to take action. This is just the sort of offender who might have been certified as a moral imbecile under the Mental Deficiency Act, were it not for the defects in the definition of a moral imbecile which I have already pointed out.

4. *Epilepsy*. A certain proportion of sexual assaults are undoubtedly committed by epileptics. While the most obvious symptom of epilepsy is the epileptic fit, the fit is merely an acute episode which brings to a focus a fundamental characteristic of the epileptic's nervous constitution, viz. explosive activity. On the mental side, the epileptic displays a personality quite in keeping with his nervous constitution. He is liable to passionate outbursts, which are sometimes of extreme violence. He is also liable to states of aberration in which he may commit all sorts of impulsive acts, including sexual assaults. What proportion of offences against children are committed by epileptics it is difficult to say in the absence of detailed information; for, when an offender is known to be an epileptic, he is usually brought under the category of either insanity or mental defect according to his mental status.

5. *Sexual perversion*. A perversion is a persistent form of sexual behaviour which deviates from the natural sexual behaviour of a mature adult in one or both of two respects, viz. (1) the nature and quality of the sex act, (2) the nature of the sex-object. Thus exhibitionism is a perversion affecting the nature and quality of the sex act, while homosexuality is a perversion affecting the nature of the sex-object. From what I have already said regarding sexual offences against children, it will have been gathered that many of these offences are essentially perverse in character. Indeed, if I am correct in my conclusions regarding the relative frequency of the various classes of offence, it would appear that the majority of offences are committed by perverts.

According to recent views, the various perversions have their origin in ideas and tendencies which are to some extent natural among normal children, but which, under certain conditions and in certain individuals, become grossly exaggerated and persist into adult life in a distorted form. Perversions are thus essentially primitive and immature forms of sexuality, resulting from a failure on the part of the sex instinct to undergo the normal process of development. Such an arrest of development on the part of the sex instinct is always found to be accompanied by defects in character formation, which compromise the pervert's capacity of self-control, so far at least as the perverse tendencies are concerned. In consequence, these perverse tendencies acquire a certain compulsive quality, which can hardly fail to be recognized by those who have devoted sufficient study to the subject.

The fact of a sexual offender being a pervert is not regarded in law as affecting the question of his responsibility, or as entitling him to be regarded as a pathological case. If, however, perversions are due to an arrest of development on the part of the sex instinct, it is difficult to see why the pervert should not be put in the same category as the mental defective so far as responsibility is concerned. If the mental defective suffers from a general failure of development chiefly affecting his intellectual status, the pervert suffers from an equally serious failure of development—one affecting not only the sex instinct, but character itself. In the present state of the law, it is only in rare cases that perverts can be dealt with under the provisions of the Mental Deficiency Act. It would seem appropriate, however, that perverts should be regarded as falling under the category of "moral imbecile"—a category outside which most of them fall at the present time. In my opinion, it is high time that changes were made in the law to permit of perverts as a class being brought within this category.

In what I have said regarding perversion as a factor predisposing offenders to commit sexual assaults upon children, I have so far been considering only those classes of offence which would be generally recognized as perverse. Assuming, however, that I have established my point regarding these particular classes of offence, I now venture to suggest that *the category of "perversion" should be extended to include all classes of sexual offence committed by adults against children, even when the offence involves an otherwise normal sex act,* except only when the victim is a maturing adolescent of opposite sex to the offender, and the act is otherwise normal. I submit that, since a child does not constitute a natural object of overt sexual behaviour on the part of an adult, such behaviour in itself constitutes a perverse act.

2. The Treatment of the Offender

If I have little to say regarding the treatment of the offender, this is not because I regard the subject as unimportant. It is rather because what I have to say is already implied in what has gone before. If I am justified in my view that sexual assault committed by an adult upon a child (other than a normal sex act committed against a maturing adolescent of opposite sex) is itself a form of perversion, then the following conclusions seem to be legitimate:

1. Offenders should be treated from a medical rather than a penal standpoint.
2. All offenders should have the advantage of such therapeutic measures as are best calculated to promote the cure of their condition.
3. Offenders who cannot be cured should be segregated under other than penal conditions.

Even if I am wrong in my suggestion that the sexual assault of a child by an adult is itself a form of perversion, there can be no doubt that a large proportion of offenders are definitely abnormal. I therefore regard it as a minimum requirement that *every adult who commits a sexual assault upon a child should be submitted to a routine medico-psychological examination* by a competent authority.

5. THE NERVOUS CHILD

You have heard from previous speakers in the Series of Lectures about various groups of *problem children*—(1) mentally defective, (2) physically defective, (3) blind, (4) speech defects. Today I am to speak about the Nervous Child. The nervous child differs from most of the children comprised by the other groups, and conspicuously from those belonging to the *mentally defective* group in a very important respect, namely *curability*.

A great deal can be done—and ought to be done—for all these groups of children, but mental defect and blindness, for example, are incurable conditions. These disabilities can certainly be alleviated and, to some extent, compensated for; but they can never be cured.

Nervousness in children, on the other hand, is essentially curable. I do not say that the nervous child can be cured of nervousness under existing conditions. But in so far as the nervous child cannot be cured, this is largely because *facilities* for such cure are practically *non-existent*.

In itself nervousness in children is essentially a curable condition. The problem of the nervous child is, therefore, of supreme *importance*. However, the importance of the problem has not received the recognition which it deserves. For example, it is almost impossible to take up a newspaper without seeing some *reference to mental defect*.

Public authorities throughout the country provide special schools and special institutions at enormous expense. Yet there is no provision made for the nervous child.

This fact constitutes an *anomaly* of the most serious kind. For the mentally defective is necessarily bad material; while the nervous child is often exceptionally *good material*. Some of the greatest men in history have been nervous children: no great man has ever been a mentally defective child. Yet, while public authorities in Great Britain spend thousands of pounds annually upon defective children, they spend nothing upon nervous children.

This anomaly is all the more serious because nervous children appear to be more numerous than mentally defective children. From my personal observation at the Psychological Clinic[1], of the first one hundred children I found:

Nervous Symptoms in 51%
Mental Defect in 11% } 19%
Low Borderline in 8% }

Thus a relatively *small* group of *useless* children, who must be a burden on society, are given preferential treatment over a relatively *large* group of children who, although a drag upon Society on account of disability, are *potentially valuable* members of the community.

It is time that the anomaly of this situation should be brought home to the social conscience. The fact is that the community has neglected the nervous child. The remedying of this public scandal is a task which should appeal specially to the *women* of the country. I should appeal above all to those women in whom a social consciousness is most developed. I am, therefore, particularly glad of the present opportunity to present the problem of the nervous child to a branch of the National Council of Women.

DEFINITION

At this stage, I should like to define what is meant by the term "Nervous Child". There is this virtue in definitions that, the attempt to frame a definition helps us to clear up confusion in our own minds and leads us to concentrate upon *main issues*.

What do we mean, when we apply the epithet "nervous" to a child? We mean the same thing as when we say "Mrs So and So is very nervous in traffic", or when we ask a friend "Do you think you would be nervous in an aeroplane?"

When we use the term "nervous" in such sentences, we mean "anxious". We mean that "Mrs So and So is very *anxious* in traffic", or "Do you think that you would be *anxious* in an aeroplane?" The "Nervous Child" is then the "Anxious Child", that is the "Child suffering from Anxiety".

What in turn is *anxiety*? Anxiety is a form of *Fear*. It is a *chronic* or sub-acute form of Fear. Fear is an acute emotional state which we are all liable

[1]The original Psychological Clinic at Edinburgh University was established by Dr Drever in 1923. A Psychological Clinic for Children and Juveniles was established under the auspices of Professor Robertson (see Introduction to Part II, page 159). It was opened on February 18th 1931. Fairbairn worked at both clinics 1927–1935. But he was particularly associated with the latter. It was Professor Robertson's interest in Fairbairn's earlier work which resulted in his inauguration of the clinic for Children and Juveniles in 1931.

to experience in face of sudden *danger*. It is accompanied by an impulse to *escape*. When danger passes or escape is affected, fear normally subsides.

If the danger is very sudden and very great, Fear takes an extreme form, which we call "panic", this is a familiar phenomena when, for example, there is a fire in a theatre, or a volcanic eruption! If, however, we are subjected not to a sudden and acute danger but to a *prolonged threat* of danger, i.e., a *chronic* or persistent danger, then our fearful emotion, while still present takes a modified form. It takes the form of anxiety.

Anxiety is always liable to develop into Panic when a threatened danger materialises. So-called "Night Terrors", to which nervous children are liable, are examples of Panic occurring when dangers underlying habitual anxiety materialise in a dream.

The relationship of anxiety to panic may easily be understood when we consider a passenger on a liner, who would experience panic in a wreck, and who would ordinarily experience only anxiety in a storm. There are persons, of course, who experience anxiety if they are on a ship at all even in an open sea in calm weather. We call such people "nervous people". They are people for whom even quite ordinary experiences constitute *sources of danger*. Such people are specially liable to fear reactions. An apparently *remote threat* of danger is sufficient to rouse in them that state of apprehensiveness, short of actual fear, which we designate as anxiety.

Similarly, the nervous child is a child who acts as if he lived more or less constantly under a threat of danger, even when there is, in our eyes, *no obvious source* of danger present.

"THE NERVOUS TEMPERAMENT"

Now that we have before us a clear definition of what is meant by the term "nervous child", we are in a position to pass to the consideration of the problems which he presents. Obviously the first question to be settled, if the subject is to be dealt with intelligently, is whether nervousness is *an inborn characteristic*. We hear a lot about "The Nervous Temperament". Is there really such a thing?

This is an important question. If nervousness is inborn there is only one radical cure—eugenic breeding. If, however, nervousness is not inborn, then it should be possible to prevent it from developing by *modifying the conditions* which produce it, and to alleviate it by modifying the conditions which maintain it.

In attempting to answer this question of nervous temperament, we must recognise in the first place, that *individuals vary* enormously in their innate endowments. This is certainly true as far as *physical characteristics* are concerned—height, etc. Individuals are also known to vary in such *mental* endowments as *Intelligence.*

It is only reasonable to assume that they vary equally in mental endowments of an *instinctive* character, for example, aggressiveness and the *Instinct of Escape* from danger. We must assume that people differ in their *sensitiveness* to danger, their liability to the emotion of *fear*, and the readiness with which they take to flight. But, given the existence of temperamental differences in these respects, does it therefore follow, we may ask, that persons in whom the fear mechanism is sensitive are necessarily "nervous" or "anxious". To this question, the *best modern researchers* give the answer "No".

To make this clear, let us take an analogy from the sphere of physical disease—the liability to the emotion of fear may be compared to the liability to a disease like tuberculosis. It used to be thought that *tuberculosis* was inborn in certain individuals. This was assumed to be the case because it was noticed how frequently children of tubercular parents were tubercular. It is no longer believed that tuberculosis is inherited. The fact that tubercular parents so often have tubercular children is explained in other terms:

1. The *susceptibility* to tuberculosis may be inherited.
2. Children of tubercular parents are often infected by their parents *after birth.*

The fact that nervous children are so often children of nervous parents may be similarly explained:

1. Sensitiveness of fear-mechanism may be inherited.
2. Children may be made anxious through being brought up by anxious parents after birth.

Let us examine these two considerations in more detail.

1. The Susceptibility to Danger Situations and the Sensitiveness of the Fear-Mechanism May Be Inherited

One of the most remarkable effects of the Public Health Movement has been the fall in the death rate from tuberculosis. For not only has the death rate from T.B. decreased, but the incidence of the disease has decreased. This improvement in Public Health has been effected, *not* by preventing tubercular persons having children (eugenics), but through the *removal of the sources of infection*:

a. The radical *treatment* of those actually suffering from T.B.
b. Preventive measures of a general kind, e.g., the improvement in the purity of the milk supply.

The incidence of *nervousness* in children could be enormously reduced through similar measures:

a. Satisfactory *treatment* for those suffering from anxiety symptoms.
b. The *modification of conditions* which tend to produce anxiety.

2. That Children May Be Made Anxious through Being Brought Up by Anxious Parents after Birth

When a nervous child is brought for examination, it is common for the mother to say, by way of explanation of the child's condition—"You know, doctor, he (or she) was a "*War baby*". There is a general impression among mothers that children born during War tended to be nervous.

What truth is there in this popular theory? The idea in the mother's mind seems to be that the child could be affected before birth by war conditions in some obscure way. Some mothers it is true seem to relate the child's nervousness to their own anxiety. But they usually regard the influence at work as ante-natal. There is no real evidence that anxiety can be communicated from mother to the unborn child. But there can be no question about the influence of the mother's anxiety upon the child *after* it is born. The truth of the "war baby" theory would seem to be that the anxious mother communicates her anxiety to the child through her attitude to it, and her treatment of it during infancy. The anxious mother makes an anxious child.

There is a *common fallacy* that the infant is *too young* to take on impressions of the environment. Nothing could be further from the truth. The *younger the child is, the more impressionable it is.*

It is a commonplace that, for grown-up persons, that *first impressions* of, for example, a new place, or new person are particularly difficult to change. It should not cause us surprise, therefore, if the child's first impressions of the world are the most difficult to change of all impressions throughout life.

The *infant's environment* is a restricted one. His social environment may be said to consist almost exclusively in his *relationship to his mother.* He *depends on* Mother for satisfaction of all his requirements; and consequently his emotional life comes to centre upon his contacts with her. *His loves, his hates, his fears* are all related to her person. *Consequently* the child is particularly *sensitised* to his mother's own emotional attitude. Nothing in the mental sphere is so *infectious* as the *emotional attitude* of those with whom we are in contact. This is the secret of "crowd psychology".

It is difficult to avoid being infected by the emotional attitude of the group in which we find ourselves—we experience joy, sorrow, anger, fear. For the infant, the *mother largely takes the place of the crowd, the group, the society.* Thus the child readily assimilates the Mother's emotional state. The sensitivity of the infant may be appreciated when we consider how readily a child cries when a stranger lifts him. This is because he senses something unusual about the way he is lifted. Similarly the manner in which the mother habitually handles the child does not fail to make an impression on it. In this way the Mother's anxiety becomes communicated to the child.

These considerations should make us *careful about ascribing nervousness* in children *to an inborn "nervous temperament"*. The assumption that the nervous child is nervous because it is born with a nervous temperament certainly provides the *easiest explanation* of his nervousness. It also simplifies the problem of treatment. If the child is nervous because he is born nervous, then there is little to be done; *the child is nervous and that's that*, anything that we do for him must follow the lines of what we do for the defective child.

This solution, however, falls under suspicion just because it is simple. It *relieves us too easily of responsibility* in the matter of the nervous child. It allies itself too readily to a *policy of despair*. From what I have said, however, it will be seen that we cannot shelve our social responsibility for the nervous child by regarding his nervousness as simply the expression of an inborn temperament.

So far as the "nervous temperament" goes, the most that we can assume is the *presence in certain children of an undue sensitiveness* of the fear mechanism, an *unusual intolerance of danger*. It does not follow from this that such children must necessarily develop into "nervous children". For this to happen, there must be *factors present to set the fear mechanism into operation* and to maintain it in operation.

It is to such factors that we must look for the origin of nervousness in children. It is to such factors that we must turn our attention if we desire either to apply remedial measures to the child who has become nervous, or (still better) if we desire to prevent children becoming nervous.

ENVIRONMENTAL FACTORS IN THE GENESIS OF NERVOUSNESS

The *real situation* with which we are faced then is this—some children by nature provide *more suitable soil* than others for the development of anxiety. If the *seed of anxiety* is to develop, however, it requires to be sown. It thus becomes a problem of mental and social hygiene; we need, so far as is possible, to prevent that seed being sown. Similarly, it becomes a problem of therapeutics to eradicate, so far as possible, the seed that has already begun to sprout. Our attention thus becomes directed to the influence of *environmental factors* in the life of the child.

When we leave the thorny and disputed territory of heredity, and turn our attention to the more familiar and better explored territory of environmental influence, we approach a region over which we have a measure of control. It will be time to tackle the problem of the nervous child from the standpoint of heredity, *when* everything possible has been done to eliminate environmental causes of nervousness in children, through the education of parents, who are the main determining agents in the environment of the child, and by modification of conditions outside the home.

When we come to consider the part played by environmental factors in producing nervousness in children, *two important considerations* must be borne in mind. These two considerations find apt expression in two familiar proverbs:

1. "One man's meat is another man's poison".
   We must avoid judging children by adult standards.
2. "There is no smoke without fire",
   i.e., There is no fear without a source of danger.

1. We must avoid judging children too much by adult standards. What is *alarming to a child is not necessarily alarming to us;* the reverse, of course, also holds good—what is alarming to us is not necessarily alarming to a child, e.g., a Mills bomb, or "Blissful ignorance". Children and adults assess danger by different standards. What it is most important to realise is that situations which seem trivial to us may seem to be full of danger to the child.

This fact is largely due to the *limited experience of the child*, and to the *immaturity of his intelligence*. It is characteristic of the child that he is unable to appreciate the *remote consequences* of events. His mental life is essentially of a "here and now" character. The meaning which things and events have for him corresponds to the impression which they make upon him from this restricted point of view. His attention is concentrated upon *immediate effects*. This fact may be illustrated in relation to the *visit of a doctor*.

We know, that, if we have a sore throat, it is important for our own welfare that our throats should be examined; and we call in the doctor to examine us and to prescribe treatment, which may be unpleasant but which we are willing to submit to, because it will save us suffering in the end. Such rational considerations do not weigh with the child. To the child the doctor is liable to be regarded simply as a strange, and therefore, potentially *dangerous person*, who comes in and always does unpleasant things. To the child, even such a simple operation as the examination of his throat is taken at face value and interpreted as an *assault*.

To us it seems stupid of the child to cry and struggle and to show signs of fear over a simple medical examination. This is simply because a medical examination *does not mean the same thing* to us as it does to the child. To understand the child's reaction, we must feel ourselves into the *child's point of view*. If we do this, we shall find that many situations which appear ordinary enough to us are situations full of danger to the child.

2. "There is no smoke without fire". In assessing the importance of environmental factors in the production of nervousness in children, it is important to go upon the assumption that *every fear has a cause*. We are familiar with the phrase "groundless fears". In a sense, there is no such thing as a groundless fear. Where there is anxiety, we must assume the existence of a *source of danger*.

As a matter of fact, the phrase "groundless fear" covers two different meanings which must not be confused:

1. A fear arising without any source of danger.
2. An *irrational* fear.

Now it is important to realise that, whereas many fears (perhaps most fears) are groundless in the second sense, no fears are groundless in the first sense. A fear may be irrational, but no fear arises without a source of danger. If there is no obvious cause for fear, this merely means that the cause is hidden; but there is some cause, if we can find it.

That an irrational fear is not really groundless may be illustrated in the case of the *savage's fear* of an eclipse of the sun. Such a fear seems absurd in the light of modern scientific knowledge. We know that an eclipse of the sun is simply due to the moon passing between the sun and ourselves—a perfectly harmless and natural event, an event as harmless and natural as a man passing between ourselves and the sun. It must be remembered, however, that the savage frequently experiences a sense of danger if the shadow of another person falls upon him. We only regard the eclipse as harmless in virtue of a *background of modern science*. Science offers us a natural explanation of eclipses and makes it possible for the occurrence to be foretold. For the savage, however, an eclipse has quite a different background. For him the background is a *world of capricious and easily offended spirits*. He is ignorant of the real cause of the eclipse and he cannot predict it. It takes him unawares. He does not know what it may lead to. Believing as he does that all events are due to the action of spirits, he interprets an eclipse as a sign of a spirit's displeasure. The eclipse is thus a danger signal and he is very naturally afraid.

It is for similar reasons that the savage is afraid of another person's shadow. He is afraid of the shadow because he believes that the shadow can transmit an evil influence from the other person.

The *fears of the child* fall into the same category as those of the savage. His mental processes are of a similar character; and, like the savage, he is largely *ignorant of the real causes of events. His fears like those of the savage are frequently irrational*. Even *civilised adults* are not altogether free of irrational fears. For superstitions are simply fears of this kind, for example, it is seen as unlucky to walk under a ladder, or to seat thirteen people at a table. *Ignorance and the primitive mentality of the child* favour the development of irrational fears. That such fears, however, are *not without an adequate cause* may be gathered from the study of the case of a nervous child.

The case of Margaret Smith—whose symptoms were: *Fear of going to school* and *Anxiety Attacks*:

- —there was nothing in her life at school which seemed adequate to account for her anxiety
- —her mother was overanxious and fussy: the girl had been delicate and her life had been despaired of in infancy
- —when the child was a few weeks old her mother had been removed to hospital
- —the child was sent to a Baby Home where she was neglected
- —when the baby returned home she was very ill: she required the greatest care and was very dependent

Interpretation

This was not a case of fear of school, but of fear of leaving home; her fear of leaving home was her fear of losing her mother.

Objection

The child was old enough to know the unlikelihood of this.

Reply to the Objection

She had already lost her mother at an age when she could not understand the real situation; for when a mother leaves the room, the infant has no guarantee that she will return. When a child is hungry he has no guarantee of being fed any more than a traveller lost in the desert has. The present child *had* lost her mother. She experienced discomfort and bad treatment in the absence of her mother, and had received constant attention on her return.

Early experiences are forgotten so far as conscious memories are concerned, but traces persist in the depths of the mind.

The truth of the interpretation of this girl's case is substantiated by subsequent events:

- —the child was unwilling to go to Sunday School
- —her parents went out for a walk on Sunday afternoons
- —the parents made attempts to persuade the child
- —the child said that she would not go, unless the mother stayed in, saying "If you aren't in, I'll think something has happened to you."

The study of such a case as this ought to convince us that, *however irrational* the anxiety of a child may seem, it is *not really groundless*, if we consider the *child's point of view*. *Where there is anxiety, there is always some source of danger* for the child.

The fact that what constitutes the source of danger to the child may not constitute a source of danger to us is beside the point. It is the child's point of view that we must consider, if we desire to gain any understanding of the problem of nervousness in children.

SUMMARY OF FUNDAMENTAL CONSIDERATIONS

It has been my endeavour to make plain to you the fundamental principles which must underlie any intelligent attempt to understand the problem of nervousness in children. Let me summarise them:

1. The nervous child is simply the anxious child. Nervousness is a state of anxiety; and anxiety is just a chronic modified form of fear, a persistent apprehensiveness of danger.
2. Nervousness is not an inborn characteristic. The only intelligible meaning attaching to the conception of the "nervous temperament" is that some children are born with a more sensitive fear-mechanism than others.
3. Many situations which are not ordinarily sources of anxiety to the adult are quite naturally sources of anxiety to the child; this is due to the immaturity of the child's mental processes, his lack of experience and his limited knowledge.
4. There is no fear without a cause. All fear is a reaction to danger; and the appearance of anxiety in a child is itself proof of the presence in the child's life of some source of danger, however irrational this may seem from the adult point of view.

The recognition of these principles is, in my view, essential to the understanding of the problem of the nervous child. Their recognition is also essential to the success of all measures directed towards the prevention and cure of nervousness in children. If I have convinced you of this, I shall feel that the purpose of this lecture has been served.

SOURCES OF ANXIETY IN CHILDREN

Before I close, however, it seems desirable that I should give some indication of the *sources of anxiety* in children. It is unnecessary for me to draw attention to the *more obvious and unusual dangers*, which, in certain cases, threaten a child and cause a fear-reaction—for example, overt cruelty on the part of drunken parents; sexual assaults on young girls; or starvation.

It is not only in children subjected to such extreme and real dangers that anxiety states develop. On the contrary most of the children who suffer from anxiety states are brought up under *apparently ordinary conditions.* It is therefore important to consider the *less obvious sources of danger* which may arise for the child.

One extremely significant fact which commonly escapes attention is that the *manner in which the child enters the world* is one calculated to produce a fear-reaction. Experience of birth is probably the most alarming experience of life, and he responds to this experience, very naturally and appropriately, by *crying.*

It seems likely that, throughout life, we are all unconsciously *striving to regain that state of security and bliss* which characterise ante-natal, as contrasted with post-natal, life. This is most evident in the young child, whose life is dominated by a striving to *attain the equivalent* of the ante-natal state of bliss in a hard and unsympathetic world.

There appear to be *two great equivalents* which the young child seeks in life, to *create the illusion* of the Garden of Eden from which he has been expelled—(1) Security and (2) The affection of his parents. Any situation which seems to *threaten his security* or to threaten him with the *loss of love* is a potential source of danger to the child. Here it is important also to recognise that what matters is *not so much the situations*, with which he is faced, in themselves as the *nucleus* which these situations provide *for phantasies.* The conditions for the weaving of such *phantasies* are provided by the imaginative character of the child's mental life and his ignorance of reality. The result is that, out of an incident which seems ordinary enough to an adult, the child may weave all manner of imaginary dangers. All situations, which appear to the child as threats to his security or as indications of loss of his parents' love, become the material of extravagant phantasies of an anxiety type such as nightmares.

There are certain *common situations* which provide specially favourable material for phantasy formations of an alarming kind. A few of these *classic situations* deserve special mention:

1. The *birth of another child* and the apparent transference of Mother's affection.
2. Special claims made by Father upon Mother's life—where Father is seen as a *rival*, owing to his privileged position; this situation is specially liable to affect boys.
3. *Harshness* and excessive discipline—in other words the unnecessary *thwarting* of the child's natural impulses.

These situations, unless carefully handled, are liable to generate phantasies of a disturbing kind which are a fruitful source of anxiety. The *effects of such phantasies* are, unfortunately, not exhausted at the time of their formation. As a matter of fact, they are usually forgotten. But they tend to *persist, as an unconscious background* to the child's mental life, influencing his whole reaction to the world. Indeed his whole life may be lived under the influence of *anxiety deriving from the presence of this unseen background* conjured up during childhood by his imagination.

The fact that nervousness throughout life may be the sequel of anxiety during childhood should impress upon us how important it is that provision should be made for the prevention and treatment of nervousness in children.

In closing, I desire to stress two facts: (1) that the nervous child can be *cured*; and (2) that, in so far as we can *prevent* anxiety developing in a child, we are guaranteeing him against the risk of his becoming a nervous child in the future. Any constructive attempt to deal with the problem of the nervous child must rest upon the recognition of these two basic facts.

6. IMAGINATION AND CHILD DEVELOPMENT

INTRODUCTION

It is a commonplace that childhood is an age of imagination. It is not everyone, however (even among those who are concerned with the care of the young), who has clearly formulated ideas as to the exact part played by imagination in the mental life of the child. There are still fewer people who think of asking why childhood should be so characteristically an age of imagination and why every human being should pass through such an imaginative phase at all. The fact that these things are so is usually accepted as a matter of course.

THE ATTITUDE OF ADULTS TO IMAGINATION IN GENERAL

Here are two groups with distinct attitudes which are clearly distinguishable:

1. Those who depreciate and decry imagination
   - —with a passion for what they believe to be "facts"
   - —the tendency to regard imagination as wrong (falsehood and lies)
   - —they would positively discourage phantasies of children
   - —they would banish fairy stories from the nursery bookshelf and substitute the Encyclopaedia
   - —the influence of this attitude may be traced in the Montessori System
2. Those who regard imagination as the meat and drink of life
   - —such people, so far from discouraging the phantasies of children, would actively encourage them
   - —unable perhaps to believe in fairies themselves, they yet retain

their childish interest in them, and indulge this interest vicariously by encouraging the phantasies of children
- such individuals, if in charge of children, would be inclined to establish a forcing house of phantasy in the nursery or the school
- exploitation of the child's imagination by an adult for his or her own ends

If the first class of persons tends to depreciate imagination, the second tends to *overvalue* it. These two groups represent two extreme attitudes to the imaginative processes which are so typical of childhood.

THE ATTITUDE OF THE AVERAGE PERSON

This is not intermediate or noncommittal. It is a combination of both attitudes. Thus they may

a. remark to the frightened child: 'It's only imagination'
b. criticise a dull poet or prosaic person as 'Lacking in imagination'

Imagination is thus simultaneously regarded as

a. something undesirable involving the acceptance of what is unreal and, therefore, false
b. something desirable which gives zest to life

THE INNER AND OUTER WORLDS

This dual attitude towards imagination and phantasy appears inconsistent, but their consistency is based on the co-existence in the mind of two scales of value, each of which has a psychological justification. The tendency to depreciate imagination is based upon an acceptance of the external world of reality as the criterion of inner thought, impulse and feeling. From this point of view, a belief is rejected if it does not correspond to actual fact. While the tendency to value or exalt imagination is based upon an acceptance of the inner world of thought, impulse and feeling as the criterion of the external world. From this point of view, a fact is rejected if it is unacceptable.

Both the outer and inner worlds, of course, are realities—that is, both exist. Unfortunately, however, there is an incompatibility between them. Each world makes its claim upon the other; but the claims of the two are only too liable to conflict. The inner world consists essentially of instincts, desires, wishes, feelings and emotions dependent ultimately upon the endowment with which we are born. From the point of view of the internal world taken in isolation, the sole criterion as to whether these inner impulses should be satisfied is the existence of a need, for example, hunger or thirst. A need knows no criterion except itself and it demands instant satisfaction. External reality may not be prepared to satisfy our needs however, for example, thirst in the desert. Alternatively, external reality may require us to defer satisfaction of our needs, for example, thirst after a surgical operation, or the case of a baby on 4-hourly feeds, who is hungry an hour too soon, or the girl who wants a doll may have to wait till Christmas. Again external reality may require us to do something before our needs can achieve satisfaction, for example the young man who wants to be a doctor has to put in five years hard work at University, or the child who wants 6d from his father may only obtain it on condition that he does an hour's weeding in the garden, while most men have to work for their daily bread. Each of us, therefore, is confronted throughout life with constant Conflict between demands of the inner and outer worlds. Our success and happiness depend largely upon the extent to which we adapt the one to the other.

To a small but varying extent, the individual is able to harness the external world to the satisfaction of his inner needs and impulses. To a much larger extent, he has to learn to modify his needs and impulses to meet the conditions imposed by the environment, including the social environment. If Smith or Jones wants to become one of the world's dictators, it is just remotely possible that, given the capacities and the opportunities of Mussolini, he may become one. It is very much more probable, however, that he will have to content himself with a minor dictatorial function in the office, home or nursery. A third possibility is that he may imagine himself to be Mussolini within the shelter of the nearest mental hospital, behind walls which shut out disturbing, disillusioning facts.

Throughout life, everyone is faced with the unwelcome necessity of having both to check his natural impulses and desires and to modify them in such a way as to meet the conditions imposed by the outer world, including, of course, the social environment. It is only by inhibiting and modifying his impulses that he is enabled to obtain such partial satisfactions as the nature of things permits.

I speak of real satisfactions; but it is always possible, in the absence of real satisfactions, to have recourse to imaginary satisfactions. I have spoken of possibilities open to the would be Mussolini. We can deliver ourselves up to phantasy, build castles in Spain, retreat like Mary Rose to a magic island to consort with fairies instead of men.[1] In so far as we do this, however, we

[1]*Mary Rose* is a play by J. M. Barrie, the Scottish playwright and author of *Peter Pan*. He became Chancellor of Edinburgh University in October 1930. Fairbairn saw the play in June 1930. In this a young married woman disappears on a Hebridean island. She returns about twenty years later and does not recognise her child (nor it must be said the other members of her family). The

are turning our footsteps in the same direction as the would be Mussolini in the mental hospital, albeit he has travelled so very much further. We are turning our back on Reality, like Mary Rose (who did this so effectively that she did not recognise her own child when she returned). It is only with a certain group of insane persons that outer reality is wholly ignored in favour of the phantasy world; but, on the other hand, there is no one whose face is wholly turned towards outer reality.

There are all intermediate degrees between the two extremes; but, to be normal, an individual must have a fairly strong Reality Sense. In general, it may be said that successful adaptation in life depends upon the extent to which the reality sense is developed. Unfortunately, human beings are not born with a reality sense. It is something which has to be acquired. Further, it has been found that the degree of reality sense, which any given adult possesses, depends mainly upon the extent to which it has been acquired in early childhood. Early childhood is the period during which the reality sense develops. Indeed, if we may regard growing up as an educational task, the development of a reality sense is the great task of early childhood.

DEVELOPMENT OF THE REALITY SENSE

The newborn babe has no reality sense. He is unable to draw any distinction between himself and outer objects. His own feelings or sensations constitute his universe. Another characteristic of the infant is a natural tendency to prefer the pleasant to the unpleasant. What is pleasant satisfies him and he soon learns to seek it. What is unpleasant makes him dissatisfied and he seeks to avoid it or to replace it by what is pleasant, for example, hunger is unpleasant so he cries; while feeding promotes satisfaction which is real. Contrast the state of things when the infant is hungry but not fed, he will seek imaginary gratification through sucking movements, or sucking his thumb. Imaginary satisfaction is unreal and transient, hunger returns. The illustration which I have given shows, however, how imagination is exploited as a method of dealing with unsatisfied impulses.

The infant learns in time, however, that the wish is *not* as good as the deed. The imaginary feed is no real substitute for the actual feed. In learning this, he has taken the first step in developing a reality sense. He has learned that there is something outside himself to be reckoned with in seeking the

play does seem to have symbolic connections with two themes in Scottish Fairy Tales where (1) naming is of particular significance e.g., "Whuppety Stoorie" (the story of which is essentially the same as Rumpelstiltskin); and (2) magical disappearances and reappearances, after a prolonged period of time, which are effected by 'people of another world'. In the case of Mary Rose it is the island itself which calls her and for which she has a special affinity.

satisfaction of his desires. He thus comes gradually to realise the breast or bottle is not part of himself, but external objects to be reckoned with. Later, he comes to appreciate the existence of the mother or nurse as external objects also, much more important objects, but objects much more uncertain in their behaviour, much more difficult to conciliate and control. So, step by step, throughout childhood the outer world is built up.

As the reality sense develops, the child's behaviour gradually changes in character. By nature, he tends to avoid the unpleasant and to seek the pleasant. This is "behaviour according to the pleasure principle". At this level of behaviour, every impulse seeks instant satisfaction. As the reality sense develops, the child's behaviour becomes more adaptive. He learns, to some extent, to content himself with such satisfactions as the nature of the world around him permits, to endure the postponement of satisfaction and even to submit to the complete frustration of some of his impulses. This lesson is hardly learned however. It is never completely learned by any of us, though some of us learn it better than others.

In the face of disappointment and when we are thwarted and frustrated in our efforts, there is always a temptation to resort to the unreal world of imagination and to seek in phantasy what is denied to us in reality. This is a regressive process. In the adult, this resort to phantasy tends to compromise adaptation in life, if it goes too far. In moderation, however, it helps to tide us over crises which might otherwise overwhelm us. We are all liable also to have recourse to phantasy when we retreat at night from the strain and stress of the real world in sleep; for dreams are simply phantasies which occur when sleep dulls the reality sense. In the case of the artist and the writer, imagination may even be exploited as a profession and thus be converted into a means of adaptation. It must be admitted, however, that there are artists and writers who employ their imaginative gifts, not in the interests of adaptation, but as an escape from reality.

THE PLACE OF IMAGINATION IN THE MENTAL LIFE OF THE CHILD

In assessing the part normally played by imagination in the mental life of the child, we are not justified in applying the rigorous standard which we feel to be appropriate in the case of an adult. Judged by adult standards, the most normal child is mad. For example,

1. "Don't sit on that chair, or you'll squash the baby."
2. "Oh Daddy, you've stood on my dog."
3. "I'll throw the baby out of the window."

Why do we judge children and adults by such different standards in these matters? The answer of the man or woman in the street would be, "Because children are so imaginative".

This brings us back to one of the questions with which we started, "Why are children naturally imaginative?" The answer is "Because they have not yet developed a mature reality sense". They have not yet completely emerged from the stage when

a. a wish is as good as a deed
b. a phantasy is as good as a fact
c. Aladdin's ring is a guarantee of the instant fulfilment of every wish, no door can resist the cry of "Open, Sesame", and the magic carpet can take you anywhere in the twinkling of an eye.

No child, of course, is completely without a reality sense, except the newborn babe. The relentless asperities of the actual world obtrude themselves too forcibly upon attention from the moment of birth, to be altogether neglected or denied. The development of the reality sense is a gradual, and normally a progressive, process throughout childhood. Other things being equal the older the child, the greater his reality sense. If the child of one year old seems less imaginative than a child of four, this is because we know so much less about what is going on in his mind.

1. He is unable to give adequate expression to his thoughts in speech.
2. His phantasies are so much more real to him that he does not require to support them to the same extent by imaginative play.

Here it may be remarked that the imaginative play of children is essentially an intermediary or stepping-stone between pure phantasy and stark reality. The play of children is largely make-believe, that is to say, they attach their phantasies to reality, as a garment is hung on a peg. Thus the hearthrug becomes a boat and two chairs become a railway train. As children grow older, play becomes more realistic. This is to say play gradually becomes more adapted to the conditions of the outer world. Play thus exercises an important function in the development of the child. It provides a series of stepping-stones between the world of imagination and the world of reality.

I have said that the development of the reality sense is normally a progressive process throughout childhood—other things being equal. Unfortunately other things are not always equal. There are times when life deals hardly with the child and reality is particularly difficult to face—for example, the

—birth of another child
—death of a parent

—adoption by a parent of a repressive and exacting attitude out of proportion to the child's capacity of adjustment
—intolerance on the part of adults of the child's play
—or, a surgical operation

At such times, the child's powers of adaptation may be unduly strained, with the result that the child is forced back into the world of phantasy. That is regression to a more infantile phase in face of serious frustration and thwarting. At such times, if the child is provided with special facilities for imaginative play, and afforded opportunity to express his phantasies in concrete material, regression may be arrested and the child's footsteps guided back along the path to reality. This principle provides the rationale of play techniques employed in psychological clinics for maladjusted children.

It is important, in such cases, that the child's remedial play should be supervised by an *experienced person,* who adopts benevolent neutrality:

1. neither praising nor blaming his phantasies
2. not interfering with the child's expression of his phantasies
3. not exploiting the child's phantasies

The therapeutic effect of imaginative play in the case of maladjusted children thus reveals the fact that imaginative play is not only an expression of the child's bondage to the world of phantasy, but also a stepping-stone between the world of phantasy and the world of reality. As the child becomes older, his play becomes more realistic, that is to say, more adapted to the conditions of the outer world. Play is thus a form of activity, whereby the child's energies become gradually directed along realistic channels, and whereby the child becomes fitted for adult life in the real world. This fact indicates the practical educational importance of providing the child with facilities for imaginative play suited to his level of development at various stages of childhood. In this way, his energies may be harnessed to the tasks of life in later years, instead of meeting with frustration and being turned back again into channels of phantasy.

The considerations which I have advanced regarding the development of the reality sense thus have a practical application. The child should be given every facility for the expression of his phantasies in imaginative play. On the other hand, care should be taken to ensure that the expression of the child's phantasies is spontaneous and that his imagination is not exploited, consciously or unconsciously, by adults who are tempted to seek vicarious expression of their own phantasies through the medium of the child.

On the theoretical side, it is now possible to add something to the

Ronald Fairbairn with his mother and children in Edinburgh in 1934

statement that the imaginativeness of the child is due to a lack of reality sense. Imagination also constitutes a means whereby the bitter wind of reality is tempered for the 'shorn lamb'. The hard facts of life involve constant disappointment, constant thwarting of our impulses, constant frustration of our dearest wishes. What the grown-up person seldom realises is that the disappointments and frustrations, which the child has to endure, are so much more cataclysmic and shattering than any which the adult is called upon to face.

The professional man may on occasion be called upon to face financial ruin; the withholding of a favourite toy may, from the child's point of view, be an even greater disaster; yet it is a common experience in the nursery. The unemployed workman may be faced with privation for himself and his family; but the hungry infant, with his meagre knowledge of reality, has no guarantee that he will ever have another feed. A disappointment in love may cause a nervous breakdown in an adult; but, every time a child's parent is angry, the child is faced with what appears to him a loss of love, which, for all he knows, may be permanent. The adult is occasionally required to endure the sorrows of bereavement; and, for many wives, the War [1914–1918] consisted of four years of anxiety, during which every ring of the bell might be the herald of bad tidings. The child is more or less constantly in the position of the soldier's wife. If the infant's mother or nurse goes out of the nursery, he has no guarantee that she will ever come back. The possibility, from the child's point of view, of the Mother not returning is one of the chief factors in the child's fear of being left alone.

The part played by such ideas as these in the child's mind may be illustrated by a concrete case.

The Case of Margaret Smith

The symptoms exhibited by this child were *fear of going to school* and *anxiety attacks*:

- —there was nothing in her life at school which seemed adequate to account for her anxiety
- —her mother was over anxious and fussy: the girl had been delicate and her life had been despaired of in infancy
- —when the child was a few weeks old her mother had been removed to hospital
- —the child was sent to a Baby Home where she was neglected
- —when the baby returned home she was very ill: she required the greatest care and was very dependent

This was not a case of fear of school, but of fear of leaving home; her fear of leaving home was her fear of losing her mother. It could be said that the girl was old enough to know the unlikelihood of this. However she had already lost her mother at an age when she could not understand the real situation; for when a mother leaves the room, the infant has no guarantee that she will return. When a child is hungry he has no guarantee of being fed any more than a traveller lost in the desert has.

This child had lost her mother. She had experienced discomfort and bad treatment in the absence of her mother, and had received constant attention on her return. Early experiences are forgotten so far as conscious memories are concerned, but traces persist at deeper levels in the child's mind.

The truth of the interpretation of this girl's case is substantiated by subsequent events:

- —the child was unwilling to go to Sunday School
- —her parents went out for a walk on Sunday afternoons
- —the parents made attempts to persuade the child
- —the child said that she would not go, unless the mother stayed in, saying "If you aren't in, I'll think something has happened to you."

Consideration of such a case should convince us that, *however irrational* the anxiety of a child may seem, it is *not really groundless*, when we see it from the child's point of view. Where there is anxiety, there is always some source of danger for the child.

From what I have said, it will be seen that the child is constantly faced by emotional crises; by dangers, disappointments and frustrations, which it is difficult for the adult, with his knowledge of real people and things, to comprehend. This being so, the harshness of the world around the child might well prove too much for him, if his imagination did not provide him with refuge in distress. His imagination softens the blows of fate, takes the edge off his bitter disappointments, mitigates his sorrows. Through the agency of imagination, the child thus becomes reconciled to life and is enabled to carry on with life's great task of adaptation to reality.

CONCLUSIONS RESULTING FROM OUR STUDY OF THE PART PLAYED BY IMAGINATION IN THE MENTAL LIFE OF THE CHILD

Our, admittedly inadequate, study of the part played by imagination in the mental life of the child has now provided us with sufficient material to understand both why childhood should be so characteristically the age of Imagination and why every human being should pass through such an imaginative phase at all:

1. Childhood is the age of imagination "par excellence", because the child has not yet developed a reality sense, or is only in the process of developing it. He has not yet come to terms with outer reality on the one hand, and with his own imperious impulses and desires on the other. He has not yet effected a sufficient reconciliation or compromise between these two incompatibles. Accordingly, when denied satisfaction through the medium of reality, he seeks it through the medium of imagination. From this point of view, the imaginativeness of the child is a limitation imposed upon him by reason of his immaturity.

2. Imagination promotes adjustment and adaptation to life on the part of the child, by functioning as a sort of buffer or shock-absorber. Just as a shock-absorber enables a motor-car to travel over rough roads without undue jarring and jolting, so the imagination protects the child, as he sets out upon the uneven road of life, by absorbing to some extent the shocks which he encounters.

A tender plant which requires a high temperature for its early growth may often be acclimatised to open air conditions by being passed through a series of glass-houses of decreasing temperature. Substitute "the child" for "the plant" in our metaphor. Substitute "imagination" for "temperature" and "stages of childhood" for "glass-houses"; and we have a fair picture of the indispensable part played by imagination in the early phase of life. From another point of view, therefore, the imaginativeness of the child is an aid to mental development.

In the light of these conclusions, it is evident that there is something to be said both on the side of those who regard imagination a source of danger to the child, and on the side of those who hold it to be a source of life. It is a source of danger in so far as it leads the child away from reality and compromises adaptation. It is a source of life in so far as it robs reality of such uncompromising features as would strain the child's powers of adaptation to the breaking point.

It should be added that imagination is also a means of salvation to the child in so far as it absorbs natural urges and impulses which, under the restrictions imposed by social life, would otherwise find no form of expression. In this capacity, imagination functions as a sort of safety-valve for forces which would otherwise be dammed back until they reached a state of explosive tension and became liable to burst out in some form of anti-social conduct. This last consideration (viz. the "safety-valve" function of imagination) opens up an interesting train of thought which I have not hitherto broached, but which I do not feel that I have time to embark upon tonight. To embark upon it would involve considering the part played by unconscious phantasies and by projection of phantasies upon the external world in such a way as to distort reality for the child. These are subjects which would require separate treatment.

PRACTICAL RECOMMENDATIONS

As parents and teachers, you are doubtless specially interested in the practical application of psychological ideas to the upbringing and education of the young. As regards our present subject, you will perhaps expect me to offer some practical suggestions as to how the child is to be safeguarded against the dangers of imagination and enabled to employ his imaginative powers in the interests of adaptation. At the risk, therefore, of "teaching my grandmother", I shall venture to submit for your consideration two guiding principles, which appear to arise out of what has been said:

1. Every effort should be made to prevent reality being too difficult for the child. Here it is important to distinguish two modes of pressure exerted upon the child by outer reality: (a) physical and (b) mediated by the social environment.

a. Physical pressure of the environment. It is universally recognised that the child requires special protection against physical dangers; such protection is provided by the average parent. There are limits, of course, to protection which can be afforded against earthquakes, etc. Much can be done, however, to safeguard the child against (i) accidents and (ii) disease.

The child requires not only special protection, but also special care so far as concerns the supply of his physical wants, e.g., food, warmth, and shelter. The necessity of modifying the pressure of reality upon the child in all these physical respects requires no elaboration. It is to be noted, however, that even the physical protection and care of the child involves a social factor.

Thus, for the infant, protection against danger means essentially the security of his mother's arms. Similarly, satisfaction of his hunger involves a most intimate relationship with his mother.

b. Social pressure of the environment. The necessity of tempering the child's social environment to suit his immaturity is to some extent realised, e.g., we require less of a child than of an adult in the way of social manners. The fact remains, however, that the difficulties presented to the child by the social environment are most inadequately realised. In actual practice, the asperities of reality which bear hardest on the child are those mediated by the social environment, e.g., the birth of a new brother or sister. This does not mean that the ideal family consists in an only child. It does mean, however, that every precaution should be taken to remove such grounds for jealousy as are not inevitable.

The example which I have just given illustrates how closely the child's disappointments and frustrations are bound up with his relationship to Other persons. The most important persons in the child's social environment are, of course, the parents, and parent figures or deputies. It is by the parents that children are thwarted most often and most seriously in things that matter to them. The effect upon children of the actions of their parents is very inadequately realised by the parents themselves. What children desire above all is to be loved by their parents. Every occasion on which they are frustrated by their parents or compelled by their parents to do something they do not want to do is interpreted as evidence of a loss of parental love.

As a matter of fact, in the early phases of childhood it is mainly due to a desire to ensure the love of their parents, a fear of losing this love and a desire to regain it when apparently lost, that children learn to do what they are told and to restrain their wayward impulses. In so far as a desire to be loved by his parents provides the child with a motive for self-control in the interests of others, it is undoubtedly the most important factor in promoting his social adjustment and fitting him for life in a community later on.

A certain amount of frustration is inevitable, if the child is to learn that others have to be considered beside himself. The amount of frustration a child has to put up with is, however, far greater than the average parent can possibly realise. Thus the fact that Mummy and Daddy sleep in the same room and he sleeps in another room means, from the child's point of view, that they love one another more than they love him—a bitter thought. The parents' bedroom thus becomes a Garden of Eden safeguarded from the child's intrusion by an angel with a flaming sword. Here is food for phantasy.

Both parents are, of course, love-objects for the child, but it is usual for the parent of opposite sex to be the chief object of affection. In so far as this happens, the parent of the same sex becomes a rival. Thus the boy tends to be jealous of his Father and to react to him as a rival for his Mother's love. Similarly, the girl tends to be jealous of her Mother. This triangular situation is undoubtedly the most difficult which the child has to face. It requires very little in the way of provoking circumstances to release in the child a flood of impotent hate towards the rival parent. This hate is impotent for many reasons, amongst others because the rival parent is simultaneously loved and simultaneously feared. The child's hate has therefore to find its chief expression in phantasy. Thus the boy readily imagines himself a Perseus slaying the dragon which comes out of the sea to devour the beautiful Andromeda.

The moral to be drawn from all this is *not* that fathers should be abolished from the environment of boys and mothers abolished from the environment of girls. The moral is that the utmost care must be taken to prevent the triangular situation becoming unduly acute. Enough has now been said to indicate the kind of difficulties which the child finds himself up against in his social environment. Difficulties of this sort are implicit in the nature of things, but the well-advised parent will seek to prevent anything happening to aggravate the inherent difficulties of the child's social environment.

Now we come to the second guiding principle to which I should like to draw attention.

2. Young children should be provided with adequate facilities for expressing their phantasies. The provision of such facilities should be one of the aims of parents and teachers. It must be taken for granted that all children have a phantasy life of some sort. In the case of some children this may not be obvious. It does not follow, however, that a child is free of phantasies because he does not express them. On the contrary, there is a class of maladjusted children, whose dull and unimaginative appearance covers a feverish phantasy life. Such a state of things is the result of two sets of circumstances, (a) circumstances which over-stimulate phantasy formation and throw the child back on the phantasy world, e.g., (i) undue frustration, (ii) undue indulgence; (b) circumstances which prevent the child's phantasies gaining expression.

Two main factors which prevent phantasies gaining expression are (a) fear of parental disapproval, on account of the nature of the phantasy; (b) inner conflict regarding phantasies, in so far as Guilt comes to be attached to them. Here it may be pointed out that, when the child's wishes and desires are frustrated by parents, the effect is to make such wishes and desires Guilty for the child. In consequence, phantasies embodying forbidden wishes tend to be denied expression not only on account of Outer Obstacles represented by the parents, but also on account of an Inner Obstacle in the form of guilt.

There are certain classic and universal phantasies of this sort, for example, phantasies embodying hostile wishes to the rival parent, and to brothers and sisters. Such phantasies occur in every nursery, for example,

> "I'll throw the baby into the ash-bucket".
> "Daddy I'll cut off your head".

It is often maintained that when children say these things, they do not mean them. Nothing could be a greater mistake. Children *do* mean them, although they seldom mean to execute them. Occasionally cases occur in which they do try to carry them into effect, for example, the case of a boy who tried to strangle a baby, etc. In the ordinary way, however, such phantasies engender so much mental conflict in the mind of the child who entertains them, that they become repressed or banished from consciousness. Unfortunately, banishment from consciousness is not equivalent to banishment from the mind. Repressed phantasies thus tend to persist in an unconscious but active state. The more active and intense such phantasies are, when they are repressed, the more likely they are to cause trouble; for the fact that they have been repressed provides no guarantee that their influence will cease. On the contrary, their repression immobilises them and prevents their being dissolved. Under certain conditions, they may eventually be translated into action and thus give rise to anti-social conduct and even crime. Under other conditions, they may express themselves in a more disguised fashion, for example in various nervous and mental disorders. Under happier conditions, repressed phantasies may provide material for imaginative writings and works of art.

These various possibilities cannot be discussed in detail; but sufficient has been said to indicate the importance of preventing phantasies becoming repressed and imprisoned in an active state in the child's mind. The repression of active phantasies is to some extent inevitable; but precautions should be taken to prevent this process occurring to excess. Of precautionary measures, perhaps the most important is, as I have already indicated, to control the child's environment and to prevent the occurrence of situations which overtax the child's powers of adjustment and thus throw him back too much on phantasy. This measure is, of course, directed against phantasy-formation.

It is only next in importance, however, to deal with phantasies which have already been formed, and to take steps to prevent their imprisonment in the child's mind under conditions of repression. To this end, it is desirable to provide adequate opportunities for the discharge of those impulses which energise the child's phantasies. These impulses cannot, of course, be allowed to translate themselves into deeds in the ordinary way, for example in the case of a death-wish towards a rival. In any case, the young child is physically incapable of realising many of his phantasies, such as cutting off his father's head. The child is thus largely impotent to realise his phantasies. The child's impulses must, accordingly, be afforded some alternative form of expression; some form of expression whereby inner tension may be relieved without awkward consequences.

What is required is a means of expression with a certain quality of the unreal, such as "make believe" and symbolism. Imaginative play exactly fulfils these requirements. (a) Play is real enough to the child, but it can always be prefixed by an unspoken, if not spoken, "Suppose". While remaining real, Play thus becomes only "Pretend Real". (b) While play is real, it need not be literal.

The child's play expresses far more than he actually does. Thus, when a little girl plays at cooking a dinner, she does not actually cook a dinner; but she goes through certain symbolical acts, which may have any degree of likeness to the real process. Similarly a boy can make a railway train by putting a few chairs together and go to London by sitting on them. The child's play thus takes advantage of symbolism; one act may represent a totally different act; one person may represent a totally different person. His use of symbolism makes it possible for a child to express a guilty phantasy without committing a guilty act. In this way a child is able to get his more embarrassing phantasies "off his chest", and to avoid the contingency which leads to their repression.

This applies not only in the case of phantasies consciously entertained by the child, but also in the case of unconscious phantasies which have been repressed. Symbolism may be unconscious, as well as conscious. Symbolism thus provides a channel whereby repressed phantasies, which would never be consciously expressed or even entertained, may find a disguised form of expression. By taking advantage of symbolism, Imaginative Play is able to exercise an important cathartic function in the economy of the child's mind. Through imaginative play the pressure of unconscious phantasies may be reduced, and inner tension consequently relieved. For example, a game of soldiers may help to relieve the small boy of the consequences of throwing the baby out of the window (even in phantasy); while throwing stones into the water may reduce some of the guilt of shooting his father.

7. ADOLESCENCE

DEFINITION OF ADOLESCENCE

Firstly I shall give some rough definitions of what we mean by adolescence:

a. The period of "youth" intermediate between the periods of "childhood" and "adulthood".
b. The period of "growing up". This then is the period during which the child becomes a man or a woman; it is an Age of Transition.

Before a more precise definition is attempted, certain important considerations must be emphasised:

1. Adolescence is a phase in the life of a *living* organism.
2. Adolescence is a phase in the life of a *growing* organism.

The importance of these considerations is that, in dealing with a being which is living and growing, we cannot make hard and fast distinctions between the various phases. Neither are the phases themselves rigid; on the contrary they are elastic periods.

These facts hold true of adolescence as much as of any other phase of life. Consequently, any satisfactory definition must be compatible with the following facts:

1. No fixed and definite boundaries can be set either to the onset or to the termination of adolescence. Thus the onset and termination of adolescence are both gradual; with the pre-adolescent period shading off into adolescence and adolescence shading off into adulthood.
2. Adolescence does not begin at any definite age. Thus the age of onset varies in different individuals. There is also a variation in the onset of adolescence in different races with earlier onset in tropical countries.

3. The duration of adolescence varies from individual to individual. On the whole the general principle involved is that, the earlier adolescence appears, the shorter it lasts.

Another important consideration to bear in mind is that the onset of adolescence is related to puberty.

PUBERTY

This is the age at which the reproductive organs in either sex begin to be functionally active as organs of reproduction. Here it must be remembered that the reproductive glands have another function besides the reproductive function, namely the endocrine function. The endocrine function of the reproductive glands is present even prior to birth. As endocrine organs, they produce and pour into the blood important secretions. These secretions have an influence on both physical and psychological development:

a. they influence the growth of the body, especially to those bodily characteristics which differentiate the sexes.
b. they influence temperament, especially with reference to those psychological features which differentiate the sexes, for example, pugnacious tendencies in men, and maternal instincts in women.

In contrast to the endocrine function of the reproductive glands stands their strictly reproductive function. While the endocrine function is present before birth, the reproductive function first manifests itself at puberty. The appearance of the reproductive function in girls is indicated by the onset of menstruation. It is indicated in boys by the formation and discharge of seminal fluid. It is the emerging capacity for reproduction that constitutes puberty.

The significance of puberty for the psychology of adolescence lies in the fact that the onset of adolescence has a definite relationship to puberty. If puberty is early, adolescence begins early; if puberty is late, adolescence begins late. The onset of adolescence and the appearance of puberty are not, however, contemporaneous. The phenomena of adolescence, as a matter of fact, begin to manifest themselves about two years before puberty.

The reason for this is that actual puberty is the climax of a gradual process in the course of which the reproductive function comes to maturity. This process of maturation is called “Pubescence”. It is a process lasting about two years. Thus adolescence begins when pubescence begins about two years before puberty. Therefore, it is the onset of pubescence that determines the onset of adolescence. Bearing these facts in mind, adolescence may be defined in terms of the following statements:

1. It is the period of transition between childhood and adulthood.
2. It is ushered in by the onset of pubescence about two years before puberty.
3. While the age at which adolescence commences is subject to considerable variation, the average age at which it commences may be taken to be twelve years for boys and eleven years for girls.
4. The average duration of adolescence is about six or seven years.

THE PSYCHOLOGY OF ADOLESCENCE

To understand the psychology of adolescence, it is important to keep in mind the relationship of adolescence to puberty. The importance of this relationship is being increasingly recognised by modern writers on adolescence. From this point of view, all the characteristic features of adolescent psychology are directly related to the changes of puberty. They are all dependent upon the emergence of the reproductive function. This fact has only just begun to be recognised.

Formerly it was believed that adolescence witnessed the emergence of a number of separate characteristics, which had remained latent during the early years of life. This view was propounded by Stanley Hall (1904). Stanley Hall was a pioneer of the psychology of adolescence at John Hopkins University, and his book on the subject still remains the standard work [in 1930]. It is a mine of information about adolescence. It was the first book of moment on the subject and is still indispensable as a work of reference. Various influences have, however, combined to undermine his general theory of adolescence.

Stanley Hall's theory is based upon the principle that individual development repeats racial development. He regarded adolescence as corresponding in the individual life to a great transition period in the history of the race, when extensive readjustments had to be made owing to great changes in the natural conditions of the earth. Assuming such an epoch to have occurred in the past, it is obvious that a period of instability would occur, while old adjustments were being exchanged for new ones. According to Stanley Hall, this is reflected in the proverbial instability of youth. In the process of readjustment, which was necessary if the race was to escape extinction, Stanley Hall surmises that the highest characteristics of present day humanity arose. Man became a social animal in the interests of self preservation, and acquired all the characteristics necessary for the higher social life which is a distinctive feature of humanity as we know it. Stanley Hall believed that in adolescence we have a recapitulation of this phase of racial history. He held that adolescence witnessed the emergence of the various traits which appeared in the race during a past period of readjustment. He thus described it as a period of new birth.

Now it is perfectly true that adolescence is a period of new birth, and it is undoubtedly a period of readjustment. But it is being increasingly recognised that the readjustment, which takes place in adolescence cannot be described as a mere echo of the readaptation of the race to a change of conditions in the past. On the contrary it is a readaptation which is demanded of each individual to a change of conditions in himself or herself. The phenomena of adolescence are coming to be interpreted as due to the readjustment which is demanded of every individual as a result of the changes of puberty. From this point of view, only one new function emerges in adolescence, namely the capacity of reproduction.

The physiological capacity for reproduction is accompanied by a corresponding psychological urge. The reproductive urge must be regarded as *the primary factor* in the psychology of adolescence. All the other psychological features which distinguish adolescence from preceding periods of life must be regarded as *secondary* to the fundamental factor. It is only when this is realised that the psychology of adolescence can be properly understood. Apart from the emergence of the reproductive urge and the reinforcement of related tendencies, which is involved, we must regard the psychological development which occurs in adolescence as merely a continuation of the orderly and progressive development which characterises childhood.

The child is born immature. During childhood, there is a gradual growth and unfolding of those physical and mental characteristics which form the hereditary endowment of the child. Adolescence is merely the last stage in the journey from immaturity to maturity. In all this there is nothing which essentially differentiates the psychology of adolescence from the psychology of childhood. All that is distinctive of adolescence arises from the appearance of the reproductive function and the strengthening of those tendencies which are relevant to it. Although, ultimately, this is all that distinguishes the psychology of adolescence from that of early phases, it is sufficient to give the psychology of adolescence a very distinct character of its own.

This will be best understood if we consider the biological significance of the reproductive function in respect of the:

1. break with ties to the old family
2. foundation of a new family

This leads to the abandonment of a life of dependence; and the necessary adaptation to a life of independence. The emergence of the function of reproduction thus involves a complete reorientation of the individual's life. It involves a biological revolution in the mind. Justification is thus provided for Stanley Hall's statement that adolescence is a new birth.

The full significance of this biological reorientation of adolescence is obscured in civilised society, owing to the fact that the progress of civilisation has been accompanied by a postponement of the age of marriage. The postponement of the age of marriage is largely due to the operation of economic factors. The adolescent boy cannot support a wife under modern conditions; thus the age of marriage is progressively postponed as the standard of living rises. This fact introduces complications in the psychology of adolescence, because it means that a fundamental biological urge is prevented from achieving satisfaction. To understand the real significance of

The schoolboy at Merchiston Castle School

the emergence of the reproductive urge, we must consider its implications in a primitive and relatively simple society.

The foundation of a new family in an unsophisticated society involves the activity of several important instinctive tendencies:

1. Mating; that is, the operation of the sex-instinct
2. Food-seeking activities; food is no longer provided, it has to be actively sought for the family
3. Aggression or pugnacity
   a. the winning of a mate by the male
   b. competition for food
   c. defence of the family
4. Parental instinct
5. Orientation of interest to the outer world as opposed to the old home.

None of these activities emerge for the first time in adolescence. This holds true even of the sex and parental instincts. The sex instinct is now recognised to be present in childhood in an immature form. The parental instinct also manifests itself in childhood, for example, a girl's interest in dolls. While none of the tendencies in question emerge for the first time in adolescence, they are enormously reinforced with the emergence of the function of reproduction. If we keep in mind the biological implications of the reproduction function and consider the tendencies which are necessarily reinforced to render it effective, it is easy to understand how pubescence gives rise to all the distinctive phenomena of adolescent psychology.

Some of the most important phenomena may be enumerated:

1. *The Tendency of Pugnacity*; this is reinforced (especially in boys), and manifested in
   a. Horseplay and bullying among boys
   b. Interest in competitive games
   c. Revolt against authority (partly)
   d. Delinquency.
2. *The Tendency of Self-assertion*; this is reinforced, and manifested in
   a. Revolt against authority (partly)
   b. Exploits and daring crimes (partly)
   c. New interest in personal appearance
   d. Boasting and bragging.
3. *The Tendency of Food-seeking*; this is reinforced, and manifested, in civilised societies as interest in a career.
4. *The Sex-instinct*; this is reinforced.
   Of all instinctive tendencies, this [the latter] is the one which

receives most marked reinforcement in adolescence. That this should be the case is easily understood in view of its intimate association with the reproductive urge. So marked is the reinforcement of the sex instinct in adolescence that it is frequently regarded as now manifesting itself for the first time.

This is the view adopted by Stanley Hall (1904). Modern investigation tends, on the other hand, to show that sex tendencies manifest themselves in one form or another in early childhood. The fact remains, however, that, with the dawn of the function of reproduction, the sex tendencies receive reinforcement in adolescence. This fact gives rise to grave difficulties of adjustment in civilised society, in which the manifestation of sex tendencies is discountenanced in the young. Evidence of this is to be found in the prevalence of self-abuse among adolescent boys and girls.

The difficulties created by the manifestations of the sex instinct in adolescence made a profound impression upon Stanley Hall. In his writings he sounds a definitely alarmist note on the subject. He pictures the sex instinct emerging for the first time at adolescence and sweeping all before it. By his account, it is difficult to see how a pathological issue is to be avoided. Those who regard the sex instinct as present in early childhood view the situation with more equanimity. From this point of view, if adjustment has been reached in early life, it is likely to be reached in adolescence, in spite of any temporary disturbance of equilibrium.

5. *The Parental Instinct*; receives reinforcement in adolescence
The operation of this instinct in adolescence is easy to observe in primitive societies where puberty is the signal for marriage. In civilised societies its operation is very much obscured. Its activity may, however, be traced in unexpected directions. The natural object of the parental instinct is the child. Where the natural expression of the instinct is denied, it tends to find its expression in activities devoted to the care and welfare of others. This leads us to the consideration of another and most important phenomenon of adolescence, namely,

6. *The Development of Higher Sentiments*
Under this heading are included social, moral and religious sentiments. According to Stanley Hall, these higher and most distinctively human sentiments emerge in adolescence for the first time. This point of view is difficult to accept. Observation seems to show the germs of these sentiments to be present even in quite young children, and that these undergo gradual development and expansion throughout childhood. There is no doubt, however,

that the higher sentiments undergo a particularly marked development during adolescence. Adolescence indeed is the "golden age" for their development. In this phenomenon we appear to witness the operation of a process which has become familiar to modern psychology under the name of "Sublimation".

Sublimation is a process by which instinctive impulses are diverted from their natural ends to ends which are:

a. socially tolerable }
b. socially valuable } e.g., sublimation of pugnacity in games

It is a process which occurs when an instinctive tendency is thwarted or frustrated. Unfortunately it is not the only fate which may befall a thwarted or frustrated tendency; but it is the only satisfactory fate for society. It would appear that the enormous development of the higher sentiments in adolescence is due to sublimation of instinctive tendencies which are frustrated. Of all the tendencies, which are reinforced at adolescence, those which are most subject to frustration are—(a) the sex instinct and (b) the parental instinct.

Frustration of the sex instinct is brought about by the increasing taboo regarding sex matters which characterises the advance of civilisation. Frustration of the parental instinct is the inevitable result of the postponement of the age of marriage in civilised countries. It would appear that the enormous development of higher sentiments in adolescence derives much of its energy, by means of the process of sublimation, from the sex and parental instincts. This fact is important for religious and social workers to realise; for, though sublimation cannot be produced to order (being an unconscious process), yet social and religious workers have a unique opportunity to provide the conditions under which it is possible for sublimation to occur.

The importance of the sublimation of the parental instinct for the formation of higher social and moral sentiments deserves particular notice. Its importance is due to the fact that it is the most disinterested of all instincts. Its natural end is the unselfish and devoted care of the helpless child. If given an opportunity for sublimation, it thus lends itself conspicuously to the development of that sentiment of unselfish devotion to the welfare of others, which is the keynote of Christian morality.

8. MALE PSEUDO-HERMAPHRODITISM

Sir, —I have read with the greatest interest the account by Drs. D. C. Beatty, C. J. Champ, and G. I. M. Swyer (1953) of "A Case of Male Pseudohermaphroditism", since a case which conforms fairly closely to the clinical picture which they describe has come under my own observation, and forms the subject of a chapter ("Features in the Analysis of a Patient with a Physical Genital Abnormality") in my recent book (Fairbairn 1952b, pp. 197–222). My interest in the case was primarily psychiatric, the individual in question having been referred to me by "her" family doctor for psychotherapy on account of symptoms of anxiety and periodic depression. Accordingly, my reference to the physical aspects of the case is only incidental—which is perhaps unfortunate from the standpoint of general medicine, since I understand that only a few such cases have been described in the literature. It is also unfortunate from this standpoint that I found it necessary to withhold certain interesting data from my account and to leave others intentionally vague for reasons of discretion. My account is subject to further limitations in consequence of the fact that, although it was not published until 1952, it was written in 1930 for a meeting of the British Psycho-Analytical Society on January 21, 1931; for at that time knowledge regarding the sex hormones was less advanced than it is to-day, and laboratory facilities for their investigation were comparatively undeveloped. Also, I did not feel it justifiable to seek confirmation of the nature of the gonads by subjecting the patient to exploratory surgical intervention solely in the interests of scientific curiosity, especially since the effect of such intervention and of discovery of the data thereby revealed might well have inflicted a psychological trauma upon the patient, whose mental equilibrium was already precarious. The interested reader will perhaps desire to refer to my published account; but I take the opportunity to draw attention to certain of the data which it contains.

The patient to whom I refer had always been regarded as female, even after the discovery of her abnormality by her family doctor, whose introductory letter included the following statement:

> She appeared to be a perfectly normal child until she reached the age of puberty. She began then to grow unduly tall, but did not menstruate, but kept perfectly well. When she was about 20 I was consulted, and made an examination. I found . . . only a pin-head opening as a vagina which led nowhere. As she felt perfectly well, nothing further was done.

Accepting the doctor's account, I took no steps to initiate a more detailed physical investigation before proceeding with psychotherapeutic treatment. As treatment proceeded, however, I began to entertain doubts not only regarding the adequacy of his account, but also regarding the sex to which "she" properly belonged. Accordingly, I arranged for the patient to be examined by a distinguished gynaecologist, who reported it as his impression that the case was one of male pseudohermaphroditism, and who described his findings in the following terms:

> The general development is strongly masculine; the chest is very broad, but the mammary development is, if anything, more suggestive of the female type in that the tissue is soft and slightly dependent. The pubic hair is normal in its distribution for the female, and the more superficial organs are quite definitely female—namely, labia, mons, clitoris, vestibule, and urethra. The hymen is completely closed, and is represented by a series of small bands crossing the site of the normal depression. Rectal examination was not easy, but . . . no cervix or uterine body was made out. These, under ordinary circumstances, are usually made out with perfect ease by this route. At the same time the examination was not sufficiently complete to exclude the presence of an imperfectly developed organ. The general impression which I have formed is that we are dealing with a condition of essential masculinity with the presence of male gonads accompanied by secondary characters of a female type.

It may be added that, in spite of his diagnosis, the gynaecologist agreed with my opinion that it would be inadvisable to acquaint the patient with the nature of his findings. Doubts were, however, subsequently cast upon the diagnosis when a specimen of the patient's urine was examined for oestrin and gonadotropic content, and reported upon as follows:

> Oestrin—at least 20 mouse units per 24 hours. Gonadotropic content—less than 100 mouse units of follicular maturation hormone per 24 hours. These excretion results are similar to those usually obtained in a female subject, and the oestrin excretion is higher than would be expected in a male. The results suggest the presence of female secretory gonads.

In the light of this report I considered it all the more desirable to continue, for practical purposes at any rate, to regard the patient as a female.

The case in question differs interestingly from that described by Beatty, Champ, and Swyer (1953) in the facts that pubic hair was present and that the patient was abnormally tall (about 6 ft. 4 in. – 1.93 m.). Another interesting feature was that during adolescence she was subject to recurrent rectal haemorrhages which lent themselves to interpretation in terms of vicarious menstruation, and which were actually mistaken for proper menstrual periods. These were followed later in life by periodical bouts of epistaxis, which lent themselves to a similar interpretation. It is also a striking fact that, while under my observation, she always spoke quite spontaneously of her periodic attacks of depression as "being unwell," and would also speak of "missing a turn" when an attack was deferred for longer than usual. The case conformed to the description of Beatty, Champ, and Swyer in that she had a definitely female mentality and displayed no evidence of Lesbian characteristics; and it may be added that her libido was highly developed towards men, and that men seemed to find her singularly attractive.

In conclusion it is of interest to record that an identical abnormality was present in several of her numerous sisters, the remainder of whom were normal women, married, and the mothers of children.

I am, etc.,
W. Ronald D. Fairbairn

III

EARLY CONTRIBUTIONS TO PSYCHOANALYTIC THEORY AND PRACTICE

INTRODUCTION TO PART III

The papers in this section are briefer communications. Two of them are included because they give an historical comparison of Fairbairn's understanding of psychoanalysis in 1929 and in 1945. The 1929 statement, 'Principles of Psychoanalysis: 1929,' is a succinct statement of agreed-on principles, a classical rendering of Freud. It allows us to see Fairbairn's jumping-off point for later theorizing and includes some of the reservations Fairbairn was already developing.

In the paper, Fairbairn draws attention to the capacity of a theory of the unconscious to give continuity to mental life and to provide an explanation for a diversity of behavioural phenomena. Fairbairn's discussion of repression and its contents is conventional. More importantly for future developments, Fairbairn specifically rejects Freud's reduction of libido to the sexual, substituting instead the term *sensuous*. This substitution later lets him dispense with the need for a theory of erotogenic zones (as in Chapter 3, 'Libido Theory Re-evaluated'), but already here, by using the word *sensuous*, Fairbairn moves our focus towards the wholeness of the early experience of the baby in relation to its mother. Fairbairn goes further here, however, when he redefines libido as the biological life impulse. By means of this redefinition Fairbairn begins the process of releasing psychoanalytic theory from the Freudian strictures of an all-encompassing sexual motivation, towards a more integrated account of human development.

Fairbairn's criticism of libido theory for broadening the concept of sexuality beyond its usefulness is interesting in view of his eventual adoption of *libido* as the term for the more general role he describes here as the biological life-impulse in the personality out of which specific sexuality is differentiated.

The next three papers deal with the role of anxiety and of aggression. They form part of the lexicon of Fairbairn's evolving clinical and theoretical thought. 'The Psychology of Anxiety', published in 1929 in *The British Journal of Medical Psychology*, demonstrates the importance of the intellectual context within which Fairbairn worked, and it highlights his uneasiness at the separation of the two disciplines of psychology and psychoanalysis. In the late 1920s and up to the late 1930s Fairbairn saw himself as a medical psychologist with strong adherence to Freudian ideas and methodology, and he directed considerable energy towards the promotion of a close association between psychology and psychoanalysis. By the late 1930s and 1940s, the status of psychoanalysis in Britain as an independent discipline had been established. Its fate lay in the hands of the British Psycho-Analytic Society, where the development of ideas was complicated by the arrival of eminent European psychoanalysts with a shared commitment to Freud's theory as they interpreted it. Fairbairn's mature contribution was therefore considered against a more restricted background than his early work.

The interdisciplinary flexibility of Fairbairn's early work remained a powerful resource for his own contributions to psychoanalysis. In this paper he utilizes Drever's insights into the psychic origins of affect in conjunction with Freud's ideas in a way which points to the vital role which affect is to fill in his own later theory. He detaches himself from the doctrinal attachment to defence mechanism and supplies the alternative formulation of an escape mechanism, another pointer to his later work. The discussion of the relationship between fear, the need to escape painful situations, and anxiety leads him to a brief original discussion of dissociation as a defence.

The next two papers reflect the attention paid to the issue of aggression in British psychoanalytical circles in the 1930s. The first paper, given in October 1932 to the Scottish Branch of the Royal Medico-Psychological Association at Bangour Mental Hospital as 'The Role of the Aggressive Instinct in Manic-Depressive Insanity and Allied Conditions', is published here for the first time as 'The Psychopathology of Aggression'. Despite the use of *instinct* in the title of the paper, Fairbairn is clearly discussing object relationships. This is clear in the content of the cases which he uses as clinical evidence. His main emphasis involves the oral nature of the symptoms exhibited in manic depression and associated conditions.

'The Role of Aggression,' published in 1939, is a well-honed summary of ideas about aggression which accepts Freud's dual instinct theory and argues for aggression as an irreducible factor. The formulation is interestingly at odds with Fairbairn's later understanding of aggression as reactive, although inevitably present in response to the frustrations met by all infants. Sutherland (1989) puts this paper into the context of the general antipathy to psychoanalytical ideas exhibited by the professors of psychiatry and psychology at Edinburgh which was personally focused on Fairbairn. In 1938, Fairbairn's old colleague and chief, Drever, delivered a paper attacking the unscientific status of psychoanalytic ideas (Sutherland 1989). Fairbairn replied by agreeing to give this paper at the same venue in 1939. Considering the content of the paper and its adherence to instinct theory which was at variance with his own earlier papers, Sutherland says, 'I have a strong suspicion that Glover or Ernest Jones might well have suggested his participation following a request for someone to put the psychoanalytic standpoint' (p. 58). Naturally, in such circumstances it would be necessary to adhere to the Freudian view.

Both of Fairbairn's papers reflect the particular emphasis which Jones himself put upon aggression, while in a wider context, the attention devoted to the subject of aggression was a distinguishing feature of theoretical differences between London and Vienna in the 1930s. The British Psycho-Analytic Society was interested in the pathogenic role of aggression and its origins in the inner world of early childhood, while the Viennese concentrated upon phallo-centric conceptions of early female development and the development of the superego in relation to the Oedipus complex (King, in King and Steiner 1991). Such a divergence was another example of the problems Freud's dualism of the life and death instincts raised for psychoanalysis, as we have discussed in the introduction to Part III.

The bias exhibited by Jones toward the role of aggression, or the 'death instinct,' in the mental economy was a factor in his support for Melanie Klein's work. Her interpretations of aggression at preconceptual levels of child development expressed in the inner world of infantile fantasy exerted an immense influence upon psychoanalytic practice in Britain. Although her position was couched in terms of object relations, she retained the idea of instincts as the source of psychic dynamism. Jones was therefore able to accept her formulations. It was thus possible for Fairbairn to draw on her work in this paper, although whether he did so for unacknowledged political reasons is unclear.

In 1938, Edward Glover asked a number of prominent analysts to answer an extensive questionnaire about their technique, which he used in writing his textbook on psychoanalytic technique. We have included in this section Fairbairn's answers to Glover's questionnaire—here titled 'Practicing Psychoanalysis'—which Fairbairn saved. The answers to the questionnaire provide the only extant guide to how Fairbairn saw his own method at that time. Besides having a note of flexibility and a tendency towards more personal availability in the analytic relationship than some analysts, Fairbairn's technique comes across as being fairly classical. We have included Fairbairn's review of the 1955 second edition of Glover's textbook in the last section of this collection, an interesting follow-up on the view of his practice provided by the questionnaire.

The 1939 paper 'Sexual Delinquency,' is of interest because of Fairbairn's extensive experience in this area. This paper suggests Fairbairn's growing sophistication in his consideration that relationships between the self and the other should not be entirely dependent upon instinctual gratification. In his focus upon the objects of sexual interest he presages the idea of dynamic internal objects. He also addresses the persistence of infantilism in sexual practices in which objects are seen solely as objects of gratification. These objects then define an infantile adherence to part-objects, and this trend becomes part of a pervasive structure of infantilism in the personality of these patients. He describes ways in which external manipulation utilizing projection can make ordinary people attribute all sorts of enormities to stereotyped cultural groups, for example, Jews, Muslims, or African Americans. This type of process characterizes these groups solely by means of one common feature, such as religion or race. In other words, each individual is turned into an object for gratification—in this case not of sex, but of aggression. Although Fairbairn does not address the issue of other modes of infantile part-object gratification, he does provide a starting point for formulations about torture and atrocities in general.

'Phantasy and Inner Reality' was Fairbairn's contribution to the 'Scientific Discussions' held at the British Psycho-Analytic Society during the period 1942–1945, now known as *The Freud–Klein Controversies* (King and Steiner 1991). It was read by Edward Glover at the Second Discussion, in Fairbairn's absence. The Scientific Discussions were designed by Glover as a means of elucidating the validity of the new psychoanalytical theories emerging in Britain at that time. But behind this aim lay two main issues:

1. *The status of psychoanalysis.* In 1929 the British Medical Association had granted professional status to psychoanalysts, defining psychoanalysis as 'the techniques devised by Freud and the theory which he has built upon his work' (King in King 1991, p. 12). Thus the status and independence of psychoanalysis depended on its adherence to Freudian theory.

2. *Training analysts.* At this time, conflicting views of psychoanalytic development were emerging within the Society. In the interests of the Society in particular, and psychoanalysis in general, it was deemed necessary to maintain a balance of power between such groups. This entailed the validation of the theoretical views held by training analysts and the control of numbers of training analysts representing the various factions. This was intended to maintain a balanced representation of the validated but disparate views held by members of the Society (source: undated proceedings of the British Psycho-Analytic Society in Fairbairn archives). It was essential to demonstrate the Freudian genesis and scientific basis of new ideas under the aegis of the Society to validate the two emerging conflictual points of view and their right to train new analysts (King and Steiner 1991).

In 'Phantasy and Inner Reality' Fairbairn uses Stout's (1927) psychological analysis of mental processes to present a flexible methodology designed to provide a scientific base from which to assess the role assigned to fantasy in psychoanalysis. Fairbairn's use of Stout began in 1930 (see Introduction to Part I). His critique of Freud in 'Libido Theory Re-evaluated' (Chapter 3), involved his use of the experimental research carried out by James Drever into appetitive and reactive instinctual tendencies associated with Stout's theory of mental levels (pp. 228–231) with the intention of providing an explanation of human psychic development and an elucidation of psychoanalytical terms such as *phantasy*. Fairbairn quotes Drever's distinction between appetitive and reactive instinctual tendencies, where appetitive tendencies relate to internal situations and reactive tendencies relate to external situations. Appetitive tendencies respond to bodily organic needs, while reactive tendencies respond to the outer world and are primarily adaptive in character. The feeling-state associated with the activation of appetitive tendencies is craving, while that induced by the reactive tendencies is object interest. Appetitive tendencies are characterized by the need for immediate satisfaction, while reactive tendencies can better tolerate delayed satisfaction.

Fairbairn (1930) thought that the correspondence between the reactive behavior and activity determined by the reality principle could be enhanced by Stout's concept of mental levels. At the perceptual level only traces of past experience are accessible, while at the ideational level the capacity exists to revive past experiences explicitly in the form of images, and at the higher ideational levels novel combinations of elements derived from former experience occur. At the highest level, the conceptual level, it is possible to apprehend the relationships of situations and objects which are either perceived or ideally represented. Fairbairn emphasized that both the appetitive and reactive tendencies occur at the perceptual level, but as the reactive tendencies are concerned with external situations and object interest, a degree of adaptation to reality is already occurring even at this level of mental life.

Thus, Fairbairn gave an account of mental development that presupposed an integral individual identity—an ego or self—where fantasy is merely one human capacity. This background allowed him to say, 'It would appear to be wrong to say that fantasy plays no part in the mental life of infancy . . . but it is . . . equally wrong to say that infancy is the period of life during which fantasy manifests itself most characteristically' (pp. 423–424).

Fairbairn's claim that the concept of fantasy is obsolete is his most challenging statement. He could nevertheless substantiate it later by pointing out that where object interest is characteristic of an adaptive reactive tendency operating at the earliest perceptual level, affective feeling states would be incorporated into the personality in the earliest stages of mental life. The inner world of the child is in the process of development from the beginning. The development of the ideational and conceptual levels consolidates the dynamic personality at a later time. As reactive tendencies are adaptive mechanisms, external reality and the child's reaction to its experience of object relationships will be incorporated early. Therefore, actual affective experience motivates ego splitting. While the child interprets external events erroneously from its immature point of view, such interpretations on the part of the child contribute to the activation of defensive mechanisms such as repression. But for the analyst to interpret erroneous understanding on the part of the child as fantasy is misleading and unnecessary. The inner world determines the child's experience of its early object relationships and is the basic determinant of the dynamic personality of the adult, not a previously developed set of fantasies free of external world influence.

Barbara Low, the only person who responded directly to Fairbairn's paper, spoke during the Third Scientific Discussion, questioning his distinction between fantasy and inner psychical reality. Quoting Fairbairn's words, 'the concept of fantasy has now been rendered obsolete by the concepts of psychical reality and internal objects' she asked what the differences were between the two concepts, and 'by what process does fantasy develop (or has developed) into inner psychical reality?' (King and Steiner 1991, pp. 391–392). Unfortunately Fairbairn was unable to reply, and therefore Susan Isaacs later replied to these questions. In her response, given from a Kleinian perspective, Isaacs repudiated Fairbairn's notion that the concept of psychic reality had replaced that of phantasy and ignores the question of levels of mental functioning:

> I have not declared myself in support of Dr. Fairbairn's notion that the concept of phantasy has been rendered obsolete by the concept of psychic reality and internal objects. I would not subscribe to such a view. Neither the concept of psychic reality nor that of internal objects is a new one. Both are Freud's discoveries. Dr. Fairbairn, to my mind, overemphasizes and distorts part of Mrs. Klein's theories to the point of caricature. He over-substantifies internal objects and makes them far too independent, leaving wishes and feelings and the id generally out of account. Dr. Fairbairn's position is not to be taken as representing Mrs. Klein's work or conclusions. [Isaacs in King and Steiner 1991, p. 458]

'Psychoanalysis: 1945' is a statement of the purview of psychoanalysis given after Fairbairn had developed his main contributions. While he carefully avoids listing his own deviations from Freud, the list he gives of those elements of psychoanalytic theory which are common to all who see themselves as consistent with Freud—as he does himself—is of interest. In addition, Fairbairn is now openly concerned with the scientific standing and the scientific method of analysis. He states, 'Psychoanalysis should be judged by its scientific rather than by its philosophical achievements' (p. 229). As we have seen, he elaborated on the importance of this theme for a philosophy of science and for the influence of educational and social problems in several later papers.

9. PRINCIPLES OF PSYCHOANALYSIS: 1929

Psychoanalysis is a subject about which considerable misunderstanding exists at the present day, not least in medical circles. No excuse seems, therefore, to be required for presenting what appear to be its fundamental principles to a medical audience, least of all when the audience is composed of younger men. It is a subject to which a minimum amount of attention is devoted in the standard medical curriculum. Indeed, that whole region in the universe of medicine, in which, as a matter of history, psychoanalysis arose, is itself relatively neglected, so far as the medical curriculum is concerned. The region in question is, of course, that of functional nervous disease. Little instruction is provided upon this subject in the medical course, except in relation to the differential diagnosis of functional from organic disease. Even in the question of differential diagnosis, importance is attached to the organic rather than to the functional. There is a tendency to regard functional disease as something to be excluded, as one might strain impurities out of a liquid, rather than something to be isolated, as one isolates lighter from heavier oils by fractional distillation. There is a tendency to regard functional nervous disease as simply "not organic," which comes to mean "not interesting, not worth serious attention."

It is easy to see how this attitude has arisen. It has arisen, in part at least, through a very proper effort to prevent the diagnosis of serious organic disease being missed by inadequate examination of the patient. While, however, the importance of differential diagnosis between functional and organic disease is incapable of exaggeration, the prevailing attitude to functional disease, when once it has been diagnosed, is unfortunate for two main reasons:

(a) The rôle of functional nervous disease in the busy doctor's practice is by no means proportionate to the small amount of attention devoted to it in the medical course. I know of no statistics bearing on the subject, but most general practitioners would agree that their life would be considerably eased, if they had no so-called "nervous" patients.

(b) Of the two classes of nervous disease, the functional is more amenable to therapeutic procedure than is the organic. Whereas functional nervous diseases are, on the whole, curable, organic nervous diseases are, on the whole, incurable. The day may not be so far distant, therefore, when it will be organic and not functional nervous disease that is filtered off as a foreign body so far as therapeutic effort is concerned.

The interest of psychoanalysis lies in two claims which are made for it by its adherents. 1. The first claim is that it offers a coherent and comprehensive theory of the nature and etiology of the various functional nervous diseases. 2. The second claim is that it provides the most effective cure for many of these conditions.

The first claim was originally put forward in relation to the neuroses and psychoneuroses only, but psychoanalysis now offers an etiological theory of the psychoses also. Psychoanalysts have come to regard many forms of insanity as belonging to the same family of functional diseases as hysteria and obsessional neurosis, although, of course, to a different genus. Certain forms of insanity of which there is known to be a definite physical cause are naturally excluded from this etiological scheme. General paralysis of the insane is known to be due to the invasion of the central nervous system by spirochætes; and confusional insanity is proved to be of toxic origin. No attempt, therefore, is made to explain the genesis of these or other similar conditions on psychoanalytic principles; but an etiology has been worked out for manic-depressive insanity, paranoia and dementia præcox, to take the chief examples.

As regards the second claim made for psychoanalysis—namely, the therapeutic claim: this has not been seriously extended to the field of the psychoses, though possibilities have been envisaged in this direction. It is probable, however, that psychoanalysis will content itself, so far as the insanities are concerned, with a preventive rather than a therapeutic rôle. Its supporters believe that the application of psychoanalytic principles to the social environment of the young would effect a removal of those conditions which favour the subsequent development of insanity—as indeed of the less serious forms of functional nervous disease. The future applications of psychoanalysis, both as regards psychoses and psychoneuroses, are, therefore, more likely to be preventive than therapeutic in character. This is, of course, in line with a general tendency in modern medicine.

The two claims made on behalf of psychoanalysis are reflected in the use of the word "psychoanalysis" itself. The term is used in two different senses. (a) It is used to denote a method of medical treatment with a special technique originated and developed by Professor Freud of Vienna. (b) The word is also used to denote a body of theory which has grown up round this technique as applied by Freud and his followers. This body of theory has been elaborated in the attempt to explain the phenomena which the technique reveals and to give a rationale to the technique itself.

Of these two meanings of "psychoanalysis," it is important to remember that the first is the original. In other words, psychoanalysis was a method of treatment before it was a theory: a fact sometimes forgotten by Freud's critics. It was the therapeutic success of the method in cases of functional nervous disease that led Freud to seek a theoretic explanation of the results obtained. However far psychoanalytic theory may seem now to have travelled from its original starting-point, it has undoubtedly been elaborated in close relation to the clinical facts of psychoneurosis and insanity. This fact is easily obscured for us when we see psychoanalysts plunging boldly, for instance, into the apparently foreign seas of anthropology. It must be remembered, however, that to study the taboos and superstitions of animism and totemism it is unnecessary to sail to the South Sea Islands. All we have to do is to visit the wards of the nearest asylum.

The present structure of psychoanalytic theory is the gradual product of, roughly speaking, forty years of investigation on the part of Freud and the adherents whom he has gradually collected in various countries. The characteristic features are almost solely attributable to Freud himself, who is undoubtedly a man of considerable genius; but important contributions have been made by some of his followers, notably Ferenczi of Buda-Pest, Abraham of Berlin and Jones of London. In spite of the numerous additions and modifications which psychoanalytic theory has undergone, the main principles have remained more or less unaffected from the time of their formulation. Let us devote ourselves for a short time to the consideration of the most fundamental of these principles. These are:

1. The theory of the Unconscious.
2. The theory of Repression.
3. Freud's Libido Theory.
4. Freud's theory of Symptom Formation and of Dreams.

THE PSYCHOANALYTIC THEORY OF THE UNCONSCIOUS

There is a common tendency to equate mental life with consciousness, and to assume that "unconscious" necessarily means "non-mental." The existence of unconscious mental processes, however, is a fundamental part of psychoanalytic theory. If their existence cannot be directly proved, it is held that it may be legitimately inferred from the facts of conscious life. If phenomena occur which we are accustomed to regard as characteristic products of mental life, and if these phenomena cannot be traced to any *conscious* processes, it seems not unreasonable to attribute them to the activity of *unconscious* mental processes. Thus, if I give a friend a problem to solve and he comes back in half an hour with the solution, I assume that the solution is the result of mental work. If, on the other hand, I have vainly sought the solution myself and go to bed with the problem still unsolved in my mind, and, if I wake up in the morning to find the solution awaiting my return to consciousness, why should I not attribute the solving of the problem to a mental process in my own case as much as in the case of my friend? We all have had experiences of this nature, and "Sleep on it" has become proverbial advice to those who cannot come to a decision. While in the first case quoted the process is conscious, in the second case it is unconscious; but does it necessarily cease to be mental on that account? It is sometimes urged that such phenomena should be explained in purely physiological terms, but no physiological explanations so far available give us such insight into what actually occurs as an explanation in terms of mental process. In the example given the simple statement "He worked it out in his sleep" is more illuminating than any available explanation in terms of neurons, synapses, and reflexes, although it is idle to deny that some related physiological process does occur. In view of the fleeting and changing nature of the content of consciousness and the interruptions to which it is subject in sleep, the hypothesis of unconscious mental processes makes it possible to give a continuity to mental life which is otherwise lacking. It thus makes possible the application to mental life of those laws of causation which have been applied so successfully by science to the physical world.

Once the existence of unconscious mental processes is admitted, an explanation may be sought in terms of mental process for innumerable phenomena which it is impossible to explain in terms of conscious processes alone. Take such a simple phenomenon as a "lapsus linguæ." This may be regarded as due to the influence of a chance association or to a failure of physiological innervation, but neither of these views is illuminating. Freud was the first to show that many slips of the tongue, so far from being accidental, are intentional acts. The intention, however, is unconscious. It is because the intention is unconscious that they are usually regarded as accidental. An example will make this clear. Dr A was discussing Freudian doctrine the other day with Dr B, who had previously criticised Dr A publicly for supporting it in certain aspects. To A's surprise, B appeared unusually conciliatory in his attitude toward Freud during the conversation. A's surprise was, however, modified when B concluded the conversation with this remark, "With Freud we must, of course, collect the *chaff* from the *wheat*": a transposition of words which suggested that the apparently conciliatory attitude of the speaker covered a more fundamental opposition. The same principle holds true of many acts of forgetting. Most of us feel somewhat resentful if a person who knows us well forgets our name. If the theory of unconscious mental processes holds true, perhaps our resentment is not always unjustified. The forgetting of our name may be an unconscious slight. Similarly in the case of a man who forgets the hour of an appointment with his fiancée. Without being a psychoanalyst, the lady is probably justified when she tells him, as doubtless she will, that he does not love her. These examples are representative of a large class of facts, which are difficult to explain except in terms of unconscious mental processes.

There are, however, other phenomena of the same order, which are of more interest than these to the medical world. Instances of such phenomena are irrational fears and doubts, obsessive thoughts and acts, hallucinations and delusions. Why is one man afraid of open spaces, another of closed spaces, another of heights, another of water? Why is one woman afraid of fire, another of horses, another of rats? Why do certain people feel compelled to read the number on every tram ticket, and why do they get into a panic afterwards in case they should have read it wrongly? Why have some people an overpowering impulse to wash their hands almost incessantly, although they know that their hands are quite clean? Why are some the victims of a delusion that they are being persecuted by the Red Muffler Gang? Why does the humble milliner believe herself to be a queen, displaced by the "usurper" in Buckingham Palace? According to psychoanalytic theory, the answer to all these questions lies hidden in the unconscious of the victim.

It is to Freud that we owe the discovery that phenomena of this class have a definite meaning, and that the key to their meaning is to be sought in the unconscious. It is to Freud also that we are indebted for a technique, which makes it possible to unmask the contents of the unconscious. This technique is the "method of free association." The object of this technique is to induce the patient to indulge in purely undirected thought with relaxed attention, and to record faithfully every item that comes into his consciousness. Under favourable conditions, it is found that many items become conscious, which the patient either had never consciously realised before, or had forgotten so completely that he could conscientiously have denied all knowledge of them. This at once raises in the inquiring mind the question, "If these things are capable of being brought into consciousness at all, why does it require a special technique?" Put in another form, the question is, "Why is the Unconscious unconscious?" The answer to this question brings us to the second fundamental principle of psychoanalysis: viz., the theory of repression.

THE THEORY OF REPRESSION

The importance of the concept of repression for psychoanalysis may be judged by the following sentence written by Freud in 1914: "The doctrine of

Repression," he writes, "is the foundation-stone upon which the whole structure of psychoanalysis rests" (1914b, p. 247).

The importance of repression may best be gathered from considering the facts which led Freud to the formulation of the conception. While working with the Viennese neurologist Breuer, in the early stages of his career, Freud's attention was drawn to a case of hysteria in Breuer's practice. The patient was a young woman, whose symptoms included a hysterical paralysis of the right arm and dissociated states in which she mumbled certain words. Breuer treated the case by hypnotism, and during the course of treatment the girl revived forgotten memories of the occasion on which the symptoms first became manifest. The revival of these memories was followed by relief from the symptoms. This remarkable fact intrigued the interest of Freud, and, in later years, when he began to practise for himself as a neurologist in Vienna, he employed the hypnotic method in hysterical cases; he did this with the object of reviving pathogenic memories in the interests of cure. Up to this point all that had been discovered was the importance of memories, which had become unconscious, upon the formation of hysterical symptoms. As time passed, however, difficulty arose over the fact that there were some patients whom he found himself unable to hypnotise. In attempting to revive memories in these unhypnotisable patients he found himself compelled to exercise a certain element of pressure; and this fact led him to the conclusion that there must be some force in the patients' minds actively opposing his efforts—a force which he named the "resistance." This conclusion was an important one, but not so striking as a further conclusion to which he was led shortly afterwards, when the idea came to him that the force which prevented the revival of memories was the very force that had originally rendered the memories unconscious at all. The idea that the disappearance of such memories was due not to a process of passive lapsing, but to a highly active process was a novel one, and it led Freud to formulate his theory of repression. "Repression" was the term which Freud employed to denote the newly-discovered process whereby memories are rendered unconscious. Its distinctive features *as a process* were found by Freud to be four in number:

1. It is an *active* process giving the impression of embodying an immense amount of energy.

2. It is an *unconscious* process. That is to say, the patient was never aware that the process was going on. The memories were not banished by deliberate acts of will, but by an automatic process outside conscious control.

3. It is a *continuous* process. It is not a case of "once repressed, repressed for good." The memories which are made unconscious by repression are kept unconscious. They only remain unconscious through the persistence of repression. It is for this reason that the therapeutic attempt to revive the patient's hidden memories is met with the phenomenon of "resistance."

4. Repression is a *purposive* process, despite its unconscious nature. It gives the impression of being directed towards an end.

Such being the four characteristics of repression as a process, the next question that arises is, "What purpose does the process serve?" Further research on the part of Freud into the nature of repressed memories led him to three conclusions which throw light upon the *function* of repression.

1. Freud found that, when he succeeded in overcoming the resistance by the technique which he employed, he invariably came upon memories with a *sexual* bearing. This does not mean that every repressed memory is a sexual memory, but it does mean that all repressed memories which are not sexual are repressed because they have associative links with memories of a sexual import. It is on account of these associative links that it is possible to recover the fundamental repressed memories at all. Their recovery is possible, because the non-sexual repressed memories have not only associative links with the repressed sexual memories, but also with unrepressed non-sexual memories which are available to consciousness. It is owing to this fact that the free-association method makes it possible for a patient, who associates freely to conscious non-sexual memories, gradually to recover his repressed non-sexual memories, and these in turn, once they have become conscious, make it possible eventually to recover the more deeply repressed sexual memories.

2. The second conclusion which Freud reached through his investigation of repressed memories was that they are exceedingly *unpleasant.* When the repressed memories were revived it was found that the patient was invariably embarrassed, discountenanced, or ashamed. He made every effort to avoid disclosing the memories which he had regained. When he did disclose them, it was evident that the task of doing so caused him acute discomfort. It was in this fact that Freud found the significance of repression. It is a means of getting rid of memories which are so unpleasant that they cannot be endured. They are too firmly fixed to be banished from the mind, and, since they are intolerable to consciousness, they are banished to the unconscious. Repression, therefore, appears to be a mental expression of the fundamental biological tendency of the living organism to withdraw from the noxious and unpleasant. Assuming this to be correct, the further question arises why all unpleasant memories are not repressed. It is a patent fact, of course, that many unpleasant memories are freely accessible to consciousness. Why should repression restrict itself to some memories only, and why should these memories be predominantly sexual or associated in some way with sexual memories? Freud's answer to this question is to point to the attitude of human society as a whole to sex. It is a fact of ordinary observation that no subject is so hedged with social taboos. Freud draws the inference that it is this social taboo that is responsible for the repression of sexual memories. So far as the individual identifies himself with society, he also accepts the social taboo.

Being brought up in society, he quite unconsciously incorporates the taboo into the structure of his own personality. It is on this account that sexual memories prove so painful. They conflict with the individual's social sentiments; and the *raison d'être* of repression is that it provides a method of dealing with this conflict. It spares the patient mental distress by relegating one of the combatants to the unconscious, just as the police might stop a street fight by removing one of the fighters to the cells. The influence of the social taboo on the individual is only possible, of course, so far as the individual identifies himself with the attitude of society. Of all the factors which lead the individual to make this unconscious identification with society, by far the most effective and important is the influence of parents upon their children at an impressionable age. This brings us to the third conclusion that Freud drew from the study of repressed memories.

3. Freud's third conclusion was that the nucleus of the unconscious is constituted by the repressed memories of *early childhood*. He was led to this view by the fact that, when the free association method was employed with sufficient patience and assiduity, it was found to lead back invariably to memories of early years. These were only reached after more recent repressed memories had been explored, but Freud was led by his investigations to believe that, at the back of all adult and adolescent repressed memories, lay a nucleus of childish memories, which formed the initial material for repression, and constituted the very heart of the unconscious. This discovery had a momentous implication. Unless Freud was to abandon his whole theory, it involved him in a still further conclusion: the conclusion, namely, that the history of the sexual life must be extended backwards to include the earliest years of childhood. This conclusion Freud did not hesitate to draw, and the result was his so-called "libido theory."

THE LIBIDO THEORY

By "libido" Freud means that fundamental biological urge, the aim of which is to ensure the propagation of the species, and which expresses itself most characteristically in sexual activity. Freud's libido theory may be taken as the third fundamental principle of psychoanalysis. Probably no part of psychoanalytic theory has received more criticism, and it is responsible for most of the opposition which psychoanalysis has met. It is impossible to-day to enter into any discussion of its validity, or to attempt to differentiate between parts of it which are valid and parts of it which are dubious. All that can be attempted is to indicate the essential nature of the theory. Its main purport is to the effect that the history of the sexual life begins not at adolescence, as is generally supposed, but in early infancy. The startling nature of this proposition is somewhat modified by three considerations which ought to be borne in mind:

1. If the theory is to be even considered as worthy of discussion, it involves an enormous broadening of our conception of what is to be called sexual. It is perfectly plain that, in the ordinary every-day use of the word, sexuality is foreign to the life of the young child. Freud, however, is not blind to this fact; and indeed he deliberately and with avowed intention extends the concept of sex to include all manner of activities and tendencies not ordinarily regarded as related to it.

2. It is also to be borne in mind that the attempt to trace back the history of the complex phenomenon of adult sexuality to simpler elements at an earlier stage is but an example of the genetic standpoint, which is so characteristic of modern scientific thought. It is the adoption of the genetic standpoint involved in the acceptance of the theory of evolution that has contributed more than anything else to the advance of modern science. The principle of continuity has been applied with success in all fields of thought. Freud applies it to the sexual life. If it is difficult to envisage a continuity between adult sexuality and phenomena of child life, it is no more difficult than to appreciate a continuity between the activities of civilised man and those of his prehistoric ancestors.

3. A third consideration to be borne in mind is that, although it is only at puberty that the gonads give evidence of their activity as externally secreting reproductive glands, the endocrine function of both ovaries and testes is now known to assert its influence from the earliest age. These three considerations should all be borne in mind in forming an estimate of the validity of Freud's libido theory.

Freud was led, as we have seen, to consider early childhood in relation to the sexual life through tracing back repressed memories to that period of development. Another factor that contributed to the formulation of his theory came from a study of the perversions. In his practice Freud came upon a number of patients who were found to be addicted to perverse practices. Eventually the idea came to him that there was a striking analogy between these sexual perversions and certain innocent phenomena of childhood. Relating the two together, he drew the double inference: (a) that the perversions were due to the persistence in undue strength of certain characteristics normal in childhood; (b) that these childish characteristics were of a sexual quality. By way of illustration, it may be recalled that in certain gross perversions (such as Fellatio and Cunnilingus) sexual satisfaction is sought through activities connected with the mouth. Freud relates this to the fact that at a certain stage of the infant's life pleasure is associated almost exclusively with the oral activity of sucking. He would, therefore, describe the perversions in question as due, in part at least, to a fixation of interest at the oral stage of libido-development in childhood, and would describe the satisfaction which the child derives in sucking as sexual in character.

One cannot help feeling that Freud would have been better advised to describe the satisfaction which the child derives from sucking as "sensuous" (i.e., "of the senses") rather than as "sexual." The pleasure derived from childish activities such as sucking is essentially due to the satisfaction of appetite, in the sense in which psychologists use this word. In the psychological sense of the word, "appetite" is not restricted to the food-seeking tendency, but applied to all tendencies demanding immediate bodily satisfaction. All pleasure afforded by the satisfaction of appetites is essentially sensuous pleasure, whatever the nature of the appetite concerned. Since the fundamental activities of the infant are all appetitive the satisfaction derived from their indulgence may be described as sensuous. To call it sexual, as Freud does, entails a mistaken narrowing of the conception involved. Sexual satisfaction is merely one form of sensuous satisfaction. The truth seems to be that in infancy sensuous satisfaction is undifferentiated, and that it is only as development proceeds that it becomes differentiated into sexual, alimentary and other forms. For similar reasons the "libido," if this unfortunate and misleading term is to be retained, should be regarded as the biological life-impulse, from which, in individual development, the sex-instinct is differentiated, rather than as something strictly sexual from the start. Freud, however, regards the libido as sexual from the outset, because the adult sex-instinct develops from it. It is for the same reason that he regards the appetitive activities of childhood as sexual, namely, because they are later integrated into the sexual impulse.

According to the libido theory, there are various zones of the body, from the stimulation of which a child is capable of experiencing so-called "sexual" satisfaction. These Freud calls "erotogenous" zones, and they include the lips, breasts and excretory passages as well as the genitalia themselves. During individual development interests in these various zones are held to be gradually organised under the supremacy of the reproductive impulse towards the ends of mating and procreation. That their influence is not without effect upon adult sexual life is illustrated by the phenomenon of kissing, which is avowedly at once an oral and a sexual activity. The history of the process whereby these diverse interests become modified, organised and integrated into adult sexuality is, according to Freud, the history of the libido. This process of organisation is normally complete before puberty, when the function of reproduction becomes physiologically possible and interest begins to develop towards members of the opposite sex outside the family. It would thus appear, if Freud is right, that behind the maturing of the adult sexual organisation lies a long and complicated history involving the co-ordination and organisation of a considerable number of different tendencies. This is the real significance of the libido theory. The complexity of the process makes it easy to see how abnormalities of development may occur. The possibility of abnormal development is increased by the fact that the first objects of a child's affection are parents or parent-substitutes, whereas the proper objects of adult sexual life are persons of the opposite sex outside the family. Freud was led by the study of his patients to the conclusion that there is a continuity in the history of the individual's affections, similar to that which he found to exist in the organisation of the libido. In tracing back the history of the affections he found a continuity between adult sexual love at one end of the scale and the emotional bond which unites an infant to its mother at the other end of the scale. He, therefore, extended the concept of the sexual to cover the relationship of child to mother. Between the two extremes in this scale of love he found a series of intermediate object relationships. Thus change in the objects of the affection accompanies the change in the nature of the libido itself. Here, again, we may accept the continuity of development upon which Freud lays emphasis, while reserving judgment as to his use of the word "sexual."

It is thus evident that, for a normal adult sexual life to be possible, a complicated series of developmental phases have to be successfully passed through, not only as regards the organisation of the sexual impulse, but as regards the love relationship also. If this be so, it would surprise us if we did not find a rich pathology of the sexual life and its antecedents. Where are we to look for the clinical manifestations of this pathology? According to Freud, we find them in the perversions, neuroses, psychoneuroses and psychoses, and also in dreams. This brings us to the fourth fundamental principle of psychoanalysis.

THE PSYCHOANALYTIC THEORY OF SYMPTOM-FORMATION AND DREAM

According to psychoanalytic theory the symptoms of all functional nervous disease are to be explained in terms of two factors. These factors are: (a) The repressed tendencies in the unconscious; (b) the forces of repression. The interaction of these two factors admits of a manifold symptomatology. What actual symptoms shall develop in any given case is held to depend partly on the nature and strength of the repressed tendencies, partly on the strength of the repression and the time of life at which it comes into being. Variations and combinations of these elements in definite proportions provide both the syndromes familiar to psychopathology, and aberrant cases which do not fall into any of the familiar groups. Repression, as we have seen, is believed to be due to the fact that the child unconsciously incorporates into his personality the attitude of the parent figure towards certain of his activities. The attitude of the parent, which, when incorporated, leads to repression, is that of disapproval. The childish activities which are subjected to this disapproval are pre-eminently those diverse pleasure-seeking activities which Freud attributes to the libido. The child's mind is thus the scene of a conflict between the tendencies in question and the parental taboo which has been incorporated into the child's own personality. As the taboo becomes more firmly established, the presence of the pleasure-seeking activities itself becomes unpleasing, and the activities are subjected to a process of repression, which relegates them to the unconscious. The result is that, as development proceeds, the unconscious becomes a vast reservoir of repressed tendencies, which attract to themselves a host of related memories such as Freud found in his neurotic patients. It is the persistence of repressed tendencies in the unconscious that makes symptom-formation possible.

Repression, of course, is not a process confined to the minds of potential neurotics, nor are the tendencies which invite repression absent in the healthy child. The existence in all social groups of taboos upon the whole subject of sex and the excretory functions is ample evidence of the universality of repression; and everyone charged with the upbringing of a child is familiar with the appearance, at one phase or another, of some at least of the tendencies which Freud holds to be the subject of repression. Tendencies which can hardly escape observation are those of interest in the excretions, exhibitionism and sexual curiosity. The reticence of parents towards children in matters of sex, and their uncompromising attitude towards any manifestation of the tendencies in question makes it impossible for any child, who is not mentally defective, to escape the influence of repression. Indeed it would appear desirable that this should be so within certain limits. For it would appear that culture and civilisation depend for their existence upon a suitable degree of repression. The various perversions appear to depend upon absence of repression in respect of one or another of the tendencies ordinarily repressed. Normally, the energy with which the repressed tendencies are endowed, being denied expression along natural channels, is deflected to other interests, which are either socially useful, or at any rate socially acceptable. This deflection of interest is termed by Freud "sublimation." Thus sexual curiosity may be transformed into a veritable passion for knowledge, such as has achieved the highest attainments of science. This is an example of a socially useful sublimation. Art, in its various branches, furnishes an example of a sublimation which, if not useful, is at any rate socially acceptable. Thus exhibitionism finds an approved outlet, within certain limits, upon the stage. The greater frequency of perverse practices among artists than among an unselected group of individuals is evidence of the repressed tendencies that underlie the artistic sublimation.

The process of repression, if it is gradually established and not so intense as to prevent any appreciable outlet to the repressed tendencies, appears, therefore, to be beneficent in character. Under such favourable circumstances the repressed tendencies find a satisfactory, though indirect, outlet. In part they find expression through organisation into the adult sexual impulse, in part they find expression through the various sublimations. If, however, repression is too intense or too suddenly brought to bear, leaving the repressed tendencies no opportunity of expression, then these tendencies, endowed as they are with an immense fund of energy, remain, so to speak, "under pressure" in the unconscious. In these circumstances they come to constitute a source of danger to the personality. Through lack of expression their potential is constantly increasing throughout development, and, at any crisis of life, or even without a crisis, they are liable to burst through the shackles of repression in some abnormality of thought, feeling, or conduct. This phenomenon is described by Freud as "the return of the repressed," and it is in this way that the symptoms of insanity and functional nervous disease are held by psychoanalysts to come into being.

From this standpoint, it is easy to understand the significance of psychotic and neurotic symptoms. They are all some form of compromise between repressing and repressed elements. If any of the tendencies subject to repression have either been unusually strong or over-indulged through influences present in the child's environment, the tendencies in question are liable to be invested with an undue amount of interest. This phenomenon is described by Freud as a "fixation." A fixation may also be determined by an unduly sudden or unduly harsh repression. In this case it is the force of the taboo that invests the forbidden tendency with interest. This is but an illustration of the principle embodied in the proverb, "Forbidden fruits are sweet," and in the words of St Paul, "I had not known sin but by the Law." It is part of the theory that different tendencies come to the fore at different periods of the child's life. Thus tendencies to exhibitionism are prominent at a later age than the activity of sucking. The various fixations are, therefore, liable to occur at specific phases of development. Each of the recognised psychoses and psychoneuroses is regarded as being characterised by a fixation at some definite level of development. Where fixations occur at several levels there result those mixed types of disease which are the puzzle of the diagnostician. The general principle involved is that the earlier the level of a fixation, the more serious is the associated disease. The insanities are thus associated with the early fixations, the psychoneuroses with the later. Of all the diseases in question, it is generally agreed by psychiatrists that dementia præcox involves the most serious disintegration of the personality; and this is the disease which, according to psychoanalytic theory, is characterised by the earliest fixation. Hysteria, on the other hand, is universally regarded as relatively benign, and psychoanalysts concur with this view by associating it with the latest fixation of which their theory admits. In this case the fixation is not so much upon one of the appetitive tendencies as upon the earliest object of the child's affection, viz., the parent. Though the symptoms of the various insanities and functional nervous diseases thus differ according to the fixations involved, they all possess the common characteristic of being a compromise between the repressed forces and the forces of repression. It is characteristic of these diseases that, though repression cannot prevent the return of the repressed tendencies altogether, it can, at any rate, prevent them returning in overt form. The symptoms are, therefore, the distortions which the repressed tendencies undergo in forcing their way through the barriers of repression. It is in this way that psychoanalysis explains the whole concourse of symptoms familiar to psychopathology. Dreams are also explained as phenomena of a similar kind, and Freud describes the study of dreams as the high road to knowledge of the unconscious.

This concludes my account of the fundamental principles of psychoanalysis. I have confined my remarks to a description of the main principles, in terms of which psychoanalysis explains the nature and genesis of functional nervous disease. Psychoanalysis in its rôle as a therapeutic agent is a subject which requires separate treatment, and does not fall within the scope of this paper.

10. THE PSYCHOLOGY OF ANXIETY

The occasion for the considerations, to which the reader's attention is about to be directed, is provided by Dr Ernest Jones' (1929) article on "The Psychopathology of Anxiety." The line of thought developed by Dr Jones in this article centres round his statement that "morbid anxiety is a perverted manifestation of the fear instinct which, in the case of neurotic conflicts, has been stimulated to activity as a protection against the threatening libido" (p. 21). This statement is later supplemented by this further statement:

> We know that anxiety arises in relation to over-development of a libidinal cathexis. Now the curious thing is that the latter can happen either from direct erotic excitation or from what might be called the opposite of this, namely, a threat to the libidinal organisation. . . . A threat causes a libidinal investment of the point threatened, as though—to speak figuratively—the libido protects itself by increasing its strength. The fear reaction on the part of the ego is secondary to this increase, and clinically we find that at least as much morbid anxiety is a response to a libido excess provoked by threats as to that provoked by erotic excitation." [pp. 23–24]

While the present writer finds himself in substantial agreement with Jones' interpretation of morbid anxiety, he believes it to require supplementing by certain considerations which are mainly of a general psychological nature. It is the writer's belief that the chief need of psychoanalytic thought at the present time is that it should make closer contact with general psychology. The reasons for the lack of contact between psychoanalytic thought and general psychology need not be considered for our present purpose. Apart from such questions as the resistances which influence the attitude of psychologists to psychoanalytic theory, there are historical considerations which explain the detached attitude adopted by psychoanalysts toward general psychology. Although this divorce between psychoanalytic theory and psychology is perfectly intelligible as a phenomenon, the fact remains that it has unfortunate consequences for both sciences. Psychology is the poorer, in so far as it fails to avail itself, for the explanation of human behaviour, of that knowledge of unconscious motivation which psychoanalysis affords. Psychoanalytic theory, on the other hand, suffers from the failure of psychoanalytic workers to avail themselves of the considerable body of knowledge about the human mind which general psychology provides. The failure of psychoanalytic workers to avail themselves of this body of knowledge is largely due to a reluctance on their part to admit that psychology has any knowledge to offer which is not sterile for the interpretation of human behaviour. It is also partly due to an unfamiliarity with the more recent developments of psychological thought. The psychology against which they are in revolt is the old academic psychology based purely upon the material revealed by introspection—the psychology of the psychologist's own conscious processes. It must be insisted, however, that not all psychology is sterile, and that many of the developments of modern psychology are capable of throwing considerable light upon the theoretical problems of psychoanalysis. The psychology of instinct is a case in point.

The desirability of a rapprochement between psychoanalysis and general psychology appears to the writer to be illustrated in the discussion about morbid anxiety, to which Jones' paper was a contribution.[1] As Jones points out, the term 'morbid anxiety' or 'anxiety' for short is employed in psychopathology to designate a group of phenomena which can be distinguished from those ordinarily ascribed to 'fear.' He regards anxiety, like fear, as a reaction to danger; but, while in the case of fear, the source of danger is obvious and external, in the case of anxiety the source of danger is hidden and internal. According to Jones, what is feared in the latter case is the libido. This general point of view must be accepted as fundamentally sound; that fear is a reaction to external danger no one will dispute; and that morbid anxiety is a reaction to internal danger appears to be one of the most conclusive inferences, which may be drawn from the facts revealed by psychoanalysis. While, however, this general point of view may be accepted as fundamentally sound, our acceptance must be subject to certain important psychological considerations.

The first of these considerations is that, while anxiety is to be distinguished from fear, it is not distinct from fear. It differs from fear simply in the fact that, while fear is an acute condition, anxiety is a chronic condition. If the symptoms of anxiety differ from those of fear, so we must remember do the symptoms of any chronic physical disease differ from those of the same disease in its acute form. If conditions change somewhat, the one may pass into the other. That anxiety may pass into fear is evident in the case

[1]The paper referred to was Dr Jones' contribution to a discussion upon morbid anxiety at a Joint Meeting of the Royal Society of Medicine, Psychiatric Section, and the British Psychological Society, Medical Section, on April 9th, 1929.

of the patient suffering from a phobia. The phobia is essentially a state of anxiety related to a situation which is imagined as dangerous. The person subject to a phobia exists in a chronic state of fear oriented towards a situation which may at any time materialize. If the situation does materialize, anxiety passes into acute fear. Thus the patient with agoraphobia is in a chronic state of anxiety, because he may be called upon at any time to cross an open space (which for him constitutes a danger). If he does cross an open space, his chronic fear becomes acute and may even develop into panic—panic being a specially acute degree of fear. When the patient escapes from the dangerous situation, the acuteness of fear subsides; but fear persists in the chronic form of anxiety, because the possibility of the dreaded situation recurring is appreciated as a constant, though not imminent, danger.

The second consideration which may be advanced is that anxiety is not necessarily morbid. This follows from the view that anxiety is just chronic fear. If an individual remains in a dangerous situation over a prolonged period, we can imagine fear becoming chronic. This holds true as much when the danger is external as when it is internal. If the sole survivor of a wreck is washed ashore upon an island notorious for the savagery of its inhabitants, we can hardly blame him if he shows signs of fear when the inhabitants come out from their villages to meet him. If, however, he lands upon the same island unobserved, we can hardly regard it as abnormal, if, after spending a few days in the bushes constantly attempting to escape attention, he finds himself in a state of anxiety. The danger of his situation is chronic. Why should his fear not be chronic also? It must be admitted, however, that, while anxiety is not necessarily morbid, it is usually so—the reason being that it is unusual for human beings to find themselves constantly threatened by an external situation which justifies fear. The reason that anxiety is such a constant feature of psychopathological states is that the dreaded danger is of internal origin. It has its source in the instinctive endowment of the individual concerned; it is part of the man himself, and therefore permanent escape is never possible. The constant presence of the libido may be masked by the operation of repression; but the libido is ever striving for expression, and it thus constitutes an ever-present menace. The resulting anxiety is consequently never wholly absent.

Thirdly, the suggestion may be hazarded that anxiety over an internal menace is not necessarily fear of the libido. Fear may be occasioned theoretically by any internal tendency which presents itself as a menace. Psychoanalytic investigation appears to show, however, that, of all the tendencies which constitute the instinctive endowment of man (the 'id'), those related to the sex instinct (the 'libido') are, as a matter of fact, specially prone to occasion neurotic anxiety. Every psychoanalysis of a neurotic patient seems to reveal the libido as the danger from which escape is sought by a flight into illness.

At first sight it appears arbitrary to regard the libido as the specific danger which occasions neurotic anxiety, but it is not so arbitrary as it seems. The reason for so regarding it is to be found in the conditions under which the process of repression comes into being in the life-history of the individual. It is to provide a means of escape from the libido that repression is called into operation in the first instance. Repression ought thus to be regarded not as banishment of the repressed from consciousness so much as a *flight of consciousness from the repressed*. The reason why it is the libido from which escape is sought is that the libido conflicts with the child's early identification with the parents as frustrating figures. As Freud (1923b) points out, this identification of the child with frustrating figures forms the nucleus of that psychical organization to which he gives the name of 'superego'—an organization which, as development proceeds, attains a varying degree of independence of the main personality (Freud's 'ego'). It is because of the conflict between the superego and the libido that repression is called into being. Repression mitigates the unpleasure, which the conflict occasions, by excluding from consciousness one of the conflicting elements (the libido) in so far as it is incongruous with the other (the superego). As Freud puts it, "we know that as a rule the ego carries out repressions in the service and at the behest of its superego" (p. 75).

Freud goes on to point out, however, that in hysterical cases the process of repression comes into operation against the superego itself. Since the process of repression is a defensive mechanism (or rather an 'escape-mechanism'), this statement seems to imply that the superego may come to constitute a source of danger to the ego. If this be so, we seem justified in assuming that the superego may itself become the object of fear for the neurotic personality. It would thus appear that morbid anxiety may be determined not only by the menace of the libido but also by the menace of the superego. Jones rightly points out that a threat to the libidinal organization may cause a libidinal investment of the point threatened and thus lead to a secondary fear-reaction dependent on the increase of libidinal cathexis involved. It is, of course, a general truth about human nature that what is in danger of being lost becomes correspondingly over-valued. The threat of 'aphanasis' thus inevitably leads to an increase of danger from the direction of the dreaded libido, but there appears to be also a direct danger from the superego itself. This fact appears to be illustrated in the dreams of neurotic individuals. Take, for example, the following dream:

> I seemed to be the object of the most vindictive and relentless persecution at the hands of people whom I think of as Bolsheviks or revolutionists and whose conduct towards me was unreasonable and entirely unmerited. I found myself time and again among a big company of people, trying to mingle with them quietly and escape notice, and, just when I was feeling a

> sense of security, some one recognised me, rushed at me, and ill-treated me. I felt that to explain my innocence was useless when dealing with such bigoted people. I remember one occasion when I was sitting in a back bench and with every seat occupied like a class in school. Suddenly I was recognised by a woman in the seat in front who turned round. This person denounced me aloud and people on every side rushed at me in a hostile way. I think certain papers were taken from me and examined or something.

In the case of this dream, the dreamer was an individual in whom the superego was particularly aggressive. The 'accusing woman' of the dream was shown by free association to represent the mother-figure, which, by a process of identification, formed the nucleus of the superego. The superego is thus represented in the dream as a danger menacing the ego or organized self. It would therefore appear that the libido is not the only internal danger which occasions morbid anxiety. There is another such danger—the superego.

The stimulus for the last and *by far the most important consideration* to be advanced here is Jones' (1929) statement that "morbid anxiety is a perverted manifestation of the fear instinct" (p. 21). It is the phrase 'fear instinct' that provides the occasion for comment. The meaning of Jones' statement is perfectly clear, but the use of the term 'fear instinct' is to be discouraged, because it involves an ambiguity which is liable to give rise to a fatal confusion of thought. The term 'fear instinct' may be taken to mean "the instinct with the activity of which fear is associated," or it may be taken to mean "the instinct *of* fear." Now it is in the latter sense that many psychopathologists use this term; and it is the tendency to speak of fear as an instinct that is responsible for most of the confusion which exists concerning the nature of morbid anxiety. It must be insisted that *fear is not an instinct; fear is an emotion*. The instinct to which Jones refers is the *instinct of escape*. The emotion of fear is, of course, intimately related to this instinct; but it cannot be insisted too strongly that fear is not itself an instinct. As Jones (1929) points out, psychoanalysts have come to take a very favourable view of the capacity of mankind to resist the stimulus of external danger without fear reactions being evoked. If fear were an instinct, it is difficult to see how psychoanalysts could have come to this conclusion; for, if fear were an instinct, it would be a quite natural and appropriate reaction to danger. It is because fear is not an instinct that Jones is right when he says that "the reaction of developed anxiety is not the inevitable or in any sense the normal mode of responding to external danger" (p. 23). Now the normal mode of responding to external danger is, according to circumstances, either by aggression or by escape. Aggression and escape are instinctive reactions dependent on the existence in the organism of certain characteristic innate reaction-tendencies. It is true that they are frequently accompanied by the emotions of anger and fear respectively; but these emotions are not themselves instinctive tendencies. They are feeling-states which tend to occur when certain instinctive tendencies are active.

The intimate association between the emotions and the instinctive tendencies was pointed out long ago by Professor William James. The relationship between emotion and instinct has subsequently been studied in some detail by Professor William McDougall. McDougall (1908), whose contribution to the subject must be regarded as of supreme importance, regards the instincts as "the prime movers of all human activity" (p. 38). This point of view seems indisputable and it is in agreement with the point of view adopted by psychoanalysts—the primitive instinctive endowment, which McDougall postulates, being identical with what Freud describes as 'the id.' The relationship which McDougall believes to exist between emotion and the instinctive tendencies may be best expressed by saying that the activity of an instinctive tendency always has an affective aspect. In the case of the simpler instincts, he believes that this affective aspect of the instinctive process attains little prominence; but, in the case of the principal powerful instincts, the affective process is distinct; further, it has a characteristic quality in the case of each of the principal instinctive tendencies. Each of these characteristic affective experiences (which are generically termed 'emotions') has received a special name. They are known by such names as 'anger,' 'fear,' etc. Anger is thus regarded as the affective experience which accompanies the activity of the instinct of pugnacity or aggression, fear the affective experience which accompanies the activity of the instinct of flight.

McDougall's general point of view, to the effect that specific emotions are related to the activity of specific instinctive tendencies, recommends itself to our acceptance; but it is not so certain that he is right in his conception of the nature of that relationship. From his point of view, the activity of the instinct of flight is necessarily accompanied by the emotion of fear. Since the instinct of flight is a natural instinctive reaction to such dangerous situations as cannot be adequately met by aggression, it would follow that fear is the inevitable emotional experience in the presence of such situations. This point of view, however, conflicts with the favourable view taken by psychoanalysts of the capacity of mankind to resist the stimulus of external danger without fear reactions being evoked. If psychoanalysts are right, it would seem that there is something wrong with McDougall's conception of the relationship between the emotions and the instinctive tendencies to which they are specifically related.

That there is something wrong with McDougall's conception of the relationship between the emotions and the instinctive tendencies has been pointed out by Dr James Drever (1917) in his *Instinct in Man*—a book which has not received the attention it deserves. Now McDougall (1921) defines an instinct as:

> an inherited or innate psycho-physical disposition which determines its possessor to perceive, and to pay attention to, objects of a certain class, to experience an emotional excitement of a particular quality upon perceiving such an object, and to act in regard to it in a particular manner, or, at least, to experience an impulse to such action. [p. 25]

While Drever accepts from McDougall the fact that instinctive experience, like all experience, has a cognitive, an affective and a conative aspect, he raises the question whether the central affective aspect is correctly described by McDougall as an *emotional* excitement. That it is an excitement "with a particular quality" is unquestionable, but Drever prefers to describe this excitement as "instinct-interest." From this point of view all 'interest' is due to an appeal to some instinctive tendency, and the activity of every instinctive tendency is accompanied by 'interest.' Thus danger-situations arouse interest by appealing to the instinctive tendency of escape, and the activity of the instinctive tendency of escape involves interest in the danger-aspect of situations. It is presumably on account of this latter fact that an individual, whose tendency to escape is provoked by an inner danger, is so liable to apprehend danger from external sources—a process aided, of course, by narcissistic investment of the libido, by projection and by symbolism.

If then we regard instinct-interest as being the typical affective element in the experience of instinctive activity, how are we to regard emotion? It is impossible, of course, to deny McDougall's observation that specific emotions are associated with the activity of specific instinctive reaction-tendencies. The question, therefore, narrows itself down to this—under what conditions does instinct-interest acquire an emotional colouring? The answer which Drever (1917) gave to this question in his *Instinct in Man* was that "the affective element in instinct-experience becomes emotion, only when action in satisfaction of the instinct is suspended or checked, when interest . . . passes into 'tension' " (p. 157, 2nd edition). Thus the activation of the aggressive tendency only gives rise to the specific emotion of anger in so far as the aggressive tendency is unable to gain satisfactory expression; similarly, the activation of the instinct of escape only gives rise to fear in so far as escape is obstructed.

The interpretation of emotion which Drever (1917) elaborates in his *Instinct in Man* is further developed in *An Introduction to the Psychology of Education* (Drever 1922). In this work Drever introduces into his theory of emotion the conception of bipolarity. Starting from the generally accepted fact that all affective experience is bipolar (i.e., that all affective experience finds a place on the pleasure-unpleasure scale), he shows the necessity of regarding bipolarity as an essential feature of emotion. Joy and sorrow have usually been regarded by psychologists as specific emotions. In conformity with the principle of bipolarity, Drever comes to regard them not as independent emotions but as:

general characters of emotion, representing in the emotional phase that bipolarity which characterizes all affective experience. This means that, when the emotional phase of affective experience develops, it tends towards the joy pole or the sorrow pole, if we may speak in such terms, and necessarily so. The conditions determining either of the directions are fairly clear. So far as the underlying tendency is being delayed, obstructed, or baulked, the direction is towards the sorrow pole; so far as the tendency is meeting with sudden, unexpected, or rapid success, and particularly if the situation is such as to increase the stimulation, the direction is towards the joy pole." [p. 59]

Drever's interpretation of the phenomena of emotion accords so well with the facts that it appears to be conclusive. From this point of view, the activation of the instinct of escape is only accompanied by emotion when the instinctive tendency to escape is either obstructed or facilitated out of proportion to the intensity with which the tendency is aroused. If the tendency to escape is relatively obstructed, then we find a specific emotion of negative (unpleasant) polarity developing—the emotion to which the name of 'fear' is given. If, on the other hand, the tendency to escape is relatively facilitated, then we find a specific emotion of positive (pleasant) polarity developing—an emotion which is usually described by those who experience it as 'a sense of relief.' If, however, the activated tendency is allowed to express itself without either obstruction or facilitation, neither negative nor positive emotion is experienced, because the conditions necessary for the development of emotion are absent. The affective experience remains merely that of instinct-interest.

The bipolar theory of emotion accords perfectly with the facts revealed by psychoanalysis. It provides ample justification for Jones' statement that "the reaction of developed anxiety is not the inevitable or in any sense the normal mode of responding to external danger" (1929, p. 23). It endorses the favourable view taken by psychoanalysts of the capacity of mankind to resist the stimulus of external danger without fear reactions being provoked. The bipolar theory of emotion also enables us to understand why it is that anxiety is such a pronounced feature of neurotic disease. Anxiety characterizes the neurotic because the tendency of escape is activated out of all proportion to the means of escape available. The tendency of escape is thus relatively obstructed, and the negative emotion of fear necessarily makes its appearance. Since the danger from which escape is sought is internal, it is ever present. It is really inescapable, so long as the internal menace persists; but escape is attempted by the various unconscious mechanisms of which repression is the prototype. Freud calls these mechanisms "defence mechanisms," but, in view of the considerations advanced, it would be more accurate to describe them as *escape mechanisms*. Neurotic symptoms are the product of the effort to escape by means of these escape mechanisms from an ever-present internal danger which constantly manifests itself as 'the return of the repressed.' In this way we can understand not only the familiar fact that symptoms undergo a progressive development, but the fact that the development of fresh symptoms fails to rid the patient of anxiety except in a temporary way. The bipolar theory of emotion also enables us to understand how relief of neurotic anxiety may occur. It occurs whenever the tendency to escape is facilitated. The average medical practitioner is an expert in devising methods for facilitating the process of escape, with the result that a positive emotion of relief is temporarily experienced, whenever a new method is adopted. During the brief interlude provided by a 'rest cure' or a voyage round the world, the emotional state of the patient frequently assumes a positive polarity, which sometimes conveys the impression to the observer that the patient is passing through a phase of slight elation. These measures are, however, only palliative. Anxiety can only be permanently abolished by measures calculated to remove the element of danger from such endopsychic tendencies as have come to constitute a menace to the patient. Such measures are adopted in psychoanalytic therapy.

In conclusion, attention must be drawn to the fact that there are two factors involved in the production of neurotic anxiety—as, indeed, there are in the production of fear in general. We have seen that the emotion of fear tends to develop to the degree that the activated tendency of escape is obstructed or thwarted. The two factors involved are therefore (1) the adequacy of the *means* of escape, (2) the intensity of the *impulse* to escape. So long as these two factors vary proportionately, no emotion is experienced. The emotion of fear may, however, be produced by a suitable variation in either factor. On the one hand, it may develop because, when the instinct of escape is activated by an appropriate stimulus, the means of escape are inadequate; or, on the other hand, it may develop because the instinct of escape is abnormally easily provoked. Given the fact that an internal source of danger has once been constituted, it is easy to see that the first of these conditions is operative in the case of the neurotic. The constant presence of a powerful endopsychic menace is certain to lead to situations in which the means of escape are inadequate. On the other hand, it would seem that in certain individuals there is a definite predisposition to neurosis, which has led medical writers to postulate the existence of a nervous or neurotic temperament. This may be interpreted as signifying that predisposition to neurotic disease depends upon a congenital hypersensitivity on the part of the instinct of escape. Assuming the existence in certain individuals of such a temperamental sensitivity on the part of the escape-tendency, it is easy to understand how the various escape mechanisms, of which repression is the prototype, should come to play a specially significant rôle in their lives. From another point of view, such individuals may be described as possessing a psychical constitution which is predisposed to dissociation-phenomena; but what are dissociated in the case of the neurotic are mental functions or elements of mental content which have acquired an unpleasant polarity; and dissociation of the unpleasant is, like repression, just a mechanism of escape. It is in this direction that we must look for the truth underlying Janet's otherwise unsatisfactory hypothesis that the dissociations of hysteria are due to a "failure of mental synthesis." The failure of mental synthesis to which he refers is really a mechanism of escape from mental content and mental functions which have come to constitute a danger for the individual concerned. Freud (1915d) regards neurotic disease as originating in frustration of the sexual tendencies (libido). "Psychoanalytic work," he says, "has furnished us with the rule that people fall ill of a neurosis as a result of frustration" (p. 323). In another place he says: "Frustration operates pathogenically in that it dams up the libido, and thus puts to the test both the person's power of tolerating the increase of tension, and his manner of taking steps to release himself from it" (Freud 1912, p. 114). Presumably individuals vary in their power of tolerating the tension caused by frustration of the sexual tendencies, just as they vary in all other psychological characteristics. According to Freud, therefore, predisposition to neurosis must depend on the capacity to tolerate the internal menace constituted by the unsatisfied libido. It would appear that the inability of some people to tolerate this menace is due to the facility with which the instinct of escape is activated. Such a person's "manner of taking steps to release himself from" tension is by adopting (unconsciously, of course,) such escape mechanisms as are available for dealing with internal danger and of which repression is the most notable. Owing, however, to the fact that the menace proceeds from the innate instinctive endowment, final escape is impossible. The instinct of escape, therefore, can never achieve satisfaction; its activity is continually subject to relative obstruction. The result is that an emotional state of negative polarity inevitably develops and remains a more or less constant feature. The negative emotion of the instinct of escape is the emotion of fear. In its chronic state fear takes the form of anxiety. Hence the fact that morbid anxiety is such a universal feature of neurotic disease.

11. THE PSYCHOPATHOLOGY OF AGGRESSION

At the outset I desire to explain that in my use of the term "aggressive instinct" I do not intend to imply adherence to any particular theory of instinct. I simply use the term to describe that native tendency to aggression which is admitted on all hands to be a characteristic feature of human behaviour and which is liable to show itself more particularly in situations of frustration.

In the course of psychoanalytical practice, I have been increasingly impressed by the role of aggression as an etiological factor in the genesis of psychotic and psychoneurotic disorders. My experience corresponds to that of a large group of psychoanalysts and it falls in line with the more recent theories of Freud. It was in *The Ego and the Id* (1923b) that Freud first expressly formulated the view that the aggressive tendencies are the chief agents in the production and maintenance of psychopathological conditions. The ground had already been prepared for this thesis, however, in some of his previous writings, e.g., in a paper entitled "Mourning and Melancholia" (1917a). In this paper he had instituted a comparison between melancholia and that state of grief and melancholy which normally follows bereavement. The obvious similarity of these states suggested to Freud that they must both be reactions to a similar situation. Since grief is undoubtedly a reaction to the loss of a love-object, he concluded that loss of a love-object was also the situation provocative of melancholia.

The two states, however, are not identical; Freud set himself the task of analysing the difference between them. The chief distinguishing feature which impressed itself upon him was this: whereas in grief self-esteem remained unaffected, in melancholia self-esteem is markedly impaired. For the bereaved person the world becomes empty and impoverished; with the melancholic, however, what becomes impoverished is not the world but the ego. Belittling of the self is one of the most distinctive features of melancholia. Freud's attention was thus directed to the nature and content of the self-approaches and self-accusations of the melancholic. These he found to possess certain marked peculiarities:

1. The self-reproach of the melancholic differs from remorse and self-reproach in normal people in that it is unaccompanied by shame. The melancholic is very far from evincing that attitude of humility which would befit such a worthless person as he declares himself to be. The average person suffering from remorse tends to hide his head and avoid attracting notice. The melancholic, on the other hand, gives the impression that he is the only possible subject of interest. He talks about himself as insistently as the bereaved person talks about the lost love-object. Freud's conclusion from this observation was that, while grief and melancholia are both reactions to the loss of a love-object, in the case of the melancholic the love-object is the ego.
2. Freud (1917a) further noticed a marked peculiarity about the actual nature of the self-accusations of the melancholic. These self-accusations convey the impression that they are not really applicable to the patient himself. With very little change, however, they are found to be applicable to "some person whom the patient loves, has loved or ought to love" (1917a, p. 58).

These observations led Freud to a conclusion which, he felt, provided the key to the understanding of the clinical picture of melancholia. This conclusion was that the self-reproaches of the melancholic are really "reproaches against a loved object which have been shifted on to the patient's own ego" (1917a, p. 158).

This interpretation of melancholia, suggested by Freud in his paper on "Mourning and Melancholia" (1917a), prepared the way for the more elaborate and comprehensive theories advanced in his work entitled *The Ego and the Id* (1923b). In this work he showed grounds for believing that neurotic and psychotic suffering in general and melancholic depression in particular are due to the presence in the patient of powerful aggressive impulses which come to be turned against the self on account of the guilt involved in their being directed against others.

It is in terms of this theory that Freud explains the persistent and refractory nature of neurotic symptoms. Refractoriness of the symptoms is a marked feature of hysteria—so much so that the hysteric impresses the observer as actively clinging to illness. This impression is regarded by Freud as corresponding to actual fact; and he interprets the "clinging to illness" of the hysteric in the sense that hysterical suffering serves a definite purpose. It is the expression of an internal necessity to suffer, an unconsciously inflicted form of self-punishment. What applies in the case of hysteria applies, *a fortiori*, in the case of melancholia. In the self-reproaches and suicidal impulses of the melancholic we see the patient arraigning himself as prisoner, giving evidence against himself, declaring himself guilty, passing sentence of death on himself and carrying it, all too often, into literal execution. Underlying this more or less conscious drama Freud discerns the operation of an unconscious mental mechanism whereby repressed aggressive impulses are deflected from their primary objects so as to attach themselves to the patient's ego. This mechanism serves a double purpose in the economy of the mind. It both saves the patient from guilty acts and atones for guilty impulses below the level of consciousness by a process of self-punishment. The mechanism sometimes operates after a guilty act has actually been committed, as may be seen in those not infrequent cases in which the murder of a lover is followed by the suicide of the murderer. In such cases suicide is the outcome of a conflict between the murderer's loves and hates. According to Freud, the symptoms of melancholia are the outcome of a similar conflict.

The origin of the mechanism whereby aggression and hate are turned back on the ego is traced by Freud to the relationship of the child to parent figures in the earliest years of life—the years in which the individual's future reaction patterns are laid down. The significance of the child's relationship to his parents lies in the fact that, while they are the child's first love-objects and the source of all his welfare, they are also the chief source of frustration and prohibitions. Aggression is the instinctive reaction to frustration; and frustration is particularly bitter when it originates in those whose love and affection are most eagerly sought. Consequently, when the child is thwarted by his parents, there are generated within him hostile feelings and impulses proportionate in intensity to his craving for signs of favour and love. The simultaneous presence in the mind of both positive and negative feelings for the same person is in itself a sufficiently intolerable situation; but the situation is rendered all the more intolerable by the fact that the parent is also feared owing to his superior power and authority. Fear and love thus combine to impose an internal taboo upon aggression; and under the influence of this taboo the aggressive impulses become repressed together with the hostile thoughts and feelings which accompany them. Being deprived of their natural objects in the outer world, they have no alternative but to seek a point of attachment in the ego. Meanwhile, as the child develops, the external authority of the parents is being internalised in the form of conscience. The result is that the introverted aggressive tendencies unite with developing conscience to constitute an internal agency which both passes judgments and exacts punishments (not only, as actual parents do, for overt acts but also for secret wishes and hidden impulses).

If this is a valid account of the origin of the mechanism whereby aggressive impulses come to be turned against the ego under the auspices of conscience, it must obviously apply in the case of normal no less than in the case of abnormal individuals. This being so, the development of psychopathological conditions must necessarily be traced to special conditions attending the conflicts of love and hate in the child. This fact finds recognition in psychoanalytical theory; and Freud and his followers have attempted to determine the precise conditions under which the various psychoses and psychoneuroses result. The special conditions which are believed to determine the manic-depressive reaction cannot be entered into now; but it may be mentioned that its origin is traced to the period of early dentition following weaning. Previous to weaning, the loves and hates of the child are largely determined by the satisfactions and frustrations which the child experiences at the hands of the mother in relation to feeding activities. For a period subsequent to weaning the oral orientation of the child still persists. Since the satisfactions of sucking are now withheld, the child seeks similar satisfactions through biting. This must be obvious to any one who observes a child during the earlier phases of dentition. At this stage, therefore, the loves and hates of the child continue to be expressed at the oral level; but biting is normally substituted for sucking. This phase may, for descriptive purposes, be classed as "cannibalistic". According to psychoanalytical theory, a fixation at this phase underlies the syndrome of manic-depressive insanity. The fixation is, of course, unconscious; but it none the less exercises an influence upon the reactions of the individual when faced with situations involving love and hate.

That Freud's views regarding the psychopathological influence of aggression are not merely fanciful is amply proved by the actual findings in practical psychoanalytical work. As a result of my own experience, I am increasingly impressed by the psychopathological importance of aggression. Unfortunately, it is not often possible to conduct the analysis of a manic-depressive case. Much light upon this condition may, however, be gained from the analysis of cases which, while not conforming to the classical picture, yet include manic-depressive components. Of the two cases which I now propose to describe, one falls into this category. The other is a case which falls clinically into the category of pre-senile melancholia. I shall describe this latter case first.

Case 1

This was the case of a married man of middle age. He was suffering from a definite but not excessive degree of depression accompanied by marked anxiety and a tendency to hypochondriacal ideas but unaccompanied by retardation of thought. Such cases do not ordinarily present a good prognosis for analytical treatment; but in this case there was a long history of neurotic anxiety preceding the onset of depression, and this at any rate seemed capable of relief.

The patient was a most intelligent man who, a few months previous to the onset of depression, had been appointed to a responsible position in a business with which he had been previously connected in a minor capacity. Since his appointment he had been subject to unusual business worries. His firm had been compelled to retrench and it had been his unpleasant duty to dismiss a number of old employees, of whom many had in the past been his seniors and consequently rivals for the important post which he now held. The fact that he had been compelled to dismiss men who had stood in the way of his promotion was evidently a factor in precipitating his guilt reaction.

Analysis revealed, however, that there were more important factors at work. The head of the firm, to whom he was responsible for his department, was a hard, aggressive, uncompromising man who was found to remind him of his father. His father, who had been dead for years, had been unapproachable and unsympathetic so far as his children were concerned. A stern disciplinarian, he had been regarded by the patient with feelings of awe rather than affection. His emotional attitude to his father was well portrayed in a dream in which he looked out of his bedroom window and saw his father standing looking up at him, gnashing his teeth with rage and snarling like a wild animal about to spring upon its prey. It became clear in analysis that the patient had a deep repressed hatred for his father and that he had unconsciously transferred this hatred to the head of his firm. This transference of hatred was accompanied by the activation of guilt; and, as a consequence, the patient always felt uncomfortable in his chief's presence and believed that his every action met with disfavour.

A still more important circumstance revealed by analysis consisted in the fact that, just before the onset of depression, the patient, who was a married man, had conceived a sudden fancy for a girl whom he met at a social function. His sexual feeling was so deeply stirred that his customary scruples were overcome and he embarked upon a secret affaire. The affaire was, however, short-lived. One night he had an assignation with the girl and left his home to meet her after giving his wife some plausible excuse. No sooner had he left the house than he was overtaken by remorse. He decided not to keep his appointment, and returned home after a few hours in the state of depression in which I found him a year later. It turned out that, while the *affaire* with the girl lasted, the patient had actually entertained conscious death-wishes towards his wife. As a matter of fact, his marital relations had never been satisfactory. Though he himself was desirous for children, his wife had an absolute horror of childbirth. Contraceptive measures had been adopted against the patient's inclination and at times coitus interruptus had been practised with resultant anxiety. His wife had never been able to satisfy him sexually, and his affection for her turned out to be accompanied by repressed feelings of hatred. From his account of his emotional state during his intimacy with the girl there can be little doubt that he was in a state of mild elation. This elation was evidently precipitated by the break-through of death wishes towards his wife, which accompanied the flow of sexual feeling towards the girl. This break-through of death wishes was also responsible for precipitating the subsequent melancholic reaction. Under the influence of guilt the death wishes were deflected from his wife's head on to his own. In conformity with the reaction pattern laid down in childhood, the patient's aggressive tendencies made the ego the object of their assault.

Case 2

This was the case of an unmarried woman of middle age. Both her parents were alive and she was the eldest of a large family. She had had two brothers, but only one survived. The patient was a qualified teacher; but in her first post after qualification she had begun to find teaching a considerable strain. She was unduly conscientious about her duties and had set herself a standard of perfection which it was impossible to realise in practice. The consequence was that from the outset she experienced constant anxiety over her work. The question of discipline occasioned her considerable anxiety. She could not tolerate the least inattention or insubordination on the part of the children. In order to command their attention she taught with an intensity which left her completely exhausted at the end of the day. After school hours she would wear herself out still further by endless preparation. All she achieved, however, was to impair her own efficiency and to antagonise the children. Consequently, the standard of teaching tended to fall instead of rising. This fact was appreciated by the patient, who redoubled her already overstrenuous efforts. A vicious circle was thus established; and during the school term the patient's failure was progressive. This progressive failure was accompanied by progressive feelings of self-reproach. By the end of each term she would find her powers of endurance at the breaking point. The holidays when they came round provided a welcome period of recuperation, but at the beginning of each new term the 'whirligig' began again.

It was several years before an actual breakdown occurred. In due course, however, the patient found herself unable to survive the school term without throwing in her hand. As the term wore on, she would find her memory playing her tricks in the classroom; she would find herself at a loss for common words or would suddenly find her mind a blank in the middle of a lesson. Problems of discipline caused her special torment. The slightest inattention or insubordination on the part of a child would cause her to boil with fury, which she only mastered by supreme efforts of self-control. She felt as if she could murder a disobedient child, but, if she did inflict a punishment, she was haunted by remorse and self-reproach. Her appetite failed and sleep became more and more disturbed. When she did sleep, she was haunted by dreams of teaching; but sleep gradually became almost impossible and she would walk about for hours during the night. Her mind became obsessed by depressing thoughts and she was haunted by ideas of suicide. Eventually tension and anxiety would reach such a pitch as to render her quite incapable of teaching. She would then abandon herself to despair and ask to be relieved of her duties. As soon as she was actually relieved, a striking transformation scene was commonly enacted. Her anxiety and depression would vanish as if by magic; and she would return home to be the life and soul of the family circle.

This sudden change from a state of anxious depression to a state of mild elation is one familiar to the psychiatrist in manic-depressive insanity. The present case is by no means typical of the condition, but all doubts as to the presence of a manic-depressive element in the case were set at rest when, a few weeks after the commencement of analysis, the patient passed into an unmistakably maniacal state. Fortunately this state was not sufficiently severe to necessitate the interruption of analytic treatment; and the manic phase gradually subsided after a few weeks.

This case was full of features of most unusual interest, but only a few of these can be referred to here. Among such features was the fact that it became possible in almost every case to trace the factors precipitating the various phases which occurred during the course of analysis. There was only one definitely maniacal phase, but there were several short periods of mild elation. Periods of mild depression were much more frequent. As analysis continued, however, these became less common. They also tended to become milder in character. Above all they tended to become shorter in duration.

Indeed the short duration of some of these phases of depression proved to be one of the most striking features of the case. At the outset these phases often lasted for several weeks, but later in the analysis their duration could be reckoned in terms of days, hours, and sometimes even minutes. Still more remarkable, perhaps, was the fact that on several occasions either the onset or the termination of a phase occurred in the consulting room under my very eyes.

The part played by aggression in determining the manic-depressive symptoms in this patient became very apparent during the course of analysis. It became evident that the patient's reaction to the school situation was due in the first instance to the stirring of her aggressive impulses by refractory children. The stirring of these impulses activated the guilt with which they were suffused. This led to self-reproach and stimulated her to make heroic efforts to perfect her teaching. The failure of these efforts increased her tendency to self-reproach; and the extra demands which she made upon the children aggravated their refractoriness; this in turn provoked her aggressive impulses still further. In the vicious circle thus established aggressiveness and self-reproach increased *pari passu* until a breakdown occurred.

The intensity of the patient's aggressive tendencies was well exemplified in certain automatic acts which she performed under their influence. Just prior to one of her breakdowns she quite unconsciously upset a kettle of boiling water over a refractory child, with the result that she was consumed with remorse. Several similar dissociated acts occurred during the course of analysis. On one occasion, while she was ironing some clothes, she was pestered by a small nephew. Her fury was aroused, but she felt herself successful in controlling it by conscious effort. Suddenly, however, she heard a scream and found to her amazement that she had burnt the child's hand quite unconsciously with the hot iron, although he had been standing at a safe distance. On another occasion she burnt her mother with a hot iron under somewhat similar circumstances. Her mother had annoyed her while she was ironing, and she was quite unconscious of what she had done until her mother pointed it out to her.

The best illustration, however, of the influence of aggression in determining the patient's symptoms was provided by the circumstances attending the death of her surviving brother, which happened to occur during the analysis. Just previous to this event, curiously enough, her associations had provided material indicating the presence of repressed aggressive feelings towards the brother. This was exemplified in a dream in which the patient was represented as standing in the kitchen of her home; as she stood there, her brother entered in an undressed state and with an expression of agony and horror upon his face; she then noticed that his genital organs were exposed and presented a ghastly wound. The expression on the brother's face in the dream haunted her when she awoke and left her with a sense of great unhappiness. Underneath this unhappiness her associations revealed a definite sense of responsibility for the wound, carried over from the dream into waking life. There followed associations which indicated a current source of annoyance with the brother and a long-standing lack of sympathy between him and herself. It is interesting in the light of psychoanalytic theory to note that the patient subsequently registered the impression that the wound in the dream had the appearance of a bite. This fact reminds us of the view that aggression manifests itself in the manic-depressive at the oral level.

By an amazing coincidence, it was not long after the date of this dream that the patient's brother met a violent death under distressing circumstances. He was walking home in the dark with his wife when a passing motor-car carried him off from his wife's side and dragged him for a considerable distance. He was picked up a mangled corpse. The patient was present when her "broken brother" (to use her own phrase) was brought to her father's house; it is interesting to note her description of the impression made on her by the appearance of the body; she said it looked as if it had been mauled by a wild beast.

The patient's reaction to this tragedy was particularly significant. The rest of the family were, not unnaturally, overwhelmed by grief. Not so the patient. In view of her previous breakdowns everyone feared that the shock of her brother's death would prove too much for her. As things turned out, however, she was the only member of the family who appeared to retain equanimity. Everyone marvelled at the manner in which she appeared to rise to the occasion. She took complete charge of affairs and made herself responsible for the numerous arrangements which had to be made under the circumstances. Throughout she experienced a sense of triumphant power which contrasted with the sense of futility which oppressed the others. She felt herself capable of anything, whereas they felt capable of nothing. In a word, the tragedy which had overwhelmed them with grief had made her elated. As time passed, however, the situation established in the home by her brother's death underwent a complete transformation. As the other members of the

> family began to recover from their grief, the patient began to lose her sense of power; and by the time they had regained their equanimity she had passed into a phase of depression.
>
> The explanation of the patient's curious reaction to her brother's death is not far to seek in view of the emergence of aggressive feelings towards him previous to the tragedy. Her brother's death provided a sudden and unexpected satisfaction of her repressed aggressive impulses. The release of inner tension resulting from the sudden satisfaction of repressed aggression gave her a sense of triumph and omnipotence and precipitated a condition of definite elation. In due course, however, the guilt attaching to her aggressive tendencies asserted itself and aggression was turned against the ego, with the result that a period of depression ensued. The truth of this interpretation of the patient's reactions seems to be amply proved by the manner in which the depression lifted in the present instance. Analysis was proceeded with during the phase of depression; and the patient produced associations which made it appropriate for me to point out that her elation had been due to the sudden fulfilment of a death wish and that the subsequent depression was due to the guilt of what amounted psychologically to a murder. This explanation came at an appropriate moment and the result was most dramatic. Within a few seconds depression had completely vanished and the patient left the consulting room in a state of happiness and contentment. She described the relief she had obtained as almost incredible. She said it was the most remarkable experience of her life. It reminded her of nothing so much as the scene in Bunyan's *Pilgrims Progress* when Christian's burden of sin fell from his back as he looked at the Cross and he experienced in an instant the joys of salvation.

The account of these two cases which has now been given provides only a sample of the material which these cases alone could provide to illustrate the etiological significance of aggression in melancholic and manic reactions. Similar material could also be produced from other cases in which psychoanalytical investigation has been possible. I shall close, however, by quoting anthropological data indicating that the same mechanisms which operate pathologically in cases of manic-depressive insanity operate normally among primitive peoples. Their operation is most obvious in totemistic communities. As is well known, the totem animal is the mascot of the tribe. The tribe is called after the totem, which undoubtedly represents the ancestor or father of the community. The totem animal is taboo; and ordinarily any member of the tribe who kills or eats the animal is regarded as having committed sacrilege and is punished by death. To kill the animal is, of course, equivalent to patricide, and to eat it is equivalent to cannibalism. On prescribed feast days, however, the totem is ceremonially killed and eaten by the community. The feast is accompanied by scenes of license and the participants pass through an experience of religious exaltation which may be regarded in the light of transient maniacal excitement. In this way aggression against the father-figure, which is ordinarily guilty, obtains periodic satisfaction in just the same way that our second patient obtained satisfaction for her aggression through the death of her brother. Mania is thus due to the triumph of aggressive impulses which have temporarily broken free from guilt. Melancholia, on the other hand, is analogous to the state of the totemistic savage who has been condemned for killing and eating the father of the tribe. In the case of the melancholic, however, the condemnation is purely internal, and unconscious at that. In the melancholic as in the savage the issue is likely to be death; only, in the case of the melancholic the death takes the form of suicide. It is also to be noted that in the totemistic community the eating of the totem animal is capable of mediating both guilt and exaltation. This fact recalls the second patient's dream of the bitten brother and the impression that his dead body looked as if it had been mauled by a wild beast. It also reminds us of the psychoanalytical theory that the pathogenic aggression of the manic-depressive derives from the oral level of development.

12. THE ROLE OF AGGRESSION

The subject of today's symposium is *The Concept of Aggression*; and no subject could be more appropriate to contemporary conditions. For, whilst it will be one of the conclusions of the present, and introductory, paper that aggression is 'always with us', it would be safe to say that at no period in the world's history have the evidences of aggression been more manifest. Not only does the efficiency of modern means of communication ensure that the news of yesterday's aggression throughout the world shall be brought daily to our breakfast table, but modern science places at the disposal of aggression weapons unparalleled in their destructiveness and enables it to be organized on a scale hitherto unknown. The topical interest of our subject makes it singularly appropriate that, at a gathering of psychologists of all persuasions, some consideration should be given to an aspect of human nature which has failed to receive the attention it deserves from psychologists in general, but to which considerable research has been devoted by the psychoanalytical school.

Subsequent speakers will discuss in further detail the part played by aggression in childhood and in social life; but, by way of introduction to these somewhat specialized aspects of our subject, we shall first consider how to answer the more general question, 'Is aggression an irreducible factor?' Since, however, this question is most conveniently approached by way of the psychology of instinct, our present enquiry will resolve itself into an attempt to determine how far, and in what sense, aggression is to be regarded as a primary instinctive tendency.

Whatever disagreement there may be among such contemporary psychologists as have attempted to formulate a theory of 'instinct', it has been their common aim to analyse human behaviour into its simplest components, so far as this can be done without deserting the field of motive for that of mechanism. The characteristic product of this endeavour is a list of behaviour tendencies varying considerably in number according to the particular point of view of the psychologist concerned; and in such a list a place is commonly, if by no means invariably, found for an instinct of aggression, although the harshness of the term 'aggression' is generally avoided by the substitution of some paler alternative like 'pugnacity'. Furthermore, it is common for the instinctive tendencies included in such a list to be regarded as essentially *reactive* tendencies, i.e., as characteristic modes of response to more or less specific situations or elements in situations. It is to be noted, however, that Drever (1917) distinguishes a group of instincts, which he regards as falling outside the category of reactive tendencies, and which he describes as 'appetitive tendencies'. These tendencies he regards as being determined by a 'feeling of uneasiness' (p. 167), and as being 'evoked by experiences which are disagreeable or agreeable, and, as it were, because of the disagreeableness or agreeableness, while the end sought has reference merely to this disagreeableness or agreeableness' (Drever 1922, p. 50). Drever's conception of the 'appetitive tendencies' provides a stepping-stone between such a theory of instinct as McDougall's and the corresponding psychoanalytical theory, in which no place is found for 'reactive tendencies' in the strict sense.

One of the distinctive features of Freud's theory of instinct in all its phases is that his classification of the primary instinctive tendencies has always remained upon a dualistic basis. It is true that Freud seeks to safeguard himself against the charge of over-simplification by speaking of 'groups of instincts' rather than of 'instincts'. Nevertheless the results of psychoanalytical research have tended increasingly to confirm the essential dualism of Freud's theory. The two groups of instincts recognized in his final formulation are (1) the life instincts, comprehensively designated as 'the libido', and (2) the death instincts or destructive instincts. As the term implies, the life instincts are oriented towards the promotion and enhancement of life; and they are conceived as manifesting themselves both in the self-regarding tendencies and in such tendencies as involve regard for external objects. Similarly, the death instincts are conceived as manifesting themselves, not only in impulses oriented towards the establishment of a state of dissolution in the subject himself, but also in impulses oriented towards the destruction of external objects, i.e., in aggression. According to Freud's formulation in *Beyond the Pleasure Principle* (1922), the primary manifestation of the death instincts is to be found in the urge to dissolution. He found a biological basis for this view in the fact that both bacteria and body cells *in vitro* produce substances destructive of their own life; and, on the psychological plane, he discovered a parallel to this biological phenomenon in the urge to suffering and illness, which characterizes the psycho-neuroses and psychoses in general and the suicidal tendencies of the melancholic in particular. In conformity with this point of view, he interpreted aggression as a diversion of death impulses outwards towards external objects at the instance of the demands of the life instincts, in so far as these latter express themselves in the form of self-preservative impulses. In recent years, however, there has been a tendency among psychoanalysts, particularly those of the British school, to regard aggression as the primary psychological manifestation of the death instincts, whatever be its status from the philosophic standpoint. This view is in part determined by psychotherapeutic necessities arising out of the consideration that the psychoneuroses and psychoses represent the expression of death impulses. Nevertheless, it finds theoretic support, not only in the deep analysis of the adult, but also in the analysis of children (now rendered possible by the development of a special technique). Undoubtedly the most remarkable, if also the most disconcerting, finding of psychoanalysis in recent years is the enormous part played by aggression in infancy and early childhood. The disposal of his aggression is the chief problem which the child is called upon to face in the course of his emotional development; and it is largely by the direction of aggression inwards that a solution of the problem is attempted. Whilst this method of disposing of aggression is found to provide the basis of all psychopathological developments, it nevertheless represents a process universally operative; and it thus has the effect of obscuring the fundamental part played by aggression in human affairs.

Quite apart from its classificatory dualism, the psychoanalytical theory of instinct differs fundamentally from all theories based upon the conception of 'reactive tendencies'; and, consequently, what the psychoanalyst understands by 'aggression' is something quite unlike what such a psychologist as McDougall understands by 'the tendency of pugnacity'. The 'reactive tendency' is conceived as a mode of response to a specific situation or to a specific element in situations; and, although, of course, such modes of response are regarded as conforming to biologically determined patterns, the conception is essentially based upon the supposition of a stimulus-response system, in which the response is only elicited by an appropriate stimulus originating in an outer situation. In psychoanalytical theory, on the other hand, the instincts are conceived more after the manner of Drever's 'appetitive tendencies'. So far as they are interpreted as modes of response at all, they are modes of response, not to outer, but to inner, situations. It is not a question of an inwardly conditioned reaction to an outer situation, but of an outwardly conditioned reaction to an inner situation—the exploitation of an outer situation for the relief of internal tensions of biological origin. This may be exemplified in the case of the most primal activity of the infant, viz. his oral behaviour. According to the psychology of the 'reactive tendencies', the oral behaviour of the infant is a response to visual, tactile and olfactory stimuli provided by the breast. According to psychoanalytical conceptions, on the other hand, the breast is an external object exploited by the infant for the relief of inner tensions. The correctness of the latter view should be obvious from the fact that, under the pressure of internal tensions, the infant will suck almost anything at all. He only comes to attach greater significance to his mother's breast than to his own thumb, because he finds that the breast provides a more enduring means of satisfaction. Nevertheless, a good feeding bottle can fulfil the same function; and, when it is found to do so, it is correspondingly valued.

Such a conception of the nature of instinct finds special support in the study of the phenomena of phantasy—phenomena which are left almost entirely out of account by the psychology of the reactive tendencies. According to psychoanalytical findings, the life of the child is largely dominated by phantasy; and, although, as the individual develops, he tends to become increasingly realistic, it is found that his thoughts and behaviour continue to be influenced at unconscious, if not at conscious, levels by phantasies persisting from his early childhood. These phantasies, it should be noted, are not simply ideational phenomena. Although their content is derived from data provided by outer situations, their proliferation is out of all proportion to any external stimuli. They are thus essentially dynamic and represent an exploitation of experiential data for the satisfaction of inner needs. In so far as they do not issue in overt behaviour, they themselves provide an alternative to such behaviour; and they can only be satisfactorily interpreted as the product of internal tensions created by the pressure of biological drives.

Considered from the psychoanalytical standpoint, accordingly, the instincts are fundamental biological drives or urges, manifesting themselves characteristically, so far at least as man is concerned, in psychological phenomena. These drives are conceived as having a definite direction, but a low degree of specificity. In seeking their goal, they exploit, not only the organic functions of the individual himself, but also external objects and external situations. Since, however, all members of the same species possess similar organic functions and encounter similar situations, the instinctive drives tend to manifest themselves according to similar patterns in every individual. The 'reactive tendencies' described by such psychologists as McDougall are thus simply common patterns in the manifestation of the primary instinctive urges, and not in any sense irreducible instinctive tendencies themselves. Further, since the various 'reactive tendencies' all represent modes of activity capable of expressing both the groups of instincts envisaged by Freud, they can no more be regarded as *simple* tendencies than as *primary* ones. This consideration applies even to McDougall's 'tendency of pugnacity'. For, whilst libidinal activities may themselves provide a vehicle for aggression, aggressive behaviour may equally provide the means of libidinal satisfaction. Thus, the indulgence of curiosity is often as much an aggressive as a libidinal activity—and is commonly treated as such by those concerning whom curiosity is displayed. On the other hand, war, which would appear at first sight to represent aggression in pure culture, is found upon closer inspection to have its libidinal components. Otherwise, why should the British soldier in the late war [First World War] have spoken, almost affectionately, of the German as 'Fritz', and of the Turk as 'Johnny'? And why should he have been as careful to collect souvenirs from his dead enemy as from the girl he left behind him? The fact is that, in the case of any given behaviour tendency, aggression and the libido may be represented in any proportion and in any degree of fusion. What is significant, therefore, is not the pattern of behaviour itself, but the extent to which the primary instinctive drives are represented in it. According to psychoanalytical findings, such drives fall into two, and only two, groups, distinguished by the direction in which they are oriented. There is one group oriented towards life, viz. the libido; and there is another group oriented towards destruction, viz. aggression.

It may now be asked whether, having carried the analysis of the instincts to a point at which only two primary instinctive drives are recognized, we may not carry the process of analysis a step further and resolve these two drives into manifestations of one single drive. In taking such a step we should, of course, be aligning ourselves with the libido theory of Jung, who interprets every tendency and every activity as a manifestation of the libido. Jung considers it to be characteristic of the libido, however, that, in its manifestations, it should differentiate into pairs of opposites. Thus, life can only manifest itself as an antithesis to death, and love as an antithesis to hate. He also adopts the view that, since the libido is dynamic, it must destroy when it does not create, and that, when an undifferentiated function sinks to a low level in the unconscious, it necessarily becomes destructive. According to Jung, therefore, aggression is a manifestation of the libido.

In contrast to Jung, Freud has always resisted the temptation to convert his theory of the libido into a theory of mental energy. Although faced with this alternative on several occasions in the history of his thought, he has always been deterred by the reflection that it is impossible to conceive of an irreducible dynamic factor operating against itself in mental conflict. In this respect his position is somewhat analogous to that of the Christian theologian, who, when confronted with the problem of evil, has always found it necessary to qualify the omnipotence of God by postulating the existence of the Devil. The original formulation of Freud's libido theory was, of course, based upon the discovery that the phenomena of the psycho-neuroses provide a link between adult sexuality and such activities of childhood as the oral behaviour of the infant; and subsequent investigation led Freud to bring more and more mental phenomena under the category of libidinal manifestations. Nevertheless, when he first found himself confronted with the necessity of formulating a working theory of instinct to account for the phenomena of mental conflict, his classification took the form of a dualism, in which a group of instincts designated the 'ego instincts' was distinguished from the libido. Subsequently, when his formulation of the concept of narcissism was found to involve the inclusion of the 'ego instincts' within the category of the libido, he was led, by considerations already mentioned, to supply the gap left in his dualism by introducing the concept of the death instincts. This concept has been in no sense compromised by the recent tendency to regard the death instincts as manifesting themselves primarily in aggression; and, as time has passed, psychoanalytical research has only served to establish the view that aggression is essentially incapable of being resolved into a libidinal manifestation. Although the course of a clinical analysis reveals that the libido is eminently labile in its modes of expression, there is no convincing evidence of the conversion of aggression into libido. If only some such evidence were forthcoming, it would be welcomed by the practising analyst; for, not only does the disposal of the patient's aggression always remain a major problem, but even such difficulties as attend the disposal of his libido are found to be mainly due to the fusion of libido with aggression. In the light of psychoanalytical investigation, accordingly, there is no alternative but to regard aggression as a primary instinctive tendency, and therefore as an irreducible factor in the economy of human nature.

Whilst it would be difficult to exaggerate the theoretic importance of the conclusion that aggression is an irreducible factor in the qualitative sense, from the point of view of applied psychology, it is perhaps even more important to determine how far aggression is to be regarded as a quantitatively irreducible factor. It may not be out of place, therefore, to conclude with some reference to this allied problem. If, then, we exclude from consideration such eugenic possibilities as the selective breeding of less aggressive types, it remains for us to make some attempt to assess the extent to which native aggression is amenable to environmental influences.

In so far as aggression is provoked by outer situations, it must undoubtedly be regarded as a reaction to frustration of impulse. The appropriate stimulus is provided, however, not by the outer situation involved, but by the inner state of frustration, which occurs in the presence of the outer situation. That the appropriate stimulus of aggression resides in an inner state of frustration may be illustrated by the well-known fact that the aggressiveness of a beast of prey depends largely upon the length of time which has elapsed since its last meal. It is also illustrated in the case of the paranoiac, whose aggression leads him to interpret innocent actions on the part of those around him in the sense of a persecution justifying retaliatory measures. A similar phenomenon is to be observed in every patient who undergoes psychoanalytical treatment; for, in spite of the adoption of a detached attitude by the analyst, he invariably becomes the target of quite unprovoked aggression on the part of the patient. This aggression is found to issue from an inner situation; and it is because the analyst is the nearest object, when the inner situation is explored, that the patient's aggression comes to be directed vicariously towards him. It is found also that the intensity of the aggression displayed in such circumstances is a fair measure of the extent to which an endopsychic state of frustration prevails. In the case of those of maturer years, this state of frustration is associated with phantasies which date from early childhood, and in which the parents are represented as bad objects. In such phantasies the 'badness' attributed to parent figures originates for the most part through the projection of the child's own aggression upon his parents; and it is out of all proportion to any actual frustration which the parents impose. Nevertheless, it is by no means wholly out of proportion to the sense of frustration experienced by the child.

The amount of frustration encountered by young children varies, of course, within wide limits; but no child is exempt from the experience of almost intolerable frustration—even under the most favourable conditions. Thus no child is ever spared the experience of hunger during the phase of infancy, in which his whole emotional life is centred upon oral gratification, and in which the satisfaction of his oral impulses presents itself as a matter of life and death; and, similarly, no parent is capable of satisfying completely the child's intense craving to be loved. Here it should be clearly understood that it is in relation to the satisfaction of his more highly charged libidinal needs and of his craving to be loved that the child feels frustration so intolerable. It is not simply a question of the child being prevented from doing exactly as he likes; for, significantly enough, the child who is allowed to do exactly as he likes tends to become an anxious child. This is because his ego is still too weak to exercise control over his aggressive impulses and, if parental figures do not help him to control them, he has no guarantee against the destructive consequences of their indulgence. As the child grows older, the external control exercised over his impulses by his parents is replaced by an internal control exercised by his superego (a part of the mental structure modelled largely upon the child's phantasies of his parents as frustrators). The impulses of the individual in later life are thus subject to an inner frustration corresponding to the state of frustration experienced during the helpless phase of childhood. It must be recognized, accordingly, that every individual contains within himself factors calculated to act as both constant and powerful stimuli of aggression.

If we are philosophically minded, we may permit ourselves to reflect, moreover, that a certain element of frustration is inherent in the ever-recurring state of desire, with the consequence that desire as such is liable to be characterized by a certain quality of aggressiveness. This consideration applies with special force to the desires of infancy, in the case of which there is found to be a considerable fusion between primary aggression and the libido. The product of such a fusion is what the psychoanalyst employs the term 'sadism' to denote; and it is in the sadistic quality of infantile desire that repression finds its rationale. The effect of repression, however, is not only to perpetuate sadistic impulses in the unconscious, but also to intensify their aggressive component owing to the frustration which repression entails. It is when we contemplate the essentially sadistic quality of infantile impulse that our minds are chiefly assailed by doubts regarding the modifiability of aggression; and, when we proceed to consider the part played by the inevitable frustrations of childhood in fostering aggression, these doubts only become more firmly established. Moreover, they receive additional confirmation in the reflection that the endopsychic situation established in childhood would seem to be perpetuated at a somatic level in enduring modifications of the endocrine balance.

So far as applied psychology is concerned, it is to be noted that, in conformity with the point of view now outlined, human aggression only appears to admit of modification in two ways: (1) in an economic sense, by regulation of the channels along which it is distributed, and (2) in a dynamic sense, by mitigation of the frustrations which provoke it. Of these two methods of control, the economic is the more important historically; but it is significant that the very measures whereby the disposal of aggression has been regulated in the past have been largely such as to involve considerable frustration and thus to intensify the very factor which they were designed to control. This holds true, not only of such mental mechanisms as repression and superego formation, by means of which the disposal of aggression is regulated within the individual mind, but also of the various social institutions (conventional, religious, legal, political, economic and otherwise), whereby individual aggression is regulated from without. Such mental mechanisms and social institutions have achieved a certain success in controlling the aggressive impulses of the individual. The precarious nature of the control which they exercise is evident, however, from the prevalence of such phenomena as delinquency, social unrest and war; and in the present condition of the totalitarian states we find eloquent proof of the extent to which the controlling agencies themselves may become exploited by the aggression which it is their function to control.

There remains, of course, the possibility of effecting a certain quantitative reduction of aggression by mitigating the frustrations which provoke it. This method has made its appearance comparatively recently in human history; but it would appear to be the method most appropriate to the present stage of human culture. It is likely to be most fruitful in its results when applied to the conditions of infancy and childhood; for, as we have seen, it is during infancy and childhood that frustration has its most significant effects. Nevertheless, such a method offers no prospects of exercising any influence upon primary aggression, which represents a fundamental and inborn instinctive tendency in human nature.

13. PRACTISING PSYCHOANALYSIS

This is a transcript of the Questionnaire as it was sent by Dr Edward Glover to 24 practising psychoanalysts throughout Britain in 1938 with Fairbairn's actual replies reproduced in italic script. See the Introduction to Part 3 (p. 225) and Fairbairn's critical review of Glover (1955) Chapter 28, entitled 'The Technique of Psychoanalysis' on pp. 439–442.

QUESTIONNAIRE (1938)

1. INTERPRETATION

Form—do you prefer?

1. short compact interpretation
2. longer explanatory interpretation
3. summing up type interpretation

I prefer (2) but also employ (1) and (3) after the ground has been previously prepared by (2).

   a. trying to *convince* by tracing development of a theme
   b. proving (or amplifying by external illustration)

I prefer (a) to (b), but occasionally introduce external illustrations.

Timing—what is your favorite point of interpretation?

1. early in the session
2. middle or before the end (allowing a space for elaboration)
3. at the end: "summing up" fashion

(2) is preferred and usually employed; (1) never employed, (3) is employed as well as (2), but to a less extent, under the following conditions, (a) with intelligent patients possessing good insight and in normal cases, (b) when associations are slow but a drift is clear, (c) when interpretations seem likely to interrupt the flow of significant associations.

Amount	
1. general: as a rule do you talk much or little? 2. early stages: how long do you usually let patients run without interference? how soon do you start systematic interpretation? 3. middle stages: is your interpretation on the whole continuous and systematic, or do you return from time to time to the opening system of letting them run?	*(1) little; (2) until such time as (a) the procedure of association is understood, (b) the initial resistances are weakened, (c) a recognisable transference situation is established. The period involved is necessarily variable, but is rarely less than a month, sometimes several months; (3) I frequently return to the opening system of letting a patient's associations run—until either new material emerges or there are signs that the relevance of previous interpretations is being lost sight of.*
4. end stages: do you find your interpretative interference becomes incessant?	*(4) No, in the last stages I prefer to gradually reduce the amount of interference.*
Depth	Please state individual definition—
(This can be thought of in terms of degree of repression, conscious accessibility and readiness or in terms of stages, e.g., pregenital as compared with genital interpretation, etc.)	*I interpret "depth" in terms of stages—developmental level.*
Do you have a standard level of deep interpretation for all cases, or do you have an optimum depth varying for clinical conditions e.g., in (a) anxiety, (b) obsessional, (c) characterological, (d) psychotic, (e) normal cases	*No, I have no standard level for all cases. All cases require interpretation at the genital level, but many cases require further interpretation at deeper levels, certainly (b), (c) and (d). Optimum depth depends on level of fixation.*
On the whole do you favour deep interpretation in early, middle or late stages?	*Middle stages.*
Do you favour deep interpretation as the ideal criterion—or deep interpretation in terms of the reality circumstances: (1) infancy, (2) childhood, (3) puberty, (4) adolescence, (5) adult life?	*I favour deep interpretation in terms of reality circumstances, ultimately those of infancy and childhood.*

2. SPECIAL PROBLEMS

The problem of anxiety.
What is your favourite method of dealing with this? e.g., by rapid interpretation of

a. 'repressed' content, or
b. 'repression' factors, or by slower expansion of the emotional state combined with a degree of reassurance (postponing deep interpretation till later).

I favour slower expansion of the emotional state combined with a degree of reassurance. In exceptional cases, however, where anxiety is very acute, I have employed rapid interpretation of the 'repressed' content—with considerable success in most instances. The latter method, however, involves the risk of the analyst failing "to knock the nail on the head". Such failure merely aggravates the situation.

3. USE OF TECHNICAL TERMS: explanation of mechanisms

What practice do you favour, e.g., do you talk about introjected objects or organs or do you use 'superego' nomenclature?

I adopt 'superego' nomenclature, but employ a minimum of technical terms. The number I employ depends on the intelligence and intellectual status of the patient. For the actual concept of "superego" I employ the term "ego-ideal" as being more easily understood and less likely to savour of the mystical.

Technical explanations or orientation

Do you usually act as a source of information (reality) on

a. sexual
b. non-sexual subjects?

I act as a source of information on sexual subjects only when the patient holds misleading ideas or is handicapped by ignorance either actual or emotionally determined. On non-sexual subjects I only give information in reply to questions on the patient's part.

4. "FORCED" PHANTASY

The term 'forced' (Ferenczi) is not very satisfactory: the interpretation of an incest phantasy is equally 'forced.'

Do you, on the strength of isolated words or actions, without waiting or hoping for confirmation in associations, expound phantasy systems affecting—

Almost invariably I wait for confirmation in associations before expounding phantasy systems affecting both (a) or (b). But (a) on rare occasions, when an acute situation has arisen affecting adaptive conduct in the face

a. reality relationships b. transference relationships	*of reality, I have departed from my rule, e.g., in the cases of a schizophrenic patient refusing food and a paranoid patient having alarming quarrels with his father. Such departures I have found to be amply rewarded by the results. (b) I have also occasionally departed from my rule in expounding phantasy systems underlying a particularly stubborn resistance [with less success than in the case of (a)].*
Do you abandon the association rule in certain instances holding the patient to one thread until you have constructed a phantasy piecemeal?	*I not infrequently abandon the association rule in order that a phantasy system may be brought more fully to consciousness.*
Do you ask direct questions	*I ask direct questions under certain conditions —*
a. about matters of fact, e.g., family history	*a. about family history when the intelligibility of the associations would suffer from the absence of the information sought*
b. about matters of phantasy	*b. about phantasies when a patient records behaviour upon which light may be thrown by the recording of accompanying phantasies; e.g., I might enquire as to the occurrence and nature of phantasies accompanying masturbation*
c. about emotional reactions	*c. about emotional reactions when a patient records experiences without indicating his emotional reaction*

5. 'ACTIVE' DEVICES

To avoid lengthy definition, this may be taken in 'Ferenczi' sense	
Preliminary: apart from laying down the association rule do you give any general or specific recommendations re suspending personal habits (masturbation, etc.) before analysis commences?	*I content myself with laying down the association rule and requiring the patient to record his dreams.*

During analysis: do you employ prohibitions or positive injunctions

1. aimed at symptom habits, phobias, obsessions
2. aimed at psycho-sexual habit—
   masturbation
   perversion
   fetish
   intercourse
   a. marital
   b. extramarital
   promiscuity
3. aimed at social habit.

If practice varies, give indications for your policy in different cases.

1. *I employ neither prohibitions nor injunctions.*
2. *The only prohibitions I employ relate to sexual intercourse (*when such is abnormal*) and active homosexuality. Otherwise I employ neither prohibitions nor injunctions.*
3. *As regards social habits, I rarely employ prohibitions. I do so occasionally, when a patient's conduct appears likely to lead to serious consequences either to himself or society, e.g., I have forbidden a patient to drive a motor-car when he was liable to unconsciously motivated accidents; I have forbidden a patient, who proposed to spend his holiday in a house in the country with a slum woman and her two daughters (aged 17 & 18), to carry through his plan; I have forbidden a patient who was a University lecturer to cultivate ill-judged affaires with female students in his class. I occasionally advise patients regarding the resumption of work, when this has been interrupted and resumption has been unduly delayed.*

6. TERMINATION OF ANALYSIS:

What are your criteria
a. symptomatic
b. psychotic
c. social

Criteria: vide item 1 (pp. 281–282)—Interpretation pages 1 and 2 (pp. 272–273)

Are your criteria mostly intuitive?

How long do you think an analysis ought to last?	*Duration of analysis—analysis should last until main active elements in the unconscious have been exposed; its length must necessarily vary depending on (1) degree of repression, (2) level of fixations, (3) difficulty of reality-situations to which adjustment must be made. 6 months may be adequate; 4 years inadequate; I consider it undesirable that analyses should be prolonged beyond 3 years unless this is unavoidable (as it frequently is).*
Have you an average period for all cases? In this matter do you differentiate between a. anxiety b. obsessional c. characterological d. psychotic e. normal cases	*Average period—I have no average period for all cases. I differentiate between the different types of case—* *a. 1 to 2 years* *b. 3 to 3.5 years* *c. uncertain* *d. 4 years* *e. 1 year and, according to purpose of analysis. NB. I feel that the figures given are very arbitrary. I find it difficult to predict the duration of analysis in any given case.*
Do you set a terminal period: if so, does it vary with each case?	*Setting of period to analysis, I sometimes set a period during the course of analysis, though never at the outset.*
If you set a period do you stick to this decision?	*In most cases I stick to the decision but not invariably.*
Do you favour a discontinuous analysis as a terminal device?	*Discontinuous Analysis—I do* not *favour it as a terminal device*
Do you favour a discontinuous analysis as a general policy? e.g., after the reduction of superficial symptom constructions?	*I do* not *favour it as a general policy but only as a "second best" in selected cases where continuous analysis is impossible.* *In some cases I consider it dangerous (where* death *impulses are strong).*

7. THE NEUTRALITY OF THE ANALYST: lay figure concept

Do you ever admit to the patient the possibility of being wrong?

Yes, I consider it a mistake for the analyst to act as if he claimed divine attributes.

Do you ever admit to the patient the possibility of 'not knowing'?

Do you lay emphasis on the cooperative nature of analysis, as distinct from the phantastic cooperation demanded in transference?

Yes, particularly at the beginning of analysis.

Do you believe in giving some indication of a positive friendly attitude as distinct from the friendliness implied in 'professional interest'?

Yes. I consider a general *friendly attitude desirable in the analyst. Absence of such an attitude is too Olympian. Cordiality, etc., are of course to be avoided, but the analyst's detachment should give the impression of being well disposed. Otherwise the patient is liable to feel relegated to the status of the "experimental animal".*

8. FEES: do you have a standard rule re payment for non-attendance?

Yes, I charge fees when non-attendance is determined by the analytical situation, but not otherwise. Thus I do not charge, if, e.g., the patient is laid up with influenza or has to go away from home on business.

Do you keep to it?

My observation of this rule is not absolutely rigid.

Do you ever raise fees during analysis?

No.

If so when?

Do you accept presents from patients?

If so, on what system?

It is very exceptional for me to accept presents. I only accept them when, for some good reason, I treat a patient gratis. Such patients are invariably medical students or doctors. I do not prevent *patients sending* small *presents to my children, e.g., at Christmas, or flowers to my wife if a patient knows her socially already.*

9. EXTRA ANALYTICAL CONTACT:

a. beginning and end of sessions:	
Do you shake hands before or after?	*I do not shake hands before or after.*
Do you use small talk?	*I use it occasionally as a patient leaves.*
Do you permit small talk?	*I permit it as a patient leaves.*
Do you lend books, etc?	*No.*
b. Extra Mural:	
Do you meet patients socially?	*Only when the meeting is fortuitous (= No).*
Do you avoid meeting patients socially? If so why?	*I avoid meeting them as much as possible—* *1. because I believe social contact complicates the analytic situation, and* *2. it embarrasses the patient.*
c. Family Contact:	
1. Do you interview members of family (a) with, or (b) without the patient's knowledge?	*I do not encourage interviews with members of a patient's family, but I do not refuse to interview, e.g., a parent, husband, wife or guardian on such subjects as, e.g., prognosis, attitude to be adopted towards patient, fees, etc. I prefer such interviews to be with the patient's knowledge, but in psychotic cases it is sometimes necessary to keep such interviews secret. When the interview is with the patient's knowledge, I usually inform the patient of the subject of the interview.*
2. Do you analyse patients who have emotional ties (friendships, etc.) to your own friends or family? Or who are related to or friendly with individuals in any way dependent on you?	*I avoid analysing patients with emotional ties to my own friends or family so far as possible; but it is impossible to be rigid in this matter in a place like Edinburgh—* *1. because Edinburgh is relatively small and one knows so many people in such a town,* *2. because of the dearth of analysts in Scotland.*
3. On these matters have you any guiding principle?	*I am guided mainly by—* *a. the closeness of the tie,* *b. the urgency of the case.*

10. RELATION OF THEORY TO PRACTICE

Do you approach each case with a preconceived theoretical outline of development to which you expect the case to conform?

Or do you approach each case with a preconceived outline modified by your knowledge and valuation of clinical features (diagnostic or prognostic criteria)?

It is difficult to avoid approaching a case with a preconceived theoretical outline of development, but my preconceived outline is always modified by my knowledge and valuation of clinical features. I think it important to realise that living processes, as such, can never be expected to conform to a rigid and cast iron schema.

Do you have preferences in regard to pathogenicity of instinctual elements: e.g., value the factor of aggression more than the factor of primitive sexuality?

I attach increasing importance to the part played by the factor of aggression. I consider that primitive sexuality alone is incapable of becoming pathogenic (as against 'perverse') without aggression, whereas aggression alone is theoretically capable of becoming pathogenic.

Do you regard the genital (phallic) Oedipus complex (positive or inverted) as the main factor in—

a. neurosogenesis — *a. Yes.*
b. the genesis of psychosis — *b. Usually not, but sometimes.*
c. characterological cases — *c. No.*

Do you regard pregenital phantasy systems as being secondary (regressive, defensive) products relating to genital Oedipus traumata?

I regard pregenital phantasy systems as usually primary, but sometimes secondary. I regard recoverable cases of psychoses as being cases in which the regressive element is strong.

Do you regard castration anxiety

a. as the only anxiety factor of significance in treatment — *a. No.*
b. as one of a number of anxiety situations — *b. Yes.*

c. as a cover for pregenital anxieties?	*c. Frequently, but by no means always. Not in hysteria. See item 2 Special problems below.*
Do you favour the view that mechanisms of projection and introjection are (from the therapeutic point of view) more important than the mechanisms of repression, regression, etc.?	*In general, yes.*
If so do you believe this applies in all cases, e.g., in the analysis of a hysteric as well as in the analysis of a psychotic character?	*No, I do not think it applies in the analysis of a hysteric.*
11. PLEASE ADD A LIST OF YOUR SPECIAL PROBLEMS IN TECHNIQUE AND OF QUESTIONS YOU WOULD LIKE TO HEAR DISCUSSED.	*See items 5. Active devices and 6. Termination of Analysis.*

CRITERIA FOR THE TERMINATION OF ANALYSIS

Since it is the desire to get rid of symptoms that drives most patients to seek analysis at all and to pay the analyst fees which would otherwise be grudged, it is usually incumbent upon the analyst to content himself with a strictly therapeutic aim rather than to strive after a complete analysis. In a sense, therefore, I feel it necessary to give *symptomatic* criteria the first place. On the other hand, it is the duty of the analyst to see that the underlying causes of symptom-formation are removed; otherwise the disappearance of actual symptoms is no guarantee that fresh symptoms will not appear in the future. Consequently I find it necessary to employ *psychosexual* criteria and *social* criteria as well.

While one's impressions of a patient's state often defy analysis, I should not like to rely on intuitive criteria alone. My chief *objective* criteria are:

1. Symptomatic
   a. freedom from disabling symptoms and general anxiety;

   b. evidence that reality relationships are not unduly determined by unconscious phantasies, e.g., of omnipotence, father hatred, etc.
2. Psychosexual
   a. presence of free libido capable of attachment to heterosexual objects at the genital level or (in the case of married persons) investment of partner with libido at the genital level, or a socially satisfactory sublimation of freed libido
   b. relative absence of pre-genital and phallic components in the patient's relation to sexual objects
   c. the absence of ambivalence towards sexual objects
3. Social
   a. ability to meet occupational demands without undue anxiety and interest in occupational pursuits
   b. ability to take part in social life without anxiety and without being influenced unduly by inhibitions
   c. some display of a desire to seek social contacts

ANXIETY

I regard anxiety as a chronic form of fear. Fear is an acute reaction to a danger situation, and anxiety is a prolonged reaction to a continued danger situation. Sources of anxiety may be classified as follows:

Outer Dangers

1. Threat to Ego
   a. real, e.g., illness; loss of money; loss of employment
   b. phantasy: "Aphanasis", e.g., castration; loss of nipple; "theft" of faeces
2. Threat to Love Objects
   a. real, loss of e.g., husband; wife; child; friend
   b. phantasy, e.g., loss of father figure or mother figure

Inner Dangers

1. Threat to Ego
   Libido
   1. direct threat: anxiety neurosis

   2. indirect threat: vengeance of the superego (Strafbedürfnis); aphanasis (including *castration*)

2. Threat to Objects
   Aggression
   1. direct threat: destruction of love objects (ambivalence)
   2. indirect threat: vengeance of the superego (Strafbedürfnis) leading to aphanasis including *castration*

14. SEXUAL DELINQUENCY

The chief purpose of the present paper is to emphasize the importance of a psychological approach to the problems of sexual delinquency. It would be unreasonable, of course, to deny the value of other paths of approach; but it may be claimed with some confidence that no adequate appreciation of the real nature and significance of sexual delinquency is possible in the absence of some knowledge regarding its psychological motivation. The present paper will accordingly be devoted in the main to a comprehensive, if brief, review of the motives which appear to prompt the individual to anti-social behaviour of a sexual nature. Since, however, such behaviour is obviously characterized by an absence of proper self-control, some account will also be given of the means whereby impulse is ordinarily controlled within the individual mind, and of the conditions under which the capacity for self-control becomes compromised.

At the outset it should be noted that the attitude adopted by the community towards sexual offences varies according to the nature of the offence in question. On the one hand, it is usual to regard offences like rape and seduction as the expressions of a more or less normal sex-impulse, which is either unduly strong or inadequately controlled. On the other hand, such offences as homosexuality and incest are commonly attributed to the influence of mysterious and inexplicable tendencies, which from time to time obtrude themselves for no obvious reason into the mental constitution of certain degenerate individuals. According to social criteria, sexual offences thus fall into two separate and apparently unrelated groups: (1) a group of offences involving the performance of an otherwise normal act of intercourse under anti-social conditions, and (2) a group of offences involving the performance of a sexual act which is inherently abnormal and "perverse", either because it is not a normal act of intercourse, or because it involves a relationship with an unnatural sexual object.

This division of sexual offences into two distinct groups is quite intelligible from the point of view of society; for it represents a distinction between sexual acts which conform to a biologically determined reproductive pattern and sexual acts which either fail to conform to such a pattern or (as in the case of incest) only conform in a manner calculated to undermine the very basis of society. In spite of the social and biological value of such a distinction, however, its maintenance is incompatible with a scientific approach to the problem of sexual delinquency; and its only effect is to prejudice any real understanding of the subject. A mere inspection of the phenomena in question should in itself be sufficient to suggest that there is no necessary connection between the sexual and the reproductive functions. The existence of such a necessary connection is, of course, commonly regarded as almost axiomatic; but in reality the two functions are by no means identical. The truth would seem to be that the sexual function manifests itself earlier in life than the reproductive function and that, in so far as the two functions come to be merged, this is only because, in the course of normal development, the sexual function is, so to speak, annexed by the dawning reproductive function, and exploited in the interests of the biological aim which reproduction serves.

Within the psychological field, we are indebted to Freud for our present knowledge regarding the relationship of the sexual and the reproductive functions; for it was Freud who first pointed out the real significance of such sexual activities as have no reproductive aim. Setting out, as he did in the first instance, to investigate the nature of hysteria, he became impressed at an early stage by the disturbances of the sexual life which characterize hysterical patients. Upon further investigation he then discovered in the hysterical patient traces of perverse sexual tendencies, of which the patient was quite unconscious, but which could be seen to exercise a determining influence upon the nature of the symptoms manifested. Since these perverse tendencies were found to be totally unacceptable to the patient's moral standards, it was concluded that they had been rendered unconscious on this very account through the operation of a mental process, to which the term "repression" was applied; and the appearance of symptoms was attributed to the persistence of such tendencies in an unconscious realm of the mind. More specifically, the symptoms were interpreted as the disguised expressions of perverse tendencies, which were prevented from expressing themselves overtly owing to the inhibitory influence of a deeply-rooted moral sense. Considered from a social point of view, the symptoms were also seen to provide a means whereby the tension of socially unacceptable tendencies could be relieved without any open or conscious infringement of the social standards accepted by the individual.

Another important discovery made by Freud was that the symptoms of hysteria were bound up with forgotten incidents of childhood, in the revival of which considerable emotion was released. It was further discovered that the emotional significance of these forgotten memories was derived from their association with a mental conflict over tendencies very similar to the perverse tendencies already mentioned. It was accordingly concluded by Freud that hysterical symptoms have their origin in a conflict during childhood over sensuous activities, which, owing to their historical connection with perverse sexual tendencies in the adult, must be regarded as essentially sexual, but which, manifesting themselves as they do in early childhood, are obviously independent of any reproductive aim. This conclusion has proved to be of vast importance for psychopathology in general; but it was accompanied by another conclusion of equal importance for the psychology of sex. This was to the effect that the mature sexual impulse is not one which emerges fully developed at puberty, but one which is the final product of a long psychogenetic process beginning in earliest infancy. This psychogenetic process was found to derive its significance from the fact that there exist in the young child a number of more or less unrelated sexual activities, which, in the course of normal development, become modified, fused and integrated under the dominance of strictly reproductive activities in such a way as to promote reproductive aims. Even in the case of the most "normal" individuals, the result achieved by this developmental process must always be regarded as failing short of an optimum. Nevertheless, failure of development may occur in any degree; and in some cases there is such an arrest of psycho-sexual development that infantile sexual tendencies of one sort or another acquire a dominance which compromises the emergence of the mature sexual impulse.

An arrest of psycho-sexual development affects not only the nature of the sexual impulses, but also the choice of sexual objects; for, where the sexual impulses remain infantile, the choice of sexual objects tends to remain infantile also. Now the persons in relation to whom the child's sexual impulses manifest themselves are naturally the persons who are emotionally significant for him; and, since these are inevitably members of the family circle, his sexual impulses take a direction which becomes essentially incestuous, if maintained in adult life. Ordinarily, of course, the strength of the incest taboo is sufficient to ensure the repression of all overtly incestuous impulses; but there are cases in which a marked failure of repression results in actual incest. Such cases are probably commoner than is generally realized, especially under conditions of inadequate housing.

Another feature of the child's choice of sexual objects is that it shows less discrimination than that of the normal adult between heterosexual and homosexual objects. The first person to attract the love of the child, whether boy or girl, is undoubtedly the child's mother; and consequently the sexual life of the girl is initiated upon a homosexual basis. At a later stage the child's father also becomes emotionally significant; and, in so far as this holds true in the case of the boy, his sexual orientation must be regarded as homosexual likewise. Thus the sexual life of children of both sexes is seen to be characterized by the presence of a considerable homosexual component, which varies in accordance with the respective rôles played by the child's mother and father in the family situation. It will be readily understood, therefore, how an arrest of psycho-sexual development may lead, under certain circumstances, to an overweighting of the homosexual component. It would be a gross over-simplification, however, to say that overt homosexuality in later life was simply the result of a lingering preference for the parent of similar sex in childhood. As a matter of fact, overt homosexuality in later life is commonly found to be preceded in childhood by the presence of unusual hate and fear, in conjunction with love, for the parent of similar sex. When such is the case, one of the determining factors would appear to be an attempt on the part of the child to overcome his hate and fear of the parent in question by converting this parent into a sexual object and so effecting a *rapprochement*. Such a procedure may at first sight appear difficult to understand. Nevertheless, analogous phenomena may be observed in international affairs; for the *rapprochement* with Germany sought by Czechoslovakia after the recent crisis was unquestionably motivated by hate and fear.

Another important consideration regarding the choice of sexual objects arises out of the fact that, before the child becomes interested in those around him as persons, his interest is focused upon such parts of their bodies as possess special significance for him. Thus, long before the infant learns to love his mother as a person, his emotional life is centred round her breast as a means of providing him with an all-important gratification; and this same pre-occupation with significant bodily organs shows itself at a later stage in sexual curiosity. It is only in the course of a gradual process of development that the child comes to substitute persons (or "whole objects") for bodily organs (or "part objects") as sources of emotional satisfaction. Special importance must be attached to this substitution, because it represents a transition from the valuation of an object as a means of gratification to the valuation of an object for what it is. In other words, it represents a renunciation of purely sexual objects in favour of love objects. In so far as there is an arrest of psycho-sexual development, however, the transition is compromised and sexual life remains oriented towards part objects. The individual then continues to treat those who make a sexual appeal to him, not as persons eliciting love and respect, but simply as objects providing a means of gratification. Such an attitude, combined as it is in cases of psycho-sexual arrest with a persistence of crude sexual tendencies, is highly favourable to the development of sexual delinquency.

It now becomes relevant to consider the relationship of aggression to infantile sexuality. In view of what has already been said regarding the part played by hate in promoting homosexual tendencies, it will hardly surprise us to learn that there is an intimate connection between sex and aggression in childhood. Aggression is unquestionably the child's natural reaction to frustration; and, in accordance with this fact, any marked frustration of his sexual impulses provokes in the child a considerable degree of aggression towards the object from which he vainly seeks gratification; and, consequently, whatever gratification is eventually obtained is accompanied by a release of aggressive impulses. Under conditions which render the child constantly liable to excessive frustration or cause him to suffer from a general sense of insecurity, such an association of sexual and aggressive impulses becomes pronounced, and his sexual impulses thus acquire a permanently sadistic colouring.

In the light of all these considerations regarding the nature of infantile sexuality and the development of the adult sexual impulse, we are now in a position to appreciate the real nature of sexual delinquency. Sexual delinquency is essentially due to a failure of psycho-sexual development involving (1) the persistence of infantile sexual trends, (2) the persistence of an infantile attitude towards sexual objects, and (3) the persistence of a sadistic type of sexuality acquired in infancy. It must not be inferred, however, that the mere persistence of infantile sexual trends, oriented in an infantile manner and endowed with a sadistic quality, is sufficient in itself to explain sexual delinquency; for investigation shows, not only that such a state of things exists to some degree in everyone, but also that it exists in many individuals in an accentuated form without the development of any marked proclivity to sexual delinquency. The fact is that the majority of individuals whose psycho-sexual development is markedly arrested save themselves from sexual delinquency either by developing character-traits of a substitutive or compensatory nature, or else by contracting a psycho-neurosis or psychosis. It is not an easy task, in the present state of knowledge, to determine with any precision the factors which differentiate the sexual delinquent from members of this other group. Nevertheless, sufficient is already known to justify the statement that these factors are to be sought in that part of the mind which is concerned with the control of instinctive impulses.

Recent study of the controlling element in the mind has led to the recognition of a number of mental mechanisms designed to deal with recalcitrant impulses. These mental mechanisms, it may be remarked, are essentially unconscious, and they represent the more primitive methods of control. The most familiar is repression—an inhibitory process, the most obvious manifestation of which is to render unconscious what would otherwise be conscious, but the chief function of which is to imprison in the depths of the mind impulses which would otherwise express themselves overtly. The operation of this mechanism rarely meets with complete success; but, in so far as it succeeds at all, it tends to arrest offending impulses *in nascendo*, and to modify their manifestations, either by imposing upon them the need for disguise, or by enabling them to be diverted along substitutive and socially acceptable channels. Repression has grave limitations, however; for repressed impulses tend, on the whole, both to remain qualitatively unchanged and to undergo a quantitative increase in face of the barriers opposing their discharge. Repression thus tends to perpetuate at unconscious levels of the mind the very impulses which it is designed to control; and, in times of stress, these impulses are liable to break through in their original form. Such is the case when sexual delinquency suddenly manifests itself later in life in individuals whose previous record provides no precedent for such a phenomenon.

Another and more primitive method of dealing with disturbing trends is provided by the mechanism known as projection. Projection is a mental process which enables trends belonging to the individual himself to be attributed to persons in the outer environment and so treated as external. It is a mental process which the rulers of Germany have exploited to the full in persuading their followers to attribute all sorts of enormities to the Jews and the Czechs. One of its greatest disadvantages is that, whilst depriving the individual of insight into his own mental trends more effectively than any other mechanism, it provokes in him an attitude of intolerance proportionate to his own weaknesses, and a tendency to retaliate against others for what he repudiates in himself. It plays a large part in determining the purely punitive attitude of the average citizen towards the sexual delinquent, and in enabling such a punitive attitude to be substituted for an attempt to understand the true nature and origin of sexual delinquency. Projection is also largely responsible for the tendency of the sexual delinquent in turn to regard society as his enemy, and to consider himself justified in anti-social behaviour.

A controlling mechanism of a more advanced kind is the process whereby the individual, instead of projecting his own disturbing impulses upon others, adopts the opposite expedient of internalizing the inhibitory and restrictive influences in his environment. Evidence has now been accumulated to show that, at a very early stage in development, the child begins to install within his own mind counterparts of those persons in the environment who frustrate his impulses and attempt to exercise control over them. Such persons are, of course, almost exclusively parents and parent-figures; and the inner representatives of these figures form the nucleus of what is known as "conscience". To begin with, the child's conscience is of a very primitive nature; for his impressions of his parents are inevitably ill-judged, and are elaborated imaginitively in terms of his own fears. The nature of the conscience which eventuates depends, however, in no small measure upon whether and to what extent the child comes to regard his parents as loving or aggressive figures. In so far as his parents appear to him in the light of predominantly aggressive figures, his conscience will acquire an exacting and uncompromising character; and the inevitable conflict between his conscience and his primitive impulses will engender both an excess of anxiety and an excess of guilt. In all cases, however, a reinforcement of the process of repression is an invariable accompaniment of the development of conscience in the child's mind; and, indeed, the child's conscience soon becomes the chief agent of repression. In a sense, however, it may be said that the primitive conscience itself becomes repressed; for the painful nature of the child's moral conflict leads to an exclusion from consciousness of the disturbing dictates of the inner mentor together with the offending impulses themselves. Thus it comes about that in later life the primitive conscience of childhood persists side by side with the repressed impulses at unconscious levels of the mind. As he grows older, of course, the individual normally absorbs from his environment standards which provide a nucleus for the conscious and more rational conscience of his adult years. Even so, however, his unconscious conscience continues to exert a profound, if subtle, influence upon his mental life. Curiously enough the persistence of a very relentless and uncompromising unconscious conscience does not always have the effects which might be anticipated. It is liable, in any case, to promote psycho-neurosis and certain forms of psychosis owing to the intensity of the inner conflict engendered; but, if the unconscious conscience is particularly overbearing, the resulting tension may be such as actually to impel the individual to commit crimes to redress the balance of uncompensated guilt. This is the deeper truth underlying the commonplace that those who are the most strictly brought up are by no means invariably the most moral; and this truth applies no less in the special sphere of sexual delinquency than in the sphere of delinquency in general. It may be added that the presence of an exacting unconscious conscience provides no guarantee of adequate development on the part of the conscious conscience. On the contrary, there are many delinquents, both sexual and otherwise, in whom the strength of the unconscious conscience is only equalled by the weakness of the conscious conscience, with the result that unconscious morality becomes the measure of conscious immorality.

Consideration of the controlling function of conscience leads us by a natural transition of thought to consider what is by far the most important factor in the control of impulse, viz. the ego or central core of the personality (the "self" in the strictest sense). At birth the child is a creature of unorganized impulse, ignorant of the nature of outer reality, and incapable of adapting his impulses to the inexorable necessities of life except at a very primitive instinctive level. His mental organization conforms to hereditary biological patterns and is thus extremely simple compared to that of the adult. In the course of post-natal development, however, the individual's mental organization becomes increasingly complicated in response to the impact of both external stimuli and internally generated impulses. Experience becomes organized in the form of knowledge; a certain order becomes introduced into the emotional life with a view to the avoidance of conflicts of feeling; and instinctive impulses become modified and inhibited in such a way as to make behaviour better adapted to the conditions of life. These changes are all the work of the developing ego, which is, so to speak, the structural precipitate of the mutual impacts of inner impulse and outer reality, and which arises essentially as a means of regulating impulse in conformity with environmental requirements. Such being the nature and function of the ego, it becomes obvious that the success with which the individual's impulses are regulated in deference to social demands will depend chiefly upon the extent to which the development of the ego follows a satisfactory course. It is the structure assumed by the ego that determines the capacity of the individual to acquire insight into his own motives, to assess correctly the nature and demands of outer reality, to tolerate the frustration of his desires, to modify his impulses in the light of outer circumstances, and generally to adapt his behaviour to the conditions of life. The individual, whose ego has developed satisfactorily, thus becomes less dependent for the regulation of his life upon such primitive and precarious mental mechanisms as repression and projection. He is able to control and modify his impulses on a realistic basis, instead of simply rendering them unconscious by repression, or distorting his picture of society by projecting them upon other people. He is also less dependent for the control of his impulses upon the dictates of a primitive unconscious conscience. In the case of the sexual delinquent, however, there is reason to suspect the presence of a defect in the structure of the ego resulting from an unsatisfactory process of mental development. It is for this reason above all that his sexual impulses, retaining the imprint of various infantile patterns as they do, are also distinguished by an absence of adequate control. The persistence of some form or forms of infantile sexuality in undue strength, and a lack of control dependent upon a defect in the structure of the ego, would appear sufficient to explain the occurrence of sexual delinquency in a large percentage of cases. In other cases, however, it would appear as if some form or forms of infantile sexuality actually become incorporated in the structure of the ego; and it is on such a hypothesis that the overt sexual perversions are most satisfactorily explained. Such a hypothesis enables us to understand, at any rate, why the confirmed homosexual, to take an example, should actually be proud, instead of ashamed, of his perverse tendency. The case of the homosexual should remind us, however, that, whilst the appearance of a sexual perversion seems to depend upon an incorporation of some form of infantile sexuality in the ego, such a process of incorporation appears to involve a definite structural elaboration of the particular form of infantile sexuality concerned.

In conclusion it may be remarked that, in the time available for this paper, it has only been possible to give a very general outline of the psychological factors upon which sexual delinquency appears to depend; but perhaps enough has been said to indicate both the direction in which we must look for an explanation of the various problems involved, and the direction in which future research into these problems may be prosecuted with the greatest hope of profit.

15. PHANTASY AND INNER REALITY

It seems to me that, in considering the role of phantasy in mental life and the stage at which it comes into operation, we can help to clarify our ideas to some extent by taking into account the general classification of mental processes which emerges from the non-psychoanalytical 'analysis' of mental processes undertaken by G. F. Stout (Stout 1927). Highly intellectualised and preoccupied with the conscious as Stout's approach is, he must nevertheless be credited with a remarkable capacity for analysing psychological phenomena into their elements and reducing these elements to order. According to Stout, mental activity manifests itself in three modes and at three levels. The three modes which he distinguishes are (1) cognition (knowing), (2) affection (feeling), and (3) conation (doing); and the three levels which he describes are (1) the perceptual, (2) the ideational or imaginative, and (3) the conceptual. These two classifications may be profitably combined in a table such as the following.

Table 15-1

	Cognitive	*Affective*	*Conative*
Perceptual Level	Perception	Emotion	Impulse
Ideational Level	Imagination	Sentiment	Desire
Conceptual Level	Conception	Ideal	Purpose

Actually all these levels and modes are represented in some measure in all human mental activity, but with the emphasis varying both as regards level and mode according to circumstances in the adult. In the infant, mental processes are conducted predominantly at the perceptual level; and mental growth consists in a gradual development from the perceptual through the ideational to the conceptual level. At the same time, although the mental life of the infant belongs characteristically to the perceptual level, it is not altogether devoid of ideational, and even conceptual, elements. From this point of view it may, therefore, be claimed that phantasy, which is an ideational process, is present in some measure from the outset of life, although it is only when infancy is succeeded by early childhood that, with the establishment of the ideational level proper, phantasy reaches its zenith—only later to become submerged in part by processes belonging to the conceptual level as this becomes consolidated.

In terms of the above classification, one of the distinctive features of psychoanalytical thought is seen to lie in the importance which it attaches to mental processes belonging to the ideational level. Such a classification also enables us to understand how it comes about that analysts may differ regarding the stage at which phantasy makes its appearance. The fact would seem to be that phantasy is already operative in embryonic form from the earliest days of infancy, and that, as an ideational process, it plays an increasingly important part in mental life as the ideational level is reached. It would thus appear to be wrong to say that phantasy plays *no* part in the mental life of infancy. At the same time it would be equally wrong to say that infancy is the period of life during which phantasy manifests itself most characteristically and exercises its chief effects.

In conclusion, I cannot refrain from voicing the opinion that the explanatory concept of "phantasy" has now been rendered obsolete by the concepts of "psychical reality" and "internal objects" which the work of Mrs. Klein and her followers has done so much to develop; and in my opinion the time is now ripe for us to replace the concept of "phantasy" by a concept of an "inner reality" peopled by the Ego and its internal objects. These internal objects should be regarded as having an organised structure, an identity of their own, an endopsychic existence and an activity as real within the inner world as those of any objects in the outer world. To attribute such features to internal objects may at first seem startling to some; but, after all, they are only features which Freud has already attributed to the Superego. What has now emerged is simply that the Superego is not the only internal object. The activity of the internal objects, like that of the Ego, is, of course, ultimately derived from the impulses originating in the Id. Nevertheless, subject to this proviso, these objects must be regarded as having an activity of their own. Inner reality thus becomes the scene of situations involving relationships between the Ego and its internal objects. The concept of "phantasy" is purely functional and can only be applied to activity on the part of the Ego. It is quite inadequate to describe inner situations involving the relationships of the Ego to internal objects possessing an endopsychic structure and dynamic qualities. It would still seem legitimate, however, to speak of "phantasies" in the plural (or of "a phantasy") to describe specific inner situations (or a specific inner situation), so long as this limitation of meaning is appreciated.

16. PSYCHOANALYSIS: 1945

INTRODUCTORY REMARKS

Firstly I would like to say how sensible I am of the privilege of addressing you today. It is this sense of privilege which prompted my acceptance of your invitation to give this address, especially as it is the exception to your general rule to invite "Original Contributions only". As far as I was concerned this was not possible on this occasion due to the pressure of other commitments. I am, however, delighted that this present occasion provides me with the opportunity to formulate some general considerations regarding Psychoanalysis.

PSYCHOANALYSIS AS A SUBJECT

Psychoanalysis does not lend itself readily to popular presentation. This is because it deals with mental processes which are obscure and which remain unconscious; such mental processes are unconscious just because they are unacceptable to consciousness. Popularisation of psychoanalytical ideas is not desirable as this renders them superficial. The influence of psychoanalysis is most profitably exerted through its impact on psychiatry and other sciences in the present stage of the development of thought within these disciplines.

However, psychoanalysis has influenced contemporary thought in wider fields. Popularisation of psychoanalysis by "hangers-on" through the medium of general literature, and especially by novelists, has taken place. In this way considerable misunderstandings regarding the nature and aims of psychoanalysis have led to misinterpretations of the discipline.

MISINTERPRETATIONS OF PSYCHOANALYSIS

1. A system of thought which provides sanctions for the removal of inhibitions: When viewed in this light, psychoanalysis appears to validate the

abolition of controls upon, and the unrestricted indulgence of, "Instinctive" tendencies: in particular that system of thought sanctioning sexual licence and sexual perversions. Psychoanalysis has been exploited in this sense by many modern novelists who are critical of existing values or adopt a destructive attitude towards them. Psychoanalytical thought has been similarly exploited by certain modern novelists with the urge to give literary expression to their own abnormalities.

The same misunderstanding is prevalent among members of a very different, and indeed opposite, group, namely moralists and traditionalists of various persuasions; by members of this group psychoanalysis is regarded as exercising an influence which is *socially disintegrating and destructive of cultural institutions* in general.

2. Another misinterpretation is to regard psychoanalysis as, in effect, a mystical cult.

a. it is regarded as such by a large group of scientists, e.g., psychologists—"Not psychology, but psychosophy".
b. it is regarded as a mystical cult by a group of devotees. Psychoanalysis is thus a *magical* means for enabling the devotee to free himself of all difficulties, both internal and external, and to become immune to the vicissitudes of human existence.

Psychoanalysis is none of these things. Well, what is it? The term is used in a number of senses with a historical basis.

1. A Method of Treatment: for functional nervous disorders (Freud). Based upon observation by Freud that the revival of forgotten memories had a therapeutic effect. At this stage Freud was employing hypnotism to achieve this end. But his attempt to revive memories took precedence over hypnotism, resulting in Freud's development of the method of "free association". The aim of which was the promotion of maximum spontaneity of thought and feeling.

2. The Attempt to explain Theoretically how such Results were achieved: through observations it was found that:

a. memories were unconscious
b. resistance to the revival of memories was present
c. memories were highly emotionalised, unpleasant on balance, and traumatic
d. memories were of childhood

The rationale of therapeutic effect was thus found in the overcoming of resistance to the revival of unconscious memories, which were both significant and unpleasant, and which belonged essentially to childhood.

3. The Attempt to explain Theoretically the Origin of Symptoms: inferences drawn by Freud were:

a. If the revival of memories was therapeutic, the forgetting of memories had a pathological effect.
b. Resistance was due to repression.
c. Unpleasantness pointed to conflict (since experiences commonly involved an element of pleasure).
d. Childhood represented a clash between *the spontaneous and "instinctive" behaviour of the child and the attitudes adopted by grown-ups (parents)* towards the child and his behaviour—thus *frustrating* and *rejecting* attitudes to a child are "bad".
e. Conflict is due to the child *wanting to please his parents and to be loved by them, and so coming in part, to adopt the attitudes of the parents to his own spontaneous behaviour*—that is, to judge its own behaviour, and even its desires, by parental standards.
f. In the last resort, *repression is directed*, not against memories, but against *instinctive tendencies*. Also repression is *instigated by partial identification of the child with the parents, and the adoption into the child's personality of parental attitudes and standards.*
g. Symptoms *are due to the pressure of repressed instinctive tendencies*, which demand expression *in defiance of adopted standards*, but which can only express themselves in a *disguised form* owing to the influence of those standards. Such symptoms develop in individuals in whom the *repressed tendencies are strong and the adopted standards uncompromising*. The symptoms are unpleasant because:
    1. the expression of the repressed tendencies is in conflict with accepted standards
    2. the repressed tendencies are unable to achieve their natural satisfaction

4. The Body of Psychological Theory: developed by Freud and other psychoanalysts in an attempt to determine the principles governing human behaviour in general, and to provide a systematic explanation of the emotional life of Mankind. As we have seen, psychoanalysis originated as a method of psychotherapy. Then it developed into a system of psychopathology; and subsequently became a system of general psychology.

It was not a complete system because a complete system would embrace (i) cognitive, (ii) affective and (iii) conative aspects of human psychology; psychoanalysis has confined itself to the *affective* and *conative*.

The psychoanalytical method does not lend itself to the investigation of cognitive processes, except in so far as these are influenced directly by affective and conative factors. The special concern of psychoanalysis is *motivation* and covers the motivation of the behaviour of the *normal* as well as the *abnormal*. This extension of field was the result of observations indicating that no definite distinction could be drawn between the one and the other. *The same factors were at work in the "normal"*:

a. Dreams

   i. forgotten memories—especially those of early childhood
   ii. repression
   iii. conflict
   iv. the same processes were involved in dream formation as in symptom formation—namely disguise

b. Fairy tales, myths, etc.: enshrine the same themes as do symptoms and dreams
c. Anthropological phenomena: these demonstrate the use of, e.g.:
   —*taboos*—indicating repression and *avoidance*
   —breaking of taboos has a connection with *phobias*
   —while *superstitions* relate to phobias and obsessions
   —*rituals* show the use of compulsions and obsessions
d. Cultural Patterns
   —Patriarchal system
   —the arts
   —aestheticism and homosexuality
   —"Group Psychology and the Analysis of the Ego"
e. The Psychopathology of Everyday Life
   —slips of the tongue demonstrate the influence of repressed motives
   —forgetting

5. The Philosophy of Life: that based upon psychoanalytical findings and which is conformable to psychoanalytical theories, e.g., theories of human nature. Theories regarding the significance of cultural institutions are contained within Freud's "Metapsychology" which is at the borderland of metaphysics. The general trend of the philosophy of life represented, for example, by Freud's "Metapsychology", is in line with the standpoint of scientific humanism as described, for example, in a recent [March or April 1945] broadcast by Julian Huxley.

Of all the senses in which the term "psychoanalysis" is used, the last is the least satisfactory. No metaphysics which ignores the findings and conclusions of psychoanalysis can be regarded as satisfactory. This is especially so since psychoanalysis has something to say regarding metaphysics itself as the product of the human mind. Nevertheless, the psychoanalytical method cannot, in itself, be regarded as providing a sufficiently broad basis for erection of a philosophical system.

It is true that biological considerations exercised a profound influence on Freud in the construction of his metapsychology. But his metapsychology remained uninfluenced, for example, by the more recent developments of physics. It may be surmised that there is more to be said about the question of *values*, which is eminently a philosophical question, than has been said in any psychoanalytical contribution to date. I would, therefore, suggest that Psychoanalysis should be judged by its Scientific rather than by its philosophical achievements.

Psychoanalysis originated as a method of psychotherapy. Successes obtained were sufficient to attempt to understand *the rationale of the method* and to put the use of the method onto a scientific basis. This led, in turn, to the attempt to provide a scientific explanation of the origin of the symptoms found to be influenced by psychoanalytical treatment. The result of this was the development of a scientific psychopathology conceived in psychoanalytical terms. This led in turn to the development of a scientific psychology conceived in similar terms.

The significance of these developments was that psychoanalysis ceased to be merely a method of treatment, and became a *method of scientific investigation within the psychological field.* This method is based on certain assumptions:

1. All behaviour and all physical phenomena have a *meaning*
2. All behaviour and all physical phenomena are capable of *explanation*
3. All behaviour and all physical phenomena are *motivated*
4. Necessary data can only be obtained under *conditions of maximum spontaneity*

This method soon proved to have a much wider application than at first appeared. It proved to be capable of profitable employment within the whole group of *psychological* and *sociological sciences*. So employed, it has given rise to a body of theory which has increasingly influenced all these sciences and seems likely to continue to influence them increasingly. Its influence is still greatest within its original field, viz. psychopathology; but it is making itself felt in general psychology, and to a lesser extent in the various sociological sciences. In its practical applications, its influence is likewise greatest in the treatment of pathological states; but it is capable of being applied in other directions—most notably perhaps in the *upbringing* and *education of children*. At the same time it is capable of contributing to the solution of innumerable *social* problems, for example, those of international warfare, and social unrest.

What I desire to stress, however, is this—that Psychoanalysis is essentially and above all a scientific method. It constitutes a certain method of approach to human problems. This method of approach has led to various conclusions embodied in a system of thought, in which certain hypotheses play an important part. But these hypotheses and the system of thought are in *no sense final*. They merely represent the best results achieved up to date, through the application of the psychoanalytical method. But it is really the method that counts and it is that which constitutes psychoanalysis.

If you want me to go on and give some further account of current psychoanalytical theories, I find myself in a dilemma. This dilemma arises out of the fact that, in recent years, I myself have developed a number of original views which have not so far found general acceptance among psychoanalysts.

The explanation is this, when I refer to "psychoanalysts", I refer to those who have *not* made a violent break with Freud. Therefore, I do not include those who follow the tradition of Jung or Adler; both of whom did make a break with Freud. Whilst I continue to regard myself, and continue to be regarded, as a psychoanalyst in the strict sense, my recent views represent a development which puts me in rather an isolated position theoretically. Not that there is complete unanimity of thought among other psychoanalysts; for several schools of thought may be detected within the psychoanalytical group, albeit the tradition of Freud is maintained by all these schools. But my views involve a more extensive revision of classical psychoanalytic concepts that has hitherto been attempted by any of these schools. Thus my views cannot be regarded as really representative. And it would be misleading if I sought to expound them on an occasion such as this. On the other hand, I find it difficult to expound views which I myself have come to regard as inadequate and as needing revision.

However, there are certain salient features of psychoanalytic theory to which I might draw attention without any fear of giving a false impression either of my own views or of those of other psychoanalysts.

COMMON FEATURES WITH A BROAD SIGNIFICANCE

1. The Unconscious as dynamic
2. Defence
3. Repression—is itself an unconscious process
4. Conflict *in* the unconscious
5. Division of the psyche—
   "Id" (Spontaneity)
   "Superego" (operating v. Spontaneity)
   "Ego" (Central & Conscious).

6. Conflicting attitudes
   Ambivalence—"libido" and "aggression"
7. Inner tension
8. Phantasy
   "wish fulfilment" and "inner reality"
9. Internalised situations of childhood
10. The problem of adaptation to reality

IV

APPLIED PSYCHOANALYSIS

INTRODUCTION TO PART IV

This group of papers demonstrates Fairbairn's capacity to apply analytic ideas to various fields: sociology, educational and social policy, and the mental health aspects of disciplines which could learn from psychoanalysis like education and dentistry.

'Psychoanalysis and the Dentist' (1933) presents an interesting discussion well suited to a general audience and gives several clinical illustrations not published elsewhere, including dreams of dental themes. The emphasis on the potential traumata of surgical and dental procedures is of potentially broad interest.

'Arms and the Child', published in January 1937, gives a capsule restatement of principles of child development with an emphasis on the way aggression is heightened by deprivation of parental care, early rejection, neglect, and an over-burdening with anxiety. This, said Fairbairn, leads to the heightening of childhood neediness in adults which predisposes them to rely on dictators and demagogic governments. The pooled aggressiveness in such populations could then be understood as an attempt to control these shared inner states of deprivation. There is no such thing, Fairbairn said, as the overly loving mother, for the mother who loves and gives is the best assurance against a war mentality. Echoes from this paper can be heard in the work by John Bowlby (1958) twenty years later.

In 'A Critique of Educational Aims', given to the Fife Head Teachers Association in November 1936, Fairbairn draws upon the educational content of his first degree in Mental Philosophy. One section of the course was devoted to theories of education from Plato to Montessori (1870–1952), and the syllabus included the works of Rousseau (1712–1778), Pestalozzi (1746–1827), and Froebel (1782–1852). In effect, the syllabus stressed the ideas of universal child-centered education that have been incorporated into current theory by writers such as Fairbairn, and have thus contributed to our present day appreciation of the psychological needs of childhood. It was against this background that Fairbairn demonstrated that psychoanalysis and a knowledge of child development could offer a radical critique of educational practice, enabling him to offer sensible recommendations designed to enhance the educational facilitation of growth and development.

'Psychoanalysis and the Teacher' was probably presented as the inaugural lecture to the Psychology and Education Society in October 1931. In this lecture, Fairbairn presents psychoanalysis in terms of instinct theory, while at the same time he discusses the effects of object relationships—in this case, the relationships between the teacher and the pupil. In his discussion, he portrays aggression as the result of frustration in object relationships, rather than as an instinctual drive. He is at pains to present an understanding of psychoanalysis as a potential aid to the teaching profession through its contribution to child psychology. As the child's relationships with his or her parents are to a large extent unconscious, behaviour exhibited by the child at school reflects these unconscious relationships. If the teacher understands the psychological processes of child development, he or she will be better able to further the task of educating the child. Moreover, if the teacher understands typical sources of problematic behaviour, which Fairbairn identified as anxiety and frustration, he or she may take steps to mitigate the entrenchment of antisocial behaviour. Fairbairn also argues that punishment is counterproductive and damaging. In addition, he emphasizes the dynamics which arise between the teacher and the child as a result of unresolved psychological conflicts in the unconscious of the teacher. Such conflicts, he argues, can produce behaviour on the part of the teacher which may exacerbate antisocial behaviour in the child.

While these comments have much in common with other enlightened analysts of the time, such as Anna Freud, who addressed themselves to problems of education, they are noteworthy for Fairbairn's signature of attention to the influence of relationships on educational and developmental processes.

'Psychotherapy and the Clergy', a talk given in 1958, juxtaposes psychotherapy and religion. The paper includes three cases illustrating the three main groups of patients seeking help. Although this is an incomplete statement, we have included it here because the juxtaposition of psychotherapy and religion is an important example of applied psychoanalysis, and because the topic is of considerable interest in view of Fairbairn's own youthful intention of entering the church.

Although Fairbairn's early religious education was strongly Presbyterian, his view of salvation was not that of Calvinistic predestination. While it could be suggested that a Christian missionary attitude is demonstrated in Fairbairn's didactic efforts to promote the understanding and utilization of psychoanalytic insights in the wider fields of interest, as represented by the papers in this section, it would be more accurate to see this as an expression of the good citizen, an example of the cultural effects of the Scottish Enlightenment. Whatever the source of Fairbairn's impetus towards didacticism, it is notable that the papers in this section rely heavily upon the interpretation of anthropological phenomena which Fairbairn used to consolidate the claims of psychoanalysis as a universal truth employed to throw light on the earliest aspects of human behaviour. The basic assumption is, of course, that rituals and ceremonies can be understood fully by members of an alien culture, and that such rituals and ceremonies are ahistorical. This attitude, common to psychoanalytic observers of the time, is not common to all religious believers.

During his life Fairbairn's attitude to Christianity became increasingly skeptical. Initially the problem as he saw it focused on its dualistic account of human nature in general and of sexuality in particular (Sutherland 1989). Fairbairn judged that Freud had provided a more adequate account of human nature than Christianity's doctrine of original sin. Even so, Freud's dualism of libido and death instincts was too close to the Christian dualism of good and evil, and both were incompatible with Fairbairn's view of psychic dynamism and the integral ego. In addition, the Church's neglect of worldly social justice could not fail to raise formidable questions in the mind of a man committed to theory based upon early social object relationships, and for whom the future mental health of the population was dependent upon the introduction of psychoanalytically enlightened practice in the education of children and the treatment of offenders. But while Fairbairn substituted belief in psychoanalytic ideas as a force for good, for those of orthodox religious belief, he nonetheless felt that the search for salvation was the primary motivation for patients who sought psychoanalytical help. He often said, 'They are looking for a Messiah, not an analyst,' and he continued to feel that the work of the clergy and the psychoanalyst had a great deal in common.

'The Study of Mental Abnormality' (1928) is a well-constructed statement of a dilemma which still dogs modern psychiatry: the propensity to split the search for the holy grail into the pure neuroscience study of the brain and chemistry (the outcome being drug therapy), as opposed to the inclusion of social and psychological research and therapy, which is currently less in favour on both sides of the Atlantic. Fairbairn argued, with an eloquence which remains timely, that ultimate progress in this area demands the inclusion of both areas of research.

17. PSYCHOANALYSIS AND THE DENTIST

At the outset, let me say how sensible I am of the honour of being invited to read a paper before the Odonto-Chirurgical Society of Scotland. I imagine that it is unusual for a psychologist, even for a medical psychologist like myself, to receive such an invitation.

I have an uncomfortable suspicion that I have accepted your kind invitation under false pretences. I have the feeling that you expect me to offer you some practical hints on the management of patients. If so, I fear that I shall disappoint you; for I have no hints to offer. As a matter of fact, I have been much impressed by the skill with which dentists actually manage their patients. They have a difficult task, however; and I wish I could provide some practical advice to make it easier. I wish, for example, that I could describe a simple technique for inducing in the average patient a positive relish for visits to the dentist, and for producing in certain other patients an admission that there is absolutely nothing the matter with their teeth. I wish I could describe a simple method of suggestion by means of which patients could be made incapable of forgetting appointments and compelled through an internal necessity to report at regular intervals. Unfortunately I do not find myself in a position to offer you hints of this practical nature. I think, however, that, as a medical psychologist, I may be able to contribute something to your understanding of the reaction of patients to dental procedures and to the person of the dentist himself.

Psychology is a young science, and medical psychology a still younger; but medical psychology does appear to have reached a stage at which it is in a position to throw some light upon the mental processes underlying the patient's attitude to the dentist and to the operations which he performs. If therefore my remarks are barren of practical hints, I trust that they will at least prove to be of some theoretical interest. I even venture to hope that they may turn out to possess some practical value, if only in promoting the dentist's peace of mind when he deals with cases presenting a psychological problem.

I take it that among the many cases which give the dentist trouble and anxiety, it is just those cases in which the problem is psychological rather than odontological that prove most baffling. I imagine also that this special group of problem-patients falls into two classes: (1) patients who shun the dentist, and (2) patients who haunt the dentist.

I shall endeavour to explain why these two groups of patients exist, and also what lies behind their respective attitudes. Incidentally, I hope also to explain why the ordinary man in the street has such a peculiar horror of the dentist—a member of society who, if reason reigned supreme in the human heart, ought to be regarded as one of the chief benefactors of mankind.

It cannot be regarded as abnormal to dislike going to the dentist. I feel convinced that dentists themselves share the common prejudice, when the rôle of dental patient is thrust upon them; for all dental procedures are at best unpleasant, and many of them are extremely painful. There is an inborn tendency in all living creatures, other things being equal, to avoid the unpleasant and to seek the pleasant. Human beings are no exception to this rule. Even animals, however, are capable of enduring great unpleasantness if a sufficiently strong motive is present. Thus, when driven by hunger, an animal will endure considerable hardship in the search for food. Such endurance of hardship at the instance of hunger may, of course, be interpreted in the sense that the unpleasantness of hunger is greater than the unpleasantness of the hardships involved in satisfying it. Behaviour of this type may be described as following the path of greatest satisfaction, or as obeying the law "The strongest motive at the moment wins." Psychoanalytical writers describe it rather aptly as behaviour according to the "pleasure principle." This type of behaviour is characteristic of the animal and of the human infant.

The situation is complicated, however, in the case of the human being, owing to the high level of intelligence attained by man. The high level attained by human intelligence is bound up with certain capacities: (1) A great capacity of learning by experience; (2) the capacity to foresee the results of possible behaviour; (3) the capacity of communicating the results of experience to others.

In virtue of these capacities every adult of normal intelligence in a civilised community is aware that to neglect dental trouble in the present is simply to lay up greater trouble for the future. He also knows that by attending a dentist regularly he may greatly reduce the risk of suffering from dental causes. Man is thus in a position to save himself greater discomfort in the future by enduring lesser discomfort in the present. When he takes advantage of this position, his behaviour is determined by *rational* motives. The essence of such behaviour is its *adaptive* character. It is adapted to the facts of life and not simply determined by the feeling and impulse of the moment. It is described by writers of the psychoanalytical school, in contrast to behaviour according to the "pleasure principle," as behaviour according to the "reality principle." The infant is quite incapable of such adaptive behaviour; if he cries for the moon, he expects to get it. His demands upon life are determined not by what reality is prepared to offer him in the way of satisfaction, but by his own inner wants. As, however, the child develops and his intelligence increases, his conduct becomes increasingly adapted to the demands of reality. He learns to some extent to content himself with such satisfactions as the nature of things permits, to endure the postponement of satisfaction and even to submit to the frustration of impulse.

Unfortunately this lesson is never completely learned. Even in the adult the reality principle is very far from reigning supreme as the determinant of conduct. Under the influence of Greek philosophy, it has been believed for centuries that man is a completely rational being. This assumption has been shown to be completely false by modern psychological research. It is being shown with increasing clearness that man's feelings and impulses elude rational control in innumerable ways. Man's intelligence enables him to penetrate the secrets of nature and, through the application of scientific knowledge, to harness natural forces for his own purposes; but his use of the powers thus acquired is largely determined by feeling and impulse. Where feeling and impulse are concerned, his intelligence is easily blinded. It is for this reason that, in an age distinguished for scientific achievement, human intelligence finds itself bankrupt in the solution of problems involving human relationships—be these problems of economics, of politics, of social organisation, or of international co-operation. When it comes to controlling his own desires and feelings, man is inclined to exploit his intelligence in the interest of his inclinations, by finding specious reasons for having things as he wants. This process of finding arguments in favour of beliefs held for emotional reasons is described in modern psychology by the term "Rationalisation." The most marked feature of rationalisation is that it deceives the subject himself even more than it deceives others. It is largely as the result of this psychological process that psychology itself has lagged so far behind the physical sciences. The backwardness of psychology is in the main due to the reluctance of man to recognise the irrationality of his own motives. Of recent years, however, psychology has at last begun to bestir herself; and the present advances in the subject are characterised by an increasing recognition of the part played by feeling and impulse in human behaviour.

Perhaps the most important of all psychological discoveries is the discovery of the part played in human behaviour by motives which are *not conscious*. This discovery has resulted from the study of neurotic symptoms, and credit for it is mainly due to the work of the psychoanalytical school. Investigation has shown that neurotic symptoms are not simply results of a failure of cerebral function, but *motivated* phenomena. The patient, however, is quite unaware of the motivation lying behind them. The motivation is *unconscious*. This discovery has opened up the way to a vast and hitherto unsuspected realm of mental processes which are ordinarily cut off from consciousness. This realm of mental processes is, for convenience, described as "the unconscious."

Once the existence of this hidden realm of mental processes is recognised, the natural question that emerges is: "Why is the Unconscious unconscious?" The answer which has been given to this question has had a revolutionary effect upon medical psychology. It has been found that the unconscious is unconscious because its contents are incompatible with and unacceptable to our conscious mental life. The unconscious is thus made up of ideas, memories, feelings and impulses which have been, so to speak, rejected by the conscious self. This process of rejection, which itself occurs quite unconsciously, is called "repression."

The remarkable fact about the "repressed" elements in the mind is that, although they are unconscious, they influence behaviour and conscious mental life in subtle and unsuspected ways. The most obvious examples of unconscious motivation are to be found in certain acts of forgetting. It is ordinarily believed that forgetting is due to a failure of our mental processes. This is by no means invariably true. The truth is that in many instances we forget because we do not really want to remember. This fact is sometimes appreciated in everyday life. If a young man forgets an appointment with his fiancée, she does not as a rule interpret his omission sympathetically and condole with him as the victim of a failure of cerebration. On the contrary, she senses a motive behind his lapse of memory and tells him that he cannot really love her. Similarly, the dentist is justified as a rule in inferring that, when a patient forgets an appointment, it is because he does not really want to keep it. A like inference may usually be drawn when a patient turns up late. The patient who turns up late is in the habit of justifying himself by all manner of rationalisations—"There wasn't a tram," "My watch must have been slow," "Someone called at the last minute." The real reason of the patient's lateness, however, is in most cases reluctance to keep the appointment—a reluctance which the patient's rationalisations are framed to conceal as much from himself as from the dentist.

Whilst the motivation behind the forgetting of appointments is essentially unconscious, the most obvious motive at work, viz.: the avoidance of unpleasant experience, is not far removed from the level of consciousness. If, however, we desire to grasp the full significance of dental operations for the patient, we shall require to delve considerably deeper into the unconscious. It was along the path provided by the investigation of neurotic symptoms that the exploration of the unconscious was originally conducted. As exploration proceeded, however, more accessible paths began to be discovered. Among the various features which were found to characterise the unconscious, two may be mentioned as having provided finger-posts to new channels of approach. Unconscious mental processes were found to be (1) primitive, (2) infantile. It thus came to be realised that the nature of the unconscious may best be studied in the phenomena of primitive and infantile mental life. The chief sources for the study of these phenomena are three: (1) the thought and behaviour of the child; (2) thought and behaviour among primitive peoples; (3) dreams (which are the products of primitive thought inasmuch as they occur when the higher mental processes are obscured by sleep).

In what follows I propose to dip for a few minutes into each of these fields of mental life. I shall do so with the object of throwing some light upon the significance, for the unconscious, of teeth, dentists and dental operations.

1. THE THOUGHT AND BEHAVIOUR OF THE CHILD

It is a characteristic feature of the young child that he is unable to appreciate the remote consequence of events. His mental life is essentially of a "here and now" character; and the meaning which things and events assume for him corresponds to the impression they make upon him from this restricted point of view. His attention is concentrated upon immediate effects; and consequently, even such a simple operation as the examination of his throat is assessed at its face value and interpreted in the light of an *assault.* This naïve attitude persists in the unconscious in later life and underlies the apparently unreasonable attitude adopted by many people to surgical and dental operations.

The significance of an operation for a young child and the emotional effects which it engenders may best be illustrated by the quotation of an extreme case of such emotional effects. Take, for example, the case of a young man who was sent to me suffering from symptoms of insanity, and who had been subject for years to distressing nightmares in which he was haunted by a female figure whom he described as "the white sister." The source of these nightmares was traced to an operation for the removal of tonsils and adenoids, performed upon him when he was a young child. When the nurse came to get him ready for the operation, he became terrified about what was going to happen to him. His terror was increased by the fact that the doctors were late in arriving and the period of painful anticipation was thereby prolonged. Unfortunately the nurse who attended was lacking in understanding and tried to control the child by adopting a harsh and threatening attitude. She employed force to put him upon the table for operation and she held him down with violence while the anaesthetic was being administered. The result was that, though the incident was apparently forgotten, a psychical trauma had been inflicted; and this trauma was preserved in the unconscious in association with a hidden memory which came to expression periodically in anxiety dreams.

The traumatic effect of operations acquires a special colouring when the patient is female and the operator male. Under these circumstances the operation is liable to assume the special emotional value of a sexual assault. This fact again may best be illustrated by an extreme case—the case of a girl who was brought to me by her parents on account of the difficulty which they experienced in persuading her to eat. In spite of her parents' persuasions she had starved herself so successfully that her body was skin and bone. The onset of this symptom had followed a surgical operation performed a year previously. The operation had been for appendicitis; but there was reason to believe that no disease of the appendix had been found at the operation. In the light of another case, which came under my notice when I was in general practice, I have a strong suspicion that the symptoms suggestive of appendicitis in this girl's case were due to the escape of menstrual blood along the Fallopian tube into the abdominal cavity. If this be so, it is not difficult to understand the operation acquiring the emotional value of a sexual assault. In any case, menstruation was just becoming established; and this in itself was sufficient to render the girl particularly sensitive to the symbolism of forcible entry into the body. That a similar symbolism attaches quite unconsciously to manipulations in the mouth has been made clear to me by the dreams of certain female patients; and this is undoubtedly a factor entering into the emotional reaction of women to male dentists.

2. THOUGHT AND BEHAVIOUR AMONG PRIMITIVE PEOPLES

The most remarkable features of mental life among primitive peoples are (a) the prevalence of *magical* ideas and practices, and (b) the system of taboo.

Let us consider for a few minutes the magical outlook on life. Magic, like science, is concerned with the causation of events. Both have come into being through the operation of similar motives. The aim of both is to bring the course of events under control. Magic differs from science, however, in that, while science is based upon rational considerations, magic is based upon superficial resemblances and superficial connections. Thus the would-be murderer in many savage communities burns an image of his enemy in the belief, or at any rate in the hope, that his enemy's body will waste away like the image in the fire. It is also believed that the possession of what has been in close contact with, or has come from the body of another person, confers power over that person. Thus, in the Banks Islands, for example, it is common for one man to try to injure another by charming hairs or nail-parings from his body.

Where magical thought prevails, the sense of security conveyed to the individual by magical procedures is balanced by the fear of magical influences originating in others. It is believed that what happens to any of the dejecta, or to any detached part of the body, will happen to the body as a whole. For this reason it is a common practice in primitive communities to bury or, so far as possible, to destroy all that comes from the body—including the products of excretion, nail-parings, hair-clippings and teeth. I understand that even today in certain parts of Europe it is customary to bury broken fragments of teeth to prevent them falling into the hands of witches. In such customs we may trace the origin of many sanitary practices which have subsequently been justified on scientific grounds. Whatever justification such a practice may have from the modern scientific standpoint, we must always remember its magical origin if we would properly understand the complexities of human behaviour, for the magical attitude still lingers on in the unconscious, even among civilised men. It is for this reason that the modern workman who does not hesitate to outrage the laws of scientific hygiene by spitting in the street will yet magically efface his sputum by crushing it under his foot.

The persistence of magical ideas in the unconscious has a great deal to do with the attitude of patients to dental procedures. I take it that most dentists, when they extract a tooth, consider that they are simply performing a necessary operation in the patient's interests. The patient may reflect so, too; but his emotional reaction all too often belies his conscious reflections. This is because magical conceptions still reign in the unconscious under the veneer of civilisation. Deep down in the patient's mind the dentist has all the emotional value of a magician. In allowing the dentist to remove and take possession of a tooth, the patient is putting himself in the dentist's power and so exposing himself to the most terrible dangers. Even minor dental operations involve the risk of magical influence: for the drilling of a tooth may be the magical symbol of a more widespread mutilation; and in filling a tooth, the dentist is introducing into the patient's body a substance which may be the vehicle of a dangerous spell.

There is another aspect of magical thought which merits our consideration owing to the important part which it plays in the unconscious. It is an aspect of magical thought closely related to that system of taboo which, as I have pointed out, constitutes the second great feature of the mental life of primitive peoples. Taboos are prohibitions which have a religious rather than a legal validity, and which are universally observed in the community. The violation of a taboo is regarded as a sin rather than as a crime; and it is visited with appropriate penalties. It is immaterial whether the violation is intentional or unintentional, or even if it is quite unconsciously committed. It is also immaterial whether the violation is discovered by human agencies; for the savage lives in a world of spirits, and punishments which fail to be exacted by a human agency will inevitably be exacted by an offended spirit. Misfortune and disease thus readily come to be interpreted as punishments for the violation of a taboo. In order that further punishment may be averted, guilt must be atoned. Accordingly, atonement is sought by the magical virtues of sacrifices. The motive behind sacrifice is to ward off the risk of serious loss or suffering by the deliberate endurance of minor loss or suffering. In this way the demands of conscience are satisfied and the anxiety of guilt is relieved.

Sacrificial rites are sometimes precautionary rather than expiatory in the strict sense. This is obviously so in the case of hand-selling and initiation ceremonies. A good example of such precautionary rites is provided by the rite of circumcision, which is widely practised among different races. This rite is sacrificial in character, because it involves sacrifice of part of an organ as a precaution against the effect of a possible violation of taboo. The Yorubas accordingly call circumcision "the cutting that saves." In some tribes the rite of circumcision is performed in infancy. In others, however, it forms part of the initiation ceremonies of puberty; and this is almost certainly the original practice. Circumcision is not the only form of ceremonial mutilation known to the anthropologist. In Malaya, for example, the teeth are filed, and among many Australian and South African tribes one or more teeth are knocked out at the initiation ceremony of puberty.

The conceptions of magic and taboo which underlie such practices appear foreign to the conscious life of civilised man; but the practice of breaking a bottle of champagne on the bows of a new ship at the launching ceremony serves to remind us that they are not really so foreign after all. The fact is that such conceptions constitute the stock in trade of the unconscious, which preserves intact all the characteristics of primitive mental life. It is in this direction that we must look for an explanation of the curious behaviour of those patients who haunt the dentist and solicit dental operations in spite of the assurance that no dental trouble is present. As a matter of fact, there *is* trouble present, although the trouble is not dental. The trouble is psychological; and it arises from the presence in the unconscious of thoughts, feelings and impulses which violate unconsciously accepted taboos. On this account there exists in such patients a constant internal necessity to seek relief from anxiety through the sacrifice of parts of the body which lend themselves to the purposes of symbolic expiation.

3. DREAMS

Dreams are the product of thought during sleep. They are imaginative thought-processes occurring when the highest mental processes characteristic of waking life are in abeyance. It is a general biological rule that the higher functions of the living organism exercise an inhibitory influence over the lower functions. When the higher functions are withdrawn, the lower functions manifest themselves more clearly. Thus the knee-jerk reflex, which depends upon the functions of the lower motor neurones, becomes exaggerated when the upper motor neurones are injured and their inhibitory influence withdrawn. In a similar fashion dreams reveal levels of mental life ordinarily inhibited or repressed during waking hours.

Dream thought has certain well-marked characteristics. Of these, only one need be mentioned for our present purpose—its symbolic character. Dream scenes are symbolic: that is to say, behind the manifest content lies a latent content, which represents the real meaning of the dream—a meaning hidden from waking consciousness by the form of the manifest content. One marked feature of symbolism is its universality. There are certain themes which occur with great frequency in dreams. Dentists, dental operations and teeth unite to provide symbols for one of these common themes. To give you some idea of the significance of dentistry for the unconscious, I shall mention a few dreams with dental themes which have been recorded by patients.

Here, for example, is the dream of a middle-aged unmarried woman with a history of anxiety and depression: "I thought I had discovered a big tooth in my mouth quite rotten. I was feeling its cavities with the head of a darning needle to estimate the damage. I pictured it as quite a shell, and black. I remember saying, 'I am *sad, sad* to think that my tooth is so bad.' My anxiety about it was very great. . . . "

This dream was followed by another dream, which it may be of interest to quote in view of the fact that dreams of the same night have been found to express similar dream thoughts, even when the manifest content is different. The second dream runs as follows: "A young man is chasing a lad. I feel the lad, if caught, will receive most dreadful punishment. . . . The boy has done something very wrong . . . and the man's anger is just. Yet the boy is smiling. . . . I feel the man is quite right, yet I admire the lad. . . . "

The patient was asked to think of the dream about the tooth and record the thoughts which arose in her mind in association with it. Among other things, the dream made her think of a story she had heard about a man whose life changed completely after one of his teeth fell out at breakfast. This man had suddenly realised that he had reached a time of life at which his powers had begun to decay. The dreamer also recorded that she experienced an extreme horror and disgust for the tooth in the dream. This directed her thoughts to a current feeling of anxiety, as to the source of which she felt herself in ignorance. She sensed, however, that her anxiety was about some disclosure which she would have to make to me. The idea then occurred to her that the tooth represented something vile in herself which ought to be removed. That in turn suggested to her the idea of undergoing the operation of oöphorectomy.

It is unnecessary for the present purpose to enter further into the significance of the dream; it is sufficient to point out that the tooth in the dream represented something in the dreamer herself of which she was unconscious, but to which guilt was attached none the less. It was something which would cause her shame if it emerged into consciousness; and its threatened emergence created in her a state of anxiety of which the real source was hidden. It was something, however, which, she felt, ought to be removed.

The significance of dental dreams may be illustrated further by reference to two of the dreams of another patient, a young unmarried woman, who also suffered from anxiety and depression. One of the dreams runs as follows:

> There was a fierce man who had committed a murder for the sake of some pearls. . . . He and I and another person were down in a cellar . . . and he was counting the spoils. The pearls suddenly fell and were scattered and we two helped him to pick them up. I kept some back, about five, hidden in my hand, because I knew he was going to cheat us. . . . We were only pawns in his game. . . . The pearls were like teeth—shaped like baby's teeth . . . But something suddenly made me decide not to cheat, whatever he might do to us. It may have been that I funked the consequences. He wouldn't hesitate to kill me if he found out.

There are several points to note about this dream:

1. There is an equivalence between "pearls" and "teeth." Teeth thus represent something of great value for the dreamer—something desirable in itself and actually desired.
2. The pearl teeth are represented in the light of *stolen* treasure. They are of the nature of forbidden fruit. To possess them means for the dreamer to be guilty and renders her liable to the death penalty at the hands of the "fierce man."
3. We get a hint of the significance of the dentist for the unconscious in the figure of the "fierce man," who insists upon having the pearl teeth at all costs, even if it means committing murder.

Here is another of the same patient's dreams:

> I was with a man, a dentist, having my teeth pulled or prodded at—some injection I was to have that made everything cloudy and the poison that was in me, or the power that shouldn't be there . . . show up in a dark opaque mass. . . . I had very mixed feelings. Principally I was frightened and

> unsure about this great cloud inside me. It was something to do with sex feelings . . . that made me anxious and ashamed.

It will be noticed that this dream, like the former dream, gives expression to the idea of something desirable in itself but forbidden and guilty—"the power that shouldn't be there." In this case, however, the dream makes plain that the desired but forbidden thing has to do with sex feeling and that the anxiety expressed in the dream is due to the simultaneous presence of desire and guilt. It is also to be noted that, whereas in the former dream the assault of the "fierce man" is punitive in character, in this dream the dental operation is represented in the light of a sexual assault.

The consideration of the second patient's dreams makes it possible to amplify what has already been said in connection with the dreams of the first patient. It is clearly indicated that, for the second as for the first patient, teeth have a high symbolic value. This symbolic value relates to the presence in the unconscious of two distinguishable and conflicting factors: (1) repressed material in the form of potential thoughts, feelings and desires; (2) guilt attaching to this repressed material. In the second patient's dreams, however, the figure of the dentist is introduced. "The dentist" also has symbolic value for the unconscious; and his symbolic value is determined from the same two sources as the symbolism of "teeth." In the second dream, he is represented as a sexual figure introducing into the patient's body "the power that shouldn't be there" and appealing to repressed feeling and desire. In the first dream, the figure corresponding to the dentist is a punitive figure capable of rewarding guilty feelings and desires with the extremest form of penalty. "The dentist" is thus seen to signify for the unconscious both the object of guilty impulses and the avenger of hidden guilt. In both these rôles he is a figure of anxiety and even terror.

All the dreams so far quoted have been the dreams of women. I shall now quote the dream of a young man suffering from neurasthenic and hypochondriacal symptoms:

> Mother and I . . . go with other people to a low restaurant. . . . A girl near me . . . chats to me, warning me of the sleek young owner of the place. Shortly afterwards this man appears. He looks at my new suit and fingers it inside and out. . . . I do not wish him to know that I have any money on me, but he feels all over the suit and adroitly takes all my money. By a mere accident I detect him and demand the money back. He gives me some of it. . . . "Come on, we leave," I say to mother and hurry out. She does not seem to follow. Have I left her in his clutches? Well, I cannot help it and I dare not go back. I run home, clutching my notes under my arm. I know the evil man is following me. I run through dirty streets and reach a hut, which I enter in order to count the notes. Suddenly it dawns upon me that I am in

> *his* hut. . . . The man comes in. It is father. He grins savagely and makes a grab for the money. . . . I strike him on the head with a hammer. . . . Father is buried up to the neck in the hut. . . . I jump on his face. . . . His jaw is on the ground. His teeth drop out. . . . He is dying. . . . I ask him to forgive me, but he says "No! It is my revenge," and tries to kick me. . . . He dies grinning.

It does not require much imagination to recognise in this dream the expression of hostile feelings on the part of the dreamer against his father. It is equally plain that the dreamer's hostility towards his father is related to jealousy of his father as a rival for his mother's affection. Such feelings of jealousy and hatred were quite foreign to the dreamer's conscious attitude; but investigation showed that they had been far from foreign to his consciousness in childhood. The guilt which naturally attaches to such feelings even in childhood had led to their repression; but their persistence in the patient's unconscious was revealed by the constant occurrence of dreams in which his hostile feelings for his father achieved an imaginative gratification, which was only possible when the higher mental functions were abolished by sleep.

The chief interest of the dream for our present purpose lies in the symbolic significance of the loss of teeth. For the dreamer's unconscious the knocking out of his father's teeth symbolised the infliction of a deadly injury. There is, however, another important feature of the dream to which attention must be drawn, viz.: the appearance at the end of the dream of the *motifs* of guilt and paternal vengeance. The dreamer asks his father to forgive him, but his father says "No, it is my revenge," tries to kick the dreamer, and dies with a grin on his face. In view of this ending, it is quite appropriate that the dream should have had a sequel four nights later. The sequel was to the following effect: "At a swimming bath. . . . I am worried. My left canine tooth comes out. It had been filled by Dr. Grundy (an imaginary name), but the filling had rotted away. The tooth has a dry, shrivelled root. I show it to ______ but I want it back."

Thus, in the second dream, the patient's father is given his revenge, on the principle of the primitive talion law—"An eye for an eye and a tooth for a tooth." There is even a suggestion that this revenge is mediated by the ministrations of the dentist. While the dreamer's father is granted his revenge, however, it is to be noted that the dreamer still wants his tooth back. This means that, at the mental level from which the dream springs, the loss of a tooth is too serious a matter to be accepted with equanimity.

It will be noted that in this patient's dreams, as in those of the other two patients, we find signs of a desperate conflict waged in the unconscious between repressed desires and attendant guilt, between magical wishes and ingrained *taboos*. Where such conflict is unduly severe, the issue is neurosis;

but not even the most normal person is completely free from unconscious conflicts. Their presence undoubtedly complicates the emotional reaction of normal as well as of neurotic patients to dental operations and to dental operators. In the case of the neurotic, however, the intensity of the emotional reaction is proportionate to the intensity of the conflict. The emotions engendered by dental procedures are only in part due to the actual dental situation. They are derived in large measure from unconscious levels. Emotions natural to the real situation thus become complicated by emotions appropriate to the state of conflict in the unconscious. This complication is due to the symbolic character of unconscious thought, according to which, the actual situation in the dentist's room is utilised as a mere setting in which the dramas of unconscious phantasy may be staged, in defiance of the reality principle. For, as I have tried to point out, the mind of the civilised adult includes unconscious mental levels which preserve intact all the primitive characteristics of his childhood and his ancestry.

DISCUSSION

Mr. J. Douglas Logan said he had listened to Dr. Fairbairn with interest and, he hoped, some profit. We sometimes failed in our treatment of a patient, or rather failed to satisfy, not because of lack of skill, but because of some prejudice, some psychological vagary of the patient which we cannot overcome, and which we cannot even discover in many instances. We all know the patient who, after being given a set of artificial teeth, comes to us a week later with the dentures in the mouth and volubly declares, with clear enunciation, that she cannot speak with the new teeth. Whether this is a case of ill-balance of mind or mental unreason, or simply an impairment of the sense of hearing, it is difficult to say, but the patient appears to believe what she says. Patients like us or dislike us, believe in us or disbelieve in us, because they have some psychological stimulus for thinking they know something that they are entirely and assuredly ignorant of, not so much that they do not know, as that they think they know. Hence for these reasons we lose patients, and by the same token we gain others. Mr. Logan was glad to hear Dr. Fairbairn say that man is not a perfectly rational animal, for it confirmed his own conclusions in the study of mankind, and theology teaches that man is not perfect in mind, body, or estate. Particularly are man's senses imperfect and unreliable. What one hears and what he thinks he hears, what he sees and what he thinks he sees, what he does and what he thinks he does, are frequently in each instance so different, that in a court of law, evidence of the senses is heavily discounted.

Mr. Dunn remarked that most of his psychological knowledge of treatment of children was derived from Dr. Cameron's book, "The Nervous Child." He said that probably the chief feature of the book was the responsibility of the adult mind being communicable to the child. Fear and timidity were conveyed to the children, in a country walk, by the nurse afraid of cows. This was further illustrated in many instances, by parental anxiety for the only child, the child being also anxious and nervous. The health of the child was psychological as well as physical.

Dr. F. G. Gibbs asked why in persons undergoing general anaesthetics some people have the same dream every time, even when different drugs are used, e.g., (a) weeping over the removal of a piece of furniture; (b) feeling of drowning, and they let out with scissors kick. Then there was another type of patient who firmly believed he was awake, and said he heard remarks (which were quite correct and often rude).

Dr. Fraser said:

> As Dr. Fairbairn's paper was so exhaustive and technical, it must appear that any remarks of mine may be frivolous. I would say, however, that I think he overstressed the fear that the majority of patients have when coming to the dentist. Some actually like coming! In dealing with children, the right type of lady assistant is very important. Some of us feel that we have not the right kind of personality to deal with certain types of patient. Can we acquire this? A mastery of the psychology of the various patients would help us to achieve success. How is it to be arrived at? Temperamentally, we are often unable to give the patient what he wants.

Mr. Sanderson thanked Dr. Fairbairn for his paper, but had to confess there were parts of it beyond him. He had met patients, who came to him the first time, with their minds badly prepared. One patient came and had two teeth taken out. He suggested filling three small cavities. However, when the patient returned, she said, "My uncle said, 'It is very painful to have teeth filled,' so I won't have it done." Not a very good preparation for a dental operation; but she was amenable to treatment and had them filled. Another patient, who was very neurotic and jumpy, gradually began to improve and Mr. Sanderson asked her what had caused the change. "Well," she said, "when I was in the chair I used to sit and think it was going to be very bad. Now I say to myself, 'It isn't bad,' and it really makes a great difference." He asked Dr. Fairbairn what was to be done when patients did not allow operation. Should we use force?

Dr. Primrose Walker said:

> I have much pleasure in adding my quota of thanks to the essayist for his instructive and highly educative paper. Dr. Fairbairn has stated that psychology is a very young science. I cannot agree with him, because, years ago, Fielding, in "Jonathan Wilde," wrote: 'that a man's greatness depends on

> his homicidal capacity.' Surely he was a psychologist. If by chance we read our Bible or our History, we learn that every great man belonged to the psychosthenic class. Take Dr. Johnson—supposed to be a delicate boy; supposed to have scrofulous glands, but lived until he was over 70; had no other T.B. manifestations, probably only had nits in his hair—was taken before Queen Anne in front of all her court to be touched. From that day he became psychosthenic until the end of his life. The fright he received probably caused the upset of his mental equilibrium. Beethoven comes under the same category. What interests us, as surgeons, is that we must be extremely careful not to inflict pain on children, particularly the nervous type, otherwise we may throw the child off its balance and ruin it for life. Thank goodness today we have anæsthetics—general and local—at our disposal, by which means we are able to eliminate pain.

Dr. Menzies Campbell, after thanking Dr. Dodds Fairbairn for his most interesting and instructive paper, mentioned that, although the address dealt with the outlook of the patient, nothing had been said about the psychology of the dentist. He then cited the case of a "difficult" child brought to consult him about carious primary teeth. Two visits were spent in gaining the child's confidence; on the next, and succeeding visits, fillings were completed. He was therefore surprised, on the day of the next appointment, to receive from the child's mother a letter stating that she had decided not to have any more fillings done. Dr. Campbell said he was mystified, but a mutual friend later supplied the reason. The child's father had, in conversation, told another dentist about his little boy having a number of first teeth filled. This particular dentist commented on the absurdity of filling teeth which would later be lost, and added that anyone who filled temporary teeth was simply looking for work. The speaker added that what really distressed him was that, having surmounted difficulties in order to do what he knew to be right for the child's welfare, he should be regarded as having been actuated by ulterior motives. Dr. Menzies Campbell concluded his remarks by saying that the dentist in question was supposed to be an ethical individual. Could Dr. Fairbairn offer an analysis of this particular mentality?

Mr. Cubie (the chairman) said:

> There is no doubt that one of the most fascinating subjects of late years is psychology, which was formerly known by the appellation of metaphysics. Tonight, we have been carefully guided along the labyrinthine ways of the subject in its relation to dental practice by an eminent exponent of medical psychology, from whom we have gained a considerable amount of information. Professor Fairbairn has treated us to a real intellectual discourse, and gone pretty deeply into some of the psychological processes, principally as they concern medical practice, and endeavoured to show their application in dentistry. In the discussion, various speeches have emphasised various

points, chiefly concerning the handling of patients, some attention being given to the management of the child. The successful handling of patients comes about to a great extent through careful observation and experience, which enable us to apply—consciously or unconsciously—psychological principles. A point which I always stress with students is to endeavour to read their patients from the very first moment of meeting them. This is important in many ways, viz.: in their successful handling; in gaining a knowledge as to their mental attitude to the dentist; also, as to how his services will be appreciated. Very much useful information can be gained in this way. Fear on the part of the patient is one of the problems with which the dentist is daily confronted, and it should be his endeavour to use every means in his power to mitigate it. Sometimes the discovery of a topic of mutual interest during the course of conversation is sufficient to displace the idea of fear for the time being from a patient's mind; or by observing a tactful and sympathetic attitude, the same desired result may be achieved. There is no doubt that fear can, in many cases, be greatly modified and held under control by careful training or education, and also by attention to the laws of health. There is, however, another aspect of the subject that is apt to be overlooked. What about the dentist himself? If he wishes to succeed in imparting confidence to his patients, and pave the way for dispelling ideas of fear from their minds, then he also must attend to the laws of health and keep fit. In all likelihood the question of psychology in dentistry will receive more attention in the future, when attempts may be made to systematise it. In conclusion, I wish to thank Professor Fairbairn most cordially for his extremely interesting paper.

Dr. Fairbairn, in reply, said that he desired to thank the Society for the most kind reception which his address had received. He regretted that it was impossible for him to deal adequately with all the questions which had been raised by the various speakers during the discussion. Several speakers had referred to the problems presented by the psychology of the dentist himself. It would, of course, have been possible to have made some reference to the psychology of the dentist in the course of the address, but it had seemed preferable to concentrate in the present instance upon the psychology of the patient. It would also have been possible to have discussed the practical management of patients from the psychological point of view. He (Dr. Fairbairn) had assumed, however, that most members of the Society had acquired considerable skill in the management of patients as the result of their own experience, combined with a working knowledge of human nature. Indeed, he was much impressed by the success with which most dentists seemed to achieve their difficult task. He had, therefore, thought it desirable to confine himself to a description of the deeper emotional significance of dental operations for the patient—a significance of which, as a matter of fact, the patient himself was quite unconscious. This was a subject with which he (Dr. Fairbairn) had had special opportunities to familiarise himself, owing to the intimate study of neurotic patients which his own work involved.

Dr. Gibbs had asked why some patients experienced the same dreams (usually of an anxiety type) every time they underwent general anæsthesia. The reason was that the anæsthetic abolished the higher mental functions before the lower ones—with the result that, in the stage of partial anæsthesia, the deeper mental strata had an opportunity to assert themselves in an unwonted way and with a minimum of modification. The dreams of the partially anæsthetised patient thus gave an indication of the more or less permanent emotional significance of operative procedures for the deeper levels of the patient's mind. The fact of a patient dreaming, e.g., that he was weeping over the removal of a piece of furniture, showed that, however clearly he might recognise the desirability of an operation at the levels ordinarily dominant in consciousness, deep down in his mind it meant for him the loss of something which he valued. The recurrence of similar dreams on different occasions indicated how permanent such deep emotional values were. In this connection, it might be noted that the experience of being anæsthetised, with the sense of suffocation which so frequently accompanied it, was itself reminiscent of the first and perhaps the most terrifying experience of life—viz., that of being born. It was seldom realised how alarming birth must be to the child who had hitherto experienced nothing but the serenity of uterine life. Although the anxiety of the birth experience was one which none of us could recall as a conscious memory, it was an experience which could hardly fail to leave a permanent impression upon the mind, and to condition the emotional reaction of the individual to all subsequent experiences involving similar sensations. It was in this sense that the recurrence of dreams of drowning recorded by Dr. Gibbs's patients was to be understood; for no available experience provided a better symbol for the trauma of birth than that of struggling in water.

Although the problems presented by the psychology of the dentist fell outside the scope of the present paper, they were closely related to the problems presented by the psychology of the patient. It was interesting to note how many speakers had recognised this relationship. Dr. Fraser had pointed out how some dentists felt that they did not possess the right type of personality to deal with certain types of patients. This feeling was undoubtedly justified. Dentists, for example, in whom the aggressive instincts were strongly developed, would be unlikely to appeal to those patients whose reactions were predominantly determined by a fear of attack; on the other hand, they would make a strong appeal to patients actuated by unconscious motives, demanding suffering and sacrifice. Similarly, dentists whose psychological constitution rendered them particularly solicitous over the infliction of pain would appeal less to the latter class of patients than to those dominated by fear of attack.

Another aspect of the relationship between the psychology of the dentist and the psychology of the patient had been pointed out by Mr. Dunn, who had remarked upon the possibility of the dentist communicating his own anxiety about a case to the patient. The communication of emotion from one person to another was a well-known psychological fact. Children were specially susceptible to the contagion of anxiety; and apprehensiveness on the part of the parents promoted nervousness in their children. One of the reasons for only children being so often nervous children was that the parent of the only child tended to be unduly solicitous. It was not uncommon to find nervous adolescents, whose mothers explained their nervousness on the grounds that they were "war babies." The truth of the "war baby" theory seemed to be that anxiety provoked in the mother during the war was communicated by her to the baby after birth.

In reply to Dr. Sanderson, he desired to guard against a misunderstanding. He did not wish to be interpreted as deprecating dental operations on the grounds of their traumatic effect. While it was true that all operations, both surgical and dental, were emotional traumata, most of them would appear to be obligatory. It was important, however, that their traumatic effect should be taken into account, and so far as possible mitigated.

Dr. F. G. Gibbs submitted three X-ray negatives as a Casual Communication: (1) Fractures of the left body of mandible and ascending ramus, with hemi-facial paralysis. Paralysis due to a complete tear of the facial nerve and auditory nerve at the base of the skull. No fracture of the base showed up in X-ray photographs, but it was undoubtedly present. Consciousness was never lost. (2) A sequestrum of complete angle of the mandible, following acute alveolar abscess, demonstrating advisability of removing the tooth concerned and establishing drainage at earliest opportunity. (3) An unerupted lower wisdom tooth, situated in the ascending ramus of mandible, where symptoms were entirely occipital headache. Removal of tooth was followed by cure.

18. ARMS AND THE CHILD

In an article by Lord Allen of Hurtwood (1936), there are two passages which may well serve as text for the remarks to follow. In the first of these passages Lord Allen expresses the belief "that it is the psychological factor which in these days will increasingly determine whether we are to go to war or pursue the policies which will lead to peace" (p. 105); and in the second passage he ventures the statement that "the evils of the Treaty of Versailles may perhaps have been due not only to what happened in the mirrored hall of a French palace, but to life in an ill-ventilated nursery, ruled over by a tired nurse, visited by a preoccupied father, or brooded over by a too-loving mother" (p. 108).

The essential truth embodied in these opinions is that the problem of peace and war is a problem of child psychology. We hear a great deal nowadays about the issues of peace and war; but most of what we hear must be accepted with considerable reserve. We hear, for example, that the only hope of peace lies in the redistribution of colonies among the great nations of the world. It would be nearer the truth, however, to say that the only hope of peace lies in the redistribution of toys among the small inhabitants of the nursery. We hear too that war is the result of economic pressure; but, if so, it is chiefly the economic pressure of an inadequate milk supply upon the infant. At the same time it is very far from my intention to imply that war could really be abolished by such measures as the redistribution of toys in the nursery and the provision of a satisfactory milk supply for infants. The situation is not so simple as all that; but I do feel convinced that, in seeking a solution of the problems of peace and war in the nursery, we should be turning our attention in the right direction. The reactions of a nation to the situations in which it finds itself placed are, after all, the common reactions of its individual citizens; and the political reactions of these individuals are determined by their reactions to the circumstances of early childhood. It is, therefore, of the utmost importance for the peace of the world that these circumstances should be satisfactorily controlled.

It is not by any means only a question of circumstances, however. If it were, it would be possible to adopt a very much more optimistic attitude towards the problems of peace and war than is justified by the real facts. Unfortunately the real facts are highly unpalatable; and it is on this account that they are so generally ignored; for there is a universal tendency in human nature to ignore unpleasant facts unless they are so obtrusive that it is utterly impossible to ignore them. Moreover, this tendency is particularly obstinate when the unpleasant facts in question are facts about human nature itself. The optimists, who hope to abolish war by redistributing colonies and raw materials, are ignoring psychological facts; and above all they are ignoring the fact that the ultimate source of war lies in the incorrigible aggression of mankind. The truth is that the hereditary endowment of man includes powerful aggressive instincts which, being hereditary, are for all practical purposes incapable of modification.

The fact that the aggressive instincts have a hereditary basis seems to render the prospects of peace so precarious that it is no wonder the optimists seek to ignore it; but there is an even stronger motive for ignoring the real nature of these instincts. When the average psychologist speaks of "an aggressive instinct," he means an innate tendency to react in an aggressive way to situations involving danger; but that is an inadequate conception. He would be nearer the truth if he meant an innate tendency to react in an aggressive way to situations which are *felt* to be dangerous—which is a very different thing; for a situation may be felt to be dangerous, when it is not really dangerous at all. Yet, even so, he would fall short of the whole truth; for the study of functional nervous and mental disorders has provided us with evidence to show that the aggressive instincts are profound biological urges which surge up inside human beings and seek expression in destructive behaviour. Worse than that, there is evidence to show that these destructive urges are present in the child from birth. Indeed it is in early childhood that they manifest themselves most clearly; for in early childhood the mental mechanisms designed to control them are only in process of being established. Fortunately, early childhood is a period of life in which physical weakness, lack of knowledge and lack of opportunity render the destructive urges relatively innocuous. If, however, the playbox included a few gas-bombs and flame-throwers, we should require little convincing about the aggressive instincts of children.

Fortunately, there is another side to the picture. The aggressive instincts are balanced by another group of instincts, which may be conveniently described as "the love instincts." If the aggressive instincts are destructive in character, the love instincts forge emotional bonds between individuals and manifest themselves in activities calculated to preserve the objects towards which they are directed. These love instincts are socially the most important part of the hereditary equipment of the child. Like the aggressive instincts, they are not mere reactive tendencies, but spontaneous biological urges; and it is to be noted that they operate in the opposite direction to the aggressive instincts. Whilst the aggressive instincts drive people apart and give rise to enmities and wars, the love instincts draw people together and make for social stability and peace.

I have said that, since the child is born with aggressive instincts which demand expression, the ultimate source of war can never be removed. This does not mean, however, that we can do nothing to avert war. Indeed, we can do a great deal, once we realize what we are up against; but it is only through a knowledge of child psychology that we can hope to do anything effective; and it is in the nursery that the necessary measures must be taken. Enough has already been said to indicate the general character of these measures. We must so order the life of the young child as both to facilitate the expression of his love instincts and to reduce to a minimum those factors which stimulate and foster his aggression. The question is "How is this to be done?"

In order that we may be in a position to put these measures into effective operation, it is important for us to realize that in the restricted world of the nursery the child's aggression and his love impulses are both directed towards the same persons. In accordance with this fact, it is found, not only that the child entertains contrary impulses of love and hate towards the same person at the same time (an attitude described as "ambivalent"), but that there is also a considerable fusion of love and hate impulses in his mind. It is on this account that children so often destroy their favourite toys and sometimes even bite their mothers in an outburst of affection. Ambivalence and fusion of the love and hate impulses are features of the child mind which tend to disappear, if development proceeds satisfactorily; but no individual grows out of them completely and all too few grow out of them sufficiently. When we consider the fox-hunter's affection for the fox which he kills, we can form some estimate of the unfortunate zest imparted to war by a persistence of the attitude in which love and hate impulses are fused; and the great danger to peace arising out of a persistence of ambivalence is that in ambivalent people the balance between love and hate is so delicately poised that in a crisis a straw may make the balance dip heavily on the side of hate—particularly if such hate receives the endorsement of dictators or political leaders.

Undue dependence upon dictators and political leaders is itself evidence of the persistence of a childish attitude into adult life; for the child is essentially a dependent creature. He is dependent on his parents for the fulfilment not only of his physical needs (e.g., his need for food and shelter), but also of his emotional needs. What he seeks above all from his parents is the assurance of love and moral support; and it is essential for satisfactory development that his demands should be satisfied. Whilst the importance of satisfying the child's physical needs is universally acknowledged, the equal importance of satisfying his emotional needs receives all too little recognition. Indeed it seems a common belief that such needs should only be satisfied sparingly if the child is to attain a desirable degree of independence. This, however, is a misconception. It is as natural for the young child to be dependent as it is desirable for the adult to be independent; and, if the child does not get the assurance of love and support which he demands, the result is that his craving for it is increased, instead of diminished, and he is confirmed in the dependent attitude. It is in this direction that we must look for an explanation of the suggestibility of the masses towards the propaganda of dictators and political leaders generally. This suggestibility becomes a grave source of danger when the aggression of the individual, which is ordinarily repressed and subjected to social prohibitions, is exploited by the propaganda of political leaders enjoying the status of parental figures; for, as the result of such suggestibility, a nation may be rushed into war before there is time for sober reflection.

I have just indicated that, when the child's emotional needs remain unsatisfied, his dependence upon parental figures is increased instead of being diminished; but that is not all. When adequate assurance of parental love and support is not forthcoming, the child experiences an intolerable sense of frustration and loss. A child finding himself in such a situation tends to react in two ways—(1) with anxiety, and (2) with aggression. He reacts with anxiety because, from his point of view, loss of love and support represent a danger-situation. That this is so may be best understood in the case of the infant. With his ignorance of the world the infant has no guarantee, when his mother goes out of the room, that she will ever come back again. When he becomes hungry and his mother is not there to comfort him, he feels utterly deserted; he feels as if his whole world had been destroyed. If he remains unfed and uncomforted, an aggressive reaction begins to manifest itself; and his cry of anxiety becomes a cry of rage. The result is that, when food and comfort do eventually come to him, he satisfies his hunger in an aggressive way, i.e., the situation of suckling, which for the infant represents the epitome of love, is accompanied by manifestations of infantile hate. Here then we have the primary and classic instance of love and hate being directed simultaneously towards the same person—and an all-important person at that. This situation involves the child in an emotional conflict of the most distressing kind; for it involves him in the intolerable position of entertaining destructive impulses towards the very source of the love and support for which he craves—the position of, so to speak, cutting off the branch on which he sits. The next step is not difficult to imagine. When the infant now finds himself hungry and uncomforted, he feels as if his state of deprivation were the result of his own destructive impulses. In the interests of mental peace he is thus faced with the necessity of coming to terms with his own aggression and disposing of it otherwise than by directing it towards his love-object. One of the most significant methods of disposal which he adopts is to disown his aggression and attribute it to his love-object or to other objects outside himself—a procedure technically known as "projection." This procedure is admirably illustrated in the fairy tale of "Little Red Riding Hood"—the wolf representing the child's own aggression, which, although originally directed against the grandmother, becomes projected upon the grandmother and then appears to be directed against the child. Through the agency of projection the child's world thus becomes peopled with terrifying objects, which seem to threaten him with destruction.

From what has been said, it will be seen that the child is the prey of considerable neurotic anxiety, i.e., anxiety having no basis in actual dangers; and this anxiety is of threefold origin. It includes—(1) primary anxiety resulting from deprivation of the love and support which the child seeks; (2) anxiety over the imagined effect of his aggression upon his love-objects; and (3) anxiety over the imagined effect upon himself of the aggression which he projects. These three anxieties combine to drive him into reliance upon parental figures. He is driven to rely upon parental figures (1) for love and support; (2) for authoritative control over his aggressive impulses; and (3) for protection against the apparent outer dangers resulting from the projection of his own aggression. The relevance of all this to the problem of war should now be obvious. The more emotionally childish the individual remains, the more subject he remains to childish anxieties, and the more he tends to rely upon dictators and political leaders for the ordering of his daily life. In subjecting himself to dictatorial leaders, he obtains the approval and support of parental figures; he obtains the moral advantages of having his aggressive impulses controlled by powerful external authorities of a parental type; and he obtains an approved outlet for his aggression by projecting it upon the supposed enemies of the parental authorities whom he serves. The resulting situation is well portrayed in the present state of Europe, of which the most striking feature is the electrical atmosphere of anxiety engendered by the mutual suspicion of a handful of totalitarian states. The internal security of these states is purchased at the price of international insecurity; for it depends upon the projection of aggression upon other states and the maintenance of a mass-delusion of persecution. The most unfortunate feature of this projection of aggression is that it does not really dispose of individual aggression at all; for the resulting anxiety provides an apparent justification for real aggression against the imagined persecutors. Hence the contemporary armament race in Europe and the ever-present threat of war.

Within the scope of the present article it has been impossible to do more than to indicate broad outlines; but perhaps enough has been said to show that, if the problem of war is to be solved at all, it must be solved in the nursery. This does not mean, of course, that we must ban toy soldiers from the play-box. That would be too superficial a remedy; for, if we ban toy soldiers, we must also ban ninepins and, even if we ban ninepins, it is always possible for the child to mobilise a few dolls and a box of bricks in the interests of aggression. The child is born with aggressive instincts; and, if his aggression does not find an outlet in play, it will inevitably find some other and less satisfactory outlet. It is safest that it should find an outlet in play; for one of the great functions of play is to relieve emotional tension. If we honestly desire to lay the foundations of lasting peace in the world, our best course is to provide our children with the assurance of love and support which they demand, and to remove to the best of our ability all sources of emotional frustration in their lives. This does not mean, of course, that we must let them do exactly as they like; for the child requires the support of parental authority against his own aggression. At the same time it is only through the assurance of parental love that the pressure of the child's aggression and anxiety can be reduced, and that the child can achieve that sense of security which provides the basis of emotional independence and realistic thought in adult life. Since the pressure of aggression and anxiety in the individual is the prime cause of war, and since emotional independence and realistic thought in the individual are the surest guarantees of peace, the promotion of the day when every child shall have the assurance of love ought to be the chief aim of all peace-lovers. The social worker who spreads the knowledge of this fact throughout the homes he visits may thus prove a better apostle of peace than the parent who spends his leisure hours attending pacifist meetings instead of playing with his children.

I have quoted Lord Allen as saying that the evils of the Treaty of Versailles might be due more than anything else to "life in an ill-ventilated nursery, ruled over by a tired nurse, visited by a preoccupied father, or brooded over by a too-loving mother." Personally I should not be inclined to blame the ill-ventilated nursery so much as the over-tired nurse and the preoccupied father; for neither of these parental figures is likely to provide the child with the assurance of love which he requires. As regards the too-loving mother, I have yet to be convinced of her existence. I feel sure, however, that what Lord Allen has in mind is really the *over-anxious* mother, whose anxiety so readily assumes the disguise of maternal love. She, of course, is the product of the system that makes wars; and her influence is a powerful factor in perpetuating the system. On the other hand, the mother whose love provides, not a masquerade for her own emotional conflicts, but a means of satisfying her child's deepest emotional needs, is anything but a war-maker. On the contrary, it is in such mothers that the surest hopes of peace rest.

19. A CRITIQUE OF EDUCATIONAL AIMS

CONCEPTION OF CHILDHOOD

Our educational aims must necessarily depend in large measure on our conception of childhood. From a biological point of view, childhood is essentially a phase of immaturity. Strictly speaking, the period of immaturity includes three distinguishable phases:

1. Early childhood (1-6)
2. Childhood (7-12)
3. Adolescence (13-18)

Education is concerned more particularly with the second phase. But it is also concerned, to an increasing extent, with the first and third phases.

There is a tendency on the part of educationists, and not educationists alone, to regard childhood as a period not so much of immaturity as of preparation. This tendency is not so strong now-a-days as in the Victorian epoch, but it is still strong. Even when it is not explicitly formulated it is yet implicit in the prevailing educational outlook. While there is no question of the biological fact that childhood is a period of immaturity, the idea that childhood is a period of preparation is an assumption which we are justified in questioning. There are two good reasons for questioning the validity of the idea that childhood is essentially a period of preparation.

1. If we assume that childhood is a period of preparation, the child inevitably comes to be regarded as material to be educated, as grist for the educational machine. We are thus faced with a situation similar to that which has arisen in the industrial world with such distressing results at the present time.

Industrialism originated as a tool to enable the community to provide the individual with means of satisfying the elemental needs of life—food, clothing, shelter, etc. The industrial machine was thus created as a servant of man. Once created, however, it has become a Frankenstein which tyrannises over its creator. Created to feed men, the industrial machine now feeds upon men. The interests of the industrial worker have become subordinated to the demands of industrialism.

Similarly, a complicated educational machine has been created to enable children to be educated; and the result is that the interests of children are now largely subordinated to the interests of the educational machine. Thus, the preparation of children for examinations has become one of the chief aims of education, to the neglect of the personal needs of individual children.

2. There is another good reason for questioning the assumption that childhood is primarily a period of preparation. We are not entitled to make this assumption until we have answered the question "What is childhood a preparation for?"

The obvious answer is, of course, that childhood is a period of preparation for *adult life*. If we are in Socratic mood, however, this answer only raises the further question—"What is there about adult life (as contrasted with the life of childhood) to justify us in regarding childhood as merely a period of preparation for it?" Let us be more specific. What are the aims of adult life?

One of the most obvious aims of adult life is to earn a living. For the task of earning a living under modern conditions considerable preparatory training is undoubtedly necessary. If we are permitted to remain in a Socratic mood, however, we may next ask ourselves "Why earn a living?" The answer to this question is, of course, "In order to live." This being so, we are left with the paradox that we earn a living in order to live and live in order to earn a living. Someone will protest, however, that we live to earn a living not only for ourselves but also for others. We marry and have children and we have to earn a living for our wives and families. Here is another aim of life—to marry and have children. Yet there is no aspect of life so completely neglected in the modern educational system as marriage and all that it involves.

It would not be an exaggeration to say that modern education provides no useful preparation whatever for the demands of marriage and the upbringing of children. Apart from this consideration, however, we do not escape from paradox, when we say that we earn a living in order that we may marry and have children. We are merely faced with a fresh paradox—the paradox, namely, that we are educated in order to earn a living so as to produce more children to be educated, and educated by methods which provide no preparation for parenthood. Someone will doubtless point out that we have still another object in earning a living—viz. to provide for our old age.

Here is a fresh paradox. We wear out our vital powers when we are in our prime in order to ward off death for a little, when we already have one foot in the grave.

After all the aim of life is to live and to live more abundantly.

On any other assumption it is impossible to attach any meaning to the teeming life of the universe. It seems mysterious to us in our reflective moods that myriads of insects should spend weeks and months in larval and pupal forms only to enjoy a few hours perhaps of adult life. But this is only mysterious to us men because our moralising leads us to lose sight of the fact that the aim of life is the joy of living. Once we recognise this fact, instead of seeking an escape from facts in abstract conceptions, we can no longer rest content with the idea that childhood is a period of preparation for adult life. On the contrary, we shall recognise that every period of life provides its own justification and, so to speak, has its own rights. Indeed, if it is life that matters, it would be more rational to prize the rights of childhood more highly than those of any other period of life; for it is in childhood that the sheer joy of living is at its maximum.

THE RELATIONSHIP OF CHILDHOOD TO ADULT LIFE

If we abandon the idea that childhood is essentially a period of preparation for adult life, we are next confronted with the task of defining the relationship of childhood to adulthood. We have seen that childhood is essentially a period of immaturity. This immaturity is shown not only in the physical realm but also in the mental realm. So far as the mental realm is concerned, it is hardly necessary to stress the fact that the intelligence of the child is immature. But the immaturity of the child shows itself also in the life of feeling and action (i.e., in the emotional and conative fields, which constitute the dynamic aspects of mental life).

Here it becomes necessary to point out that childhood is not only a period of immaturity but also a period of growth.

The results of the intelligence tests devised by modern psychological research show that the growth of intelligence may be measured up to the ages of 14–16 at least. If our knowledge of the intellectual development of the child is due to the research of academic psychology, our knowledge of the development of the dynamic aspects of the child's life is due chiefly to psychoanalytical research. As Freud pointed out, the behaviour of the infant is determined exclusively by what he describes as the "Pleasure Principle".

This means that the child is essentially impulsive, his wishes and desires of the moment seek gratification irrespective of the suitability of the occasion and the possibility of satisfaction under the circumstances prevailing: i.e., his impulses seek satisfaction simply because it is the nature of an impulse to seek satisfaction.

From the point of view of the infant then, the presence of a need is absolute warrant for its direct and immediate satisfaction irrespective of any conditions imposed by external reality—of the nature of which, indeed, it is almost wholly ignorant. Thus if an infant wants its mother, it demands her instant presence. It knows nothing about the rival claims of household duties upon her time and, indeed, if it did know, it would not care.

The nature of the pleasure principle as a determinant of behaviour is well illustrated by a recent statement of Mussolini—"No power on earth will stand between the Italian people and its will." The nature of reality is such, however, that the infant's impulses are constantly frustrated.

When the satisfaction of impulse is withheld from the child, it tends to react to frustration in two distinguishable ways:

1. He bursts into tears and flies into a rage, the emotion he experiences being misery and anger.
2. Failing the actual satisfaction of his impulses, he resorts to phantasy and imagines them gratified. This explains why the hungry child, after crying loudly for a time, often suddenly becomes mysteriously quiet. When this happens, the anxious parent often creeps up to him to see what has happened to make him suddenly cease crying. It is then found that the child is going through movements of sucking and that he has a smile upon his face as if he were really satisfying his hunger. He is indulging in a wish-fulfilment phantasy. This resort to phantasy affords, of course, only a fleeting gratification, for his organic hunger is not really satisfied and his hunger pains reassert themselves in due course.

Behaviour according to the pleasure principle is essentially unadaptive.

1. It is directed towards the immediate satisfaction of impulse irrespective of the possibility of satisfaction.
2. It involves a demand for immediate gratification regardless of ultimate welfare.

So far as the life of emotion and behaviour is concerned, growing up consists essentially in the gradual abandonment of the primitive pleasure principle as a determinant of behaviour and its replacement by another principle—the "Reality Principle".

As the child develops, he begins to discover three important facts of life:

1. Reality only gratifies his impulses under certain conditions and in varying degrees.

2. The satisfaction of his impulses has often to be deferred, if satisfaction is to be attained at all.
3. Phantasy gratification is no adequate substitute for actual gratification.

Under normal conditions, the child gradually learns to abandon the pleasure principle in favour of the reality principle, which is (or ought to be) the principle determining adult behaviour. Here it must be noted, however, that the abandonment of the pleasure principle is never complete and it would be safe to say that there is no grown-up person in existence whose behaviour is wholly determined by the reality principle. The 100% determination of behaviour by the reality principle is an ideal of adulthood rather than an actuality. At the same time, the extent to which the pleasure principle is abandoned and the reality principle adopted is a measure of how far the individual has grown up emotionally.

If the pleasure principle is essentially unadaptive, the reality principle is essentially adaptive. Behaviour according to the reality principle consists essentially in the adjustment of individual demands to what reality permits. It involves:

1. Learning to endure unpleasant experiences when these are unavoidable.
2. Learning to endure the complete frustration of some impulses and desires.
3. Learning to submit to the postponement of the satisfaction of other desires.
4. Finding substitutive satisfactions for a number of impulses and desires. The process of finding substitutive satisfactions for natural impulses is known as sublimation.

As civilisation becomes more complex, sublimation becomes more and more important. Here it is perhaps necessary to point out that the social environment of the individual constitutes part of the outer reality to which he has to adapt his impulses. Thus, the more complex civilisation becomes the more difficult is the task of adaptation.

The chief difficulties which face the child in his task of learning to adopt the reality principle are as follows:

1. The imperiousness of his own impulses and desires.
2. The uncompromising nature of the frustration he has to endure.
3. The child's ignorance of reality.

The great task of education properly understood is to enable the child to deal with these difficulties and gradually to wean him from the pleasure principle to the reality principle.

THE ORIGIN OF EDUCATION

The historical origin of education is to be found in the Initiation Ceremonies of puberty, which are a feature among all primitive peoples. In primitive communities all the significant events of life are made the occasion of ceremonial rites. Such rites are specially associated with occasions marking the beginning of an activity or the performance of an act for the first time; i.e., the majority of such rites are really handselling ceremonies. Even in civilised communities similar rites are still a feature of some of the major events of life, e.g., birth, marriage, death. Vestiges of such rites are also to be found in New Year celebrations, house-warming parties and the "coming of age" parties, which are a feature of life in the U.S.A. The American "coming of age" party is a relic of the primitive initiation ceremony of puberty.

Puberty, of course, is an event of vast biological importance for it represents the emergence of the reproductive function. Its biological importance receives special recognition among primitive peoples, who regard puberty as marking the transition from childhood to adulthood. This transition is celebrated by impressive ceremonies, which are most characteristic in the case of boys. At these ceremonies the boy is initiated into manhood and accepted into the community of men.

The initiation rites are oriented in two directions:

1. They are intended to bind the young adult to the community. They exact from the adolescent a pledge of loyalty to the adult community, i.e., they put him under a social obligation.
2. They are intended to confer upon the adolescent the privileges of manhood.

There are two features of the initiation rites of puberty which demand our attention.

1. The initiation ceremony is preceded by a preparatory educational period lasting a few weeks or months. In this preparatory educational period the boy is given instruction in the following subjects:
   a. the customs governing the life of the community
   b. the lore of hunting, fishing, care of domestic animals, cultivation, etc.
   c. the art of war
   d. biological facts of sex (so far as they are known to the community)
2. The initiation ceremony itself involves a trial by ordeal, during which some form of mutilation is practised upon the adolescent

boy. This ceremonial mutilation takes such forms as circumcision, the removal of a tooth, etc.

It is important to realise that these mutilation practices are not simply meaningless and unintelligible acts. On the contrary, they have a deep, though doubtless unconscious, meaning.

1. They represent the ceremonial exaction of a penalty inflicted upon the aspirant to adulthood by the adult community. There are two aspects to the infliction of this penalty.
   a. From the point of view of the adolescent, it is an act of revenge on the part of adults directed against a new rival for the privileges of adulthood.
   b. From the point of view of the adults it is a penalty paid by the adolescent for adulthood, for entering into rivalry with his elders.
2. The mutilation rites are also precautionary.
   a. From the point of view of the adult these mutilations are a symbolic precaution against the rivalry of the adolescent, who is symbolically crippled and thus rendered harmless.
   b. From the point of view of the boy they are a symbolic precaution against the consequences of his own rivalry with his elders.

The rites of trial by ordeal and mutilation are, thus, primarily an expression on the part of the adult community of fear and hatred of young rivals. The community dare not, of course, kill or seriously disable the young rival, because the new aspirants to manhood strengthen the resources of the community, which depends upon its manpower for survival. The community, therefore, contents itself with symbolic mutilation. This mutilation serves to work off the concealed hatred of the grown-up for the young on the principle of catharsis. On the other hand the mutilation rites serve the secondary purpose of enabling the child to deal with an internal conflict over his own hostile wishes towards his elders. In growing up the child is encroaching upon the rights of his parents, and the initiation rites serve the dual purpose of providing him with an atonement for his guilt over this encroachment and symbolically removing his capacity to encroach.

The preliminary period preceding the initiation rites of puberty among primitive peoples is historically continuous with formal education in civilised communities. Modern formal education differs, however, from pre-initiation education in several respects:

1. The relationship of education to puberty has become obscure.

2. The length of the educational period has been extended so as to encroach increasingly upon childhood on the one hand and upon adolescence on the other.
3. The subjects of instruction have undergone a marked change, which may be summed up in the statement that education has lost much of its practical bearing.

While it is not difficult to trace the historical connection between modern formal education and the pre-initiation educational period in primitive communities, it is less obvious that traces of trial by ordeal and mutilation still persist. Their persistence is, of course, not consciously realised, but deep psychological investigation reveals indubitably that they exercise no small influence upon educational practices.

1. Trial by ordeal has been replaced by trial by examination. The persistence of the examination system, in spite of all the disadvantages which recent investigation has proved to attach to it, is undoubtedly due to reluctance on the part of the adult community to abandon the principle of trial by ordeal. It is to be noted that the anxiety which the adolescent in the primitive community must feel over the trial by ordeal is reflected in our own times in the anxiety to which children are subjected over examinations.

2. The principle of trial by ordeal is also illustrated in the teaching of subjects for their disciplinary value. The retention of the classics as a subject of school instruction undoubtedly receives its main support from this principle. The effort involved for the child in learning the classics is out of proportion both to their utilitarian and cultural values. The arguments brought forward to prove their value are simple rationalisations, which conceal unconscious motives of a completely irrational kind. To teach subjects for their disciplinary value is simply to teach it because it imposes hardship—in other words to make the subject an ordeal to the child.

3. The principle of mutilation is perpetuated in the practice of physical punishment. Again the arguments advanced in favour of physical punishments are simply rationalisations to justify a savage practice, which is perpetuated owing to the presence in a civilised community of the same motives which underlie the mutilation rites of primitive communities. It is true that, in a civilised community at any rate, these motives are unconscious, but they are none the less operative because they are concealed.

The retention of the practice of physical punishment is a special feature of Scotland. It has been dispensed with in most civilised countries without detriment to the well-ordered conduct of schools. This fact alone shows that the arguments advanced in favour of it are rationalisations. Doubtless the continuance of the practice in Scotland is favoured by the influence of Calvinistic tradition which sets such a high valuation upon the infliction and enduring of suffering. The continuation of the practice is indefensible under modern conditions for several reasons:

a. It has been proved by the experience of other countries to be unnecessary.
b. Most of the physical punishments inflicted are inflicted upon a small group of children who are repeatedly punished. This fact alone shows the inefficacy of the practice, otherwise the same children would not require to be punished again and again.
c. It is an appeal to the pleasure principle in the child since it tends to make the avoidance of suffering the motive for good behaviour.
d. It provides a gratification of concealed aggression and hatred in those who inflict the punishment.

THE AIMS OF AN ENLIGHTENED EDUCATIONAL POLICY

In the light of our review of the general nature and development of childhood and our survey of the historical origin of education, let us now consider what ought to be the aims of an enlightened educational policy.

A. Prevailing Aims to Be Eliminated

To begin with, it is necessary to eliminate from educational practice all prevailing aims which are out of place in an enlightened community. Such aims are almost exclusively unconscious aims. But it is the fact that they are unconscious that makes them so insidious and which makes it necessary that attention should be drawn to them.

1. In the first place it is necessary to eliminate all such magical aims as receive their classical embodiment in the primitive rites of mutilation and trial by ordeal. In the ultimate resort these rites have their origin in two groups of emotions prevailing in the adult community:

a. concealed hatred and jealousy of the young
b. fear of the young

The fact that educational practices influenced by such motives are accepted with such comparative acquiescence by children is no justification for their continuance. During my experience of work in a psychological clinic, I could not help being impressed by the remarkable acquiescence of children in the irksome and irrational features of the educational system. Their acquiescence is to be explained by the fact that the child is afraid not only of the authority of adults but also of his own aggressive impulses. It is because repressive measures provide the child with a means of dealing with his own rebellious impulses that he accepts them so readily; but it by no means follows that such measures are calculated to promote the best interests of education.

2. It is desirable to eliminate from educational practices such features as serve the purpose of satisfying the emotional needs of the teacher rather than promoting the best interest of the child.

In the course of my clinical work I have had the opportunity of treating several teachers suffering from nervous breakdowns and thus to familiarise myself with the deep unconscious motives which express themselves in teaching. I am under the impression that nervous breakdowns are particularly frequent among teachers, and I cannot help feeling that this fact must be associated with the nature of the work, which is particularly liable to intensify prevailing emotional conflicts in the individual.

THE CASE OF C.E.L., PRESENTED WITH THE FOLLOWING CHARACTERISTICS

- inner conflict between primitive, repressed urges of an aggressive kind and an uncompromising ego-ideal.
- externalisation of the inner conflict in the schoolroom situation. This is particularly liable to occur in teachers, because their position necessarily forces them into the position of representing standards of conduct to their pupils.
- projection onto the children of rebellious impulses, which then have to be dragooned in the presence of the children. Children thus become scapegoats, vicarious substitutes for repressed impulses.
- this patient was unable to tolerate any inattention, any imperfection of work or any restlessness in the children. The children had to be perfect. Her over-disciplining of the children was quite unconsciously undertaken in an attempt to achieve inner perfection.

What took place in extreme form in the case of this teacher is liable to take place to some extent in the case of all teachers, owing to the nature of their occupation.

B. Positive Aims

It is time for us to consider the positive aims of an enlightened educational policy. Perhaps it will be inferred that, in criticising the assumption that childhood is a period of preparation, I am completely undermining the rationale of education. This, however, is far from being the case. I have stressed the fact that, as an expression of the life impulse childhood is, so to speak, the peer of adulthood and ought to enjoy equal rights.

I have also stressed the fact that the object of life is the joy of living rather than, for example, earning a livelihood. Reality considerations, of course, impose upon the adult the necessity of earning a livelihood; but earning a livelihood ought, under ideal conditions, to be one of the characteristic channels through which the joy of living asserts itself. A man's work ought not be simply an unpleasant task undertaken simply to enable him to enjoy his leisure. It ought to be satisfying in itself; it ought to provide direct as well as indirect satisfactions.

The same holds true of education in the case of the child. Just as a man's occupation ought to promote a fullness of life so a child's education ought to promote fullness of life—and fullness of life not only in future adulthood, but in childhood itself. In a sense being educated corresponds to a man's occupation. It is the child's job.

Strictly speaking, however, a child's real job is "growing up"; and the true function of education is to help him to make a satisfactory job of his job. I have had occasion to point out that, so far as the dynamic aspect of life is concerned (and after all the dynamic aspect of life is the essence of life), "growing up" consists essentially in the progressive replacement of the pleasure principle by the reality principle as the determinant of behaviour. The chief aim of education, therefore, ought to be to help the child to take this great step and ensure that the transition is effected with a minimum of

Father and son: Ronald Fairbairn and Nicholas at Gifford 1949–1950

emotional disturbance. It is essential that the process should be a gradual one, if it is to be well-ordered. The cold wind of reality must be tempered to the shorn lamb; or rather the temperature of the wind must be gradually reduced, if acclimatisation is to take place.

Two dangers must be guarded against:

1. On the one hand, if the demands made on the child's powers of adjustment are too great, the child will regress to the pleasure principle. When regression occurs, the chief source of difficulty is usually found to lie in the home environment; but regression may also be precipitated by factors in school like

a. Over-disciplining
b. Excessive demands upon the child in school work; i.e., demands in excess of the child's capacity
   i. excessive standards of work
   ii. excessive hours of work
   iii. the practice of homework (which in my opinion ought to be abolished)
c. Curriculum and methods of teaching, which fail to make a direct appeal to the child's natural interests

There are two common factors in these various situations, which are liable to cause regression in the child:

a. Frustration of the child's natural interests and impulses in excess of his capacity to endure frustration.
b. The enforcement of standards of behaviour in excess of the child's capacity to respond.

Both factors are fruitful causes of anxiety in the child. And here it must be noted individual children of any given age differ both in their capacity to endure frustration and the capacity to satisfy any given standard imposed on them. The children who find their way to Child Guidance Clinics are children in whom these capacities are weak.

The symptoms which manifest themselves, when these capacities are over-strained, fall into three groups:

a. Nervousness or anxiety
b. Over-conscientiousness, which is always accompanied by some degree of anxiety
c. Naughtiness, which, as a matter of fact, is often accompanied by anxiety also.

Perhaps it may not be out of place to add a word about naughtiness in children. One of the most surprising findings of modern psychological research among children is that the naughty child is really an anxious child and that the anxious child is a frustrated child. When I speak of "naughtiness", of course, I am not referring to simple "high spirits". I refer to the sort of naughtiness that constitutes a child seen as a "problem child".

When a child is unduly frustrated and put into the position of having to conform to standards in excess of its capacity anxiety is the inevitable result. If it identifies itself sufficiently with the standards imposed upon it, it also becomes over-conscientious. On the other hand, if it identifies itself with its frustrating impulses, it becomes naughty. In either case, anxiety is in the background. Anxiety always accompanies failure of adjustment. Since the child is still to a large extent under the dominance of the pleasure principle, failure of adjustment favours regression to behaviour and thought of the "wish-fulfilment" type. It encourages phantasy, which then either finds behaviouristic expression in naughtiness or, on the other hand, leads to a withdrawal of interest from the outer world of reality and absorption in the inner world of imagination.

2. I have pointed out that the great task of education is to wean the child from the pleasure principle to the reality principle and that it is of paramount importance that this weaning process should be carefully graduated. I have also stressed the dangers that arise when this weaning process is speeded up beyond the capacity of the individual child for adjustment.

There is, however, an opposite danger, which is equally deleterious to the child's welfare—viz. the danger of making the weaning process too slow and thus allowing the child to remain too long under the dominance of the pleasure principle. If the child is allowed to remain too much and too long under the dominance of the pleasure principle, his capacity to adopt the reality principle becomes compromised. The child then becomes habituated to the inner world of wish-fulfilment. Such a child is commonly known as "a spoiled child". Curiously enough, the result in such a case is very similar to the result in the case of the child who is unduly frustrated and upon whom excessively severe standards are imposed. As a matter of fact, the "spoiled child" is so much dominated by the pleasure principle that any frustration at all becomes an intolerable frustration.

Since it is impossible to avoid some degree of frustration in life, the spoiled child is also liable to excessive anxiety. He inevitably becomes nervous, and, like the over-repressed child, he is liable to become either naughty or over-conscientious according as he identifies himself with his own natural impulses or such minimum standards as he finds it necessary to conform to. As in the case of the over-repressed child, so in the case of the spoiled child the chief sources of trouble are usually to be found in the home.

At the same time, a number of factors in school life may precipitate regression in the 'spoiled' child:

a. Needless to say, all the factors which operate unfavourably in the case of the over-repressed child operate in the case of the 'spoiled' child: —viz. over-disciplining; excessive standards of schoolwork; and curricula and methods of teaching, which fail to make a direct appeal to the child's interests.
b. Over-indulgent school methods also have a bad effect upon the 'spoiled' child.
    i. As regards discipline, libertarianism (as practised, for example, at Dartington Hall School in Devon) is psychologically unsound; for it involves a complete surrender to the pleasure principle.
    ii. Excessively low standards in schoolwork exercise a similar influence. Besides, a child who is asked to work below his capacity becomes bored and, through lack of opportunity to exercise his capacities, he becomes frustrated.
    iii. Any form of education which is based upon exploitation of the child's imagination is deleterious. There is nothing to be said, of course, for any form of education that cramps the child's imagination. It is essential that the child's imagination should have free play; for the child's creative powers first express themselves in the world of imagination. At the same time, a wise educational policy must provide the child with well chosen opportunities to correct its phantasies by a reference to reality and to gradually harness its creative powers to the demands of reality. Above all, it is fatal for education to exploit the imagination of the child and to convert the schoolroom into a hothouse for phantasy.

My statement that the chief aim of education ought to be to wean the child from the pleasure principle to the reality principle implies, of course, a criticism of the present intellectualistic bias in education. This intellectualistic bias is all wrong.

As I have pointed out, the job of the child is to grow up; and growing up is mainly an emotional rather than an intellectual process. If, as I hold, the educational system ought to be regarded as a tool for the purpose of enabling the child to grow up, the product of education ought to be not a mind well stored with facts, but a character well balanced and well adapted to the demands of reality. The criterion by which the educational product ought to be judged is not success in examinations, as at present, but successful adaptation to life in general.

At the same time, I do not wish to be thought to imply that the intellectual aspect of education is to be neglected. On the contrary, the adoption of the reality principle necessarily involves a knowledge of reality; for it is impossible to adapt to reality, if you don't know what reality is. On the intellectual side, therefore, it ought to be the aim of education to help the child to enlarge his knowledge of reality.

This raises the problem of the *School Curriculum.* The great question to decide in framing the school curriculum is "What aspects of reality is it most important for the child to learn about?" The answer is "Those aspects of reality which are most important for life". Bearing this principle in mind, I venture to suggest that the ideal school curriculum would embrace the following subjects:

1. Means of communication: English; English Language; reading; writing; for older children at least—modern languages (not classics).
2. Knowledge of properties of numbers, in so far as such knowledge is relevant to everyday life.
3. Elementary knowledge of the nature of the Inorganic World—physics; chemistry; geography; astronomy.
4. Elementary knowledge of the nature of the Organic World—nature study; physiology; hygiene; laws governing the care of children (especially for girls); laws governing preparation of food (especially for girls); laws governing the care of house and clothes (especially for girls).
5. Elementary knowledge of the laws governing human relations—history; sociology (features of national life in this and other countries); "The British Constitution".
6. Cultural subjects (with wide range of choice)—religion; art; anthropology; hobbies.
7. Occupational subjects—for older children.
8. How to use the body—physical education; games and sports.
9. How to think clearly—*Not* formal logic; *not* geometry and algebra; rather—knowledge of significant psychological processes, e.g., "projective mechanism"; training in the detection of fallacies of thought.

Possible criticism—the inclusion of such a wide range of subjects in the curriculum would overload it unduly and involve that very strain upon the children, against which I have issued a warning.

In reply to such criticism, I would advance for considerations:

1. Under the system I contemplate, the standard of attainment expected in all the subjects taught would be adapted to the capacity of the individual child.

2. Since under the system I contemplate examinations would be abolished, both child and teacher would be relieved of the strain involved in reaching examination standards and the teacher's efforts could be devoted to making the subjects taught interesting to the child.
3. The wide range of subjects, which I envisage, is calculated, owing to its variety, to relieve the child of monotony and harness his interest to the task of learning.
4. Such a wide range of subjects would be in keeping with the manifoldness of life and would militate against that divorce between education and life, which is such a feature of the present system and which represents such a departure from the original aim of education as a historical institution.

A word now regarding *Educational Method.* The ruling principle behind Educational Method ought to be that education is made for the child, and not the child for education. At present, as I have already pointed out, the interests of children are largely sacrificed to the interests of the educational machine. This must be altered.

1. Take the physical welfare of the child alone. At an age at which the growing child requires a maximum of air, sunshine and exercise, and a maximum of protection from disease, we confine him for a large part of the day in a classroom among a crowd of other children under conditions admirably calculated to promote the risk of infection. We do this quite contentedly in the interests of education; but we seldom stop to ask ourselves how far this is in the best interests of the child. We look with horror upon the period, not so far removed from our own times, when the children spent their days in factories and coal mines; but perhaps the more sensitive, hygienic conscience of a future generation may look with equal horror upon what we accept as a matter of course.

2. If we turn to the intellectual needs of the child, there is still more occasion of heart-searching. Let us give concrete form to our heart-searching by asking ourselves a series of questions:

a. Is the existence of classes containing forty or fifty children determined by the needs of the individual child or the demands of the educational system?
b. How far is it due to the demands of a rigid educational system that children of widely differing degrees of intelligence are lumped together in the same class?
c. If the needs of the individual child were made paramount would the system of class teaching be maintained or would some system like the Dalton plan be substituted?

If we answer these questions sufficiently conscientiously, I think we must admit that the present system is determined more by the demands of the educational system than by the needs of the child.

3. The *Emotional Needs* of the child are infinitely more important than his intellectual needs. This is due to the intimacy of the connection between emotional needs and the dynamics of behaviour. Emotional satisfaction depends upon the satisfaction of instinctive impulses; and, on the cognitive side, these instinctive impulses manifest themselves in natural interests. It follows that the real driving-force in education must come from the natural interests of the child.

Under an enlightened educational system, teaching methods would not be dictated or influenced by such aims as bringing children up to examination standards or instilling into them a prescribed amount of knowledge. On the contrary, the aim inspiring teaching methods would be to present the subjects taught in such a way as to intrigue the interest of the child.

The young child is distinguished by an amazing gift of natural curiosity. His passion for knowledge, however, usually meets with little encouragement on the part of his parents. On the contrary, it is usually sternly repressed. This, of course, is lamentable from the educational standpoint; for the child natural curiosity is an asset of inestimable value for education. It ought to be one of the educationist's main endeavours to revive and foster the repressed curiosity of the child. When we reflect upon it, the capacity of the child to learn out of pure interest is amazing. The child learns more out of pure interest in his pre-school years than he learns during the whole period of formal education.

The fact that so much can be achieved through the spontaneous expressions of the child's natural interests is a most significant psychological fact. It justifies us in believing that an educational policy based unreservedly upon a direct appeal to the child's interests would not only prove more satisfying to the child, but would also prove more efficient than any other policy. The wholehearted adoption of such a policy would, of course, involve changes of a revolutionary character in the present educational system. But, if it is worth educating children at all, it is worth educating them properly in the light of modern psychological knowledge.

And I venture to suggest that an educational policy such as I have attempted to indicate would provide the child with a "liberal education" in the best sense of the term.

20. PSYCHOANALYSIS AND THE TEACHER

My reasons for the choice of subject:

1. Psychoanalysis is a subject I know something about and the members of this society are for the most part prospective teachers.
2. Psychoanalysis is a topic of current interest (witness the modernity of the word), but one about which considerable ignorance and misunderstanding prevails (also witness the modern novel).
3. Psychoanalysis is already exercising noticeable and growing influence upon the intellectual life of our time. Thus—In *Outline of Modern Knowledge* (Rose 1931), it is one of twenty-four subject treatments, i.e., 1/24th of the volume is devoted to it. The movement has met great opposition, and is likely to continue to do so because many of its theories are unwelcome. The fact must be recognised, however, that, in spite of opposition, the psychoanalytic movement has now been established on a stable basis. For better or worse, the psychoanalytic movement is a factor to be reckoned with.
4. While psychoanalytic writers make no claim whatever to speak authoritatively on questions of education as such, they have a great deal to say which is highly relevant to the subject of education. Indeed if there is any grain of truth whatever in psychoanalytic theory, the educator can hardly remain indifferent to it.

I. How does Psychoanalysis come to have anything to say upon the subject of Education at all?

Psychoanalysis arose originally as a method of treating functional nervous disease. The success of the method led to the formulation of a body of theory

a. to explain how the method operated and achieved its results
b. to explain the mechanism of symptom formation

Later it was found that hypotheses found necessary for these purposes involved questions which were of vital importance for the proper understanding of human behaviour in general. Their relevance for education arises out of several findings, of which two may be selected for our present purpose:

1. Investigation traced the origin of functional nervous disease to situations of childhood.
2. It was found that the same factors which led to the production of nervous illness were also involved in the production of a number of certain important character traits, e.g., obstinacy, orderliness.

II. On what grounds does the psychoanalyst claim to be in a position to teach the teacher anything about children that he does not already know?

The teacher spends most of his time dealing with children. Surely he ought to know more about them than anyone else! There is a tendency on the part of teachers to assume that they are in a better position to acquaint themselves with the fundamentals of child psychology than another class—witness their attitude to Psychological Clinics. It is disconcerting for them to be told that, in the absence of psychoanalytic knowledge, their knowledge of children is relatively superficial. Yet this claim would be made by psychoanalysts.

How would psychoanalysts justify this claim? On three grounds:

1. Because the teacher is not a passive observer, who is of necessity always interfering with the spontaneous reactions of the child. This is not a criticism of teachers. It is a teacher's job to interfere, to influence the child's reactions. He is not a simple observer, he is an educator. The psychoanalyst, on the contrary, makes it his business to be as passive an observer as is humanly possible, to eliminate his own reactions and to refrain from passing judgements.
2. The psychoanalyst has found reason to adopt the view that the child's character has been almost completely determined before the child reaches school age. The formative influences which determine character would thus escape the teacher's observation.
3. The psychoanalyst has found reason to believe that much of the conduct of the child is determined by unconscious motivation. This motivation it is claimed remains unrecognised in the absence of the special method of observation adopted in psychoanalysis.

The two points so far considered relate to the general claim of Psychoanalysis to have a special contribution to make the understanding of the child's mind. I will now pass on to consider certain specific points which emerge from psychoanalytic theory.

III. In the third place, therefore, I shall draw your attention to a phenomenon to which great importance is attached in psychoanalytic thought—amnesia which prevails in later childhood and in adult life for events of infancy and early childhood.

It is a striking fact how little the ordinary person remembers of the first five or six years of life. The explanation ordinarily offered is that the child is too young to remember. He is not too young, however, to learn and retain more knowledge about the world in his first quinquennium than in any subsequent quinquennium. He is not too young to learn the fundamentals of language and to retain them as a basis for communicating with others.

Further, such memories as remain are often detached memories of the most trivial incidents. The more significant and intimate of memories of childhood are thus held from consciousness. Two at least of the laws of memory, those of Primacy and Vividness, are thus defied by the Amnesia of Childhood. It can be shown, however, that many "lost" memories of childhood are not lost but merely withheld from conscious recall.

1. Recall in delirium.
2. Recall under hypnosis.
3. Recall by the process of Free Association, e.g., associations to dreams.

By similar methods, it may be shown that many actual memories which survive really represent "cover memories".

In view of the phenomenon of infantile amnesia, it is evident that any ordinary psychology of conscious processes must underestimate the importance of the first five years of life.

IV. Fourthly, I would draw attention to the importance attached by psychoanalytic thought to Unconscious Motivation and to Unconscious Mental Processes in general.

Psychoanalysts have found reason to believe that amnesia of childhood is motivated amnesia. The events of childhood are forgotten not because the child is incapable of remembering, but because there is a motive for forgetting. Similarly, it is found that what are forgotten are not the least important events, but the most important events. The burglar is fairly safe in presuming that the strength of the lock of a safe is some index of the value of the contents. Psychoanalysts have found that the greater the difficulty in reviving a memory, the more significant it usually is.

The phenomenon of forgetting has been studied by Freud in connection with the normal amnesias of everyday. His finding was that—we are inclined to forget that which there is motive for not remembering. Thus we are liable to forget disagreeable appointments rather than agreeable ones. Also we are not so liable to forget an unpleasant appointment if there are external circumstances present for keeping it. The motive is avoidance of the unpleasant.

Freud's general formula is that *the unpleasant tends to be forgotten*. This formula has been disputed by some psychologists—conspicuously Wohlgemuth. Such criticisms are largely based on a misunderstanding of Freud. "Unpleasant" in Freud is applied to mental content, which is unpleasant on account of a *conflict of feeling* within the ego. The significance of a conflict of feeling is that it represents *conflict of impulse*. Imagine what a young woman engaged to a young man would think if he forgot an appointment with her. Her inference would be—he is no longer undivided in his allegiance. The reason we forget an unpleasant appointment is not so much its absolute unpleasantness but because we are divided in our own minds about keeping it. One part of us says "I won't go", the other part says "I must go".

The "active forgetting" to which Freud refers is the forgetting of mental content which is unpleasant because it is associated with a conflict of impulse. Such mental content, according to psychoanalytic theory, tends to be kept out of consciousness. The process whereby consciousness is guarded from such content is termed "Repression". Owing to the operation of repression, mental content which is relevant to inner conflict tends to be excluded from consciousness. The fact that, under certain conditions (e.g., hypnosis, in delirium, by free association), it can be recalled to consciousness shows that such material has not been obliterated in the mind. It is therefore spoken of as persisting in the *Unconscious*.

It is thus that the psychoanalytic concept of "The Unconscious" has arisen. In the early days of psychoanalysis "Unconscious" was believed to consist simply of buried memories. It has now come to be recognised that buried memories come to be repressed owing to their association with conflicting impulses and trends in the mind. It is these conflicting impulses and trends that are now regarded as the essential constituents of the Unconscious. It is against them that Repression is primarily directed. Memories are only repressed in so far as they represent situations involving repressed trends and impulses. Owing to association of ideas in the mind, however, operation of repression tends to be extended to mental content associated, however remotely, to critical situations in the past. Extensive amnesias are thus created.

The most extensive amnesia found in normal individuals is the amnesia which prevails for events of early childhood. It is held by psychoanalysis that the amnesia of childhood is the classic instance of an amnesia produced by repression.

The greater the conflicts of early childhood, the greater is the operation of repression; and the greater the operation of repression, the greater the amnesia.

V. In the fifth place, we shall now consider the Nature of the conflicts of Early Childhood, as conceived by psychoanalytic theory.

The child at birth is a creature of impulse. He is endowed with powerful instincts, which demand satisfaction. The child cannot bear the frustration of impulse. Demands made by the child upon reality are determined by the nature and strength of his instinctive impulses—irrespective of all considerations as to whether the external world is disposed to provide satisfaction of these impulses or not.

This is what Freud means when he says that we are primarily actuated by the pleasure principle. The child has to learn to adapt himself to conditions prevailing in the external world. In Freud's terminology, the child has to learn to replace the pleasure principle by the reality principle in his conduct. He has to learn to be guided in his life by the reality principle. The child has to learn to endure the frustration of natural impulses, to find satisfaction of instinctive impulses along lines dictated by external circumstances. This task is imposed upon the child in the first five years of his life.

The first phase of his education thus consists of:

a. In cognitive sphere, learning the nature of the real world.
b. In the affective and conative spheres, learning to adapt his feelings and impulses to demands of the outer world.

This phase of the child's education must be regarded as being by far and away the most important. It occurs in the earliest and most plastic period of life, and, in this plastic period, the foundations of the individual's character are almost completely determined by the age of five. If this claim is true, it follows that the child's personality has already been formed by the time he reaches school age.

Here lies an important implication for the teacher. The implication is that the teacher must abandon all hope of moulding the character of his pupils. All the teacher can do is to make the best of material which comes to him ready-made. What the teacher can do for the child is thus already determined and limited by the adaptations achieved by the child before he comes to school. Many teachers have come to this conclusion as a result of their own observations. The distinctive contribution of the analytic school is that the character of the child is determined by the issue of inner conflicts to which his mind is subject in the first five or six years of life.

The nature of the fundamental conflict in the child's mind has already been indicated. Two factors in this conflict are:

1. Instinctive impulses
2. The demands of reality

As regards (1), I do not propose to embark upon a discussion of the nature and constitution of the child's instinctive tendencies. As regards (2), however, it is essential to consider how demands of reality present themselves to the child.

The demands of reality present themselves to the child above all in the persons of parents (or parent substitutes). To a lesser extent, they are presented to the child through the medium of such brothers and sisters as he may possess. The importance of parents as representatives of reality to the child depends upon a biological fact—namely the utter dependence of the human child. The contrast between the human child and the young of animals is:

a. the extent of dependence
b. the duration of dependence

The child is dependent for satisfaction of every need upon the mother-figure—e.g., food, warmth, comfort, protection. The child soon learns to associate the person of the mother with the satisfaction of needs. He thus early begins to form a sentiment for the mother. His desire for her soon comes to exceed actual demands of physical necessity and need for self preservation. He comes to demand above all signs of affection from her. From his point of view, the signs of affection are:

1. satisfaction of his needs
2. her constant presence and attention

It is not, however, practicable, or even possible, for the mother to arrange for the instant satisfying of the child's slightest need or to devote her whole life exclusively to his service. Nor does she consider it desirable for his own welfare to do so. In so far as she fails to do this, however, she is thereby acting as frustrator of his cravings and desires.

The mother-figure thus comes to play a double role in an infant's life as the

1. source of the infant's every satisfaction
2. source of the infant's every frustration

In so far as the mother-figure satisfies the child's wants and desire, he comes to feel he is loved by her and learns to love her in turn. On the other hand, in so far as she withholds satisfaction, he comes to interpret her action as due to lack of love. Such frustrations arouse his anger; and in so far as his mother behaves as a frustrating figure, he learns to hate her. In this way there arises within the child's mind a state of emotional *ambivalence* towards the most important figure in life. By "ambivalence" is understood the *simultaneous* existence of positive and negative sentiments for the same person. The behaviour of the mother-figure towards the child largely determines his future emotional development.

Overindulgence has among its possible effects:

1. making the child unduly dependent
2. impairing the child's capacity for adapting himself to reality

Undue frustration has among its possible effects:

1. Intensifying the child's infantile desires, on the principle that what is withheld comes to be unduly longed for. The result is that the child is driven to seek, in fantasy, an imaginary satisfaction for those desires which reality satisfies all too sparingly. His interests thus tend to be diverted from the outer world to the inner world of imagination.
2. Creating an attitude of resentment in the child, provoking aggressiveness and strengthening sentiments of hate.
3. Maintaining and exaggerating an ambivalent attitude towards important figures in his environment. Ambivalence is characteristically an infantile and childish emotional attitude, and if it survives into later life it tends to have most crippling effects. It is associated with mental conflict from the beginning and its persistence in later life leads to constant reactivation of the conflicts which distress the earliest years of childhood.

We have seen that factors involved in the primary conflict of life are:

1. instinctive impulses demanding satisfaction
2. the constitution of an external world which constantly denies satisfaction of impulse

In the light of developments which I have just described, it will be evident that primary conflict between Impulse and reality soon develops into a conflict between sentiments of (a) love and (b) hate.

So far as I have sketched development of the second great conflict in the child's life, I have considered only the child's relationship to the mother-figure. This single relationship gives rise to a sufficiently complex situation in the child's mind. But the situation is rendered much more complex by the presence of other important figures in the child's early life:

1. in most cases, other children of his own parents
2. the Father

1. Consider first the situation which arises when the child is not the only child in his home. The child does not have to be very old before he realises, however dimly, that brothers and sisters are formidable rivals for the mother's love and attention. Feelings of jealousy are all too easily provoked, particu-

Father and son: Ronald Fairbairn with Cosmo 1937, on holiday in the Lake District

larly if there is an actual favouritism on the part of the mother. One special situation in which jealousy is particularly liable to be stirred is—when a new baby is born before the child has achieved any marked independence of his mother, and the mother's chief interest becomes suddenly transferred to the new arrival.

Unless parents exercise discretion, the birth of a new baby may constitute considerable emotional trauma for the young child. Some degree of jealousy is almost inevitable; in all cases hostile wishes are entertained towards the newcomer. The intensity of these wishes depends largely upon the opportunity afforded the child to identify himself empathetically with his mother in her attitude to the baby. In so far as he is able to identify himself with the mother in feeling, baby becomes his own and the sentiment of love develops at the expense of hate. It is rare, however, for this desirable result to be achieved without some degree of conflict.

2. It is time to consider the relationship of the child to his father. Important as are conflicts which arise in his mind over his brothers and sisters, they are as nothing compared to the conflict which arises over his father. If the mother-figure constitutes the most important element in the child's environment, the father-figure is easily the second in importance. Like the child's brothers and sisters, his father is essentially a rival for the mother's interest and love. Father, however, is a much more formidable rival

1. because the father enjoys a greater intimacy with the mother
2. on account of the father's authority and power in the home

To the child, weak, undeveloped and inexperienced as he is, both parents must appear almost omniscient and omnipotent. In most households, however, the authority and prestige of the father are greater than those of the mother—at least in a patriarchal civilisation like our own.

He is normally possessed of greater physical strength. He is appealed to by the mother as a great upholder of discipline. He is relieved of most of the menial tasks which the mother performs for children. He comes and goes apparently of his own sweet will. His comings and goings are like the appearances and disappearances of the Greek gods.

The child comes to hate the father as a rival for the mother's love and to fear his father's power and authority, but he also admires and reverences his father on account of this same power and authority. He craves his father's love—all the more, perhaps, because he sees so much less of him than of his mother. Just as he learns to love his mother, so he learns to love his father too.

It will thus be seen that the young child's attitude to both parents is characterised by *ambivalence,* and, further that the child's conflict of feeling over one parent is complicated by his relationship to the other. The situation is still further complicated by the sex of the child. Thus the male attitude of the boy tends to reinforce the bond to the mother. The female attitude of the girl leads to transference of some of the positive feeling originally entertained for the mother onto the father, and some of the negative feeling originally entertained for the father onto the mother.

From what has now been said, it must be evident that the earliest years of childhood witness a series of most poignant mental conflicts in relation to parental figures. What are popularly supposed to be the years of carefree happiness and innocence are haunted by frustrations of impulse, fears of the loss of love, humiliations of fruitless anger and fears of revenge and punishment. Underlying all these lies the fundamental conflict between the inner forces of love and hate. According to psychoanalytic theory, it is to spare us from the contemplation of this powerful turmoil that repression draws the comforting curtain of amnesia across the stage of our early childhood.

VI. In the sixth place, I propose to give some indication of the way in which repression is conceived as coming into operation and as achieving its goal.

The great lesson which the child has to learn in the earliest years is to endure frustration of impulse and to find his satisfactions along lines and under conditions dictated by reality—i.e., along lines and under conditions mainly dictated by his parents.

The first frustrations at the hands of the parent are "negative" frustrations for the most part—withholding of means of satisfaction. Before the child is very old, however, he experiences frustrations of a much more positive kind—e.g., active interference with his activities, a host of prohibitions and taboos, which are enforced by punishments and threats.

The child has to learn to make conduct conform to standards imposed by parents. In imposing these standards, in issuing prohibitions and in enforcing taboos, parents are representatives of society. The attitude of the individual in later life to demands and restrictions of society depends largely upon reactions provoked in him as a child by exactions, prohibitions and punishments experienced at the hands of his parents.

In learning the difficult lesson of adapting his conduct to standards imposed by his parents, the child is at first influenced by their superior power, i.e., at first he only refrained from satisfying his impulses because he is prevented. Later he comes to be influenced by the fear of punishment and the fear of losing his parent's love by disobedience. At this stage he becomes able to refrain from indulging his forbidden impulses even in the absence of his parents—through the influence of fear. If his conduct remained at this level the fear of being found out would remain throughout life the highest motive for self-control.

Even the young child does learn, however, to exercise self-control in the absence of risk of being found out in wrongdoing. How does this come about? According to the psychoanalytic school, it comes about in this way—because the child not only reacts to parents as outer objects, but is also capable of feeling himself into the attitude of the parents and imagining himself in their place. This process appears to be akin to "empathy". In psychoanalytic terminology it is described as the process of "identification". Much of the so called "imitative behaviour" of children would appear to have its origin in this process. The most important result of Identification is that the child comes to adopt the same attitude towards his own wayward impulses as he imagines his parents to adopt towards them. The parents as frustrating figures become introjected or internalized, and there arises in the child's mind a more or less distinct institution which exercises critical, inhibiting and punitive functions and retains all the prestige of parental authority.

This institution is described in psychoanalytic terminology as the "ego-ideal" or "superego". It is regarded as performing functions of a primitive "conscience" and as forming the nucleus of the developed "conscience" of the adult. With the appearance of the ego-ideal, a change occurs in the nature of mental conflict.

The original conflict was between (a) Instinctive impulse and (b) reality (here affect is unpleasure). In due course, there emerged great conflict between (a) Love and (b) hate—a conflict between sentiments (here affect is anxiety). And now this conflict in turn becomes obscured by a conflict between two distinguishable components of the self—(a) Instinctive nature and (b) the ego-ideal (here affect is guilt).

In this great conflict, it is held that the tension between the two conflicting components is experienced as a special form of anxiety—viz. guilt. According to the more recent developments of psychoanalytic theory, it is particularly to protect the ego from the conscious experience of guilt with all its poignancy, that the process of repression comes into operation.

Such instinctive impulses as conflict with the standards of the ego-ideal come to be repressed on account of the sense of guilt which their conscious expression would engender. There is also evidence that the primitive ego-ideal of childhood accompanies the repressed impulses in their descent into the unconscious, apparently because of its close association with the experience of guilt.

The unconscious (in the psychoanalytic sense) thus consists of two distinguishable elements—(a) the repressed and (b) the ego-ideal. The unconscious is thus regarded as comprising both the elements of inner conflict of early childhood. From this it follows:

1. that the unconscious retains in after life all the essential features of the infantile mind
2. that the primitive conflicts of the young child are carried on in the unconscious, even after the work of repression has been completed

It is believed that the work of repression has been practically completed in the average child by the age of five or six years. This age, be it noted, corresponds to the age at which the educationalist has come to regard the child as sufficiently stabilised to be amenable to the discipline of school. By this age, according to psychoanalytic findings, the average child has reached—if not a *solution* of his classic emotional conflicts, at any rate an *adjustment* to them. In so far as the conflicts have not been resolved by adjustments in the real world the scene of conflict is now transferred to the unconscious. It is extremely doubtful whether it is ever possible for a *complete* resolution of these primary conflicts to be reached by adjustments in the outer world. For such an achievement we must await the super-child. In the average child, a considerable degree of unconscious conflict persists, but it must be recognised that, in so far as it does so, efficiency in life is impaired. Where conflict in the unconscious remains excessive, definite abnormality is to be expected. We may perhaps hazard the *formula* that, other things being equal, adjustment to reality in life varies inversely with the persistence of unconscious conflict.

VII. In the seventh place, I desire to draw attention to the fact that the psychoanalytic conception of the unconscious is dynamic.

The unconscious is conceived as the battleground of highly energised psychical components:

1. repressed impulses struggling for expression and energising hidden factors
2. primitive ego-ideal based on infantile ideas of parental authority and energised by intense emotional values which have been created by the child's early relationship to his parents

The fact that these highly dynamic constituents of the unconscious are withheld from consciousness is not regarded as preventing them from influencing behaviour. On the contrary, their chief significance is held to lie in the fact that they *do* influence behaviour. Much emphasis thus comes to be laid upon *unconscious motivation* by psychoanalytic writers. Because constituents of the unconscious are dynamic, they are constantly struggling for expression. While repression may prevent their overt emergence in consciousness, it cannot prevent them from influencing the conscious processes and from influencing behaviour in roundabout ways.

There are countless phenomena in which this subtle influence may be detected. Dreams provide a classic instance of the influence of unconscious factors upon the thought-processes. So far as conduct is concerned, I shall content myself with pointing out one particular phenomenon, which appears specially significant for my present purpose. I refer to the compulsion which we all suffer, to a greater or lesser extent, to reinstate our primitive conflicts in relation to current situations. The unconscious expresses itself, so to speak, by exploiting current situations. The result is that we tend to restage our childish conflicts in the setting of everyday life, and thus to reproduce in our outward conduct the situation which exists in our unconscious. In this way, for example, our attitude to persons in authority provides a clue, for those who know how to read the clues, to our relationship to our parents in infancy; and the nature of our own repressed tendencies is revealed in our attitude to similar tendencies in others. Our unconscious life provides the scene in which our unconscious stages the old play with a new setting.

VIII. Lastly, I come to the question—What is the significance of all these ideas for the teacher?

The significance is manifold, but I shall content myself with emphasising two points:

1. If the psychoanalytic interpretation is correct, the child repeats at school unresolved conflicts of his nursery years.
   a. The child's reaction to the teacher is determined by factors operative before he comes to school.
   b. The teacher is the parent-figure. The child's parents are his first teachers; and it is equally true that his teachers are his second parents.
   c. For the child, the teacher is the parent-substitute, parent-sur-

rogate. It is in the light of this fact that the teacher must learn to interpret the child's reactions. It will help him to understand why one child should be cowed, another rebellious; why one child should be mischievous and another over-conscientious.

It must be remembered, of course, that the faithfulness with which the child will reproduce his early conflicts in relation to the teacher will depend partly on the extent to which the teacher possesses characteristics in common with one or other of the child's parents.

d. Similarly, the child's reaction to schoolfellows is largely determined by his early relationships to brothers and sisters, his place in the family and similar factors.

2. If psychoanalytic interpretation is correct, the teacher's reaction to his pupils is also powerfully influenced by the situation in his own unconscious.

This holds particularly true of the teacher's attitude to questions of discipline and punishment.

A strict disciplinarian and strong advocate of physical punishment may convince himself and others that he is acting solely in the interests of his pupils. He should beware, however, lest his arguments are mere rationalisations concealing from him the real nature of his own motives. It is always possible that in punishing a child he is merely venting upon an innocent victim feelings which he once longed but did not dare to vent upon his father.

Or perhaps the child is a vicarious substitute for the teacher's young brother whose arrival made him jealous long ago in the days comfortingly veiled by the amnesia of early life.

Or yet again, the child whom he punishes may be but an unfortunate symbol for the teacher's own repressed infantile impulses projected outwards. His righteous indignation will then be a measure, not so much of the shortcomings of the child, as of his own inner guilt. The comfortable mechanism of projection will thus enable him to satisfy the relentless demands of his own hidden conscience by inflicting punishment upon the person of another. In this manner he will, for the psychoanalytic eye, be but another recruit for the army led by the great persecutors of history.

21. PSYCHOTHERAPY AND THE CLERGY

Religion and Psychotherapy are very closely related. Religion is the earliest and original form of psychotherapy. Psychotherapy as such may be said to have developed out of religion as the result of an attempt to establish the cure of psychological troubles on a scientific basis.

The concrete problems with which religion and psychotherapy deal have much in common, albeit the two disciplines deal with these problems in different ways; the approach of psychotherapy being characteristically medical, whereas the approach of religion is characteristically spiritual. The problems with which both religion and psychotherapy are concerned are predominantly emotional, although problems of conduct and thought are also involved, especially where religion is concerned. Thought in particular would appear to assume greater importance in the religious than in the psychotherapeutic field in view of the emphasis laid on belief.

From the psychotherapeutic standpoint, thought is regarded as powerfully influenced by emotion, as is obvious in the case of phantasy; and phantasy represents a large proportion of the material with which psychotherapy is concerned. However, the role of ideology cannot be ignored, even within the realm of psychotherapy. Indeed the psychotherapist himself may be influenced to a greater extent than he realises by belief, cf. Glover's inquiry (recorded in *The Technique of Psycho-Analysis,* 1955, pp. 439–442). It must be remembered, however, that from a psychological standpoint belief must be regarded as profoundly influenced by emotional factors.

There seems to be a general impression among members of the ministry and priesthood that the psychology of Jung is more compatible with a religious outlook than the psychology of Freud. Whilst there is a certain truth in this view, it is not so true as is commonly supposed; and indeed it is based partly upon a misconception.

As is well known, Freud wrote a book in which he described religion as an illusion, namely *The Future of an Illusion* (1927). His view was that religion is an illusion based largely upon the Wish-Fulfilment Principle; and that is a manifestation of an infantile part of the personality persisting in the unconscious into adult life. Freud thus regarded religion as incompatible with a mature adult attitude, and as springing from the same inner sources as nervous symptoms in that individual.

For Jung, on the other hand, the religious outlook is an integral feature of human nature and represents an approach to life as indispensable in the adult as in the child. In his view, it is also a safeguard against nervous symptoms. This does not, however, affect the fact that, for Jung, religion is just as much a subjective phenomenon as it is for Freud, and that he takes no account of the questions of religious truth. In other words Jung treats religion as a purely psychological and not as a cosmological phenomenon. It must be added, however, that, from the point of view of psychology as a science, it is impossible to treat any psychological manifestation as other than psychological. Cosmological questions must thus be regarded as lying outside the sphere of psychology as a science. Freud's scientific approach to religion was, of course, essentially reductive. At the same time it is impossible to ignore the presence in him of a personal antagonism to religion, which can only be regarded as emotionally determined. It is thus that he came to speak of 'The Lie of Salvation'. Actually, I think there can be no doubt, in the light of the recent biography of Freud by Ernest Jones, that Freud had an intense internal conflict over religion. And it is a striking fact that the man who spoke of 'The Lie of Salvation' should have devoted his life in no small measure to the attempt to provide something remarkably like a *means of salvation* in the form of psychoanalytical therapy.

In my own personal opinion, it is something very like *salvation*, rather than medical cure, that the average patient is seeking when he embarks upon a course of psychotherapy. From a religious, or at any rate a Christian point of view, what man seeks salvation *from* is sin, estrangement from God, spiritual death, and that fear which is cast out by "Perfect Love."

Correspondingly, from a psychotherapeutic point of view, what (in my opinion) the patient seeks salvation *from* is anxiety, guilt, his own aggression and the bad persecuting parental figures which haunt his inner world as the result of his experiences in childhood. What he seeks, accordingly, would appear to be something very like the forgiveness of sins and the casting out of devils.

The psychotherapist does not, of course, aspire to the priestly function of absolution and exorcism. But he does make it his endeavour to help selected patients to achieve some mitigation at least of such features of his mental life as anxiety, morbid guilt, aggression and the persecutory nature of parental figures in his inner world.

There must be very few ministers or priests of experience who have not come across individuals in whose case they detected an element of morbidity which seemed to place them beyond the reach of an ordinary spiritual approach. It may, therefore, be useful to give some indication of the types of patient who find their way to the consulting-room of the psychotherapist, or to the psychotherapeutic clinic. In general, such patients may be said to fall into three main classes:

1. Those suffering from Psychoneuroses, or, in popular language, cases of "Nerves". Examples:
   - Anxiety states
   - Physical symptoms of psychological origin, e.g., certain cases of sinusitis
   - Phobias, e.g., fear of going out alone
   - Obsessions and compulsions, e.g., an irrational fear that whatever one has done is wrong; the compulsion to go back to make sure that one has made no mistakes; compulsive cleansing rituals; etc.
2. Those suffering from Psychoses, or in popular language, "mental" cases. Examples:
   - Morbid depression
   - Morbid elation
   - Conditions characterised by delusions and hallucinations
3. Those suffering from character disorders, exhibiting abnormal personalities. This class covers a *wide range* of disorders, of varying degrees of seriousness. At one extreme there are psychopathic personalities, e.g., individuals with criminal propensities. While at the other extreme there are people with personal difficulties which compromise their success in life, e.g., men who find themselves unable to follow an occupation; students who persistently fail exams, although not lacking in the necessary intelligence; also included under this category are alcoholics or sexual perverts.

1. A CASE OF PSYCHONEUROSIS

A woman of 50.

She has been hyperconscientious since the age of 15 years; and is subject to a morbid sense of guilt without knowing what she is really guilty about. She has anxiety dreams about not having done some work which she ought to have done.

Her sense of guilt became worse after her father's death when she was 26 years, and still worse after a motor accident in which a friend was killed two years later.

Subsequently she had a bad illness, originally diagnosed as T.B. and later found to have no physical basis. She gets tired unduly easily.

She is a fairly High Church Anglican, and has gone regularly to Confession since the motor accident. She can think of no sin she has committed, which is sufficiently bad to account for her intense sense of guilt. She has derived temporary relief from Confession; but her relief has never lasted. She developed an infatuation for a priest to whom she confessed for years, and eventually ceased attending the church of which he was incumbent on this account.

She has had several romantic friendships with women friends, including the friend who was killed in the motor accident.

2. A CASE OF PSYCHOSIS

A woman aged 48 years. Married with children. Presbyterian.

According to the husband, the marriage was happy and followed an undisturbed course for fifteen years. Then one day she told her husband that the assistant minister of the church which the family attended had given her new faith.

Thereafter she began saying that she was at last growing up and began using cosmetics for the first time. She also wanted her husband to grow up too, and become elevated to a higher social plane. She added that there were people at work helping them to grow up and attain a higher social status, and in particular the minister and his wife, and various elders and their wives. She expressed the belief that one of the reasons why these people were helping them was that her daughter was going to marry the brother of a school friend, and that there was going to be a society wedding which necessitated the social status of the family being raised to that of the young man's family. These ideas were complete rubbish; but she insisted that she had got them from God.

She also announced that her husband and the minister's wife were shortly going to die, and she was going to accept the minister's love; and she wrote to the minister to this effect.

About this time a presentation was made to the minister by the congregation; and he wrote about this in the church magazine saying that the congregation had given him something more precious than the actual presentation; and she interpreted this as referring to her love.

She says that her marriage can't be the same now since her husband does not believe in her idea.

3. A CASE OF ABNORMAL PERSONALITY

A young man aged 26 years. Unmarried. University student.

He has been at several Universities, and has difficulty in settling. He is always failing exams, although he is of good intelligence. He drinks too much.

He developed the idea that he had acquired V.D. from a girl with whom he had an affair. Medical tests proved this idea to be false; but the idea persisted; and he believed for a time that his landlady and his fellow-students knew that he had venereal disease and talked about it with one another. During this period he was also depressed.

His delusion about V.D. and his depression represented a transient psychotic phase; but the total picture was that of a psychopathic personality. He finds great difficulty in bringing himself to study, and indulges in bibulous social activities well into the night with boon companions, and spends much of the day in sleep and thus misses classes.

It may be added that in conformity with the general picture, he failed to keep his first appointment with me.

22. THE STUDY OF MENTAL ABNORMALITY

In the British Medical Journal dated 14th January 1928, there appeared a plea by Professor R. J. S. Berry of Melbourne in favour of a National Laboratory for the study of mental abnormality. This project deserves encouragement from all interested in the welfare of the Empire, and it is to be hoped that before many years elapse the proposal may have aroused sufficient interest to make its realisation a reasonable expectation. For some reason the study of mental abnormality has conspicuously failed to fire the imagination or enlist the support of the British public. This fact is all the more remarkable in view of the appeal which this study appears to make to the citizen of the United States. There the subject is not only held to be important but receives practical support; here neither general interest nor support are forthcoming. In consequence there is no institution in this country really comparable to the Psychopathic Hospital in Boston. It is true that in London, through the generosity of the Commonwealth Fund, the problems of mental reactions in children are about to be attacked on a large scale, but even here the impetus appears to originate in the United States. In view of this unsatisfactory state of affairs, Professor Berry's plea comes none too soon and ought to be a trumpet call to others who share his desire to see a national disgrace removed. While, however, the establishment of a national laboratory for the study of mental abnormality is an urgent need, the proposal would be incomplete without further discussion of the line upon which it ought to be established. Many who have read Professor Berry's plea will agree with the present writer that the basis upon which he would have it established is too narrow to ensure its being of optimum value to the community. It is true that, when he deplores the lack of co-operative effort between non-correlated specialties in the past and advocates unity of study in the future, he lends an apparent atmosphere of breadth to his proposals. To discover how essentially narrow they are, however, we have only to ask how this unity of study is to be achieved. Though it is never explicitly stated, the general trend of Professor Berry's paper leaves the reader no doubt as to the answer which he would give. Towards the end of the paper he makes the following definite statement:

> The first place to seek for mental abnormality of all kinds, and certainly those which are commonly classified as antisocial, are the cells of the human cerebral cortex, and this study demands co-operative national effort. That there has not hitherto been any co-operative effort to study the mental abnormalities appears to be due to a lack of appreciation of the simplicity of the great principles underlying the construction of the vertebrate neuraxis. . . . [p 47]

He represents the study of the nervous system at the present day as being illogically divided between neurology and the psychological sciences on an anatomical basis. Neurology is represented as concerning itself with the receptor and effector neurons, psychology and psychiatry as concerning themselves with the internuncial neurons in their normal and abnormal functioning respectively. He then goes on to make this statement—"To divide a functional entity, like the neuraxis of man, into a series of water-tight, non-correlated specialities appears to be unscientific and calculated to breed error. It is rather unity of study which is so essential" (p. 47).

As the earlier and greater part of Professor Berry's paper is devoted to the interpretation of human conduct in terms of neurons and their development, it would seem that he believes unity to be best attained by substituting for all the partial, non-correlated specialities the study of the physiology of the nervous system. It is presumably to this study alone that, in Professor Berry's view, the proposed national laboratory is to be devoted. It is with the object of drawing attention to the dangers of a spurious attempt at comprehensiveness in the study of mental abnormality and in the hope that discussion will favour the adoption of a genuine comprehensiveness, that the present writer submits the following observations.

1. The functional entity to be studied in problems of mental abnormality is not the neuraxis of man but man himself as a psychological organism. If it is unscientific to study the receptor and effector neurons in isolation from the internuncial neurons and *vice versa*, it is at least equally unscientific to isolate the neuraxis from the rest of the organism. The neuraxis has definite functions to fulfil, but it is no more a real functional entity than the liver. The neuraxis may indeed be considered for purposes of science in relative isolation—as, indeed, neurology does consider it. But, if we desire to establish a comprehensive science, the functional entity with which we shall concern ourselves will not be the neuraxis but the organism. That the neuraxis is meaningless apart from the rest of the body is evident when we ask ourselves what significance the neuraxis has for mental abnormality in

isolation from the endocrine organs. Professor Berry has made the interesting statement that "75% of those social reactions against which society seeks to protect itself, and known as 'crimes', are directed against the person or the property—sex and acquisition" (p. 47). But what meaning can we ascribe to crimes of sex in terms of a neuraxis conceived apart from the gonads? What significance have crimes against property or the steps taken by society to prevent them, if we regard the neuraxis in isolation from the pituitary and adrenal glands—the former intimately associated, as it is, with the disposition of self-assertion, and the latter, as Cannon has shown, with the dispositions of self-preservation, attack and defence. Further, if the neuraxis is physiologically meaningless in isolation from the rest of the body, it has even less meaning when divorced from psychological processes. Anti-social reactions are completely unintelligible in terms of brain cells alone. They can only be adequately understood if we introduce the psychological conceptions of instinct, motive and purpose. The crime of rape is not simply the failure of a few pyramidal cells to inhibit the functions of the infragranular cortex, it is also the behaviour of an organism whose sexual impulses have not been subordinated to the social sentiments in the process of development. Of these two ways of conceiving it, the latter is the more significant and the more fruitful. If, then we are seeking a real functional entity on which to base a comprehensive science of human behaviour, whether normal or abnormal, there is only one such entity to be found—the entity which behaves, and this is nothing short of the human psycho-physical organism.

2. Since the functional entity in all behaviour is the psycho-physical organism, it follows that neither physiology nor psychology nor any other science that considers but one aspect of the organism can claim to offer a comprehensive study of either normal or abnormal reactions. In actuality no such unifying science exists, but, if it did, it would partake of the nature of biology. Doubtless such a science will eventually be elaborated; but in the meantime there are insufficient data for this establishment. Such data can only be accumulated at the present stage of knowledge by allowing the various biological sciences to work unrestrictedly in their own fields, and to compare their various findings with one another. This being so, division of the field between the various special sciences is not a matter for regret. On the contrary, the advance of modern knowledge has been characterised by a multiplication of partial sciences. Only by restriction of the field can advance in knowledge take place. The history of science is the history of the birth of new sciences. The finitude of the human mind necessitates increasing specialisation as knowledge accumulates. Even 2,000 years ago it was only possible for Aristotle to cover the whole ground of human knowledge because he was the greatest genius in history. Today it would be impossible even for him to compass the field of human behaviour, which, for purposes of study,

is divided between partial sciences. Comprehensive study of human reactions is not to be obtained by substituting for the individual sciences, like neurology and psychology, one single science, but by correlating the results of individual sciences with one another. The study of mental abnormality is therefore most likely to be furthered by allowing physiology, neurology, psychiatry, psychology and other biological sciences to pursue their own goals independently, and by then attempting to relate the various results obtained in each field with one another. To attempt to obtain comprehensiveness in the study of mental abnormality by allowing the physiology of the nervous system to usurp the fields of the other biological sciences would be a procedure at once retrograde and barren of results. To devote a laboratory to such an attempt would be of little value to the community.

3. Assuming that the various sciences capable of throwing light upon the problems of mental abnormality are to be allowed to proceed unrestricted in their own fields, we must be careful to see that the various fields are properly delimited and the boundaries between them accurately drawn. Otherwise clarity of thought is impossible and confusion is the inevitable outcome. An allocation of the field such as that which Professor Berry believes to exist at the present day is above all to be avoided. If the boundaries were actually drawn where he believes them to be drawn, there would be some justification for his advocacy of the physiology of the neuraxis as final arbiter in questions of abnormal human reactions. Fortunately the fields are not delimited in the manner which he represents. According to Professor Berry, neurology concerns itself with the receptor and effector neurons of the neuraxis, and psychology and psychiatry concern themselves with the internuncial neurons in their normal and abnormal aspects respectively. The unifying science whose cause he pleads would, on the other hand, concern itself with the whole neuraxis as a functional entity. The science which concerns itself with the neuraxis as a whole is, of course, the physiology of the nervous system. As regards the other sciences concerned, the boundaries are in reality drawn as follows. Neurology restricts its outlook for clinical reasons, in two respects; it restricts itself to the neuraxis in isolation from the rest of the organism, and it further restricts itself to the consideration of the neuraxis in its anatomical aspects so far as these are affected by disease. Psychology takes as its subject matter not the internuncial neurons but the psycho-physical organism as a whole. It restricts itself, however, to one aspect (part) of the organism, viz. the normal behaviour of the organism so far as that can be interpreted in terms of mental process. Psychiatry resembles psychology in concerning itself with the behaviour of the organism interpreted in terms of mental process, but, being a clinical science, it has a narrower field and, for practical reasons, restricts itself further to such abnormal behaviour as indicates a gross lack of adaptation to reality. Physiology (which, so far as it is neurological, Professor

Berry would set up as *the* comprehensive science) resembles psychology in that it adopts as its subject matter the behaviour of the whole organism, but it differs from psychology in excluding those aspects of human behaviour which can be interpreted in terms of mental process, and restricting itself to those aspects which can be interpreted in physical and chemical terms only. Within the boundaries indicated each of the sciences concerned is entitled to complete autonomy and is justified in attempting to push its conclusions as far as they can be carried without inconsistency. Any attempt, however, on the part of one of these sciences to usurp the field belonging to another is to be resisted in the interests of consistency and clarity of thought. To claim for physiology of the nervous system the right to annex or even to establish a protectorate over the territory of the adjoining sciences is to make a claim which will not bear examination. Any laboratory for the comprehensive study of mental abnormality which may be established in the future must therefore be prepared to admit to its precincts every science which is able to make a significant contribution to the solution of the problems of the subject.

4. Lastly, attention must be drawn to the futility of any scheme for the study of mental abnormality which fails to recognise the claims of the psychological sciences. There is an unfortunate tendency in some medical circles to depreciate the psychological in the interests of the physiological sciences. Since modern medicine is based upon physiology, it is easy to see how this tendency arises. But the result is an unnecessary impoverishment of medicine. The belief that the first place to seek for mental abnormality is the cells of the cerebral cortex appears to be bound up with wrong conceptions of the provinces of the various sciences, such as have already been discussed. It is, of course, quite legitimate for the physiologist to seek a solution of the problems of mental abnormality in terms of the cells of the cerebral cortex, if such a solution is consistent with other physiological facts. But it is equally legitimate for the psychological sciences to seek a solution of these problems in terms of mental processes. Both attempts are legitimate; but a survey of the last twenty-five years suggests that the remarkable advance which has taken place in the understanding of mental abnormality during that period has derived its impetus mainly from the side of the psychological sciences. Certain contributions have undoubtedly been made by neurological physiologists. The work of Pavlov and his followers may be cited as evidence of work in the physiological field which has thrown light upon the problems of human reaction, and theories of the psycho-neuroses have been elaborated which make the "conditioned reflex" the basis of their explanations. The conception of conditioned reflexes only explains human conduct in a superficial way, and in any case, it really offers no explanations that have not already been elaborated in terms of psychological conceptions.

The work of Pierre Janet and Henry Head might also be legitimately cited as having received its inspiration from the direction of neurological physiology. The great value of Janet's conception of dissociation and of Head's work upon the problems of sensation and of aphasia is indisputable, but it is a question how far this is not to be attributed to the fact of their bringing psychological conceptions to bear upon the problems before them. This is particularly noticeable in the case of Head's (1926) researches on aphasia which have thrown a flood of light upon a field rendered barren and obscure by a succession of workers dealing with narrow anatomical and physiological ideas. In the case of Janet the influence of psychological conceptions is also noteworthy, and the further interesting fact appears that not only the value but the limitations of the dissociation theory depend upon his psychological ideas. The limits of Janet's views are the limits of his sensationist psychology. It is the abandonment of sensationist psychology and the adoption of a dynamic psychology that has led in recent years to such advance in the understanding of mental abnormality. For this application of dynamic psychology to the facts of mental abnormality credit is mainly due to the psychoanalytic school.

The liability to errors, which an attempt to understand human behaviour purely in terms of brain cells involves, may be illustrated by a statement in Professor Berry's paper. Discussing the effect of environmental stimuli upon brain growth, he says—"If, for example, the acoustic exteroceptive stimuli be completely cut off, the child becomes a deaf-mute, with a thinner acoustic cortex and a correspondingly diminished general intelligence" (p. 47). In this statement it is assumed that a failure of development of the acoustic cortex necessarily implies a corresponding diminution of general intelligence. This is just the sort of assumption to which an exclusive preoccupation with "brain cells" is liable to lead. It may be true, or it may not be true, but proof or disproof of such assumptions is only possible when the psychologist is permitted to produce his evidence also. Reference may here be made to an investigation of the general intelligence of deaf-mute children, which is at present being conducted at the George Combe Psychological Laboratory of Edinburgh University by Dr Drever and his workers. Though the results of this investigation are still incomplete and thus not available for publication, the results so far obtained would seem to emphasize the surprisingly slight degree to which the general intelligence of deaf-mutes is affected by their disability. Mental defect is certainly not a feature of deaf-mutism, though mental defectives naturally occur in deaf-mutes as they do among hearing children. As judged by the performance tests used in this investigation (language tests being impossible), the deaf children scored remarkably high; they proved to be retarded by less than one year of mental age, as compared with a control group for hearing children. In view of the enormous disability which a deaf-mute suffers both as regards deprivation of valuable cortex and loss of the main channel for the acquisition of human knowledge, it is a striking fact that his general intelligence should seem to be so little affected. At any rate, the results of such investigations indicate the danger of pronouncing upon questions of mental reactions, normal or abnormal, if brain cells alone are studied and psychological factors neglected.

Many instances could also be quoted of problems for which consistent explanations of a psychological nature have been offered, but upon which the study of the supragranular cortex can throw little light. What explanation can be offered in terms of brain cells for the fact that a hysterical patient suffers from, e.g., fear of open places; an obsessional case from, e.g., a compulsion to wash his hands every time he touches a door handle; and a paranoiac from a delusion of persecution? Perhaps, all depends upon which part of the supragranular cortex is effected by some hypothetical pathological process; but no one knows what the pathological process is, which neurons are affected, or what connection there is between these hypothetical lesions and the symptoms. Any explanation of this sort is completely barren. Yet for the differences between the symptoms of hysteria, obsessional neurosis and paranoia psychological explanations have been offered, which, whatever criticisms may be passed upon them, introduce order and intelligibility into a difficult and obscure field.

In conclusion, the hope may be expressed that, when the national laboratory for the study of mental abnormality comes to be founded, it will be founded upon a basis broader than the study of the neuraxis and its neurons. On the contrary, every precaution ought to be taken to provide facilities for the inclusion of every science that is capable of throwing light upon the problems at issue—not excluding the physiology of the nervous system. It is in the hope that Professor Berry's most valuable suggestion for a national laboratory to study mental abnormality may not be prejudiced by too narrow a conception of its functions that the above observations are submitted to the medical profession.

V

TOWARDS A PSYCHOLOGY OF ART

INTRODUCTION TO PART V

These papers are among those which are now little known, but which were significantly in advance of their time in applying psychoanalysis to an important intellectual area. Fairbairn had a considerable interest in art and in applying psychoanalytic theory to the understanding of the creative process. He published these two major papers on the subject in 1938 in *The British Journal of Psychology*. The first, 'Prolegomena to a Psychology of Art', is written largely from the standpoint of the pleasure principle. These aspects seem particularly dated, but the emphasis on object relations and Klein's idea of intrapsychic restitution are important and are pertinent to later developments in the psychology of art. The second paper, 'The Ultimate Basis of Aesthetic Experience', is imbued with Fairbairn's capacity to set things in relational perspective and stands as a milestone in the application of object relations to a theory of aesthetics.

In the 'Prolegomena' Fairbairn recognized the four areas of aesthetic influence, namely, the work, the creative artist, the audience, and the technique. While he focused on visual art, he meant this psychology to be applicable to all creative artists, regardless of their medium. He noted that most aesthetic theory had concentrated on the reaction of the audience and used Herbert Read's notion of art as a solitary activity to confine his remarks to the psychology of the individual artist. Art is only a solitary activity, however, if it is undertaken in a particular way within a particular cultural milieu. Non-individualistic, communal artistic activity is common in tribal societies. Other examples which spring to mind include medieval schools of painting, or rugmaking in Iran. So from the outset Fairbairn narrowed his consideration to the individual artistic endeavor. Relying on Freud, Fairbairn described art as play; thus artistic activity is making something for fun. By using childish creation as an example, he asserted that anything which has been created is a work of art. Fairbairn then used Freud's account of dream work to concoct the analogous notion of 'art work'. However, art work is a product of motor activity, while dream work requires its suspension. Thus by means of motor activity the internal unconscious content of the artist's psyche is outwardly expressed. Using the surrealist artists as examples of failed art work, Fairbairn argued that without repression, no high achievement in art is possible. He then introduced the concept of internal objects through Klein's notion of the destructive impulses of infants and suggested that artistic reassembly is a means of restitution. Fairbairn combined his notion of art work as a function of the ego with the principle of restitution as a means of obeisance to the superego, a notion derived from Klein (1929). This combination allowed him to view art work, like dream work, as a positive process in which the work of art becomes an external expression of the resolution of conflict in the artist's psyche.

The work of art as a restored object is an idea which was ultimately given fuller expression in Kleinian theory. It has been used by Peter Fuller (1988), who uses the ideas of Klein, Segal, Fairbairn, and Guntrip in his discussion 'Venus and Internal Objects'.

While Fairbairn retained Freud's notion of the opposition of the pleasure and reality principles, he tried to focus on the artist's object relationships, or inner reality, at the same time. He suggested that the motive for creativity comes from the process of restitution through which the artist's ego makes atonement to his superego for the destruction implied in the presence of repressed destructive impulses. This formulation, dependent as it is on impulse theory, lacks the subtlety of Fairbairn's later theory of endopsychic structure, where atonement would be conducted at an unconscious level between all the ego structures including those with superego function. It remains within Klein's world of object relations, before the addition of Hanna Segal's (1981) seminal work on aesthetics and symbol formation.

Fairbairn also pointed to a method through which the personal iconography of the artist could be understood. In his reductive methodology, Fairbairn was unable to take account of the symbolic nature of cultural iconography. At the time when Fairbairn wrote 'Prolegomena', the major concern in aesthetics was to forge a theory which could give an adequate account of the relationship between form and content. Despite its methodological inadequacy, Fairbairn can be seen to be addressing this issue. The reduction of his conclusions to the inner world of the individual without the help of a theory of symbolic formation in object relationships renders the paper not altogether convincing, leaving him to posit that the purpose of art is to do something for 'fun', an idea based on the pleasure principle. Twenty-five years later, Winnicott (1971) transformed the idea of fun embedded in the pleasure principle to the idea of 'play' as the child's—and the artist's—work, where play becomes the capacity to move back and forth in an ambiguous transitional space in which the physical space between infant and mother represents the internal space between self and object. Read in this way, Fairbairn's concept of artists' doing their work principally 'for fun' moves towards the more sophisticated meaning elaborated by Winnicott.

In 'The Ultimate Basis of Aesthetic Experience', published in October 1938, Fairbairn arrived at a more sophisticated conclusion. The function of art became a psychological one in which the artist combines the dual role of the creator and the beholder. By this means Fairbairn consolidated the subjective views of the artist and viewer into a single psychology. This enabled him to concentrate upon the psychology of the artist, to provide an adequate symbolic account of the battle between libido and destrudo, and its subsequent resolution by means of restitution of the object in the form of the work of art which, itself, must resonate with the psychical experience of the beholder. Such resonance can perform two functions, the first of which is the dissolution of the gap between the creator and the beholder. This fits with the later object relations idea that the personality itself tends towards reintegration despite its inherent struggle with splitting and anti-integration undertaken under the threat of frustration to its human objects. Second, the evidence of such correspondence was used by Fairbairn to validate the credentials of the work itself.

This paper still has methodological problems, but it made a contribution to aesthetic theory at the time of its publication, breaking new ground in the description of the psychology of the 'found object' as dependent upon the act of discovery, a spontaneous event wherein the 'found object' has an emotional significance for the finder. Although Fairbairn saw this as an example of wish fulfilment, which is dependent on Freud's pleasure principle and dream theory, we can now see that the 'found object' must represent inner objects or part-objects, explaining its capacity to draw forth the affective response associated with this part of the viewer's inner world.

In these papers, Fairbairn moved towards an object relations methodology even though he was still only able to approach aesthetics in a piecemeal way. The novelty in his exploration is evident in his explanation of creative restitution and of meaning of the 'found object,' and in his juxtaposition of the experience of the artist and of the beholder who meet symbolically at the interface between inner and outer worlds. This discussion has a most interesting parallel with Winnicott's (1953) description 15 years later of the transitional object and its 'discovery by the baby' in a way that produces just such a blending of inner and outer reality, and which Winnicott later (1971) came to think was the ultimate basis of all creative experience.

Fairbairn's attempt to develop an adequate psychology of art was ambitious, but his failure to understand the way visual relationships operate within the mind of the artist and the beholder limits the development of his thesis. It is the relationships and the spatial juxtaposition of one form to another which determine the affective content of the work and which elicit our response. Temporal relationships are similarly vital to literary works. The form of the succession of marks on the page indicates the continuum of time, while descriptive passages evoke affective response, and dialogue itself deals in time and dramatic character interaction. Music is similarly active in time and dramatic emotional interaction.

The failure to understand these matters probably contributed to Fairbairn's obvious and personal dislike of surrealist art, which is evident in both papers. Surrealism becomes his whipping boy for bad art—that which is under- or over-repressed and therefore not susceptible to the feeling that the artist-beholder could achieve integration of the repressed. There is an irony here. In the same way that Freud had begun the process of proposing new understanding of human relationships in ways which shocked people, the surrealists, like Fairbairn himself or like the physicists Heisenberg or Einstein, were seeking new ways of explaining and expressing relationships. The influence of psychoanalysis on the surrealists and on André Breton (1924, 1929, 1936a, b) in particular was the impetus for their idea of reaching the truth about man and the working of his mind (i.e., a universal truth) through an art which followed Freud's methods and reflected the content of dreams. This idea of a universal 'sur-réalité' was utilized by Breton in his attempted promotion of international understanding and was thus seen as a potential weapon in the campaign to abolish war. The surrealists utilized a new way of expressing spatial relationships as dream space allied to shocking images, emotional and symbolic relationships which might have appealed more to Fairbairn if he had considered their intentions more fully.

23. PROLEGOMENA TO A PSYCHOLOGY OF ART

I. THE ARTIST

The term 'Art' is ordinarily employed to describe a social phenomenon embracing three component elements: (1) The *Work of Art*, (2) The creative *Artist*,[1] (3) The *Percipient* or Audience. In addition to these three factors there is, of course, the fourth factor of *Technique*, which provides the means whereby the artist is enabled to embody his conceptions in actual works of art. A complete psychology of art would thus have to be based upon the study of a fourfold field comprising (1) the artist, (2) the percipient, (3) the work of art, and (4) technique. The psychological aspects of technique must, however, be regarded as falling outside the province of the general psychologist, except in so far as they are determined by the emotional make-up of the artist. Consequently the general psychologist is left with the artist, the work of art and the percipient as the material for his study. Whilst a complete psychology of art would involve bringing each of these three elements under review, it is a matter of importance to decide which of them ought to be made the starting-point for investigation; for it is always possible that one of them may provide a clue, which the others do not, to the real significance of art as a psychological phenomenon. If this be indeed the case, we may at once dismiss the work of art, since the only possible concern of the psychologist with the work of art arises out of its capacity to express the purposes of the artist and to produce effects in the mind of the percipient. The psychologist is thus left with a choice between the artist and the percipient in deciding where to seek a foundation for the psychology of art.

[1]In what follows, the word 'artist' will be understood not in the narrow sense of 'painter' (so familiar in common parlance), but in the general sense of 'artistic creator' (irrespective of the department of art in which artistic creation manifests itself). It is true that the thesis of the present paper has been illustrated almost exclusively by examples drawn from pictorial art; but this fact is determined solely by considerations of expository convenience. It must in no sense be regarded as restricting the application of the argument to any one department of art.

In the past the choice of the psychologist has usually fallen upon the percipient—with the result that hitherto the psychology of art has been largely a psychology of art-appreciation, i.e., a psychology of 'aesthetics'. That this should have been the case is not difficult to understand in view of the historical preoccupation of the general psychologist, at first with purely introspective methods, and later with those of the laboratory; for it is obvious that art-appreciation lends itself to the application of such methods in a way in which artistic creation certainly does not. This concentration of psychological interest upon the percipient has, however, been attended by such a remarkable barrenness of results that one is inevitably driven to the conclusion that it has led the psychology of art into a cul-de-sac. That it should have done so might have been predicted from the first; for obviously it represents an attempt to base the psychology of art upon a relatively unessential element in the total phenomenon concerned. Assuming that the shipwrecked Robinson Crusoe was an artist, it would be ridiculous to maintain that there was no art in the Juan Fernandez island until the arrival of the man Friday. Whereas art is unthinkable in the absence of either the artist or the work of art, there is at least no theoretical difficulty in conceiving of art in the absence of an audience.

Once we reach the conclusion that no secure foundation for a psychology of art is to be found in the study of the percipient, the issue becomes simple. We are left with no alternative but to approach the psychology of art by way of the psychology of the artist—a path of approach, it will be noticed, that has always been taken by adherents of the psychoanalytical school of thought. In his recent book entitled *Art and Society*, Herbert Read (1937) makes the statement that "art begins as a solitary activity"; let us amend this statement by saying that art begins as a solitary activity *on the part of the artist.* It then becomes our first task in the present enquiry to determine the general nature of artistic activity. In performing this task, it will be noted, we shall be killing two birds with one stone; for, since artistic activity can be defined only with reference to the work of art, the work of art must obviously be the complement of artistic activity; and it follows that, in determining the nature of artistic activity, we shall also be determining the nature of the work of art.

II. TYPES OF ACTIVITY

Activities may be regarded as falling into two great classes: (1) activities undertaken for their own sake, i.e., activities undertaken for the satisfaction provided by the activities themselves; (2) activities undertaken for ulterior ends, i.e., activities undertaken as a means of providing satisfactions independent of those inherent in the activities in question. Another way of drawing the distinction would be to say that, whereas activities of the first class are undertaken 'for fun', those belonging to the second class are 'serious' activities. Or again, employing psychoanalytical terms, we may describe activities of the first class as predominantly determined by 'the pleasure principle', and those of the second class as predominantly determined by 'the reality principle'. It would also seem that we should be justified in regarding the distinction between the two classes of activity as corresponding (roughly, at any rate) to that between 'play' and 'work'. Games as such provide an obvious example of the first class of activity; for we 'play' games for 'fun' at the instance of 'the pleasure principle'. On the other hand, in so far as occupational activities are undertaken with the object of earning a living, we must regard them as belonging to the second class; for they are 'serious' activities determined by 'the reality principle'; and they fall under the category of 'work'.

Any given form of activity may, of course, fall now into the one class, now into the other. Thus, whereas people hunt foxes for fun in England, in the Hudson Bay country fox-hunting is a serious business. Furthermore, any given activity may fall into both classes at once in varying proportions; i.e., it may fall at any point on a scale, at one end of which lies the 100% 'play' activity, and at the other end of which lies the 100% 'work' activity. Indeed, most activities would seem to fall at an intermediate point on this scale. So far as artistic activity is concerned, we must regard it as falling into the 'play' class in proportion as the artist seeks the pleasures of artistic creation; but it must be regarded as falling into the 'work' class in proportion as the artist harnesses his art to some ulterior motive such as making a living, gaining social prestige, or propagating a cause. To judge by the majority of opinion recently expressed by art-critics, the portrait-painter Winterhalter would appear to have been more influenced by ulterior motives and would, therefore, fall nearer the 'work' end of the scale than such portrait-painters as Titian or Velasquez, whose pictures bear the impress of the pure joy of artistic creation. It may perhaps appear anomalous at first sight to apply the term 'play' to the 'work' of the latter artists. Nevertheless, pure artistic activity, which is free from all ulterior motives, is seen to fall automatically into the class of play-activities under the present classification.

III. ART AS A PLAY ACTIVITY

That artistic activity is essentially a play-activity could hardly be better illustrated perhaps than in G. K. Chesterton's essay entitled 'The White Horses' (1911). In this essay, Chesterton describes how he spent a day motoring, with a silent man of peasant stock as his chauffeur, round the traditional battlefields of Alfred the Great. In the course of his pilgrimage he passed three of the numerous white horses carved out by prehistoric men on the chalk hill-sides of the Southern Downs; and he tells us how the sight set him wondering, "Why did barbarians take so much trouble to make a horse nearly as big as a hamlet; a horse who could bear no hunter, who could drag no load?" The answer came later. "As I rolled away out of that country", he continues, "I was still cloudily considering how ordinary men ever came to want to make such strange chalk horses, when my chauffeur startled me by speaking for the first time for nearly two hours. He suddenly let go one of the handles and pointed at a gross green bulk of down that happened to swell above us. 'That would be a good place', he said." Chesterton's chauffeur had entered into the spirit of the prehistoric artist. He wanted to carve white horses on the hillside for fun.

Once we come to regard artistic activity as falling essentially within the class of play-activities, it is not a difficult task to discover what differentiates it from other members of its class; for artistic activity is not just 'doing something'; it is also '*making* something'. *Artistic activity* may, therefore, be defined forthwith; it consists simply in *making something for fun.* On the basis of this definition, we are also in a position to define 'a work of art' and 'art-appreciation'. A *work of art* is something that is made for fun; and, conversely, *anything that is made for fun* must be regarded as a work of art. *Art-appreciation* consists in *perceiving something that has been made for fun.* And furthermore, *aesthetic pleasure* may be defined as *the fun of perceiving something that has been made for fun.*

The conception of art implied in these definitions is doubtless unfamiliar. It certainly involves an enormous enlargement of the sense in which the term 'art' is conventionally accepted. In accordance with this conception, for example, we must regard as works of art the 'bird's nest' effects produced by the child of three years of age in his first attempts to use a pencil for the fun of making something.[2] It also follows that the sandpies which the child makes on the beach and the ordered arrangements of stones and tins which he makes in the garden are no less genuinely works of art than the sculptures of Michael Angelo.[3]

In accordance with our definition, a work of art may also be an object appealing to any of the various sense departments. Conventionally the term 'work of art' is used in a sense which restricts its application almost exclusively to objects appealing to the visual and auditory senses. The reasons for this

---

[2]Compare with the "bird's nest" effects produced by the child such a Surrealist picture as S. W. Hayter's 'Work in Progress' (Read, (1936), Plate 38).

[3]Compare the arrangement of objects in the 'Poème-object' by the Surrealist, André Breton, illustrated in Herbert Read's (1936) *Surrealism*, Plate 13.

restriction cannot be considered in the present paper. Suffice it to say that it is part of the general cultural process whereby the senses of sight and hearing are exalted at the expense of senses, like taste and smell, which are more closely related to the libidinal gratifications of childhood, and, further, that this cultural process is intimately related to the process of repression in the individual mind. In spite of conventional restrictions, however, it must be recognized that, if anything made for fun is a work of art, such an object does not cease to be a work of art because its appeal is to the gustatory or olfactory sense, rather than to the sense of sight or hearing. Consequently there is no justification for denying that aesthetic pleasure enters into the experience of the gourmet, or for withholding the title of 'artist' from the *chef* who derives satisfaction from making his *soufflés* dainty, ephemeral as these works of art may be.

IV. THE PURITAN ATTITUDE TO ART

However unfamiliar the conception of art now suggested, its substantial accuracy is borne out by a consideration of the puritan attitude towards art. The essence of puritanism lies in an extreme intolerance of all forms of activity inspired by pleasure-seeking motives. Consequently the puritan is an arch-enemy of fun; like the melancholic, he is so obsessed with guilt (or, to use psychoanalytical terms, so much under the domination of a tyrannical superego) that, in his eyes, all fun is equivalent to sin. If he is not, like the melancholic, quite incapable of being happy, he feels, at any rate, that to be happy is to be wicked. The fact is that he recognizes no activity as legitimate unless it is undertaken for such ulterior motives as 'edification' or the salvation of his soul. Since, therefore, artistic activity consists in making things for fun and aesthetic pleasure consists in the fun of contemplating things made for fun, it follows that art has no place in the *Weltanschauung* of the puritan; and it is on this account that, if puritanism has one eloquent Milton to its credit, most of its Miltons are admittedly mute and inglorious.

V. ART AND THE DREAM

Having proceeded sufficiently far in our enquiry to reach some conclusion regarding the general nature of artistic activity, we must now examine in greater detail what artistic activity involves. At this point it will serve our purpose best to focus our attention upon the work of art and to attempt to reach some understanding of the psychological significance of the work of art in terms of the psychology of the artist. Our best prospect of reaching such an understanding seems to lie in comparing the work of art with another product of mental activity, about which we already know something, and to which the work of art is, without any question, closely related—viz. the dream. We know that Coleridge's 'Kubla Khan' was the embodiment of a dream in poetry; and, if a dream is not a work of art in itself, the recorded dream bears all the marks of a work of art, whether it be embodied in a drawing or simply in a written narrative.

As Freud has pointed out, the dream is the product of unconscious trends, which are repressed and thus denied not only direct expression in action, but also direct access to consciousness. The cognitive equivalents of the repressed urges consist in phantasies, which are likewise repressed. With the relaxation of repression which occurs in sleep there is a relative increase in the pressure of the repressed urges, which then mobilize sensory impressions and memory traces in such a way as to enable these to become the disguised expression of repressed phantasies. The resulting product is, of course, described by Freud as 'the manifest content' of the dream; and the mental processes, whereby the disguise is effected, are described as 'the dream work'. The work of art is distinguished from the dream above all by the fact that it is a product of motor activity. In the state of sleep motor activity is ordinarily precluded; and, consequently, it is impossible for the product of dream-work to be embodied in outer reality. If, however, it cannot be embodied in outer reality through the agency of motor activity, the product of dream-work is none the less exteriorized through the only alternative channel open to it. It is exteriorized as a sensory phenomenon. The manifest content of the dream thus acquires hallucinatory vividness and provides the dreamer with the temporary illusion of experiencing outer reality. The work of art, on the other hand, is a product of motor activity and is thus enabled to find an actual place in outer reality, in contrast to the illusory reality of the dream-world. Apart from its embodiment in outer reality, however, the work of art bears a remarkably close analogy to the dream; and it is for this reason that we are conscious of no incongruity, when we see a mediaeval Gothic cathedral described in the guide-books as 'a dream in stone'.

According to Freud's theory of dreams, the primary function of the dream is to provide some means of expression for the repressed urges of the dreamer and, by relieving their pressure, to reduce psychical tension. We must regard the work of art as fulfilling a similar function in the mind of the artist. Freud has pointed out, of course, that, if the repressed urges received undisguised expression in the dream, sleep would be interrupted owing to the anxiety which would result from such a contravention of the standards accepted by the ego. Hence the necessity for dream-work, which enables a compromise to be reached between the satisfaction of the repressed urges and the need for sleep. Pursuing the analogy between the work of art and the dream, we must postulate a process of 'art-work', which performs a function in relation to the work of art similar to that performed by dream-work in relation to the dream. Like dream-work, art-work must be regarded as essentially unconscious. It precedes the emergence of the creative phantasy into the artist's consciousness; and the creative phantasy which emerges is thus analogous to the 'manifest content' of the dream. It is through the agency of art-work that the repressed phantasies of the artist, in the form of 'manifest content', are placed at his conscious disposal for embodiment in works of art—and here it should be noted that the artist's conscious disposal of such manifest content is in turn analogous to the process of 'secondary elaboration' which Freud ascribes to the conscious mental activity of the dreamer. Art-work thus provides the means of reducing psychical tension in the artist's mind by enabling his repressed urges to obtain some outlet and satisfaction without unduly disturbing his equanimity; and it is in virtue of this function of art-work that we are justified in regarding the work of art as something that is made 'for fun'. It must be recognized, however, that, just as dream-work can fail, so can art-work; and, when art-work fails, we may expect the equanimity of the artist to suffer. We may expect the quality of the resulting work of art to suffer also; for, since the character of the work of art is determined by art-work, the quality of the art-work must necessarily affect the quality of the work of art. That we are justified in our expectations may be illustrated by reference to the work of the painter Sims, who committed suicide in a state of unsound mind in 1928. This artist's pictures showed progressively less evidence of art-work as his mental condition deteriorated; and the quality of his art suffered accordingly.

A further analogy between the work of art and the dream may be observed. In the case of the dream, the complexity of the dream-work depends upon the relative strength of the repressed urges and the factors responsible for repression. In the case of the work of art, the complexity of the art-work is similarly determined. This at once becomes obvious, when we compare, say, the Madonna by Leonardo da Vinci in the Hermitage at Leningrad with a picture entitled 'Maternity' by the Surrealist, Joan Miró.[4] In both pictures maternity is the theme; but, whereas the former shows considerable evidence of art-work, the latter, like most Surrealist works of art, shows comparatively little. It requires no very profound study of Surrealist works of art to convince us that the comparative poverty of the art-work which they display is directly related to pressure of unconscious phantasy combined with weakness of repression. For it is the avowed purpose of the Surrealist school to break down the barriers existing between the world of the unconscious and the world of outer reality; and it was in conformity with this

[4]This picture by Miró is illustrated in Herbert Read's (1936) *Surrealism*, Plate 54.

purpose that in the recent Surrealist exhibition in London (1936) a place was found for examples of asylum art. Although it is hard to believe that all the criticism levelled against the Surrealists is based upon strictly aesthetic considerations, the comparative poverty of their art-work seems to justify the view that Surrealism does not provide us with art of a very high order. Our previous conclusion that anything that is made for fun is a work of art does not permit us to say that in the complete absence of repression there would be no art at all; but there can be no doubt that art-work, like dream-work, is dependent upon repression, and that without repression no high achievement in art is possible.

VI. INSPIRATION

Mention of the Surrealist school makes it now relevant to consider the nature of the unconscious urges in which the 'inspiration' of the artist has its source; and, in view of the unconscious nature of these urges, we must turn for our knowledge of them to such information as the psychoanalytical study of the unconscious provides.

Here let us remind ourselves that, according to psychoanalytical findings, human nature is governed by two great groups of incompatible urges springing from unconscious levels. The first group, described as 'the libido', consists of impulses embodying the life principle and expressing themselves characteristically in the fields of self-preservation, sex and love, whilst the second group consists of aggressive and destructive impulses, which represent a denial of the life principle. The co-existence in the individual of these two incompatible groups of impulses inevitably leads to a mental conflict of the most distressing kind; for in early childhood both the libidinal and the destructive impulses are in large measure directed simultaneously towards the same persons—either separately (i.e., ambivalently) or in a state of fusion (i.e., in the form of sadism). At the level of object-love, of course, the destruction of love-objects occasions intolerable guilt; but, even at a narcissistic level, it occasions intolerable anxiety, since it involves the removal by the individual's own agency of his own sources of libidinal satisfaction. It is to deal with the anxiety and guilt engendered by destructive phantasies regarding love-objects that repression is originally instituted in childhood; and it is owing to the persistence of such phantasies in the unconscious that it is maintained in adult life. Nevertheless, whilst the rationale of repression lies in a need to safeguard the ego against the consequences of destructive urges, the intimate association of libidinal with destructive urges in early life inevitably results in a considerable repression of the libido.

Since artistic activity is essentially creative, we should expect art to be determined by exclusively libidinal urges; and it was in this light that art was originally regarded by psychoanalysts, before the importance of the destructive urges had been appreciated, and the significance of ambivalence and sadism had been properly understood. In the light of more recent psychoanalytical discoveries, however, it becomes evident that the destructive impulses must play an important part in the phenomenon of art. It becomes evident, for example, that art may be a channel for the expression of sadistic phantasies; and that this actually happens may be seen in the pictures of Goya and of the Surrealists.[5] Of course, the sadism of Goya and the Surrealists is expressed chiefly in the subject-matter of their pictures; but sadism may be expressed in the brushwork of a picture, even when it is absent in the subject—as in the case of Van Gogh.[6]

The influence of the destructive urges within the field of artistic activity is by no means confined, however, to the embodiment of sadistic phantasies in works of art and the expression of sadistic impulses in their execution. No investigator has done more to enlighten us regarding the prevalence and strength of destructive phantasies in the unconscious than Melanie Klein; but Melanie Klein (1929) has also shown that these destructive phantasies are characteristically accompanied by compensatory phantasies of restitution. These phantasies of restitution arise as a means of alleviating the guilt and anxiety engendered by destructive phantasies. Their function is to provide some reassurance regarding the integrity of the threatened love-object; and, since the preservation and enhancement of its objects of attachment is the great concern of the libido, we must regard phantasies of restitution as libidinal manifestations in spite of the fact that they owe their origin to the presence of destructive urges. The cultural importance of phantasies of restitution can hardly be exaggerated; for, once the operation of the principle of restitution[7] has been recognized, it can be seen to underlie all the strivings of man after the perfect, the ideal and the absolute. It is this principle that spurs him on in his search after truth, goodness and beauty; and it is this principle that turns his steps towards religion. From the point of view of our present enquiry, of course, what concerns us particularly is the part played by phantasies of restitution in art. If art provides a channel of expression for sadistic phantasies, we have equal reason to believe that it provides a channel of expression for phantasies of restitution. Indeed, since the chief source of inner tension is found to lie in the pressure of destructive urges, and since

[5] *Vide* 'Tampaca' ('Desastres de la Guerra', No. 36) by Goya and 'Spanish Night' by the Surrealist, Francis Picabia (Read 1936, Plate 76).

[6] Consider, for example, Van Gogh's 'The Cypress Tree'.

[7] The term 'principle' is not used in any mystical sense either here or in what follows. Psychologists who are suspicious of the phrase '*principle* of restitution' may, if they so desire, substitute '*motive* of restitution' without altering the writer's meaning. Cf. Freud's 'pleasure *principle*'.

artistic activity both relieves this inner tension and is essentially creative, we are justified in concluding that the principle of restitution is the governing principle in art.

Within a considerable area of the artistic field the dominance of the principle of restitution is easily appreciated. Greek art perhaps provides the most obvious example; for it is hard to imagine any more convincing attempt to establish the integrity of the object than that represented by the symmetry of Greek architecture and by the perfection of form and purity of line, which are such obvious features of Greek sculpture.[8] The work of the Dutch painter Vermeer also provides an obvious illustration of the principle of restitution; for the tranquillity of his interiors and the meticulousness of his painting give us a very definite impression of the integrity of the object. These examples, of course, are drawn from art imbued with the so-called 'classical' spirit, in which the principle of restitution might be expected to be more obvious than in 'romantic' art. To convince ourselves, however, that the principle of restitution also reigns within the field of romantic art, we have only to reflect for a moment upon the atmosphere which pervades the great religious art of the Middle Ages in Europe.[9]

When we turn to some of the moderns, we find a very different state of things. In many pictures by such artists as Paul Klee and Picasso (even in his pre-Surrealist period) the objects represented give the impression of having been either grossly distorted or broken up into fragments—or else subjected to both these mutilating processes.[10] Pictures of this nature very naturally produce in the man in the street an impression of chaos; and they must be regarded as giving expression in no uncertain terms to that sadistic, 'tearing in pieces' tendency, to which Melanie Klein (1935) has drawn attention. Even in such pictures, however, we can find evidence of restitution—as when, for example, the parts of an apparently dismembered figure are found to have been reassembled, albeit in an unfamiliar way. Further, while such pictures may represent objects reduced to fragments, the ordered arrangement of these fragments in the composition must be regarded as a form of restitution.

The same combination of sadism and restitution may be illustrated in the case of the Surrealist painter Dali, in whose work the sadistic, 'tearing in pieces' tendency is often expressed with considerable licence. Take, for

[8]Consider, for example, the Apollo Sauroctonus (after Praxiteles) in the Louvre. Even the fragment of the Aphrodite (Zouaglia) in the Louvre conveys the impression of 'the integrity of the object'.

[9]Consider, for example, the statues of 'Church' and 'Synagogue' to be seen at Strasbourg Cathedral.

[10]Consider, for example, Paul Klee's 'Dynamics of a Head' (Read 1936, Plate 44) and Picasso's 'The Woman with the Golden Breasts' (Read 1936, Plate 78).

example, his picture 'Spectre du sex-appeal'.[11] Here we see the minute figure of a boy contemplating a colossal female figure, whose head merges into a rugged mountain mass in the background. The figure is deformed, contorted and mutilated; and various parts of the body are missing. Yet, apart from the unifying effect of the composition, evidences of restitution are not wholly lacking from the subject itself; for the figure is propped up by crutches and the missing parts of the trunk are at any rate replaced by sacks. In certain other pictures of Dali's the human body is represented as partly constituted by a tier of half-opened drawers, out of some of which the contents are seen to dangle (*vide* Read 1936, Plate 25). Here again we have an expression of the 'tearing in pieces' tendency. Yet the theme of restitution is not wholly absent; for, if a drawer may be opened for the removal of its contents, it may also be shut again with the contents replaced.

VII. SYMBOLISM

These pictures in which part of the human body is represented as a chest of drawers bring us back to the question of art-work; and they direct our attention in particular to the part played by symbolism. The substitution of the conception of opening a drawer for that of tearing the contents out of a body obviously represents a certain amount of art-work. In spite of the sadism of the phantasy represented, the occurrence of such a substitution is evidence that repression is not altogether inoperative. It indicates that some degree of disguise is necessary to enable the artist to express his sadistic phantasies without undue guilt and anxiety. The art of Dali provides particularly favourable material for the study of art-work, because, when his pictures are surveyed as a whole, all the various stages of symbol-formation are found to be represented. If these various stages are placed in series, we obtain a bird's eye view of the process of symbol-formation. Thus in one of Dali's pictures we may find a disembowelled body, in another a body containing a tier of half-opened drawers and in yet another a chest of drawers detached from the body altogether. Having studied such a series, we are then in a position to state categorically that, when a chest of drawers appears in one of Dali's pictures, it represents a body.

Sometimes the emergence of the symbol may be studied within the scope of a single picture of Dali's, e.g., in the picture entitled 'Le sevrage du meuble aliment' (a title which may perhaps be translated as 'Being weaned

[11] *Vide* Dali, 1935, 'La Conquête de l'Irrationel', Plate 1.

from Nutrient Furniture').[12] The background of this picture is a land-locked bay; and on the shore in the foreground we see receding to the left a row of four boats with the bows pointing out to sea. In the forefront of the picture, on the right of the boats and in series with them, is the seated figure of a woman, whose back is half-turned towards the spectator, and whose outstretched legs lie parallel to the boats. Her bowed head is swathed in a bandage; and a large rectangular block is missing from the trunk of her body, which is supported by a crutch. Just beyond the feet of the woman is a rectangular bedside-pedestal consisting of a cupboard surmounted by a drawer, which is half-open. A study of this picture makes it obvious that the rectangular pedestal represents the missing portion of the woman's body, which is also rectangular. Further, since the body of the woman is in series with the boats, it becomes obvious that the boats are equivalent to the bodies of women; and this is confirmed by the fact that the boat nearest to the woman has attached to it a cable corresponding to the crutch that supports the woman's body. From a study of this one picture we are thus enabled to infer that, when boats and bedside-pedestals occur in other pictures by Dali (as they frequently do), they represent a woman's body.

The interest of Dali for our immediate purpose lies in the fact that his art lends itself in a special degree to a study of the genesis of symbols under the influence of art-work. His pictures, like those of most Surrealists, cannot be regarded as representing a very high level of artistic achievement. There is, so to speak, a low coefficient of repression in relation to the strength of the unconscious urges expressed; and the result is that the art-work is comparatively meagre. It is for this very reason, however, that Dali's art is of such psychological interest. In the case of the more classical, as well as the more conventional, artists, the art-work has already reached such a stage of elaboration in the unconscious that, by the time the symbol emerges into the artist's consciousness, both its origin and its significance have become obscured. In the case of Botticelli's 'Birth of Venus' the title of the picture gives us a clue to the fact that the shell, above which Venus stands poised, must represent a maternal body. Otherwise the significance of the shell would be impossible to interpret in the absence of such special knowledge as the psychoanalytical study of dream-symbolism provides. It would be impossible to interpret, because Botticelli's art-work is so much more elaborate than that of Surrealist artists. It is only when art-work is relatively undeveloped that we are in a position to trace the origin of art-symbolism. This is just what we should expect on the analogy of dream-symbolism; for the knowledge of dream-symbolism which we owe to psychoanalysis is dependent on the fact that, as repression is overcome in the course of psychoanalytical treatment,

[12] *Vide* Gascoyne 1936, p. 32.

dream-work becomes progressively simplified until a point is reached at which the significance of the symbol becomes apparent.

VIII. ART-WORK AND THE PRINCIPLE OF RESTITUTION

It is now time for us to consider the relationship between art-work and the principle of restitution. Art-work, as we have seen, is analogous to dream-work; and, according to Freud's original formulation, dream-work is the means whereby repressed phantasies are modified, or disguised, in such a way as to enable them to escape repression and to express themselves under hallucinatory form in a dream. Whilst this formulation must be accepted as correct so far as it goes, it can hardly be regarded as adequate, in that it leaves us in some doubt as to the source of the dream-work. It must be assumed, however, that Freud laid the *onus* of the dream-work upon the impulses investing the repressed phantasies, since, for explanatory purposes, he represented the operation of repression under the figure of a hypothetical 'censorship', which the repressed impulses could only elude by adopting a disguise. The conception of the 'censorship' was, of course, only a stop-gap conception pending further investigation of the agency of repression; and, when Freud subsequently formulated his theory of psychical structure, the function of the censorship was attributed to the 'ego-ideal' or 'superego'. In the light of Freud's eventual theory of psychical structure, the source of dream-work at once becomes clear. Dream-work is seen to be a function of the ego, which thereby modifies phantasies engendered by the instinctive id-impulses in deference to the demands of the ego-ideal. Once this conception is reached, it necessitates a significant change in Freud's original dream-theory; for it implies that dream-work is not merely a negative, but also a positive process. Dream-work ceases to be merely a means of disguise, whereby repressed impulses evade an internal censorship, and becomes also a positive gesture on the part of the ego towards the ego-ideal. Art-work must be regarded in a similar light. It is an activity of the ego performing a dual function in the economy of the artist's mind. On the one hand, art-work modifies repressed phantasies in such a way as to enable them to elude the vigilance of the ego-ideal and so to become available for embodiment in works of art—by this means affording the repressed impulses an opportunity for expression and relieving the *tension between the repressed impulses and the ego*. On the other hand, art-work enables the ego to convert phantasies unacceptable to the ego-ideal into positive tributes to its authority and so relieves the *tension existing between the ego and the ego-ideal*. Through its dual function, art-work is thus the means of producing that general relief of tension which the artist experiences, when he produces a work of art.

So far as the psychoanalytical study of art is concerned, attention has been hitherto largely concentrated on the first function of art-work; and this fact has given rise to the criticism that, while psychoanalysis may shed some light on the nature of the unconscious urges prompting artistic activity, the central problems of the psychology of art fall outside its purview. This criticism ceases to apply, however, once the second function of art-work is envisaged. In virtue of this function, art is seen to be not only a sublimated expression of repressed urges, but also a means whereby *positive values* are created in the service of an ideal, viz. the ego-ideal; and the creation of positive values is an act of restitution on the part of the ego.

We have seen, of course, that, even at a narcissistic level, phantasies of restitution occur as a means of relieving the anxiety engendered by destructive phantasies regarding love-objects. We must, therefore, envisage a form of art consisting simply in the embodiment of such restitutive phantasies; and the simpler and more primitive forms of art lend themselves to interpretation in this sense. We must so regard the earliest artistic efforts of the child and such examples of prehistoric art as consist simply in the outline of an animal or of a figure scratched upon a rock. Nevertheless, it is doubtful whether, either in the history of the individual or that of the race, art can be regarded as attaining a very high standard until the level of ego-ideal formation is reached. Once this level is reached, it is natural that restitution should take the form of a tribute to the ego-ideal; for the ego-ideal originates through an imaginative internalization or introjection of the love-objects threatened in destructive phantasies. Within the sphere of morals, the tension created by the pressure of the ego-ideal upon the ego is experienced as 'the voice of conscience'; and it is accompanied by an urge in the individual who experiences it to *do* something by way of restitution for destructive acts committed or destructive impulses harboured. Within the sphere of art, the tension created by the pressure of the ego-ideal is experienced as an itch to *make* something; and the creation of a work of art thus becomes a means of restitution analogous to the moral act.

At first sight it may not appear easy to relate the conclusions which have now been reached regarding the restitutive function of art to our previous conclusion that a work of art is something that is made for fun. It seems desirable, therefore, that some attempt should be made to clarify their relationship. As already indicated, the more primitive forms of art would appear to belong essentially to a level of development antecedent to that of ego-ideal formation. Since, therefore, at this level the work of art cannot be regarded as a tribute of restitution paid to the ego-ideal, it must be regarded simply as an embodiment of restitutive phantasies; and the satisfaction

Ronald Fairbairn and Ellinor, 1939

afforded by its creation must be attributed to a relief of the inner tension occasioned by repressed destructive impulses. In this connexion it is not without significance that, when the young child is asked what his earliest and apparently incoherent drawings represent, it is usually found that they are intended to represent such objects of his destructive phantasies as 'Mummy', 'Daddy' and 'Nanny'. This fact accords with the restitutive nature of the child's artistic activity; but the further fact that the child's explanation is commonly accompanied by a laugh indicates that the drawings are at the same time made 'for fun'—the 'fun' being due, of course, to the relief of inner tension effected by the act of restitution. At this primitive level restitution would appear to be made to the object represented by the work of art itself; and in this connexion it is interesting to note not only that such art is characteristically representational in spirit, but also that the earliest examples of prehistoric art consist for the most part in representations of animals hunted by primitive man (cf. the theory that such representations had the magical intention of promoting the fertility of the animals in question). Once the level of ego-ideal formation has been reached, it is only natural that the restitution effected by artistic activity should be made to the ego-ideal instead of to external objects; for the replacement of external by internal objects has been shown by Freud to constitute the essence of ego-ideal formation. This substitution does not, however, affect the essentially restitutive nature of artistic activity. Neither does it affect the essential nature of the satisfaction which artistic activity provides. For, in so far as the act of restitution is determined by a need for the relief of inner tension, the creation of a work of art must be regarded as 'making something for fun'.

Once we come to recognize the essentially restitutive nature of artistic activity, we find ourselves in possession of a clue to a number of further problems, among which the vexed question of the artist's audience is by no means the least important. At an earlier stage in the present paper an attempt was made to show that the essence of art lies in the creative act of the artist quite irrespective of any effect produced by the work of art in the percipient, and that, in so far as this is so, the artist requires no audience. This conclusion must now be qualified by the admission that artistic creation does seem to require an audience *of a kind* after all. The audience for which the artist creates is not, however, the conventional percipient. It consists in the objects to whom restitution is made, whether, as in the case of primitive art, these be external objects (actual or phantasied), or, as in the case of more advanced art, they be the internal objects represented in the artist's own superego.

24. THE ULTIMATE BASIS OF AESTHETIC EXPERIENCE

I. INTRODUCTION

The present paper may be regarded as the sequel to a paper entitled "Prolegomena to a Psychology of Art". There I pointed out that, whilst no psychology of art could be regarded as complete unless it were based upon the study of both the artist and the beholder,[1] nevertheless artistic activity can occur, theoretically at least, in the absence of any beholder, and that, therefore, the psychological problems of art can be approached with profit only by way of the psychology of the artist. Adopting this path of approach and taking into account the results of recent psychoanalytical research, I proceeded to consider the significance of the work of art as a product of artistic activity. In the present paper I shall pass from the psychology of the artist to the psychology of the beholder and consider the significance of the work of art as a source of aesthetic experience. The argument will, however, presuppose the conclusions of the earlier paper.

II. UNWARRANTED ASSUMPTIONS IN AESTHETICS

In my former paper I provided a background for the present attempt to determine the nature of aesthetic experience. The importance of such a background is not difficult to appreciate, when we consider the confusion which reigns in aesthetics, both as to what constitutes a work of art and as to what is implied in the conception of 'the beautiful'. Owing to its misleading

---

[1]The term *beholder* is employed throughout this paper to signify *the subject of aesthetic experience.* Although the argument is developed with special reference to pictorial forms of art, it is intended to apply to every form of art quite irrespective of the particular sense department involved. The term 'beholder' is now chosen in preference to the wider term 'percipient', which appeared in my former paper, to signify a percipient who is undergoing aesthetic experience.

associations, the term 'aesthetics' must itself be regarded with suspicion. The term is now employed almost exclusively in the secondary meaning for which Baumgarten (1750) is responsible, and which is defined in *The Shorter Oxford English Dictionary* as "The philosophy of taste, or of the perception of the beautiful". Such a definition provides an interesting example of the presence of unwarranted assumptions in aesthetics. According to the definition, it will be noticed, 'taste' is equated with 'the perception of the beautiful'. Herein lie two assumptions: (1) that 'the beautiful' is something objective, which has only to be perceived to give rise to aesthetic experience; and (2) that it is the necessary function of a work of art to be beautiful. These, however, are assumptions which can hardly be allowed to pass unchallenged; for they present us with the alternative of either denying the status of 'work of art' to all such professed products of artistic activity as are not universally acknowledged to be beautiful, or of so modifying the conception of 'the beautiful' as to enable products of artistic activity, about which there is no such consensus of opinion, to be admitted to this category. The fact is, of course, that there is no general agreement as to what is beautiful; and consequently standards of beauty provide no criterion of what constitutes a work of art. It is only when we seek our clue to the psychological significance of art in artistic activity (i.e., in the motives of the artist) that it becomes possible to establish a definite criterion by which to differentiate between what is a work of art and what is not. Such a criterion is to be found, however, in the conclusion reached in my previous paper that anything that is 'made for fun' is a work of art. This conclusion, together with the conclusion that the work of art represents a tribute of restitution paid by the artist's ego to his superego, provides a means of surmounting the difficulties inherent in prevalent conceptions in aesthetics.

III. THE BEAUTIFUL IN ART AND IN NATURE

Before we proceed further, it seems desirable to make some attempt to clarify the relationship between the beautiful in art and the beautiful in nature. The phenomena of nature, to which we commonly ascribe beauty, are not, of course, works of art in the ordinary sense. Nevertheless, it is interesting to note how generally the presence of beauty in nature has been cited in support of the teleological argument for the existence of God. The beautiful in nature always gives the impression of something that does not depend simply upon the operation of natural laws, something that is not absolutely necessary, something that is *added to* natural phenomena. In other words, it gives the impression of something that is there 'for fun'. Here we are reminded of the definition reached in my previous paper, that anything that is made for fun is a work of art. It would appear, accordingly, that, if the beholder does not regard every work of art as 'beautiful', he nevertheless tends to regard everything 'beautiful' as a work of art.

IV. THE WORK OF ART AS A 'FOUND OBJECT'

This conclusion provides a convenient starting-point for the investigation of one of the later developments of Surrealism—a development following the invention by Dali of what is described as 'the surrealist object'. (A special Exhibition of Surrealist objects was held in London in the autumn of 1937.) Surrealist objects are defined by David Gascoyne (1936) as "objects functioning symbolically" (p. 108). These objects are for the most part constructed by the artist out of a strange medley of materials, which appear to him significant. One such object constructed by Dali consisted in a hairdresser's bust of a woman, from whose neck two Indian corn cobs were suspended by means of a collar, and upon whose head was laid a loaf of French bread surmounted by a metal inkstand representing Millet's *Angelus*. This Surrealist object is illustrated, under the title of "Retrospective Bust", by André Breton. According to Gascoyne (1936), "These objects typify the more recent ideas of surrealism, which conceive super-reality as existing in the material world, objectively, as well as subjectively in the automatic thought of the unconscious" (p. 109). In the light of this statement, it is easy to understand the next development of Surrealism, which consisted in an enlargement of the conception of 'the surrealist object' such as to enable it to include so-called 'found objects'. The 'found objects' of the Surrealist consist in external, and for the most part natural, objects, in the appearance of which he discovers a hidden symbolic significance, and which he therefore preserves and, so to speak, 'frames'. They represent to those who 'discover' them a union between the world of outer reality and the inner world of the dream; and in virtue of this fact they are regarded as possessing a certain 'super-reality', which obviously resides in their capacity to act as symbols of wish-fulfilment. Their 'discovery' is accompanied by an intense emotional experience, which is evidently of an aesthetic nature, since it leads their discoverer to regard them as essentially 'beautiful'.

The interesting thing about the Surrealist's emotional attitude to his 'found object' is that it represents *an intermediate point between the attitude of the artist and that of the beholder*. In so far as the artist is not responsible for the existence of the object, but simply 'finds' it, he may be said to play the role of a beholder as much as any member of the general public who 'finds' such an object in a Surrealist exhibition. On the other hand, in so far as he is the person who discovers a hitherto unrealized significance in the object and 'frames' it by isolating it from its environment, he may be regarded, in a quite intelligible sense, as the creator of the object. As regards the 'found object' itself, the interesting thing is that it is just a work of art and no more. It is really *a work of art approximating quantitatively to a zero value*—a minimal work of art.

V. THE HISTORICAL ORIGIN OF ART

Considered from the point of view just indicated, the 'found object' of the Surrealist may well throw some light upon the historical origin of art. As we are reminded by Herbert Read (1937), it has been found that in many of the earliest cave-drawings the objects represented are drawn round some projection or other natural feature forming part of the cave-wall itself. Such natural features are comparable to the 'found objects' of the Surrealist. They evidently suggested to the prehistoric artist the figures (usually animals) which he felt impelled to portray. Like Surrealist objects, they were 'objects functioning symbolically' and represented a union between the outer world of reality and the inner world of wish fulfilment; but, instead of just framing them as the Surrealist frames his 'found objects', the prehistoric artist went a step further and made them the nucleus of a picture in the accepted sense. Considered from the quantitative point of view, the resulting work of art thus represented a considerably greater departure from a zero value than does the 'found object' of the Surrealist; and it was only a further departure from this zero value, when the prehistoric artist created a picture which required no natural object as its material nucleus.

VI. THE GENESIS OF THE WORK OF ART

a. The Discovery of the Object

The relationship between the 'found object' and the work of art in the accepted sense may be illustrated with reference to a picture entitled "Visage Paranoiaque" by the Surrealist artist Dali (1935, Plate 30). Hung in the horizontal position, this picture is seen to represent a group of natives sitting before an African building covered with foliage in a desert setting; but, if the picture is rotated clockwise through 90°, the building with the natives sitting before it assumes the appearance of a human head. In the absence of knowledge regarding the circumstances which led to its composition, this picture appears little more than a practical joke played upon the public by the artist. It appears in a different light, however, when the following circumstances are taken into account. At a time when Dali was specially preoccupied with a certain period of Picasso's painting, he was sitting at his desk one day preparing to formulate his reflexions in writing; and, while looking through his papers for some notes, he came across a picture post-card, which had been sent to him some time previously. As his eye fell upon the post-card, he immediately interpreted it as representing a picture of a head by Picasso; and it was only later that he recognized it to be a photograph of an African village with natives sitting outside their huts (see Gascoyne 1936, p. 101). In the light of his original interpretation, however, the post-card had all the significance of a 'found object'; and this 'found object' provided the nucleus of the picture.

b. Wish Fulfilment

As a matter of fact, what really inspired Dali to paint the picture, to which reference has just been made, was the discovery of the process of discovery itself; and it is thus integral to the picture that the relationship of the 'found object' to the resulting work of art should be unusually obvious.[2]

This fact, together with the history of the composition, provides us with an exceptional opportunity to study the genesis of a work of art. The artist is confronted in the course of his daily experience with an object in which he discovers a symbolic significance. This significance is not inherent, however, in the real nature of the object. It is due entirely to the fact that the object happens to possess features which enable it to represent for the artist a fulfilment of his emotional needs—a 'wish fulfilment'. For the artist concerned, the discovery of such a significance in an object is tantamount to the discovery of a new object. The object thus acquires the quality of a 'found object'; and the artist seeks to preserve and perpetuate what he has found in the form of a work of art. At the same time, the 'found object' is not simply something that was there all along and is now revealed; for, since its significance is dependent upon its capacity to represent a wish fulfilment, it does not exist apart from the act of discovery. It is created by the discovery itself; and the discovery represents a creative act on the part of the artist. It is but a further elaboration of this creative act when the artist embodies his discovery in a formal work of art.

The process described may be taken to represent what happens in all artistic creation, Surrealist or otherwise. If the universality of the process is not obvious at first sight, this is perhaps chiefly due to the fact that it is not always easy to isolate the 'found object'. There need be no real difficulty, however, unless we interpret the 'found object' in an unduly restricted sense.

[2]It is a common practice of Dali to portray in his pictures the processes underlying artistic creation, and in particular the process of symbolization.

The 'found object' may be anything in the external world, which serves the purpose of wish fulfilment for the artist. In the case of representational art, the 'found object' is the object depicted—not, of course, the object as it exists in outer reality, but the object in its emotional significance for the artist. In the case of expressionist art (and Surrealism, it may be noted, is really a development of expressionist art), the 'found object' may be derived from the combination of a number of objects, which are quite unrelated in outer reality, but which have an emotional relationship in the artist's mind. The same applies even in the case of abstract art; for, even when art is at its most abstract and is concerned solely with the arrangement of lines, planes, surfaces and colours, the composition represents a combination of emotionally related elements derived from the artist's experience of the external world.

c. The Need for Disguise

In the light of my previous paper, we must, of course, regard the emotional needs, which determine the significance of the 'found object' for the artist, as predominantly unconscious. It is true that the Surrealist appears to be conscious to an unusual degree of the nature of the appeal made to him by his 'found objects'; but the case of the Surrealist is exceptional in this respect, that it is his conscious aim to effect a union between the world of reality and the world of the unconscious. As I pointed out in my previous paper, the comparative poverty of the art work in Surrealist works of art is evidence of a relative failure of repression. Consequently, it is only to be expected that in the case of Surrealist art the 'found object' should represent the demands of unconscious urges with an unusual poverty of disguise. In the case of most schools of art, however, the incidence of the 'found object' is determined by a greater need for disguise; and, consequently, it is usual for the ultimate significance of the 'found object' to be unconscious, although, of course, the fact of the object's appeal is consciously recognized. Even for the Surrealist, indeed, a certain amount of disguise appears to be necessary to enable any object to function as a 'found object'. At least this seems to be the meaning of André Breton (1936a), the leading exponent of Surrealism, when he says, "One's pleasure is always partly accounted for by the lack of resemblance between the desired object and the *discovery*" (p. 42).

VII. THE NATURE OF AESTHETIC EXPERIENCE

Taking as our starting-point the attitude of the Surrealist to his 'found objects', we have now considered the discoverer of the 'found object' in the role of *artist*; and the conclusion which we have reached is that all artistic creation involves the discovery and perpetuation of a symbolically significant object, i.e., an object which symbolizes for the artist the fulfilment of unconscious emotional needs. If now we consider the discoverer of the 'found object', no longer as artist, but simply as *beholder*, we seem justified in concluding that aesthetic experience represents a specific emotional reaction, which occurs when a symbolically significant object is discovered in the external world.

Aesthetic experience may accordingly be defined as *the experience which occurs in the beholder when he discovers an object which functions for him symbolically as a means of satisfying his unconscious emotional needs*. Although, of course, the fundamental emotional needs of mankind are shared by all, nevertheless in the case of any given individual they are influenced by a considerable number of factors; and, in consequence, individuals vary both in the precise nature of their emotional needs and in the amount of disguise necessary to enable an object to function symbolically for them, i.e., to function as a 'found object' and not as an actual object. This fact enables us to appreciate the subjective character of the aesthetic judgement.

VIII. THE WORLD OF ART AS A WORLD OF 'FOUND OBJECTS'

The aesthetic character of the experience, which occurs in the beholder in the presence of a 'found object', remains unaffected, whether the 'found object' belongs to the world of nature or belongs to the world of art. The world of art differs, however, from the world of nature in that it is composed specifically of 'found objects', whereas in the world of nature the 'found object' is only incidental. It does not follow, of course, that every work of art will appear beautiful to everyone. Indeed, we have already seen that the contrary is the case. Nevertheless, we must assume that every work of art must appear beautiful at some time to someone—if only to the artist who creates it.

If the world of art represents a world of 'found objects', the artist is evidently a person who is specially good at discovering such objects. A capacity of this nature is by no means the sole qualification of the artist, however; for, in the mere discovery of a symbolically significant object, the artist is as yet little more than a beholder, although he may have the capacity for discovery—the gift of 'vision'—in an unusual degree. The beholder only becomes an artist when he isolates or frames the significant object and gives it a certain permanence by, so to speak, converting it into a monument. The task of so doing constitutes artistic creation.

The most primitive form of artistic creation is represented by the 'found objects' of the Surrealist. In this case the 'found object' is merely framed more or less as it is found. A slightly more complex product of artistic creation is represented by such 'surrealist objects' as are constructed out of a variety of actual objects. It is but a further step along the path of artistic creation when symbolically significant objects come to be represented in pictures and sculptures. Once this stage is reached, the range of 'found objects' which can be so represented becomes, of course, enormously enlarged. The whole gamut of natural phenomena is placed at the disposal of the artist; and the possibilities of artistic creation are thus made more commensurate with the range of the artist's vision.[3]

The role of the beholder of a work of art is to discover for himself the objects which the artist has already discovered and isolated for him; and it is for this reason that the element of *surprise* is integral to the aesthetic experience. It is to this element that Herbert Read (1931) refers when, speaking of the frame of mind in which the beholder ought to approach a picture, he says

> All that is necessary is that he should have a perfectly *open* mind. . . . He just walks round a corner, thinking of nothing in particular, and comes to a standstill before this object. . . . Many theories have been invented to explain the workings of the mind in such a situation, but most of them err, in my opinion, by overlooking the instantaneity of the event. [pp. 17, 18]

The importance of the 'open mind', to which Herbert Read refers, resides, of course, in the fact that the open mind is a precondition of discovery; and the 'instantaneity of the event' is characteristic of the act of discovery itself. In walking round a corner and finding himself confronted with a work of art, the beholder is thus placed in a position to 'discover' a symbolically significant object. It is true that the object is already a 'found object' in that it represents what its creator (the artist) has already discovered. Nevertheless, it is a new discovery for the beholder. In making his discovery, the beholder shares the experience of the artist who made the discovery in the first instance; and, by identifying himself with that artist, he shares the satisfactions of artistic creation himself.

---

[3]It seems permissible to speculate that the psychological processes, which led primitive man to immortalize 'found objects' in the form of works of art, may also have led him to immortalize such objects in the form of specific sounds, and that it is to this fact that we must look for an explanation of the origin of *language*. If this speculation is correct, then language must be regarded, not only as providing a medium for literary art, but as having originally constituted a form of art in itself. Indeed, in much of what is known as "Modern Verse" language would appear to have reverted to just such a status.

IX. THE FAILURE OF AESTHETIC EXPERIENCE

a. Over-symbolization and Under-symbolization

It is always possible, of course, for the beholder of a work of art to fail to identify himself with the artist who created it. When this happens, as it frequently does, the work of art fails to present itself to the beholder as a 'found object' and no discovery takes place. Such a phenomenon may be simply due to a lack of technique on the part of the artist—as when, for example, a painter lacks sufficient mastery over his material to know how to produce the effects which he desires. It may occur, nevertheless, even when the technique is good. In this connexion I am reminded of a visit which I paid to the Royal Academy of 1936. As I went round the gallery, it so happened that I kept step with a clergyman; and I noticed that, each time he came to a picture by Stanley Spencer, he turned to his companion and expressed an unfavourable verdict in unmeasured terms. His final outburst was to this effect: "Did you ever see anything so dreadful? This isn't really art at all. And the worst of it is that the man can paint!" Obviously Stanley Spencer's pictures did not present themselves to this particular beholder as 'found objects'—and this in spite of the fact that he could not help recognizing the artist's mastery of technique.

When such a situation arises, the reason why the work of art does not appear in the light of a 'found object' is that there is a disparity between the total emotional needs of the artist and those of the beholder—'*total* emotional needs' because it is a question, not only of the expression of repressed urges, but also of the demands of the superego and of that need for 'restitution', to which reference was made in my previous paper. This being so, the failure of a work of art to appeal to the beholder as a 'found object' may be due to either of two causes:

1. It may be that the censorship of the artist's superego is so rigorous, and necessitates such an elaborate disguise of the urges expressed, that the work of art is deprived of almost all symbolic significance for the beholder. In such a case the work of art makes no emotional appeal. It falls flat. It conveys the impression of sterility. It provokes the criticism that the artist 'has nothing to say'. The beholder looks at it and makes no 'discovery'. Such is the impression created upon the artistically educated of the present generation by such Victorian works of art as the pictures of Lord Leighton.

2. The inability of a work of art to present itself as a 'found object' may occur for a totally opposite reason. So far from being due to excessive censorship on the part of the artist's superego, it may be due to a relative failure of such censorship. When the artist's superego is weak and his

repressed urges are really 'urgent', these urgent urges express themselves in the work of art with a minimum of disguise. The effect of such a work of art is to provoke an excessive emotional reaction in any beholder whose superego is more exacting than that of the artist, and whose need for the disguise of repressed urges is greater. So far from saying too little, such a work of art says too much. It says more than the beholder's superego will tolerate. Consequently, under the pressure of impending anxiety, the beholder rejects it with feelings of disgust or indignation. In the presence of such a rejection, of course, the work of art cannot present itself as a 'found object'. The experience of 'discovery' is precluded because the object represented actually fails to convey the impression of symbolic significance to the beholder; and the reason of this failure is that the object is not sufficiently symbolic to pass the censorship of the superego. It is, so to speak, too like the real thing. This applies, so far as most people are concerned, to Surrealist works of art in general.

b. Form without Content, and Content without Form

It is to be noted that, in both cases instanced, the reason why the work of art fails to present itself as a 'found object' is that it lacks symbolic significance for the beholder concerned. The reason for this differs, however, in the two cases. The work of art lacks symbolic significance in the former case owing to an *over-elaboration* of disguise, which precludes any appeal to the repressed urges, in the latter case owing to an *inadequacy* of disguise, which leaves the requirements of the superego unsatisfied. It lacks symbolic significance in the one case because it is so over-symbolized that its symbolic reference becomes completely obscured, and in the other case because it is so under-symbolized that it has not reached the stage of being symbolic at all. To express the same thing in other terms, we may say that in the former case the symbolism has form without content, and in the latter case it has content without form. It is only in such a reference, at any rate, that any useful meaning can be attached to the contrasted terms of 'form' and 'content', which have long been a source of confusion in aesthetics.

c. The Optimum of Symbolic Significance

At this point an observation of considerable significance may be recorded. Whilst there is a marked difference in the emotional reactions produced in the observer by the over-symbolized and the under-symbolized works of art respectively, yet both tend to provoke a common criticism. Both are equally liable to call forth the comment, "This isn't really art at all". This fact is important because it indicates that, for any given beholder, the work of art depends for aesthetic value upon the degree to which it approximates to an *optimum of symbolic significance* lying at an intermediate point on a scale between over-symbolization and under-symbolization. In other words, a work of art only acquires an optimum of aesthetic value for the beholder in so far as it enables both his repressed urges and the demands of his superego to obtain a maximum of satisfaction.

X. THE PRINCIPLE OF RESTITUTION

a. The Work of Art as a 'Restored Object'

The duality of satisfaction which we have just found to underlie aesthetic experience is now seen to correspond to the duality of satisfaction provided by artistic activity; for, as was pointed out in my previous paper, artistic activity performs the double function of providing a means of expression for the repressed urges of the artist and of simultaneously enabling his ego to pay a tribute to the supremacy of his superego. It was also pointed out in my previous paper that, in so far as the work of art consists in a tribute paid by the artist's ego to his superego, it essentially represents a means of restitution, whereby his ego makes atonement to his superego for the destruction implied in the presence of repressed destructive impulses. In pursuance of the analogy between the emotional needs of the beholder and those of the artist, we may now infer that the aesthetic appeal of a work of art will depend upon its capacity to represent a restitution for the beholder also. The aesthetic experience is thus seen to be an experience that occurs when a person finds himself confronted with an object which presents itself to him, not simply as a 'found object', but also as a *restored object.*

Now that a work of art is seen to depend for aesthetic value upon its capacity to function as a 'restored object' for the beholder, we can understand better how it comes about that aesthetic experience should be compromised in the presence of both under-symbolization and over-symbolization. The under-symbolized work of art fails to produce the effect of restitution, because the impression which it gives is one of more or less unmitigated destruction and, consequently, the demands of the superego remain unsatisfied. On the other hand, restitution is meaningless apart from the presupposition of destruction; and, consequently, over-symbolization precludes the effect of restitution by excluding the impression of destruction too rigorously.

b. The Optimal Synthesis

Here we are at once reminded of the central conception of Hegelian philosophy—a conception summarized by Edward Caird (1901) in the statement that "the highest unity is to be reached only through the full development and reconciliation of the deepest and widest antagonism" (p. 42). Taking advantage of this philosophic conception for descriptive purposes, we may say that aesthetic experience depends upon the resolution of an antinomy created by the simultaneous operation of the libido (the life principle) and the destructive urges (the death principle). In the resolution of this antinomy the demands of the libido may be said to constitute the thesis, the pressure of the destructive urges the antithesis, and restitution the synthesis. What conditions aesthetic experience within the field of art is the capacity of the work of art to represent such a synthesis for the beholder. For a complete synthesis to occur, there must be an optimum proportion in the relationship between thesis and antithesis. It is only in so far as such an optimum relationship exists that the work of art becomes a 'restored object'. In a work of art characterized either by under-symbolization or by over-symbolization the proper relationship is absent, and the aesthetic experience is accordingly compromised.

XI. AESTHETIC THEORY

It is to the dependence of aesthetic experience upon the satisfaction of a need for restitution in the beholder that we must look for the rationale of that type of aesthetic theory which seeks the clue to 'beauty' in a certain 'perfection' or completeness in the object. This type of theory has, of course, played an enormous part in the history of aesthetics. It is true that it has had fewer advocates in recent years, as psychologists, anthropologists, art critics and even artists themselves have increasingly invaded the field of aesthetics, formerly so largely monopolized by philosophers. Nevertheless it has always made a special appeal to the more philosophically minded; and it has undoubtedly dominated the field of aesthetic theory in the past. Its most concise formulation is perhaps that of Aristotle (1931): "The essential characters composing beauty are order, symmetry and definiteness" (xii, 3). Such a formulation is representative of a widespread tendency in aesthetics to regard the 'beauty' of a work of art as residing in its capacity to convey the impression of something *intact*, *whole*, *complete* or *perfect*; and the presence of this tendency may be regarded as confirming the correctness of the view that aesthetic experience depends upon the satisfaction of a need for restitution in the beholder.

In the history of aesthetics there is evidence, however, of a contrasting line of thought—a line of thought perhaps best epitomized in Croce's (1931) claim that "expression and beauty are not two ideas but one" (p. 243). Expressionist theories of aesthetics seem to make a special appeal to the modern mind, characterized as it is by a tendency to question time-honoured values. That they are no novelty, however, may be illustrated by reference to Aristotle himself; for, in spite of his 'perfectionist' theory of aesthetics in general, we find Aristotle (*Poetics*, 1993) ascribing the appeal of tragedy to its capacity to effect a catharsis of the emotions of pity and fear—an essentially expressionist interpretation. Considered in isolation, such a theory is hopelessly inadequate to explain the aesthetic value of tragedy, since the emotions of pity and fear in themselves tend to compromise aesthetic values rather than to enhance them—the reason being, of course, that pity and fear imply a sense of uncontrollable destruction at work. The tragedy which simply releases pity and fear is thus comparable to the under-symbolized picture. Its effect is to produce a state of distress or horror in the beholder, and to provoke a reaction of rejection on his part. On the other hand, a tragedy which fails to release pity and fear in the beholder is rejected as emotionally unconvincing. It appears trite or ludicrous, because it fails to convey any impression of destruction at all, thus excluding the possibility of restitution. Such a tragedy is comparable to the over-symbolized picture.

It becomes evident, therefore, that it is only when a tragedy complies with perfectionist as well as expressionist standards that it acquires aesthetic value. To impress the beholder as in any sense 'beautiful', a tragedy must not only release the emotions of pity and fear, but at the same time produce an impression of completeness and perfection—an impression of 'the integrity of the object'. The fact is that the expressionist and perfectionist theories of aesthetics each represent a half-truth—the whole truth being that a work of art can only appear 'beautiful' to the beholder in proportion as it satisfies the particular conditions demanded by his need for restitution. To satisfy these conditions (i.e., to appear beautiful), the work of art must be able above all to produce in the beholder an impression of the 'integrity of the object'; but, in order to do so, it must at the same time provide a release for the emotions which imply the destruction of the object. Otherwise the conditions of restitution remain unsatisfied; and aesthetic experience is accordingly precluded.

VI

BOOK REVIEWS, LETTERS, AND AUTOBIOGRAPHICAL MATERIAL

INTRODUCTION TO PART VI

The four brief reviews and three examples of correspondence which make up this final section offer a reprise of the breadth of Fairbairn's interests and scholarship and of the way he was influenced by diverse fields and individuals, while at the same time offering responses which could further their contributions.

'On Working in the Gap' is a review of *On Not Being Able to Paint* by Joanna Field, now known to be the psychoanalyst Marion Milner. The book articulated material unattended to by Fairbairn in his own writing about art. The tone of the review makes it evident that he has enormous sympathy with the book, so his comments provide a supplement to his own earlier theorising. As Milner discusses her own experience in terms of object relationships without resorting to 'impulse' theory in the way that Fairbairn's own papers on art did, she succeeds in filling out some of Fairbairn's earlier formulations. It is particularly relevant to Fairbairn that Milner's identification of the 'creative interplay between dream and external reality' (p. 420) enabled her to produce artistic work reconciling the ambivalences of human experience which, in Fairbairn's theory, necessitate early ego-splitting. Fairbairn also identified with Milner's comments on 'traditional educational methods', which 'have the effect of stimulating the inner anxieties of the child and actually encouraging a resistance to the educational process itself' (p. 420). The introduction by Milner of the 'gap', or the space 'to provide the framework within which the creative forces could have free play' (p. 421), a notion derived from Winnicott's ideas on transitional phenomena (Winnicott 1953), is associated by Fairbairn with the 'sort of willed effort' demanded of patients by psychotherapists. This conjunction highlights the need for greater therapeutic attention to the experience of 'how it is to be in the real world' in order for reconciliation between the patient's inner and outer worlds.

In his earlier writing, Fairbairn (1938a, b) appeared to regard all art created by the child as representing 'objects of his destructive phantasies', an assumption more consistent with Klein's version of object relations than with

Fairbairn's own formulation a few years later. The main thrust of Fairbairn's work would lead us in a different direction, to a view of drawing, and indeed of all play, as functions of the need to relate to self and others, in the service of both creativity and reparation. In the aesthetic realm, it is through drawing that both child and artist identify shapes and express spatial and emotional relationships. So it is fitting that Fairbairn quoted Milner with approval on her hard-won capacity to reconcile 'the general human concern arising out of "being a separate body in a world of other bodies which occupy different bits of space" ' (p. 419).

'Psychoanalysis and Art', Fairbairn's review of *Psychoanalytic Explorations in Art* by Ernst Kris (1952), provides a brief update of Fairbairn's thinking on art fifteen years after his major essays on the topic, which are printed and discussed in Part V. After setting the book in the context of Kris's background, he relates it to his own object relations approach. In this succinct statement of his own views Fairbairn raises the issue of aesthetic value, arguing that 'the nature of artistic activity will . . . come to be described, . . . as an attempt to reconcile the primitive expression of a repressed id-structure with the requirements of a conscious ego-structure orientated towards external objects in a social milieu' (p. 429). This can provide for a scale of aesthetic values which Fairbairn felt had been badly missing in psychoanalytic writings about art: 'The aesthetic failure of a work of art depends upon a comparative failure to effect . . . reconciliation' (p. 430).

Thus, a work of art which fails to convince the perceiver is either over-symbolized or under-symbolized. However, Fairbairn still insists on retaining his formulation from the 'Prolegomena' (Chapter 23) that artistic creation is 'for fun', despite his work in the ensuing years describing endopsychic structure, in which it is the *unsatisfying aspects* of the child's early object relationships which are split off and rendered unconscious. To be consistent with his own object relations formulation, he might have said that what motivates an artist's creativity is the dissatisfaction associated with the 'allure' of rejecting bad objects and with those exciting objects with which there are also painfully dissatisfying relationships. While he urges that we understand reconciliation as the process which leads to artistic satisfaction and value, serious art seems hardly to be something undertaken merely 'for fun'. In the light of Winnicott's extensive work (1971) of the importance of play as the work of the child, rather than simply fun, this idea seems less frivolous, and if we were able to press Fairbairn on this matter, perhaps he would have defined serious 'fun' as the 'relief of inner tension through restitution' (1938a, p. 395), reconciling his early grounding in Freud's pleasure principle with object relations by viewing artistic creativity as a synthetic activity of the central ego.

'The Origins of Berkeley's Philosophy,' Fairbairn's review of *The*

Unconscious Origins of Berkeley's Philosophy, by John Oulton Wisdom, was published in 1955. Berkeley's philosophy was one of the topics on which Fairbairn had lectured at Edinburgh University between 1927 and 1935. The review documents Fairbairn's abiding interest in philosophy, even in the absence of specific papers of his own in this area. In this review, Fairbairn specifies the philosophical underpinnings of his own theory of internal objects as offering a structure which simultaneously represents the internalization of experience and a part of the self which modifies the meaning of experience as it continues to encounter it.

The review forms a small evocative bridge between psychoanalysis and philosophy, a bridge which Freud, Wisdom, and many modern philosophers have traveled more specifically, but one to which Fairbairn's theories make an important contribution. The final sentences of the review raise an issue of supreme importance to analysis:

> Psychoanalysis has thrown a flood of light upon psychopathology . . . but almost no light upon that most characteristic group of human achievements so appropriately described as 'the Humanities'. Does this perchance mean that, in its present phase at any rate, psychoanalysis is better qualified to throw light upon the negative than upon the positive aspects of human nature? [pp. 437–438]

As we have noted in previous introductory comments, two major philosophical assumptions made by Freud had negative connotations. The first was that of the Helmholtzian conservation of energy in which energy is divorced from structure, and in which physical bodies seek a state of inertia. For Freud, this meant that the mind had to have an external energy source—the instinctual forces residing in the id allied to the necessity to seek a state of inactivity. Fairbairn wrote in 1930 (see Chapter 3, pp. 121–122) that it was illogical to say that a living being could be defined as moving toward a state of inertia or death. Each person must be active to survive.

Second, Freud assumed that Man was by nature antisocial and defensive, seeking freedom from intrusion by others rather than seeking participation (see *Civilisation and Its Discontents*). Hobbes (*The Great Leviathan*, 1651) developed the psychology of the defensive individual, which was incorporated by Locke into classical liberal philosophy. The liberal bourgeois culture, of which Freud was a member, participated in this view which remains the dominant mode of English and American culture today. For Freud, resistance to knowledge by the self and by others was the major factor in his theory of the unconscious, making resistance the primary characteristic of the defensive individual, a characterization embedded in the heart of Freud's theory.

Fairbairn was a member of a similar culture. Consequently, his use of the terms *repression* and *resistance* seem commensurate with those of Freud.

However, for Fairbairn the avoidance of unpleasure was primarily determined by the need to avoid anxiety in relation to the object, rather than by the need to deny instinctual forces. Where Freud's world was dualistic, Fairbairn's was a holistic one in which Man seeks the development of a potential which is dependent upon his participation in human endeavors. The philosophical basis of this view stems from a definition of human nature as seeking the 'freedom to' participate rather than a 'freedom from' others. As we have seen, Fairbairn himself did not explicitly explore the philosophical origins or implications of his reorientation, but its effect is readily identifiable in the papers in this collection.

'The Technique of Psychoanalysis,' Fairbairn's review of the second edition of Glover's textbook *The Technique of Psycho-Analysis* (1955), provides an interesting, late follow-up on the view of his practice provided by his answers to Glover's questionnaire on clinical technique twelve years earlier (see Chapter 13). The review establishes Fairbairn's areas of agreement with the 'classical' approach to analysis, especially since, as he notes, Glover was antagonistic to the Kleinian view on the importance of introjection of the analyst as a major therapeutic factor. Fairbairn is in agreement with the broad span of Glover's picture of analytic technique, respectful of Glover's experience, scholarship, and questioning attitude towards the decisive factors in psychoanalytic treatment. However, Fairbairn finds weakness in Glover's advocacy of a central role for 'exact interpretation' in psychoanalysis, pointing to Glover's admission that relatively comparable results could be obtained by analysts of different stripes who used different techniques. He quotes Glover: 'In the deeper pathological states a prerequisite of the efficiency of interpretation is the *attitude*, the true unconscious attitude of the analyst to his patients' (Glover 1955, p. 372). For Fairbairn, this meant that Glover himself had raised the question as to whether it was not after all the 'actual relationship between the patient and the analyst in the analytical situation which is not the decisive factor' (p. 442). By now, of course, Fairbairn had concluded this to be so and was to record these views at length (*see From Instinct to Self: Volume I*, Chapter 4).

Three letters written between 1942 and 1954 are included as the final contributions to this section. They demonstrate Fairbairn's consistent willingness to address issues raised by others and the vehicle of exchange of ideas with his colleagues. It is clear from this small sample that he was prepared to give his time and a courteous, thoughtful response to any requests on his views, whether it be from a like-minded colleague such as Brierley, or one whose work was a considerable distance from his own interests. The final letter is particularly interesting because it is on a subject he was later to write about, and because it was written to his disciple and close friend, John Sutherland, who did so much to extend the range and influence of Fairbairn's views.

25. ON WORKING IN THE GAP

On Not Being Able to Paint. By Joanna Field. (Pp. 173, with 50 illustrations by the author.) London: William Heinemann Ltd. 1950.

It must have been just shortly after the publication of Joanna Field's first book, *A Life of One's Own*, in 1934 that a copy was lent to me. On reading it, I can remember, my reaction was rather critical on the grounds that the author showed a lack of that psychoanalytical orientation which seemed to me necessary to enable her to do justice to the very practical endeavour which she had undertaken, viz. 'to find out what kinds of experience made me happy'. At the same time I admired her courage and was sufficiently intrigued by what I read to buy a copy of the book for myself for future reference. As things turned out, the volume remained in my bookcase undisturbed (except for an occasional dusting) until 2 years ago, when, under the influence of a sudden impulse which can hardly have been fortuitous, I took it down from its shelf and read it again. On this occasion I found myself not only fascinated, but also much less critical. Since then I have read both of the author's subsequent books—*An Experiment in Leisure* (1937) and the recently published volume which is the subject of this review.

In each of her three books Joanna Field's method is essentially the same—that of selecting a problem of personal importance to herself whilst at the same time involving issues of equal importance to everybody, and then attempting to feel her way towards a solution by means of introspection aided by such theoretical knowledge as she already possessed, an unusual capacity for insight and an exceptional determination to face inner facts. In the preface to *A Life of One's Own* she writes: 'The form of the book follows from the nature of the experiment. I have tried to show the development of the problem by giving actual extracts from my diaries. I have tried always to keep to the facts as I saw them in order to show how I gradually pieced together the hints and clues which led to my final conclusions'. The same description applies to the form of the two subsequent books, with the qualification that in the present volume reproductions of a number of her own drawings accompanied by an account of the 'stories' of these drawings (based on contemporary free association) take the place of excerpts from her diaries. Thus in each book we find a historical account of the mental processes which led her to her conclusions regarding the particular problem in question. The problem with which her first book was concerned has already been mentioned. Of the problem which is the subject of *An Experiment in Leisure*, she writes: 'I have tried to find out by simple observation just what this particular mind (I hesitate to call it mine because during the course of this experiment I came to feel less and less possessive about it) seems to find most interesting'. *On Not Being Able to Paint*, however, embodies an inquiry of a somewhat different nature—one arising out of certain misgivings which she experienced in connexion with the results of a 5-year-scientific study of the way in which children are affected by orthodox educational methods. Ever since her own childhood she had entertained a special interest in learning to paint; but, in spite of such technical efficiency as she had acquired (evidently considerable), she felt that her efforts 'had always tended to peter out in a maze of uncertainties about what a painter is really trying to do' (p. xvii). However, it now occurred to her that, if only she could discover how to set about learning to paint, this would throw light upon the wider problems of learning with which education is concerned—and particularly so if, as she surmised, these problems are really aspects of the general problem of psychic creativity. Accordingly, it is with such wider implications of the psychological problems involved in 'learning to paint' that the book is concerned. From what has just been said it will be appreciated that the problems in question lend themselves readily to be described in psychoanalytical terms as problems of libido and resistance; and it is undoubtedly in this sense that they are conceived by Joanna Field. It is not to be inferred, however, that the book is in any sense a formal psychoanalytical treatise; for it is characterized by a studied avoidance of technical terms. Whilst thus obviously intended to reach readers who are not professional psychotherapists, it is nevertheless the embodiment of profound psychoanalytical thought and insight, and therefore deserves to be taken seriously from a scientific standpoint. In this connexion a comparison of the three books becomes a matter of interest. In the first the knowledge of psychoanalytical theory and practice displayed by the author is that of an interested and well-informed outsider; but it is to be noted that her initial 'experiment', like those which follow, is based essentially upon the technique of free association. The second book conveys the impression that she is now speaking with inside knowledge of psychoanalysis. And now on the cover of the third volume it is expressly stated that the author's pen-name covers the identity of a practising psychoanalyst. The trilogy thus acquires special interest as representing a psychological pilgrimage towards an overtly psychoanalytical standpoint. The outlook associated characteristically with the name of Melanie Klein has obviously exercised an important influence upon the author's thought; but it is interesting to note that the originality which characterizes all her books has been enriched rather than compromised by this circumstance. For, quite apart from an identity of methodological approach, there is the same subtle quality about *On Not Being Able to Paint* that originally intrigued me when I read *A Life of One's Own*. This particular quality is rather difficult to analyse; but my guess is that it springs from a highly developed sense of positive values. The old criticism that psychoanalysis is all analysis and no synthesis certainly does not apply here.

The whole theme of the book springs out of Joanna Field's personal discovery that by adopting the method of 'free' drawing ('letting hand and eye do exactly what pleased them without any conscious working to a preconceived intention', p. xvii) she was able to produce pictures which possessed greater artistic value than those produced by deliberate effort. This discovery proved disconcerting in so far as it seemed to threaten not only traditional beliefs regarding the importance of consciously exercised will-power, but also the sense of personal identity associated with the exercise of this function. However, it seemed to have a bearing on her investigation of the effects of orthodox educational methods, based as these are upon demands for willed effort to achieve preconceived standards, whether within the intellectual or the moral sphere. Her misgivings were confirmed by the further observation that pictures produced by the free method often displayed evidence of a creative ordering of material far superior to that achieved by deliberate effort. Another important observation was that, so far from the significance of the free drawings being confined to the light which they threw on unconscious 'complexes', the drawings also represented a form of personal visual comment upon the problems of living. Such observations contributed to a growing realization that the painter's basic concern with 'the feelings conveyed by space' was simply a manifestation, within a particular field, of the general human concern with problems arising out of 'being a separate body in a world of other bodies which occupy different bits of space' (p. 12). Pictorial composition thus resolved itself into an attempt on the painter's part to deal with all the problems involved in object-relationships, viz. problems concerned with such vital issues as separation and 'ways of being together', loving and hating, having and losing, taking and withholding, innocence and guilt, freedom and slavery, security and insecurity, etc. It followed from the nature of these problems that their solution necessitated a reconciliation of opposites, an integration of differences; and in the particular case of the artist it depended on his success in effecting a reconciliation: (1) between his own imaginative dream and the actual subject of his picture, and (2) between his own active effort to objectify his dream and the physical attributes of the medium which he employed for this purpose. However, as Joanna Field discovered from personal experience, artistic success has no positive relation to conscious efforts either to follow the rules expounded in art schools and textbooks about art (and so to be a slave to authority) or to be faithfully naturalistic in the representation of objects (and so to be a slave to the object). On the contrary, the motivation of such effort was traced to inner anxieties over allowing instinctive forces to be expressed, and over-externalizing internal situations; and it was the influence of such anxieties that was found to account for the phenomenon of 'not being able to paint'. In reaching this conclusion Joanna Field is obviously drawing attention to the part played by 'resistance' within the field of art, albeit she refrains from describing it so technically. She is not content, however, to leave it at that, but proceeds to direct attention to the converse fact that the cultivation of an attitude of mind which attaches supreme importance to a willed effort to follow the rules has the effect of actually mobilizing and intensifying inner anxieties and resistance, and that the attempt to be meticulously representational has a similar effect. This observation is shown to have important implications, since it applies not only to painting, but also to the whole field of life; and it has an application of special importance in the field of education. Traditional educational methods are thus seen to have the effect of stimulating the inner anxieties of the child and actually encouraging a resistance to the educational process itself.

On the constructive side, the direction in which Joanna Field looks for the establishment of educational methods upon a sounder psychological basis lies in a deeper understanding of 'the human predicament'. As she points out, this predicament may be formulated in various ways arising out of the fact that it has a variety of aspects which may each be made the basis of formulation; but, whichever aspect is considered, it can only be surmounted by a reconciliation of differences. The essential 'difference' which underlies the human predicament is that between self and 'other'; but it also presents itself as a difference between, e.g., subjective and objective, internal and external, emotional and intellectual, imagination and action, dream and reality, illusion and disillusion, independence and dependence. As Joanna Field points out, these various aspects of the difference underlying the human predicament have been made the subject of special study on the part of psychoanalysts; but, speaking as an analyst herself, she records that the particular feature of the human problem which psychoanalysis had not previously made clear to her was the importance of 'creative interplay between dream and external reality' for its solution. Such creative interplay may be studied with special profit in the activity of painting; for the resulting picture is not just a dream, nor yet is it an external object independent of the artist's dream. The essential difficulty which confronts such creative interplay has its ultimate source in the disturbing experiences of childhood through which the individual becomes so painfully aware of 'the difference between what one would like and expect people to do and what they do do'. The trouble is that, having once learned to differentiate these opposites, the individual is tempted to go to extremes and keep them too rigidly apart, whilst all the time never ceasing in the depths of his being to aspire to a restoration of the original situation which existed before the difference was experienced. The effect of this is not only to produce emotional difficulties for the individual in social relationships, but also to compromise creative activity on his part; and such unfortunate developments are fostered not only by the intellectual bias of traditional educational methods and the rigidity of traditional moral codes, but also by that demand for objectivity which characterizes the modern scientific outlook. There are, of course, dangers of an opposite kind arising out of a failure to maintain an adequate distinction 'between dream and external reality'; but, if that way madness lies, the maintenance of too rigid a distinction breeds a madness of its own which tends to rob outer reality of real significance (since it is 'dream' that confers significance). For, as Joanna Field shows, it is possible to be 'seduced by objectivity'. What it is vital to recognize is that both the internal dream and the external reality have each a value in their own right—but only provided that they are not kept rigidly apart. It is also important to recognize that they never permanently coincide, but only interact. The 'way of detachment, of analysis' must be supplemented by 'the way of fusion, becoming one with what is seen'; the way of intellectual knowledge must be supplemented by the way of intuitive knowledge; the narrow focus of attention must be supplemented by the wide focus of attention. But, if this is all true, where does the function of will-power and conscious planning come in? This is a question which lies very near the heart of Joanna Field's inquiry; and the answer only emerged when she came to realize that, although the actual activity of her drawing was 'free', there arose a necessity 'to impose action according to plan, at least to the extent of forcing oneself to go on drawing in spite of not knowing what was going to appear' (p. 104). She also found that an effort of will was required 'to maintain the kind of attention which created a gap ahead in time and a willingness to wait and see what was emerging to fill the gap' (p. 104). Her conclusion, therefore, was that the true function of willed effort was to 'plan the gap . . . to provide the framework within which the creative forces could have free play' (p. 104). Psychotherapists will at once recognize that this is the sort of willed effort which is demanded of their patients; and they will find it profitable to read for themselves all that Joanna Field has to say in elaboration of the theme which I have tried to outline.

On Not Being Able to Paint acquires added interest from the fact that the book itself provides an example in illustration of its own theme. 'Thus', the author writes in the Postscript, 'the book is not the retrospective account of a creative experience which had happened independently and was then written about, it is itself an attempted embodiment of the process of creating. And

Cosmo Fairbairn at Fountains Abbey, Yorkshire, 1949

what had been created, not just by the activity of making the free drawings without preconceived purpose, but also by writing the book without fore-knowledge of where it would lead, was finally a new certainty of belief' (p. 145). These remarks strike a special note of conviction in me, since, when I venture to write, I also write without fore-knowledge of where it will lead and without any conscious planning, except for 'planning the gap'; and I agree with Joanna Field that planning the gap affords full scope for the exercise of will-power. Another feature of the book which impresses me is that the problems which it discusses are discussed wholly in terms of object-relationships. This feature appears to be quite spontaneous, and not to be due to any theoretical considerations; and it is all the more impressive on this account. It is refreshing to read a book so much concerned with the psychological processes involved in art and never to come across the term 'sublimation'. Sublimation is, of course, a concept which has its roots in impulse-psychology; and it is difficult to find a place for it in a psychology of object-relations. In this book the artist's problem is discussed essentially in terms of the artist's relationship with his objects; and, so far as the psychology of object-relations is concerned, the book seems to me to represent an important contribution. I hope I may be forgiven for ending this review on a personal note; but I can hardly forebear to remark that Joanna Field's observations *from inside* regarding the mental processes involved in painting appear to confirm some of the conclusions which I recorded in two contributions to the psychology of art in 1938 on the basis of an *objective* approach.

26. PSYCHOANALYSIS AND ART

Psychoanalytic Explorations in Art. By ERNST KRIS. (Pp. 358, with 79 illustrations.) New York: International Universities Press. 1952.

As the author states in the Preface, the preparation and publication of the fourteen essays which this book comprises extended over a period of considerably more than twenty years. The essays here collected together for the first time have all appeared previously elsewhere; and it would seem that they have been left largely unchanged except in the case of the first essay, which combines material from two earlier publications, and which has been largely rewritten and expanded in the light of recent advances in psychoanalytic knowledge. In the case of the other essays revision has been mainly confined to the addition of references to recent literature, and to the indication of the bearing of the more recently published views of others upon the author's formulations. The author originally planned the essays with a double purpose in mind. The first of his purposes was to apply the special insight derived from the growth of psychoanalytic ego-psychology to the problems which have traditionally belonged to the province of the humanities. The attempt to implement this purpose revealed the difficulty of subjecting to psychoanalytic interpretation data which had been collected without a psychoanalytic perspective in mind; and, with a view to meeting this difficulty, the author has set himself the task of developing a new type of interdisciplinary contact based upon a critique of sources. This is a task for which Kris is specially well equipped; for, not only was it in the field of the humanities that he received his own earlier training, but, as the reader will not take long to realize, he displays a special capacity for appreciating the requirements of interdisciplinary research. This fact prepares us for the second purpose which Kris has sought to implement in the essays here collected—a purpose based upon the realization that the study of art and of 'creative processes' in general is capable of making a most important contribution to psychoanalytic psychology itself. Accordingly, these essays not only represent the fruits of the application of a high degree of psychoanalytic insight to the field of cultural studies, but also embody important contributions to psychoanalytic theory derived from research within the cultural field. The author is thus no less concerned with what psychoanalysis can *learn* within the field of cultural studies than with what it can teach. Happily there are signs that this is an attitude which is beginning to make itself felt more effectively within the psychoanalytic movement than was at one time the case; and the present volume will doubtless play no small part in promoting the development of this auspicious attitude.

The book is divided into five parts. The first, which is entitled 'Introduction' and consists of two essays, is succinctly and aptly described on the dust-cover as dealing with 'the actual and potential contributions of psychoanalysis to the study of art and creative processes, and to a sociologically based psychology of the artist, his audience and his biographer'. The second part is devoted to 'The Art of the Insane'; and it includes studies of the artistic productions of a psychotic medieval cleric (de Canistris) and a psychotic sculptor of the eighteenth century (Messerschmidt). In the third part of the book the nature of the comic comes under consideration; and the author devotes special attention to the psychology of caricature, to the relationship of the comic to ego-development, and to laughter as an example of expressive behaviour. In the fourth part the author displays considerable originality in discussing problems of literary criticism from a psychoanalytic standpoint; and the essay on 'Aesthetic Ambiguity' (in collaboration with Abraham Kaplan) strikes the reviewer as among the most original and impressive in the book. Originality and impressiveness also characterize the fifth and final section of the book, devoted as this is to the 'Psychology of Creative Processes', and comprising as it does two essays—one 'On Inspiration', and the other 'On Preconscious Mental Processes'.

Three of the essays contained in the book have been written in collaboration with others. That written in collaboration with Kaplan has already been mentioned. The others are 'The Principles of Caricature' in collaboration with E. H. Gombrich, and an essay in which Else Pappenheim is associated with Kris in a study of the function of drawings and the meaning of 'the creative spell' in the case of a schizophrenic artist. Questions of co-authorship apart, Kris takes an opportunity in his Preface to acknowledge a special debt to the thought of H. Hartmann, to whom, as he says, 'the development of psychoanalytic ego psychology owes much', and with whom he has been closely associated 'over the decades'.

Reference to influences which have contributed to the author's formulations makes this a convenient point at which to register a minor criticism regarding his use of the pronoun 'we', which occurs with great frequency in the text, and which appears to be employed in three different senses. In the case of the essays of which he is joint author, the significance of 'we' is usually obvious. Elsewhere, however, the first person plural appears to be used sometimes to signify a consensus of psychoanalytic opinion and sometimes to signify the author's own individual views. This latter usage, which is obviously stylistic, is not quite in conformity with recognized literary custom in English; and doubtless it would be in the interests of clarity if in future editions the pronoun 'we' were replaced by the pronoun 'I' when this is appropriate to the meaning. The reviewer also feels that the mode of expression employed by the author is sometimes a little cumbrous, and that in some places a more direct manner of statement would make the reader's task easier. However, such minor criticisms pale into insignificance beside the impressive intellectual calibre of the book.

Perhaps what impresses itself most readily upon the reader is that this is a very learned book—or, more properly speaking, that it is a book written by a very learned author. The wide range of his literary knowledge and the catholicity of his cultural interests, although never obtrusive, are everywhere obvious; and a bibliography containing well over six hundred references provides a measure of his familiarity with the technical literature. For those of lesser accomplishment such a wealth of references is capable of proving rather overwhelming; and such a one might perhaps be pardoned for wondering whether (to take liberties with the proverb) the wood does not obscure the view of some at least of the trees.

Some eager readers will doubtless share a certain disappointment experienced by the reviewer on reading in the author's Preface the following warning against undue expectations: 'In this volume no psychoanalytic psychology of art is offered. I do not feel that the time for a systematic presentation of this type has yet come' (Preface). Instead of such a systematic presentation, what we find is the detailed exploration of a number of relevant fields with a view to the formulation of promising research-hypotheses and the development of a valid methodology for further investigations; and within the limits which the author has thus deliberately set himself the important task which he has undertaken has been brilliantly performed. Any initial disappointment experienced by the reader who expectantly awaits the advent of a systematic psychology of art is thus quickly overborne by admiration of the prospects of investigation and exploration which are opened out before his eyes as he reads on.

At an early stage in the first essay ('Approaches to Art') Kris takes the opportunity to draw attention to, and dissociate himself from, a hitherto prevailing tendency to simplify or abbreviate psychoanalytic thinking on the part of those who have discussed the problems of art in the light of psychoanalysis. In particular, he points out that, while psychiatrists are accustomed to assess the demands of specific environmental situations in their clinical work, there is a tendency to neglect the 'reality' in which the artist creates. Thus, even in the case of Freud's (1910b) famous study of Leonardo da Vinci, the central problem of Leonardo's genius evaded elucidation; for, whilst Freud penetrated deeply into the psychological secrets of this great artist, he provided no real answer to the question why an individual with the particular infantile experience and pattern of defences which he was able to reconstruct in Leonardo's case should have been fated to become specifically a masterly artistic creator. As Kris points out, art is not produced in an empty space. The artist is always involved in a specific tradition and is driven by his individual incentives to create in a structured area of problems imposing certain 'stringencies'. The degree of the artist's mastery within such a framework and, in certain periods at least, his capacity to modify its stringencies must be important factors in the assessment of his artistic achievement; but as yet psychoanalysis has contributed little to an understanding of the framework itself and of the real significance of artistic style (perhaps the most challenging of all problems for the psychology of art). 'We do not at present have the tools which would permit us to investigate the roots of gift or talent, not to speak of genius', says Kris; but he adds, 'However, recent advances in ego psychology enable us better to focus on this gap in our knowledge and suggest enquiries which promise to improve our understanding' (p. 20). And he himself is inclined to the view that 'what psychoanalysis may have to offer will probably depend on our ability to view the phenomena of style in art at least in part in terms of the processes of discharge which they stimulate in artist and public' (p. 22). He also attaches great importance to the influence which the innate endowment of the personality may exercise on experience, 'and particularly the role endowment may play in facilitating the detachment of certain ego functions from conflict, in establishing autonomy in certain activities' (p. 21).

Another theme broached by Kris in his first essay and later developed in illuminating directions is based upon an appreciation of the implications of the impression registered by Freud that the psychoanalytic approach was only differentiated from that of the intuitive psychologists among the poets by an attempt at vigorous scientific thinking. Agreeing with this impression, Kris points out that it is only by means of psychoanalysis that it is possible to establish the interaction between elements derived from various stages of awareness (conscious, preconscious and unconscious). In this connexion he draws attention to the comparison which psychoanalytic investigation has made it possible to establish between dream work and 'what one might call the "art work" '.[1] He proceeds, however, to point out that the significance of this

[1]Incidentally 'art work' is a concept which was formulated and developed as the basis of a general theory of the psychology of art by the reviewer (Fairbairn 1938a).

comparison lies not so much in the similarities as in the differences between art work and dream work; and the differentiating feature to which he attaches supreme importance is that, as Freud demonstrated in the case of wit, so in the case of art the ego remains in control of the primary process whilst permitting a regression to the level at which this process functions. The theme of such controlled regression to the level of the primary process may be regarded as providing *the basic concept* underlying all the investigations recorded by Kris in the present volume. He does not claim, of course, that the phenomenon in question is specific to art; for not only does he quite deliberately borrow it from Freud's conclusions regarding the nature of wit, but also, as we have seen, he disclaims any attempt to establish a specific psychology of art. At the same time he makes this phenomenon the basis of a series of explorations in various directions within the artistic field and the foundation upon which his various illuminating research-hypotheses are constructed. He regards it as an essential, albeit not specific, feature of the characteristic equipment of the artist that he should have the capacities to gain easy access to id material without being overwhelmed by it, to retain control of the primary process, and to make appropriately rapid shifts from one level of psychic functioning to another. Kris recognizes, of course, that the capacity to gain easy access to id material must bear some relation to psychopathological conditions in which id material intrudes upon the ego; and it is in conformity with this fact that one section of the book is devoted to 'The Art of the Insane'. In this section the conclusion reached may be briefly summarized to the effect that, in so far as the artist is 'normal', his ego remains in control of the primary process, and, in so far as he approximates to the psychotic, the primary process dominates his ego. Art as an aesthetic, and therefore as a social, phenomenon is thus seen to be closely linked with the integrity of the ego.

Another feature of the characteristic (albeit not specific) equipment of the artist, to which Kris attaches great importance, and which he is inclined to ascribe to native endowment, is the (already mentioned) capacity to detach certain ego functions from conflict and thus establish autonomy in certain activities. Relevant to the existence of such a capacity is the question of 'sublimation'. As Kris points out, Freud's use of this term is far from consistent, with the result that it retains a variety of shades of meaning in psychoanalytic usage. Kris himself draws a clear distinction between (a) 'the displacement of energy discharge from a socially inacceptable goal to an acceptable one', and (b) 'a transformation of the energy discharged'. Both these processes are ordinarily included in the concept of 'sublimation'; but Kris restricts the connotation of this term to the former process, and adopts the term 'neutralization' to describe the latter—his reason for doing so being that the two processes are not necessarily synchronous. He also regards the transformation of energy involved in 'neutralization' as applying to aggression no less than to libido; and he considers that 'neutralized energy' is not necessarily identical with what Freud has described as 'bound energy'—on the grounds that energy may retain the hallmark of libido or aggression to various degrees even when it is fully bound and under the control of the ego. 'Sublimation', as he understands it, may be characterized, he feels, both by fusion in the discharge of instinctual[2] energy and a shift in psychic levels; and he regards 'neutralization' as having the effect of providing conditions favourable for fusion and thus for the mastery of instinctual demands.

At this point it would seem not out of place to remark that the whole concept of 'sublimation' (in the more comprehensive sense which includes 'neutralization') presents considerable difficulties for those who, like the reviewer, adopt a psychology of object-relations based upon the principle of dynamic structure. To those of this way of thinking, both the concept of the displacement of energy from a socially unacceptable to a socially acceptable goal and that of the transformation of energy itself assume a somewhat artificial complexion, since they imply an approach based upon a divorce of energy from structure. In terms of the principle of dynamic structure, the displacement of energy from a socially unacceptable to a socially acceptable goal would resolve itself, where the field of art is concerned, into a change in the relationships existing between the artist and those objects who constitute society for him; and similarly, the transformation of energy would resolve itself into a complex change (a) in the relationships of internally differentiated ego-structures not only with internal objects, but also with one another, and (b) in the relationships of the conscious ego-structure with external objects. It would, of course, be grossly unfair to Kris to suggest that he is indifferent to structural considerations; for his concern with these is evident throughout the whole book—and indeed the explorations which he records are quite deliberately designed to bring recent advances in ego psychology to bear upon the psychology of art. At the same time, it is evident that he inherits from Freud that dichotomy between energy and structure which Freud himself inherited from nineteenth-century physics; and there is a growing number of those who regard this dichotomy as imposing a serious limitation upon the advance of psychoanalytic research, especially within those fields in which sociological implications are more obvious. The question of the validity of this dichotomy has an important bearing on the distinction between the primary and the secondary processes—a distinction which Kris makes so basic to his re-

[2]The reviewer has never ceased to wonder why the perfectly good English adjective 'instinctive' has come to be so characteristically replaced in psychoanalytic writings by the coined word 'instinctual', which appears to be only a less euphonious synonym. Is it a case of an alignment with 'sensual' and 'sexual'? But, if so, why not 'aggressual' too?

searches. There is no need, of course, to stress the illuminating nature of this distinction originally drawn by Freud, or the rich fruits of psychological insight for which it has been responsible not only at the hands of Freud, but also at the hands of his successors; and in the present volume we find Kris employing the distinction in so masterly a manner as to open up vast new vistas of insight into the psychological problems of art. At the same time, there is a case for the claim that still greater insights could be achieved if the concepts of primary and secondary processes were revised in terms of a psychology of object-relations based upon the principle of dynamic structure. That, in spite of theoretical assumptions, such a psychology is often implicitly adopted by Kris in his researches seems to be implied in such statements as, 'It will not be found that the same equipment, the same psychological proclivities will in all periods of history make for success—in any given medium or in artistic creation in general' (p. 29). It also seems to be implied in the statement, 'Our starting point will be the function of art as a specific kind of communication from the one to the many' (p. 31) (a conception with which the published views of both Herbert Read and the reviewer are in agreement). However, when, in another passage, Kris commits himself to the statement that sexual functions presuppose 'regressive patterns' involving a suspension of ego control, it would appear that the dichotomy between energy and structure, instinctive impulse (id) and ego, reasserts itself. According to the principle of dynamic structure, it is not a case of a structural ego being differentiated under the pressure of the impact of external reality out of an original id which is relatively formless, so much as of the id being a structure with primitive characteristics which is differentiated from an original (and relatively primitive) ego-structure under the influence of repression; and it can be seen that, once such a differentiation has occurred, the repressed id-structure will retain primitive features (and acquire exaggerations of such features under the influence of repression), while that part of the ego which remains conscious and in touch with external reality will be free to develop under the influence of relationships with external objects. In the light of such a conception, the primary process will present itself as a characteristic feature of the activity of the repressed id-structure, and the secondary process as a characteristic feature of the activity of the conscious ego-structure; and the nature of artistic activity will then come to be described, not as an ego-controlled regression to the level of the primary process, but rather as an attempt to reconcile the primitive expression of a repressed id-structure with the requirements of a conscious ego-structure orientated towards external objects in a social milieu. Such a description of the nature of artistic activity does not, of course, in itself suffice to define the specific nature of artistic activity as such. It only indicates the class of activity into which it falls. Its specific nature can, however, be defined by the further statement that the reconciliation between the expression of the id-structure and the requirements of the conscious ego which it is the specific aim of the artist to establish is one accomplished through the specific activity of making (creating) things—and making them not primarily for utilitarian purposes, but (as the reviewer attempted to establish in 1938 [Fairbairn 1938a]) primarily 'for fun'. One advantage of the conception of artistic activity just indicated is that it finds a place for a *scale* of aesthetic values; and the extent of this advantage may be judged by the fact that failure to make provision for such a scale of values has always been the greatest weakness of psychoanalytic writings about art. According to the conception in question, the aesthetic failure of a work of art depends upon a comparative failure to effect the reconciliation to which reference has been made. Such failure may be brought about in either of two ways—either through a failure on the part of the artist to make the expression of the id-structure conform sufficiently to the requirements of the conscious ego (as exemplified by the wilder productions of the Surrealists), or through the requirements of the conscious ego proving so exacting as to preclude the expression of the id-structure from endowing the work of art with a sufficiently dynamic quality to render it convincing (as exemplified by much of Victorian art and other forms of art characterized by excessive formalism). These two types of failure have been described by the reviewer elsewhere (Fairbairn 1938a, b) as 'under-symbolization' and 'over-symbolization' respectively; and what appear to be corresponding phenomena on the side of the audience have been described by Bullough, who is quoted with approval by Kris, as 'underdistance' and 'overdistance'. On the other hand, the success of a work of art depends upon the extent to which reconciliation approximates to the optimal. The optimal itself does not, of course, represent any fixed standard. What is optimal for one artist may not be optimal for another. Similarly, what is optimal for one audience may not be optimal for another audience; and what appears optimal in terms of the ethos of one age or culture may appear anything but optimal to those of a succeeding age or of a culture which is alien. Hence the notorious subjectivity of aesthetic judgements. The greatest works of art, however, are those which have the most universal aesthetic appeal. It should be added that the reconciliation upon which the aesthetic value of a work of art depends would appear to be one characteristically effected at a preconscious level, although the artist's conscious contribution to the moulding of his creation must have an important influence upon its final form; and doubtless in the case of the greatest artists there is a happy combination between conscious and preconscious activity.

In making this excursion into the implications of the principle of dynamic structure for the psychology of art, the reviewer may appear to have strayed somewhat from his allotted task. It is to be hoped, however, that the excursion may appear justified as a form of critical comment which it would have been difficult to condense without sacrificing intelligibility. Although the principle of dynamic structure is not one which Kris theoretically accepts (and is indeed one which he might very well theoretically disown), there is, as has already been indicated, some reason to think that it is one which at times he implicitly adopts. Short quotations which seem to support this interpretation have already been cited; but another may now be added—'Instead of accepting the division of form and content . . . psychoanalytic orientation suggests the value of establishing their interrelation' (p. 22). This sentence is all the more significant in view of the fact that in another passage, after quoting Bühler's characterization of psychoanalysis as 'content-bound', he goes on to remark, 'Without contradicting this statement we may say that ego psychology tends to suggest a number of points where problems of formal elaboration become accessible' (p. 105). There is still another relevant passage which bears quotation—one which occurs in the essay 'On Preconscious Mental Processes'. After making reference to the development of Freud's views on this subject, Kris proceeds as follows, 'One might therefore well take the view that the systematic cohesion of psychoanalytic propositions is only, or at least best, accessible through its history. The clearest instance of such a reformulation was the gradual introduction of structural concepts. The introduction of these new concepts has never fully been integrated with the broad set of propositions developed earlier' (p. 304). From the standpoint of the psychology of dynamic structure, this statement is unexceptional and may be whole-heartedly endorsed, especially where the last sentence is concerned. The only question is whether Kris himself has really succeeded in integrating the newer structural concepts with 'the broad set of propositions developed earlier'. His discussion of the function of the preconscious mental processes is extremely illuminating, as is his brilliant essay on 'Aesthetic Ambiguity', in which he demonstrates how greatly the aesthetic appeal of poetry depends upon that multiplicity of meanings which characterizes the dream-symbol, and which has its roots in the primary process. At the same time, in spite of his insistence on the importance of structural concepts, his own formulations remain largely conceived in terms of the disposal of energy—sufficiently so to lead him to speak of 'the appropriateness of describing thought processes in terms of cathexis and discharge' (p. 314). It would thus appear that his thought still remains basically under the influence of Freud's original dichotomy between energy and structure; and the conclusion that this is so seems to be borne out by his treatment of his central theme. This theme is to the effect that artistic activity essentially involves an ego-controlled regression to the level of the primary process, and that aesthetic experience also involves a corresponding regression on the part of the audience; and his treatment of this theme impresses the reviewer as being conceived almost exclusively in economic terms. As applied to art, the theme itself also appears to involve him in a certain contradiction in that it makes it difficult for him to account satisfactorily for the art of children and prehistoric peoples. This contradiction may be illustrated by the fact that, whilst he describes art as involving a regression to the level of the primary process controlled by the ego, he also describes the graphic art of the child as 'to a great extent controlled by the primary process'. In the light of such a contradiction we are reminded of the fact that Kris disclaims from the outset any attempt to offer a psychoanalytic psychology of art. The most that he claims to do is to analyse some of the processes involved in artistic activity and (to a lesser extent) aesthetic experience; and indeed he goes so far as to say, 'The quest for what is specific to the psychological processes connected with art . . . constitutes a problem that we can hardly hope to solve' (p. 31). Perhaps, however, what is specific to art and differentiates it from other activities involving the processes which Kris describes so well is not after all to be sought in the nature of the processes involved. Perhaps, as has already been suggested, it is to be sought in the fact that these processes are manifested within the field of creation—in the act of *making things* in so far as these things are made, not for utilitarian purposes, but for the sake of making them, viz, in so far as they are made (so to speak) for fun.

27. THE ORIGINS OF BERKELEY'S PHILOSOPHY

The Unconscious Origin of Berkeley's Philosophy. By John Oulton Wisdom. (Pp. xii + 244, 1 illustration.) London: Hogarth Press and Institute of Psycho-Analysis. 1953.

This book is concerned, as the author states in the Preface, both to interest psychoanalysts in philosophy—which he describes as 'perhaps the strangest of all the creations of the human mind'—and to interest philosophers in psychoanalysis. Whether he will succeed in the second aim so well as in the first is perhaps open to doubt; for it may well be that the philosopher will content himself with the conclusion that the strangest of all the creations of the human mind is psychoanalysis. There can be no doubt, however, about the interest which the philosopher will take in the scholarly exposition of Bishop Berkeley's philosophy to which Part I of the book is devoted. To provide such an exposition is undoubtedly one of the author's purposes. However, his main purpose is to provide the psychoanalytical interpretation of Berkeley's philosophical conceptions which appears in Part III; and, in aid of this purpose, Part II is devoted to a consideration of all such historical aspects of Berkeley's life as are considered relevant. Fortunately, the details of Berkeley's adult life are well documented; but, apart from such meagre details as might be of interest to a registrar, all that is known about his early life appears to be contained in a single statement of his own, viz. 'that I was distrustful at 8 years old'. This absence of knowledge regarding Berkeley's early life has an unfortunately compromising effect upon the value of Wisdom's psychoanalytical study; for his attempted reconstruction of the emotional sources of Berkeley's philosophy in early life is thereby rendered purely speculative—a fact which remains unaffected by his explicit denial (in the Introduction) that such is the case. The grounds of this disclaimer are that 'the interpretations, even though not phrased in a form suitable to use with a patient, are in general of a well-recognized clinical type'; but it would be a rash analyst who would interpret the details of a patient's early emotional life in the complete absence of any associative material regarding his childhood. Such interpretations would infallibly develop a resistance in the patient; and it would hardly be surprising in the present instance if a resistance should develop in the reader. In the light of these considerations it will be noticed that Wisdom's study of Berkeley the philosopher stands in marked contrast to Freud's (1910b) study of the artist Leonardo da Vinci; for the value, no less than the interest, of the latter study depends upon the manner in which Freud attempts to throw light upon certain features of Leonardo's art in terms of known facts regarding the artist's childhood. By contrast, Wisdom's reconstruction of the conflicts of Berkeley's childhood, to the influence of which the particular form assumed by his subsequent philosophy is attributed, conveys the impression of an elaborate exercise in deductive reasoning from general psychoanalytical principles—among which, incidentally, the concepts of introjection and projection occupy a prominent place. It is only fair to add, however, that, in forming his conclusions, Wisdom takes extreme care to sift the details of Berkeley's later life for indications of his unconscious motivations.

Wisdom's description of Berkeley's philosophy takes full account of the most recent scholarship on the subject, and in particular the researches of A. A. Luce and T. E. Jessop. He accordingly draws a distinction between Berkeley's 'considered philosophy' and the solipsistic interpretation of his philosophy which has acquired historical importance through its influence upon Hume and other thinkers.[1] Berkeley's considered philosophy was based essentially upon an immaterialist theory of perception which he condensed into the classic formula '*Esse* is *percipi*'. This theory embodied a rejection of Locke's contention that ideas are representations or copies of something outside the mind; and it was combined with an attack upon the abstract idea of Matter accepted by Locke. Whilst rejecting Matter as the source of what is perceived, Berkeley recognized that the existence of what is perceived does not depend solely upon the perceptual activity of the human percipient; and he therefore concluded that what is perceived has an immaterial source in God. His considered philosophy thus represents a theocentric interpretation of the natural world. The solipsistic interpretation is, of course, based upon Berkeley's theory of perception considered in isolation, and is to the effect that, in terms of this theory, the external world depends wholly for its existence on the mind of the percipient. The scepticism implicit in such solipsism is, as Wisdom points out, completely alien to the spirit of Berkeley's considered philosophy, which began as Theocentric Phenomenalism and later assumed the form of Pantheism—'the doctrine that God is neither the world,

[1]Hence the relevance of Sydney Smith's quip, 'Bishop Berkeley destroyed this world in one volume octavo; and nothing remained, after his time, but mind; which experienced a similar fate from the hand of Mr Hume in 1739'.

nor separate from the world, but that the world is in him'. However, it is Wisdom's view that the solipsistic interpretation is not entirely arbitrary, but corresponds to a trend in Berkeley's own mind, which, although later submerged, was fairly explicit in his early *Philosophical Commentaries* (not intended for publication).

Wisdom is careful to avoid the error of regarding Berkeley's philosophy as a phenomenon isolated from the philosophical background of his age and so denying validity to 'explanations' conceived within the framework of the history of philosophy; but the framework within which his own 'explanation' is offered is strictly psychogenetic and psychoanalytical. Within this framework he accordingly suggests that a world governed by Berkeley's principle that '*esse* is *percipi*' is in no way distinguishable from a dream world; and he regards Berkeley's philosophy as representing essentially the embodiment of a phantasy. Berkeley's attack upon Matter, which later merged into an attack upon freethinkers, deists and mathematicians, is then interpreted as representing an attack upon a projected internal persecutor constituted (1) by faeces, and (2) at a deeper level, by milk from the bad breast. The '*esse* is *percipi*' principle thus resolves itself into an attempt to eliminate projected internal 'poison'. The accompanying substitution of God for Matter as the source of perceptions is then interpreted as an attempt on Berkeley's part to replace the dangerous poison by something good, and at the same time to alleviate his guilt over poisoning the outer world by the projection of his aggressive faeces.

The fact that, as Berkeley passed middle age, his enthusiasm for the immaterialist 'New Principle' as a key to the problems of life came to be subordinated to an almost fanatical belief in the medical virtues of tar-water is interpreted by Wisdom in the sense that the locus of the dreaded poison had shifted from the external to the internal world; and to this development he relates the chronic ill-health from which Berkeley began to suffer after the shipwreck of his cherished project to establish a college in Bermuda for the education of the New World. The shipwreck of this project, due largely to the political chicanery of Walpole (then Prime Minister) in refusing to implement a grant in aid of the scheme voted by the House of Commons, created in Berkeley a profound sense of disappointment, and, in Wisdom's opinion, had the effect of disillusioning him regarding the efficacy of the 'New Principle' as a means of denying the external existence of poisonous Matter (now incarnated in the perfidious figure of Walpole). The deterioration in Berkeley's health following this disillusionment is interpreted by Wisdom as a reaction of a predominantly psychosomatic nature. How far this interpretation is justified is difficult to determine on the available historical evidence, which is to the effect that Berkeley suffered from 'cholic', 'a bloody flux' and 'hypochondria'. That Berkeley became increasingly preoccupied with his health in later life there can be no reasonable doubt; and the term 'hypochondria' may be interpreted in this sense, although it would be a mistake to read into this descriptive term the technical meaning imparted to it by modern psychopathology. As regards the 'cholic' and the 'bloody flux', there is one passage (p. 139) in which Wisdom ventures the diagnosis that Berkeley suffered from 'disorder in the urinary system and the bowel'. From a medical standpoint, however, it seems unlikely that he suffered from simultaneous disorders of the urinary and intestinal systems; and the most probable hypothesis is that the complaint from which he suffered was either colitis or urinary calculus. The former alternative is certainly compatible with the psychosomatic hypothesis; but, if he suffered from urinary calculus (and there are strong indications in favour of this alternative), it would be rash to attach a categorically psychosomatic label to his complaint. Whatever views may be held regarding the part played by psychosomatic factors in inducing the metabolic changes to which the formation of urinary calculi are ultimately due (e.g., through the medium of phosphaturia), such psychosomatic influences are very remote from the established condition, which once it has reached the stage of giving rise to renal colic, is inherently preoccupying. The fact remains, however, that Berkeley became progressively 'hypochondriac'; and the total syndrome of his ill-health is interpreted by Wisdom as predominantly psychosomatic—an interpretation which he makes the occasion for submitting a revised theory of psychosomatic disorder in general.

It is interesting to note that, whereas in a passage to which reference has already been made (p. 139) Wisdom diagnoses Berkeley's complaint as 'disorder in the urinary system and the bowel', in the chapter entitled 'A Theory of Psychosomatic Disorder' he reduces the diagnosis to 'a disorder of the intestinal tract' alone (p. 194); and one cannot help wondering how far this simplification of the issue is due to the influence of his theoretical view that 'faeces and food constitute the primary and typical bad objects of which others are only derivations' (p. 178). Be this as it may, the general form assumed by his theory of psychosomatic disorder may be gathered from the following concise statement: 'A purely psychological disorder is one in which the imagination conducts basic conflicts in terms of projective [viz. visual and auditory] images; a psychosomatic disorder is one in which the imagination conducts basic conflicts in terms of tactile or kinaesthetic sensations' [the term 'sensation' as used here being intended to include 'images' in the accepted sense] (p. 206). Involved in this formulation is the dubious assumption that, whereas tactile and kinaesthetic images can give rise directly to physiological changes in the bodily organs, visual and auditory images cannot. It is also argued that projective images fulfil a defensive function in virtue of their capacity to represent dangerous objects as at a distance from the body, and that the experience of tactile and kinaesthetic images represents a failure of this defence in so far as it implies that such objects are in contact with or inside the body. This theory, although interesting, bears such a striking resemblance to Berkeley's celebrated theory of vision (to the effect that visual perceptions function essentially as signs of potential tactile experience) that one cannot help wondering how far the author has here come under the influence of the subject of his study.

By contrast, Wisdom's view that faeces and food constitute 'the primary and typical bad objects' implies an emphasis on Matter which is the complete antithesis of Berkeley's immaterialism; and indeed, according to Wisdom, the unconscious aim of Berkeley's immaterialism was precisely to deny the existence of these bad objects. However, there are many psychoanalysts who, without endorsing an immaterialist philosophy, regard the primary objects of the infant, both good and bad, as constituted by his mother and her breast; and there are some at least who attach primary importance to the personal relationship of the infant to his mother. Readers who adopt such ways of thinking will doubtless be impressed by the paucity of reference to Berkeley's relationship with his mother—and indeed by the comparatively inconspicuous part which personal object-relationships in general appear to play in the author's basic conceptions.

However intrigued the reader may be by the ingenuities of the author's psychoanalytical study of Berkeley and his philosophy, there are certain questions about which he will remain as ignorant when he lays the book down as when he took it up; for, if he is curious to know by the agency of what mental processes a man beset by bad objects, now introjected and now projected, became (1) a philosopher at all, and (2) one of the greatest figures in the history of philosophy, his curiosity will remain unsatisfied. It may also be a disappointment to him to find that he has learned nothing about that strange alchemy of the mind whereby an Irish clergyman's preoccupation with faeces should have led him to anticipate Keynes's economic theories and Mach's criticism of Newton's mathematics by roughly three hundred years. These are all questions to which the author does not claim to have provided an answer; and indeed he expressly disclaims any attempt to have done so. But, unless the present study is to be regarded simply as representing the analysis of another psychoneurotic, these are the interesting questions. Similar considerations apply, of course, to Freud's (1910b) study of Leonardo da Vinci, which, however intriguing, throws no light (as indeed Freud himself was the first to point out) upon the questions (1) why Leonardo became an artist at all, (2) what made him one of the greatest of the great masters, and (3) what conferred upon his artistic creations that ineffable and individual quality by which they are distinguished. Psychoanalysis has thrown a flood of light upon psychopathology, no inconsiderable light upon the somewhat allied discipline of anthropology, some light upon the less closely allied discipline of sociology, but almost no light upon that most characteristic group of human achievements so appropriately described as 'the Humanities'. Does this perchance mean that, in its present phase at any rate, psychoanalysis is better qualified to throw light upon the negative than upon the positive aspects of human nature?

28. THE TECHNIQUE OF PSYCHOANALYSIS

The Technique of Psycho-Analysis. By Edward Glover. London: Baillière, Tindall and Cox. 1955. Pp. x + 404.

This volume, like Caesar's Gaul, is divided into three parts. Part One consists in an expanded version of the book published by the author in 1928 under the same title as the present volume and comprising six lectures delivered as a training course at the London Clinic of Psycho-Analysis in the days before systematic instruction in psychoanalytical technique had been initiated. The original book was published at a time when Freud's ego-psychology had only comparatively recently been formulated and his concepts of the superego and the id were still novel; and, in view of the considerable developments which psychoanalytical theory has undergone since that date, the author has had to consider how far the general outline of the original book could be preserved. In deciding to preserve it, he has been influenced by the consideration that, whatever complications may have been introduced into the technique of interpretation by theoretical developments, the 'analytical situation' as such and the phenomena of 'transference' continue to be governed by a few simple laws. He has also been influenced by the consideration that the practical difficulties experienced by students of psychoanalysis remain more or less constant. Part Two comprises an analysis of the results of a questionnaire concerning the details of psychoanalytical technique completed by twenty-four practising British psychoanalysts in 1938. The results of this research were originally published in 1940 under the title, *An investigation of the Technique of Psycho-Analysis;* and they may be regarded as providing a representative picture of the practice of members of the British Psycho-Analytical Society at the date of the Questionnaire. Part Three contains three papers of varying dates, each of which has already appeared in *The International Journal of Psycho-Analysis;* and each represents a contribution towards an attempt to determine what is and what is not to be regarded as psychoanalytical treatment in the strict sense.

The book as it stands represents the most systematic and comprehensive study of the technique of psychoanalysis known to the reviewer; and, if the disquisition in Part One may appear to the reader somewhat *ex cathedra*, it must be remembered that this part originated as a lecture course for students of psychoanalysis seeking authoritative guidance in a field beset with difficulties. The reader can hardly fail to be impressed by the complexity of the problems which confront the psychoanalyst, and by the high standard of knowledge, training, judgement and skill required of him. However, Dr Glover takes pains to discourage any tendency to regard psychoanalysis as an esoteric cult, and to disillusion such as may be inclined to accept the myth of the psychoanalytical superman. As he makes clear, the psychoanalyst is merely an ordinary human being who, through his own analysis, has acquired an unusual degree of insight into the nature of unconscious mental processes and has achieved an appreciable mitigation of his own inner conflicts. In his view, any extravagant claims for the superiority of the analysed person were administered a *coup de grâce*, once and for all, by Freud's discovery of the id as an integral part of human nature; and he deprecates any inclination on the part of the analyst to identify himself with 'the all-powerful parent who knows everything and does no wrong'. He likewise makes it plain that, whilst the analyst must necessarily be dispassionate in his approach to his patient's problems and avoid the pitfalls of the counter-transference, he must never fail to maintain a human approach. Considerable space is naturally devoted to problems of interpretation, this being the main therapeutic instrument of the practising analyst; and emphasis is laid on the general principle that 'interpretation of unconscious phantasy must as a rule be timed to take effect when the defensive systems have been really weakened' (p. 65).

The problem considered in Part Three, viz. that of differentiating psychoanalytical therapy proper from other forms of psychotherapy, obviously makes a special appeal to Dr Glover. Among the criteria of psychoanalysis to which he attaches special importance are (1) integrity and non-tendentiousness of interpretation, and (2) the maintenance of an attitude of detachment or neutrality on the part of the analyst. He also considers it as distinctive of psychoanalytical treatment that it aims not so much at strengthening ego-defences as at penetrating them with a view to unmasking unconscious processes which distort 'normal ego-defences', and that, in pursuing this aim, it abjures both suggestion and any unchecked exploitation of rapport. He further claims that any interpretative technique which is not based upon unreserved recognition of such fundamental Freudian concepts as repression and infantile sexuality culminating in the Oedipus situation forfeits all claim to be called psychoanalysis, and that the same applies to any form of psychotherapy which dispenses with analysis of the transference.

According to Dr Glover any therapeutic effects produced by 'inexact interpretation' must be regarded as dependent upon suggestion; and, indeed, he appears to regard suggestion as a form of therapy based upon an exploitation of inexact interpretation. It may well be asked, however, how far the effects even of 'exact' interpretation can be regarded as wholly independent of the authority and the general attitude of the analyst; and such a query is all the more justified in view of the fact, revealed by the results of the Questionnaire, that, whilst 'a number of orientated and practising analysts holding to the fundamental principles of psychoanalysis varied in their methods in every imaginable way', the therapeutic results obtained appeared to be 'much the same' (p. 373). This remarkable finding is perhaps less remarkable than a conclusion registered by Dr Glover regarding the perplexing problem of the length of psychoanalytical treatment, viz. 'that the earlier analysts were accustomed to conduct analysis of six to twelve months' duration which as far as I can find out did not differ greatly in ultimate result from the results claimed at the present day by analysts who spin out their analyses to four or five years' (p. 383). This conclusion may well give rise to some heart-searchings. The obvious doubt which it raises in the critical mind is whether what the earlier analysts did and what contemporary analysts do are really the same thing. This is a question which it is difficult to answer on the basis of available data, owing to what Dr Glover describes as 'the curtain of uncommunicativeness behind which psychoanalysts are only too prone to conceal their technical anxieties, inferiorities and guilts' (p. vii); and it should be noted that Freud himself provided comparatively little information regarding the technical details of his handling of patients. However, it is difficult to see how this question can be satisfactorily answered until more light is thrown upon the more basic question how psychoanalytical treatment produces its effects. The view current in the earlier days of psychoanalysis was that the therapeutic effects of analysis were produced by the dissolution of more or less localized 'complexes' combined with abreaction of the affects bound in these complexes; but this was in the days before Freud's ego-psychology had been formulated. The view most widely held in contemporary psychoanalytical circles and endorsed by Dr Glover himself is that the therapeutic effects of analysis depend upon (1) modifications of ego-defences such as to enable the ego to develop more satisfactory methods of dealing with id impulses (the id itself being, of course, by hypothesis incapable of modification), and (2) modifications of the superego such as to render it less primitive and less exacting in its demands upon the ego. However, among those influenced by Kleinian thought there is a tendency to attach therapeutic importance to the introjection of the analyst as a good object. The importance of this factor is regarded by Dr Glover as having been exaggerated. He is, of course, well known to be unsympathetic towards the Kleinian school; but he himself describes 'the humane relation of the transference' (p. 370) as a factor in the therapeutic process, and makes himself responsible for the suggestion that 'in the deeper pathological states a prerequisite of the efficiency of interpretation is the *attitude*, the true unconscious attitude of the analyst to his patients' (p. 372). All this suggests that the analyst does not merely fulfil the dual functions of a screen upon which the patient projects his phantasies and a colourless instrument of interpretative technique, but that his personality and his motives make a significant contribution to the therapeutic process. Dr Glover himself says in one place, 'It is obvious that many people cure themselves through their unconscious human contacts' (p. 372); and the question therefore arises whether the actual relationship between the patient and the analyst in the analytical situation is not the decisive therapeutic factor. If this be so, it may partly explain not only why analysts using varying methods obtain similar results, but also why the results obtained nowadays in analyses lasting four or five years are no better than those obtained in analyses of six to twelve months by the earlier analysts. For it may well be that the attitude of the contemporary analyst, steeped as he is in ego-psychology and impressed as he cannot fail to be by the inherent difficulties of effecting a lasting alteration in mental structure, makes a less therapeutic impact upon the patient than the more naïf attitude of the earlier analyst who regarded his task as comparatively simple and really believed that psychoanalysis provided an answer to all human ills. At any rate, it would appear an urgent demand that Dr Glover's masterly study of the technique of psychoanalysis should be supplemented by some more profound research than has hitherto appeared into the fundamental problem how psychoanalysis really works.

29. THREE LETTERS

A. LETTER UNDATED 1942 TO DR MARJORIE BRIERLEY

Letter undated, which is part of a correspondence with Marjorie Brierley on the subject of his theoretical change from an 'instinct'-based account of psychical development to one of 'object-relationships'. The exchange of letters took place in 1942, against the background of the 'Freud–Klein Controversies' in the British Psycho-Analytic Society. This letter is also a reply to Brierley's paper entitled 'Some Observations on the Concept-Internal Object' *read before the British Psycho-Analytic Society on 18 February 1942. Brierley's paper was published later (see refs: Brierley (1942) for details). In this she quotes WRDF's paper* 'A Revised Psychopathology of the Psychoses and Psychoneuroses' *(1941) published in* International Journal of Psycho-Analysis *22(3, 4):250–*279 *(see also Psychoanalytic Studies of the Personality, pp. 28–58).*

Dear Dr Brierley,

Thank you so much for your letter of 6th March, and for the copy of your paper. It is good of you to say that I may keep the latter; and I shall be very glad to do so. I may say that I very much appreciate your letting me have a copy. I should have acknowledged receipt sooner if your letter had not been delayed en route owing to its being treated as Departmental Correspondence and delivered at the Ministry of Labour Office on the other side of the Crescent. In spite of this contretemps, it has now arrived safely.

So far I have only had time to glance over your paper rather hurriedly. I am, therefore, hardly in a position to embark upon any detailed apologia on behalf of my particular method of gold-mining, although I should like to find time to do so later. At the same time I cannot refrain from recording the opinion that I have struck rather a rich seam; and I am afraid I feel quite unrepentant, although I admit that I might have expressed my views rather differently if I had realised the extent to which the Society is now riven into "political" camps, each with a different scientific legend upon its banner. It was only after I had written the paper that Dr Glover initiated me into some of the mysteries of the Society's internal politics and so disturbed my innocence; and it is only since the era of Extraordinary Meetings was ushered in that the scales have finally fallen from my eyes and the present sordid scene has presented itself in all its nakedness to my somewhat bewildered gaze.

The point of view which I have developed is admittedly of Kleinian lineage, although privately I regard it as a definite advance beyond the Kleinian standpoint. I understand from Dr Glover, however, that the Klein group disclaim any paternity—or should I say "maternity"? I feel, therefore, somewhat of an orphan. Perhaps I have been disinherited as too independent-minded a child, whilst at the same time suffering from the disadvantage of my lineage in the eyes of those who look askance at it. At the same time, the last thing that I contemplated when I wrote the last paper was that I should be caught up in the maelstrom of any political struggles within the Society. That, of course, was just the inevitable, and I think pardonable, ignorance of a country bumpkin innocent of the wiles of the great Metropolis.

Be that as it may, I still cling obstinately to my "internalised objects", although I see now that I shall have to define what I meant by these monstrous forms. If I have not defined them already, this is not because I had been transported into fairyland in blissful ignorance that I had been bewitched. I have always thought that the Klein group ran the risk of being bewitched without knowing it; but I have always felt at the same time that it was their familiarity with fairyland that enabled them to make such an important contribution to our knowledge about that part of the mind (ordinarily unconscious) for which fairyland matters most. It did not occur to me that, in trying to add to the knowledge which they had acquired, I should be under any obligation to prove that I was not bewitched also. But then, as I have already said, I was unaware both of the extent to which sorcery had been introduced into the Society from the faery world by the Klein group, and of the extent to which the Vienna group had set their faces against traffic with fairyland. I have thus fallen between two stools—indeed between three, because I seem to have rather missed the boat so far as the Middle Group are concerned; and it is with the Middle Group that I should certainly align myself politically, if it is to become a question of politics. I remain quite unrepentant about my views, however, because I feel that they represent a genuine contribution. I still remain convinced of the paramount importance of object-relationships; and I feel that a failure to recognise their paramount importance has imposed a definite limitation upon psychoanalytic thought and practice in the past. So far as practice is concerned, I have found that, in several cases in which considerable progress had been made on a basis of interpretations in terms of instincts and gratification, but in which the analysis had begun to drag and show signs of inconclusiveness, the analysis acquired a completely new lease of life after I began to interpret in terms of object-relationships, and that it can only be adequately dealt with in the light of this problem. I feel that a lot of unnecessary resistance is provoked by a too exclusive insistence on gratification interpretations owing to a sense of injustice which they engender—and naturally engender, as I think. Not that interpretations in terms of object-relationships fail to stir resistances. There would be something wrong if that were so; but I find that by far the deepest and most profound resistances are revealed by such interpretations. The deepest resistances of all is, in my opinion, the resistance to the unmasking of bad internal objects. I think I have enough clinical material to prove that—and to prove that resistances based on guilt are trivial in comparison. It is no small measure to the consideration of resistance-phenomena that I trace the origin of my present views in retrospect.

I agree with you in some measure at least about the desirability of correlating the new with the old. This is, in my opinion, a task which the Klein group have never faced. What they have done, so far as I see it, is to adopt new views while retaining old views so far as these suited them without considering how far the two sets of views are compatible, the result has been a considerable amount of confused thought, even amounting at times (e.g., in some of Melanie Klein's sentences) to complete nonsense. In my paper I have tried to remedy this, even when it involved a considerable amount of scrapping of the old. Thus, in my opinion, the line of thought initiated by Melanie Klein is incompatible with the classic libido theory; and in the development which I have pursued my choice has lain with the former. There would also seem to be a considerable incompatibility between the Klein theory in its logical implications and any high estimation of instinct theories; and here again my choice has gone against instinct theories. In my exposition, however, I have tried to be systematic where the Kleinians tended to be muddle-headed.

Where I would tend to disagree with you about the correlation of the new with the old is in the fact that my views (and Kleinian views too) involve as complete a reorientation as was involved in the supersession of Ptolemaic astronomy by Copernican. In my opinion the view that the libido is essentially object-seeking and the view that it is essentially pleasure-seeking cannot be squared. It is the case of one or the other; and, if the former is adopted, all its implications must be accepted—and these implications are found to affect every aspect of psychoanalytic theory. They involve, for example, a knell of the "death-instinct". They also impose a severe limitation upon the value of instinct theories.

I have not much time to read nowadays; but, on dipping into Freud here and there since I wrote my paper, I have been struck by two facts—(1) how little I have said which is not implied, if it is not explicitly stated, in Freud's works, (2) how frequently Freud just misses the point owing to the influence of his original libido theory and his concept of instinct. In my opinion all that is valuable in his instinct theory (and for that matter in any instinct theory) is concentrated in that passage in the "Ego and the Id" where he says that the libido binds men together and the aggression drives men apart. If he had only gone a step further and said that it is the *function* of libido to bind men together and the *function* of aggression to drive men apart, his statement would have been complete. But the preconceptions of the libido theory made it impossible for him to take this extra step.

You well point out in your paper the dependence of the individual scientist's conceptions, so far as their actual form is concerned, upon the scientific background of his period. Freud's libido theory was formulated upon the basis of the 19th century conception of Matter and Energy—both constant in quantity constituting a Universe in which the ultimate state is one of complete equilibrium and a cessation of movement. This is also the basis upon which theories of instinct are characteristically founded. Modern physics has upset that apple-cart, of course, Matter and Energy are now regarded as convertible; and quantity has become meaningless except in terms of direction. In conformity with this general scientific reorientation, the original libido theory inevitably becomes old-fashioned; and, in order that it may be modernised, the conception of object-seeking (direction) must be introduced to replace that of gratification (seeking equilibrium).

I have become appalled by the length which this letter has assumed; and I just hope it will not prove too great a tax upon your patience. As I have written it in several spasms, its posting will be delayed beyond my original expectation, I fear. However, better late than never.

I hope that you have now recovered completely from your flu. I am just recovering from an attack of the same complaint.

As Gifford has been more or less continuously under snow since New Year's Day, I have not always had free access to my new home in the country;

but there are now a few signs of spring which encourage great hopes for the summer.

I hope the Extraordinary Meeting, which should be already over as I finish this letter, has passed off with reasonably satisfactory results for the Moderate Group to which, like you, I firmly adhere.

B. LETTER DATED 24 SEPTEMBER 1953 TO DR DENIS HILL

Letter dated 24 September 1953 in reply to one from Dr Denis Hill (dated 14 August, 1953, written from the Maudsley Hospital, London) in which he asks for WRDF's views on questions relating to a paper which he is preparing and which is entitled 'Interrelationships between Psychotherapy and the Physical Methods of Treatment in Psychiatry'.

Dear Dr Hill,

I must apologise for having taken so long to reply to your letter of 14th August, in which you ask for my views on 4 questions bearing on the theme of the "Interrelationship between Psychotherapy and the Physical Methods of Treatment in Psychiatry". The fact is that I was on holiday when your letter arrived, and that I have been very much occupied since my return with the preparation of a paper of my own in addition to routine work. This has left me with little time to consider the problems involved in your questions.

I am afraid I do not feel very qualified to express opinions on the subject of these questions, as I have little personal experience of the physical methods of treatment now employed in psychiatry. However, I shall endeavour to answer your questions briefly in the light of (1) my theoretical views and (2) my experience of patients who have been treated by physical methods and have come under my observation:

1. I should certainly regard psychoanalysis as impossible in the case of a patient undergoing pre-frontal leucotomy (a) because pre-frontal leucotomy interferes with the emotional expression which it is one of the aims of psychoanalysis to promote, and (b) because a case selected for pre-frontal leucotomy is unlikely to be a suitable case for psychoanalysis in any case. I also consider that psychoanalysis is incompatible with electronarcosis and insulin coma therapy because of the divergence existing between the aims of the latter physical methods and the aim of psychoanalysis: for one of the

main psychological functions of these physical methods is, as it seems to me, to enable the patient to submerge and repress the conflicts which it is the aim of psychoanalysis to bring into the open and help the patient to face and work through. As regards E.C.T., however, I consider it quite possible for psychoanalytic treatment to be conducted concurrently with it, since the convulsion induced by E.C.T. is a discharge phenomenon, and the discharge of libidinal and aggressive tension is included among the therapeutic aims of psychoanalysis. From the psychoanalytical standpoint, it would, of course, be preferable for the discharge to be affected through the weakening of psychological defences and for the discharge to be accompanied by insight into the nature of the forces discharged and the inner situations involved. But, on the other hand, a large proportion of cases selected for E.C.T. may be presumed to be cases in which the defences are particularly stubborn and resistant to psychoanalytical influence.

2. I consider that a history of pre-frontal leucotomy consitutes a contraindication to subsequent psychoanalysis owing to the impairment of the capacity for emotional expression produced by leucotomy, if for no other reason. Such impairment of the capacity for emotional expression is bound to have an adverse effect upon the prognosis for psychoanalytical treatment—one reason being that a patient who had been treated by these methods would be encouraged to expect a passive solution of his inner difficulties, viz. one effected through the intervention of an outside agency, and would thus be encouraged to seek an escape from the task of facing these difficulties on the basis of cooperative effort.

3. I regard pre-frontal leucotomy as having the effect of precluding genuine psychological adaptation owing to the impairment of the capacity for emotional expression which it produces. I also consider that the other forms of physical treatment [i.e., electronarcosis, insulin coma therapy and E.C.T.] compromise the capacity for psychological adaption in that, as indicated in my answer to question 2, they encourage the patient to expect a passive solution of his inner difficulties based on external intervention in the absence of cooperative effort.

4. It would be difficult to formulate my personal experience in such a manner as to illustrate my answer to the previous questions concisely—except perhaps for an observation about the effects of pre-frontal leucotomy. As regards this method of treatment, my experience is that the endopsychic situation prevailing in the leucotomised patient remains unaffected except in so far as emotional expression is concerned. Thus I have found that patients with delusions which have rendered them difficult to manage retain their

delusions in unmodified form after leucotomy. What is affected is their capacity to experience the emotions appropriate to their delusional systems and their capacity to act in accordance with these emotions. Thus a leucotomised patient whose previous behaviour has been violent under the influence of his delusion may give voice to his delusions in a completely detached manner, perhaps with an irrelevant smile. Such an attitude, when organically determined (as by leucotomy), seems to me to preclude the capacity to face the realities of internal conflict in the manner required in psychoanalytical treatment.

Hoping that my answers will prove of some interest and value to you in the preparation of your paper, and with kind regards,

I am,
Yours sincerely,
WRDF

C. LETTER DATED 27 JANUARY 1954 TO DR J. D. SUTHERLAND

Letter to Jock Sutherland dated 27th January 1954 relating to a manuscript by Macalpine and Hunter submitted for publication. The letter also refers to Macalpine and Hunter's work on the Schreber case (see also Memoirs of My Nervous Illness *by Daniel Schreber [1955]).*

My dear Jock,

Having been unable to shake off a most unpleasant cold which has been afflicting me for a week or two, I knocked off work yesterday to give myself a chance of getting over it; and, on the "ill wind" principle, this has had the advantage of enabling me to study the Macalpine/Hunter Ms. sooner and at greater leisure than would otherwise have been the case. I have also been able to read carefully their previous article on "The Schreber Case". The result is that I have been favourably impressed by both papers; and I certainly think you would be doing the right thing in accepting "Observations on the Psycho-analytic Theory of Psychosis, etc." for the Journal.

The argument in both papers is substantially the same; but whereas in the published paper it is worked out in relation to Freud's [1915a] study of Schreber, in the M.S. it is worked out in relation to Freud's [1923a] study of Christoph Haitzmann in "A Neurosis of Demoniacal Possession in the

Ronald Fairbairn, Jock Sutherland, and Winifred Rushforth, Edinburgh, 1960.

Seventeenth Century". You will perhaps recall that I made some reference to this case in my paper, "The Repression and the Return of Bad Objects"; and it was you who drew my attention to Freud's paper on the subject as one which would be of special interest to me—for which I owe you a debt. Macalpine and Hunter quote my paper in their M.S., as you will see, and they draw attention to the remarkable fact that my reference to this paper of Freud's is the only reference to it which they have been able to find in the whole of psychoanalytical literature. They also note the extraordinary fact that this paper should have been completely ignored by other analysts whereas Freud's study of the Schreber case, to which it is highly relevant, has become almost canonical (not their actual words, but what they imply). I think this illustrates the tendency of analysis in general to accept much of Freud's work quite uncritically; and one of the virtues of the M.S. paper is that it raises the question of the validity of certain of Freud's formulations—and, what is more, does so convincingly. The particular "doctrines" upon which they throw doubt are (1) the view that paranoia represents a specific defence against repressed homosexuality, and (2) the view that the explanatory principles which apply in the case of the psychoneuroses apply equally in the case of the psychoses. I consider that they succeed in substantiating their case on both issues by the evidence which they produce. Also their argument is clear, lucid, well presented, and well documented with references to psychoanalytical and anthropological literature.

Their argument (a) that it is arbitrary and misleading to regard the explanatory principles which have been applied with comparative success to the psychoneuroses as applying equally to the psychoses, and (b) that the attempt to explain the psychoses in the same terms as the psychoneuroses has held up understanding of the former, is of special interest to me, as I indicated in my last letter; for one of my main points in my "Revised Psychopathology" [1941] paper was that, whereas the psychoneuroses were the product of specific defences, schizophrenia and depression represented psychopathological disasters which the psychoneurotic defences were designed to avert. It is to be noted, however, that I interpreted paranoia as representing the operation of a specific defence, and therefore as falling into line with the psychoneuroses (as against the psychoses). What Macalpine and Hunter have to say about the Schreber Case falls into line with this view; for they show that Schreber's paranoid symptoms, upon which Freud concentrated his attention, were secondary to his main illness, which was schizophrenic, and that the homosexual issue involved in these symptoms was likewise secondary. Indeed what they say in this connection is substantially to the effect that the homosexual issue and the paranoid symptoms connected with it essentially represented a defence against what was involved in Schreber's schizophrenia.

Their central contention is that Schreber's and Haitzmann's psychoses were both characterised by (a) the irruption of pregenital, pre-Oedipus, non-sexual, essentially intestinal "procreation phantasies" into the field of the ego, and (b) a resulting uncertainty regarding maleness or femaleness on the part of the two men; and they quote Bleuler to the effect that these features are pathognomonic of schizophrenia. In my opinion they prove their point quite conclusively. The moral which they point is, of course, that it is hopeless to try to explain such phenomena in terms of the Oedipus situation and libidinal conceptions based upon it—which fits in with my main contentions in the "The Revised Psychopathology" [1941].

Another of their theses is that the irruption of such archaic phantasies manifests itself essentially in the somatic sphere, with resulting hypochondriacal tendencies; and they show convincingly how inadequate and unilluminating psychoanalytical conceptions of hypochondria have been up to date. They also draw back the veil; which has hitherto masked the psychopathological defeatism embodied in the conceptions of "actual neuroses" and "organ neuroses"—for which I think we may be grateful to them. They also raise the whole question of the significance of the psychosomatic factor, and the difference between conversion-phenomena and hypochondriacal delusions—a very important issue. These issues I find very interesting—especially since the difference between "fear of illness" and "conviction of illness" has formulated itself very vividly in my mind lately with reference to certain patients, and particularly P. It occurs to me that the difference between psychoneurotic and psychotic factors, which Macalpine and Hunter stress so much, has relevance to the negative therapeutic reaction which is so commonly found in hysterics. It may well be that this negative therapeutic reaction is due to the presence of a psychotic factor inaccessible to orthodox interpretations couched in terms of the Oedipus situation and allied libidinal conceptions. My views regarding the essential unity of hysterical dissociation and schizoid splitting are, of course, apposite here.

The chief weakness of the M.S. paper from my point of view is the lack of reference to internal object-relationships, but I do not consider this at all serious. Their view is that, whereas the psychoneurotic is concerned with *inter*-personal situations, the psychotic is concerned with *intra*-personal situations. They leave it at that; but in doing so, they leave open the question as to what is involved in "intra-personal" situations. This problem could, of course, be developed by some one else, if not by them, in terms of internal object-relations.

I hope that you will find these comments of some help in evaluating the paper. Personally I should strongly recommend publication of the paper in the Journal, as I consider it a most important contribution.

Yours ever,
R.F.

P.S. I shall let you have my review of Wisdom's book on Berkeley's philosophy in due course. I may say that I am not greatly impressed by it from a psychoanalytical standpoint.

R.F.

Father and sons at Fairbairn's house in Duddingston, 1959.

30. IMPRESSIONS OF THE 1929 INTERNATIONAL CONGRESS OF PSYCHO-ANALYSIS

The notes of Fairbairn's impressions of the 1929 International Congress of Psycho-Analysis included here are of historic interest. Within Fairbairn's subjective account of his personal introduction to the international psychoanalytical scene, he identifies the dominant issues for psychoanalysis in 1929.

It was at this Congress that Fairbairn met Ferenczi. At a Conference entitled "Ferenczi Rediscovered," held at the Institute of Psycho-Analysis in London in October 1993, the papers presented emphasised Ferenczi's move from a 'one person' psychology to a 'two person' psychology. Ferenczi's shift of focus included an awareness of the participatory nature of the mother–infant relationship and ideas of 'narcissistic splitting', with a potentially pathological outcome, resulting from infantile deprivation.

As we can see from Fairbairn's account, major topics of debate included the 'nature and aims' of psychoanalysis and the practical application of its 'method'. In general, Ferenczi saw the analytical relationship as an active one, implicitly questioning the idea of transference as a one-way phenomenon and introducing the issue of countertransference as an active phenomenon. Apparently Ferenczi also suggested that the psychoanalytical encounter in which the analyst maintains a strictly detached attitude might be potentially pathogenic. Fairbairn addresses all these issues in his later papers (1952a, 1957a and 1958a; Chapters 5, 3 and 4 in Volume I). In our view, it is significant that Fairbairn only addressed these methodological issues after his own reorientation of psychoanalysis was virtually completed (i.e., in 1952).

It was stated in a paper presented by Dr Tonnesmann (1993) that, in his lecture at the 1929 Congress, Ferenczi discussed inaccessible memories originating from a period 'before thought developed'. Dr Tonnesmann related this phenomenon to Winnicott's 'frozen memories'. Fairbairn himself (1930) addressed this absence of memories, which he describes as 'periods of silence' in this paper here entitled "Libido Theory Re-evaluated" (Chapter 3 of this volume) (see p. 144). Fairbairn returned to this issue in 1952a and 1958a (Volume I, Chapters 5 and 4). Other issues concerning the psychoanalytical encounter are also covered in Fairbairn 1957a (Volume I, Chapter 3).

Father and daughter on holiday in Angus, 1930.

IMPRESSION OF PSYCHOANALYSTS

Absence of Freud, his daughter Anna Freud was present. The leading figures:

Ferenczi (Budapest)
Jones (London)

The British Group:

- Edward Glover was intellectually the most impressive
- Interesting to note the presence of Leslie Stephen and Strachey
- About 26 members (of which 8 were women)
- About 31 associates (of which 12 were women)
- Attitude was distinctly Freudian
- Psychologists—Flugel and Susan Isaacs

Representatives from most European nations and USA:

- Mainly from German-speaking countries (Germany and pre-war Austria)
- Holland well represented
- Least Freudian among national groups—Holland and USA (most congenial)

- –France – several representatives. Only moderately Freudian. Princess Buonaparte
- –Enormous percentage of Jews (noticeable even in British group). What is cause of special appeal to Jews? (father complex; introverted race; persecution; Jews as doctors on continent)
- –Large percentage of women (increasing)
- –General impression – Psychoanalysts as a whole are well adjusted/ intelligent

IMPRESSIONS OF THE PSYCHO-ANALYTIC MOVEMENT

1. Psychoanalytic movement is now on a firmly established basis, for better or worse, with teaching centres in, e.g., Berlin, Vienna and London. In this way psychoanalysis has become a permanent factor in social organisation.

2. The Psychoanalytic movement has a markedly international character. This international character is even more marked than in the average scientific movement. Is the reason for this a result of the psychoanalytic view of complexes leading to nationalism and war?

3. The exclusive nature of psychoanalysis: here Fairbairn notes that Oxford is unaware of the Congress, that its deliberations are not reported in the press [this is against the accepted background of press reporting of psychological and other 'technical' lectures in Edinburgh].

4. Increasing number of lay analysts. The Psychoanalytic movement in general has accepted the principle of admitting lay-analysts to its fold, however, this principle has only been adopted after considerable discussion. The movement to admit lay analysts has arisen mainly as a result of two facts:

(1) The fundamental principle of analytic technique nowadays is that nothing must be done by analysts to complicate the transference phenomenon.

Transference must be the natural product of the patient's own reaction to the analytic situation. The analyst must remain absolutely detached, even formalities of social greetings and leave-taking dispensed with. Emotional reactions of analyst are to be reduced to minimum. Otherwise there is a risk of – (a) fixation on analyst, (b) increasing of resistance, on the part of the patient. This becomes the fundamental difference between analytic and suggestive therapy, where the latter exploits Transference.

The tendency of analysts to avoid physical examination of patients as a preliminary to treatment relies on the belief that such examinations are seen as likely to complicate the phenomenon of transference, by compromising the detached attitude to the patient cultivated by analysts.

Similarly, preliminary psychiatric examination of patients tends to be avoided. Such examination is held to satisfy the curiosity of analyst, and thus to create an emotional attitude to the patient. Analysts thus tend to refer cases for preliminary examination to neurologists and psychiatrists. This procedure thus reduces the necessity for the medical training of the analyst.

(2) Psychoanalysis is no longer restricted to the study of medical problems.

Psychoanalysis originated as a form of medical treatment, where the necessity of interpreting phenomena exhibited by patients led to construction of psychoanalytic theory. The development of psychoanalytic theory led to application of psychoanalytic principles to cultural problems—anthropology, art, myth and legend, etc. Cultivation of these fields led to the realisation that more was to be learned from them, than from strictly medical investigations, for interpretation of psychoneurotic and neurotic symptoms. This being so, it was argued that a general cultural training formed a better background for psychoanalytic practice than a medical training.

Fairbairn noted that the movement to admit lay analysts has had less support in Great Britain and USA than in other countries.

5. Increasing number of women analysts. Younger adherents were largely women.

6. Development of child analysis. This has developed in recent years. Recently child analysis has shown signs of becoming a definite branch of analysis, which appears to have been undertaken exclusively by women. The leaders are—Anna Freud (Berlin), and Melanie Klein (London).

These two schools conform to different principles:

1. Melanie Klein—the same principles are adhered to as in adult analysis; viz. the analyst does nothing which increases the transference. The technique is modified, however, to meet the capacities of child. As free association is impossible—Play technique is used.
2. Anna Freud—uses exploitation of the transference, where the transference of child to analyst is used to reinforce explanations made by the analyst.

The former technique is more approved by leading analysts.

7. The most important feature of the modern psychoanalytic movement is best approached by considering the question "What is a psychoanalysis?"

The aim of psychoanalytic theory is

1. To provide a rationale for psychoanalysis as method of treatment, and to enable analysts to understand what is happening in psychoanalytic treatment.

2. To provide indications for determining the direction of development of the psychoanalytic technique.
3. To provide an explanation of certain aspects of human behaviour—in terms of unconscious or endopsychic processes.

The aim of psychoanalytic practice has changed in recent years.

—Original historical aim—to rid patients of symptoms.
—Modern aim is hard to define—but is best described as "to produce a completely analysed person".

Old aim of ridding patient of symptoms is suspected [as]

—A concession to the primitive "pleasure principle"
—It implies that the analyst is himself ruled by the pleasure-principle, i.e., that he is unable to bear unpleasure in self or others (by identification)

Similarly the aim of "doing good" is suspected as

—It implies that the analyst is dealing with his own inner conflicts by projecting them on to patients and attempting to solve them in the person of his patients instead of by internal adjustment.
—It also implies in the analyst narcissistic fantasies of omnipotence.
—It implies that, instead of working out his own salvation, he is trying, substitutively, to save others.

Modern aim of psychoanalytic procedure is

—To produce "completely analysed person", i.e., a person who is completely aware of the motivation of all his acts.
—Motivation of whole behaviour must be accessible to consciousness.
—Consciousness, from biological point of view, is an adaptive mechanism.
—Consciousness leads to control.
—Consciousness leads to adaptation.

Complete consciousness of motives would thus lead to complete adaptation.

—It would make men "masters of their fate" and "captains of their souls". There is something morally impressive about this aim. It must be recognised, however, that "the completely analysed person" is not a "normal human being" but a Superman. We are reminded of the philosophic development, which is represented by Schopenhauer, von Hartmann and Nietzsche. It is interesting to note how both in this philosophical development and in the history of Psychoanalysis,

> the theory of the Unconscious has led to the doctrine of "The Superman".

Certain *limitations* characterise the modern psychoanalytic ideal:

1. Its impracticability. The psychoanalytical ideal does, however, impose limitations of a profound kind upon psychoanalytic *practice*—for there is no limit to plumbing of unconscious motivation.

a. If [the] ideal is to be approximated, it means that no psychoanalysis would ever be finished. Every psychoanalysis is necessarily incomplete. Lifelong analysis is impracticable [so a] compromise is necessary.

It has resulted in prolonging of the duration of psychoanalytic treatment. Psychoanalytic treatment of patients tends to last 2–3 years, while some analysts have themselves been analysed for 10 years. The most "completely analysed person" at the Conference was not the most attractive.

b. Psychoanalysis is necessarily limited to the few due to the time and expense involved in undergoing such treatment. Psychologically speaking, the restriction of psychoanalysis to the few can be seen as a necessary corollary of the idea of a 'Superman'.

The saving element in the situation is that psychoanalysts themselves are aware of the dangers of the "Superman Ideal". Leading analysts frequently stress that it is unanalytical for analysts to allow themselves to adapt an attitude of superiority to others on grounds of—(a) resolutions of their own conflicts; (b) Insight into the motivation of others.

2. It is a question whether unlimited contact with the primitive mind as revealed in analysis may not be detrimental to the higher mental processes. In certain forms of insanity, e.g., dementia praecox, we find a breaking through of the primitive mind, usually imprisoned in the unconscious, so that consciousness becomes dominated by what is ordinarily unconscious. The impression given by these patients is of something sub-human.

Another fact of interest is that the insane are often better interpreters of character and behaviour of asylum staff than the sane, e.g., comments of maniacs are the best source for home truths. The reason is that their own unconscious motivation is familiar; thus they are experts at interpreting unconscious motivation of others.

The question thus arises whether making available to consciousness the total sources of unconscious motivation may not have a deteriorating effect. The psychoanalytical ideal is to make available to consciousness, and so amenable to control, motivation which is unconscious and which operates in the form of compulsion (concealed rationalisation). This ideal is good as it leads to freedom of will.

It is obviously inadvisable that people's behaviour should be unduly influenced by motives which are unconscious and so operate compulsively.

On the other hand, we have to consider that there may be good as well as bad reasons for the Unconscious being unconscious. According to psychoanalytic theory, the Unconscious is unconscious on account of repression. An individual is unable to tolerate awareness of certain tendencies in self. On the other hand, it is recognised by psychoanalytic thought that culture depends upon the operation of repression. Repression is the sine qua non of sublimation.

The study of anthropology suggests that what constitutes the Freudian unconscious was largely conscious at one phase of human development, e.g., phallic symbolisation—e.g., phallic worship was probably once an overt cult. Phallic symbolisation now, in the normal individual, is unconscious.

If much that at one phase was conscious is now unconscious, perhaps the biological justification of the relegation of much mental life to unconsciousness is that it was incompatible with higher mental processes in process of development.

In so far as the unconscious tyrannises over human beings, it seems desirable to make unconscious motivation accessible to consciousness. But it seems possible for the unmasking of the unconscious to go too far. It seems possible for consciousness to become monopolized by processes ordinarily unconscious, with the result that characteristically conscious processes may become overwhelmed or suffer depreciation.

Prima facie, psychoanalytic thought sets so high a valuation on consciousness as an adaptive mechanism, that consciousness is believed capable of reaching an adjustment with regard to whatever unconscious processes are brought into consciousness.

There is a risk, however, of this impressive ideal defeating its own end. The risk is that instead of consciousness gaining control of unconscious processes, unconscious processes may come to depreciate consciousness.

It must, therefore, be recognised that there is a danger attached to the present phase of the psychoanalytic movement. I have no doubt that this danger will be recognised in time by psychoanalysts themselves. However, the danger of the "completely analysed person" has not been recognised.

It, therefore, seems relevant to insist upon the recognition of two facts, which are in danger of being lost sight of:

1. It is possible to be over-analysed. The completely analysed person is a Superman. It seems as if psychoanalysis will have to be content *not* to aim at producing Supermen, *but* at removing the disabilities of those whose domination by the unconscious assumes pathological form. The object must be to render those, whose social efficiency is impaired as a result of compulsive motivation from the Unconscious, capable of playing the part in social life which is characteristic of the normal individual.

2. While theoretically it may be unjustifiable to make relief of symptoms the aim of psychoanalysis, after all that is what the psychoanalyst is paid for doing by his patients. Relief of symptoms may not be best effected, if that is made the aim of treatment. It is often easy to relieve symptoms; but what is wanted is removal of the cause of symptoms. At the same time, it seems unjustifiable to ask a patient to pay to become a fully analysed person, once the cause of actual disability is removed.

8. Tendency of psychoanalysis to become a cult (religious). This is shown in several ways:

1. Freud's "ipse dixit".
2. Secrecy—lack of advertising.
3. Lack of controversy on fundamental "doctrines".
4. Membership of Psycho-Analytic Association [where] Analysis is a sine qua non of membership—i.e., "Initiation".
5. Analogy between process of analysis and 'conversion', where the process leads from the old life of subjection to the tyranny of the Unconscious to the new life of freedom and control—i.e., "salvation"—where the "completely analysed person" is the saved person.

31. AUTOBIOGRAPHICAL NOTE

I was born in Edinburgh on 11 August 1889; and I have lived in Edinburgh for most of my life, although from 1941 to 1957 my home was at Gifford in East Lothian. It will be noted that I was born during the reign of Queen Victoria; and I have retained considerable affection for the Victorian régime, which has been subsequently so much maligned, and, as I think, misrepresented. I had no objection to going to church on Sunday mornings; but I disliked Sunday afternoons when ordinary activities were suspended and there seemed to be nothing to do. During the Victorian period I was accustomed to see working class children going about in the streets in bare feet—which was not so good: but life in the streets was much more interesting then than it is now. For example, there were German bands, barrel-organs, one-man bands, performing bears and Punch and Judy. Vehicles were all horse-drawn, of course; and there was the periodical excitement of seeing horse-drawn fire-engines dashing along the street with the horses galloping and smoke and flames bellowing forth from the chimney of the fire-engine—an impressive sight.

My early education was obtained at Merchiston Castle School, Edinburgh. I started in the lowest class in the Preparatory School and ended in the top class of the Upper School. So Merchiston Castle was my only school. After leaving school I went to Edinburgh University, where I took the degree of M.A. with Honours in Philosophy in 1911. My original intention had been to become a lawyer; but my study of philosophy had the effect of imbuing me with more idealistic notions. The result was that I devoted the next three years to the study of Divinity and Hellenistic Greek. During this period I studied not only in Edinburgh, but in the Universities of Kiel, Strasbourg and Manchester. Then came the First World War, during which I served as a Territorial in the Royal Garrison Artillery. To begin with, I was stationed on the Forth defences; but, after volunteering for service overseas, I served in Egypt and Palestine under General Allenby. During the Palestinian campaign I took part in the capture of Jerusalem; and I actually spent Christmas Day,

Me and my dog: Ronald Fairbairn, 1891.

1917, in Jerusalem, where my battery had a gun-position at the time. During the course of the war, I decided to go in for medicine with a view to specializing in psychotherapy; and after demobilization I entered the Medical Faculty at Edinburgh University. After a somewhat abbreviated course I obtained the degree of M.B.Ch.B. in 1923; and in 1929 I obtained the qualification of M.D. I also obtained the Diploma in Psychiatry at Edinburgh University.

After obtaining my medical qualification I was Assistant Physician at the Royal Edinburgh Hospital for Mental Diseases from 1923 to 1924. Thereafter I began psychoanalytical practice in private; but I combined this practice with various appointments. Thus from 1926 to 1931 I was Assistant Physician at the Longmore Hospital, Edinburgh; and from 1927 to 1935 I was Lecturer in Psychology at Edinburgh University. I was also Lecturer in Psychiatry from 1931 to 1932. At the same time I was Medical Psychologist at Jordanburn Nerve Hospital, Edinburgh, and at the Edinburgh University

Ronald and Marion at home, 1949.

Psychological Clinic for Children from 1927 to 1935. During the Second World War I was Visiting Psychiatrist at Carstairs E.M.S. Hospital from 1940 to 1941. Thereafter I became Consultant Psychiatrist to the Ministry of Pensions—a post which I held until 1954. During all this time and subsequently, I continued psychoanalytical practice in private. Two years ago I virtually retired; but I still have a few old patients under analysis.

I am not quite sure exactly when I was elected to Associate Membership of the British Psycho-Analytical Society; but I think it was in 1931. A few years later I was elected to full Membership.

The Autobiographical Note published here was written by Fairbairn for inclusion in a special issue of *The British Journal of Medical Psychology* (1963, vol. 36:(2)) in honour of Ronald Fairbairn and his work. This issue included contributions by J. D. Sutherland, Otto Kernberg, H. V. Dicks, R. E. D. Markillie, Jessie Sym, J. O. Wisdom, H. Guntrip and J. F. Pave.

References

Allen, Lord R. C. (1936). Of mental hygiene and international relations. *The Liverpool Quarterly* 4(1):105–111.

Aristotle. (1931). *Metaphysics* XII, 3. In *Philosophies of Beauty,* ed. E. F. Carritt. Oxford: Oxford University Press.

_____ (1988). *Politics* trans. B. Jowett, ed. S. Everson. Cambridge: Cambridge University Press, Cambridge Texts in the History of Philosophy.

_____ (1993). *Poetics,* trans. G. Else. Ann Arbor: University of Michigan. (1981). trans. D. W. Lucas. Oxford: Oxford University Press.

Baumgarten, F. (1750). *Aesthetics,* §14. In *Philosophies of Beauty*, ed. E. F. Carritt, p. 48. Oxford: Oxford University Press.

Beatty, D. C., Champ, C. J., and Swyer, G. I. M. (1953). A case of male pseudohermaphroditism. *British Medical Journal,* June 20, p. 1369.

Berry, R. J. S. (1928). Mental abnormality. *British Medical Journal,* January 14, pp. 46–47.

Blacker C. P. (1929). Life and death instincts. *The British Journal of Medical Psychology* 9 (4):277–302.

Bowlby, J. (1958). The nature of the child's tie to his mother. *International Journal of Psycho-Analysis* 39:350–378.

Breton, A. (1924). Manifeste du Surréalisme. *La Revolution Surrealiste.* 1st edition.

_____ (1929). Second manifesto. *La Revolution Surréaliste,* December 15.

_____ (1936a) *What is surrealism?* London: Faber & Faber.

_____ (1936b). Limits not frontiers of surrealism. In *Surrealism*, ed. H. Read, pp. 93–116. London: Faber & Faber.

Breuer, J., and Freud, S. (1893). On the psychical mechanism of hysterical phenomena. *Collected Papers* 1:24–41. New York: Basic Books. See also *Standard Edition* 2:1–17.

_____ (1895). Studies on hysteria. *Standard Edition* 2:300–305.

Brierley, M. (1942) Some observations on the concept—internal object. Paper presented at the meeting of the British Psycho-Analytic Society, London February 18, 1942. *International Journal of Psycho-Analysis* 23:107–112.

Caird, E. (1901). *Hegel.* Edinburgh: Blackwood.

Cannon, W. B. (1915). *Bodily Changes in Fear, Hunger and Rage: An Account into Recent Researches into Emotional Excitement.* New York: Appleton.

Carritt, E. F., ed. (1931). *Philosophies of Beauty.* Oxford: Oxford University Press.

Chesterton, G. K. (1874-1936). "The White Horses". (essay). (Possibly published in *Chesterton Calendar* (1911). London: Kegan Paul.)

Croce, B. (1931). A breviary of aesthetics. In *Philosophies of Beauty,* ed. E. F. Carritt. Oxford: Oxford University Press.

Dali, S. (1935). *La Conquête de l'Irrationnel.* Paris: Editions Surréalistes.

Dickson, A., ed. (1985). *The Pelican Freud Library Volume 14: Art and Literature.* Freud (1910) *Leonardo da Vinci and a Memory of his childhood.* Harmondsworth: Penguin Books.

Drever, J. (1917). *Instinct in Man.* 2nd ed (1921) Cambridge: Cambridge University Press.

_____ (1921). *The Psychology of Everyday Life.* London: Methuen.

_____ (1922). *An Introduction to the Psychology of Education.* London: Edward Arnold & Co.

Fairbairn W. R. D. (1928). "The Ego and the Id." Unpublished paper for University Discussion Class: November 2, 1928.

_____ (1929a). The relationship between dissociation and repression: Considered from the point of view of medical psychology. M.D. thesis submitted to Edinburgh University, March 30, 1929. [First published in *From Instinct to Self, Volume II: Early contributions and papers on applied psychoanalysis.* Northvale, NJ: Jason Aronson (1994)].

_____ (1929b). Fundamental principles of psychoanalysis. *Edinburgh Medical Journal,* June 1929, pp. 329–345.

_____ (1931). Features in the analysis of a patient with a physical genital abnormality. Reprinted in *Psycho-Analytic Studies of the Personality* (1952b), pp. 197–222. London: Tavistock Publications, Ltd., with Routledge, Kegan Paul.

_____ (1932a). Obituary—George Matthew Robertson MD, LLD, FRCPE, Hon. FRCSE. *Edinburgh Medical Journal* 39(6):397–403.

_____ (1941). A revised psychopathology of the psychoses and psychoneuroses. *International Journal of Psycho-Analysis* 22(2, 3):250–279. Reprinted in *Psycho-Analytic Studies of the Personality* (1952b), pp. 28–58.

_____ (1943a). The war neuroses: Their nature and significance. *British Medical Journal,* 1 (February 13): 183–186. Reprinted in *Psycho-Analytic Studies of the Personality* (1952b), pp. 256–288.

_____ (1943b). The repression and return of bad objects (with special reference to the war neuroses). *The British Journal of Medical Psychology* 29(3, 4): 327–341. Reprinted in *Psycho-Analytic Studies of the Personality* (1952b), pp. 59–81.

_____ (1943c) Phantasy and internal objects [originally untitled]. Paper presented by Dr. E. Glover in W. R. D. Fairbairn's absence, February 17, 1943, at the meeting of the British Psycho-Analytic Society, London. In *The Freud-Klein Controversies 1941–1945* pp 358–360. eds. P. King and R. Steiner. London: Routledge, Chapman, Hall, and Institute of Psycho-Analysis.

_____ (1944). Endopsychic structure considered in terms of object-relationships. *International Journal of Psycho-Analysis* 27(1, 2):70–93. Reprinted in *Psycho-Analytic Studies of the Personality* (1952b), pp. 82–136.

_____ (1946). Object relations and dynamic structure. *International Journal of Psycho-Analysis* 27(1, 2):30–37. Reprinted in *Psycho-Analytic Studies of the Personality* (1952b), pp. 137–151.

_____ (1949). Steps in the development of an object-relations theory of the personality. *The British Journal of Medical Psychology* 22(1, 2):26–31. Reprinted in *Psycho-Analytic Studies of the Personality* (1952b), pp. 152–161.

_____ (1951a). A synopsis of the development of the author's view regarding the structure of the personality. Reprinted in *Psycho-Analytic Studies of the Personality* (1952b), pp. 162–179.

_____ (1951b). Critical notice on "On Not Being Able To Paint." *The British Journal of Medical Psychology* 24(1):69–76.

_____ (1952a). Theoretical and experimental aspects of psycho-analysis. *British Journal of Medical Psychology* 25(2, 3):122–127.

_____ (1952b). *Psycho-Analytic Studies of the Personality.* London: Tavistock Publications, Ltd., with Routledge, Kegan Paul.

_____ (1954a). Observations on the nature of hysterical states. *British Journal of Medical Psychology* 27(3):106–125. Reprinted in *From Instinct to Self,* vol. I. Northvale, NJ: Jason Aronson.

_____ (1954b). Critical notice on "The Unconscious Origins of Berkeley's Philosophy" by John Oulton Wisdom. *British Journal of Medical Psychology* 27(4):253–256.

_____ (1956a). Critical notice on *The Technique of Psychoanalysis* by Edward Glover. *British Journal of Psychology* 47(1):65–66.

_____ (1956b). A critical evaluation of certain basic psycho-analytical conceptions. *British Journal of the Philosophy of Science* 7(25):49–60. Reprinted in *From Instinct to Self,* vol. I. Northvale, NJ: Jason Aronson.

_____ (1957). Freud, the psycho-analytical method and mental health. *The British Journal of Medical Psychology* 30(2):53–61. Reprinted in *From Instinct to Self,* vol. I. Northvale, NJ: Jason Aronson.

_____ (1958). On the nature and aims of psychoanalytical treatment. *International Journal of Psycho-Analysis* 39(5):374–385. Reprinted in *From Instinct to Self,* vol. I. Northvale, NJ: Jason Aronson.

_____ (1963) "Synopsis of an Object Relations Theory of the Personality" *International Journal of Psycho-Analysis* 44:224–225.

Field, J. (Milner, M.). (1934). *A Life of One's Own.* London: Chatto & Windus.

_____ (1937). *An Experiment in Leisure.* London: Chatto & Windus.

_____ (1950). *On Not Being Able to Paint.* London: Heinemann.

Fleming, J. A. *Report of the Departmental Committee on Sexual Offences Against Children and Young Persons in Scotland.* (1926). Scottish Office, HMSO: Command Paper Refs. no. 6 MD 2592.

Freud, S. (1893a). "Charcot." *Collected Papers* 1:9–23.

_____ in collaboration with Breuer, J. (1893b). On the psychical mechanism of hysterical phenomena. *Collected Papers* 1:33. (Same material as Breuer & Freud, 1893).

_____ (1893c). Some points in a comparative study of organic and hysterical paralysis. *Collected Papers* 1:42–58.

_____ (1894). The defence neuro-psychoses. *Collected Papers* 1:59–75.
_____ (1896a). The aetiology of hysteria. *Collected Papers* 1:183–219.
_____ (1896b). Further remarks on the defence neuro-psychoses. *Collected Papers* 1: 155–182.
_____ (1898). The psychical mechanism of forgetting. *Standard Edition* 3:287–297.
_____ (1900). *The Interpretation of Dreams,* trans. A. A. Brill. Revised Ed. 1915. London: Allen and Unwin. New York: Macmillan.
_____ (1901). *The Psychopathology of Everyday Life,* trans. A. A. Brill. London: Fisher Unwin. New York: Macmillan. See also *Standard Edition* 6:1.
_____ (1904). Freud's psycho-analytic method. *Collected Papers* 1:265–271.
_____ (1905a). *Three Essays on the Theory of Sex. Standard Edition* 7:135–245.
_____ (1905b). My views on the part played by sexuality in the aetiology of the neuroses. *Collected Papers* 1:272–283.
_____ (1905c). *Three Contributions to the Theory of Sexuality,* trans. A. A. Brill (with introduction by J. J. Putnam). In Nervous & Mental Disease Monograph series No 7. (1925): New York: Nervous and Mental Disease Publishing Co.
_____ (1907). *Delusions and dreams in Jensen's Gradiva* (See also Freud 1917b.) *Standard Edition* 9:1–95.
_____ (1910a).Psychogenic visual disturbance according to psycho-analytical conceptions. *Collected Papers* 2:105–112.
_____ (1910b). Leonardo da Vinci and a memory of his childhood. *Standard Edition* 2:57–137.
_____ (1911). Formulations regarding the two principles in mental functioning. *Collected Papers* 4:13–21.
_____ (1912). Types of neurotic nosogenesis. *Collected Papers* 2:113–121.
_____ (1914a). On narcissism: An introduction. *Collected Papers* 4:30–59.
_____ (1914b). On the history of the psycho-analytic movement. *Collected Papers* 1:287–359.
_____ (1914c). The Moses of Michelangelo. *Standard Edition* 13:209–236.
_____ (1915a). A case of paranoia running counter to the psycho-analytical theory of the disease. *Collected Papers* 2:150–161.
_____ (1915b). Instincts and their vicissitudes. *Standard Edition* 14:109–140.
_____ (1915c). Repression. *Collected Papers* 4:84–97.
_____ (1915d). Some character-types met with in psycho-analytic work. *Collected Papers* 4:113–121.
_____ (1915e). The unconscious. *Collected Papers* 4:98–136.
_____ (1916–1917). *Introductory Lectures on Psychoanalysis*, books I, II and III. *Standard Edition* 15, 16.
_____ (1917a) Mourning and melancholia. *Collected Papers* (1924) 4:152–170.
_____ (1917b) Delusions and dreams in Jensen's *Gradiva*: New York: Moffat, Yard, trans. H. M. Downey. (This edition includes a translation of Jensen's *Gradiva. Standard Edition* 9:1–95 does *not* include Jensen's story.)
_____ (1922). *Beyond the Pleasure Principle*, trans. C. J. M. Hubback. London & Vienna: International Psycho-Analytic Press.
_____ (1923a). A neurosis of demoniacal possession in the seventeenth century. *Collected Papers* 4:436–472.

_____ (1923b). *The Ego and the Id,* trans. J. Riviere, (1927). London: Hogarth Press and the Institute of Psycho-Analysis.

_____ (1924). *Collected Papers* vol. I. London: Hogarth Press.

_____ (1927) The Future of an Illusion. *Standard Edition* 21:1–56.

_____ (1930). *Civilization and Its Discontents,* trans. J. Riviere. London: Hogarth Press and Institute of Psycho-Analysis. New York: Cape & Smith. See also *Standard Edition* 21.

Fuller, P. (1988). *Art and Psychoanalysis.* London: Hogarth.

Gascoyne, D. (1936). *A Short Survey of Surrealism.* London: Cobden-Sanderson.

Glover, E. (1955). *The Technique of Psycho-Analysis.* London: Bailliere, Tindall & Cox.

Glover, J. (1926). The conception of the ego. *International Journal of Psycho-Analysis* 7(3, 4):414–419.

Goethe, J. W. (1840). *Theory of Colours.* London: John Murray. Reprinted Cambridge, MA. and London: MIT paperback, 1970.

Hall, G. S. (1904). *Adolescence, Volumes 1 & 2.* New York: Appleton.

Hart, B. (1926). The conception of dissociation. *British Journal of Medical Psychology* 6(4):241–263.

_____ (1927). *Psychopathology.* Cambridge, England: Cambridge University Press.

Head, H. (1926). *Aphasia and Kindred Disorders,* vols. 1 and 2. Cambridge: Cambridge University Press.

Healy, W., Bronner, A. F., and Bowers, A. M. (1930). *The Structure and Meaning of Psycho-Analysis.* New York: Knopf.

Herbart, J. F. (1816). *Text Book of Psychology,* trans. M. K. Smith. New York: Appleton.

Hitler, A. (1934). *Mein Kampf.* London: Gollancz.

Hobbes, T. (1651). *The Great Leviathan,* ed. C. B. Macpherson (1982). Harmondsworth: Penguin Books.

Isaacs, S. (1943). The Nature and Function of Phantasy. In *The Freud-Klein Controversies 1941–45 (1991),* eds. P. King and R. Steiner. London: Routledge, Chapman, Hall, and the Institute of Psycho-Analysis.

James, W. (1891). *Principles of Psychology. Vol 1.* London: Macmillan. Cambridge: Harvard University Press.

Janet, P. (1907). *The Major Symptoms of Hysteria.* London and New York: Macmillan.

_____ (1911). *L'Etat des Mental Hysteriques.* Paris: Rueff et Cie.

Jones, E. (1926). The origin and structure of the super-ego. *International Journal of Psycho-Analysis* 7:303–311.

_____ (1929). The psychopathology of anxiety. *British Journal of Medical Psychology* 9(1):17–25.

Jung, C. (1917). *Collected Papers on Analytical Psychology,* trans. C. E. Long, 2nd. ed., p. 288. London: Bailliere, Tindall & Cox.

_____ (1923). Psychological Types. In *Collected Works,* vol. 6.

_____ (1928). *Two Essays on Analytical Psychology.* London: Baillière, Tindall & Cox.

Kant, I. (1781). *The Critique of Pure Reason,* trans. J. M. D. Meiklejohn. London: Bell, 1924.

King, P. (1991). Introduction. In *The Freud–Klein Controversies 1941–45,* eds. P. King and R. Steiner. London: Routledge, Chapman, Hall, and the Institute of Psycho-Analysis.

King, P., and Steiner, R., eds. (1991). *The Freud–Klein Controversies 1941–45*. London and New York: Tavistock, Routledge.

Klein, M. (1929). Infantile anxiety situations reflected in a work of art and in the creative impulse. In *The Selected Melanie Klein,* ed. J. Mitchell. Harmondsworth: Penguin, 1986.

_____ (1935). A contribution to the psychogenesis of manic-depressive states. In *The Selected Melanie Klein*, ed. J. Mitchell. Harmondsworth: Penguin, 1986.

_____ (1948). *Contributions to Psycho-Analysis* (with an introduction by E. Jones). London: Hogarth Press, International Psycho-Analytic Library.

Kris, E. (1952). *Psychoanalytic Explorations in Art.* New York: International Universities Press.

Leibniz, G. W. (1705). *New Essays on Human Understanding*. Oxford: Clarendon Press.

Macalpine, I., and Hunter, R. A. (1954). Observations on the psycho-analytic theory of psychosis: Freud's "A Neurosis of Demoniacal Possession in the Seventeenth Century." *The British Journal of Medical Psychology* 27:175–192.

Maeterlinck, Comte M. (1898). *Wisdom and Destiny*, trans. A. Sutro. London: G. Allen.

McDougall, W. (1908). *An Outline of Social Psychology*. London: Methuen, 1928. 21st and (1950) 30th editions are indentical.

_____ (1921). *An Introduction to Social Psychology*. London: Methuen.

_____ (1926). *Outline of Abnormal Psychology*. London: Methuen.

Mitchell, T. W. (1921). *The Psychology of Medicine.* London: Methuen.

Prince, M. (1910). *The Unconscious.* New York: Macmillan, 1916.

_____ (1919). *The Dissociation of a Personality.* New York: Longman, Green.

Read, H. (1931). *The Meaning of Art.* London: Faber & Faber.

_____ ed. (1936). *Surrealism*. London: Faber & Faber.

_____ (1937). *Art and Society*. London: Heinemann.

Rivers, W. H. R. (1923). *Conflict and Dream.* London: Kegan, Paul, Trench, Trubner.

_____ (1924). *Instinct and the Unconscious.* Cambridge: Cambridge University Press.

Rose, W., ed. (1931). *Outline of Modern Knowledge*. London: Gollancz.

Schopenhauer, A. (1819). *The World as Will and as Idea*, (1969 edition: Trans. E. F. Payne. New York: Dover.

Schreber, D. P. (1955). *Memoirs of my Nervous Illness,* trans. and ed. I. Macalpine and R. A. Hunter. London: William Dawson & Sons.

Segal, H. (1981). *The Work of Hanna Segal: A Kleinian Approach to Clinical Practice.* New York: Jason Aronson.

Shand, A. F. (1920). *Foundations of Character-Mind.* Volume 5. Oxford: Oxford Journals.

Stout, G. F. (1927). *The Groundwork of Psychology.* London: W. B. Clive.

Sutherland, J. D. (1989). *Fairbairn's Journey into the Interior*. London: Free Association Books.

von Hartmann, E. (1869). *Philosophy of the Unconscious.* Berlin: Duncher. trans Cupland in 3 vols 1884. (1931 edition, London: Ogden)

Winnicott, D. W. (1953). Transitional objects and transitional phenomena. *International Journal of Psycho-Analysis* 34:89–97.

_____ (1971). *Playing and Reality*. London: Tavistock.

Wisdom, J. O. (1953). *The Unconscious Origin of Berkeley's Philosophy*. London: Hogarth Press and the Institute of Psycho-Analysis.

A W. R. D. Fairbairn Bibliography

(1927). Notes on the religious phantasies of a female patient. In *Psychoanalytic Studies of the Personality* (1952), pp. 183–196. London: Routledge & Kegan Paul, Henley Boston: Henley.

(1928a). The study of mental abnormality. *British Medical Journal* I:566–568. In *From Instinct to Self: Volume I* (1994).

(1928b). The ego and the id. Paper presented at Edinburgh University Psychology Discussion Class November 12, 1928. A section of this paper is published in the Introduction to Volume II of *From Instinct to Self* (1994).

(1929a). The relationship of dissociation and repression: considered from the point of view of medical psychology. M.D. thesis, submitted to Edinburgh University March 30, 1929. First publication in *From Instinct to Self: Volume II* (1994).

(1929b). Fundamental principles of psychoanalysis. *Edinburgh Medical Journal* June 1929, pp. 329–345. In *From Instinct to Self: Volume II* (1994).

(1929c). Some points of importance in the psychology of anxiety. *British Journal of Medical Psychology* 9 (4):303–313. In *From Instinct to Self: Volume II* (1994).

(1929d). What is the super-ego? Paper presented at the meeting of the British Psychological Society (Scottish Branch) on November 2, 1929. First published in *From Instinct to Self: Volume II* (1994).

(1929e). Is the super-ego repressed? Extension of "What is the super-ego?" (1929d). First published in *From Instinct to Self: Volume II* (1994).

(1930a). The psychology of adolescence. Lecture given as part of a Vacation Course for Missionaries at the Missionary College in Edinburgh April 14, 1930. First published in *From Instinct to Self: Volume II* (1994).

(1930b). The libido theory and the theory of the pleasure principle interpreted in terms of appetite. First published in *From Instinct to Self: Volume II* (1994).

(1930c). Impressions of the 1929 International Congress of Psycho-Analysis held in Oxford. Paper presented to the British Psychological Society (Scottish Branch) in Edinburgh on November 25, 1930. Published in *From Instinct to Self: Volume II.*

(1931a). Features in the analysis of a patient with a physical genital abnormality. In *Psychoanalytic Studies of the Personality* pp. 197–222.

(1931b). Psychoanalysis and the teacher. Probably presented as the inaugural address to the Psychology and Education Society in Edinburgh on October 21, 1931. Published in *From Instinct to Self: Volume II.*

(1932a) Obituary—George Matthew Robertson, M.D., L.L.D., F.R.C.P.E., Hon F.R.C.S.E., *Edinburgh Medical Journal* 39(6):397–403.

(1932b). The nervous child. Lecture given to the National Council of Women (Edinburgh Branch) and Edinburgh Women Citizens on December 14, 1932. First published in *From Instinct to Self: Volume II* (1994).

(1932c). The role of aggression in manic-depressive insanity and allied conditions. Paper presented to the Royal Medico-Psychological Association (Scotland) on October 28, 1932 at Bangour Mental Hospital. First published in *From Instinct to Self: Volume II* (1994).

(1933). Psychological aspects of dentistry. *Dental Record* 53:10. In *From Instinct to Self: Volume II* (1994).

(1934). The place of imagination in the psychology of the child. Lecture given to the PNEU School in Edinburgh February 1, 1934. First published in *From Instinct to Self: Volume II* (1994).

(1935a). Medico-psychological aspects of the problem of child assault. *Mental Hygiene* April, no. 13, pp 1–16. In *From Instinct to Self: Volume II* (1994).

(1935b). The sociological significance of communism considered in the light of psycho-analysis. *British Journal of Medical Psychology* 15(3):218–229. In *Psychoanalytic Studies of the Personality* pp. 233–246

(1936a). The effect of a king's death upon patients under analysis. *International Journal of Psycho-Analysis* 7(3):277–284. In *Psychoanalytic Studies of the Personality* pp. 223–229.

(1936b). A critique of educational aims: a medical psychologist's reflections on education. Paper presented to the Fife Head Teachers Association June 11, 1936. First published in *From Instinct to Self: Volume II* (1994).

(1937a). Arms and the Child. *The Liverpool Quarterly* 5(1):27–41. Liverpool Council of Social Services. In *From Instinct to Self: Volume II* (1994).

(1937b). Communism as an anthropological phenomenon. *Edinburgh Medical Journal* 44(7):433–447.

(1938a). Prolegomena to a psychology of art. *British Journal of Psychology* 28(3):288–303. In *From Instinct to Self: Volume II* (1994).

(1938b). The ultimate basis of aesthetic Experience. *British Journal of Psychology* 29(2):167–181. In *From Instinct to Self: Volume II* (1994).

(1938c). Questionnaire. Answers to Glover for *Textbook on Psychoanalysis* (1938). First published in *From Instinct to Self: Volume II* (1994).

(1939a). The psychological factor in sexual Delinquency. *Mental Hygiene* 5(2):1–8. In *From Instinct to Self: Volume II* (1994).

(1939b). Is aggression an irreducible factor? *British Journal of Medical Psychology* 18(2):163–170. In *From Instinct to Self: Volume II* (1994).

(1939c). Psychology as a prescribed and as a proscribed subject. In *Psychoanalytic Studies of the Personality*, pp. 247–255.

(1940). Schizoid factors in the personality. In *Psychoanalytic Studies of the Personality*, pp. 3–27.

(1941). A revised psychopathology of the psychoses and psychoneuroses. *International Journal of Psycho-Analysis* 22(2, 3):250–279. In *Psychoanalytic Studies of the Personality*, pp. 28–58.

(1943a). The war neuroses; their nature and significance. *British Medical Journal* 1:183–186. In *Psychoanalytic Studies of the Personality*, pp. 256–288.
(1943b). The repression and return of bad objects (with special reference to the "war neuroses"). *British Journal of Medical Psychology* 19(3, 4):327–341. In *Psychoanalytic Studies of the Personality*, pp. 59–81.
(1943c). Phantasy and internal objects. Paper presented by Dr. Glover on February 17, 1943 at the British Psycho-Analytical Society in London in reply to Susan Isaacs's paper "The Nature and Function of Phantasy." Published in *The Freud-Klein Controversies 1941–45*, (1991). Ed. P. King and R. Steiner. Routledge Chapman Hall and The Institute of Psycho-Analysis, pp. 358–360. In *From Instinct to Self: Volume II* (1994).
(1944). Endopsychic structure considered in terms of object-relationships. *International Journal of Psycho-Analysis* 27 (1, 2):70–93. In *Psychoanalytic Studies of the Personality*, pp. 82–136.
(1945). Psychoanalysis. Paper presented to the Edinburgh Cosmopolitan Club on April 22, 1945. First published in *From Instinct to Self: Volume II* (1994).
(1946a). Object-relationships and dynamic structure. *International Journal of Psycho-Analysis* 27 (1, 2):30–37. In *Psychoanalytic Studies of the Personality*, pp. 137–151.
(1946b). The treatment and rehabilitation of sexual offenders. In *Psychoanalytic Studies of the Personality*, pp. 289–296.
(1947a). Revision de la psicopatologia de las psicosis y psiconeurosis. *Revista de Psicoanalisis* 4 (4):751–781.
(1947b). La represion y al returno de los objetos malos. *Revista de Psicoanalisis* 4 (4):202–225.
(1947c). Las estructuras endopsiquicas consideradas en terminos de relacione de objeto. *Revista Psicoanalisis* 5 (2):346–395.
(1949). Steps in the development of an object-relations theory of the personality. *British Journal of Medical Psychology* 22 (1, 2):26–31. In *Psychoanalytic Studies of the Personality*, pp. 152–161.
(1951a). A synopsis of the development of the author's views regarding the structure of the personality. In *Psychoanalytic Studies of the Personality*, pp. 162–179.
(1951b). Critical notice of "On not being able to paint," by Joanna Field (1950). *British Journal of Medical Psychology* 24 (1):69–76. In *From Instinct to Self: Volume II* (1994).
(1952a). Theoretical and experimental aspects of psycho-analysis. *British Journal of Medical Psychology* 25 (2, 3):122–127. In *From Instinct to Self: Volume I* (1994).
(1952b). *Psycho-Analytic Studies of the Personality*. London: Henley & Boston: Tavistock and Routledge & Kegan Paul.
(1953a). Critical Notice of *Psychoanalytical Explorations in Art* by Ernst Kris. *British Journal of Medical Psychology* 26 (2):164–169. In *From Instinct to Self: Volume II* (1994).
(1953b). Male pseudohermaphroditism. *British Medical Journal*, July 11th, 2:94. In *From Instinct to Self: Volume II* (1994).
(1954a). Observations on the nature of hysterical States. *British Journal of Medical Psychology* 27 (3):106–125. In *From Instinct to Self: Volume I* (1994).
(1954b). Critical notice of *The Unconscious Origin of Berkeley's Philosophy* by John Oulton

Wisdom. *British Journal of Medical Psychology* 27 (4):253–256. In *From Instinct to Self: Volume II* (1994).

(1955). Observations in defence of the object-relations theory of the personality. *British Journal of Medical Psychology* 28 (2, 3):144–156. In *From Instinct to Self: Volume I* (1994).

(1956a). Critical notice of *The Technique of Psychoanalysis* by Edward Glover. *British Journal of Psychology* 47 (1):65–66. In *From Instinct to Self: Volume II* (1994).

(1956b). Considerations arising out of the Schreber case. *British Journal of Medical Psychology* 29 (2):113–127. In *From Instinct to Self: Volume I* (1994).

(1956c). A critical evaluation of certain basic psycho-analytical conceptions. *British Journal for the Philosophy of Science* 7 (25) 49–60. In *From Instinct to Self: Volume I* (1994).

(1957a). Freud, the psychoanalytical method and mental health. *British Journal of Medical Psychology* 30 (2):53–61. In *From Instinct to Self: Volume I* (1994).

(1957b). Notes and comments: Criticisms of Fairbairn's Generalisations about Object-Relations: comments on "A Critical Evaluation," by Balint, Foulkes, and Sutherland, and Fairbairn's reply. *British Journal for the Philosophy of Science* 7 (28):323–338. Included in *S. H. Foulkes: Selected Papers*. Ed. Elizabeth Foulkes (1990). London: Karnac. In *From Instinct to Self: Volume I* (1994).

(1958a) On the nature and aims of psychoanalytical treatment. *International Journal of Psycho-Analysis* 39 (5):374–385. In *From Instinct to Self: Volume I* (1994).

(1958b). Religion and psychotherapy. Paper presented at a Conference on Psychotherapy for the Clergy, May 8, 1958. First published in *From Instinct to Self: Volume II* (1994).

(1963a). Synopsis of an object-relations theory of the personality. *International Journal of Psycho-Analysis* 44:224–225. In *From Instinct to Self: Volume I* (1994).

(1963b). Autobiographical note. *British Journal of Medical Psychology* 36:107. In *From Instinct to Self: Volume II* (1994).

(1964). A note on the origin of male homosexuality. *British Journal of Medical Psychology* 37:31–32.

(1978). La trinité du moi. In *La Ça, Le Moi, Le Surmoi*, trans S. M. Abelleira pp. 171–201. Paris: Maury SA.

(1992) *Ronald D. Fairbairn: Il Piacere e L'Oggetto: Scritti 1952–1963*, ed. F. Orsucci, trans. L. Baldaccini. Rome: Astrolabio.

(1994) *From Instinct to Self: Selected papers of W. R. D. Fairbairn. Volume I: Clinical and Theoretical Papers; Volume II: Early Contributions and Applied Psychoanalysis*. Edited by David E. Scharff and Ellinor Fairbairn Birtles. Northvale, NJ: Jason Aronson.

Credits

We would like to thank the following publishers, editors, and authors for their kind permission to include in this collection material originally published by them. Full publication details are on pp. 479–482.

The British Medical Association in *The British Medical Journal*: 'Male Pseudohermaphroditism' (Chapter 8); 'The Study of Mental Abnormality: Prolegomena to the Establishment of a National Laboratory for This Purpose' (Chapter 22).

The British Psychological Society in *The British Journal of Medical Psychology*: 'Some Points in the Psychology of Anxiety' (Chapter 10); 'Is Aggression an Irreducible Factor?' (Chapter 12); critical notice on *Psycho-Analytical Explorations in Art* by Ernst Kris (Chapter 26); critical notice on *Unconscious Origins of Berkeley's Philosophy* by John Oulton Wisdom (Chapter 27); critical notice on *On Not Being Able to Paint* by Joanna Field (Chapter 25); 'Autobiographical Note' (Chapter 31). In *The British Journal of Psychology*: 'Prolegomena to a Psychology of Art' (Chapter 23); 'The Ultimate Basis of Aesthetic Experience' (Chapter 24); Critical notice on *The Techniques of Psycho-Analysis* by Edward Glover (Chapter 28).

Liverpool Council of Social Services in *The Liverpool Quarterly*: "Arms and the Child" (Chapter 18).

Mind (National Association for Mental Health) Publications in *Mental Hygiene*: 'Psychological Aspects of the Problem of Child Assault' (Chapter 4); 'The Psychological Factor in Sexual Delinquency' (Chapter 14).

Routledge, Chapman Hall, The New Library of Psychoanalysis and The Institute of Psychoanalysis in *The Freud-Klein Controversies 1941–45*, ed. P. King and R. Steiner, 'The Discussion paper on "The Nature and Function of Phantasy" by Susan Isaacs' (Chapter 15). We also thank the editors Pearl King and Riccardo Steiner for their kind permission to publish this extract.

The Scottish Medical Journal in *The Edinburgh Medical Journal*: 'Fundamental Principles of Psychoanalysis' (Chapter 9).

It has not been possible to trace the publishers of *The Dental Record*, 'The Psychological Aspects of Dentistry' (Chapter 17). This copyright has now reverted to the author (in this case the Fairbairn family).

We would also like to express our thanks to all the librarians who facilitated the research for various volumes and journals in so many ways.

Publication Details of the Papers and Lectures in Volume II

Chapter 1. This thesis was submitted to Edinburgh University on March 30 1929, under the title "The Relationship of Dissociation and Repression: Considered from the Point of View of Medical Psychology". This is its first publication.

Chapter 2. These papers on the superego are published here for the first time.

Chapter 3. This paper on libido theory is published for the first time.

Chapter 4. This paper was originally published under the title 'Medico-Psychological Aspects of the Problem of Child Assault' in *Mental Hygiene* April 1935, no. 13, pp. 1–16. It was a lecture delivered on November 1, 1933, to the Joint Committee of the Edinburgh Women Citizens Association and the National Council of Women (Edinburgh and District Branch).

Chapter 5. This lecture was entitled 'The Nervous Child'. It was given to the National Council (Edinburgh Branch) and Edinburgh Women Citizens Association on December 14, 1932. It is published here for the first time.

Chapter 6. This lecture was given under the title 'The Place of Imagination in the Psychology of the Child' to the Parents National Educational Union on February 1, 1934. It is published here for the first time.

Chapter 7. This lecture was given under the title 'The Psychology of Adolescence' to the Missionary College on January 4, 1930, as part of a Vacation Course. It is published here for the first time.

Chapter 8. This piece was originally published under the same title in *The British Medical Journal*, July 11, 1953, 2: 94–95.

Chapter 9. This paper was originally published under the title 'Fundamental Principles of Psycho-Analysis' in *The Edinburgh Journal*, June 1929, pp. 329–345. It was a paper read to the Royal Medical Society on February 8, 1929.

Chapter 10. This paper was originally published in 1930 under the title 'Some Points of Importance in the Psychology of Anxiety' in *The British Journal of Medical Psychology* 9(4):303–313.

Chapter 11. This paper was entitled 'The Role of Aggression in Manic-Depressive Insanity and Allied Conditions' and was presented to The Royal Medico-Psychological Association (Scotland) at Bangour Hospital in November 1932. It is published here for the first time.

Chapter 12. This paper was originally published in 1939 under the title 'Is Aggression an Irreducible Factor?' in *The British Journal of Medical Psychology* 18(2):163–170. It was the opening paper of the symposium given before the St Andrew's Meeting of the British Psychological Society on April 2, 1938.

Chapter 13. This piece is in the form of a reply to Edward Glover's questionnaire sent to twenty-four practising psychoanalysts in Britain in 1938. The answers were used by Glover (1955) in his *Techniques of Psychoanalysis*.

Chapter 14. This paper was originally published under the title 'The Psychological Factor in Sexual Delinquency' in *Mental Hygiene*, April 1939, pp. 1–8. It was a lecture given at the Fifth Biennial Conference on Mental Health held in London on January 13, 1939.

Chapter 15. This untitled paper was originally read by Dr Edward Glover, in Fairbairn's absence, at the Second Discussion of Scientific Controversies held at the British Psycho-Analytic Society on February 17, 1943, and published in *The Freud–Klein Controversies 1941–1945* (1991), eds. P. King and R. Steiner, pp. 358–360.

Chapter 16. This address, under the title 'Psychoanalysis', was given to the Edinburgh Cosmopolitan Club on April 22, 1945. It is now published for the first time.

Chapter 17. This paper was originally published in October 1933 under the title 'Psychological Aspects of Dentistry' in *The Dental Record* 3(10). It was read before the Odonto-Chirurgical Society of Scotland on November 10, 1932.

Chapter 18. This paper was published in January 1937 in *The Liverpool Quarterly* 5(1).

Chapter 19. This paper was entitled 'A Critique of Educational Aims: A Medical Psychologist's Reflections of Education' and presented to the Fife Head Teacher's Association on June 11, 1936. It is published here for the first time.

Chapter 20. This paper was probably presented as the inaugural address to the Psychology and Education Society on October 21, 1931 under the same title. It is published here for the first time.

Chapter 21. This paper was entitled 'Religion and Psychotherapy' and was read at a Conference on Psychotherapy for the Clergy on May 8, 1958. It is now published for the first time.

Chapter 22. This paper was originally entitled 'The Study of Mental Abnormality: Prolegomena to the Establishment of a National Laboratory for this Purpose' and was published in 1928 in *The British Medical Journal* 1 (March 31): 566–568.

Chapter 23. This paper was originally published in January 1938 under the same title in *The British Journal of Psychology*, 28(3): 288–303. It was read before the Scottish Branch of the British Psychological Society on March 6, 1937.

Chapter 24. This paper was originally published in October 1938 under the same title in *The British Journal of Psychology* 29(2): 167–181. It was based on a paper read to the Scottish Branch of the British Psychological Society on January 29, 1938.

Chapter 25. This critical notice was originally published in 1951 in *The British Journal of Medical Psychology* 24(1): 69–76.

Chapter 26. This critical notice was originally published in 1953 in *The British Journal of Medical Psychology* 27(3) 164–169.

Chapter 27. This critical notice was originally published in 1955 in *The British Journal of Medical Psychology* 28(2, 3): 253–256.

Chapter 28. This critical notice was originally published in 1956 in *The British Journal of Psychology* 47(2): 65–66.

Chapter 29. Letters

a. Letter to Dr Marjorie Brierley
b. Letter dated 24 September 1953 to Dr Denis Hill
c. Letter dated 24 January 1954 to Dr J. D. Sutherland

Chapter 30. Impressions of the 1929 International Congress of Psycho-Analysis held in Oxford.

Chapter 31. This piece was originally published in 1963 under the title 'Autobiographical Note' in *The British Journal of Medical Psychology* 36:107.

Index